World politics since 1945

World politics since 1945

Third edition

Peter Calvocoressi

WITHDRAWN

Longman

London and New York

Longman Group Limited London

Associated companies, branches and representatives
throughout the world

This edition published in the United States of America
by Longman Inc., New York.
First published in the United States of America
by Praeger

First published 1968
Second edition 1971
Third edition 1977
Third impression 1979
Fourth impression 1980

Printed in Great Britain by
Richard Clay (The Chaucer Press) Ltd,
Bungay, Suffolk

ISBN 0 582 48913 X

Contents

Foreword

A number of friends have read parts of this book. I am extremely grateful to them for the trouble they took and for their comments which have been very valuable to me. Among those who can be named I wish, here and once more, to thank Alastair Buchan, Elizabeth Monroe and Guy Wint for special kindness and helpfulness. My pupils too, perhaps unwittingly, have sometimes made me think more about things which I, no doubt rashly, had thought to have disposed of. And I am very much indebted to Rosemary Douglas who, in the course of editing the complete book for me, raised questions great and small which I would otherwise have missed.

P.C.

Foreword to the Third Edition

This book now covers a period of thirty years since the end of the Second World War. Much of the international map has changed little in these years. The USA and the USSR remain in conflict, mainly because they are still powers of a different order to every other. The essence of this conflict is the clash of power, although its nature and course have been affected by ideology, particularly on the American side, for whereas the USSR has used its power – in Europe and thereafter in the Middle East and at sea – in ways and for purposes which have been standard European power practice for centuries, the USA's major display of strength – in Vietnam – owed a great deal to the view that Russian and Chinese power must be checked because they are communist. Europe remained divided. Despite periodic reminders of the hazards of the new European order, for example in Czechoslovakia in 1968, this division acquired a certain normality and even the continuing and confirmed division of Germany itself (which would not have surprised Henry the Fowler) has been absorbed into the larger division around it. The longevity of Tito has kept Yugoslavia where it is, but the mortality of Franco began the shift of Spain out of its straitjacket and the neighbouring dictatorship was cracked by Portugal's impossible policies in Africa. Middle Eastern affairs have been persistently dominated throughout these thirty years by the Arab–Israeli fight for Palestine, the increasing appetite of the rest of the world for oil, and the uneasy and unsure manoeuvrings of the superpowers in an area which has continued to hypnotize everybody. The British empire has all but completely vanished away, leaving Britain with major problems of readjustment and vast areas of Asia and Africa (where the French, Belgian, Dutch, Portuguese and Spanish empires also dissolved) with responsibility for their own problems relieved only by the meagre help which they could wring from the rich either directly or through such bodies as the UN, the World Bank or the EEC – the last a phenomenon which seemed at first to mark a major change in the world's pattern but by 1975 faced the question whether the change was major or minor. Latin America has remained a byword for instability and inequality. There has been a lot of fighting and killing in the world but none of it nuclear. It has become accepted that the major concern of superpowers is to seek to control the nuclear arms race and this is perhaps the most significant feature of the world political map, even though the hideous complexity of the matter has prevented this mood from being transformed into more than very partial agreements. The third superpower, China, recognized as such by Roosevelt before 1945 if by few others, has displayed a reticence which should probably be attributed to greatness of a different kind, namely its great size which has enormously complicated the business of organizing the country after a major revolution which itself came at the end of a century of wars and decay. Next to the threat of nuclear catastrophe, and for most of the human race, a more present threat has been poverty, squalor and starvation aggravated for many by the helpless beholding of plenty not far away and corruption even nearer. The jarring injustices of racial discrimination have been reduced by decolonization and by changes in mood but not yet eliminated from a world in which so elementary an evil as slavery still persists.

For this edition I have brought all sections of the book up to date while trying to make it not too much longer. The principal changes are these. In the Part One I have added a new chapter on post-war Japan and have carried the story of arms control forward to the end of SALT 1 and into the incomplete SALT 2 negotiations. In Part Two I have essayed an appreciation of the cohesion of the two halves of Europe, the eastern after the invasion of Czechoslovakia in 1968 and in the light of economic stringencies and choices among the members of Comecon, the western in terms of the addition of three new members to the EEC and proposals to make it yet larger. The principal additions to Part Three concern the Arab–Israeli war of 1973 and the destruction of Lebanon. The end of American intervention in Vietnam and the secession of Bangladesh from Pakistan provide most of the new material in Part Four and the end of Portuguese empire and its consequences do the same for Part Five. Finally, to Part Six I have made few additions but have appended an overall view of Latin America in terms which have emerged from further thought about its problems. The arrival of man on the moon falls outside the scope of this book.

The main purpose of a book of this kind is to order a mass of factual detail and in that way offer explanations of what has happened: the danger is that it will ignore the general currents which are difficult to discern in a period so short as thirty years and so recent. Nevertheless some currents in which later historians may discern lasting significance may tentatively be indicated.

While war has never been absent from the annals of man (except, I believe, among Eskimoes) there have been periods which in retrospect appear remarkably pacific and others which appear remarkably sanguinary. Unquestionably war has in the twentieth century been enormously discussed as well as disastrously waged, and its causes sedulously dissected by academic and other writers while the horrible facts of war have been witnessed directly or through photography by vaster audiences than ever before. Whether warmaking has been commensurately diminished by this specialist enquiry or general impact is another matter, over which it is worth pausing briefly.

When the Second World War ended there was, first of all, an attempt to prevent its repetition by constitutional means – through the Charter of the United Nations and the obligations and institutions thereby created. Yet – and partly because the UN was not so much a new venture as a second attempt – the aspirations invested in the UN were muted from the start and the organs of the UN soon became little more than functional additions to the established machinery of international relations. More or less contemporaneously a second view about the prevention of war emerged. This was to the effect that war had become so destructive and uncontrollable that major powers, remembering the fable of the sorcerer's apprentice, would eschew it on a calculation of expediency, let alone human revulsion: that war had ruled itself out. This was the balance of terror argument which meant that no super-power could expect to defeat another without itself being laid in ruins. But this argument, which still prevails, had a serious flaw. It rested on the presumed nature of nuclear war and applied therefore to nuclear powers only. In order to broaden the argument it was necessary to add a new factor: that non-nuclear wars too would be interdicted because the nuclear powers, fearing that a non-nuclear war might develop into a war involving themselves and their nuclear armouries, would prevent lesser states from making wars or at worst stop them almost as soon as they started (thus in effect transferring to lesser power the blitzkrieg reasoning of the twenties and thirties). The spread of nuclear weapons and, more important, of nuclear technology and capacity has eroded the credibility of this theory which in any case presumed an overriding common purpose and joint action by the superpowers. It required in effect a new kind of international police function – the policing of international disputes not by the UN or by a single world power such as Britain had been but by a combination of two, perhaps later more, powers who must in the nature of things be distrustful of one another, understand one another less than perfectly and communicate with one another with all manner of hampering reservations.

There were therefore no solid grounds for supposing the elimination or significant reduction of war as a regulator of international conflict. New constitutional apparatus, however useful, was an adjunct of an international system which included war as part of the system; this apparatus was not the instrument of a new and more pacific system. In nuclear powers *raison d'état* would, in their relations with one another, take account of the destructiveness of nuclear weapons, but for the great majority of non-nuclear states the conduct of international relations remained much as it had been since the emergence of the nation-state system. In addition groups or movements which lacked the trappings of a duly constituted state were claiming, where they could, some of the prerogatives of the state, notably diplomatic recognition and the right to make war and kill people just like states do (including the age-old practice of resorting to war without a declaration of war).

But what about the impact of war on human sensibilities? This is shaky ground. Since however it is observable that the ravages of war have been unevenly spread over the centuries, it is legitimate to try to discern why this should have been so and why in particular mankind has experienced a relative immunity from war at certain times. One such period in Europe was the age which succeeded the wars of religion, an age which certainly did not see the abolition of war but did see the exercise of more control over its initation and conduct. One explanation which has been offered for this more benign state of affairs is that the excesses of the wars of religion, culminating in the appalling devastation of the Thirty Years War, so sickened observers and survivors that for a time war became rarer and milder. If there is anything in this argument, then there are grounds for hoping that the concluding decades of the twentieth century may follow this example, since the recent past has provided devastation enough. The peoples of the USSR suffered in the forties death and destruction on an appalling scale; the Japanese suffered the unprecedented shock of two nuclear bombs; China had lived through a century of mounting upheavals; and finally the United States, hitherto immune from the worst horrors of wars even though taking part in them, became involved in and responsible for the slaughter and wasting of Vietnam with retributive – and perhaps not wholly transient – humiliation and demoralization. Were these experiences of the world's leading states enough to put them off war and make them use their skills and strengths to stop other people's wars too?

There is, finally, another strand in the history of these thirty years which deserves an oblique glance. This is the feminist movement which, in various parts of the world, was marked by the advent of women to positions of power and a more general increase in the influence of women at many levels of public affairs. There are precedents for this phenomenon. In the later Middle Ages in Europe – particularly in France, England and Naples – queens became more than the consorts of kings and women have been credited with the softening of manners which changed a warrior world of straw-littered castle halls full of roistering illiterates into a gentler, more decent, more private, more considerate society prepared to give a higher place to the practice of the arts and the play of the mind. But whether women are nicer than men in these respects only when subject to men and without the temptations of power is a question which, so far as I know, remains unanswered.

Peter Calvocoressi
September 1976

Part One

The Great Powers

Chapter 1

The Cold War

1. End of Alliance

In the summer of 1945 it was known both in Washington and Moscow that Japan was ready to acknowledge defeat and abandon the war which it had begun by the attack on Pearl Harbour. In July the Americans experimentally exploded the first nuclear weapon in the history of mankind and in August they dropped two bombs on Hiroshima and Nagasaki. Japan surrendered forthwith and this clinching of the imminent American victory deprived the Russians of all but a token share in the post-war settlement in the Far East. The Second World War ended with an act which contained the two central elements in the cold war: the advent of nuclear weapons and Russo-American rivalry.

In the European theatre this conflict remained for a short time veiled. The organs and habits of war-time collaboration were to be adapted to the problems of peace, not discarded. The Russian spring offensive of 1944 had set the USSR on the way to military dominance and political authority in Europe unequalled since Alexander I had ridden into Paris in 1814 with plans for a concert of victors which would order the affairs of Europe and keep them ordered. The nature of mid-twentieth century great power control was a matter for debate – how far the powers were collectively to order the whole world, how far each was to dominate a sector. The Russians and the British, with the reluctant assent of President Franklin D. Roosevelt (and the dissent of his Secretary of State, Cordell Hull), discussed the practical aspects of an immediate division of responsibilities, and in October 1944, at a conference in Moscow which the president was unable to attend owing to the American election campaign, these dispositions were expressed in numerical terms: the Russian degree of influence in Romania was described as 90, in Bulgaria and Hungary as 80, in Yugoslavia 50, in Greece 10. In practice these figures turned out to be rough indices of political control; although expressed as a bargain, they described a situation: 90 and 10 were polite ways of saying 100 and 0, and the diagnosis in the two extreme cases of Romania and Greece was confirmed when the British took control in Greece without Russian protest and the USSR installed a pro-communist regime in Romania with only slight British protest. Bulgaria and Hungary, only slightly less heavily weighted to the Russian side, went the same way as Romania. Fifty described a situation which could not endure but whose outcome was not at that moment to be predicted or acknowledged. Poland, not included in the calculation, might also have been rated at 50, along with Yugoslavia. Both fell shortly afterwards into the Russian sphere, so that Europe became divided into two irregular segments appertaining to the two principal victors, the United States and the USSR. These two powers continued for a while to talk in terms of alliance, and they were specifically pledged to collaborate in the governance of the German and Austrian territories which they and their allies had conquered. The few surviving neutrals had no impact on this developing pattern. In 1948, however, Yugoslavia challenged the pattern and asserted a new kind of neutralism which, supported by Nehru's India and later adopted by Nasser's Egypt, was to play an increasing role in the evolving politics of the cold war. In the forties, however, the focus of international politics was Europe and the dominating event was the ultimate division of the continent by the abandonment of German unity and the creation of two new German states. Thereafter Europe remained territorially stable and politically almost so.

The position of the USSR in these years was one of great weakness, offset by the weakness and war-weariness of others and above all by the rooted disinclination of the United States to use bombs (it is not known how soon after Nagasaki a third bomb was ready) in order to coerce a state which, though regarded as devoted to a universal and malevolent conspiracy, had been so recently an ally against the uncontestable evils of nazism. For the USSR the war had been a huge economic disaster accompanied by loss of life so grievous that its full extent was probably not disclosed. The Russian state was a land power which had expanded generation by generation within a zone which presented a persistent German threat. In the Soviet phase of history Russian external politics were further characterized by a diplomacy which led to isolation and so, in 1941, to the threshold of total military defeat. The USSR had been saved by its extraordinary geographical and spiritual resources and by the concurrent war in the west in which the Germans were already engaged before they attacked the USSR and which became graver for them when, shortly afterwards, Hitler gratuitously declared war on the United States of America. For Stalin, however, the anti-fascist alliance of 1941–45 can hardly have appeared to be more than a marriage of convenience and limited span; nor did it look any different when seen from the western end, at any rate by governments, if not in the popular view. With the war over, the purpose of the alliance had been achieved, and there was little in the mentalities and traditions of the allies to encourage the idea that it might be converted into an entente: on the contrary, the diplomatic history of all parties up to 1941 and their respective attitudes to international political, social and economic problems suggested exactly the reverse.

The elimination, permanent or temporary, of the German threat coincided with the explosion of the first American nuclear bombs. For the first time in the history of the world one state had become more powerful than all other states put together. The USSR, no less than the most trivial state, was at the mercy of the Americans if they should be willing to do to Moscow and Leningrad what they had done to Hiroshima and Nagasaki. There were plenty of reasons for supposing that they were not so willing, but no government in the Kremlin could responsibly proceed upon this assumption. Stalin's only prudent course in this bitterly disappointing situation was to combine the maximum strengthening of the USSR with a nice assessment of the safe level of provocation of the United States, and to subordinate everything, including post-war reconstruction, to catching up with the Americans in military technology. He possessed a large army, he had occupied large areas of eastern and central Europe, and he had natural allies and servants in communists in various parts of the world. At home his tasks were immense: they included the safeguarding of the USSR against a repetition of the catastrophe of 1941–45, and the resurrection of the USSR from that catastrophe which had cost something like 20 million lives, the destruction or displacement of a large part of its industry and the distortion of its industrial pattern to the detriment of all except war production, and the devastation and depopulation of its cultivated land so that food production was almost halved. To a man with Stalin's past and temperament the tasks of restitution included the reassertion of party rule and communist orthodoxy and the reduction therefore of the prominence of the army and other national institutions and the reshackling of all modes of thinking outside the prescribed doctrinal run. In matters of national security, in economic affairs and in the life of the spirit the outlook was grim. At home artists and intellectuals were regimented, victorious marshals were slighted and the officer class persistently if quietly purged, while the first post-war five-year plan prescribed strenuous tasks for heavy industry and offered little comfort to a war-weary populace. Externally Stalin made it clear that the protective acquisitions of 1939–40 were not for disgorging (the three Baltic states, the eastern half of Poland which the Russians called Western Ukraine and Western Byelorussia, Bessarabia and northern Bukovina, and the territory exacted from Finland after the winter war); elsewhere in eastern and central Europe all states must have governments well disposed to the USSR, a vague formula which seemed to mean governments which could be relied upon never again to give facilities to a German aggressor and which came after 1947 or thereabouts to mean governments reliably hostile to the United States in the cold war. Such governments must be installed and maintained by whatever means might be necessary. During the wartime conferences between Stalin, Roosevelt and Churchill parts of the USSR were still occupied by German forces, and during the war and its psychological aftermath (a period of indefinable duration) Stalin was no doubt obsessed with his German problem. The cold war first substituted the

Americans for the Germans as the main enemy but then, after the re-armament of Western Germany, combined the two threats as a new American–German one. These developments, to which Stalin himself contributed by his actions in eastern and central Europe, may nevertheless have been a disappointment to him if, as seems possible, he had entertained at one time a very different prospect of Russo-American relations.

To Stalin during the war the Americans were personified by Presi-dent Franklin D. Roosevelt who made no secret of his desire to get on well with the USSR or of his distrust of British and other western im-perialisms. Moreover Roosevelt wanted a Russian alliance against Japan and did not seem at all likely to do the one thing which Stalin would have feared, i.e. to keep troops permanently in Europe and make the United States a European power. On the contrary, Roosevelt was not much interested in post-war Europe and showed, for example, none of Churchill's concern about what was going to happen in Poland and Greece. Whereas Russo-British relations came near to breaking-point over Poland, Russo-American relations did not; and Stalin, whether out of genuine lack of interest or calculated diplomacy, avoided serious disagreement with Roosevelt over problems of world organization (such as the representation of Soviet republics in the UN) in which Roosevelt was seriously interested. On the basis that the United States would be remote from Europe and in some degree friendly towards the USSR Stalin was prepared to moderate his support for European com-munists in order not to alarm the United States. He could not foresee that by abandoning Greece to Britain he was preparing the way for the transfer of Greece to the United States within three years. His failure to help the Greek communists may have been principally a result of a calculation that they were not worth helping, but he may also have reflected that helping them would alarm and irritate Americans in Roosevelt's entourage. He was continuing a line of policy applied in Yugoslavia during the war when he restrained the Yugoslav com-munists' desire to plan and prosecute their social revolution while the war was still in progress, and urged them to co-operate with other par-ties, even monarchists. Again he persuaded the Italian communists to be less anti-monarchical than the non-communist Action Party; it was the communist leader Palmiro Togliatti who proposed, after the fall of Mussolini, that the future of the Italian monarchy should remain in abeyance until the war was finished. By that time, however, Roosevelt was dead and whatever Stalin's policies towards the United States may have been, they could no longer be based on his relations with Roosevelt and his estimate of Roosevelt's intentions. Even if Roosevelt had survived, his policies might have been radically altered – as Truman's were – by the successful explosion of two nuclear bombs and by the evolution of Stalin's policies in Europe.

For Stalin, confronted in August 1945 with the evidence from Hiroshima and Nagasaki, the outstanding fact was that the USSR possessed no strategic air force and could not deliver a direct attack on the United States. The best that Stalin could do was to pose a threat to western Europe which might deter the Americans from attacking the USSR. The Russian armies were not demobilized and they were not withdrawn from the areas which they had occupied in the last campaigns of the war and which included the historic capitals of Budapest, Prague, Vienna and Berlin. Thus Stalin created a glacis in advance of his vulnerable heartlands and at the same time forced the exhausted and tremulous Europeans and their American protectors to ask themselves whether the Russian advance had really been halted by the German surrender or might be resumed until Paris and Milan, Brest and Bordeaux, were added to the Russian bag. This policy, like the American counter-policy which it evoked, was a rational response to an ill-defined threat which could not be ignored, but – also like the American counter-policy – it may have been unnecessary. The Americans did not attack the USSR, and it is highly improbable that they ever intended to do so. Stalin succeeded in immunizing his country while he turned it into a nuclear power (Stalin's successors later allowed the Chinese to do the same thing), but it cannot be proved that he needed to keep a huge army in being and to reduce most of central and eastern Europe to vassalage while Russian money and Russian brains were producing the Russian bomb. Moreover, although the outcome was atomic parity of a sort by 1954, Stalin's road to national security accentuated the American hostility which he had cause to fear, since the creation of the satellite empire and attempts to gain control of the whole of Germany created the appearance of an aggressive imperialism even more dangerous and hardly less brutal than Hitler's.

Nuclear parity was an almost inescapable objective for the Kremlin after 1945, but there was in theory an alternative which the Americans tried to bring within the scope of practical politics. This was to sublimate or internationalize atomic energy and so remove it from inter-state politics. One of the first actions of the United Nations was to create in 1946 an Atomic Energy Commission. At the first meeting of this commission Bernard M. Baruch presented on behalf of the United States a plan for an international Atomic Development Authority which would have exclusive control and ownership in all potential war-making nuclear activities and would also have the right to inspect all other atomic activities. Upon the inauguration of effective international control the United States would stop making nuclear weapons and destroy existing stocks. But the United States could not destroy its advanced technological knowledge and it would therefore retain a huge advantage over the USSR which, by accepting the Baruch Plan, would inhibit its own advances in nuclear physics. In addition the USSR disliked the plan because it involved the abrogation in this field of the veto, the principal symbol and guarantee of national sovereignty as opposed to international government, which the USSR was even less disposed to countenance than any other state. A. A. Gromyko proposed instead a treaty banning the use of nuclear weapons, the destruction of existing stocks, and an international control commission subordinate to the Security Council (and therefore subject to the veto); he opposed the creation of a new international authority and was only prepared to allow international inspection of those plants which had been declared to have ceased nuclear production and were offered for inspection by the government of the country in which they were situated. These positions were irreconcilable and although the debate continued for a while the UN Atomic Energy Commission eventually decided in 1948 to adjourn indefinitely. The Russian rejection of the Baruch Plan was an additional factor in persuading the administration of Harry S. Truman, who had become president on the death of Roosevelt in April 1945, that the USSR was no longer an ally but an adversary.

American policy-makers had theoretically more freedom of choice than their Russian counterparts. Endowed with a mighty technical superiority, which they may have regarded as permanent, they were in a position in which they could strike or threaten or wait and see. To strike – to start a preventive war – was in practice impossible because they were unable to summon up the will to do so. A preventive war is a war undertaken to remove a threat by a people which feels threatened, and the Americans were not threatened by the Russians and did not feel threatened by them. In these circumstances a preventive war by the Americans was an abstract intellectual concept. (For the Russians it was substantive but also suicidal.) The Americans therefore pursued policies which combined threats with waiting to see.

The nuclear bomb was a military weapon which had been used to bring the war with Japan to an end in a particular way. It was also a political weapon which, in fact, had an effect on American and on Russian policies and, arguably, was deliberately used by Truman and his advisers for definite political purposes, notably to shackle and reduce Russian power in central and eastern Europe. Whatever the intentions of American policy-makers at the end of the war, the outcome of a complex of factors was that the United States became a major power in Europe with considerable military forces in Europe. These factors included the American nuclear bomb and Stalin's regimentation of the countries near his borders, but the attempt to describe either factor as a consequence of the other oversimplifies the political process and seeks to identify a cause and an effect where in reality both factors were operating causes and effects in a chain of interactions and reactions.

All weapons have political implications and the biggest weapons have the biggest implications. A weapon which is too frightful to use has the most implications, since its possessors will want to put it to political use in order to compensate for the anomalous limitations on its military usefulness. Truman's position was automatically different from Roosevelt's as soon as Hiroshima had been destroyed. The question was not whether he was to make political use of the new weapon, but to what political end he should use it. The relationship between the

United States and the USSR had been altered: how should this alteration be exploited? The context in which this question first arose was not Asian but European, for it was in Europe that the principal political issues were arising. The United States, unlike the USSR and Britain, disliked the idea of spheres of influence. It also disliked the prospect of exclusive Russian control over half Europe and believed that the Russians were moving towards such control in contravention of pledges to install democratic governments in the countries liberated from German rule. Since Russian designs were uncertain – Stalin seemed content at first to accept coalition government in these countries and to interpret democratic as meaning anything which excluded fascists (only a moderately ambiguous term in the prevailing circumstances) – the United States wished to exert pressure on Moscow in two directions: to make the coalitions more rather than less democratic in the sense of being proportionately representative of the popular will, and to allow American and British representatives on the Control Commissions in liberated countries to have more rather than less authority in relation to their Russian colleagues. And the pressure to be used in the pursuit of these aims included the fact that the nuclear bomb should make Russian leaders think twice before adopting opposite policies.

On the American side that intangible but none the less real factor called the climate of opinion was changing at this juncture for more reasons than the accretion of nuclear power. New men impart new ideas and new ways of handling existing problems. Truman was a very different man from Roosevelt and conscious of the differences: an American of some eminence but in no sense a world figure, a man respected for the qualities which go with simpleness and directness rather than with subtlety, a man in whom political courage would have to take the place of political sophistication, a man typically American in his attachment to a few basic principles and ideologies where the less typical Roosevelt had generally preferred the modes of thought of the pragmatist. Truman in the last resort played politics by precept and not by ear, and where Roosevelt had been concerned with the problem of relations between two great powers Truman was more influenced by the conflict between communism and an even vaguer entity called anti-communism. Again, so far as these generalizations are pardonable, Truman was the more representative American of the late forties and more inclined to regard the meeting of Americans and Russians in the middle of Europe as a confrontation of systems and civilizations rather than of states. Reports of indiscipline and barbarities by Russian troops, often described in this context as Asian or mongoloid, increased this propensity. (Europeans too, if they had to choose between a host of rapists and a host of seducers, not only preferred the latter but also stood in fear of the former as something alien as well as terrifying.)

The United States had some cause to believe that the implications of Hiroshima for Europe were not lost on the Russians. Elections in

Hungary in October and November 1945 were held without coercion and gave the communists only a minor share in the government of the capital and the state. Elections in Bulgaria were postponed on American insistence and against Russian wishes. In Romania the United States aligned itself with the anti-communists and the king against the prime minister, Petru Groza, whom the Russians had installed when they entered the country in 1944. But the crucial testing ground was Poland where coalition government, under a socialist prime minister, was maintained until 1947 but gradually transformed in that and the following year – the years which saw the prevailing of the east wind over the west in central and eastern Europe, the failure of the American attempt to resist the partition of Europe into spheres of influence and the formalization of the cold war.

In these years American policy veered away from the attempt to maximize American influence throughout Europe in favour of the lesser aim of giving the USSR to understand that further territorial advances in Europe were forbidden. This prohibition was to be enforced and institutionalized by a series of open political arrangements, backed by military dispositions. The overwhelming power of the United States would be used obstructively but not destructively. In so far as the USSR presented a material menace, it would be contained by physical barriers; in so far as it presented an ideological menace, it would be countered by democratic example, money and the seeds of decay which westerners discerned in the communist system (as Marxists did in capitalism). American policy was also constructive and reconstructive. The UN Relief and Reconstruction Agency (UNRRA) was mainly financed by American money; its help was enormous, especially to the USSR and Yugoslavia. In March 1947 the United States took over Britain's traditional and now too costly role of keeping the Russians out of the eastern Mediterranean: Truman took Greece and Turkey under the American wing and promised material aid to states threatened by communism. Three months later the United States inaugurated the Marshall Plan to avert an economic collapse of Europe which could, it was feared, leave the whole continent helplessly exposed to Russian power and communist lures. The offer of American economic aid was made to the whole of Europe including the USSR but Moscow refused for itself and for its satellites. For a second time – the Baruch Plan being the first – the Russians rejected a generous overture from Washington rather than accept collaboration which would have enabled Americans and others to go up and down in the USSR and observe its true plight. Separate development of western and eastern Europe was affirmed and the American initiative in restoring western Europe killed Russian hopes (if any) of victories in the west.

Thus a line was drawn. The coup which substituted communist for coalition rule in Prague the next year made it starker. Gloom and fear descended upon European politics. Although there was no fighting except of a local, sporadic and unacknowledged kind, everybody concurred in describing the situation as a war. Then, in Germany, where the major powers had joined hands in 1945 and had established a joint administration, the struggle for the only important piece of Europe outside the two camps produced a challenge and a counter-challenge which seemed bound to lead to shooting.

2. Germany

At the end of the war the United States, the USSR and Britain were in apparent agreement on two fundamental propositions about Germany, both of which they failed to maintain. The first of these was that Germany should be kept under constraint, and the second was that it should remain a single unit. Within a decade Germany became divided into two separate states, each – particularly the western one – playing an increasingly effective part in international politics. The reasons for this outcome included the inability of the victors to agree on other aspects of the German problem, the intrinsic importance of Germany itself, and external circumstances of which the Korean war was the most important. So Germany too was partitioned, like Europe as a whole, as a consequence of Russo-American rivalry in the conference chamber and on the ground in Europe and beyond. The bipolarity of post-war power politics led inevitably to delineation and demarcation – even, in a celebrated and late episode, to the building of a wall, a tactic reminiscent of such antique devices as the attempt to bar the Golden Horn to ships or the isthmus of Corinth to armies. When bipolarity began to shift and the Cold War to wane the biggest obstacle to the revision of Russo-American relations was Germany.

The principal victors were initially agreed that Germany should be disarmed and denazified, divided administratively into zones of occupation but treated economically as a single unit which would pay for imported necessities out of current production. Dismemberment, which had been discussed and may have lingered on in some French minds, was tacitly abandoned without being officially repudiated, and the territorial amputations suffered by Germany were the loss of east Prussia to the USSR and of all other territories beyond the Oder and Western Neisse rivers which were left under Polish administration pending the final delimitation of the German state by the peace conference which never took place. Churchill opposed the designation of the Western as opposed to the Eastern Neisse as the western limit of Poland's sphere (the Western Neisse flows northward into the Oder at a point where the upstream line of the Oder turns sharply eastward) but he felt unable to persist in a seemingly anti-Polish attitude. The Potsdam decision on Germany's frontiers, although expressed in provisional terms, was in reality a victory for the Russians. Germany lost nearly one quarter of its pre-1938 territory.

The victors were divided in their views on the economic policy of the occupation and on the future structure of the German state. The general principles of economic unity and the balancing of imports and production, adopted at Potsdam, were traversed by the problem of reparations which had been inconclusively discussed at Yalta and then shelved at Potsdam. It was agreed at Yalta that the sum of $20,000 million should be taken as a basis for further discussions, half of this sum being claimed by the USSR for itself and Poland. At Potsdam the Russians, whose need for reparations in kind or cash was intense, secured agreement for removals from their zone of occupation to meet Russian and Polish reparation claims but nothing was settled about the extent of these claims. The western allies were likewise to be entitled to dismantle and remove property in their zones in order to meet their claims and those of the remaining allies. This arrangement was bound to make nonsense of the principle of economic unity since the various zones were economically dissimilar both in regard to manufacturers and to agricultural production. It also made nonsense of the principle of paying for imports out of current production, since it permitted the occupiers to destroy the sources of production. Germany could to some extent be looted or milked, but it could not for long be both looted and milked. The western allies soon found that dismantling left them with an obligation to provide their zones with imported goods which had to be paid for by their own taxpayers since German production was unable to foot the bill. Moreover, Russian dismantling and removals on a vast scale, coupled with severe shortages in the USSR itself, placed upon the western occupiers and their taxpayers the additional burden of supplying the Russian zone with essential foods and goods. Although the Americans might have been willing to help the Russians directly with equipment for reconstruction, they resented the roundabout way in which the Russians helped themselves to German equipment at eventual American expense, while for their part the Russians were happy to take from Germany what their *amour propre* prevented them from accepting from the Americans.

This conflict was accompanied by related disagreements about the political structure of Germany and, subsequently, about its political attachments. The British were pragmatically predisposed in favour of a unitary rather than a federal structure, for economic rather than political reasons. The main Russian concern was strategic: to maintain their position in eastern Germany. This was the essential minimum to which they subsequently adhered unfalteringly. It was strengthened, in November 1945, by the first significant political event in the reviving post-war Europe – the elections in Austria in which the communists were decisively defeated. If, compatibly with the aim of holding fast to eastern Germany, Russian power could be extended to the whole of Germany, so much the better; but this wider aim can never have seemed more than problematical after the first few disordered months of peace. So long, however, as it remained a possibility, the Russians favoured a strong central government for Germany in the hope that it would be captured by the Socialist Unity Party (SED – an attempt to create a left wing party under communist control and prevent the operation of a distinct socialist party). They only abandoned this sub-policy after it bécame evident that a united Germany would no more be a communist Germany in the nineteen-forties than it had been after 1918. They thereupon switched not to a federal solution for Germany as a whole but to a two-Germanies policy. The supporters of federation, meaning thereby a federation with a weak central government, were the French. Incapable themselves of imposing any control over Germany and dubious of their allies' capacity to do so for long, the French wanted a weak German state, disarmed and disabled by internal political fragmentation. They also wanted coal for their own reconstruction plans and the Saar. Their changes in policy came in stages: first, Georges Bidault, when foreign minister, reluctantly acknowledged the hostility between the USSR and the western allies, threw France's lot in with the latter and accepted the establishment of a new western German state, including the French zone; next, Robert Schuman sought, in a wider European context, to win German friendship rather than insure against German hostility, and René Pleven, in the same context, accepted the rearmament of Germany; finally de Gaulle, developing Schuman's policy of reconciliation without the European framework, concluded with Schuman's old colleague, Konrad Adenauer, a bilateral Franco-German alliance.

In the three years after the Potsdam conference the occupiers, having failed to produce a coherent German policy, drifted away from the notion of Germany as something to be constrained to the notion of Germany as something to be acquired, from a basically collaborative to a basically competitive position. Two conferences of foreign ministers in 1947, at Moscow in March and at London in November, failed to elaborate the peace treaty which was supposed to emerge. In the same year, which was also the year of the Truman Doctrine and the Marshall Plan, the American and British zones were fused (January) and endowed with an economic council of fifty-four members (May). In the next year the Americans and the British moved determinedly towards turning their joint zone into a solvent and autonomous parliamentary democracy. The economic council was doubled in size and given a second chamber; a plan was produced for the internationalization of the Ruhr in order to counter the fears of those who found it difficult to stomach the reappearance of a sovereign German state; in June the Americans and the British devalued the mark in their zones, a long discussed and necessary reform which the Russians had obstructed by appealing to the principle of economic unity; in September a constituent assembly met in Bonn. These steps were supplemented in April 1949 when the French zone was joined with the Anglo-American. But meanwhile the Russians decided to challenge the whole western policy of separate development of a western German state. They chose Berlin where their position was special and strong.

Berlin had been excluded from the zonal system and placed under a

separate, joint allied authority, the Kommandatura. For practical purposes the city was divided into four sectors but these sectors did not
have the administrative autonomy of the zones. But the Russian position in Berlin was distinct for two reasons. It was the Russians who first
entered the city, occupying it a few days before the German surrender
and setting about the business of clearing rubble, organizing rations,
installing new local authorities and establishing a police force before
the arrival of American or British units; and secondly, the drawing of
the zonal boundaries left Berlin an enclave within the Russian zone and
separated by 260 kilometres from the nearest point under British control. Subsequently there was much debate about the lack of foresight
and political sense of the western allies in allowing the Russians to
reach Berlin first and in accepting the virtual isolation of the city
without even securing clearly and formally defined rights of access to it.
Although something must be allowed for the temper and exigencies of
wartime collaboration (which had to be preserved to the last at almost
any cost), there can be little doubt that the Americans and the British
would have driven a different bargain if they had realized that they
were in effect handing Berlin over to the Russians subject only to the
right to be imprisoned within it.

Berlin was the central point of a Russian attempt to gain control of
Germany which, having started with auspicious expedition, quickly ran
into trouble. The socialists refused to submerge themselves in a single
party with the communists and promoted instead an anti-Russian
coalition which, in elections in October 1946, thwarted the Russian
design to place the city's administration in communist hands. In 1947
Ernst Reuter, an ex-communist socialist, was elected mayor in a symbolic contest in which the non-Russian occupiers were clearly, if still
discreetly, aligned with Reuter against the Russians and the communists. The independent political life of the city had revived before the
Russians had been able to impose a throttling substitute so that, while
the Russian strategic position remained strong, the Russian political
position had not thriven commensurately and the western occupiers
found themselves indebted to the anti-Russian activities of Berliners. In
return for this uncovenanted aid the western occupiers later felt obliged
to commit themselves to the maintenance of the independence of Berlin
from the Russian zone and its successor, the east German state or German Democratic Republic.

The steps taken by the western occupiers in 1947–48 to establish a
west German state threatened the Russian ambition to keep Germany
whole and turn it communist. They also foreshadowed the revival of an
independent German power in world politics, armed and hostile to the
USSR. The Russians decided to make a major issue of these
developments and to resort to force to stop them. They cut the road,
rail and water routes by which the western occupiers communicated
with Berlin and stopped food, electricity, gas and other necessities from
being supplied regularly to the western sectors from the east. The legal

right to use the routes uninterruptedly was vague – and also irrelevant in what was clearly a trial of strength. The western occupiers, having considered and rejected the possibility of asserting their rights by sending an armed convoy to force its way along the road from the British zone to the boundary of the city decided instead to pierce the Russian siege by air, thus placing the Russians in the position of having to fire a first shot. They also imposed a counterblockade on the Russian zone, and the Americans moved part of their long range bomber force to airfields in England. Between July 1948 and May 1949 the American and British air forces carried over 1.5 million tons of food, fuel and other goods into Berlin (the highest load in one day exceeded 12,000 tons), thus ensuring the needs of the entire civilian population of the blockaded sectors as well as their western guardians. This doubly extraordinary feat – extraordinary for what it did and extraordinary for doing it without leading to open hostilities – defeated the Russians, who abandoned the blockade in May after 318 days in return for a promise of one more conference on Germany (which was held in Paris but achieved nothing). After elections in August the German Federal Republic came into being on 20 September with its capital in Bonn and Dr Konrad Adenauer as its chancellor. Adenauer thereby agreed to postpone German reunification by joining the western camp. An occupation statute and a series of agreements (the Petersberg agreements) defined the relations between the new state and the western powers and imposed certain restrictions on its sovereignty, but these detailed provisions were of no importance compared with the transcendent fact that the greater part of Germany had been removed from the joint control of its conquerors and attached to a new anti-communist western alliance. Exactly a year after the inauguration of the Federal Republic its rearmament became a live issue: as a result of the outbreak of war in Korea in June 1950 the Americans persuaded themselves and, with more difficulty, their British and French allies and Adenauer (who was initially opposed) that the Federal Republic should contribute to the armament of the west.

3. The Frigid Fifties

The western alliance which was created to wage the cold war came into existence on 4 April 1949, during the blockade of Berlin. Two years earlier such an alliance would have seemed to most Europeans and Americans impossible because of the strength of the communist parties of France and Italy, but during 1947 communists were excluded from the government of these two countries and the belief that they were ungovernable without communist participation was proved false. The North Atlantic Treaty was an association of twelve states which declared that an armed attack on any one of them in Europe or North America would be regarded as an attack on them all, and that each would in such an event go to the help of the ally attacked by taking such action, including the use of force, as it deemed necessary. The area covered by the treaty was defined as the territories of any signatory in Europe or North America, Algeria and islands, vessels or aircraft of any signatory in the Atlantic north of the tropic of Cancer; the treaty would also be brought into operation by an attack on the occupation forces of any signatory in Europe. Greece and Turkey joined the alliance in 1952 and the German Federal Republic in 1955. The creation of Nato was an affirmation of the dissolution of the wartime alliance. It was a defensive gesture by the principal western powers based on fear of Russian aggression, revulsion against the fact and the nature of Russian domination in eastern Europe, frustration turning to hostility in German affairs, the exposure of western Europe as a result of war damage and demobilization, and the failure to internationalize the control of atomic energy.

In 1945 the American war-making capacity had been supreme even without nuclear weapons, but in the next years a new pattern was created by American demobilization. While American supremacy was guaranteed by the nuclear bomb, the Russians, by not demobilizing, established a superiority in mobilized land power in Europe. Thus, all future attempts to disarm were bedevilled by the impossibility of comparing like with like; the defence of western Europe became dependent on nuclear power and nuclear strategy and ultimately the collective defence of western Europe provoked dissension about inter-allied control over nuclear weapons. Whereas in 1945 there had been some qualms and, on the Russian side, some hopes of an American retreat from Europe, four years later the United States was formally committed to a dominant role in European affairs for the next twenty years. Realizing too late what had been brought about, Stalin proposed in 1948 the withdrawal of all foreign troops from Germany, but his offer was regarded as a mere device to make the Americans take a long journey from which they would not return while the Russians remained within striking distance of Germany. So long as Germany was debatable ground the United States would remain on it. Hence western Germany's eventual place in Nato alongside its recent enemies.

The cold war was a very short episode in the history of Europe but it assumed at the time an air of permanence owing to the metaphors of frigidity and rigor in which it was discussed. Its two principal features were apparent in 1946 in the speeches by Churchill at Fulton, Missouri, in February in Truman's presence and by Truman's Secretary of State, James F. Byrnes, at Stuttgart in September. These speeches showed that the tripartite wartime alliance was being replaced by a new pattern of two against one and that the United States, so far from turning its back on Europe (and in spite of the reduction of American forces in Europe from 2.5 million men to fewer than half a million at the date of the Fulton speech), regarded Europe as an essential American sphere of influence. Although Truman had to accept virtual exclusion from central and eastern Europe, he secured by the Truman Doctrine of March 1947 a foothold in the Balkans and the Middle East at the time when he was preparing to consolidate anti-communist and anti-Russian positions in western Europe by a combination of economic aid and military alliance – embodied in the Marshall Plan and the North Atlantic Treaty. These were the beginnings of the policy of containment, designed to curb Russian power and change the Russian mood, but little more than a year after the signing of the North Atlantic Treaty this essentially European policy was complicated by a distant event, the outbreak of war in Korea, which became a drain on the forces available for containment in Europe and converted containment from a European to a more nearly global policy.

The Korean war also embittered the atmosphere. In the United States it was treated as evidence to fortify the myth of a masterly communist conspiracy to conquer the world. Senator Joseph McCarthy, alleging that this conspiracy extended into the United States government itself and other centres of influence, conducted a buoyant and repellent smear campaign in which he and his associates intimidated important segments of the public service by denouncing as communists (or homosexuals) anybody who did not subscribe to their extreme views of how loyal Americans ought to think: a number of Americans were driven into exile and some to suicide, and the formulation and conduct of American external policies were corrupted and demoralized before McCarthyism was anaesthetized by a few bold individuals, by its own excesses and by the residual good sense of the American people – without much help from their more supine elected leaders. This atmospheric pressure affected the American election campaign of 1952 in which the Republicans, in their bid to recapture the presidency for the first time since 1932, adopted General Eisenhower as their candidate. The principal Republican spokesman on foreign affairs was John Foster Dulles, soon to be Secretary of State.

McCarthyism apart there were grounds for questioning the Democrats' foreign policies. The United States was engaged in a grievous war; the USSR was not; containment seemed to mean peace for the Russians who, although prevented from expanding, remained unconstrained in their treatment of their satellites, whose fate bore uneasily on the American conscience. In his election speeches Dulles gave the impression that the Republicans would come to the aid of the enslaved people of eastern Europe and somehow liberate them from Russian domination. Containment was decried as negative and immoral. The Republicans won the election and the policy of liberation was rapidly forgotten. Instead Dulles proceeded with the policy of containment, filling the gap between Nato and the American position in Japan by fostering Seato (the South East Asia Organistion) and the Baghdad Pact. He also tried to escape from the frustrations of containment, which he had criticized for being a series of responses to Russian initiatives, by evolving a strategy of massive retaliation to be applied at times and places of American choosing. But when in Indo-China in 1954 the United States had the choice between massive retaliation and acquiescence in an ally's defeat it chose the latter and so acknowledged that massive retaliation contained a large element of bluff.

In Europe the cold war continued to revolve round the related themes of Germany and European security – the latter phrase being a cover name for the prevention of a war either by a renascent Germany or between the two blocks on account of it. The Americans successfully pursued their policy of annexing western Germany to Nato, accepting as a corollary the impossibility of dislodging the Russians from eastern Germany, which was turned into a satellite communist adjunct of the Russian empire in Europe. After passing through similar stages – an economic council, a parliament, a constitution, the election of a president (Wilhelm Pieck) and prime minister (Otto Grotewohl) – the eastern zone became in March 1954 a separate state under the name of the German Democratic Republic. The integration of western Germany into the western camp involved the end of the occupation and the negotiation of agreements which would both ally the Federal Republic with other western states and allow the latter some control over German rearmament. The three principal western powers offered to terminate their occupation of the Federal Republic if it would join a European Defence Community in which national forces would be subject to international control, and in May 1952 a convention was signed at Bonn ending the occupation and a European Defence Treaty was signed the next day. Elections in 1953 gave Adenauer's Christian Democratic Union and its Bavarian counterpart the Christian Social Union, a two to one victory and in 1954 the Federal Republic ratified the European Defence Treaty. The French parliament, however, refused to ratify the treaty and a fresh scheme had to be elaborated. The Paris agreements of October 1954 created a Western European Union (Britain, France and the Benelux Countries, which had been associated by treaty since 1948 and were now joined by Italy and the Federal Republic); and, with the ending of the occupation confirmed, the Federal Republic joined Nato. With the necessary ratifications of these agreements in May 1955 the Federal Republic became an almost fully fledged member of the western alliance. It foreswore the manufacture of nuclear, bacteriological and chemical weapons and accepted a form of inspection over industrial concerns. In return it got a reiterated pledge on reunification, the recognition of the government in Bonn as the government of the whole of Germany, and the privilege of contributing twelve divisions to Nato's forces.

These developments were strenuously opposed by the Russians who tried a variety of expedients to prevent the adherence of the Federal Republic to Nato. In 1952 they were willing to accept a degree of German rearmament if it were accompanied by neutralization; they proposed, to a sceptical west, a mutual withdrawal from Germany. In June 1953, however, shortly after Stalin's death, risings in the eastern sector of Berlin and in cities in the eastern zone, directed against too much work for too little pay and against political imprisonments, found the east German régime so helpless that it had to be helped and preserved by Russian troops. The USSR became therefore committed to the maintenance of the men whom it had salvaged, and at the same time aware of the hopelessness of supposing that any sort of Germany would be pro-Russian. The rising and its suppression strengthened the argument for holding on to what one had.

Upon the death of Stalin in March 1953 Churchill thought he saw an opportunity to arrest the collision course of the two alliances. In keeping with his own predilections in international diplomacy he proposed a personal meeting of heads of government, but the temper of the times was inimical, the Americans (and many in Britain) cool, the west Germans suspicious, and Churchill himself soon afterwards suffered a stroke. The rising in eastern Germany in June encouraged those in the west who preferred to wait for the USSR to get into deeper trouble, and presumably discouraged those in the USSR who may have been disposed to try more conciliatory policies.

Stalin's successors were faced with crucial decisions in defence policy. The growth of Russian nuclear power had outmoded the Stalinite reliance on a satellite glacis and large non-nuclear forces, but there was no settled doctrine about the best way to exploit and deploy nuclear power or about its economic consequences. G. M. Malenkov, Stalin's successor as prime minister, argued that nuclear weapons had made war impracticable and that more should be spent on consumer goods. N. S. Khrushchev, the first secretary of the Communist Party and Malenkov's rival, argued, from conviction or because he wanted military support, that everything must be subordinated to strengthening the retaliatory striking power of the armed forces. In 1955 a new Air Defence Command was created and in the succeeding years the strength of the army was cut from 5.8 to 3.6 million men. A further cut of 1.2 million men was announced on 1 January 1960 but in 1961 policy was changed and the reduction postponed, presumably as a result of military pressure. This was therefore a period of debate, reorganization and consequent vulnerability. The corollary was a cautious and comparatively amiable foreign policy. The German and Austrian problems were brought to the conference table, as were also Korea, where an armistice had been signed in July 1953, and Indo-China. Bulganin and Krushchev made their peace with Tito, surrendered Porkkala in Finland and Port Arthur, put forward new disarmament proposals, visited India, Burma, Afghanistan (the first non-communist recipient of Russian aid) and Britain, and repaired in July 1955 to a meeting at Geneva with the American president and the British and French prime ministers. This so-called summit meeting was a demonstration in favour of relaxing the cold war. It produced some euphoric notions – a non-aggression treaty between Nato and the Warsaw pact, proposed by the USSR; a free-inspection zone, proposed by Eden; and an open-skies survey, proposed by Eisenhower. An ancillary conference of foreign ministers, designed to give point and precision to the Geneva atmosphere, was a failure and this first attempt to thaw the cold war was brought to nought by the Polish and Hungarian revolts of 1956. But the leaders had met and had set an example of decent manners and the pursuit of tolerance.

In relation to Germany Stalin's successors toyed with schemes for reunification, evacuation and neutralization, but in the knowledge that the Americans were committed to two propositions unacceptable to the USSR: reunification by means of free elections and not by sticking the two Germanies together (which the Russians wanted and which entailed treating the Federal Republic and the much smaller and undemocratically constituted Democratic Republic as equals), and freedom for the reunified state to make alliances (i.e. to join Nato). At a conference in Berlin at the beginning of 1954 Eden and Molotov produced plans which demonstrated the impossibility of reaching agreement. Eden proposed reunification in five stages: free elections, a constituent assembly, a constitution, an all-German government and a peace treaty. Molotov seemed ready to agree to elections on certain conditions but wanted also a fifty-year European security treaty (with, it was later explained, the United States as a party) with a ban on joining other alliances; that is to say, he dropped the earlier Russian method of reunification in a bid to secure the dissolution of Nato. When this plan failed the USSR even suggested that it should join Nato. In 1955 Bulganin and Khrushchev agreed to the evacuation and neutralization of Austria, and by the State Treaty of that year Austria recovered its full sovereignty within its January 1938 borders, subject only to two prohibitions: no *Anschluss* with Germany and no alliance with either side in the cold war. (Since by the Warsaw treaty of the same year the USSR acquired the right to station troops in Hungary and Rumania, it lost nothing strategically by renouncing its post-war rights in occupied Austria and the concomitant rights of access through adjacent territories.) But Bulganin and Khrushchev secured no comparable arrangement for Germany, even though they recognized the Federal Republic and exchanged ambassadors with it. The attempt to stop the rearmament of the Federal Republic as a part of the anti-Russian alliance had failed. In the same year the Russians created a counterpart to Nato by the Warsaw treaty and in 1956 the German Democratic Republic became a member of it.

In the fifties both sides exploded a thermonuclear or hydrogen bomb, the Americans in November 1952 and the Russians (who had exploded their first atom bomb in 1949) nine months later. Despite the Russian advances the Americans retained their supremacy until about 1953 owing to their superior capacity to deliver, by aircraft or rockets, the atomic weapons which both sides now possessed. The Russians, however, rapidly developed their means of delivery so that a mutual deterrence ruled the mid-fifties and by 1958 the USSR was leading in the race to produce long-range missiles. American stocks, however, were at all times very much greater than Russian stocks. In order to meet the Russian superiority in non-nuclear weapons – a superiority which threatened to force the Nato powers either to suffer defeat in a non-nuclear war in Europe or to turn it into a nuclear war – the Americans pressed their allies to rearm and become the non-nuclear segment of the alliance. At a meeting in Lisbon in May 1952 the Nato council adopted a plan to create forces, including German units, capable of fighting a prolonged non-nuclear war, but the plan was never implemented and was replaced from 1954 onwards by the equipment of Nato units with small nuclear weapons. This change in strategy was made possible by the invention of smaller, so-called tactical nuclear weapons and by the elaboration of a doctrine to the effect that these weapons could stop a non-nuclear attack without starting a full-scale nuclear war, bombs and all. This doctrine had a short life and became discredited at about the time (1961) when tactical nuclear weapons were coming into service with units in Europe in effective quantities; by then they were adjudged to be more nuclear than tactical and likely to evoke nuclear responses of greater and greater weight. The debate on them in the late fifties served only to distract attention from the need for non-nuclear forces and to leave Nato at the end of it still dependent on the threat of massive retaliation by the heavy nuclear forces of the American Strategic Air Command, which was not itself part of Nato.

The creation of Nato, the western victory over Berlin and the establishment and arming of a western German state were accompanied by the abandonment in 1953 of the pretence that disarmament discussions were serving a practical purpose; they were dropped. Palliatives were sought in disengagement, demilitarization and other forms of arms control. Disengagement, i.e. putting a distance between opposing war machines by a mutual retreat from advanced positions, was attractive for a variety of reasons: it might minimize the risk of unpremeditated clashes, it might prove to be a successful experiment in local disarmament which could be repeated on a larger scale, and it might lessen political tensions in the centre of Europe and so lead towards a solution of the German problem. In 1955 Eden proposed limitations on forces in Germany and (unnamed) neighbouring states together with a system of inspection and verification controlled by a reunited German state and its four previous occupiers. Eden also proposed a European experiment in demilitarization, beginning with a zone along Germany's eastern borders, and added a few days later as an experiment in arms control a plan for mixed inspection teams on both sides of the division between eastern and western Europe. These ideas were not well received by the Americans or the west Germans whom Eden apparently failed to consult in advance and who objected to the implied recognition of the German Democratic Republic. Russian proposals presented by Gromyko in 1956 and 1957 for a zone of limitation and inspection were rejected on the same grounds. Similar plans were advanced by the leader of the British parliamentary opposition, Hugh Gaitskell. He proposed a gradual thinning out of foreign forces in the two Germanies, Poland, Czechoslovakia and Hungary and a ban on nuclear weapons throughout the same zone; the two Germanies would be reunited, the Federal Republic would withdraw from Nato and the three eastern states from the Warsaw military alliance. Finally, in 1957 the Polish foreign minister Adam Rapacki, with Russian backing, proposed at the General Assembly (and later elaborated in written form) a plan to prohibit the manufacture and presence of nuclear weapons in both Germanies. He promised that Poland would follow suit, and the Czechoslovak government promised to do so too. The Rapacki plan dealt only with nuclear weapons in a specified area and did not overtly attack the surrounding political issues – the reunification of Germany, the freedom of Germany to join alliances, the presence of considerable American and Russian forces in central European states, the balance of American and Russian power in Europe which would be unsettled by the removal of American nuclear forces without a corresponding withdrawal of Russian non-nuclear forces. It was rejected by the United States in May 1958. Disengagement was thereupon dropped from the political agenda. It had been defeated by the entirely opposite trend of arming the two Germanies as separate contributions to the strength of the forward positions of the two rival blocks, by western fears of the USSR's large non-nuclear forces, by the Nato policy of putting nuclear weapons into forward positions, and by inexperience and distrust of methods of inspection and verification. The fortification of the alliances had priority over the dismantling of them.

4. The Thaw and Cuba

In the USSR Stalin's death in 1953 was followed by an interlude of three years. The communist party had held its nineteenth congress in the previous year after an unconstitutional delay of thirteen years, probably occasioned by the simple fact that the party leaders needed time after the war to set many houses in order. Although nobody knew how nearly Stalin's death was approaching, the succession was inevitably uppermost in all minds. By his handling of the congress's business Stalin indicated a definite preference for G. M. Malenkov who, having outlived A. A. Zhdanov, looked like outpointing his most serious rival N. S. Khrushchev. Zhdanov's death in 1948 had been followed in 1949 by a purge of his associates; the older men had been regressing for some years and the two most eminent among them, Molotov and Mikoyan, had lost their ministerial posts (though not their other positions) in 1949; Lavrenti Beria too, the police chief, seemed somewhat less favoured and less powerful in the early fifties despite his control over a police force of 1.5 million men and a militia of

300,000. Then in January 1953 nine doctors, seven of them Jews, were accused of complicity in the death of Zhdanov. This so-called doctors' plot, which was itself declared to be a baseless plot after Stalin's death, combined anti-semitism with an attack on Zhdanov's enemies, and it was no secret that Zhdanov's principal enemy was the man who had most markedly profited by his death, Malenkov. When therefore Stalin died in March 1953 Malenkov's position was less promising than it had seemed a year ealier, but it was still strong enough to ensure his succession to the top posts in both government and party. The evidence suggests that Malenkov's initial victory was secured in alliance with Beria but it did not last long. Malenkov and Beria may have had some similar ideas, notably in helping the consumer industries at the expense of heavy and armaments industries, but Beria was an exceptionally unpopular man, personally and *ex officio*, and for Malenkov the support of the country's chief policeman was offset by the hostility of the armed services which disliked both Beria's private army and Malenkov's economic policy. Soon after the end of the war Stalin, who did not see himself as a Bonaparte and did not want any Bonapartes around, had set about putting the army and its leaders safely back in a position of subordination to the civil power but in the struggle for power after his death the army was inevitably a major counter and Krushchev, who had military friends from his days as a commissar on the Stalingrad front, decided to use it.

At first he did not have to. The devolution of Stalin's entire position on any one man was more than any of the principal civilian leaders, except Malenkov himself and possibly Beria, was prepared to tolerate. Power was almost immediately divided. Malenkov was forced to choose between being head of the government and head of the party. He chose the former and ceded the latter post to Khrushchev. The antagonism of the two men was thus institutionalized. Two teams of five faced one another. Malenkov and four others formed the top layer of government while Khrushchev and four others constituted the party secretariat. This position lasted until 1955 when Khrushchev defeated Malenkov, partly by reviving rumours of Malenkov's complicity in Zhdanov's death and the subsequent purge and by accusing Malenkov of conspiring with Beria to establish personal instead of collective rule on Stalin's death – charges which alienated party feeling from Malenkov – and partly by manufacturing a war scare which created the alliance between himself and the army. In February 1955 Khrushchev secured the removal of Malenkov and the substitution at the head of the government of Bulganin who was destined to stay there as long as Khrushchev felt it inopportune to claim the post for himself. Bulganin was succeeded at the ministry of defence by Marshall G. K. Zhukhov. Other changes were made at top ministerial level where there seemed to be a shift from political veterans to technical experts, although the chopping and changing of these years more probably reflected uncertainties and inconsistencies in economic planning.

Khrushchev's victory was secured in spite of mistakes on his part and not owing to their absence. After Stalin's death he had been put in charge of agriculture and had turned to central Asia for a solution of the USSR's most consistent failure. His policy of exploiting the virgin lands of Kazakhstan was radical and sound but disastrously applied in the short run. Nevertheless his political acumen and mobility enabled him to survive both this setback and, for several years thereafter, the disfavour and machinations of his colleagues who, after forcing Malenkov into the shadows, discovered that Khrushchev was at least as keen on personal authority and impatient with the committee system. The elder statesmen in the party decided therefore to remove Khrushchev from his position at its head. They secured a large majority against him in the presidium of the central committee, but he succeeded in appealing to the central committee itself, where, with the help of his continuing alliance with the army, he got the vote reversed. His enemies, who were united in little except dislike of him and his methods, were publicly attacked and demoted. Even Molotov, the oldest of old bolsheviks and the man who was second only to Stalin among the civilians who had directed the war against the Germans, was disgraced and virtually exiled along with other veterans like Voroshilov and Kaganovich. Malenkov's decline was further precipitated and Khrushchev's mastery was so complete by 1957 that he felt able to drop Zhukov from his government.

In 1956 the congress of the communist party of the Soviet Union, assembled for its twentieth session, was astonished to hear, first from Mikoyan and then from Khrushchev, wide-ranging and vehement denunciations of Stalin and Stalinism reaching back to what Lenin's wife had said more than thirty years earlier and to the murder of Kirov of 1934. This repudiation of the past, which did not long remain secret and included a specific undertaking to revise the USSR's relations with its satellite neighbours, encouraged anti-Russian feeling and contributed to risings in Poland and Hungary. In Poznan there were strikes for better wages in June and admissions of social unrest. At the same time a conflict arose within the Polish communist party between the faction of Boleslaw Bierut, who had died earlier in the year, and the more nationalist or Titoist faction led by Wladyslaw Gomulka, who had recently been released from a prison to which he had been consigned after being disgraced in 1949. In July Khrushchev, Bulganin and other Russian leaders went suddenly to Warsaw and vehemently invaded discussions in the Central Committee of the Polish party. They were, however, unable to prevent the victory of the Gomulka faction. Gomulka was appointed first secretary and the Russians, discovering that they must choose between allowing Gomulka to take over the government and using force to prevent it, chose the former course and accepted changes which included the dismissal of the defence minister, the Russian Marshall Rokossovsky.

In Hungary the nature of the disturbances and their outcome were different. In July the established rulers, Matyas Rakosi and Erno Gerö, went to Moscow to urge reforms in order to forestall trouble. In October demonstrators demanded better wages and liberty. Hungarian police and Russian troops failed to prevent these demonstrations from turning into an anti-communist revolution. Imre Nagy, who had been prime minister from Stalin's death to 1955, was reinstated. Mikoyan and Suslov arrived from Moscow to direct operations and decided to back Janos Kadar, the reasonably well-regarded first secretary of the communist party who represented a compromise between the Rakosi/Gerö team and Nagy, but the revolution gained strength and at the same time the Russians found themselves confronted with the risks and opportunities of a war in the Middle East provoked by the Anglo–French attack on Nasser. After withdrawing their troops from Budapest for tactical reasons they resorted to full-scale military measures to suppress the revolution. Faced with this turn of events Kadar sided with the Russians while Nagy named a new coalition government, promised free elections, proposed to take Hungary out of the Warsaw Pact and appealed to the outside world for help. With the western powers enmeshed at Suez and the USSR vetoing UN action, the revolution was extinguished in the first week of November. The reality of Russian power was underlined by the fact that the American administration not only took no action but never looked as though it might.

These events were a setback both for Khrushchev and for the policy of east-west rapprochement. Both, however, recovered. In June 1957 Khrushchev was attacked by Malenkov in the presidium of the communist party and defeated on a vote, but he resiliently summoned a meeting of the central committee which expelled Malenkov from the presidium together with Molotov and Kaganovich. In October Zhukhov was replaced by Marshal Malinovsky. This year saw the triumph of Khrushchev over his adversaries and over the doctrine of collective leadership. In March 1958 he became prime minister as well as first secretary and he remained predominant until his unexpected fall in October 1964. He reaped the benefit, in external affairs, of the dramatic appearance – in August and October 1957 – of the first intercontinental ballistic missile and the first earth satellite (sputnik). From a platform thus fortified, and observing the alarm in the United States at the thought that the American technological lead had been eliminated, Khrushchev adopted peaceful co-existence as a general description of his intentions. Peaceful co-existence was a benevolent and reassuring (but not new) political slogan of vague purport and useful variability. It could indicate a greater or lesser degree of rapprochement at any given moment and was used by Khrushchev as a tool in a strategy of avoiding major conflicts, reducing prices at home, winning goodwill in the non-aligned countries and softening opinion within the United States. Since peaceful co-existence was a slogan rather than a policy it was liable to recede at moments of special opportunity or special nervousness – at the appearance, for example, of the enticing prospect of turning Cuba into a Russian missile base in 1962, or when American reactions looked alarming over Syria in 1957, Iraq in July 1958 and China in September 1958.

The Berlin crisis of November 1958 is not easy to interpret in this context. The forcing of the issue may have owed something to Chinese insistence. Throughout the year exchanges about and between the two Germanies had been clouding the atmosphere and the Poles, disappointed by the failure of the Rapacki plan and unable to rid themselves of their German phobia, were urging the Russians to find a way of preventing the Federal Republic from becoming a nuclear power and osbtructing its potential capacity for making mischief in association with Nato. Khrushchev himself was anxious to secure wider recognition of the German Democratic Republic in order to stabilize the map of Europe and so facilitate the reduction of Russian military commitments abroad and the progress of his policy of rapprochement. He chose to threaten to transfer the USSR's authority in Berlin to the German Democratic Republic unless a solution of the German problem were found within six months. The western occupiers contented themselves with controverting the USSR's right to act as it proposed, and the ultimatum was first toned down in March 1959 and then died a natural death at the end of May.

The failure of this gambit, coupled with Khrushchev's growing conviction that the United States did not intend to attack the USSR, and with the presentation to the twenty-first congress of the Communist Party in January 1959 of a seven-year economic plan which depended to some extent on switching funds from guns to butter, led to the second attempt to thaw the cold war. After a visit to Moscow by vice-president Richard Nixon, Khrushchev visited the United States, conferred privately with Eisenhower at Camp David, presented a plan for general and complete disarmament in four years to the General Assembly of the UN, and announced the second major cut in Russian military manpower. The centrepiece of the détente of 1959–60 was to have been a second summit conference in May 1960 but it was ruined by the shooting down of an American reconnaissance aircraft over Russian territory on 1 May. Reconnaissance flights by U-2 aircraft flying at great heights between bases in Norway and Pakistan provided the United States with militarily valuable information at no political risk so long as the aircraft were not intercepted and their missions not made public by either side. The American president either did not know about the flights or had not thought of cancelling them in the pre-conference weeks, and the Russian government either had not thought of telling its defences to stop trying to shoot them down in this delicate period or – a plausible alternative view – had ordered them to do so. False statements in Washington about the aircraft's mission only compounded the American discomfiture because they were quickly exposed by the Russians who had captured the pilot alive and with his spy kit. After the consequent failure of the Paris conference Khrushchev repeated, in Warsaw and Moscow, his belief in the policy of rapprochement, but for the time being practical progress had been halted by the U-2 as surely as it had been halted in 1956 by the Hungarian revolution and it was arguable that Khrushchev had deliberately engineered this stop on his own policies, possibly in response to pressures from military and pro-Chinese lobbies. His rapprochement with the United States affronted the Chinese, who did not share his view about American aggressive intentions, resented and feared Russo-American confabulations, and refused to be mollified when he went to Peking on his return from the United States. These views found some echo in the Kremlin. Further, Khrushchev's defence policy of relying on nuclear missiles and cutting non-nuclear forces was too bold for some of his colleagues and advisers. Although a Rocket Force Command was established under Marshal Nedelin (later succeeded by Marshal Moskalenko), the second cut was cancelled and at the twenty-first congress in October 1961 Malinovsky stated that he did not see eye to eye with Khrushchev. (This tussle was resumed in 1963–64 when cuts were again proposed and again opposed: Khrushchev was forced to promise that the cuts would be reasonable but his persistence was probably one of the causes of his downfall.) Finally, Khrushchev had discovered that his attempt to secure recognition of the German Democratic Republic by raising the Berlin question could be turned against him by the Americans, who proceeded to couple a settlement in Berlin with a general Russian withdrawal in Europe for which neither Khrushchev himself nor the ruling group in Moscow as a whole was yet ready.

After the dismal experiences of the fifties the next decade opened with mixed signals. The Russo-Chinese quarrel had become public property (it is examined in the next chapter) and was held to be an incentive to Russo-American accords. In Washington the Eisenhower era closed and was succeeded by the short presidency of John F. Kennedy, whose youth and intellect provided the greatest contrast to what had gone before and promised to reverse the decline in leadership and purpose which had depressed the fifties. A cease-fire was arranged in Laos, but in an encounter with Khrushchev in Vienna Kennedy made no great mark and may even have left Khrushchev with the impression that the omens were propitious for an anti-American stroke. At any rate Khrushchev gave permission for a new essay in Berlin.

The government of the German Democratic Republic was threatened with collapse. Its citizens were escaping from it at the rate of 1,000 a day, which was economically and psychologically ruinous. Its boss, Walter Ulbricht, had to act urgently in order to maintain his régime, while Khrushchev was probably persuaded that if he did not support Ulbricht the crisis in the German Democratic Republic would lead to a war in Germany. He accordingly gave his consent to the erection of a wall between the eastern sector and western sector in Berlin so that the eastern sector should become a part of the German Democratic

Republic and the western sector might be made too uncomfortable for continued western occupation. In the night of 12-13 August the wall was built and the flow of refugees virtually stopped. Kennedy had told Khrushchev a few weeks earlier in Vienna that the United States remained committed to the use of all necessary forces to defend the status and freedom of Berlin. The building of the wall was a provocative act which the United States accepted and which may have influenced Khrushchev's estimate of how far it was safe to provoke the United States: he himself was to venture much further than the east Germans in the next year in Cuba.

Kennedy inherited from his predecessor a Cuban problem which was initially a chapter in the relations between the United States and Latin America but not a chapter in the cold war. Its origins are described in Part Six of this book. In April 1961 Kennedy, pursuing a venture designed by the Eisenhower régime, aided an attempt by refugees to invade Cuba and overthrow Fidel Castro. It was immediately and totally unsuccessful. At some point thereafter Khrushchev, who was already giving Castro financial and diplomatic aid, decided on an audacious throw. Instead of merely helping Castro to remain in power, he decided to use Cuba to help the USSR, to convert it into a Russian base directly threatening the United States with Russian missiles. Surface-to-air missiles were despatched in the summer of 1962, followed by MiG 21 fighters, Il.28 jet nuclear bombers and ground-to-ground (i.e. offensive) missiles, of which forty-two out of a projected sixty-four arrived in late September or early October. The installation of these weapons put the United States for the first time under fire from close range and would have nearly doubled the number of bases or cities threatened by the USSR. Within three weeks of the beginning of the operation the Americans became aware of it, although it was not at first clear to them that the Russians were doing more than strengthening the defence of Cuba. The Russians assured Washington that this was indeed the case and that they had no offensive intentions, and in spite of disturbing tales from refugees close reconnaissance produced no contraverting evidence until the middle of October. On 14 October photographs showed a launching pad and one missile. Kennedy decided at once on his objective: the complete removal of Russian nuclear weapons from Cuba. The vital problem was how to achieve this objective without starting a nuclear war. It was assumed in Washington that action must be taken within about ten days. The obvious retort was an air strike but the objections were serious. Apart from the strong disinclination to open hostilities by using nuclear weapons in whatever circumstances, the president and his advisers were heavily conscious of the dangers of escalation and also of a Russian counterstroke against Berlin. Many of the Russian weapons were still on their way to Cuba by sea, and the secretary of defence, Robert McNamara, supported by the attorney-general, Robert Kennedy, proposed a naval blockade to prevent them reaching their destination and to force the Russians to remove what had already arrived. After long debate this plan, which had immediately appealed to the president, was adopted. It was explained by him to the public in a televised address and to his allies by special emissaries, and American ships of war moved into the path of the vessels bearing the Russian missiles westward. The first Russian response was to repeat that the weapons were defensive and to denounce the blockade. A clash seemed imminent. Then the president, on the suggestion of his close friend the British ambassador, Lord Harlech, moved his line of interceptors southward in order to give Khrushchev a little extra time to think and act. Khrushchev decided not to accept the challenge. The leading ships were reported slackening speed. One innocuous tanker was allowed to pass through the line unsearched and proceed upon its way. The other ships turned back. In the Security Council Adlai Stevenson confronted the Russian and other delegates with photographic proof of the threat against which the United States had acted. On the high seas and in the council chambers of the world the triumph of the United States was complete.

It was also controlled. In the choice of method and in the ensuing diplomatic exchanges Kennedy was careful to leave Khrushchev the openings for the retreat which the Americans aimed to enforce. The dramatic element was intense to the end. Khrushchev signified his surrender in a letter to Kennedy in which he averred once more that the deliveries of arms were a defensive measure; he said that they had been completed and that, if the United States would promise not to invade Cuba and would raise the blockade, the USSR would see no need for a Russian presence in Cuba. Here was the recognition of the Monroe Doctrine which the Americans wanted. But almost at once a second message arrived from Moscow. In it Khrushchev demanded not only an American undertaking not to attack Cuba but also the removal of American missiles from Turkey in return for the removal of Russian missiles from Cuba. Kennedy wanted no bargaining, only a clear cut decision on the Cuban issue in isolation. After a brief period of consternation the attorney-general suggested that the second letter was in reality an earlier one which had got delayed and should be ignored. The president accordingly replied to the first letter, accepting its general tenor and agreeing to open negotiations on the basis that all construction work in Cuba be stopped. This message, sent on 27 October, was accepted on the next day by Khrushchev who agreed to ship the Russian missiles back to the USSR.

The Cuban crisis of October 1961 coincided – perhaps not fortuitously – with a Chinese attack on India, and both these operations contributed to the deterioration of Russo-Chinese relations. The Chinese accused Khrushchev of foolhardiness in Cuba, and the Russians were embarrassed by Chinese action against the most important of the neutrals which the USSR was wooing. Khrushchev, who had already delivered a public attack on China in October 1961 during the 22nd Party Congress, was therefore less deterred than he may have been in 1960 from pursuing a rapprochement with the United States in spite of China and China's friends in the Kremlin. Moreover the demonstrations of American intransigence over Berlin and determination over Cuba were not the only reasons for reverting to a soft line. The assumption in the late fifties that there was a missile gap – i.e. that the Russians had gained a quantitative advantage over the Americans – was by 1961 known to be false not only by the Russians themselves but also by the Americans whose air reconnaissance had laid bare Russian deployment; and although Major Yuri Gagarin was cast into space in April 1961 ten months before the first American astronaut Colonel John Glenn, the early sixties were marked by a considerable expansion of American nuclear power as Polaris and Minuteman rockets came into service. The principal effect of the myth of the missile gap had been to intensify American efforts with the result that the American stock of intercontinental missiles had risen by the end of 1962 to about 500 as against a presumed Russian stock of about 75, and the United States had therewith become capable of threatening military targets instead of (the less credible threat) centres of population. The Americans were in the lead and staying there, and an aggressive Russian policy was more likely to increase the lead than diminish it. The argument for more butter and fewer guns gained ground, since it seemed more practicable to reduce western strength and deployment in Europe by negotiation than by an arms race. The circumstances were once more propitious for a détente. It took the form, at Russian suggestion, of purposeful disarmament discussions which achieved a modest success.

5. Disarmament and Arms Control

The history of post-war disarmament discussions is one of futility until the end of the fifties. In 1946 the United States propounded the Baruch plan for the complete international ownership and control of the sources of nuclear energy and the transfer of American stocks to an international body. The UN Atomic Energy Committee reported that such a plan was technically practicable. It was, however, politically unattainable at that date. In the same year the USSR presented its counter-proposals for a ban on the manufacture and use of nuclear weapons and the immediate destruction of existing ones (which were exclusively American). The Russian demand for immediate destruction was unacceptable to the Americans who insisted that the creation of international machinery must come first. The American and Russian plans were also irreconcilable in other respects. The USSR accepted the principle of international control but rejected international ownership. The USSR conceded that an international authority created to supervise international control should proceed in some matters by majority vote and without a veto, but it insisted that any proposed enforcement action must be subject to a veto. In the Russian view an international convention should be reinforced by domestic legislation in each of the states signing the treaty but not by any transfer of sovereign powers to an international organ empowered to carry out inspections and to observe whether the convention was being honoured. Inspection was not entirely ruled out by the USSR but was to be limited to the inspection of proclaimed nuclear establishments, excluding any search for clandestine activities. These attitudes reflected the strategic realities of the moment. So did contemporary controversy over the reduction of non-nuclear weapons, the United States wishing to link disarmament of this kind with an agreement on nuclear weapons, while the USSR urged a proportionate reduction of forces (by one third) which would alter the level of armaments without disturbing the relative strengths of states in these types of armament. In 1949 the USSR exploded its first nuclear weapon and in the next year it abandoned the UN Disarmament Commission (created in 1948 by fusing its Atomic Energy and Conventional Armaments Commissions). There were now two nuclear camps and the one – perhaps under the distracting impact of Mao Tse-tung's victories in China and the Korean war – was displaying a marked lack of interest in international discussions about disarmament. Nevertheless in 1951 the United States, Britain and France tried to revive these discussions. The Baruch plan was tacitly dropped but the Russians spurned western proposals, maintained their opposition to international intervention in their internal affairs and seemed still resolute in preserving their advantage in non-nuclear armaments. In 1952 the three western powers proposed quantitative limits for the armed manpower of all states, but it was not until after the death of Stalin, the end of the Korean war and the explosion of the first Russian hydrogen bomb that any progress was discernible. By this time advancing technology and, in the United States, the search for a new strategy by a new administration had produced a diversification of nuclear weapons, large and small, and intensive testing of them. These tests led in turn to worldwide alarm about the effects of radio-active fallout, especially after American tests in the Pacific in 1954 which were believed to have killed some Japanese fishermen, poisoned vast numbers of fish and infected an area of some 7,000 square miles. In 1954 Britain and France proffered a new graduated plan which was designed to reconcile the differing American and Russian priorities in a step-by-step disarmament process. This initiative had the effect of restarting negotiations. In the next year the Russians proposed a plan beginning with a reduction in conventional forces and then in nuclear stocks and leading to the elimination of bases on foreign soil, a cut-off in nuclear production, a ban on the use of nuclear weapons and a conference on a test ban treaty. The USSR also accepted quantitative manpower ceilings, thereby embarrassing the United States whose worldwide commitments demanded larger forces than those envisaged. The United States proposed in return higher ceilings (which would nevertheless have required some reduction in American forces) and an 'open skies' inspection licence whereby each side would keep the other under permanent observation from aircraft or satellites in orbit round the globe, but continued to press for an international control organ – even if subject to a veto – and rejected the idea of a ban on the use of nuclear weapons and the destruction of existing stocks. In the American view the time for prohibiting the use of nuclear weapons had gone by. The attempt, initiated by the Baruch plan, to insulate the science of war from the latest advances in physics had to be abandoned.

The negotiations of 1955 had no immediate outcome, partly because of preoccupations with the rearming of western Germany. This was followed in 1956–57 by abortive discussion of various plans for local disengagement in Europe (opposed by Adenauer) and arms control schemes advanced by the United States (for example, a cut-off in fuel production, reductions in force levels, controls over vehicle tests, an early warning system to be gradually extended to cover the whole world). Both sides offered surprisingly wide zones for aerial inspection and the Russians dropped their extreme demands for the removal of foreign bases, but for the western powers the allurements of disengagement and arms control were not sufficient to persuade them to arrest the re-arming of western Germany, shackle Nato's freedom of choice and put in issue the American presence in Europe. There was, however, in 1957 a cessation by tacit agreement of nuclear tests – partly a consequence of the satisfactory conclusion of series of American and Russian tests at this time – and some preliminary examination of the possibility of a more formal and permanent ban. Here too there was a serious gap between what was acceptable to the United States and what to the USSR: on the constitution of a control organ and the voting within it, on the manning of control posts by observers of foreign nationality, and on the number of onsite inspections to be carried out in any year in a specified area in order to ensure compliance with the ban. On all these matters the gaps between the protagonists were narrowed during discussions in 1958–60 but insufficiently to produce agreement before the destruction of the American U-2 reconnaissance aircraft over the USSR in May 1960 and the abandonment of the summit conference of that month temporarily ruffled the Russo-American rapprochement.

Concurrently with their approach to a test ban the two principal powers sponsored plans for general and complete disarmament. These totaly unrealistic and possibly dangerous schemes occupied a certain amount of debating time to the detriment of more fruitful topics but they may have had the compensating virtues of bringing attention back to the discredited subject of disarmament in general and of giving people new hope and new incentives. From the Russian point of view they were useful, and from the opposite point of view consequently embarrassing, because they focused popular opinion on favourite Russian objectives such as the withdrawal of foreign troops and bases rather than on the less spectacular topics of control and verification with which American and British negotiators were more particularly concerned. The Russian plan, presented by Khrushchev to the General Assembly of the UN in September 1959, was followed in March and June 1960 by two American statements. A ten-nation disarmament conference at Geneva in 1960 was shortlived but also the occasion for a joint Russo-American initiative in the shape of a series of recommendations elaborated by John J. McCloy and V. Zorin. No conference was held in 1961. The Americans and Russians agreed a set of principles but failed to agree on a statement about controls submitted by the Americans; both sides produced draft treaties on general and complete disarmament (the Russian was a revision of an earlier draft) in time for the autumn session of the General Assembly.

The high-water mark of these negotiations was the McCloy-Zorin recommendations. These consisted of a set of principles to govern continuing disarmament negotiations, beginning with the acceptance of general and complete disarmament as an ultimate goal. This document was in effect an agreed statement of what had to be agreed. It clarified the issues but did not resolve them. It predicated the need to establish reliable procedures for the peaceful settlement of disputes and the maintenance of peace; the retention by each state of adequate non-nuclear forces for the preservation of law and order; the disbanding of superfluous forces and the elimination of all nuclear, chemical and bacteriological weapons, all means of delivering weapons of mass destruction, all military training institutions and all military budgets; an agreed sequence of stages in the disarmament process, subject to verification at the conclusion of each stage; balanced measures to ensure that neither side secured a temporary advantage as disarmament proceeded; and strict and effective international control of the process and thereafter through an International Disarmament Organization within the framework of the UN. This visionary package required agreement on the order in which different operations would be carried out, agreement on the equivalence of different types of armament, and agreement on the nature and modes of operation of an inspectorate. Agreement on these and other points required a degree of trust which no political leader felt or could perhaps have evinced without incurring plausible charges of gambling with national security. The Russians, for example, accepted at one stage the principle of inspection, but it transpired that what was to be inspected was weapons destroyed and not weapons surviving; they were reluctant to disclose what was left through fear of having it attacked and destroyed. Ingenious schemes for circumventing this difficulty, such as Professor Louis Sohn's proposal to divide national territory into zones and give inspectors the right to search only a limited number of zones at defined intervals, did not suffice to overcome nationalist conservatism.

The crucial feature of the revived disarmament discussion was the problem of inspection and verification (an element which had not obtruded in earlier negotiations such as those which preceded the Washington Treaty of 1922, though it had engaged the attention of the disarmament conference of 1932, which proposed a Permanent Disarmament Commission with powers of inspection but no powers of enforcement). The evolution of nuclear weapons had enormously increased the dangerous consequences of allowing a party to a disarmament agreement to cheat and to conceal; he might by doing so gain the mastery of the world. But concealment was also regarded as one of the conditions of survival. To any power inspectors were potential spies who were licensed to discover and might then reveal how the inspected territory could be denuded of its defences at a blow. The impulses of politicians who took up disarmament for one reason or another were therefore continually countered by more cautious and short-term questionings which prevented the conclusion of any except partial agreements.

Partial agreements were, however, made. The cessation of nuclear tests in the atmosphere was an early example, which was matched in the same year by an agreement to neutralize the Antarctic continent. Tests were resumed by the Russians unilaterally in September 1961, chiefly because they had proceeded to a point at which they had something new which needed testing, but 1963 produced – in the aftermath of Cuba – a new and more extensive test ban agreement (as well as the installation of a direct and permanently open, or 'hot', line of communication between the White House and the Kremlin). When the Russians announced the resumption of tests, the Americans and British offered to conclude a treaty banning atmospheric tests without any provision for inspection, but the Russians were not to be deterred from their new series of tests and shortly afterwards the Americans resumed testing too. At the end of the year the Russians proposed a treaty banning all tests, subterranean as well as atmospheric, without inspection; this proposal was immediately rejected, and the three powers reported to the UN their failure to agree and the abandonment of their attempts to do so. Alarmed by this breakdown the UN resolved to convene yet another disarmament conference, this time with eighteen members including eight neutrals, an innovation inasmuch as neutrals had not previously participated in test ban discussions but only in discussions on general and complete disarmament. The French, who were in the earlier stages of developing a nuclear armoury of their own and had therefore no wish to ban tests, took no part in the proceedings, but the neutrals (Brazil, Burma, Egypt, Ethiopia, India, Mexico, Nigeria, Sweden) proved themselves valuably persistent in devising compromises and keeping the discussions going. The debate on inspection was resumed between the nuclear powers and was narrowed down to a question of numbers, the western powers ultimately refusing to go below seven a year and the Russians refusing to concede more than two or three. In the early part of 1963 the failure of the talks was generally expected but was avoided and then converted into success largely by the unobtrusive pertinacity of the British prime minister Harold Macmillan. Early in July Khrushchev hinted in a public speech that a partial ban might be agreed, and later in that month Averell Harriman and Lord Hailsham went to Moscow where the three powers agreed on the terms of a treaty banning nuclear tests in the atmosphere, in outer space and under water for an unlimited period but subject to the right of any party to withdraw from its undertakings if its supreme interests were jeopardized by extraordinary events connected with the subject matter of the treaty. Many other states adhered to the treaty. They did not include China or France.

The conclusion of this treaty raised the question of what to try next. It gave a fillip to the partial approach and therefore to the search for parts ripe for tackling. Lyndon B. Johnson, who had become president in the United States upon the assassination of Kennedy in November 1963, listed some topics early in the next year. They included an antiproliferation programme to include a total ban on nuclear tests, a ban on the transfer of nuclear materials to non-nuclear states and inspection of peaceful nuclear activities; a chain of observer posts to guard against surprise attack; a verified freeze on missiles; a verified cessation of the production of fissile material; and a ban on the use of force to alter boundaries or otherwise transfer territory from one state's control to another. Proposals from other quarters included a bomber bonfire (applying to B.47s and Tu.16s) and percentage cuts in military budgets. In Poland Gomulka recast and revived the Rapacki plan by proposing, in December 1963, a nuclear freeze in Europe, which however the Americans disliked partly because they attached little value to controls over the location of weapons unaccompanied by controls over their production and partly out of deference to the suspicions of their German allies.

These plans bore no immediate fruit for three reasons. First, the achievement of the test ban treaty was as much as the leaders on either side could for the time being digest and make palatable in their own countries. More might become possible, but not too soon. Secondly, discussions within Nato about joint control over nuclear dispositions and nuclear weapons roused eastern fears of a nuclear Germany. The United States was caught between the desire for a continuing dialogue and rapprochement with the USSR and the desire to accord to its most effective continental ally the status and the authority in allied councils and operations which its material contributions to the alliance warranted. To the Russians the proposed Nato multilateral force (MLF – see chapter 4) was a form of proliferation of nuclear weapons, although the Americans had devised it as an anti-proliferation policy to satisfy the Federal Republic and also France with something less than independent nuclear forces. And thirdly, the increasing American involvement in Vietnam (see chapter 16) put an additional strain on Russo-American relations. The American attempt to buttress an independent and non-communist South Vietnamese state entailed war against the Vietcong which ranked in communist terminology as a national liberation movement, and war against the communist state of

North Vietnam, and something like war against the vastly more important communist state of China. For the Russians to fail to support
President Ho Chi Minh of North Vietnam would be a betrayal of communist solidarity, dangerous at any time to Russian standing in the
communist world and doubly dangerous at a time when Russian
pre-eminence and doctrinal purity were being assailed by the Chinese.
Further, for the Russians to fail to support the Vietcong was again
doubly dangerous, for if the Vietcong lost communists would blame the
Russians, whereas if the Vietcong won without Russian help Chinese
influence might rout Russian influence in Asia and the Chinese would
be proved right in their contention, against the Russians, that wars of
national liberation could be fought without escalation into nuclear war.
When by 1965 the Americans had become unconcealed principals in
the war and not merely adjutants of the South Vietnamese, the scale
and the nature of the fighting were changed and the Americans had to
face worldwide protests against the ensuing horrors. The Russians joined in the outcry. Although, therefore, the evolution of nuclear strategies
and the resurgence of China and the passage of time had combined to
put an end to the bipolar cold war, the principal adversaries were
prevented by particular crises and by habit from acknowledging the
fact and acting on in more than very tentatively; only de Gaulle did
both.

    Nevertheless, whether by understanding or as a result of blinder
forces, a significant degree of stability and tolerance had evolved on the
biggest question of the time: whether the cold war would engender a
nuclear war. In the nuclear age peace could be preserved so long as
each side relied upon the threat of retaliation to keep the other side
from attacking first. But one side might conclude that the only way to
avert an attack was to attack first. It would then, using the modern version of the pre-nuclear blitzkrieg, adopt a counter force strategy and
build up, advertise and possibly use its power to destroy the enemy's
war-making capacity at a single blow. In order to neutralize this
strategy it was necessary to protect aircraft and missiles sites so effectively as to make it incredible that they could all be destroyed by a
first-strike surprise attack. Their protection by anti-aircraft and fighter
defences had been rendered obsolete by the enormous increase in the
destructive power of each single bomb and by the vastly increased
speed of missiles. In its place two new and extremely expensive forms of
defence were developed: missiles were placed in dispersed, hardened
sites and, in the case of Polaris, under the sea in submarines; and an
early warning system gave the defence enough time to get aircraft into
the air and to save them from being destroyed on the ground. Before the
appearance of the intercontinental missile an early warning of two to
three hours was achieved by the Americans, and when this was
rendered inadequate it was improved to half an hour, at which point a
part of the bomber force was kept always in the air and a part at fifteen
minutes' readiness on the ground. These measures to ensure the sur-

vival of an effective part of the retaliatory force, bombers and missiles, caused both antagonists to concentrate on second-strike strategies as a means of security. It was essential to the success of this attitude that each side should be seen by the other to have adopted it, and it was a consoling feature of the later years of the cold war that each side succeeded (with the help of the fact that a first-strike force differed in size and composition from a retaliatory force) in transmitting to the other tacit messages to this effect. The probability and danger of a surprise attack diminished.

Nuclear forces could, however, also be used in reply to a non-nuclear attack. The use of nuclear weapons was not ruled out by the reticence and deterrence of the two principal nuclear powers in relation to one another. Both could and did threaten to use them offensively in other contexts. In January 1954 Eisenhower and Dulles spoke on separate occasions of massive and instant retaliation. The last phase of the French war in Vietnam had begun and the Americans were faced with a choice between helping the French by a nuclear strike or letting them be finally beaten. The Americans tried to make political use of their nuclear armoury while knowing that they would not use it militarily; in a display of brinkmanship Dulles used tough language in order to scare the Russians and the Chinese and prevent them moving into the battle area – and perhaps in order to scare the British too and so get them to restrain him from a course from which he wanted to be diverted in any case. In 1956 Khrushchev, faced simultaneously with a war in the Middle East and a revolution in Hungary, made vague threats of using nuclear weapons in unspecified places in order to terrify the British and French governments and peoples and gain credit in the Arab world, and after the U-2 episode in 1960 he threatened smaller nations with nuclear attack if they facilitated American reconnaissance activities. But in the event both sides reserved their nuclear armaments for each other and became increasingly concerned not merely to keep nuclear weapons out of use but also to keep them out of other nations' hands. Yet one of the more sinister consequences of the cold war was the postponement, throughout the fifties and into the sixties, of the realization of this common interest until after two other powers, France and China, had become nuclear powers and a number of others had acquired the capability and, in the absence of an international control system, were also developing the will to follow suit. During the cold war the two protagonists had developed an increasing sobriety in relation to one another, and even a sort of fearful intimacy. There was, however, no reason to suppose that other possessors of nuclear weapons would acquire sobriety with might, or – if, for example, they were Israel and Egypt – would develop this intimate understanding of the permitted limits of nuclear politics; nor was there reason to suppose that the two giant powers would find it as easy to control the conflicts of others as to control their own.

These two problems – how to prevent a nuclear war between nuclear powers and how to prevent more states graduating to the nuclear élite – were aspects of the wider problem of arms control which superseded more traditional approaches to disarmament during the sixties. Arms control, the regulation as opposed to the elimination of the use of weapons of war, was not new. It had been applied particularly to naval weapons by, for example, the Rush–Bagot treaty of 1817 which barred navies from the Great Lakes, and by the Washington treaties of 1922 and 1930 which sought to limit the naval power of one state in proportion to that of another. Interest in similar schemes was revived in the nineteen-sixties by scepticism about general disarmament, and academic discussion of arms control was taken up by politicians in Washington and Moscow who were feeling the need to communicate with one another (as in the Cuba missiles crisis) or to co-operate with one another (as in the Middle East crises of the decade). The idea that major powers had more in common than the need to avoid mutual annihilation was further fortified by their common interest in their own superiority. Neither of them wanted to see nuclear weapons in any other states' armouries and in 1968 they, together with Britain, concluded a Nuclear Non-Proliferation Treaty to which they invited all other states to adhere. The object of this treaty was to freeze the existing nuclear hierarchy, keeping France and China in the grade of second rate nuclear powers and every other state permanently excluded from acquiring nuclear weapons. France and China predictably refused to sign. From the non-nuclear but potentially nuclear states there were sounds of discontent. Before subscribing to such an act of abnegation they objected that they should not be asked to forego modern weapons without a better prospect of escaping embroilment in a nuclear war and they urged the nuclear powers to balance their enthusiasm for non-proliferation by a more serious attempt to control their own arms race.

By 1975, when a reviewing conference was held in Geneva, ninety-six states had adhered to and ratified the treaty, but the omissions were more significant than the accessions. They included France and China; Japan; Israel and Egypt; India and Pakistan; South Africa; Argentina, Brazil and Chile. It was supposed that within another decade a dozen more countries would be able to make nuclear weapons, even if they did not do so. This capacity, although restrained by cost and perhaps by opinion, continued to proliferate. The necessary technology became more widespread and so did materials and engineering plant, largely as a consequence of a misguided American generosity which supposed it possible to endow other countries with nuclear capabilities without enabling them to make weapons.

Alarm at the spread of nuclear weapons was accompanied by alarm at the development of weapons technology. The MIRV (Multiple Independent Re-entry Vehicle), whose separately controlled multiple warheads greatly increased the threat from each missile; and ABM (Anti-Ballistic Missile) systems, which could counter a first strike and so destroy the deterrent stability which rested upon the presumptive efficacy of first strike, were enormously increasing the cost of the arms race. At the same time the deadliness of new missiles which were alleged to be capable of landing within a few dozen yards of a target, combined with new defences which could destroy incoming missiles only at the cost of removing the deterrent factor which was designed to prevent their discharge in the first place, inclined the super-powers to talk about the control of the use and development, as well as the proliferation, of nuclear weapons. Strategic Arms Limitation Talks (SALT) were begun in 1969.

Strategic arms may be defined in this context as weapons which can reach targets in an adversary's territory from bases or launching sites in one's own territory or on the high seas. They include missiles or bombs carried by long-range aircraft as well as missiles launched from static or mobile land sites or submarines. The category of strategic arms is therefore a complex one and it is further complicated by the fact that a single missile with many warheads, each of which can be independently directed to a different target, is far from being the equivalent of a missile with a single warhead that can hit one target only. There are furthermore two distinct and incompatible ways of calculating the effectiveness of a nation's strategic armoury. On the one hand it may be assessed by the number of enemy targets theoretically vulnerable, an assessment which involves counting the number of independently targeted warheads deployed; on the other hand it may be assessed by the weight of explosive which can be delivered by all available launchers and aircraft on a single occasion. Finally, the category of strategic arms is not a closed one since there is argument about whether to include nuclear weapons of shorter range which are nevertheless brought within range of the enemy by being based on intermediate territory or capable of being sent there at short notice.

Given these complexities it is remarkable that, by an exercise of political will over technical intractabilities, two agreements were signed in May 1972 (and two minor agreements in the previous year). In negotiations in 1970 at Vienna and Helsinki, which occupied five months of the year, the Americans took the initiative by proposing a total ban on mobile land sites, a special limitation on particularly potent weapons and an overall numerical limit on the sum of the land and sea sites and bombers which either country might possess. Next year the two countries reached agreement on a Seabed Treaty banning the placing of nuclear weapons on the ocean floor (the treaty to be open for signature universally) and up-dated their agreement of 1963 for a hot line between Washington and Moscow by modifying it to take account of the new means of communication by satellites. The United States then proposed a standstill on the deployment of intercontinental land-based missiles and all submarine-based missiles. Concurrently the negotiators tackled the defensive as distinct from the offensive aspects of strategic nuclear war by trying to set limits to the deployment of anti-ballistic missile (ABM) systems, but the familiar problem of distinguishing a defensive from an offensive weapon bedevilled progress for a time as it was impossible to say that every missile or launcher in an ABM system could never be used except for defensive purposes.

Notwithstanding these conundrums an ABM treaty and an interim agreement on offensive missiles were concluded in 1972. The USSR had at this point an incomplete ABM system round Moscow and the United States was planning two systems for the protection of its intercontinental launching sites. The ABM treaty, of indefinite duration although subject to quinquennial review, permitted each party to deploy two systems, the one for the defence of its capital and the other for the defence of some part of its intercontinental missiles, the centres of the two systems to be not less than 810 miles apart and the radius of each no more than 94 miles; each system might contain 100 launchers, all of them static and capable of firing one warhead only. The agreement on offensive missiles was much barer. It was of limited duration, would expire in 1977 and did no more than impose a freeze on new construction subject to a proviso permitting the substitution of more modern for obsolescent equipment on land and in submarines. The United States and the USSR also agreed to begin in November a second round of SALT talks.

SALT 2 was to be concerned with what had been omitted from the 1972 agreements. This was much. The United States maintained its plea, rejected by the USSR, to ban mobile land-based launchers totally. The Russians had tried but failed to include in the interim agreement specific provisions about long-range bomber aircraft which were still a significant part of the American armoury, although not of the Russian: the Americans had over 500 such aircraft and the Russians, who wanted each aircraft to count as one launcher in an overall total, had 140. There had been no agreement about shorter-range aircraft based outside the United States: the Americans had about 300 such aircraft, capable of carrying nuclear weapons, 500 of them in Europe. Above all there was the problem of MIRVs. The USSR had, so far as was known, no operational MIRVs, although it had a larger total than the United States of intercontinental missiles. The United States, however, had begun deploying MIRVs on land (Minuteman 3) in 1970 and at sea (Poseidon) in 1971. By 1972 the USSR was believed to have 2090 strategic missiles capable of hitting that number of targets, whereas the United States had 1710 such missiles capable of reaching 3550 targets and, within a few years as re-equipment with MIRVs proceeded, over 7000 targets. The Russians were expected to begin deploying MIRVs on their operational sites in 1975, at which point the effectiveness of the Russian force in terms of targets reachable would begin to multiply while the American, already largely re-equipped, would be becoming static. So in order to retain their superiority and match the expanding number of warheads sprouting from Russian launchers the Americans would have to increase the number of their launchers above the total frozen by the interim agreement. If they did not do this after 1977 the Russians would, it was assumed, have almost twice as many American targets in their sights by 1980 as the Americans had Russian. The Americans therefore were primarily concerned to set, limits to the land-based missile capacity of each side. The Russians countered by proposing the elimination of American forward bases (aircraft bases in Europe and submarine bases in Spain and Scotland), a limitation on the number of aircraft carriers to be permitted in European waters (the Russians had no carriers of the conventional type but only carriers with helicopters or vertical take-off aircraft), and the relegation of nuclear-armed submarines to parts of the ocean from which they could not hit enemy territory. Progress in SALT 2 was in consequence laborious and negligible until Nixon visited Moscow in mid-1974 when the impasse was slightly shifted by three minor accords: a modification of the ABM treaty, an agreement to ban underground weapons tests of 150 kilotons and over from March 1976, and agreement that a new SALT treaty would extend to 1985. This last agreement was reflected in November when Gerald Ford, who had stepped into the presidency when Nixon resigned in August, met Brezhnev at Vladivostok in an attempt to prevent the steam from going out of Russo-American détente in general and SALT in particular. Ford and Brezhnev agreed that the talks should continue on the basis that each side might have up to 2400 strategic launchers of all kinds (a somewhat high ceiling) of which no more than 1320 might be fitted with MIRVs. The next year was devoted to the attempt to transpose this core into a formal agreement but with no success. The political will was there, fortified by the wish of both leaders to reach agreement before, in Brezhnev's case, the twenty-fifth Congress of the Communist Party of the Soviet Union in February 1976 and, in Ford's, the presidential campaign which would take up most of that year. But the complexities and technicalities, themselves in constant flux, overpowered the negotiators.

SALT was an aspect of Russo-American détente and détente was an aspect of the growing primacy of super-power diplomacy over alliance politics. Each of the super-powers (this term was invented when former great powers such as Britain and France did not want to abandon their titles but could no longer qualify for the top class) was concerned first and foremost with the other. Their other concerns – China, the Middle East, allies – were becoming secondary. Allies were still important in Europe where the cold war had begun and Nato and the Warsaw Treaty Organization continued to confront one another, but these alliances were fraying at the edges as a result of the passage of time, diminished fears and resentments within both camps against dominant partners (see chapters 5 and 6). Although Nato began in 1968 to propose mutual reductions in armed forces no progress was made in this direction. The main motive for these proposals was to save money but the European members of Nato were also impelled to suggest mutual reductions because they feared unilateral reductions on their own side by the United States, particularly in the context of super-power détente. The United States did not conceal its belief that the Americans were carrying an unfair share of the financial burden of Nato and when the American balance of payments became alarmingly adverse (mainly because of the war in Vietnam) the United States began seriously to look for foreign savings. In 1970 Senator M. Mansfield, the Democrats' leader in the Senate where his party had a majority, tabled a resolution urging on the government big cuts in American forces in Europe. The European members of Nato would then be obliged either to pay more themselves in order to maintain the overall strength of the alliance or to reduce the threat from the other side by persuading the Warsaw Pact countries to reduce their forces. They were not agreed among themselves and in any case the balancing of reductions – a basically statistical approach to a strategic problem full of variables – was hardly less complex than the Russo-American search for formulas to regulate the parameters of conflict at the bilateral strategic level. Nevertheless Nato repeated its invitation in 1969 and 1970 and on the latter occasion the Warsaw Pact responded, if somewhat ingenuously, by expressing interest in discussions about the thinning out of foreign forces. Talks having been begun in 1973 Nato made the first concrete proposals: a 15 per cent cut by both sides in the central sector to be followed by a reduction to 700,000 – which proportionately would be a bigger cut by the Warsaw alliance than by Nato. The Warsaw Pact proposed initial cuts of 20,000 on both sides, followed by a 5 per cent and then a 10 per cent reduction. This scheme, more proportional than numerical, reflected the Warsaw Pact's advantage in numbers, which it designed to keep. Nato on the other hand favoured a mainly numerical approach leading to a parity in numbers which it did not possess. After these opening gambits nothing much happened and nobody seemed in a hurry that it should.

What did happen in Europe was different. One effect of the cold war had been to prevent the conclusion of anything like a conventional peace treaty except with minor combatants. The post-war order in Europe had grown organically out of victory and defeat and the balance of power between the victors. In many significant respects it lacked legal sanction and, in particular, many frontiers were firmer in fact than in international law. It had long been Moscow's desire to secure general and formal recognition of these frontiers, including the frontier between the two post-Hitlerian German states, by some protocol or declaration equivalent to a treaty. Russian efforts met with little success until a Conference on Security and Co-operation in Europe which opened in Helsinki in July 1973 and closed two years later with a Final Act, signed on 1 August 1975 by every European state except Albania and by the United States and Canada. The Final Act declared that existing European frontiers were inviolable and introduced rules requiring notification of certain forms of military manoeuvre. It also prescribed norms for economic and technical co-operation and for what was called humanitarian co-operation which, intended as the *quid pro quo* for the declaration on frontiers, meant freer emigation from the USSR, freer flow of news and ideas, including better facilities for journalists in the USSR, and the like. There was to be a further conference of the same kind in Belgrade in 1977. The Final Act of Helsinki was an example of the trend towards accepting aspirations in place of obligations and its principal consequence was recrimination when non-binding undertakings were treated as such and not observed.

In all these matters of arms, allies and frontiers the two super-powers were manoeuvring for advantage in their inescapable hostility. Détente was not meant to substitute friendship, still less alliance, for this hostility. Its aim was to conduct conflict within certain limits and according to certain rules, implicitly or explicitly arrived at. As the last quarter of the century opened each super-power was more than ever on its own. If for most of the fifties China had seemed to be a huge addition to the Russian side, it was emphatically so no longer. Japan may have seemed for a period a counterweight on the American side, but Japan by 1975 was an independent power at nobody's bidding. Britain, France and western Germany all had substantial power; they were firmly on the American side if the chips were down (an increasingly unlikely event) but they were becoming more interested in each other than in the United States. There were as yet no other powers of this order. There was, however, another element: the sea.

If a great power is a power that can act in any quarter of the globe – and that is as good a definition as any – then sea power remains crucial. The United States was without question a great naval power capable of sailing all the world's oceans and of commanding passage through all but the most private waterways. The USSR was not such a power but was determined to become one and needed only time to do so. Because it was aiming to be what it had not been, its efforts roused considerable alarm. The world was not used to seeing Russian fleets in many oceans, but the universalization of Russian power required this to happen. On land the USSR had advanced little since 1945. Its hold on eastern Europe, although sometimes troubled, remained indisputable and with it the power to pose a threat to western Europe whose credibility was a constant conundrum. It had established in the fifties its rights to be considered a power in the Middle East, although in the seventies the limits of this power were exposed by its eviction from Egypt and by its negative role in the diplomacy that followed the war of 1973. Its sallies into the Congo in 1960 and the Caribbean in 1962 were failures, its role in the wars in South-East Asia marginal, the poor performances of communists in Portugal and Greece in 1974 disappointing, the illness and absences of Brezhnev in 1975 and the uncertainty of the succession a source of hesitations. Its economy and the quality of life of its peoples remained vulnerable to the vagaries of the weather and of an unwieldy bureaucratic system, both of which could perpetrate massive shocks. For all its vast strength the USSR was in one vital respect a power of a different kind from the United States, a power still confined whereas American power roamed free. The seaways, and the underseaways, offered one escape from this inferiority.

By the mid-seventies the Russian navy far surpassed the American in the number of its submarines but was distinctly inferior in every other respect. American naval manpower, including marines, was 733,000 against 500,000 Russian equivalents. The United States had 15 aircraft carriers, the USSR none other than helicopter carriers; of cruisers and destroyers with nuclear weapons the United States had 110 and the USSR 79. But the USSR had 265 submarines against 75, albeit that in nuclear-powered submarines the balance was more even at 75 Russian to 64 American. Such figures ignore a great deal and a closer comparison of the two navies would have to take account of the age of vessels, their armaments, each nation's reserves, research expenditure and other indicators of comparative effectiveness. Political effectiveness moreover is not the same as military effectiveness. What would happen if the two navies engaged one another in combat was a nearly academic question, but the effect of the appearance of a Russian flotilla of any size in, for example, the Mediterranean was not. This fleet varied between 25 and 60 surface and submarine vessels, sometimes larger in numbers and sometimes smaller than the US Sixth Fleet but without air cover, smaller than the French, much smaller than the Italian and trivial beside the combined forces of Nato in this theatre. It was none the less a portent and it made a political point. It had its effect on the conduct of relations between the USSR and Algeria and Libya, two strategically placed anti-western but not pro-Russian states. It reminded western governments that their fears, acute in the late forties, of Russian bases in Yugoslavia and Albania might yet one day be realized, with incalculable consequences for Mediterranean politics. A foretaste of these consequences was provided by the prime minister of Malta, Dom Mintoff, whose search for money for his impoverished island led him to demand from Britain greatly increased fees for the use of Malta's harbour, with more than a hint that if Britain did not care to use it at the going price the Russians would. As a result Mintoff secured in 1972 a rental of £14 million a year for seven years, of which Britain's Nato partners were to provide £8.75 million, and additional lump sums of £2.5 million from Italy and £7 million from other members of Nato. (In the longer term Malta seemed set for economic dependence on Libya.)

Throughout the three decades that followed the end of the Second World War the USSR was an assertive power. It was widely believed to be assertive because it was communist. It was more clearly impelled to be assertive because it was and remained the second power in the world, trying to become the first and never succeeding. It caused fear. The main source of this fear was simply its power which was too great for other people's comfort, but additional sources were its brutality, abated after the deaths of Stalin and Beria but still by any standards terrible, and its ruthlessness to those within reach of its punch as shown in 1956 and again in 1968 in Czechoslovakia. The USSR did not change its standards of political behaviour much between 1945 and 1975. The United States on the other hand did. In 1945 the United States, although a much greater power than the USSR, was not feared. Its power was more distant; the Americas were still for most people another world. But also its repute was fairer. Although ideologically suspect or even hated by some as the arch-capitalist state, it was also a strong fount of anti-imperialism and a country far more envied than decried. Its blemishes – chief among them its racialism at home and the crassness of its admiration of materialist success – were offset by its technical and scientific achievements and its continuing devotion to liberty. But its anti-communist crusade, extended from Europe to Latin America and Asia, altered its image within a generation. In particular the invasion of the Asian mainland (to prevent an expansion of Chinese communism which was not on the cards and existed in the American mind only as a product of ideological preconception) converted the United States in anti-communist as well as communist opinion into an imperialist nation which did not baulk at brutally dominating and devasting foreign lands; and if the Central Intelligence Agency was no Ogpu it was nevertheless discovered in the seventies by both a Senate inquiry and a presidential commission to be more akin to that exemplar of ill fame than had been supposed, a law unto itself in the worst tradition of political secret services, an organization happy to regard any means including assassination as fair practice. The standing of the United States, to the shame of some and glee of others, was further destroyed by the astonishing behaviour of President Nixon who was forced by the exposure of his chicanery and mendacity to resign his office in August 1974, after arranging for its transfer to a congressman of mediocre capacity, Gerald Ford. But loss of repute is not loss of power. How far prestige is an ingredient in power is a standard question for students of international affairs, and the common and sufficient answer is that prestige does not add much to power but does not add nothing: attempts to be more precise are unrewarding. In 1975 the standing of the United States was lower than it had been in 1945. Its power was not.

Chapter 2

The resurgence and isolation of China

1. The Triumph of Mao

In 1949, a little over a quarter of a century after its birth, the Communist Party of China gained possession of the ancient capital city of Peking. A movement had become a government. The defeated Kuomintang was reduced to the island of Taiwan (or Formosa) where its leader Chiang Kai-shek, like the last of the Ming emperors 300 years earlier, clothed himself with imperial pretences reminiscent of the French nobles and Italian bankers who wandered round western Europe in the later Middle Ages calling themselves emperors of Byzantium. The new lord of China, Mao Tse-tung, was able to declare in January 1950 with only slight exaggeration that all China was his except Tibet.

The vast lands and imperial traditions which fell to Mao after the Second World War had been going begging since just before the First. The decline of the last (Manchu) dynasty, which had exposed China to foreign intervention and had almost occasioned its partition in the latter part of the nineteenth century, had culminated in the revolution of 1911. Revolutionary groups and secret societies, partly indigenous and partly fomented among overseas Chinese, effected the disintegration of the *ancien régime*. Faced thereafter with the task of re-establishing the cohesion, dignity and power of China they failed, so that fifty years later China was still potentially a great power but not actually one.

The most notable of these successor groups was that of Sun Yat-sen (died 1925), a nationalist, a democrat and a socialist who wanted to reform China through his instrument the Kuomintang. The Kuomintang established a government in the southern capital of Nanking but it never succeeded in bringing the whole country under its obedience. The collapse of the old régime was followed, especially in the north, by the appearance of war lords who created autonomous fiefs for themselves and engaged in civil wars. Even in the south, where the Kuomintang imposed a degree of order and stability, the huge tasks of administrative reform and modernization were tackled but not mastered.

The Kuomintang looked around for outside help and accepted from the new and no less revolutionary government of the USSR the advisory services of Michael Borodin. Under the pressure of circumstances the Kuomintang began to adopt in its fight against the war lords some of the methods (the organization of the party and of party-state relations), though not the doctrines, of European communism, and it also entered into an alliance with the Chinese communist party which had been founded in Shanghai in 1922. The communists consisted of small groups in certain southern provinces. They became a part of the Kuomintang under the overall leadership of Chiang Kai-shek, but disputes between communist and other Kuomintang leaders – and between left and right non-communist factions within the Kuomintang – were endemic. There was also confusion among the communists themselves because communist committees in Shanghai gave ill-judged instructions to leaders active in the countryside, and still more because Moscow attempted to direct matters without adequate knowledge of Chinese history and conditions. At one moment Moscow had different emissaries in China advocating incompatible policies. In this atmosphere Mao Tse-tung gradually became one of the principal leaders in the countryside, often at odds with his superiors in Shanghai on political and military tactics and himself still evolving and changing his own ideas on these subjects. Disputes between communists and non-communists led to fighting. In 1931 the Japanese attack in Manchuria forced Chiang Kai-shek to send troops to the north but the confusion in the communists' ranks prevented them from taking advantage of this distraction of the non-communists and in 1934 they were decisively defeated as a result of adopting ill-chosen tactics which Mao had argued against. The communists set out on their strenuous and myth-making Long March from south-eastern China, first westward and then northward to the province of Yenan in the far north-west, where they preserved their movement and bided their time. It was during the Long March that Mao rose to ultimate authority. He had been moving away from the classic Marxist strategy of achieving power by fighting the battles of the industrial proletariat and towards annexing communism to peasant indignation (periodically a mighty subversive force in Chinese history); he proposed to set up a small peasant republic and to create peasant armies which would one day be strong enough to seize towns.

Meanwhile the Kuomintang, having disposed of the communists and made headway against the war lords (it took Peking in 1928 and secured Manchuria the next year by agreement with General Chang Hsueh-liang, the Young Marshal), was attacked by Japan, first in Manchuria in 1931 and then in China proper in 1937. From this date until 1945 the Kuomintang and the communists were rivals for the honours of effecting the revival of China as a great power and for the prize of ruling it after the Japanese had been defeated. The communist remnants which had reached Yenan grew rapidly into an army of about 100,000, attracting recruits from the peasantry and from youth generally on a nationalist anti-Japanese ticket. In 1941 the Japanese attack on the United States at Pearl Harbour merged this Far Eastern war into a general war which temporarily overlaid China's civil discords. The

Kuomintang acquired powerful allies but its fortunes were not destined to revive. It had failed to arrest economic collapse, its leadership remained narrow and cliquish, its administration became corrupt, high-handed and over-reliant on secret police, and finally its armies disintegrated. By contrast the communists rose in popular esteem. Their sojourn in the wilderness had given them glamour and concealed the seamy side of their own methods of rule. They had the reputation of fighting the Japanese more seriously than the Kuomintang and when the war ended they were ready to return from the outskirts to the centre. Only a few years later they were the government of China.

When Chiang Kai-shek was chased out of China, a generation of civil conflict came to an end and the communists were presented with the opportunity to do what no faction had been able to do since the fall of the empire, and what the empire itself had failed in and been reproached for: to make China strong and healthy enough to maintain its integrity and independence. In the past, threats to the integrity of China had come from the imperial powers of western Europe sailing across the seas, from the Russians approaching over land, and from the Japanese. By 1945 the western European powers were no longer in a position to menace anybody in the Far East, and Japan had been all but annihilated. The Russians, however, had just reappeared on the scene, while the Americans, traditional upholders of the integrity of China against interlopers, were despairing of the Kuomintang and were about to revert to an Asian policy centred on Japan such as they had pursued at the opening of the century.

The history of continuous Russian expansion into Asia begins after the Crimean War. That defeat in Europe inaugurated essays in liberalism at home and in Far Eastern adventure, both of which were sporadic. The Tsars were more or less permanently preoccupied with the problems of Poland, the Balkans and the Straits, but there was also a party at St Petersburg which made a speciality of the Far East. The sixties and seventies were a period of expansion; the great Russian pro-consul Muraviev established the Amur and Maritime provinces in 1858 and 1860 respectively; Vladivostok was founded in 1861; Sakhalin was acquired (but Alaska sold); the Kazakhs and the central Asian Khantes were subjected. By the eighties Russia, having reached the borders of Persia and Afghanistan, had been brought face to face with the British in India, while further north a warm water Pacific port and a share in the China trade stimulated imperial and financial imaginations.

War between the Japanese and the Chinese in Korea in 1894–95 brought Japan considerable gains (including Taiwan, the Pescadores and, temporarily, the Shantung peninsula and Port Arthur) and served notice of the decline of Chinese power. Russia, France and Germany intervened in defence of China, although Britain, suspicious of the Russian advance in Asia, now began its pro-Japanese policy as a counter.

The Russians, having with the French helped China to pay its war indemnity to Japan, entered into an alliance with China, took Port Arthur and planned the Chinese Eastern and South Manchurian railways. The Russians and the Japanese were now vying with each other for Manchuria. In 1904 Japan attacked Port Arthur and in the ensuing Russo-Japanese war the Russians were defeated and forced back into Manchuria and Mongolia. Japan's standing in Asia and the world was immensely increased and the Russian advance across the top of Asia was checked by a Japanese counter-force in Manchuria. The First World War temporarily eliminated Russian power, effected no Chinese revival, distracted other Europeans from Asian affairs, and left Japan in a situation where, far from curbing the Russians, it had itself to be curbed – and could be curbed by no power except the United States. The Russians recovered positions in Outer Mongolia and Central Asia in the twenties and came once more into conflict with the Japanese in Manchuria in the thirties, but they did not seriously return to the struggle for Manchuria until the final week of the Second World War.

For most of the war years Stalin was too much occupied with the Germans to pay much attention to Asia, let alone intervene there. The USSR had signed a neutrality pact with Japan in 1941 and before Pearl Harbour Japan sought and received assurances that the Russians would abide by this pact. Up to the Teheran conference of 1943 Stalin asked for nothing in the east, being in no position to ask for prizes until he was ready to give a helping hand against Japan. At the Moscow conference in October 1944 there were hints of a change in the Russian attitude, and at Yalta in 1945 Stalin's terms were set out and accepted by allies who were anxious to avoid quarrels, still overrated Japan's will and capacity to fight on, and were – except for a few initiates – ignorant of the nuclear weapons about to be used. Stalin asked his allies to reverse the verdict of the Russo-Japanese war of 1904–5 and also to guarantee him certain positions at the expense not of Japan but of China. The positions lost by the Russians in Manchuria and Sakhalin in 1905 were to be restored; the Kuriles were to go to the USSR too; and the USSR's virtual annexation of Outer Mongolia was to be recognized.

Stalin's policy in Asia was to nibble at the Chinese circumference and to prevent the establishment of any powerful central Chinese government. By declaring war on Japan he secured rights, and planted troops, in Manchuria. He was also able to carry off Japanese industrial plant, although not without incurring Chinese resentment. He had already engineered an anti-Chinese revolt in the Ili valley in Sinkiang, where a secessionist republic of Eastern Turkestan sprouted under Russian protection in 1944. Outer Mongolia, nominally under Chinese suzerainty but effectively in the Russian sphere since 1921 and conceded to the USSR by the western allies at Yalta, was abandoned by the Chinese (who had no choice in the matter) by the Russo-Chinese treaty of August 1945. It was not recovered for China when Mao succeeded Chiang in 1949.

Stalin's declaration of war on Japan had one further notable consequence in the bisection of Korea, for when the Japanese surrendered it was arranged, as a matter of convenience, that Japanese forces north of the 38th parallel should surrender to the Russians and those south of that line to the Americans.

Russian intervention in the Far East was nicely timed. As the Russians knew, the Japanese were anxious for peace; they were taking soundings in Moscow in the hope of securing Russian mediation to end the war. The first nuclear bomb was dropped on 6 August on Hiroshima by the Americans who also knew that there was an active peace party in the Japanese cabinet. The Russian declaration of war followed two days later. On 9 August the second bomb was dropped on Nagasaki. Hostilities ended on 15 August (on which day the Russians signed their treaty with Chiang Kai-shek).

Whereas Stalin wanted a weak China, worked to that end and may well have considered himself successful until the eve of his death, the Americans wanted a strong China, failed through no fault of their own during the years of transition from war to peace, and later began to see the prospect of China strong indeed but not at all to their liking.

American policies in the Far East, which began to take shape at the beginning of the century, were conditioned at the start by the acquisition of the Philippine Islands from Spain in 1898 and by suspicion of the European powers which, having turned most of South-East Asia into colonial terrain, seemed about to carve up China too. With its interests and its moral sense in happy accord Washington claimed for itself any rights or privileges which any European power succeeded in extracting from the Chinese (the policy of the open door, i.e. no commercial preferences between foreigners from different states) and stood up at the same time for the integrity and independence of China.

The American entry on this scene was unexpected and unpremeditated. The war of 1898 against Spain, which began in a muddled way in Cuba, had the incidental result of substituting American for Spanish rule in the Philippines. There ensued a considerable public debate on the politics and morality of expansionism, with the lurking background knowledge that if the United States did not assert its power in the Pacific, either the British or the Germans or the Japanese would. This debate coincided with the manifest decline of China.

The British, alarmed by the trend towards annexations, leases and special commercial privileges for particular groups of foreigners, had sought American co-operation to put a stop to this colonialist rat race in China, but Washington was not at this point interested and the British thereupon entered a game which they despaired of preventing and began themselves to mark out enclaves and take leases.

The change in the American attitude came at the end of the nineteenth century with the appointment of John Hay as Secretary of

State. Hay's first set of notes, condemning spheres of influence and advocating the open door, had little practical effect, although they were popular in the United States; a second set, at the time of the Boxer rebellion and the allied intervention under German command to which the rebellion gave rise in 1900, testified to increasing American concern; so did Washington's mediation in the Russo-Japanese war and the signing of the treaty of Portsmouth on American soil. But it was some time before American and British policies were brought into harmony. Britain, seeking an ally in eastern waters and apparently rebuffed by the United States, had turned to Japan, while the United States was becoming increasingly the protector of China and the enemy at sea of Japan. This discrepancy continued, not without damage to Anglo–American relations, until after the First World War when the Washington treaties of 1921–22 in effect eliminated the Anglo-Japanese alliance, established a three-power naval ratio of 5-5-3, and secured a nine-power guarantee of the integrity of China and the open door. (At the London conference of 1930 the Japanese ratio was raised from 3 to 3.5.) In addition Secretary of State Hughes forced the Japanese to withdraw their troops from the Shantung peninsula and Siberia, but in the thirties the Americans, undecided whether strong action would check or strengthen the expansionist factions in Japanese politics, became less effective and there was little reaction from Washington to the Japanese conquest of Manchuria, the proclamation of the state of Manchukuo in 1932 or even to the Japanese occupation of Shanghai later in the same year. Japan withdrew from the Washington and London naval treaties at the end of 1936, claiming parity with the United States and Britain, and embarked on full-scale war with China in 1937. At the same time Japan challenged the European powers by propounding a 'new order' for all eastern Asia, and when the Europeans (western and Russian) had made it plain that they wanted no troubles in the east, Washington began to negotiate with Tokyo.

The outbreak of war in Europe in 1939 gave Japan a freer hand against China and new opportunities in South East Asia. A new and more bellicose government, installed in 1940, decided to attack Indo-China as a first step but hoped to avoid American intervention. This government fell when Hitler attacked the USSR. The foreign minister, Yosuke Matsuoka, who wanted to join in the attack, was dropped, and Tojo, who wanted to attack the United States, became the most influential member of the cabinet. He also became prime minister in October 1941 and gave the order for the attack on Pearl Harbour in December.

Until the turn of the tide in the middle of 1943 the Americans were in danger of being evicted from the Far East altogether, but the turning point of the Battle of Midway and the final victory over Japan in 1945 brought them back with a unique preponderance such as no power had ever previously enjoyed.

The war forced Washington to reconsider its Far Eastern policy.

Everything combined to make Americans pro-Chinese – traditional policies, missionary connections, Japanese behaviour, and the appealing (in both senses) Madame Chiang – but the Kuomintang government was not successful and was ceasing to be worthy. Nevertheless Washington, which renounced extraterritorial rights in China in 1943 as a gesture, determined that China should emerge from the war fully sovereign in the full extent of its ancient territories (including Manchuria, Taiwan and the Pescadores) and a major power with a permanent place in the Security Council.

China was to be the United States of the Asian continent, a vast, united and liberal-democratic power: a view which Churchill, among others, regarded as romantic moonshine. When the shortcomings of the Kuomintang became more and more obvious, General Joseph Stilwell was sent to keep an eye on Chiang Kai-shek and to bolster and, if possible, reform the Kuomintang, but the general's comments on the Kuomintang were so critical that he was recalled in October 1944 at the instance of Chiang's friends. General Patrick Hurley, who had been sent to China in August as President Roosevelt's personal representative with the Generalissimo, became the principal vehicle of American policy with the new task of bringing the Kuomintang and the communists together again in a coalition. General Hurley and General George C. Marshall, who succeeded him in November 1945, made only slight headway. The Kuomintang and the communists were ineradicably suspicious of each other – the communists had had earlier experience of the Kuomintang attacking them under cover of a truce – and discussions for an accommodation broke down on the issue of the amalgamation of their two armies. When the Japanese surrendered the Americans lifted Kuomintang forces by air to take control in north-eastern China (in the event a strategic mistake), while the Russians who had just entered Manchuria gave the communists arms and opportunities in that area. Until the latter part of 1947 there was an uneasy truce, but civil war was only suspended. The Americans, by now thoroughly distrustful of the Kuomintang, withdrew their units from China but were uncertain whether to withdraw all forms of support. General Wedemeyer, sent to China in July 1947, recommended in September extensive American aid on the basis that the Kuomintang should introduce extensive reforms under American supervision, but by this time China was approaching economic and financial collapse and rioting was becoming common. Nevertheless interim aid to China was approved before the end of the year and the China Aid Act was passed in April 1948. This was supplemented by a Sino-American agreement and the Kuomintang made a belated effort to put its house in order.

But it was too late. The communists were winning battles in steady succession. All Manchuria was theirs by the end of 1948 and the next year became a rollcall of famous cities conquered for communism. Washington at last wrote off the Kuomintang. Chiang, who had made the characteristic blunder of over-committing himself in the last stages

od the civil war, resigned the presidency at the beginning of 1949 and
the Kuomintang asked – in vain – for mediation by the United States,
the USSR, Britain and France. The communists had no further interest
in coalitions or accommodations. A People's Republic was proclaimed
in September. On 18 December Mao arrived in Moscow as a head of
state.

The victory of the Chinese communists created problems for both the
Americans and the Russians. During the remainder of 1949 and the
first half of 1950 the Americans were moving towards diplomatic
recognition of the new régime, but possible negotiations to this end
were first held up by the arrest of the American consul-general in
Mukden and his imprisonment with four of his colleagues for a month
at the end of 1949, and were then rendered impossible by the war in
Korea. At some point in this period the United States decided that
Taiwan was a necessary part of a line of strategic bases and must
therefore not be allowed to fall into communist hands. This decision
was made public and it combined with the Korean war to make the
United States keep Mao's régime out of the Chinese seat at the UN and
to make the Chinese believe, first, that Taiwan was being held as a temporary refuge for Chiang Kai-shek pending an attempted reconquest of
the mainland and, secondly, that the UN was an American tool. The
Korean war also led the Chinese into an overconfident assessment of
their military strength, expressed in the picturesque but inaccurate
description of the United States as a paper tiger.

Mao's victory soon proved as awkward for the Russians as for the
Americans. The world at large supposed that the interests and policies
of the two principal communist powers must be closely allied. This
assumption owed something to the cold war, in which context the new
communist state came to birth; it was strengthened by the incidence of
the war in Korea in 1950–54 between communists and anti-communists; and it led to bewilderment and amazement when it transpired
a few years later that Moscow and Peking were quarrelling bitterly. In
fact the interests of the USSR and China were partly congruent and
partly conflicting, and the communist parties of the two countries had
no close emotional bonds; in Moscow moreover the Chinese party may
well have been regarded as only doubtfully communist in its doctrine
and in its loyalty to the world movement dominated by the Russians.
After the death of Stalin the divergence in policies became more obvious, partly because of the removal of the undoubted leader of the
communist world and partly because the passage of time allowed the
differences in the circumstances of the two countries to make
themselves increasingly felt.

Stalin, as already stated, wanted no powerful China. So long as the
government of China was non-communist it was comparatively easy for
him to pursue a policy of alliance coupled with pinpricks. The treaty of
August 1945 with Chiang had pins stuck into it, since the Kuomintang
acknowledged in effect the absorption of Outer Mongolia into the

Soviet sphere and failed to regain in Manchuria rights which now passed from Japan to the USSR. The Chinese communists were, for Stalin, another pin with which to lacerate the Kuomintang, until in 1949 they took the place of the Kuomintang and so ceased to be a mere pin. When Mao arrived in Moscow, Stalin had to devise a completely new China policy which would take into account both the USSR's desire to dominate the Asian heartlands and the inescapable expectation of fraternal love and assistance between communist parties. Given the size and potentialities of China, this was a problem which had never previously come up in Moscow.

Mao had to learn too. He had had no first-hand experience of the USSR before his visit to Moscow, which lasted two months. Its first fruits were a new Russo-Chinese treaty, concluded on 15 February 1950. This was a business measure dealing with railways, credits and similar matters. The Russians gave the Chinese a handsome present consisting of the Changchun railway and its installations. The Chinese also acquired the right to administer Dalny, though the ultimate fate of this port was to be reconsidered upon the conclusion of a treaty of peace with Japan. The USSR provided China with a credit of $300 million over five years at 1 per cent interest and repayable in 1954–63. Further agreements were concluded a month later for joint exploitation of oil in Sinkiang and joint operation of air routes in central Asia, and a general commercial agreement was signed in April. These agreements were the start of co-operation between the two countries which lasted until the late fifties and was of vital importance to China during the years of experiment and incipient modernization. They were confirmed during a visit to Moscow by Chou En-lai in August–September 1952 shortly before the announcement of China's first five-year plan, the formation of a powerful National Planning Commission under Kao Kang, and the creation of a Ministry of Higher Education all in November–December of that year). With the plan, the commission and the drive for higher education the Russo-Chinese agreements were an integral part of Mao's design for a new China.

2. The Korean War and Sino-American Confrontation

Nine months after the proclamation of the new Chinese republic war broke out in Korea. This unforeseen and, for the Chinese, extremely inopportune event had a deep effect on Asian politics and on the relations between Asians and non-Asians involved in Far Eastern affairs. It forced the Chinese to look to their defences when they should have been concentrating on their internal affairs; it dominated American policy at a moment when that policy was in the making; it raised questions concerning consultation and co-operation between the principal communist powers; it threatened to import a cold war into Asia, boosted Indian neutralism and caused Americans for a while to equate neutralism and pacifism with indifferentism and moral perversion.

The history of Korea is like the history of any small country which finds itself wedged between more powerful neighbours. Korea is a peninsula which stretches into the sea from the south-eastern corner of Manchuria until it nearly reaches the southernmost of Japan's principal islands. For a thousand years it was ruled by two dynasties separated by a brief Mongol conquest. It suffered Japanese and Manchu incursions in the sixteenth and seventeenth centuries but survived until the end of the nineteenth, by which time it had become a pawn in Sino-Japanese-Russian conflicts. Japan's victories in the war with China in 1894–95 and with Russia in 1904–05 gave Japan a free hand in Korea which was annexed in 1910. It failed in 1919 to recover its independence although a provisional government was established under the presidency of Syngman Rhee, a Korean who had acquired a doctorate in philosophy at Princeton. Independence was, however, promised by the Cairo declaration of 1943 by Roosevelt, Churchill and Chiang Kai-shek.

When therefore the war came to an end in 1945 there was no dispute over the status of Korea, but at the moment of independence an accident deprived it of unity. The Japanese having surrendered partly to the Americans and partly to the Russians, Korea was divided into two pieces along the 38th parallel. This famous line came into existence as a result of negotiations between army officers of relatively junior rank; it was not a creation of ministerial decisions. But administrative convenience hardened into political fact and thereafter all attempts to equip Korea with a single government failed. The cause of this failure was the presence of Russian as well as American troops. Contemporaneously in Poland, for which rival governments also contended, there was only one occupying army and so only one possible answer. In Korea there were two armies and so no answer.

In 1947 the United States took the problem to the United Nations which appointed a commission (UN Temporary Commission on Korea – UNTCOK) to effect unity through elections. Elections were held in the south in May 1948 but the commission was prevented from operating in the north and the result of its activities was the creation of a government which claimed to be the government of all Korea but had in fact no authority or existence north of the 38th parallel. The head of this government was Syngman Rhee, now an elderly, rough, reactionary but legendarily essential and, as it turned out, almost irremovable father figure. In 1949 the Russians (who had nurtured a rival government in the north) and the Americans both withdrew their armed forces. Korea was now a country with two governments, overhung by the Russians in Manchuria and Siberia and by the Americans in Japan and vaguely conscious of the emergence of a new China on its borders.

The first half of 1950 was occupied by new elections in South Korea and propaganda in North Korea for reunification either by elections throughout the country (from which Syngman Rhee and others were to be debarred) or by a merger of the two parliaments. When it became apparent that these gambits were unavailing northern troops crossed the border on 25 June, capturing the southern capital of Seoul the next day. It is doubtful in the extreme whether North Korean troops would have taken this action if Dean Acheson had not, in January, excluded Korea (and Taiwan) from the defence perimeter which, by implication, the United States was ready to fight to retain, and it is also extremely doubtful whether the North Koreans would have crossed the parallel without feeling assured of Russian approbation. What was perhaps unforeseeable in June was that the American attitude of January would be immediately reversed by the invasion and that South Korea and Taiwan would prove to be parts of the American defence perimeter after all.

The Security Council met at once at the request of the United States and passed, in the absence of the Russian member, a resolution requiring a cease-fire and the return of northern troops to their own side of the border. All members of the UN were asked to support these measures and President Truman thereupon instructed General MacArthur in Tokyo to give support to the South Koreans. The President also ordered the US Seventh Fleet to insulate Formosa. Two days later (27 June) a second resolution of the Security Council called on all members to help South Korea to repel the attack made upon it and to restore international peace. This resolution proceeded upon the basis, subsequently challenged by the Russians, that the fighting between north and south was an international threat, although it was not made clear whether it was international because north and south were two different states or because an admittedly internal and civil war was deemed to have international repercussions. On 6 July China protested against illegal intervention in Korean affairs.

At first the fighting went rapidly in favour of the North. The South Koreans and the UN forces which came to their help were driven to the very tip of the Korean peninsula, but in September General MacArthur, who was in command of the UN forces, landed troops at Inchon 150 miles to the north and as a result of this bold stroke South Korean and other units crossed the 38th parallel in October and pressed on to the Manchurian border. The war seemed to be over. President Truman flew to Wake Island to congratulate and confer with General MacArthur who gave his opinion that neither the Russians nor the Chinese would intervene. He was right about the Russians, who were now anxious to discountenance the war, but wrong about the Chinese, who attacked on 26 November. Exactly a month later they were across the 38th parallel and the South Koreans and their allies were once more in full retreat.

The Chinese attack was almost certainly a forestalling action. The Chinese, who remembered the Japanese attack on their country via Korea in 1931, had reason to suspect that the new American power in

Japan was about to repeat that performance. American aid to Chiang under the China Aid Act, General MacArthur's visit to Chiang on Formosa soon after the outbreak of war in Korea, the crossing of the 38th parallel by the Americans in October and their approach to the Yalu River, the open debate on American strategic interests in the Pacific islands and on the possibility of a return by Chiang to the mainland – all these things combined to alert the new régime in Peking and persuade it that the Americans intended an anti-communist campaign like the similar, albeit unsuccessful, anti-communist interventions in Russia after the 1917 revolution. So the Chinese struck first.

Chinese intervention altered the nature of the war and gave rise to a fierce debate about how it ought to be prosecuted. From the end of June to the end of November the war, although waged on one side primarily by the Americans, could be represented as an international punitive expedition. After November it became more and more a Sino-American conflict. General MacArthur wished to recognize this fact and to wage open war on China, using the most relevant and effective military means. This meant, in particular, following Chinese aircraft across the Manchurian frontier instead of breaking off pursuit when this line was reached in combat, and it meant also bombing Chinese fixed installations on the Yalu River and elsewhere. Logically this attitude to the war could lead to the use of nuclear bombs in the heart of China itself.

But General MacArthur's views did not carry conviction in Washington. The chiefs of staff shrank from the prospect of embarking on a war with China which might drag on for years, while the president and his civilian advisers were extremely loath to re-enter Chinese politics (from which the United States had very recently extracted itself) and well aware of an almost worldwide disapproval of any such adventure. Washington's allies became alarmed (Attlee flew to Washington to express this alarm, especially about the possible use of nuclear bombs in Asia for a second time) and the neutrals began to give neutralism a markedly anti-American inclination; distrust of the United States in world affairs received in these months a fillip which was very slow to fade away.

As early as July 1950 Nehru, whose government had supported both the Security Council's resolutions, made approaches to Stalin and Acheson to put a stop to the fighting. His intervention was received with bare courtesy but in December India and other neutrals appealed to both sides not to cross the 38th parallel and during that month the Indian representative at the UN, Sir Benegal Rau, had a series of conversations in New York with an emissary from Peking, General Wu Hsiu-chuan. The latter, however, left New York before the end of the year with nothing achieved; a UN cease-fire committee was rebuffed by Peking; the time for mediation was not yet.

On the first day of 1951 the Chinese launched their second offensive. UN forces were quickly forced out of Seoul and a fresh UN appeal for a cease-fire was rejected. But the Chinese advance petered out. At the UN China was declared an aggressor and in Washington in March a telegram from General MacArthur was read to the Senate in which the general in effect urged the United States to strike at China and not simply to accept the re-establishment of the 38th parallel as a boundary line. These were the alternatives, and both the declared aims of the UN and the arbitrament of war favoured the second. But it was now the Chinese turn to retreat, the UN recovered Seoul on 14 March and the South Koreans once more crossed the 38th parallel on the 25th. General MacArthur took the opportunity to issue on his own initiative a peremptory challenge to his adversaries to accept an armistice, coupled with an implied threat of massive retaliation if they did not. The challenge was ignored and President Truman warned General MacArthur that he had exceeded his powers and pursued a policy not approved by his government and commander-in-chief; he was told to stick to his own business. By way of reply the general tried once more to appeal to the Congress and people of the United States over the heads of his military and civilian superiors. He sent to the Republican leader in the House of Representatives, Joseph W. Martin, a letter which was read in the House and which recommended the strongest measures against China, including the use of Chiang's troops. On 11 April he was dismissed by President Truman.

The dramatic dismissal of General MacArthur caused such a stir that its significance was not immediately assimilated. What it meant was that the Korean war must be brought to an end by compromise and mediation. The American government rejected the alternative of complete victory obtainable only by the military defeat of China. Yet it took more than two years more of fighting and negotiation before an armistice was eventually signed in July 1953, more than three years after the initial act of aggression in June 1950.

The dragging out and winding up of the war can be briefly recorded. Fresh Chinese attacks in April 1951 were soon held and both sides began to feel their way towards a truce. A broadcast in the United States at the end of June by the Russian member of the Security Council, J. A. Malik, led to truce negotiations which were begun at Kaesong in July and later transferred to Panmunjon. These negotiations were tedious, long, fruitless and punctuated by fears of a renewal of full-scale operations and by accusations against the Americans of recourse to bacteriological warfare. The most intractable issue was the fate of prisoners of war, many of whom in southern hands were alleged to be unwilling to return to the north, but an exchange agreement was eventually signed in June 1953 (shortly after the death of Stalin, although no connection between the events can be definitely proved). The agreement was then wrecked by Syngman Rhee who released prisoners rather than turn them over to the North Koreans, whereupon the Chinese launched a major offensive. Notwithstanding these turbulent episodes an armistice agreement was signed in July.

The Geneva conference which opened in April 1954 failed to produce a final settlement and Syngman Rhee then went to Washington to try to persuade the United States to sanction a joint invasion of China by South Koreans and Chiang Kai-shek's forces. He argued that the régime in China was on the verge of collapse but he failed to win over Congress or Eisenhower or Dulles to his view. In the following year American and Chinese troops were gradually withdrawn. Korea remained bisected but it was clear that the war was over.

The year 1954 was something of a landmark in Asia's post-war history. The Geneva conference, although it failed to produce agreement on Korea, demonstrated that the country would revert to the position that ruled in 1949, bisected and freed from foreign occupation. In the same year the United States decided not to intervene at Dien Bien Phu. But also in the same year the United States concluded treaties with Pakistan and Japan and created Seato. The acceptance of the *status quo ante* in Korea and the refusal to engage in war in Indo-China did not betoken an American withdrawal from Asia. For the next eleven years – until the beginning in 1965 of the American attack on North Vietnam – the United States tried to play a major role in eastern and south-eastern Asia by displaying but not using military power. The principal object of American policy was to halt the territorial progress of communism by conquest or subversion. In Korea aggression had failed to annex southern Korea to a communist northern half, but in the American view communism was making dangerous strides elsewhere in Asia by means of subversion. In fact the opposite was the case in Malaya where the tide was running against the communist insurgents, but the growth of Chinese power, still supported by Russian aid at this date, made Washington tremble for the successor states in Indo-China and for Indonesia. American policy was thus anti-Chinese because China had become the fount of a new wave of communism, and by the same token it was ideological, claiming virtue for the stand against the evils of communism and imputing wickedness to those who refused to fight the good fight or at least applaud it.

The events of the early fifties strengthened and prolonged American links with the remnants of the Kuomintang. On the outbreak of the Korean war Truman gave Chiang Kai-shek an undertaking to keep the new Chinese régime away from Taiwan and the Pescadores. In view of China's total naval incapacity, this commitment was easy to honour but it involved Washington in courses not approved by its principal European allies and it contained an awkward ambiguity. When Chiang was evicted from the mainland he had retained control of some small islands off the coast. Did the American umbrella cover these islands as well as Taiwan itself? The question was partly a question of the extent of Washington's unwritten commitments to Chiang, became to some extent a question of asserting American steadfastness after the vacillations over Dien Bien Phu, and was often discussed in terms of whether these islands were necessary for the defence of Taiwan or not.

The offshore islands were the Tachens, Quemoy and the Matsus, situated off Amoy and Foochow and forming an offshore screen similar to the advance guard which the Pescadores provided for Taiwan on the other side of the Taiwan Strait. In 1954 resolutions in favour of the liberation of Taiwan started to be manufactured and emitted by Peking and provoked retorts from Washington showing that any attempt to attack Taiwan would have to reckon with the American fleet. In September the Chinese began to bombard Quemoy as a retort, it seemed, to the creation of Seato by the Manila Pact. The Kuomintang fired back and for several weeks this fire and counterfire looked like the beginning of a more serious encounter. In November thirteen American airmen, captured during the winter of 1952–53 when their aircraft came down in Manchuria, were sentenced in Peking to terms varying between life and four years for espionage, and in December the United States and the Kuomintang concluded a new treaty which declared the defence of Taiwan and the Pescadores to be a common interest. Whether the retention of Quemoy and the Matsus was essential to the defence of Taiwan and the Pescadores was left unmentioned. In 1955 Chiang abandoned the Tachens under fire from the mainland.

The Chinese agreed to receive a visit from Hammarskjöld who invited himself to Peking to talk about the American airmen, but the Geneva summit conference in the summer of 1955 caused the Chinese to reflate the crisis. In July they started another major bombardment of Quemoy. The Americans had meanwhile apparently decided – whether on strategic or general political grounds – that no more territory should be ceded. The new bombardment served to make this resolve clear and after it had died away like its predecessor there followed a period of easier Sino-American relations marked by exchanges at Geneva, ambassadorial conferences in Warsaw and the release of the American prisoners. By the middle of 1958 there was even talk of American recognition of Peking, but a statement from Washington in August showed that the Eisenhower-Dulles administration contemplated no such step.

This statement was immediately followed by a fresh bombardment of Quemoy. During the 1955–58 lull Chiang had moved troops into Quemoy until about one-third of all his forces was stationed just offshore from the mainland. In September 1958 Peking demanded the surrender of the islands and was met by a declaration by Dulles to the effect that the Americans would fight to protect Formosa and another by Eisenhower defining Quemoy and the Matsus as necessary for its defence. American escorts for Chiang's troops sailed within a few miles of the coast. War was feared. Washington's allies and sections of American opinion too became alarmed, and after a few days the crisis was deflated by the resumption of the Sino-American ambassadorial talks in Warsaw. Unpopular and hazardous though Dulles's policy of brinkmanship (i.e. using military power to make political threats) had been, it had achieved during these years the object of showing that the

American decision not to intervene in Indo-China in 1954 did not betoken a general American failure of will. This determination was to be further sharpened and displayed in South Vietnam where the Americans first gave the anti-communist régime economic and military aid and then engaged themselves directly in war on the Asian mainland. But this engagement changed the nature of American power and policies in the Far East. The defeat of Japan in 1945 had given the United States total dominance in the Pacific. The conflict between Truman and MacArthur and its outcome showed that Pacific dominance was still the basis of policy, buttressed as it was by garrisons in the Japanese and Philippine islands and by alliance with Australia and New Zealand (concluded in 1951 as the price of these countries' consent to the peace treaty with Japan). But the collapse of the French attempt to resume empire in Indo-China, coming as it did after the triumph of communists in China, led the United States towards a new policy of Asian rather than Pacific dominance.

3. Chinese Communism and the Sino-Soviet Split

Mao's government was pledged to end corruption in the public services, reverse the financial and economic slide which had overwhelmed the Kuomintang, make China a modern industrial power, and introduce sweeping reforms in land-holding and agriculture. These were huge tasks requiring money, authority and peace, and it was difficult to say which was the most pressing. Corruption, waste and bureaucracy were attacked in the Three-Anti campaign begun in Manchuria in August 1951 and extended to the whole of China two months later. A Five-Anti campaign followed, directed against bribery, tax evasion, fraud, the theft of state property and the betrayal of economic secrets. These campaigns seemed to betoken, on the part of the government, a real concern to secure the approbation of the Chinese people and, conversely, an equal concern to ensure that the people should not only behave correctly but think correctly. The campaigns were pursued by means of public meetings, confessions and purges. They were indiscriminate and were used for attacks on unpopular or richer classes such as missionaries, merchants and private entrepreneurs. Landlords and kulaks were also singled out, partly as an acknowledgement of the debt owed to the poorer peasants who had ensured the survival and eventual success of the communists. The dispossession of landlords and kulaks, which began in 1950, was accelerated and made horrible by the panic which spread in China during the first months of the Korean war and claimed two million victims or more: the newly installed rulers, like the leaders of the French Revolution facing the armies of émigrés and hostile powers, lived in expectation of a counter-revolutionary uprising which would be supported and exploited by the United States.

Collectivization began slowly in 1951. The example of the USSR in the thirties, and the inadvisability of disillusioning and antagonizing the peasants who had just become proprietors in place of the vanished landlords, dictated caution. Nevertheless Mao decided in 1955 to step up the pace. He had a number of reasons. After two poor years the 1955 harvest promised well; he did not want to leave the new peasant proprietors undisturbed for long for fear that a new class of kulaks might emerge from their ranks; the first five-year plan, covering the years 1952–57 (but not published until about half its course was run) was inadequately primed by the Russian pump and needed a further boost that could come only from brigading and driving the peasants into more efficient methods and greater productivity. The basic aim was to sap the peasant's resistance to the state; so long as he owned his land he would keep the will to fight, but as soon as he lost it the spirit would go out of him. In earlier years the approach to communal ownership had been cautiously prepared through a series of staging points beginning with co-operation on specified tasks at certain seasons; proceeding thence to a distribution of rewards partly on the basis of the size of a man's holding and partly on the amount of work done by him; and so leading to a final phase in which the ownership of the land would be transferred to the communal group (not the state), rewards would be calculated entirely on the basis of work done, and the group's affairs would be regulated by general meetings and elected committees. From the latter part of 1955 this progression was enormously accelerated and in something like two or two and a half years it was all but completed. The speed of this vast economic and social revolution was characteristic of the methods and outlook of China's new leaders but it also sharpened the discomforts and resentments (especially among the better-off peasants) which such a programme would have evoked in any case.

During these years Mao, whose rapid collectivization was bound to offend the more conservative, also ran the risk of disgruntling the more radical faction by wooing the intellectuals who, though suspect because of their western training and thinking, were very useful to the régime. Mao, perhaps influenced by events in Hungary, wanted to initiate a genuine debate which would engender a genuine conviction of the correctness of his policies. The intellectuals, however, were extremely chary of beginning, even after Mao, by coining the slogan of the Hundred Flowers, virtually pressed them to believe that the régime wanted them to think for themselves and express their views with more freedom and less regard for conformity than they had hitherto dared to use. When criticism was evoked, it proved to be too exuberant. The inevitable disillusion which was eroding the high hopes and self-reliant optimism of the morrow of victory had been sharpened by inflation, labour troubles, and shortages of food and consumer goods, and in this atmosphere the hoped-for discussion about how to progress along the communist path extended to more radical questioning of basic communist tenets. A few months after the first mention of the Hundred

Flowers the debate released by that slogan was abruptly closed.

It was succeeded early in 1958, at the commencement of the second five-year plan, by the Great Leap Forward and the vigorous introduction of the commune system in country and town. The Great Leap Forward (preceded by an earlier and unsuccessful Little Leap during 1956–57) was an incitement to greater exertions associated particularly with Liu Shao-chi, a leader of the more impetuous school who succeeded at the end of 1958 to the highest position in the state upon the unexpected and still unexplained retirement of Mao from the presidency. The Great Leap Forward was a short cut to greater production. After some experimentation it was ordained for the whole country in the autumn of 1958. The principal objects were to mobilize labour, set women free for industrial jobs, establish local industries as an adjunct to the larger units of production, and provide country people with an elementary introduction to industrial processes. One of the most publicized items in the programme was the making of steel in back yards (a system which produced much but poor steel), but the most important feature was the communes. These began to be formed at the beginning of 1958, were announced and explained in April, and were rapidly established throughout rural areas to the accompaniment of a propaganda barrage designed to drown criticism in a wave of enthusiasm. Property was brought into communal ownership and individuals were told to look to the community for free food, services and entertainment. In many places results went too far; even cottages, trees, fowls and small tools were turned into communal property. The vast size of China made radical reform almost impossibly difficult since the central government had only faulty machinery for ensuring that its wishes were carried out sensibly. It operated in fact through cadres, a non-communist device added by the communists to the system of government in China. These cadres were the links between the central government and the people. They were responsible for much of the inefficiency, crudity and brutality with which new policies were implemented, but without them government would have broken down and, in reverse, government would have been without any means of discovering the mood of the people.

By bad luck the inefficiencies of the Great Leap Forward were magnified by natural disasters which produced great hardships and famines, and the whole experiment, in so far as it was meant to rationalize and boost agricultural production, was abandoned. Although the communes survived as new elements in society and in government, by 1960 the small team was once more the basis of the rural economy. The revolution moreover lost face seriously during the great famine years. It had exacerbated an inevitable crisis by grave overestimates of crop production and it had experimented unsuccessfully with a new communal pattern which the Russians, sceptical about any plan for operating a society without a monetary incentive, had explicitly and correctly derided.

These failures at home were accompanied by a sharp decline in Sino-Russian relations in the course of quarrels which developed in the late fifties and were public news by 1960. One of the most startling consequences of the death of Stalin was the clash between the incompatible temperaments of Khrushchev and Mao which was superimposed upon the sometimes divergent interests of the Russian and Chinese empires and exacerbated by doctrinal dispute.

When Mao visited Stalin in 1949 there was an element of obeisance about this encounter between the Chinese leader and the man who, hyphenated with Marx-Engels-Lenin, was much more than just a Russian leader. Stalin's power had endured for a quarter of a century, his prestige had been enormously increased by the Second World War, he was a legendary figure, a little more than mortal man, a little like a long-lived and successful Chinese emperor. There was no doubt about the relationship between the two men and Mao, so far as we know, never questioned it. A Chinese leader might, in the nature of things, be a greater man than a Yugoslav or a Polish leader, or even a purely Russian leader, but in Stalin, Mao recognized a universal figure.

When Stalin died in March 1953, there was at first no agreement in the USSR about his successor and even a short-lived view that he had no single successor. A composite Stalin – Bulganin/Khrushchev – quickly replaced the committee rule of the Malenkov interlude and visited Peking in 1954. Then Khrushchev emerged as the new Russian autocrat and was assumed by many to be *ipso facto* the chief of world communism as well. To Mao, however, this proposition was not self-evident; there was no rule which said that the world's leading communist had to be a Russian nor any disposition in Mao's scholarly mind to accept a rumbustious political boss in that role. During his visit to Peking in 1954 Khrushchev had failed to establish with Mao either a hierarchical or a personal relationship.

For a while relations remained equable. China still needed the economic and technical help of the USSR and remained alive to the need for military support which the outbreak of the Korean war had dramatized. The Russians continued to help the Chinese to modernize their army; the Chinese Fourth Field Army which had entered Korea in 1950 was a part of the force which had defeated the Kuomintang and which the Chinese were anxious to transform into a more modern instrument. Resentments, such as the feeling that the Russians had done very little to help the Chinese communists before they won power, were kept in the background. In 1954, with the Korean war clearly over, the Russians left Port Arthur and handed over its installations to China – two years later than the date set in the Russo-China treaty of 1950. They also transferred to China their half share in the joint companies formed in 1945 to exploit oil, non-ferrous metals and civil aviation in Sinkiang and to operate ship building and repair in Dairen. Finally, they entered into new agreements to give economic and technical aid in the shape of financial credits and the provision of skilled technicians and know-how.

The deterioration in Sino-Russian relations set in about 1956 and acquired a concrete edge in the two following years. At the twentieth congress of the Soviet communist party in February 1956 Mikoyan, followed by Khrushchev, set about the demolition of Stalin's memory. De-Stalinization involved points of doctrine on which Mao could fairly claim to be heard, but he was not consulted and was perhaps offended by the Russians' evident assumption that such matters could be settled by Russians alone. Khrushchev was still a new man, or at any rate unconfirmed in his new apogee, and it would have been at least becoming for him to consult an elder like Mao. In external affairs too Khrushchev was showing a dangerous unsureness. One of his first initiatives had been the repair of the breach with Yugoslavia. Chinese attitudes to Yugoslavia were unsettled in the late fifties. On the one hand the Yugoslav's independence of Moscow appealed to the Chinese; on the other hand they harboured heretical notions. It would seem that the independence prevailed at first over the heresies, but that from about 1957 the heresies seemed to the Chinese more serious, especially when the independence became less pronounced and Moscow gravitated towards a Yugoslav policy of co-existence, of supping with the devil when needs must, a policy which the committedly anti-American Chinese considered reprehensible, inexpedient and silly. Furthermore, in 1955 Bulganin and Khrushchev demonstrated support for non-communists, notably Asian non-communists, by their visits to India, Burma and Afghanistan. Chinese doubts were next reinforced towards the end of 1956 when revolt occurred first in Poland and then in Hungary. In the Chinese view the Russians mishandled, or nearly mishandled, both emergencies. In the Polish case the Chinese intervened in support of the more independent communist Gomulka and restrained the Russians from the use of military force; in the case of the anti-communist Hungarian rising they urged the Russians not to withdraw their troops prematurely. But these disagreements were not lethal, and in the next year the Chinese were advising the Poles to be more amenable to the Russians.

In 1957 in a new agreement on technical aid, Khrushchev (according to the Chinese at a later date) promised China samples of nuclear material and information about the construction of nuclear weapons. This, moreover, was the year in which the Russians perfected the first intercontinental missile and launched the first sputnik. The whole world drew exaggerated conclusions from this achievement. The Russians were thought to be overhauling the Americans, perhaps even to have done so, and the Chinese expected Khrushchev to exploit this marvellous advantage. The communists had long possessed superiority in sheer numbers; now they were ahead in technology as well. The east wind, in Mao's phrase, was prevailing over the west. The Russian nuclear armoury could be used to pin the Americans to the wall, while the communist states helped their friends to power throughout the underprivileged world; in Asia, Africa and Latin America there were revolutionary movements eager to discard the yoke of capitalist imperialism with the help especially of the Chinese, whose own experiences between 1922 and 1949 had taught them more than anybody else knew about the strategy of revolution in poor, backward, agricultural countries. The Chinese, preparing for the Great Leap Forward and their second five-year plan, felt that they could also make a fresh bid to take Quemoy and make themselves felt in communist and Asian affairs.

There were several points in the Chinese analysis with which Khrushchev and at least some of his senior colleagues disagreed. They may well have been the only persons in the world who knew at this time that the Russian sputnik had not put the USSR ahead of the United States, and therefore they did not believe that they could immobilize the United States by the threat of nuclear annihilation. To some extent they were caught in the toils of their own jubilation, for the more they magnified their technical successes, the more it was supposed that they had won for themselves a much freer hand in international affairs than was really the case. While the Chinese thought them capable of preventing nuclear war, they feared it. The Chinese concluded from the Russian achievements that nuclear war had become much less likely and that therefore the communist powers could afford to try more adventurous policies. They also maintained the orthodox Marxist position that war in some form at some day was inevitable because imperialism made it so.

The Russian view of war had changed, more because the Russians approached the topic from a different angle than because of any radical revision of doctrine. They had diluted the basic doctrine of the inevitability of war not so much for reasons of pure logic but rather because their fear and awareness of the frightful consequences of the use of nuclear weapons had led them to discard so baleful a belief; they were thinking specifically of nuclear war and not of war in general. The nuclear danger also caused them to differ from the Chinese in their approach to non-nuclear wars: both Moscow and Peking endorsed wars of national liberation, but Moscow was more worried than Peking about the risks of escalation to nuclear war and therefore more cautious in any particular case. These divergences were a further consequence of the death of Stalin which, in this as in other subjects, released a stifled debate inside the USSR. In March 1954 Malenkov had pronounced that a world war would be likely to destroy all civilization; during his term of office as prime minister he stressed the imbecility of war and coupled it with his policy of increasing the supply of consumer goods. Khrushchev, while still in competition with Malenkov, attacked the latter for defeatism and for advocating co-existence with capitalists and put forward a hard policy of building up the strength of the USSR. When, however, he himself became prime minister he set out to assuage the asperities of the cold war because the USSR was technically behind the United States and because he found the Russian forces ill organized. At the twentieth congress of the communist party in February 1956 he said that war was not inevitable and might not be essential to the worldwide triumph of socialism. This view was repeated in the declaration issued in November 1957 at the end of the Moscow conference of communist parties (the Chinese included), and discussion seemed from this point to be shifting to the question whether all war, and not only nuclear war, had become inexpedient. In 1958, however, the Chinese view that the east wind was prevailing over the west turned a theoretical debate into a live tactical issue with the Chinese expecting the Russians to take positive action incompatible with the general trend of the debate since 1953.

At the same time a further cause of dispute emerged. In general the Russians and the Chinese were in accord on the need to turn Asia, Africa and Latin America away from the capitalist camp, but they differed over the means. The Chinese, intent upon multiplying the number of states under communist rule, wanted to help only communists, whereas the Russians, taking the more pragmatic attitude that any anti-western régime was an advantage, were willing to help bourgeois revolutionary movements where communists were non-existent or unlikely to succeed. At the conference of communist parties in Moscow in December 1960 this disagreement was temporarily smothered by the adoption of a compromise formula: national democracies were to be helped if they were evolving in a socialist direction.

The Russio-Chinese alliance, already ruffled by suspicion and friction in 1956–57, was completely unhinged in the next two years, during which the USSR showed itself indifferent to vital Chinese interests, or even hostile to them. Chiang's immunity on Taiwan under the protection of the American Seventh Fleet was an affront about which Peking could in fact do nothing since it possessed no fleet of its own, but his possession of Quemoy and the Matsu islands just off the Chinese coast was an even less supportable and also a less irremediable taunt. Peking resolved to make a bid for Quemoy and the Matsus by a policy of bang and bluff. A first attempt in 1955 failed and now a second also failed because Dulles refused to be rattled, and part of this failure was ascribed by Peking to the luke-warmness of Russian support. The Russians, while sympathizing with Peking's feelings about irredeemed Chinese territory, were wary of Pacific entanglements and determined not to be drawn into a war for the reconquest of Taiwan. They refused to set up a joint command for the Far East and made demands which amounted in Chinese eyes to impermissible infringements of Chinese sovereignty. Khrushchev seems to have been willing to establish nuclear bases in China but only on the basis that they would be Russian and that there would be no Chinese finger on the trigger. Some Chinese leaders, including the minister of defence, Marshal P'eng Teh-huai, apparently considered the price worth paying, but an opposite view prevailed, Marshal P'eng was dismissed and the Russian attempt (if such it was) to create in eastern Asia the same sort of strategic position as the American position in western Europe failed. To make matters worse the Russians poured cold water on the Great Leap Forward at a time when their co-operation was essential to its success, adopted a neutral attitude in China's disputes with India in 1959, continued to give large amounts of aid to Indonesia even though Peking was being driven to protest against the Indonesian government's behaviour to its Chinese population, and set out to improve relations with the United States. The Chinese were being forced to re-assess the attitudes of the USSR and the balance of the major forces in the world. Events in the Middle East may well have contributed to this re-thinking. In July 1958 the Iraqi monarchy was overthrown and the king, his uncle, his prime minister Nuri es-Said and other notabilities murdered. For a time it seemed to some observers that the Americans and the British would take up arms against this revolution and that a war of major or minor dimensions would begin. The Chinese were certainly interested in these events. At a later stage they demanded to be included in any conference assembled to deal with the situation, and their renewed bombardment of Quemoy began shortly after the Iraqi coup. They may have calculated that the Russians could be induced to use the nuclear threat against the Americans or even to become involved in fighting. If they were thinking in these euphoric terms, their disillusionment was sharp and they were forced to the profoundly melancholy view that, on the contrary, the Russians were engaging in a conspiracy with the Americans to dominate the world and prevent China from becoming a nuclear power.

When the world learned on 3 August 1959 that Khrushchev was going to the United States and would confer with Eisenhower at Camp David, the Chinese concluded that Khrushchev had rejected Peking's thesis that the USSR should put forth its strength rather than negotiate from it. Although there had been some signs of Chinese endorsement for the Khrushchev policy, a change of mind in Peking, coincident with changes in the top ranks of the Chinese communist party, had produced an unequivocally tough tone towards the United States and warnings against the naïve amateurishness of those who imagined that it was possible to lie down with imperialist lions. And not only was the Camp David spirit not shared by the Chinese leaders; the Camp David negotiations appeared to leave out Chinese interests as though China were nothing more than an impediment to a Russo-American rapprochement. In October, shortly after his return from the United States, Khrushchev went to Peking, a visit which had the almost unparalleled consequence of producing no communiqué. If his hosts asked him what he had said to Eisenhower about Taiwan, it is unlikely that he had a palatable reply, and in the new year both the foreign minister and the prime minister of China made statements which amounted to declarations of no confidence in Khrushchev's foreign policy and proceedings. At a meeting of the presidium of the World Peace Council (a communist front organization) in Rome in January 1960 the Russian delegation attacked China, and at a communist conference in Warsaw in February the Chinese were observers only, although Outer Mongolia and North Korea were full participants. In April the ninetieth anniversary of Lenin's birth provided both sides with an occasion to expound their views at intemperate length, and a powerful Chinese propaganda campaign brought the quarrelling into the open. Mao, emerging from semi-retirement, made five separate statements explaining the Chinese attitude and pouring scorn on the folly of trusting the Americans.

It was no doubt the Chinese hope to convert or unseat Khrushchev, and the Russian leader, preparing for the Paris summit conference in mid-May, may have been in some danger. The Supreme Soviet met on 5 May, there was a reshuffle in the party secretariat, and there were rumours of splits and cabals. But Khrushchev went to Paris and, despite the U-2 incident and the failure of the conference, repeated his belief in peaceful co-existence on and after his return home. At a communist conclave in Bucharest in June, Khrushchev personally attacked the Chinese in the course of a meeting which was supposed to restore harmony and in August Russian technicians in China, to the number of about 12,000, were ordered to pack up and return home, bringing with them the plans on which they had been working. This bitterly unfriendly act, coinciding with the domestic setbacks of the great famine years, seemed to the Chinese tantamount to an invitation to the Americans to invade China and to the Kuomintang to incite a rising against the communist régime.

Correspondence and propaganda continued with increasing acerbity and in November 1960 eighty-one communist parties attended another general conference held in secret in Moscow to assuage the discord. After vituperative debate this meeting produced a communiqué which too thinly papered a too large crack. The Russians had the better of the argument when it came to counting heads. By this date the Russo-Chinese alliance was non-existent and doctrinal solidarity a farce. The withdrawal of the Russian technicians was a cancellation of the economic co-operation initiated immediately after the establishment of the Chinese People's Republic, and Khrushchev's approaches to Eisenhower had revealed the strict limits of Russian support for China in external affairs. The attempt to operate a Russo-Chinese alliance in world affairs had run onto the rocks of Khrushchev's American policy.

But at the end of 1964 Khrushchev was overthrown and the second triumvirate which took over power *ad interim* (like the earlier collective leadership after Stalin's death) attempted a reconciliation. Kosygin went twice to Peking. The Chinese, however, refused to attend a conference of communist parties in Moscow in May 1965 and subsequently frustrated Moscow's plans for a world communist conference. The Russian embassy in Peking was attacked in 1967 and the next year Peking condemned the Russian invasion of Czechoslovakia and Brezhnev's doctrine on the right and duty of the USSR to act outside its borders for the defence of socialism and the socialist block as a whole. In 1969 there were incidents on the Ussuri river, where the possession of a few islands had long been a matter for (not very heated) dispute. Men were killed and there was talk about the possibility of a Russian pre-emptive strike against China before its nuclear capacity assumed deterrent proportions. Whether this talk in the world at large was echoed in the Kremlin remains unknown. In 1969–70 negotiations in Peking, to which the USSR sent one of the most senior and most able officials of its foreign office, were lengthy but unproductive. The two countries remained to all outward appearances keenly hostile, and as China emerged from the turmoils of its cultural revolution it seemed determined to resume its anti-Russian foreign policies, proclaiming that Russian and American policies were basically indistinguishable and that the world was endangered by an unholy alliance between these two super-powers who were doing no more than masquerade as enemies of one another.

4. China's Place in the World

China remained a considerable power and an even more considerable bogy. Although militarily and economically much inferior to the world's two giant powers, deficient especially in applied engineering and manufactured products, China had the strength of its size, traditions, prestige, tenacity, minerals, oil and conventional forces. It had to devise a policy for surviving and prospering in isolation through the years which it would need to become a major independent nuclear power. It was bound in these years to avoid a clash with the United States or the USSR and especially to act warily in areas close to its own frontiers about which, as its intervention in the Korean war showed, it must be specially sensitive. It was prepared to deal with neutralists, as in Burma and Cambodia, and to refrain from forcing communists into power; no Chinese armies marched into neighbouring states and no satellites of the Stalinist stamp were created. Even where action seemed comparatively easy, as in Hong Kong and Macao, it took a pragmatic and not a doctrinaire view of its own interests, and the attack on India in 1962, which might seem to belie these postulates, was not out of keeping with them when it is remembered that the object of this limited operation (see chapter 14) was probably to establish frontiers and to ensure, at their western end, communications with the outlying province of Sinkiang. Part of the aftermath of the campaign of 1962 was a fresh verbal attack, nationalist rather than ideological in tone, on Russian machinations in central Asia, where the longest of China's sensitive frontiers ran.

At the same time China was determined to become an independent nuclear power (it achieved its first explosion in October 1964) and sought to become the leader of a new international of the under-privileged. Chou En-lai, who had steadily built up China's diplomatic position in Asia from the Bandung conference in 1955 onwards, made a tour of African countries in 1963–4. China's exclusion from the United Nations, where the seat specifically allotted to China continued to be occupied by the Kuomintang's rump, may have contributed to its wish to assert its claim to a leading world role outside the UN and in defiance of the UN's principal members, even though its comparatively modest defence expenditure and its industrial growth pains made China a power of the future rather than a power to be reckoned with in the present. What China achieved in these years of travail was to project so menacing an image of its future power as to make the world take it very seriously in the present and even to be more afraid of China than of any other country in the world. This fear was not merely a consequence of adept Chinese diplomacy; it was also a product of the mysteriousness with which China was cloaked by the outside world's own determination to treat it as not just different but out of this world. It was a product in particular of confusion about Chinese attitudes towards nuclear war and a belief that China's leaders regarded such a war with equanimity on the grounds that China's vast size and few large cities would enable it to survive nuclear attack. The Chinese were in fact well aware that a nuclear war would be a universal disaster and that China and the Chinese communist party would be among the victims, and although they clung to the not implausible thesis that wars were inevitable they did not apparently regard nuclear war as inevitable. Like others they hoped to prevent a nuclear war by a policy of deterrence but, unlike others, they could not in the fifties and sixties do the deterring themselves. They had to rely on the Russians to deter the Americans, and they came to believe that the Russians, possibly out of fear or animosity towards China, were abandoning this vital role. China in this period was exposed to nuclear threats or preventive war in the same way as the USSR had been exposed between 1945 and 1949.

In this situation the Chinese, like the Russians before them and regardless of whether their ultimate intentions were malevolent or peaceable, had to resort to minor non-nuclear deterrents while being careful to avoid any disastrous provocation of a nuclear power. They challenged and exposed Asia's largest non-nuclear state, India, and came to terms with lesser countries which might have been tempted into an enemy camp. Having taken Tibet because they could and post-poned the conquest of Taiwan because they must, they pursued a policy of limited activity which fitted their limited capacities. The decision of North Vietnam to take an active part in war in the south was, it may be presumed, approved by the Moscow conference of eighty-one communist parties and by the government of the USSR, which could not resist appeals to communist solidarity and could have no objection to endorsing and even assisting a modest guerrilla war likely to prove embarrassing to the United States. Between 1960 and 1965 the Vietcong gradually established a winning position, but in 1963 the United States decided to take a leading part in the war and to raise the level of warfare in order to preserve an independent South Vietnamese state and serve a no-aggression notice on China. The Chinese, faced with a conflict between two principles – the principle that a nuclear power must not be provoked, and the principle that a national liberation movement must be helped – opted for the former.

This dominant principle was further exemplified in Europe. Albania, one of China's few friends, received little more than the rhetorical support which the Russians could be expected to put up with. In any case the Chinese were only marginally interested in Europe. They were more interested in Africa, which presented in their view excellent prospects for revolution. More broadcasting time was devoted to African listeners than even to southern Asians, but the results were disappointing for by the time that China was ready to play a full part in world affairs, most of the nationalist movements in Africa had won power and independence and, being intent on retaining their power, were anything but insurrectionary and were suspicious of Chinese intervention in their affairs. The fall of Ben Bella in Algeria 1965 was a special setback, similar to the rout and slaughter of the Indonesian communists in the same year.

China in the sixties was a country on the way to becoming a regional nuclear power but also a country which was searching in vain for a more than regional role. Its emergence as a future giant power gave notice that the bipolar world of the cold war was destined to be singularly short-lived. China's first nuclear explosion in October 1964 was followed by a second in May 1965. A year later a first thermonuclear weapon, probably one capable of use in submarines (of which China had thirty, received from the USSR), was exploded. China's first guided missile test occurred in October 1966 and its first hydrogen bomb was exploded in June 1967. It would soon be formidable for a thousand miles around; it could be expected to have a wide range, if limited stocks, of nuclear weapons some time in the seventies; and it might spring a surprise by developing ahead of expectations a submarine nuclear armoury to threaten the United States and Latin America from the Pacific ocean. But unlike the United States and the USSR it was not becoming the centre of a group. It had failed to detach more than a few, comparatively insignificant communist parties from the main body of international communism which, if faced with a choice, persisted in choosing Moscow rather than Peking, even while reducing the intensity of Muscovite control; only the distant and ineffective Albanians and New Zealanders stuck staunchly at Peking's side. Elsewhere China caught the fancy of sundry malcontents in France or Egypt or Zanzibar, but these were countries with nationalist rather than internationalist preoccupations and with discontents which were peculiar to each of them and provided no basis for common politics.

There is always a certain grandeur about isolation. Britain, Japan and the United States had all at various times dallied with its lures. Communist China made a virtue of its isolation and discounted the dangers by dwelling on a more distant future in which it would ultimately circumvent and discomfit the major powers whose hostility it had to bear in the present. China was used to having powerful enemies. Britain and Germany had been succeeded in this role by Japan, and Japan in 1945 by the United States – especially after the outbreak of the Korean war. The USSR, superficially a natural ally, had turned out within a decade to be an enemy, a foreign power upon whose goodwill China had mistakenly, if for a short space, allowed itself to become over-dependent. In this situation China's leaders seemed to veer towards a nationalism even more intense than might have been expected from a half century of impotence and revolution, and to seek reassurance in their country's vast size and splendid history, their faith in the revolution which they had made and an optimistic view of world politics. In their eyes Asia, Africa and Latin America were revolutionary, anti-colonial domains where their major enemies – the United States, the USSR and the principal western European states – would get into trouble because of their archaic political attitudes and economic contradictions. Western Europe and northern America would also develop similar revolutionary movements in which the bourgeoisie would be threatened and would finally be supplanted by the proletariat. Meanwhile China must assemble and develop its resources and – in the view of Mao himself and some of his associates – preserve the ardour of its revolution.

But in the sixties the revolution began to devour its children. China's ruling group was disrupted with a violence more familiar in the USSR than in China, where the only major communist figures to have been purged had been Kao Kang in 1954 and P'eng Teh-huai in 1959, both suspected of being too Russophile. Mao, approaching the end of his life, became obsessed by the fear that his life's work was being eroded by bourgeois backsliding and compromise. He determined to displace all those leaders whose steadfastness and fervour were in doubt and to revitalize party and populace by turning to youth. After some years of reflection and preparation he revealed in 1965 to his principal colleagues plans for a cultural revolution and appointed the major of Peking, Peng Chen, to direct it. Peng Chen, however, was soon at cross purposes with Chiang Ching, Mao's third wife, and sometime in the first half of 1966 he was dismissed. In May 1966 Mao reappeared in public after an effacement of six months and a few weeks later the cultural revolution got publicly under way with a series of rallies, demonstrations and denunciations and a much publicized swim by Mao in the Yangtse near the provincial capital of Wuhan. It so happened that at this time there was a major breakdown in the educational system which had forced the authorities to postpone for a year all entries into universities and similar institutions and so discharged millions of young people into temporary purposelessness. They were turned into Red Guards who were to replace the communist youth organization (which had supposedly gone flabby) and go to work to boost production in field and factory. From these useful, if unacademic, pursuits they were diverted to an ideological crusade and, in an exuberance of anti-revisionist spirits, demonstrated against revolutionary insufficiencies and pre-revolutionary attitudes and symbols, assaulting individuals and destroying property in a movement which spread so extensively that it disrupted communications and brought factories to a halt. Some twenty million young people were said to be involved, most of them in their teens.

The cultural revolution had its sources in internal and external problems – economic planning, devolution, consolidation versus forcing the pace of progress, attitudes to the Russians – which had troubled the party in the fifties and disrupted it in the sixties. The revolution split the party at all levels. Hundreds or thousands of leaders, from President Liu Shao-chi to much humbler officials, lost their posts. Inevitably the army advanced in power. Lin Piao, who had succeeded P'eng Teh-huai in 1959 and had invented and distributed the famous little red book, sided with Mao, thus ensuring Mao's victory and confirming the defeat of the pro-Russian faction once represented by P'eng. Lin Piao was proclaimed Mao's eventual heir. Chou En-lai, whose capacity for survival seemed a boon for his country as well as for himself, resumed his policy of making links with the Third World. Other countries too, seeing that China had not been destroyed by its civil war, began to review their attitudes to it. Canada and Italy established diplomatic relations in 1970. In the same year a majority in the General Assembly of the UN – but not the requisite two-thirds majority – voted in favour of China's membership and brought nearer the day when Peking would be recognized as the rightful incumbent of China's permanent seat in the Security Council.

But the shock waves of the cultural revolution were not so lightly extinguished. In 1971 Lin Piao disappeared. Rumour had it that he fled to the USSR in an aircraft that crashed in Mongolia, killing him. Two years later at the tenth congress of the Chinese Communist Party he was openly attacked. He was accused of plotting to assassinate Mao. His death, following unmasking and flight, was said to be accidental. He was described as a reactionary, soft on capitalism, but he seems rather to have been too persistent a champion of the cultural revolution, too much of the military man who is slow to trust or hand over to civilians, and too rigidly anti-American at a point where the more flexible Mao had decided to ameliorate Sino-American relations and receive Nixon in Peking. The tenth congress appointed a new politburo which contained five vice-chairman under Mao instead of one. The first of these was Chou En-lai who died early in 1976, preceding Mao out of this world by a few months.

At the Geneva conference of 1954, Chou had proposed discussions for a reduction of tensions. A first meeting took place in Geneva in August 1955 after China had released eleven captured American airmen, but American recognition of Taiwan as a separate state proved an insuperable obstacle and the talks were broken off by the United States at the end of 1957. They were resumed in Warsaw the next year and the United States began to give visas to American newsmen who wanted to go to China, but the three months' crisis over Quemoy and the Matsu islands intervened to freeze attitudes on both sides. In 1960 Chou proposed a Pacific non-aggression pact. For several years there was a stalemate, although contacts were maintained. In 1966 the American Secretary of State Dean Rusk said that the United States would not try to overthrow the government in Peking by force but however Peking might interpret this disavowal of Chiang's persistent hope, the war in Vietnam put an end to even the mildest sign of normal relations between Peking and Washington until the American withdrawal from South-East Asia revived the situation created in the fifties by the truce in Korea. The Americans were acknowledging the defeat of their efforts to be a continental Asian power. In 1971 an American ping-pong team which had been playing in various Asian countries was invited to China, the first recorded appearance of this sport in high politics. This move was followed by a further relaxation of the American trade embargo (there had been some relaxation in 1969). In July Nixon's adviser on national security, Henry Kissinger, went secretly to Peking and it was then revealed that Nixon himself would follow the next year. This was a sensational piece of news (for its effects in Japan see the next chapter) and the Nixon visit, duly accomplished with the Secretary of State William Rogers in attendance, heralded a stream of other highly placed visitors anxious to make their peace with China and recognise and perhaps trade with it. Already in December 1971 Mao's regime had been admitted to be the rightful occupant of China's place in the UN and China had been strong enough to come in on its own terms which included the rejection of an American-Japanese proposal to retain Taiwan as a separate member alongside China. Nixon's visit to Peking was taken, at least by the Chinese, to betoken abandonment of this short-lived two-Chinas policy.

The Mao–Nixon détente was a political demonstration made possible by the ending of the Vietnam war and valuable to both countries as a means of addressing a warning to the USSR – by the Americans, not to take Russo-American détente for granted; by the Chinese, not to make trouble on the Sino-Soviet frontiers. The demonstration had no precise content (and a visit by President Ford to Peking at the end of 1975 gave it none) but it jolted thinking about international affairs at the great power level. There was now another piece on the board and it served to confuse a game which, by all the rules of a bipolar world, allowed for two players only. In military terms, however, China was still well below super-power standards. It could not touch the United States or greatly harm the USSR. (The Sino-Russian front had been quiet since the incidents on the Ussuri in 1969 but the Russian armies in Mongolia had been built up from fifteen divisions to forty-four.) By 1975 China had set off some twenty nuclear explosions and possessed a stock of nuclear weapons estimated at 300. Some of these were in-termediate range missiles but most could be delivered only by aircraft whose range was 1500 miles.

Chapter 3

Japan

The post-war history of Japan is an object lesson in what international politics are really about. In 1945 Japan was prostrate, with its military power annihilated and its national symbol, the emperor, nullified. Within a generation Japan regained the status of a great power and it did so not by replacing its armouries but by rebuilding its industries, regaining its foreign trade and reconstituting its reserves of cash and currencies. Only after these achievements did it begin to contemplate and then to refashion its lost military might. It was the one power in the world that could be referred to as a great power but had no nuclear capacity and it was evidently more powerful than some powers – Britain, France, India – which had made nuclear explosions.

Furthermore Japan in this period lacked not only the military trappings with which states are wont to make their mark in the world; it was also conspicuously short of primary resources. It had no – or virtually no – oil, uranium, aluminium or nickel; very little coal, iron ore, copper or natural gas; and only half its requirements of lead and zinc. These shortages were made all the more acute by the great expansion of industry, an expansion which paradoxically was both essential to Japan's recovery and yet exacerbated its dependence on foreign materials. This need to secure primary products, whether by participating in exploration or by establishing commercial-political control in the places where they lay, became a major guideline of Japanese foreign policy.

In the immediate post-war years the most striking things about Japan were the physical devastation of a number of its cities, unemployment somewhere between 10 and 15 million, the almost total inadequacy of ordinary means of transport, and the American occupation.

The American share in the defeat of Japan had been so overwhelming that the United States could reduce post-war allied co-operation in the occupation to a not very polite figment. Two bodies were created: the Allied Council for Japan, located in Tokyo and consisting of the United States, the USSR, China and a representative of Britain and the Pacific members of the Commonwealth; and the Far Eastern Commission, located in Washington, with eleven members. But in fact Japan was ruled by the supreme commander, who was General MacArthur and whose ways of treating associates, subjects and problems were a cross between those of the shoguns and Lord Curzon. Retribution took the form of disarmament, demilitarization and trials of war criminals. Then came a new constitution, administrative and social reforms, and attempts to alter the industrial and cultural patterns of the country on the basis, however, of the retention of imperial rule and the emperor himself. The MacArthur régime was an exemplar of autocratic efficiency with an increasing touch of benevolence as rehabilitations took the place of demilitarization. The new constitution, drafted and imposed by the occupiers, was to a large extent backward-looking in that its authors tried to identify and eliminate factors in Japanese history that had led Japan into error. The emperor was cut down to human size, over 200,000 (most military) persons were barred from public life, the prime minister and all his colleagues were to be civilians, the great financial conglomerates or *zaibatsu* were to be broken up. More forward-looking was the American programme of land reform, again imposed from outside and one of the few examples of its kind in the twentieth century anywhere in the world to eventuate in practice as well as on paper.

None of all this stood in the way of revival when the opportunity came, and much of it was helpful. The purge may have eliminated a number of able men but it cleared the way to the top for many more who, without the purge, would not have got there so quickly: some European bureaucracies and businesses would have benefited from such a purge. The elimination of big, often absentee, landowners facilitated the modernisation and re-equipment of agriculture, established a rich rural sector alongside the reviving industrial and commercial sectors, and gave Japan the efficient food production which was vital for so densely populated a country. (At the same time a new abortion law halved the birthrate over a period of five years and stabilized the population.) As in Germany, the Americans were quickly converted from exacting reparations to repairing the Japanese economy, first in the general cold war context of anti-communism and then more specifically and far more vigorously by the Korean war. Above all war in Asia – the Korean war and later the wars in Vietnam – gave Japan the opportunity and the boost which transformed its fortunes in an astonishingly short time. Like the United States during the Second World War, Japan became an arsenal of war and a war-fuelled economy with the added advantage that it was not itself a belligerent. Europe in the same period saw nothing like the revival of Japan because hot war is better than cold war for making the wheels go round. What happened was no miracle but an unexpected opportunity allied with the determination and discipline of the Japanese people; the autocratic rule of General MacArthur, who permitted no interference by strikes or unions to the process of making goods and money; a form of central planning which regulated priorities and the allocation of resources without seeking to control operations; and a harsh capitalist competition which sent the weak to the wall but encouraged that adventurousness and vision which had characterized the nineteenth-century English merchant and industrialist before he was turned into a conservative twentieth-century financier. Finally, it was a condition of Japan's success that its new leaders should collaborate closely with the Americans who ruled in Tokyo and Washington.

New is hardly the word to describe the first of Japan's post-war prime ministers, Shigeru Yoshida, who was already seventy when he was installed in 1948 in an office which he held for six years, but Yoshida understood the constraints and possibilities and had no inhibitions about tackling Japan's alarming post-war inflation by the most familiar of deflationary tactics, killing off weak businesses and adding to the unemployed. Then he struck lucky. The Korean war came (1950–53) and prosperity boomed. MacArthur was removed by Truman but Dulles took charge of the business of turning the occupation of a defeated foe into a Japanese-American alliance. In 1951 the United States organized a peace treaty which was signed at San Francisco in September by Japan and forty-eight other states, the USSR and its associates refusing to take part. By it Japan renounced Korea (which it had ruled since 1910), Taiwan and the Pescadores (Japanese for over half a century), the northern Kuriles and southern Sakhalin (ceded to the USSR), and the mandated islands in the Pacific acquired at the end of the First World War; Japan also accepted temporary American occupation of the Ryukyus, including Okinawa, and the Bonins. These were substantial territorial losses but Japan had to suffer nothing like Germany's bisection of its heartlands. On the same day as the signing of the peace treaty Japan and the United States signed a security treaty in which Japan requested the United States to keep forces in Japan and on this basis the American occupation came formally to an end in April 1952. Japan became a member of the UN in 1956.

Japan's constitution forbade the creation of armed forces but this ban had already been partially circumvented in 1950 by the creation of a National Police Reserve and Self Defence Forces which looked and lived very like an army. These forces gradually expanded to the comparatively modest figure of 250,000 where they stayed. Defence expenditure was kept below 1 per cent of GNP (which was however rising steeply) and around 6 to 7 per cent of government expenditure, again a comparatively modest figure. By the seventies there were the beginnings of a debate about whether Japan should go nuclear: its weight in the world pointed affirmatively in that direction but there were special political as well as the constitutional obstacles. Japan signed the Partial Test Ban Treaty – although this was an act of supererogation if the constitution were to be taken at its face value – and public opinion in the land of Hiroshima and Nagasaki was ultra-sensitive to the exercise of the nuclear option. An incident in 1954 had dramatized these feelings. In March of that year a Japanese fishing vessel, the *Fukuryu Maru* or *Fortunate Dragon,* a few miles outside an area closed to fishing on account of American nuclear tests on the island of Bikini was caught in the fall out of an H-bomb. Before this terrifying fact was realized the *Fukuryu Maru* had returned to port and sold part of its catch. Panic followed. One member of the crew died. Later the United States paid $2 million by way of damages or conscience money for this terrible accident. It also had to pay a political price as Japanese opinion gathered hostility to the United States and to Yoshida as the symbol of the Japanese–American alliance.

This episode coincided with the conclusion in March 1954 of new defence, financial and commercial agreements between the United States and Japan, which included a Mutual Defence Agreement providing for mutual assistance against communism and an expansion and reorganisation of Japan's pseudo-military forces. In April Yoshida, whose régime was disfigured by scandals as well as charges of undue subservience to Washington, suffered a parliamentary defeat which he refused to recognize as such. He set out on a tour of western Europe, Canada and the United States, but on his return rifts in his own party had grown too large for repair and in December he was replaced by an old rival, Ichiro Hatoyama, whose foreign minister Mamoru Shigemitsu expressed the intention to restore normal relations with the USSR and China. But Hatoyama did not last long and was succeeded by Nobusuke Kishi, another of the Liberal Democratic Party's numerous but not harmonious chiefs. Kishi preferred to pursue the policy, initiated by his predecessors, of restoring relations with Japan's former enemies in South-East Asia rather than the Hatoyama-Shigemitsu approach to the USSR and China which, in view of Japan's continuing attachment to the United States, was still too hot a potato. Kishi also negotiated in 1960 a revised version of the Security Treaty of 1951, but the new treaty – and especially a clause making it last for ten years – was unpopular. The government was accused of involving Japan in the cold war by allowing American nuclear weapons to be held on Japanese territory. This criticism was given point by the notorious flight of the U-2 reconnaissance aircraft which was shot down by the Russians in May. There were disorderly scenes in the Japanese parliament and outside it, and although the new treaty was ratified in June a projected visit by Eisenhower had to be cancelled and Kishi resigned before the end of the year.

In 1962 Japan concluded with China a five-year commercial agreement on a barter basis. The vastness of China and its population mesmerised some Japanese industrialists but the government remained inhibited by Washington's hostility to Peking and in any case the present gains to be made in trade with China were small. Japan's trade with Taiwan was substantially larger and the 1962 agreement with China was no more than a gesture towards a vague future. The sixties were the years when Japan impressed itself on the rest of the world by annual growth rates of 10 per cent and more; when the alternation of boom and slump which had characterized the fifties seemed to have gone for good; when the new shape of Japanese industry with its emphasis on heavy industry and chemicals in place of textiles became apparent; and when its admission to the ranks of the OECD publically designated it as one of the world's economic heavyweights. These achievements were crowned by a spectacular demonstration in Tokyo in 1970 called Expo 70.

Then came a bolt from the blue. Without warning to Tokyo President Nixon announced that he had accepted an invitation to visit Peking. The Japanese government, whose policies had been moulded and constricted by the American alliance and by American policies which, in Asia, were based on hostility to China, was seized with equal astonishment and resentment. What seemed to the rest of the world a sensible move to take some heat out of an overheated quarrel betokened in Japan a reversal of alliances not unconnected with commercial and economic rivalry. Japan feared not only a political *volte face* by Washington but also the closing of American markets to Japanese goods, partly at the instance of the American textile lobby but more generally too in order to check the big Japanese surplus in the balance of trade between the two countries. Proposals by Japan to restrict Japanese exports to the United States had produced no result and Nixon then took unilateral action, including a 10 per cent surcharge designed primarily to hit Japanese trade. Japanese anger was increased when it became apparent that the rate of growth in 1971 had been reduced to 6 per cent, and this interruption in Japan's expansion was blamed on American policy and illwill. The undervalued yen, a source of complaint from all Japan's trading partners, was allowed to float in August 1971 and was in consequence revalued by 16 per cent by the end of the year. Relations between Japan and the United States became, temporarily, bad. They were not sensibly improved by the return of Okinawa to Japanese sovereignty as the agreement to do this set no limit on the use of the island by American troops and was imprecise about its use as a nuclear base. The emperor visited the United States, his first journey outside Japan since 1921, but the visit was treated as a curiosity rather than a political event. Japan joined the United States' attempt to get the United Nations to retain Taiwan as a separate member when China was admitted, but the attempt failed and Japan's part in it seemed to many Japanese to be misplaced loyalty to a shifty ally. Nevertheless the drama of Nixon's visit to Peking exceeded its immediate consequences and neither Tokyo nor Washington wished their economic disagreements to degenerate into serious political conflict. New trade agreements were signed in 1972 and in September President Nixon and Prime Minister Eisaku Sato met at Honolulu and Japan promised to make massive purchases of American (and other foreign) goods to redress the imbalance in its foreign trade. Japan's balance of payments and reserves rose again in 1972.

Sato did not long survive the Honolulu meeting. Brother to Kishi and no less pro-American he had suffered a serious decline in favour, in the country and in his party, as a result of the buffetings of the previous year and he gave way to Kakuei Tanaka who immediately went to Peking and restored diplomatic relations with China. This was no reversal of policy, for Tanaka was doing only what the United States had done the previous year and many other countries were hastening to copy. China was neither a possible ally for Japan nor a substitute for the United States as a trading partner; nor was Tanaka markedly pro-Chinese. He was in fact too unpopular to carry through new policies. He retired temporarily into the background during 1972 and was wiped out by scandals at the end of 1974 (and arrested in 1976).

Japan's main problem in the seventies was that it had become a voracious consumer of the world's products without having any sure way of getting them: one estimate at this time had it that by 1981 Japan would need one-tenth of the world's total exports, and in oil more than one-tenth of the world's total production. Britain in the nineteenth century and then the United States had had a similar problem and had solved it by a variety of means which go under the name of imperialism. The essence of imperialism from this viewpoint is not the domination of an area for glory's sake but domination in order to secure materials, whether by channelling them towards oneself or by ensuring that the producers go on producing those materials and not something else or by encouraging a bigger output. The means include investment and so partial or total ownership of minerals, crops or manufacturing industry. Japan had plenty of money to invest but there were difficulties about investing it. The whole idea of foreign investment had become suspect; however welcome investment funds might be in purely commercial terms, there was a wide and nervous awareness of possible conflicts of interest between investor and recipient and a legacy of hostility to the foreign investor who was presumed to be distorting and retarding a developing economy and indeed to be intent on doing so. Additionally Japan's standing in the closest and most obvious area of investment, South-East Asia, had not recovered from the traumas of war and spoliation, as Tanaka was able to see for himself as late as 1974 when he visited Thailand and Indonesia. Japan had paid reparations to its victims (under agreements of 1954 with Burma, 1956 with the Philippines and 1958 with Indonesia) but the revival of Japanese power had rekindled fears about the uses to which it might be put. In the special case of oil Japan's problem was aggravated by the fact that most known investment opportunities had been pre-empted by the United States or western Europeans. Nevertheless Japan began in the sixties to place some of its wealth abroad and considerably increased this flow in the early seventies, particularly to Malaysia, Indonesia, Thailand and the Philippines. It was also anxious to reduce its dependence on Middle Eastern oil (99.5 per cent of its oil was imported and 90 per cent of these imports came from the Middle East) and engaged therefore in exploration or investment in Indonesia, New Guinea, Australia and Nigeria. Japan's vulnerability in terms of oil was compounded by the fact that Middle Eastern oil bound for Japan passed through the narrow Malacca Strait and so was at the mercy of any unfriendly power in Malaya or Sumatra. The oil hunger of these years focused attention on certain small islands in the South China Sea: the Paracels, seized by China in 1975 by evicting a small South Vietnamese force, and the Spratly Island further south which was claimed by China, Vietnam, the Philippines, the Netherlands and France.

Chapter 4

World Order

So long as the state remained the basic element in international society the preservation of world order and the prevention of war could only be secured by the more powerful of these states. They had a choice of methods. Each major power might assume primary or exclusive responsibility in a given region, or all the major powers might together supervise and police the whole globe, or these same powers might equip and finance an association of other states to do the job vicariously on their behalf. After the Second World War international organization and international co-operation were theoretically based on the second of these methods after the first had been unsuccessfully advocated in some quarters; but the circumstances necessary for the success of the second method did not materialize, so that practice approximated rather to an adaptation of the third, imperfectly acknowledged and precariously pursued.

The forms of international organization were discussed during the war by the principal victors-to-be. Churchill and Roosevelt both inclined to a regional pattern, and Churchill elaborated a scheme for a number of local federations to be grouped in three regions under a supreme global council. Power would be concentrated in the three regions – European, American, Pacific – rather than above or below. This pattern did not appeal to Stalin whose suspicions of Churchill, based on his mistrust of the British governing class and on disputes over the timing of the opening of a second front in western Europe, were sharpened by proposals which included the creation of Balkan and Danubian federations in an area of special concern to the USSR: Stalin wanted untrammelled sovereignty and, so far as the two were not incompatible, a continuing association with his allies in order to avoid a return of the USSR's pre-war isolation. On the western side too there was opposition to regionalism, especially among professional politicians like Cordell Hull and Eden who feared that it would produce autarkic blocks each dominated by a particular major power and would in particular revive American isolationism. At Moscow, in October 1943, the foreign ministers of the three allies adopted the principle of a global organization based on the sovereign equality of all states and, with a minimum of incompatibility, laid the foundations for a new world organization which was to perpetuate the alliance of democracy and communism against fascism and give to the principal representatives of the former the charge for keeping the peace by the joint exercise of their allied power, this joint charge being coupled with a guarantee for each of them of immunity from any substantive interference by lesser states which were to recognize their superior power and undiluted sovereignty.

The United Nations was, in form, a revised version of the League of Nations. The principal organs of the two bodies were very similar. The authors of the UN Charter aimed, not to devise a new kind of organization, but to retain a familiar framework and insert into it more effective machinery for the prevention of war. The Covenant of the League had not proscribed war. It had bound its signatories to pause before resorting to war and to attempt to resolve their differences by one of three recommended processes. If this interposition of reason failed, there was no covenanted ban on the resort to war, and international sanctions were only applicable in the event of a resort to war in defiance of the preconditions laid down by the Covenant. In 1928 a much more radical attempt to prevent war was made by the signatories of the Kellogg-Briand Pact, who engaged themselves to dispense with war altogether except for certain limited purposes, namely the defence of the Pact itself and of the Covenant and of existing treaties, and in the exercise of the right of self-defence (the justification for the exercise of this right being left to the state claiming it): the United States and Britain also attached conditions relating respectively to the Monroe Doctrine and the defence of the British Empire. The UN Charter fell somewhere between the conceptions of war as permissible subject to a pause for taking counsel and war as impermissible subject to defined exceptions. The Charter went far towards banning war except in defence of the Charter, or in pursuance of the obligations contained in it, or in self-defence but it did not totally proscribe war. It explicitly sanctioned not only the use of international force but also the use of national force, by one state or an alliance, in self-defence. The Charter vested considerable authority in the Security Council which was empowered to determine whether a given situation contained a threat to international peace or a breach of the peace or an act of aggression and, if it so determined, to require all UN members to take action against the delinquent (except to use force, a sanction which remained voluntary to each member). On the other hand this collective authority was offset by the procedural obstacles to reaching in the first place a collective decision in the Council, namely, a majority of the Council and the assent of all its five permanent members. In the absence of such a decision it was improper for any UN member to reach an opposite decision or take measures of the kind envisaged in the Charter; whereas an affirmative decision of the Council automatically placed all members under obligation, a failure to reach a decision precluded all action under the Charter. Consequently, although the Council was in this field sovereign over the members, each of the permanent members was sovereign over the Council.

Like the League, the UN was designed as an association of sovereign states (notwithstanding that its ban in interference in the internal affairs of a member – article 2(7) – did not extend to measures for peace enforcement under Chapter VII), and like the League it attempted to assert a degree of collective judgment and a field for collective action against its constituent sovereign members in a period when these members had been massively strengthened by the growth of modern technology and of modern ways of influencing people. The state had turned the industrial and the democratic revolutions of the nineteenth century to its own advantage by annexing modern armaments and popular chauvinism to its purposes. Neither the League nor the UN was able to steal the control of armaments from sovereign states nor to create in the peoples of the world an attachment to international organizations which exceeded their purely national patriotism. Besides these general handicaps the UN saw its peace-keeping machinery rendered inoperative at an early stage of its existence. The efficacy of this machinery depended upon the unanimity of the major powers in the Security Council and the provision by all members of forces adequate for the execution of the Council's decisions. The unanimity of the major powers faded in the first breath of peace, so that the veto became a common tactical instrument instead of a weapon of last resort and the Charter's prescription for raising international forces – a series of bilateral agreements between the Security Council and members – was never implemented because the body appointed to negotiate these agreements, the Military Staff Committee, never agreed even the general nature and size of the forces required.

The veto given to the permanent members of the Security Council was a special feature of the UN. In the Council of the League every member had a veto. The authors of the UN Charter had to decide how far to depart from this unanimity rule. They decided to introduce majority voting as a general practice but subject to limited exceptions: in the Security Council, but not in other organs, special power was accorded special privileges with the result that major powers were able to prevent action against themselves or their friends, although they were not entitled to prevent discussion and criticism. No permanent member of the Council has ever objected to this principle, although particular permanent members have objected to the use of the privilege by other permanent members. During the late forties and fifties the USSR, being in a semi-permanent minority in the council, used the veto to such an extent that other members complained of a breach of the spirit, if not the provisions, of the Charter. Russians argued in return that the UN had become a tool of American policies and that these policies were basically anti-Russian – as evidenced by Truman's use of his nuclear monopoly for political purposes, by speeches of prominent western leaders beginning with Churchill at Fulton and Byrnes at Stuttgart in February and September 1946. The USSR, after an initial attempt to use the UN for its own political purposes by raising or supporting complaints about the Dutch in Indonesia, the British and French in Syria and Lebanon, the British in Egypt and Greece and western tolerance of Franco's fascism in Spain, fell back upon the veto to meet western counter-charges and then in January 1950 ceased to attend meetings of the Security Council. This retreat from the UN was, however, reversed partly because it enabled the Security Council to initiate action in Korea in June 1950 and partly because the expansion of the UN – notably in 1955 and 1960, the years respectively of a package deal admitting an assortment of sixteen blocked candidates and of the major African afflux – altered the character of the organization and offered the Russians political opportunities outweighing its fundamentally minority position in the Security Council. (It was in this period that the Russians ceased to attack the leaders of new states as bourgeois stooges and began instead to make friends with them.)

American hostility to the frequent Russian use of the veto led to two attempts to circumvent it by transferring to the General Assembly some part of the Security Council's authority. In 1948 an *ad hoc* committee of the Assembly, popularly called the Little Assembly, was established as a means of keeping the Assembly in permanent session, but the Little Assembly's powers were circumscribed and it never became an organ of any importance. The Russians were not alone in regarding it as a contravention of the Charter and it faded away. More important was the adoption in 1950 of the Uniting for Peace resolution. This resolution was sponsored by the United States which saw that the UN operations in Korea had been made possible only by the absence of the Russian member and his veto from the Security Council and which sought to ensure that their presence on a future occasion would not fatally obstruct similar action. The resolution, which was adopted by the Assembly by fifty votes to five with two abstentions, introduced machinery for calling an emergency session of the Assembly at short notice; asserted the right of the Assembly to pass judgment on threats to peace, breaches of the peace and acts of aggression when the Security Council was prevented from doing so; created a Peace Observation Committee of fourteen, available for missions of exploration and elucidation in trouble spots; also created a (stillborn) Collective Measures Committee of fourteen to study international peace-keeping machinery; and asked members to earmark forces for service at short notice in UN peace-keeping operations. The Assembly twice stigmatized China as an aggressor in Korea under this procedure and again used it in 1956 to denounce the Anglo–Franco–Israeli attack on Egypt and raise an international force to supplant these aggressors. But the legality of the Uniting for Peace resolution was always in dispute. The USSR and other members attacked it and refused to pay for operations set in motion by the Assembly within its terms of reference. In 1962 the International Court was asked to advise on this issue and declared by nine votes to five that the Security Council's responsibility for peace-keeping was primary but not exclusive.

Thus disputes of a legal nature, reflecting fundamental political disagreements, threatened to thwart the hopes of those who had sought in
1945 to produce a document and an organization which would secure
peace and order. Disharmony among the permanent members made a
mockery of the Security Council's name and turned the Council itself
into an arena for the public display of wrangling and propaganda
charges. Open diplomacy became as discredited as secret diplomacy
had once been suspect. Likewise the General Assembly became noted
for the marshalling of block votes and the trading of unattached ones,
especially after the afflux of new members had increased the number of
those who were likely to have no direct interest in a particular issue and
who would therefore vote either for ulterior reasons or not at all.
Recourse to the UN became in consequence something of a gamble
owing to the unpredictability of the attitudes of many members.

Disappointment with the functioning of the central organs of the UN
led to a recrudescence of interest in regionalism. Although the authors
of the Charter had come down on the side of centralism as opposed to
regionalism, they had not totally excluded the latter from their design.
The Charter recognized regional organizations in two ways. It affirmed
by article 51 the right of regional self-defence and in effect sactioned a
regional collective system for defence which was an alternative to the
machinery of the Security Council. This article covered regional
alliances such as Nato, whose primary purpose was not the
maintenance of peace and order within their area but the defence of it
from outside threats. Secondly, the Charter made provision in article 52
for regional organizations intended to police the region and resolve disputes arising within it. The Organization of American States (which is
more closely examined in Part Six of this book) as, however, the only
organization of this kind to achieve any significant claim to effectiveness
in the first twenty years of the UN's existence, with the result that
regionalism did not in this period offer any substantial alternative
to UN's central organs as a means of keeping the peace within a
region.

But although the Security Council failed to function as anticipated
by its authors and although regional organizations failed to step into
the gap, the UN became continuously active in security operations,
developed a variety of experimental techniques and even engaged – in
the Congo – in a major operation in which it deployed a total of nearly
100,000 men over four years. UN intervention in dangerous situations
ranged from comparatively modest missions to establish facts, lower
tension and gain time, through more complex mediatory operations involving military units but not the use of military force, to military expeditions prepared not only to defend themselves but also to attack
others. The line between one type of operation and another cannot be
precisely drawn. Thus UN intervention in Kashmir, Palestine and the
Suez war could be classified as mediatory and in Korea and the Congo
as military, whereas intervention in Cyprus could arguably be placed in

either category or in one category to begin with and in another at a later stage. But classification is no index of activity and the UN's activity in peace-keeping is not to be denied. Where the League had been criticized for passivity, the UN came to be criticized for doing too much.

In the first or pre-Korean phase of this activity the Security Council was faced with situations arising out of the war: the lingering of the Russians in Iran beyond the term set by wartime agreements, and the slowness of British and French troops to leave Syria and Lebanon. These matters were debated in the Council and resolved outside it without further ado. Precedents of recourse to the Council were quickly set. The Council declined to act on a Russian complaint of British interference in Greek affairs through British troops in Greece, but it later investigated Greek complaints of foreign aid to Greek rebels by Yugoslavia, Bulgaria and Albania. It despatched teams of observers who, after being denied access to the non-Greek sides of the frontiers in question, issued a report condemning Greece's enemies. The Council did not put an end to the fighting in progress (which was only stopped when American aid had re-equipped the Greek army and restored its morale and when Yugoslavia, after the breach with the USSR and its communist neighbours in 1948, stopped helping the rebels), but the UN had set a precedent for on-the-spot investigations and could claim that it had contributed to elucidating and holding a potentially dangerous situation until it was eliminated by other means. This function was further exemplified in Indonesia and Kashmir. In Indonesia the Council succeeded in establishing a cease-fire which temporarily halted the first Dutch police action against the Indonesian nationalists and secured a temporary agreement between the two sides through a conciliation committee. Although these achievements were at first transitory, the eventual transfer of sovereignty from the Netherlands to the Indonesian republic at the end of 1949 was mediated by international intervention. In Kashmir too the UN negotiated a cease-fire and succeeded in putting a stop to fighting, even though it failed to secure a withdrawal of Pakistani or Indian troops which had entered Kashmir or to resolve the underlying political dispute between Pakistan and India. Kashmir was the first clear example of a paradox which was later to become explicit and teasing: the fact that a cease-fire and the immobilization of hostilities could obstruct the solution of basic disputes by relieving the contestants of the urgency to come to terms in order to save lives and money. UN observers, sent to Kashmir in 1949, were still there twenty years later.

In Palestine, the final pre-Korean illustration of UN security operations, UN emissaries negotiated a cease-fire, repaired it when it was broken and helped to secure armistice agreements. The Arabs and Israel did not, however, make peace and a UN Truce Supervisory Organization found itself established in the Middle East for more years than its orginators had contemplated, subjecting both sides to the hazards of having their infractions of the truce exposed by an impartial body of observers.

The Korean war which, like other events referred to in this summary of UN activities, is described in more detail elsewhere in this book, was a test of a different kind since it arose out of an act of aggression to which there could be no effective response except the use of force. Chapter VII of the Charter was invoked and the Security Council, in the absence of the USSR, in effect endorsed American action and com- missioned the United States, which had forces available in Japan and the surrounding waters, to meet force with force. The Korean war became therefore a war conducted by an American general responsible to the American president acting as the agent of the UN. Fifteen other states, mostly allied with the United States for other reasons, sent units to the battlefield but half the ground forces engaged, 93 per cent of air forces and 86 per cent of naval forces were American, and when the Chinese invaded Korea and the war gradually evolved into a trial of strength between the United States and China (with the possibility of an even larger clash between the United States and the USSR whose aid for the communist side was not far in the background) many UN members began to feel that the UN's motives in going to war had been lost sight of and that no future UN operation ought to be conducted in the same way. For more than a decade after the Korean war it was an axiom that major powers should not be invited to make a fighting con- tribution to UN operations – an axiom only attenuated in Cyprus by the obvious advantage of using the British forces already present in the island. Korea became therefore an exception. But its part in typing the UN as an organization prepared to take action, as opposed to the League's failure to take action in Manchuria twenty years earlier, is not to be underestimated.

The next important operation – the UN intervention at Suez in 1956 – was a combined operation by medium powers set in motion by the General Assembly and placed under the executive control of the secretary-general. The force, which was recruited and despatched with astonishing speed, was equipped for self-defence but not for attack: ten nations contributed troops. Its arrival and deployment was secured in advance by agreement with Egypt (necessary, since the operation fell within chapter VI of the Charter on peaceful settlement of disputes and was not an enforcement action under chapter VII) and by the knowledge that the British and French governments would not use the power which they had to oppose it. The Anglo-French attack on Egypt having been halted by the United States, the UN was used to lever the Anglo-French forces out, to patrol the troubled areas along the Suez Canal and incidentally to clear the canal which the Egyptians had blocked when they were attacked. Peace was restored through the agency of the UN after the United States had displayed a determina- tion, which neither Britain, France nor Israel could gainsay, to stop the fighting. The role of the UN in this crisis was performed within the framework of collective security but was in fact something different. The proponents of collective security, whether in the League or the UN, envisaged the mustering, under pre-existing commitments, of overwhelming force to deter or stop a transgressor. At Suez in 1956 the transgressors were not stopped by such a collective show of force but by the United States. The collective force sent to the area could not have fought the Anglo–French or Israeli aggressors, nor was it meant to. It was intended not to push the intruders out but to keep the major powers out, and the name found for this type of activity has been preventive diplomacy. Hammarskjöld's aim was to forestall by a UN presence the incursion into the conflict zone of the Americans and Russians, and his experiences at Suez fashioned his policy in the Congo four years later. Some of the limitations on action of this kind were demonstrated when, in 1967, the UN force was removed on Egypt's abrupt demand (see Chapter 10). Others were demonstrated simultaneously with the war of 1956 when the USSR refused to allow even a personal visit to Budapest by Hammarskjöld.

Between Suez and the Congo, a period of less than four years, the UN was again invoked in the Middle East and was required to use its techniques as observer and mediator. In 1958 the Lebanese government complained of interference in its internal affairs by the United Arab Republic and called in American troops. The UN despatched a few groups of mobile observers to check and report on what was happening along Lebanon's borders and subsequently enlarged this mission to enable it to replace the American units, whose presence had become an embarrassment to all concerned, including the Americans. The UN thereby shed light on a confused situation, deflated it and finally smoothed the way for a return to normality. This was an adaptation of previous experiences. It was followed, more or less, in Laos in 1959; in West Irian in 1962–63 when a UN presence eased the transfer from the Netherlands to Indonesia; in North Borneo and Sarawak in 1963 when UN investigators reported that the inhabitants of these territories were not, as Indonesia alleged, opposed to the creation of Malaysia; in Yemen in 1963–64 when a situation as obscure as it was contentious was to some extent clarified by UN observers; and in discovering the wishes of the inhabitants of the trust territories of Togoland and the Cameroons when the administering powers were about to withdraw between 1956 and 1960.

The involvement of the UN in the Congo was a consequence of the precipitate Belgian withdrawal and the mutiny a few days later of the Congolese army, upon which the Belgians returned to protect their nationals, Katanga purported to secede and the Congolese government turned to the UN for help in keeping order, securing essential services, getting foreign forces out and holding the new state together. This involvement had therefore from the start a mixture of international and internal aspects. It was international in so far as it aimed at removing the Belgians and pre-empting the Americans and the Russians – a further instance of preventive diplomacy. But it was also internal in so far as the UN forces were filling the gap created by the mutiny or inadequacy of the Congolese government's own forces and, besides securing law and order, became involved in maintaining the integrity of the new state by preventing the secession of part of it. Hammarskjöld used his right under article 99 of the Charter to bring the matter to the attention of the Security Council. In the four years in which the UN then operated in the Congo a force which reached a strength of 20,000 and averaged 15,000 was used (at a total cost of over $400 million, of which 42 per cent was paid by the United States and none by the USSR) to keep order, prevent civil war and, more contentiously, to force Katanga to acknowledge the authority of the Congolese state. Its operations were based on chapter VI of the Charter. Chapter VII was never explicitly invoked, although shifting circumstances produced a situation very like enforcement action under chapter VII. These operations were initiated by the Security Council, but they were conducted by the secretary-general and medium powers. Once again only medium states were asked to supply combat units and the secretary-general was given executive control. He created an *ad hoc* advisory committee of representatives of the states with troops engaged, in order to help him to interpret the general directives given by the Security Council and apply them to the circumstances of the moment. Acting in this way the UN became the prime factor in preserving the unity and integrity of the new state and in preventing foreign intervention and perhaps a clash between major powers; it also alleviated human distress by containing civil war, minimizing bloodshed, helping refugees and providing a range of basic medical, administrative and other services; but in the short run it strained itself by incurring the hostility of major powers who distrusted the growth of the secretary-general's authority, sometimes disapproved of his objects and actions, and jibbed at the price which they were asked to pay towards keeping the peace. But if the major powers were not to allow and enable the UN to act in defence of international security, they would have to assume the role of policemen themselves, whether jointly or severally – or permit degrees of disorder in the world beyond the bounds of prudence. They were in fact placed in a dilemma, afraid on the one hand to tolerate too much international disorder and reluctant on the other to sanction the growth of an international peace-keeping authority with an independent competence of its own; and the only escape from this dilemma was to use the machinery of the UN which they had themselves constructed in the first place and which enabled them to act vicariously instead of directly and to keep a curb on any particular operation. The solution to their dilemma was to have a UN capable of acting reasonably effectively, but not too effectively, in keeping the peace; to have a competent but subordinate police force whose wish to become more competent would not be gratified if it entailed a serious move away from subordination. This was what the world got in 1945 and still had in 1975 and looked like having far on towards the end of the century.

Part Two

Europe

Chapter 5

The communist block

1. Stalin's Empire

The partition of Europe after the Second World War was the consequence of a trend and an accident. The trend was the decline, accentuated by war, of the European nation-states. Europe was a continent which had functioned in the form of comparatively small and comparatively strong entities, capable of maintaining separate existences because of the industrial sophistication of some and the addiction of all to the principle of self-determination. Thus the stronger European states existed because they were strong, while the weaker ones existed because it seemed right to the stronger that they should. But with the waning of the strength of the strong the basic element in the pattern of Europe disappeared and Europeans ceased to be able, for the time being, to maintain truly independent states. The question was what new forms would be imposed by dependence.

The answer to this question was determined by accident, by the fact that the precipitating cause of the war had lain in the centre of the continent – in Germany – so that the course of war meant a convergence of anti-German forces upon the centre from the sides. Despite some plans to the contrary, the Anglo-American and the Russian advances into Germany were in substance separate operations which created separate American and Russian dominances to the west and to the east of Germany. Anglo-American sea power modified this pattern by decreeing that Mediterranean Europe as far as the Aegean should fall into the American and not the Russian sphere. This new distribution of power was recognized by Stalin's abandonment of Greece to Churchill, his refusal to pay attention to the Greek communist revolt or help it, and by the subsequent attachment of Greece and Turkey to Nato. At the other end of Europe Finland fell into the Russian sphere not only because of its strategic importance for the defence of Leningrad but because Anglo-American sea power did not overlap Europe round the north as far as it did in the south. Only Germany and Austria were designated common ground and, as we have already seen, even here the new principle of Russo-American partition prevailed and created in Germany a partition within a partition which assumed crucial and critical significance in world affairs as the focus of the cold war. In the rest of Europe the Americans and the Russians let one another be, but in Germany they could not – partly because Germany was the cause and prize of war, partly because of its central position and potential power, and partly because the old notion of the nation state remained strong enough to make the division of a state seem much more unnatural than the allocation of whole states to great power spheres of influence.

It has been argued that the division of Europe and the resulting Russian overlordship in eastern Europe were the consequence not of historical accident but of agreement, notably agreement at Yalta by Roosevelt and Churchill to give Stalin a position of power which otherwise he could not have achieved. This argument cannot be sustained. Roosevelt and Churchill conceded at Yalta nothing that it was in their power to withhold. The Russian armies were already in occupation of positions in Europe from which they could not be expelled and Stalin's post-war dominance in eastern Europe derived from his victories and not from any bargain with his allies. The most that Roosevelt and Churchill could do was to try to get Stalin to accept certain rules governing the exercise of the power that was his. This they succeeded in doing by persuading him to endorse a Declaration on Liberated Countries which promised free elections and other democratic practices and liberties. When, later, Stalin ignored the engagements contained in this declaration western governments could do no more than protest. Action in eastern Europe was impossible. Only in western Europe could they do anything and steps such as the formation of a west German state were their riposte and also a further manifestation of a division of the continent which preceded, and was not determined by, Yalta.

Within the Russian sphere Stalin's problem was the nature of Russian control and its mechanisms. He created a satellite empire in which the component states retained their separate juristic identities – separate from each other and from the USSR – but were subjected to Russian purposes by the realities of Russian military power and the modalities of communist party and police rule and unequal economic treaties. There was soon little difference between former foes like Hungary, Romania and Bulgaria, and wartime allies like Poland, Czechoslovakia and Yugoslavia. This indifference was manifested at an early stage: in Poland the Lublin committee, a communist dominated group of leaders formed in July 1944 from among the Polish resistance and then groomed in Moscow, was established in Warsaw as the government of Poland in order to frustrate the London Poles who had conducted the fight against the Germans from exile; in Romania the king was compelled in March 1945 to appoint a government controlled by communists. In form the defeated enemies were equated with the allies by the conclusion of peace treaties in February 1947 and of further treaties between each of them and the USSR during 1948 (with the allies the USSR already had treaties dating from the war years). The peace treaties cost Hungary Transylvania which went to Romania, and a smaller piece of territory awarded to Czechoslovakia; confirmed Romania's loss of Bessarabia and northern Bukovina to the USSR, and southern Bukovina to Bulgaria; and gave the USSR the Petsamo area of Finland and a fifty-year lease of the naval base at Porkkala with an access corridor. The treaties of 1948 provided for mutual assistance against Germany and proscribed any alliance by the one signatory which might be construed as directed against the other.

But Stalin aimed at more than formal arrangements and by the end of the forties he had, except in Yugoslavia and Finland, transferred the machinery of government into the hands of obedient communists who were not merely conscious of the realities of Russian power but determined puppet-like to serve it. This transfer involved the suppression or emasculation of non-communist parties and the elimination from the communist ranks of communists who were more national than Muscovite. This process was successfully achieved in the short run, unsuccessful in the longer run in that it failed to secure for Moscow a trouble-free zone of influence round the USSR's European borders. Yugoslavia rejected Russian dominance in 1948, Poland and Hungary kicked against it in 1956 and Romania led a campaign against it in the mid-sixties.

In 1946 Yugoslavia, Czechoslovakia, Bulgaria and Albania had communist prime ministers: Tito, Klement Gottwald, G. M. Dimitrov and Enver Hoxha. In Hungary and Romania the post was occupied by Peasant Party leaders, in Poland and Finland by socialists. All these countries had coalition governments, although only the governments in Prague and Helsinki gave the appearance of a real distribution of power. In Finland the communists were left out of a new government formed after elections in July 1948, in which they fared badly. Elsewhere communist control was intensified during 1947–8, although in Yugoslavia the communist monopoly of power worked against and not for the Russian interest and culminated in June 1948 in the eviction of Yugoslavia from the fraternity of communist states. This section will deal with the consolidation of communist power up to the breach with Yugoslavia, paying particular attention to Poland and Czechoslovakia.

Poland's history is a struggle against neighbours, not least against Russia. Polish communism has also had its anti-Russian side: Rosa Luxemburg disputed Lenin's peasant policy, and the Polish communist party later deprecated Stalin's campaign against Trotsky. The leadership of the Polish party was wiped out in 1937–38 and the party itself was dissolved by the Comintern when Stalin was laying his plans for his pact with the Nazis. It was resuscitated in 1942 and nourished by the hideous behaviour of the Germans in Poland, which caused some revulsion of feeling towards Russians and communists. The discovery in April 1943 of the Katyn massacre (only implausibly ascribed by the Russians to the Germans) reminded the Poles that, for them, the choice between Russians and Germans was a hopeless one, but the Germans were at that time the present pest from which the Russians were future liberators. At the beginning of 1944 the Russians entered Poland in pursuit of the Germans and in July of the same year they proclaimed the Curzon Line as Poland's frontier in the east and formed the Lublin Committee, which shortly afterwards became the country's provisional government. In August the people of Warsaw rose against the Germans in the expectation of swift help from the advancing Russians, which however failed to materialize; the victims included many leaders of the resistance, national communists as well as non-communists.

The looming Polish problem was twofold: what were to be Poland's boundaries and who was to rule? The Russians wished to shift Poland to the west in order to gain territory for themselves in the east and, perhaps, to perpetuate a pro-Russian and anti-German slant by adding German lands in the west to the Polish state; the Russians were also determined to insist on a government which was wholly or preponderantly communist. At the Yalta conference in February 1945 the Americans and the British disputed the Russian plans at length but irresolutely; they recognized the force of Stalin's arguments about the importance of a reliable Poland between the USSR and Germany, they did not regard the Polish question as the most important on the agenda, and they believed that no great harm would come from leaving the composition of the future Polish government vague since they had Stalin's agreement to the broadening of the provisional government and to fair and early elections after the end of the war. Before the Potsdam conference in July the Poles had been put by the Russians in possession of German lands beyond their old western borders and at that conference Churchill's forebodings and remonstrances were uttered in vain. The British and the Americans accepted the accomplished fact provided it were called an interim measure which would be reopened upon the negotiation of a peace treaty with Germany.

Stanislaw Mikolayczyk, chief of the Polish government in exile in London and leader of the Polish Peasant Party, had been added to the provisional government in Warsaw as a deputy prime minister. The other principal figures in the government came from the Lublin group: the communist Boleslaw Bierut as president, the socialist Edward Osobka-Morawski as prime minister and the communist Wladyslaw Gomulka as a deputy prime minister. The promised elections were held in January 1947 to the accompaniment of every conceivable electoral abuse. The Peasant Party was said to have won only 10 per cent of the vote and 28 of the 444 seats in the parliament. Mikolayczyk resigned and later fled, as did many others. The rump of the Peasant Party was absorbed into the newly created Democratic Block, which took the place of the communist party. In the following year the social democrat party was led by Josef Cyrankiewicz, who had taken the place of Osobka-Morawski, into a merger with the Democratic Block which thereupon became the United Workers Party. The Americans and the British protested in vain over proceedings which they had no power to rectify. But within the communist leadership the old division between Polish and Muscovite communism, already visible in the days of Rosa Luxemburg, reappeared with Gomulka, now secretary-general of the single party, as leader of a faction which wanted to make communism more Polish, more popular and less subservient to Moscow. The quarrel between Stalin and Tito gave him an occasion to express support for Titoism, as a result of which he was gradually denuded of all his posts and disappeared into the background for the next eight years.

These events coincided with the transformation of the political scene in Czechoslovakia. Eduard Beneš, who resumed the presidency after the defeat of Germany, was the principal symbol in central Europe of the wish to conduct a state in accordance with western values and in friendship with the USSR. His government, in which the communist Klement Gottwald was prime minister, was a balanced coalition of several parties, and it is not impossible to suppose that the Russians might have found such a régime acceptable had they not been faced, early in 1948, with a menace of civil war in Czechoslovakia at the time when the quarrel with Yugoslavia was about to lead to a public breach. In February 1948 the minister of the interior, Vaclav Nosek, dismissed eight police inspectors in Prague. The cabinet voted to reverse this step but the prime minister supported Nosek and the arrival in Prague of a deputy foreign minister of the USSR, Valerian Zorin, suggested outside interest of an unusual kind. Nosek declined to reinstate the policemen and eleven ministers tendered their resignations. They were the non-communist ministers, minus however the socialists who, although they had voted with the majority of the cabinet against Nosek, were reluctant to break their association with the communists in government – despite the fact that three months earlier they had selected a new leader to replace the fellow-travelling Zdenek Fierlinger. Anti-communist demonstrations, chiefly by students, occurred in Prague. Police were brought into the capital from outside. Amid fears of increasing tumult Beneš tried to restore calm by accepting the eleven resignations. Two ministers were killed by falling from windows, one of them – Jan Masaryk – having perhaps been pushed out. In June Beneš resigned. He was succeeded by Gottwald. The mopping up operations consisted of amalgamating all Czech parties or remains of Czech parties with the Czech communist party, and likewise in Slovakia, whereupon the single Slovak party was amalgamated with the single Czech party to make the National Front. A similar attempt to extend Russian control in Finland in 1948 was dropped when it ran into difficulties.

The concurrent events in the Danubian satellites may be briefly related. In Hungary, the monarchy having been abolished in January 1946 – nearly thirty years after it had ceased to function – a coalition government was formed with leaders of the Smallholders Party as president and prime ministers (Zoltan Tildy and Ferenc Nagy). In the winter of 1946–47 rumours of a plot against the state were put about, trials were staged and the secretary-general of the Smallholders Party,

Bela Kovacs, was abducted by the Russians. The Americans and British, who were partners with the Russians in the Control Commission for Hungary, protested but were helpless. In May 1947 the prime minister went to Switzerland to see a doctor and, while he was away, was asked to stay away and resign. A new plot was discovered. Elections in August were patently rigged. Members of non-communist parties fled or were put on trial, their parties were split and partially absorbed, as elsewhere, into a single National Independence Front. Tildy resigned the presidency in July and was succeeded by a complaisant social democrat, Arpad Szakasits.

In Romania the Peasant leader Ion Maniu was accused in 1947 of plotting against the state with American and British agents. He and others were tried and condemned, and the Peasant Party was dissolved. In December the king abdicated. In the following February the social democrat party was merged with the communist party, and in March this party won 405 of the 414 seats in parliament. But before this election dissension had struck the communist party too and one of its veteran leaders, Lucretsiu Patrasceanu, was dismissed from the government, arrested, expelled from the party and, according to rumour, lodged in the Lubianka prison in Mosçow. In Bulgaria the leader of the Agrarian Party, Nicola Petkov, was arrested with others in June 1947 and executed. The Fatherland Front, product of the usual socialist-communist merger, appeared in the next year.

During this period of regimentation Moscow's central purpose was to refashion each satellite in accordance with a single general pattern and to attach each of them to the USSR by all means short of incorporation. But there was to be no incorporation. The newly fashioned states were to be People's Democracies; they were not to become Soviet Republics. Talk of incorporation was dowsed by Moscow, which made it clear that a People's Democracy was something short of a fully communist state and something different from a Soviet Republic. Communist enthusiasts with visions of admission to an extended Soviet commonwealth were disabused. The reasons for this policy may be found in Stalin's essentially cautious nature; or in his realization that these areas would, if fully absorbed, cease to be a buffer zone; or in the inability of the war-ravaged USSR to make radical changes in its structure in the mid-forties; or in the knowledge that some of the satellites had enjoyed and expected a higher standard of living and of public administration than the USSR could provide; or in Stalin's desire to avoid unnecessary provocation of the western powers and to hoodwink them by getting the substance of empire without making constitutional changes which they would not stomach.

At the same time Stalin prevented the satellites from making new political associations among themselves. Everybody visited everybody and piled up bilateral treaties of friendship and mutual assistance until almost all the possible permutations had been employed, but schemes of a more radical kind withered quickly. Various such schemes were in the air immediately after the end of the war. Czechoslovak minds reverted to the Little Entente with Yugoslavia and Romania; and Hungary, whose relations with Czechoslovakia were marred by problems of exchanges of population, riposted in some alarm with a plan for a Danubian confederation. (A Danubian conference at Belgrade in July 1948 left the Russians in effective control of half the river. The Americans, British and French, outvoted at every turn, protested that the convention of 1921 remained in force in the absence of a universally accepted substitute. The riparian states were no counterpoise to the USSR so long as they remained separate.) Downstream the notion of a south Slav federation flourished for a while and produced some talk of a Romanian-Hungarian counterweight. The south Slav federation was the least unlikely of these federative ideas, if only because it was sponsored by two leaders of the first eminence, Tito and Dimitrov. But their plans became too grandiose for Moscow's liking. In June 1947 Tito told the Bulgarians publicly that he looked forward to a monolithic entity of free Balkan peoples. In August Dimitrov, visiting Yugoslavia to sign four pacts, secretly ceded Pirin Macedonia to the Yugoslav Macedonian Republic. In December Traicho Kostov, deputy prime minister of Bulgaria, spoke of a union of all south Slavs in the near future, and a month later Dimitrov spoke in the Romanian capital of a customs union leading to a federation or confederation which would include not only the south Slavs but also the north Slavs (other than those in the USSR) and Hungary, Romania, Albania and Greece. At this point Moscow intervened, summoned Yugoslav and Bulgarian leaders to Moscow and told them that Romania must be left out of their plans, although Albania might later be added to a Yugoslav-Bulgarian state. The Yugoslavs were also told to drop plans for sending troops into Albania. No union of any kind was effected. In May 1948 Yugoslavia was expelled from the communist block. Dimitrov died in Moscow in July 1949.

2. The Yugoslav Secession

The dispute between the Russian and Yugoslav leaders was conducted by correspondence in the months of March, April and May 1948. The heart of the matter was the refusal of the Yugoslavs to accept direction from Moscow and their insistence on the right to think out their own problems in their own context and apply their own solutions in preference to Russian principles and Russian programmes. They maintained that Yugoslavia was not only separate from the USSR but different, and that communist doctrine and practice were not so rigid as to be unable to take account of the differences. In the course of the correspondence the dispute ranged over such topics as the proper organization of a communist state, the role of the communist party, agrarian policies, Yugoslavia's laxity in liquidating capitalism and the person of the Yugoslav foreign minister, Vladimir Velebit, whom the Russians accused of being a British agent. Friction was increased by the presence in Yugoslavia of Russian civilian and military advisers who seemed to the Yugoslavs to represent a Russian claim to superiority and to be paid too much; Russian attempts to put pressure on the Yugoslavs included threats to withdraw these experts. Throughout the correspondence the Yugoslavs were evidently anxious to avoid a breach, an attitude which may have strengthened the Russian resolve to exact admission of error on the points in dispute. But the outcome was a Yugoslav refusal to accept the status of pupil and in June the breach was made public by the eviction of Yugoslavia from the Cominform, the international association of communist parties which had been formed in the previous September to ensure ideological unity and conformity.

The quarrel between Moscow and Belgrade was the second major rebuff to European communist solidarity after the Second World War and the more blatant. In Berlin in October 1946 the Socialist Unity Party (a communist party) had been badly beaten because, among other reasons, its leaders saw German problems through Russian spectacles, asserted Moscow's infallibility, were intolerant of discussion, imposed police rule and insisted on centralized direction of industry instead of workers' control. In Germany this conflict was resolved in favour of the orthodox Muscovites and against the nationalists or deviationists, but the substance of it was not specifically German and it soon reappeared in Yugoslavia. Tito himself was a loyal but not an obsequious communist. He had envisaged the adherence of a Yugoslav communist republic to the Soviet Union but he had also in his younger days been disturbed by the Russian purges of the thirties, had been shaken by the Russo-German pact of 1939 and had had experience during the war of differences with Stalin and of Stalin's attitude to lesser communist leaders. In 1948 he abandoned international communism for nationalism and non-alignment reluctantly, as a victim of ostracism and as a result of contradictions between practical Yugoslav needs and general communist doctrines. Yugoslavia became an international anomaly, a communist state dependent on American and other western aid, an ally of Greece and Turkey in the Balkan Pact of 1953 and then a protagonist with Nehru's India and Nasser's Egypt of neutralism and non-alignment.

Since Tito seceded and survived, it follows that Stalin miscalculated. The simplest explanation of his mishandling of the situation is that he overrated his capacity to discipline the Yugoslav party, but this is a complex generalization embracing a number of contributory factors: his own doctrinal inflexiblity and confidence, his failure to appreciate that the less doctrinal western powers would come to Tito's aid economically, his distaste for Yugoslav deviationism in doctrinal terms and fear of its political consequences in satellite states which he had created subject but yet independent. Tito's survival was also due to a variety of factors: his genuinely national roots which distinguished him from a number of other communist leaders who had lived longer in the USSR than in their native countries, his position as a combatant leader against the Germans and Italians, the fact that Yugoslavia had no frontier with the USSR, and the parrying of communist economic blockade by western aid. The Yugoslav secession not only entailed the end of schemes for a Balkan union round a Yugoslav-Bulgarian core but also diplomatic and economic breaches with the remaining satellites and shifts in Yugoslavia's relations with its non-communist neighbours: it contributed to the defeat of the communist rebellion in Greece and the settlement by partition in 1954 of the problem of Trieste (Italy finally renounced its claim to the whole Free Territory in 1975). It dispelled the myth that a communist government not subservient to Moscow was a contradiction in terms. And it promoted a series of witch-hunts in the satellite block where the Russians felt obliged to eliminate communists who might by sympathetic to Tito or tempted to follow in his footsteps.

The removal of Patrasceanu and the decline of Gomulka bore witness to Russian awareness of the defects in Stalin's plan for ruling his satellite empire indirectly through communist satraps. The quarrel with Tito magnified the difficulties. Its most spectacular consequence was the trial of Laszlo Rajk in Hungary. The secretary-general of the Hungarian party, Matyas Rakosi, had fallen under suspicion but, having confessed to errors, survived. Then in September 1949 Rajk and other Hungarian communists were brought to trial on a compendium of charges to which they confessed and which included spying for the pre-war Horthy régime, for the Nazi Gestapo, for the United States and Britain and, more significantly, for Tito. The trial was an anti-Tito demonstration, all the more forceful in that it ended with the execution of the accused. It was repeated elsewhere. In Bulgaria the veteran communist Traicho Kostov, who had been expelled from the party in March 1949, was arrested in June and, along with others, tried and executed in December. The charges ranged from Trotskyism to Titoism; their essence was conspiracy against the state. In Albania Koci Xoxe, who had favoured a union with Yugoslavia, was eliminated by his anti-Yugoslav rival, Enver Hoxha. In Poland Gomulka lost his remaining badge of respectability by being expelled, with others, from the central committee of the party after accusations of collaboration with the Pilsudski dictatorship and the Gestapo and of nationalism and deviationism. He was not, however, put on trial. Moscow preferred to strengthen its position in the most important of the satellites by sending the Soviet marshal Konstanty Rokossovski to Warsaw where he became a Polish citizen and minister of defence. In Czechoslovakia Tito's secession and the Rajk trial were followed by a purge of suspected pro-Titoists and of communists who had spent the war years in London. The victims included the foreign minister, Vladimir Clementis, who resigned in March 1950 but was not made to stand trial. At the end of 1951 communists of the wartime Moscow group, including the party secretary Rudolf Slansky, were put on trial in proceedings which had a distinct anti-Jewish tinge and seemed intended to use Jews as scapegoats for the unpopularities of the régime.

These years were critical for Stalin's hold on the satellites – or, judging by Russian actions, were deemed by him to be critical. The rejection of the Marshall Plan in 1947 had been followed by the Russian blockade of Berlin and by more militant action by communists in western Europe (particularly in France and Italy), but these ventures had failed and their failure coincided with a challenge to Russian rule in eastern Europe which succeeded in Yugoslavia and looked like becoming contagious. Stalin's first response was harsh and practical: he stamped, where he could, on threats to Russian interests. In addition, he added to the apparatus of communist integration in two ways – by creating in Comecon an institution for economic assimilation and by creating the beginnings of military co-ordination as well. These measures, although primarily conceived as retorts to western measures and although not developed during the remainder of Stalin's lifetime, ultimately affected the nature of the relations between the USSR and its satellite neighbours.

Comecon – the Council for Mutual Economic Assistance – was founded in January 1949 as a counter to the Marshall Plan. Its founding members were the USSR, Poland, Czechoslovakia, Hungary, Romania and Bulgaria, which were joined almost at once by Albania and a year later by eastern Germany. It was in form an association of sovereign states: communist propaganda was at this time attacking the Marshall Plan as an American device for over-riding European sovereignties. But in Comecon there was for many years no question of any insistence on sovereign rights to dissent, and the dominance of the USSR was underlined by the exclusion of Yugoslavia. For ten years Comecon had no constitution, meagre quarters and a tiny staff in Moscow, and few activities. In so far as it was anything more than an anti-American gesture, it was an adjunct of the Russian policy, chiefly pursued by other means, of using planning to annex the satellite economies to Russian needs and not to develop the area as a whole in the interests of all its parts. The satellite governments were themselves in the process of adopting the rigid communist system of planning by setting national targets and instructing each separate enterprise how much it must contribute to the aggregate (a system which the head of the State Planning Commission in Moscow, Nikolai Voznesensky, was trying to reform until his dismissal by Stalin in March 1949). Until the crises of the mid-fifties Comecon occupied itself modestly with statistical research, technical exchanges and the promotion of bilateral and triangular trade treaties, but from 1956 considerable changes were introduced. Twelve standing commissions were established in different capitals, Yugoslavia and China were admitted as observers, a constitution was worked out and came into effect in 1960, an international executive was inaugurated in 1962, and meetings of these various organs became regular and frequent. Comecon organized aid for Hungary in materials and credits after the revolution in 1956, promoted joint planning and investment, and expanded satellite co-operation on a broad multilateral basis, e.g. for the distribution of electric power and in the construction of oil pipelines.

In military matters Moscow exercised control and supervision through officers in the satellite forces who had been trained in the USSR and were regarded as dependable. The despatch of Marshall Rokossovski to Warsaw was a uniquely overt and elevated gesture but one which had numerous parallels at lower levels. In 1952 this tentacle policy was supplemented by the creation of a military co-ordinating committee with Marshal Bulganin as chairman, and at a conference in Warsaw at the end of that year a combined general staff was instituted with headquarters in Cracow under a Russian general. Military facilities, involving considerable, displacements of population, were developed along the Baltic coast, in Poland and eastern Germany and round the Black Sea. The satellites were at this stage contributing something like 1.5 million men to military and security forces, were incurring a commensurate financial burden, and were being obliged to adjust their industries, their industrial revolutions and their economic planning to the military requirements of the block as assessed by the USSR. There was, however, no formal multilateral defence treaty until, after Stalin's death, the admission of western Germany to Nato prompted the inauguration in May 1955 of the Warsaw Pact. This treaty, to which the USSR and all its satellites were parties, was expressed as a regional arrangement for self-defence within the meaning of article 52 of the Charter of the United Nations. It created joint organizations with headquarters in Moscow under the command of Marshal Koniev. It incidentally regularized the presence of Russian troops in Romania and Hungary where they would otherwise had no legal standing after the termination of occupation rights in Austria by the treaty which restored Austrian sovereignty in that year. In general the Warsaw Pact was a formalization of existing dispositions and at this stage added little of substance to them. It did, however, also introduce – like Comecon – the principle of round table co-operation which the satellites were beginning to insist on and later provided the Russians with machinery for altering the nature of international relations within the block when they found themselves under pressure to do so.

The death of Stalin in March 1953 occurred in the middle of a period of active change; it did not initiate these changes but it facilitated them. Unrest was already manifest – in strikes in Czechoslovakia, for example, in 1952. In June 1953 more serious disorders broke out in eastern Germany which the government was unable to bring under control without the help of Russian tanks. In 1954 the Russians gave evidence of new thinking about their relations with their neighbours when they sold to the satellite governments the Russian share in joint companies created after the war for the control of key industrial and commercial

enterprises, and at about the same time the liquidation of Beria and
police rule in the USSR was copied further afield: in Hungary the chief
of the security police, Gabor Peter, was sentenced to life imprisonment
and the first secretary of the party, Istvan Kovacs, was forced to confess
to unjust arrests and false witness. Throughout these years the
Yugoslav example continued to influence affairs. The introduction of
workers' management in industry in 1950 and the abandonment of
collectivization in the countryside in 1953 were evidence of a lessening
of doctrinal rigidity and of a capacity for experiment which other countries were keen to imitate, and in 1955 the new rulers in Moscow paid
the first of two visits to Belgrade which repaired the relations between
the governments and the communist parties of the two countries and
further encouraged the nationalists and the intellectuals in satellite
capitals. Khrushchev's first visit to Tito, in 1955, was tantamount to a
confession of error and an apology for the Russian stand in 1948. The
second visit in June 1956, was preceded by two significant events. At
the twentieth congress of the communist party of the Soviet Union in
February, Khrushchev included in his denunciation of Stalinism an in-
dication that relations with the satellites needed to be put on a new
basis; and in April the Cominform, the body which had pronounced
the excommunication of Tito for doctrinal backsliding and obduracy,
was dissolved. This step virtually proclaimed, to all communist parties
and not merely the Yugoslav, that there might be different roads to
socialism and that the men on the spot might be the best placed to
decide which road to take. Recognizing the failures of the satellite
system Khrushchev was bent on eliminating its excessess and so
reaching a new *modus vivendi*. The international system devised by Stalin
was ominously creaking and it was necessary in the Russian interest to
replace it by something more flexible and therefore more dependable.
The problem lay in the process of transformation.

3. Discontents

In June 1956 there were strikes and riots in the Polish city of Poznan
directed chiefly against low wages for long hours. Industrial unrest
coincided with intellectual ferment and with Roman Catholic
demonstrations in August at Czestochowa, the home of a specially
venerated shrine of the Virgin Mary. A meeting of the central committee of the party in July was attended by Gomulka, and when
Bulganin and Zhukov arrived from Moscow in the hope of taking part,
they were not allowed in. The first secretary of the party, Edward
Ochab, became at some point persuaded that Gomulka must be re-
admitted to grace and power; during visits to the USSR and China
Ochab seems to have convinced the Chinese, but not the Russians, of
the need for this reversal. In October the politburo resolved to reconsti-
tute itself, admitting Gomulka and excluding Rokossovski. On 18 Oct-

ober a powerful Russian delegation arrived consisting of Khrushchev, Molotov, Mikoyan and Kaganovich, and Russian troops in Poland and eastern Germany began to move. Gomulka was included in the Polish team chosen to confront the visitors. These were not allowed to attend a meeting of the Polish central committee and after twenty-four hours they left. Hot words were spoken but rough action was stayed. Gomulka was appointed first secretary on 21 October. On 29 October Rokossovski left for Moscow. He was followed within a few days by Gomulka. The upshot of these events was that the Russians, who had presumably gone to Warsaw with the intention of checking Gomulka and his party, decided after a quick look to accept them. The alternative, a direct use of Russian forces in Poland, was too risky because Russian forces might well have been resisted by the Polish army and a fight in Poland could have led to serious trouble in other countries. Gomulka was a communist and had no illusions about Poland's need to keep on reasonably good terms with the USSR. He did not propose to take Poland out of the Warsaw Pact or to share power in Poland with non-communists. He could be lived with. If the Russians had initially feared that a new Polish government would go too far in jeopardizing essential Russian interests, they concluded on second thoughts that Gomulka would not exceed the bounds of the tolerable. In December a new treaty gave the Russians the right to retain troops in Poland.

In Hungary, however, the revolution which immediately followed the settlement in Poland, did exceed those bounds. After the death of Stalin Imre Nagy was wafted into the premiership on a wave of general relaxation and of reaction against old-school hard-liners. In April 1955, however, he was ousted by Rakosi who took over the post himself and held it until July 1956. But Rakosi was unable to stem the rising tide of opposition emanating from the Petöfi circle (the centre of intellectual debate and dissatisfaction) and from the keen dislike of Tito, his neighbour to the south. When even the party newspaper *Szabad Nep* turned against him, the Russians realized that he had become a handicap and put their money on Erno Gerö. But Gerö too was disliked by the malcontents and by Tito, and in October Nagy regained power. He was in fact, if not reinstated, at least confirmed by the Russians, who had been forced to the conclusion that Rakosi, Gerö and communists of that ilk must be expended. Military operations by the Russians against Budapest had been begun on 24 October but the next day Mikoyan and Suslov arrived in Budapest and signified their acceptance of a Nagy régime – but without knowing, perhaps, what kind of government Nagy intended to form. Everything depended on whether Nagy could shape a policy acceptable both to the Russians and to the upsurge of Hungarian nationalism. He announced his government on 27 October and included in it two leaders of the suppressed Small-holders Party, Zoltan Tildy and Bela Kovacs. On the next day a cease-fire was arranged and the day after that the Russian troops began to withdraw from Budapest. Nagy then announced the end of one-party rule and the complete evacuation of Russian troops from Hungary. Nagy had now gone much further than Gomulka and it is probable, though not certain, that he had exceeded the limits of what the Russians deemed tolerable. By 30 October it seemed that the withdrawing Russian troops were preparing to return, or at least were being redeployed with a view to a possible return. The die was cast either on 31 October when Mikoyan and Suslov were told that Hungary intended to leave the Warsaw Pact, or at the latest on the following day when Nagy made a public statement to this effect and declared that Hungary would become a neutral. On that day an alternative government was set up by the Russians under Janos Kadar and when, two days later, General Pal Maleter, Nagy's minister of defence, went to negotiate with the Russians over the withdrawal of their troops, he was kidnapped. Budapest was attacked on 4 November (the day on which Gomulka went to Moscow) and thereafter the revolution was quickly suppressed.

The suppression of the Hungarian revolution was one of those brutal acts of policy which do grave damage to the perpetrator but are undertaken none the less upon the calculation that graver damage would otherwise result. Communist parties lost members on a considerable scale and even communist governments which reckoned that Nagy had gone imprudently far shuddered at the display of Russian might. Before long they found a new cause for restiveness in the Russo-Chinese split. The Chinese were judged to have given the Russians the right advice on Poland and Hungary – i.e. to acquiesce in changes and, in Hungary, to use force only after Nagy had given the revolution an anti-communist course – and Chou En-lai visited Poland and Hungary early in 1957 to consolidate this advantage and stress the need for good Russo-Chinese relations. Khrushchev's subsequent handling of the quarrel with Peking disturbed satellite leaders who disliked the way in which Khrushchev insisted on bringing it into the open and making communists take sides. In June 1960 Khrushchev used a congress of the Romanian party to stage a demonstration against the Chinese, and although in November 1961 eighty-one communist parties (Yugoslavia alone abstaining) signed in Moscow a declaration intended to lessen strife and paper over cracks, Khrushchev continued until his fall in 1964 to conduct a public campaign against the Chinese. On this issue Romania took the lead first in persisting with attempts to resolve the disputes and then in refusing to take sides. Gheorghe Gheorghiu-Dej, the virtual ruler of the country since the end of the war (and undisputed ruler after the fall in 1952 of Ana Pauker, Vasile Luca and other Muscovite leaders), also challenged the Russians in Comecon where, in 1962, Khrushchev proposed to create a supra-national planning organ with powers to direct investment throughout the block and prescribe what should or should not be done in each member state. The Romanians, who wanted a steel mill but were cast for the role of producers of raw materials, invoked the principle of national sovereignty which the Russians themselves had made much of when Comecon was founded. They displayed their dissatisfaction by entering into a separate agreement with Yugoslavia for a hydro-electric scheme at the Iron Gates on the Danube, by proposing that China be a full member of Comecon and by threatening to leave it. Romanian leaders visited Paris, London, Ankara and other non-communist capitals. After Gheorghiu-Dej's death in 1965 his successor as party secretary, Nicolae Ceausescu, also talked of the dissolution of the Warsaw Pact and of the loss of Bessarabia to the USSR twenty-five years earlier. After a tactful visit by Brezhnev to Bucharest in July 1965 the more implausible Romanian proposals abated as the realities of the situation reasserted themselves: the satellites might have more room for diplomatic manoeuvre but Russian predominance remained.

Within this framework the cultivation of openings to the west continued. In 1967 Romania and west Germany agreed to establish diplomatic relations. While a new government in Bonn was looking for openings to the east, the main impulse came from Romania and was commercial. As the countries of eastern Europe grew more prosperous they began to need and to be able to afford badges of progress such as computers. The Romanian initiative was soon followed by its neighbours.

Potentially more disturbing to eastern Europe was, once more, the example of Yugoslavia which, after protracted public debate, adopted liberal guiding lines for the management of its economy and the regulation of its political life. The economic achievements of the fifties, during which industry had been expanded and living standards raised, were imperilled by a recession in the early sixties and while economists were considering how best to meet it a political reform, embodied in a new constitution of 1963, brought new forces into the argument and strengthened the economic reformers who wanted to relax central control and planning of industry in an attempt to get better and more efficient production. This policy courted not only ideological attack but also political risks since the criterion of efficiency was bound to deprive the more distant or ill-favoured provinces of industries which could be more profitably conducted elsewhere. In a federation like Yugoslavia the central government needed courage to allow economic activities to be distributed in accordance with economic rather than political or social needs. Opposition was strong enough to impede the new course – and ill-advised enough to operate a government within the government. The security services, for whose activities the minister of the interior Aleksandr Rankovitch was responsible, went to the lengths of bugging even Tito's private quarters. Rankovitch, disgraced but not otherwise pursued, ceased to exist as possible successor to Tito, now in his mid-seventies. New men, and new classes, were entering upon the political scene and changing it. Elections in which candidates did not have to be communists were announced and the communist party went so far as to accept the proposition that if communists failed to win a majority in a provincial assembly they would hand over to those who did. Tito seemed to be validating the criticism of his arch-enemy Mao who argued that revisionism led logically to the possibility of abandoning power.

4. The invasion of Czechoslovakia and the Cohesion of the block

It had long been accepted that no anti-communist revolution was possible in eastern Europe because the USSR would not permit one to succeed. In 1968, however, the Russians faced the more awkward problem of a revolution within a ruling communist party which seemed arguably to threaten both the security of the communist block as a whole and the permanent dominance of communists within a communist state.

If Yugoslavia had proved itself in 1948 a communist state with a difference, so too was Czechoslovakia a communist state with a difference, though less obviously so. Before the Second World War, the Communist Party of Czechoslovakia was, unlike its neighbours, neither illegal nor underground. It was the second largest political party in the country. It escaped being compromised by the general communist alliance with Hitler in 1939–41 because Czechoslovakia was already occupied by the Germans and its parties banned. It played a patriotic role during the war and emerged after it as the biggest party owing to the proscribing of the collaborationist Agrarian Party. Its leader, Klement Gottwald, was therefore the natural prime minister. He and his colleagues had operated before the war in a democratic system and they now co-operated with other parties in what was at first a genuine coalition of all anti-fascist groups. The first post-war elections endorsed Gottwald's position by giving the communists 39 per cent of the vote in a free election, the highest percentage. Moreover, when in 1948 the non-communist parties tried to undermine communist authority (a legitimate aim) by resigning *en bloc* from the government and forcing President Beneš to install a government of officials (a dubiously democratic procedure), Beneš backed Gottwald and the scheme collapsed. But so too did genuine coalition government. The communists began to make a mockery of it and to govern increasingly through tyranny and terror. Czechoslovakia became a police state. The Yugoslav secession gave Gottwald a motive and an excuse for tightening his control (there were more executions in Czechoslovakia than anywhere else) and the bleak years of the cold war with their talk of American action to liberate eastern Europe put a clamp on all meaningful criticism of the government. Although the government was distrusted, it was not seriously opposed; fear of the police stifled talk and prevented organization. Within the governing party itself debate was atrophied. Even the events of 1956 in Poland and Hungary struck no visible spark in Czechoslovakia, which came to be rated as the most docile of the satellites.

Presiding over this inertia was Antonin Novotny, first secretary of the Czechoslovak Communist Party from 1953 and president of the republic from 1957. Novotny was a Czech who despised Slovaks and did not conceal the fact. This became one item in a movement against his leadership which led to his removal from his party post in January 1968, from the presidency in March and from the party in May. He was succeeded in the first office by the first secretary of the Slovak Communist Party, Alexander Dubček, and in the second by General Jan Svoboda. The first and more important of these changes was effected by a special meeting of the central committee of the party called to resolve a deadlock in the presidium. It amounted to a reversal of power within the party, largely instigated by Slovaks. But it was much more than this. Two larger themes were breaking surface.

The first was the state of the economy. Czechoslovakia was an industrial state which was specially hampered by the drawing of the iron curtain where it was drawn. Economically its western half belonged with the western world, even if Slovakia did not. Its main role in Comecon was to produce heavy industrial goods but in order to fulfil this role it needed supplies and knowhow from the west. Overcentralization had caused confusion and torpor. Following some ineffective reform initiated in 1958 a more far-reaching programme for decentralising industrial management proposed by Professor Ota Sik was adopted by the Central Committee in 1965. Similar ideas had been discussed in neighbouring countries, including the USSR itself, and more far-reaching measures had been adopted in Hungary. There was no serious reason to suppose that the Russians would oppose them and there was an added incentive to radical change in the declining productivity of Czech industry in the mid-sixties.

But pressure for such changes was accompanied by a second kind of ferment. Decentralization of economic management was equated with liberalization of controls and worker participation (or industrial democracy) and these trends overlapped naturally with demands for more freedom generally, notably freedom of expression in the press and on the radio and the democratization of party politics and the parliament – all of which posed more serious problems for the Russian guardians of the established order. Whereas in January 1968 the Russians had apparently decided that Novotny had lost his grip and was expendable, and that Dubček was acceptable in his place (Dubček proclaimed the solidarity of Czechoslovakia with the USSR and visited Moscow immediately after his appointment), a couple of months later Brezhnev and his colleagues were becoming worried by Dubček's reform programme and perhaps also by the likelihood of Dubček being forced further in a liberal direction by the enthusiasm released by the change of government in Prague. This change had been followed by a considerable relaxation of the censorship, by a number of ministerial changes and by the prospect of political democratization as well as economic liberalization. There was talk of elections and popular pressure on Dubček to make such radical internal reforms that these would be bound to raise questions about Czechoslovakia's external relations. Dubček had taken care to make personal contacts with Russian, Polish and Hungarian leaders before meeting the slightly suspect Romanians and for a couple of months his neighbours evinced no distrust of him or his new course, but from the end of March criticisms began to appear in east Germany and Poland and it is reasonable to suppose that the Russians must have begun to ask themselves whether the changes in Czechoslovakia were not more portentous than they had at first seemed. The reformers were growing in confidence and were exciting ever greater popular expectations. Their Action Programme, produced at the beginning of April, made radical proposals concerning the reorganization of the respective functions of party and government, the rehabilitation of victims of the purges of 1949, the position of Slovakia, the revival of the parliament and some freedom for minor parties (within the national front which the communists would continue to control).

To the Russians the Action Programme was objectionable in itself and doubly objectionable in the wider context of central and eastern Europe. It brought personal and political freedom to the centre of a debate which could hardly be confined to Czechoslovakia. The first major upheaval in the post-war communist block had been caused by the example of Yugoslavia in 1948, the second by the examples of Poland and Hungary in 1956. Both had required, and in Moscow's eyes justified, recourse to violent measures including judicial assassination and force of arms. It was vital to prevent Dubček from setting a third bad example. Romania, particularly since Ceausescu's accession to power in 1965, had been making itself awkward in Comecon and the Warsaw Treaty Organization; it had ceased attending meetings of the latter. Tito was still alive and vibrant. (Both these leaders were to visit Prague in August within a few days of one another and to rapturous acclaim.) Czechoslovakia under Gottwald and Novotny had been a key element in the western sector of the USSR's European dominions, aligned with Poland and eastern Germany. The prospect of Dubček's Czechoslovakia sliding out of this sub-block and into alliance with Yugoslavia and Romania was both strategically alarming and an unacceptable display of political independence. Political changes in Prague, themselves a sequel to economic and managerial changes, might in their turn have dangerous strategic consequences.

If the Russians were becoming uneasy about Czechoslovak actions, so were the Czechoslovaks about possible Russian reactions, particularly in view of the fact that popular pressure had induced Dubček to agree to accelerate to early September the party Congress which would presumably acclaim and entrench the reform programme. At the beginning of May Dubček and other leaders of the new course went to Moscow. Two weeks later Kosygin went to Prague and so too – at the same time but separately – did Marshal Grechko, accompanied by

General Epishev, the chief of the Soviet army's political intelligence. In June the forces of the Warsaw Pact held manoeuvres in Czechoslovakia. These had been arranged a long time earlier, but they were considerably enlarged and the Russian tanks which came with them seemed in no hurry to leave. This hint or demonstration by the Russians coincided with the publication of a new liberal manifesto – the Two Thousand Words – which put further reformist pressure on Dubček and sharpened the tension between democratic and counter-reformist elements in Prague. The situation was now so dangerously charged that the French and Italian Communist Parties tried to mediate and the west Germans, equally alarmed by the turn of events, withdrew their forces from the Czechoslovak border in order to belie rumours that they and their allies were instigating a secession from the Warsaw block or were proposing to take advantage of the rifts within it.

Intervention in the affairs of a neighbour was neither new nor ideologically entirely unjustifiable, but the extreme form of military invasion was to be avoided if possible – perhaps to be eschewed altogether on some estimates of the damage that such strong-arm methods might do to international communism and the USSR's place in it. The debate on how and how far seems to have engaged the Russian leaders throughout July and half of August. A first meeting at Warsaw, not attended by the Czechs, produced a letter warning them that their proposed reforms were tantamount to allowing power to escape from the communist party. This meeting was followed by a Russo-Czechoslovak meeting at Cierna-nad-Tisou on the Slovak border on 29 July. It lasted four days and was immediately followed by a meeting at Bratislava of all the members of the Warsaw Pact except Romania. These meetings seemed to clear the air. Before the first the Russians had issued a threatening statement saying that a cache of American arms had been found on Czech soil. After the second the Russian troops in Czechoslovakia moved out and Moscow's propaganda against Prague stopped. But on 20 August the Russians accompanied by east German, Polish, Hungarian and Bulgarian units, invaded.

It is not possible to say whether the decision to do so had been taken in principle before the July meetings or whether it was taken at short notice after them. If there was a change of plan during August, then the event most likely to have caused it was the publication on 10 August of the new statutes of the Czechoslovak Communist Party which amounted to the ending of democratic centralism and the granting of substantial rights to minor parties. These statutes were to be considered at the Party Congress a month later and would certainly be adopted unless drastic steps were taken to change the party leadership once more and prevent the holding of the Congress. That the Russians invaded at short notice rather than after long and concealed premeditation is suggested by the fact that this political programme was only partially fulfilled. Although the invasion was militarily precise and efficient (the Czechoslovak armed forces offered no resistance and the Dubcek government had said they would not do so), its political tactics were palpably confused and its political aims only partially achieved. Dubček was not overthrown. He was seized, flown to Moscow under arrest, possibly tortured, but then reinstated. If, as there are many reasons to suppose, the Russians expected the presidium in Prague to displace Dubček and his associates, install a new government and issue an invitation to the Russians to validate the invasion, they were ill informed and their disposition insufficient. They came as blatant conquerors and although their power was irresistible they had to negotiate with Dubček and Svoboda.

But if Dubček remained in office, the Russians had to remain in the country. In October the Czechs signed a treaty permitting Russian troops to be stationed in Czechoslovakia, in undefined numbers. Thereafter the Russians and their allies in the Czechoslovak party worked slowly to demote Dubček, who was first sent to Turkey as ambassador and then recalled to be expelled from the party. The reformers and their reforms were progressively eliminated, but the Russians shrank from installing their extreme supporters in power and preferred instead a relatively neutral government under the Slovak Dr Gustav Husák. Whether impressed by the spirit and discipline of the Czechs and Slovaks, or by the damaging comments of the world at large, or by the hostility within the communist world to Brezhnev's doctrine that the USSR had the right to intervene in a communist state to safeguard communism generally, the Kremlin used its victory with more circumspection than might have been expected once the initial step had been taken – but without foregoing its major aim of putting Czechoslovakia back under the sort of communist system which Dubček's followers in the party had tried to reform.

The invasion of Czechoslovakia was from the Russian point of view a regrettable necessity and a well calculated action. Some western tremors notwithstanding, it created no threat to international peace and it did not halt the course of Russio-American détente: there was no more than a brief interruption in the talks that led to the opening of SALT in 1969 and the agreement with Bonn in 1970. As a crisis manager Brezhnev proved to have many of the qualities which had served Kennedy well in the Cuban crisis of 1962. But the invasion forced Moscow to proclaim an extreme doctrine about the limits of sovereign independence within the communist block and to make plain that Russo-American détente implied no loosening of the reins of power therein. The invasion and the doctrine unsettled eastern Europe by the violence of the action and the implications of the doctrine, and the use of the ostensibly anti-western Warsaw Pact against one of its own members emphasized the strains prevailing within the block twenty years after its consolidation.

These strains had two main sources: nationalism and conflicts of economic interest. Nationalism was endemic throughout the block, although weaker in some places than others. Bulgaria, at one end of the scale, endorsed the Brezhnev doctrine in a new constitution in 1971 and so elevated socialist internationalism above traditional nationalism and states' rights. This was an echo of Dimitrov's old-style international communism coupled with Bulgaria's perennial leanings towards Moscow to offset its perennially uneasy relations with its neighbours. (But in the seventies Bulgaria sought to improve its relations with Romania and Yugoslavia and even with Greece and Turkey too.) Most eastern Europeans, however, were as loath as western Europeans – or, for that matter, Arabs – to subordinate their national identity to supra-national organizations or causes. To some extent the USSR had contributed to this particularism not merely by its heavy-handedness in moments of crisis but also by obstructing regional associations within its sphere (Balkan, Danubian or other). Any association had to be all-embracing and it must of course include the USSR itself.

There were two principal organs of eastern European integration: the Warsaw Treaty Organisation and Comecon. The Warsaw Pact was little more than an expression and deployment of Russian power. Its forces were commanded by a Russian commander-in-chief and its headquarters were a departmental office of the USSR's high command. It had been created in opposition to Nato and its principal function was to face Nato's forces in Europe. But whatever their avowed purpose, the Pact's forces had other potentialities of which the invasion of Czechoslovakia was an uncomfortable reminder. The defence of eastern Europe included, according to the Brezhnev doctrine, firing shots in anger against enemies within the gates. The doctrine raised questions not about power but about sovereignty. All eastern European countries knew that they had to live with Russian power and observe the limitations which it imposed on their own freedom of action, but they wished at the same time to maintain, even if they might not always exercise, their sovereign rights. This was for the most part a vain aspiration, a kicking against the pricks exemplified by Romania's continued refusal (maintained in spite of a visit to Bucharest by Marshal Grechko in 1973) to take part in Warsaw Pact activities and by Ceausescu's symbolic visit to Peking in 1971 and his reception in Bucharest in 1972 of the presidents of the United States and western Germany.

In Comecon the strains were more concrete. Having come to life in the late fifties after a somnolent start, Comecon was endowed in 1962 with a Basic Plan of International Socialist Division of Labour. This title proclaimed the intention. In 1971 a second basic document was adopted: the Complex Programme for the Development of Socialist Economic Integration, incorporating a long-range programme reaching fifteen to twenty years ahead. (In this year Albania rejoined the organization after a gap of nine years.) Comecon's practical problems were fundamentally no different from those of any international organization trying to reconcile the good of each with the good of all. Its members had divergent views of their interests and the harmonization of these was further complicated by the immense preponderance of power of one member – a complication absent from the similar problems of the EEC. In eastern Europe the division of labour meant two things in particular: that each non-Russian member should concentrate on one or two economic activities prescribed for it by the organization as a whole, and that the resulting exchanges within the group should largely take the form of trading these prescribed manufactures for Russian primary products – notably oil: Russian exports of oil to other members of Comecon rose from 8.3 million tons in 1965 to a projected 50 million tons in 1975. Such a division of effort within a state would seem natural enough but when applied in advance of political unification it entailed a supra-nationalism which members – Romania in particular – distrusted because it removed decisions from national control (the same objections were heard in western Europe) and threatened to reduce particular members to dependence on a single industry or crop, with consequent further loss of political independence. There was also the question of payments, the fear that the terms and benefits of trade with Comecon would be manipulated to the disadvantage of the weaker brethren by arbitrary fixing of unfavourable currency parities. The 1971 Complex Programme acknowledged these fears to the extent of envisaging a common currency or convertible rouble by 1980 after a period in which separate currencies would be equitably and permanently adjusted in terms of one another.

Members of Comecon had a common interest in raising their economic performance and their trade with one another, but particular members also had an interest in trading with, and therefore producing for, countries outside the block: some of their needs could be satisfied only by buying from western countries, their trade would expand faster if they dealt with western as well as eastern countries, and there were political advantages in a commercial diversification which would reduce economic dependence on one or two neighbours. The USSR itself set an example which it could hardly denounce in others by concluding with the United States in 1972 an agreement designed to treble Russo-American trade by 1975. (This agreement was terminated by the USSR at the beginning of 1975 after the US Congress had inserted into the Trade Reform Act 1974 an amendment linking the expansion of Russo-American trade with the relaxation of the USSR's emigration policies. The author of the amendment, Senator Henry Jackson, hoped to facilitate Jewish emigration from the USSR but succeeded only in checking trade between the two countries.) From 1973 Comecon engaged in talks with the EEC about agreements between the EEC and particular Comecon members embodying quota reductions and most-favoured-nation clauses. Western countries were particularly attracted by the possibility of increasing their purchases of non-Middle Eastern oil.

But these horizons were not all fair. Increased east–west trade coincided with increased world commodity prices and increased inflation in the west. Eastern Europe, experiencing inflation in its own economies for domestic reasons including higher wages, was faced with the alternatives of importing a further measure of inflation with western goods and raw materials or of cutting back its trade. When Romania, which had redirected half of its foreign trade to countries outside Comecon, was preparing a new five-year plan in 1975, it altered its first intentions by reducing the share of its trade which it proposed to do with the west; but, loath to retreat into the closed circle of Comecon, it began to explore the prospects for more trade with the Third World and for this purpose applied for and was given membership of the conference of non-aligned states convoked to Lima in that year (but held in Colombo the next year). Even Czechoslovakia, consistently the strongest economy and a creditor country within the block, was caught in this dilemma, partly because of the vigour of its trade and industry. Its trade with the west, facilitated in some measure by the establishment of diplomatic relations with western Germany in 1973, brought in the world's goods but at the world's inflated prices, and since Czechoslovakia could not abandon incomplete projects which depended on foreign contracts it found itself having to increase the value of its exports to the west by more than 20 per cent if it was to pay for its imports by trade. But the government, unpopular since 1968 and aware of its unpopularity, lacked the nerve to go for growth in the style of the post-1970 government in Poland.

In Poland economic difficulties led to the overthrow of the government by workers' demonstrations, a phenomenon rare in any quarter of the globe and least expected in an authoritarian communist state. Increases in food prices provoked at the end of 1970 strikes and riots which the government tried but failed to control by force. Forty-five people were killed and over a thousand injured. Gomulka, who had been brought back to power in the midst of the troubles of 1956, resigned. A new government under Edward Gierek cancelled the price increases, raised wages and social security payments, imported foreign consumer goods (at considerable cost) and purged party and administration by dismissing officials at all levels and placing new men and women in half of the top positions at the centre and beyond. The press was given greater freedom (but was restricted again in 1974) and in 1972 wages and benefits were raised again – the government demanding in return harder and more punctual work – and a new parliament was elected with many new faces but also the standard 99 per cent vote for the communist candidates. By 1973 many economic indicators were so propitious that it was permissible to speak of a boom: industrial and agricultural production up, real wages up, investment up, prices stable. But the cost was a large increase in the import bill and foreign debt, as the government satisfied consumer demand and the needs of industrial modernisation by buying abroad and financing its purchases by foreign borrowing and encouraging foreign investment. By 1974 Poland, like Romania, was doing half its trade with the west. Rather than put a clamp on the boom Gierek continued to force the pace and damn the cost, buying in the west (oil from Britain, grain from the United States) when the Russians could not supply Poland's needs, but as inflation grew and shortages appeared he and his colleagues had to go on the stump in order to repress uneasy doubts whether his policy of buying now and paying later was a sound basis for real and lasting prosperity.

In Hungary decentralization in economic affairs troubled the Russians and the more conservative wing of the Hungarian communist establishment, but a visit by Brezhnev to Budapest in 1972 was taken to carry with it continuing Russian support for Kádár and cautious liberalization. Nevertheless Kádár remained harassed. Hungary's import bill rose vastly, with Russian as well as world prices increasing so much that the government, unable to bridge the gap by greater productivity and exports, was obliged to pass some price increases on to the consumer. At the eleventh party congress in 1975 Kádár himself survived criticism but his prime minister, Jenö Fock, and other senior personages had to resign and new policies of austerity and recentralization were adopted primarily in order to cope with an unmanageable deficit in the balance of payments.

Finally Yugoslavia, where the principal fact was that Tito (born 1892) lived on, a stabilising figure but also a reminder of the unsettled succession and unpredictable changes to come. Inflation was serious, freezes more unpopular than curative. A first devaluation of the dinar at the beginning of 1971 failed to check the rise in the import bill or stimulate exports. A second devaluation at the end of the same year had better effect and with the help of tourism and remittances from migrant workers the balance of payments was favourable. A new constitution, adopted in 1971, created a presidential board of twenty two members from whom a new president would be elected every year – but only after the death of Tito, who was meanwhile president for life. The constitution also gave workers in industry wider powers of local decision and control. But devolution, a specially delicate operation in a federation, did not assuage discontents which were gathering in some areas. Croats complained that their enterprises were allowed to keep too small a part of their foreign earnings. They went on strike, with the support of students and liberal intellectual dissidents. There were similar incidents in Bosnia and elsewhere. Leaders of these protests were removed from their posts and put on trial. Tito blamed foreign malevolence, which was understood to mean Russian, and spoke of the dangers of civil war. The troubles were contained but not extinguished.

In 1971 Yugoslavia resumed diplomatic relations with Albania after thirteen years – and Albania and Greece resumed diplomatic relations after twenty-five.

Chapter 6

Western Europe

1. The security of Western Europe

When the war ended in 1945 the countries of western Europe were in a state of physical and economic collapse, to which was added the fear of Russian dominance by frontal attack or subversion. Their only salvation from these dangers was American aid to enable them to restore their shattered, but advanced, economies and an American guarantee of their continued independence and integrity in the shape of a semi-permanent American occupation. During the war plans had been made for the relief of immediate needs in Europe. The UN Relief and Rehabilitation Agency was created in 1943 and functioned until 1947: a European Central Inland Transport Organization, a European Coal Organization and an Emergency Committee for Europe were established and merged in 1947 in the UN's Economic Commission for Europe (ECE). These organizations assumed that Europe's ills could be treated on a continental basis, but the cold war destroyed this assumption and, although the ECE continued to exist and issued valuable *Economic Surveys* from 1948 onwards, Europe became bisected for economic as well as political purposes.

The immediate precursors of American economic aid were the failure of the conference of foreign ministers held in Moscow in March and April 1947 and the Truman Doctrine whereby, in March, the United States took over Britain's role of supporting Greece and Turkey and rationalized it in anti-communist terms. In June General Marshall, then secretary of state, propounded at Harvard the plan which bears his name and which offered to all Europe (including the USSR) economic aid up to 1951 on the basis that the European governments would accept responsibility for administering the programme and would themselves contribute to European recovery by some degree of united effort. This American offer required the creation of a European organization; the Russian refusal of the offer, for the USSR and its dependants, turned the organization into a western European one. Sixteen countries established a Committee for European Economic Co-operation which assessed their requirements in gools and foreign exchange for the years 1948–52 and was converted in April 1948 into the more permanent Organization for European Economic Co-operation (OEEC). Western Germany was represented through the three western commanders-in-chief of occupation forces until October 1949 when German representatives were admitted. The United States and Canada became observer members of the organization in 1950 and subsequently co-operation was developed with Yugoslavia and Spain. At the American end the Foreign Assistance Act of 1948 created the Economic Co-operation Administration (ECA) to supervise the European Recovery Programme (ERP). In the following years the OEEC, using American funds, became the principal instrument in western Europe's transition from war to peace. It revived European production and trade by reducing quotas, creating credit and providing mechanism for the settlement of accounts between countries. While it was a government-to-government and not a supra-national organization, it nevertheless inculcated international attitudes and fostered habits of economic co-operation which survived the ending of the ERP. (It was replaced in 1960 by the Organization for Economic Co-operation and Development – OECD – in which the United States, Canada and Japan were full members and which extended the work of the OEEC into the developing areas of the world.)

The establishment of the OEEC coincided with the signing in March 1948 of the treaty of Brussels by Britain, France, Belgium, the Netherlands and Luxembourg (the last three compendiously referred to as Benelux from the time when they formed a customs union in 1947). This treaty, like the Anglo-French treaty of Dunkirk of 1947, was a military alliance ostensibly directed against a revival of the German threat. It contained in addition provisions for political, economic and cultural co-operation through standing committees and a central organization, and it was also seen by at least some of its promoters as a first step towards a yet broader military alliance with the United States. President Truman, speaking of the need for universal military training and selective military service in the United States, so interpreted it and the leader of the Republicans in the Senate, Arthur H. Vandenberg, proposed and carried a motion in favour of American aid to regional military organizations which served the purposes of American policy: the senator was in essence advocating a military pact between the United States and western Europe, a military counterpart to General Marshall's economic plan. The North Atlantic treaty, signed in April 1949, by the United States, Canada and ten European countries, gave the latter for at least twenty years a guarantee of their continuing independence and integrity against Russian attack by formalizing and institutionalizing the American intention to remain in Europe and play the role of a European power. At this date the Russians, like the Chinese fifteen years later, had large and frightening land forces which weighed heavily on all those within their reach but lacked a diversified, modern armament capable of engaging the United States. The North Atlantic treaty was therefore a way of bringing American air power, including nuclear weapons, to bear in order to inhibit the use of Russian land forces in the area designated by the treaty.

The European members of this new alliance were at first comparatively passive beneficiaries who, in spite of the fact that they provided 80 per cent of Nato's forces in Europe, were dependent on the far more significant American contribution, without which their own contribution was irrelevant to their main needs and fears. Although in terms the treaty was a collective security arrangement, in fact it was to begin with more like the protectorate treaties of an earlier age whereby a major power had taken weaker territories under its wing. The treaty created a permanent organization (Nato) for political discussion and military planning and some of its makers and later devotees envisaged the growth of something more than a military alliance – an entente or community or union. But nothing of the kind emerged for a variety of reasons: the enormous disparity between the power of the United States and any other member, the failure of the European members to coalesce into a political unit commensurate with the United States, the breadth of the Atlantic ocean, the unquestioning addiction of Americans to the sovereignty which seemed to them old-fashioned in others, the revival of European power and confidence, and the waning of the Russian threat half-way through the life of the treaty.

Within a little more than a year of its inauguration, the alliance was radically altered by the outbreak of the war in Korea which created fresh and substantial calls on the United States' resources and the fear of similar hostilities in Germany. Washington became therefore anxious to convert its allies from passive protégés into junior partners and to build up in Europe itself a counterforce to the Russian armies, distinct from the long-range American air power which, although based in Europe, was under exclusive American command and remained so even when a joint Nato command was created. The allies, however, were still weak. Britain and France, with much of their forces committed outside Europe, could give little help immediately and they were therefore the more easily constrained to accept an American emergency decision to rearm the Germans. The anti-Russian alliance feared by Moscow between two world wars now took shape and at the end of 1950 General Eisenhower returned to Europe as supreme commander of another grand alliance. In the same year Greece and Turkey were invited to co-operate with the allies in the defence of the Mediterranean, although they did not become full allies until early in 1952: their co-operation helped to establish an eastern flank to protect the allied central sector and to threaten the USSR from the south. Early in 1951 a new headquarters came into operation (Supreme Headquarters, Allied Powers in Europe – Shape) and a year later, at Lisbon, the Nato council approved a plan to endow this command by 1954 with ninety-six active and reserve divisions, including fifty in the central sector, and 9,000 aircraft.

These targets were never attained and in 1953 the return to power of the Republican party for the first time since 1932 increased the emphasis on a strategy of massive retaliation (i.e. the threat to use overwhelming air and nuclear power on comparatively slight provocation), coupled with the equipping of Nato divisions with tactical nuclear weapons after 1957 as a substitute for the divisions which had failed to materialize. This emphasis on nuclear weapons, at long and short range, was however partially modified after a few years because, in the first case, it ceased to be credible and, in the second, it relied on a mythical distinction, namely the existence of identifiable and specifically tactical nuclear weapons capable of fulfilling the function of non-nuclear weapons without escalating the conflict to full nuclear war. In 1957 a new plan was produced, based on thirty divisions in the central sector capable of imposing a 'pause' on an aggressor during which negotiation could take place and the significance of a resort to nuclear weapons be brought home to the Russians. But again the target was not attained because, despite the growing German assistance, Britain and France still could not do what was asked of them. Nor were the Europeans, especially the Germans, by this time content with the non-nuclear role and the doctrine of the pause, since they had come to believe that the Russians could only be deterred by the probability of American intervention upon the first exchange; they had little faith in a policy which envisaged an exchange followed by a lull, since the Russians might conclude that they might safely make a local or limited attack, accept the ensuing pause and keep their gains.

This strategic debate on how best to interdict Russian military threats in Europe coincided with the processes by which western Germany was rearmed and admitted to the alliance as a sovereign partner after the outbreak of the Korean war. In the sixties therefore the problems of the division of roles between Americans and Europeans in Europe became complicated by the question of integrating German with other European military forces and later by the further question whether, and if so how, Germans were to have a share in nuclear planning and operations.

When the argument in favour of German rearmament was accepted the French government produced a plan for bringing it about without conferring independent military power on the West German state which was destined contemporaneously to acquire sovereign status. René Pleven, the French minister of defence, proposed that German units be raised and incorporated in multi-national divisions but that western Germany be allowed no separate army, general staff or defence ministry. Adopting the pattern of the European Coal and Steel Community, which had been launched on French initiative and was about to come into existence, Pleven devised a European Defence Community (EDC) with a council of ministers, an assembly and a European minister of defence. The French aim was to minimize the German military unit and at the same time to integrate the German military contribution, both operationally and politically, in an international organization. British participation was all but essential since without it the proposed international organization would consist only of France and Germany with some comparatively trivial makeweights. For France a British commitment was the only way adequately to offset the risks inherent in the rearmament of Germany and the reappearance of a sovereign German state, but no British commitment satisfactory to France was forthcoming during the four years in which the EDC was under debate.

In May 1952 the Bonn and Paris agreements created a complex new structure: six continental European states signed a treaty creating the EDC, the three western occupiers of Germany agreed to end the occupation upon ratification of the EDC treaty, and both Britain and the remaining Nato powers entered into separate ancillary treaties promising military aid in the event of an attack upon any of the EDC partners. But the French remained uneasy and undecided. They wanted British membership of EDC and not a pledge to help it, and they disliked the provision in the EDC treaty permitting the raising of whole German divisions in place of the smaller units proposed by Pleven's plan for incorporation in international divisions. The United States and Britain brought pressure to bear on France, the former by threatening an 'agonizing reappraisal' of American policies if the EDC treaty was not ratified (which was taken to mean the cutting off of American aid to France) and the latter by giving in 1954 a further pledge of military and political co-operation with the EDC (a pledge echoed by President Eisenhower within the limits of his constitutional competence). In August of that year the French parliament finally came to a vote and refused, by 319 votes to 264 on a procedural motion, to debate the ratification of the treaty.

With this vote the EDC and all the Bonn and Paris agreements of 1952 collapsed. There was anger in Bonn, where Adenauer insisted that western Germany must have sovereignty nonetheless, and in Washington, where Dulles decided ostentatiously to cut Paris out of a tour of European capitals. In London, more constructively if belatedly, Eden set to work to put the pieces together again by diplomatic labours and a more specific pledge than Britain had so far been willing to vouchsafe. By the end of the year the Brussels treaty had been expanded to take in the German and Italian ex-enemies and renamed Western European Union (WEU); this WEU took over the non-military functions of the Brussels treaty organization and became militarily an ingredient in Nato; Britain declared that it would maintain on the continent forces equivalent to those already committed to the Supreme Allied Commander in Europe (Saceur), i.e. four divisions and a tactical air force; the occupation of western Germany was ended; Adenauer undertook not to produce atomic, bateriological or chemical weapons, long range or guided missiles, bomber aircraft or warships, except upon the recommendation of Saceur and with the assent of two-thirds of the council of WEU; western Germany was to become a full member of Nato, and did so formally the following year. One other loose European end was clutched. France and western Germany agreed that the Saar, which France had hoped ever since 1945 to annex in one form or another, should constitute a special autonomous territory embedded in WEU, but the Saarlanders rejected this arrangement by plebiscite in October 1955 and the Saar became a part of western Germany at the beginning of 1957. Thus the first post-war decade closed with Nato in existence to extend American protection over western Europe, Britain as the firmest and most effective of the European members of the alliance, and a nascent German state back in the comity of western Europe. The weak point was France.

The next decade saw a big change in the status and therewith the attitudes of France. British effectiveness waned owing to a series of economic crises and stagnation in economic life under a succession of Conservative governments led, except during the first years of Macmillan's premiership, by ailing statesmen; and to the disastrous miscalculations and deceptions of the Suez war of 1956. The American record under the two successive Eisenhower presidencies was also ingloriously lacking in nerve and intellect. In France, however, a nation marked by the humiliating defeat of 1940 and by an outstanding record of political and economic ineptitude after the war, was beginning to recover its health, its idiosyncratic temper, its taste for leadership and its capacity for clear thinking and skilful diplomacy.

France had been a major European land power and a major imperial power but had failed in the contest with England for sea power. In the nineteenth century the decline of France's position in Europe had been matched by the acquisition of a second overseas empire to replace the territories lost to Britain in the wars of the eighteenth century, but by the beginning of the twentieth century France, slipping back in the demographic and the industrial race and spiritually still divided between the heirs of the Enlightenment and the Revolution and those who accepted neither, was becoming discouraged and unnerved and unresponsive to central government. The awful sacrifices of the First World War and the hardly less awful humiliation of the second, separated by incapacity to face up to the problems of the economic crisis or to Hilter's challenge to basic values, brought France low in its own eyes until the exploits of the Resistance and the leadership of de Gaulle revived and personified the French spirit: de Gaulle's identification of himself with France and his constant use of the first person singular were precisely what was needed after the physical and spiritual lesions of a century.

When the war ended the French tried to strike out into a new world with some of the trappings of the old until they found that this would not work. They adopted a constitution and political methods unhappily reminiscent of the defunct third republic, made great efforts to retain or recover their empire in Asia and Africa, tried the old game of weakening Germany permanently, and made treaties with their traditional British and Russian allies. But they also adopted, under the lead of

Jean Monnet, centralized economic planning for the restoration of key industries and of agriculture, revolutionized their foreign policies by joining the anti-Russian western alliance even though it entailed the rearming of Germany, took the lead in devising new political structures suitable to Europe's altered place in the world, and eventually accepted the end of empire. The last of these transformations brought them, over the Algerian question, to the verge of civil war, from which they were saved in 1958 by the return to power of de Gaulle and the thwarting thereby of a right wing military plan to seize control of the capital and the state. De Gaulle tamed the generals and colonels, disposed of the politicians and the remaining colonies and, profiting from a rapidly improving economic situation, raised France from a position of pity and scorn to one of independence and attention.

De Gaulle inherited two recent decisions of his predecessors – the decision to become a nuclear power and the decision to join an economic community with avowed political implications. The first of these decisions was presumably congenial to him. He believed that France could be a major power and he believed that power must be modern. Just as he had been an expert in tank warfare when many of his colleagues were still in favour of the horse, so now a generation later he held that there was a choice between nuclear power and no power, and he held too that beyond a certain point there was little difference between one nuclear power and another: a nuclear power which reached that point became a member of the first league even if it possessed fewer or less sophisticated weapons than other members of the league. The second decision may have been less congenial to him, not so much because he eschewed all unions or harboured antiquated notions about the ability of a country like France to go it alone, but rather because his ideas on the nature of useful unions were different from those of the authors of the treaty of Rome. While aware that the independent states of Europe were no longer what they had been (even if, by becoming nuclear powers, one or two of them could stand up for themselves in the exceptional circumstances when the nuclear argument is brought into play), he did not believe that the minds of Europeans had become supranational. In his view the vast majority of Europeans still responded to the idea of the nation and he therefore based his European policies on the nation state and on associations of nation states. He differentiated between more and less powerful states and held that any association should be governed or guided by a directorate composed of the former – in this case either France, western Germany and Italy, or France and western Germany. Equality between states, with its corollary of one-state-one-vote, he regarded as a vicious pretence, whether portended in the EEC or practised in the UN General Assembly. (The directorate of the five permanent members of the Security Council, however, fitted his theory, subject to putting the right Chinese delegate in the Chinese seat.)

De Gaulle also inherited a position which he found intolerable in a

Nato which he found anachronistic. Following his doctrine of directorates, Nato should be directed by the United States, Britain and France, but it was in his view dominated by the United States with a touch of special British influence achieved by British subservience to American policies. Shortly after his return to office in 1958 de Gaulle tried to establish with the United States and Britain a triumvirate within Nato but his ideas were rejected on the grounds that the formation of an alliance within an alliance would lead to the loss of the other allies. Washington and London, moreover, under-rated France at this stage: they derided French nuclear ambitions, and did not see how France was to dispose of its Algerian incubus, and failed to see that the status of France was changing and would change more rapidly in the near future.

De Gaulle not only desired the revival of France: he rightly saw that it was happening. He also saw that Europe was changing. The cold war was over. It might be renewed one day but for the present the fear of Russian aggression which had prompted the creation of Nato was fading fast. It followed that the Americans could not be expected to stay in Europe indefinitely. Perhaps they would be gone by 1980. Again de Gaulle, taking a long view and a clear view was probably right since the development of weapons technology was converting the American presence in Europe from a strategic disposition into a political gesture, and a political gesture is more easily abandoned than a strategic position, especially if, as began to happen after 1960, difficulties with their balance of payments should cause the Americans to ask what their forces were really doing in Europe. Europeans were coming to doubt the automatic immediacy of an American response to a Russian attack since American cities first came under direct threat from Russian intercontinental missiles: either the Russians would not attack or they would do so in a way calculated to avoid an American response.

Immediately after de Gaulle's return Dulles offered France nuclear weapons in return for the right to put launching sites in France. De Gaulle refused and in 1959 withdrew the French contingent from Nato's Mediterranean fleet. He refused to be ruffled by the Berlin or the Cuba crises and was strengthened by both in his view that there was no pressing Russian danger. In 1962 when Kennedy offered France as well as Britain nuclear weapons he again refused and in 1966 he withdrew French forces from all Nato commands. This policy struck some responsive chords in the rest of Europe. The waning of the Russian threat and of the fear of economic collapse, the achievement of the prime purposes of Nato and the Marshall Plan, gave Europeans a new confidence which they translated into a desire to run their own affairs (notwithstanding that for the most part they already did so). Since western Europe had been saved by the Americans from having its affairs run by the Russians, the new mood was anti-American, for it was the Americans and not the Russians whose presence affronted a new nationalism which was further sharpened in the sixties by resentment and alarm at American economic penetration, the debit side of the American investment which gave Americans control over European enterprises and so over the hiring and firing of labour. De Gaulle's anti-Americanism, rooted in Roosevelt's partiality for Vichy and right wing French generals and admirals during the war, was not out of tune with Europe's mood – until he gave the impression that he wanted to put an end to the American alliance altogether. For this western Europe was not prepared. The cold war might be over but it might recur, and so long as there was a doubt there had better be an alliance. De Gaulle himself affirmed the need for an alliance more than once, but his desire to see the Americans at a distance from Europe created the impression that the alliance was itself in the guallist view expendable.

France in the sixties was ready to relinquish, or at any rate relax, an alliance which it had adopted in the forties out of economic necessity. The change in France's economic circumstances was at least as important as its change of ruler in 1958 in producing a change in policy. De Gaulle was not untypical of Frenchmen and many other Europeans in wishing to diminish political and strategic dependence on the United States as soon as economic dependence was no longer a fact. At the end of the war de Gaulle and other leading French politicians had wanted France to adopt an intermediate position between the United States and the USSR, but the onset of the cold war and French military and economic weaknesses forced the French government in 1947 to make a choice and to choose the American side. The need for money and for food determined French policy. The Marshall Plan offered salvation and France took it. But – like the Americans themselves – they saw the programme as a short-term rescue operation and – unlike the Americans – assumed that the consequential alignment would also be reviewed at the end of the short term.

This post-war drift from an intermediate to an aligned policy was facilitated by, and also to some extent a cause of, the dropping of the communists from the government. From their role as national heroes and active partners in the resistance to the Germans the communists had reverted to a suspect, sectarian position in which the interests of Moscow counted for more than national unity and regeneration. Even before the Marshall Plan and its rejection by the USSR their continuance in the government had become next to impossible on account of the Truman Doctrine on aid to Greece and Turkey for the defeat of communism, the decision to abandon discussions with the Viet Minh and fight it, the stern suppression of revolt in Madagascar and of strikes in the nationalized Renault works, and a wage freeze; communists had already been dropped from the Belgian and Italian governments earlier in 1947. At the end of that year the French communists tried to exploit politically serious strikes which had genuine economic sources in the financial policies of the government of Paul Ramadier, but they failed, their representatives were dismissed from the government and the party lapsed into a long period of opposition. Political power shifted to the right and even when it swung back leftward in the mid-fifties it did not re-embrace the communists and France remained for a decade an acquiescent member of the western alliance. By the sixties France was ready to reconsider its role, and it so happened that, owing to the coup of 1958, its gradual disengagements from the American alliance took place not at the instigation of communists (who remained outside the pale of government) but under the guidance of de Gaulle.

A fourth principal element in de Gaulle's heritage in 1958 – along with France's nuclear programme, the treaty of Rome and membership of Nato – was the rapprochement with Germany. The principal architects of this rapprochement were Robert Schuman and Jean Monnet on the French side and Adenauer on the German. Adenauer proposed in 1950 a Franco-German union, to which Italy and the Benelux states and possibly Britain too might adhere. De Gaulle, then in retirement, welcomed the idea and ten years later he turned it to good account by concluding a Franco-German treaty at a time when his relations with the EEC and Nato groups were strained. De Gaulle's return had coincided with a weakening of German-American relations. Adenauer's political attitudes were markedly personalist and the death of Dulles had removed the principal bond between him and Washington. He was moreover suspicious of the Camp David spirit and Eisenhower's attempts to find points of agreement with Khrushchev. Towards Britain Adenauer's feelings had been cool since, after the war, a British officer had found him unfit to be mayor of Cologne in spite of the fact that he had held that office continuously from 1917 to 1933. He did not like Macmillan, was caustic about his attempt to play the role of mediator between Washington and Moscow, and was angered by his visit to Moscow in 1959 to discuss a European settlement – affecting above all Berlin – without prior notice to Britain's German allies who were more closely affected by such a topic than anybody else. Adenauer also resented Britain's aloofness from the EEC and its attempt to block progress by forming EFTA. He was ready to turn to France and, after some initial hesitation, to find a new personal friend in de Gaulle.

In 1959 Adenauer, after ten years as chancellor and now eighty-three years old, toyed with the idea of accepting the west German presidency. For a man who was Stresemann's senior and had been considered for the chancellorship of the Weimar republic in 1921 and 1926 the end was approaching and his colleagues considered that the time had come for him to retire to a less active post. But for Adenauer the transfer was only palatable if it were to be accompanied by a transformation of the presidency from an ornamental into a executive office. He was willing to be a president like Eisenhower or de Gaulle but not a president like his own predecessors or his Italian neighbour. When it became apparent that his compatriots did not relish a presidential democracy he decided to remain chancellor. In elections in 1961 his party, the Christian Democratic Union, lost its absolute parliamentary majority and in the ensuing inter-party negotiations for a new government Adenauer was forced to accept a conditional fourth term of office as chancellor, the condition being that he would retire in 1965 at the latest. During meetings with de Gaulle at Rambouillet in July 1960 and in Paris in July 1962 – the latter was followed in September by a triumphant tour of western Germany by de Gaulle – Adenauer opted for a continuing Franco-German understanding in spite of misgivings about de Gaulle's version of European integration and de Gaulle's opposition to a European political union and the inclusion of Britain in the EEC. By 1962 he was further disillusioned with the United States under the new Kennedy administration and with Macmillan's devious approaches to the EEC, and in January 1963 he signed with de Gaulle a treaty which formalized the Franco-German entente and sought to make it the core of European politics, a working alternative to or brake upon Nato, the EEC, the Anglo-American partnership, an American–Russian rapprochement, or the American-German entente of the fifties. This treaty was a peak in de Gaulle's diplomacy but he did not remain on it, for the accord was flawed from the start. Adenauer himself was on the way out and his successors were unenthusiastic about this, among others, of his personal achievements. West Germans were the most cautious of the Nato allies in jumping to conclusions about the ending of the cold war and the least ready to dispense with or even tamper with the American alliance. De Gaulle was credited with regarding Britain as Washington's Trojan horse within the walls of Europe, but it would have been more correct to see Bonn in that role, for whereas Britain in its chronic state of economic ill health was economically dependent on the United States, western Germany remained strategically dependent on the United States. Consequently the Franco-German treaty became almost at once a dead letter. It failed to serve de Gaulle's purposes of enforcing a reform in Nato or of setting Europe on a road to integration which would not lead through Brussels and the EEC, and its failure left France diplomatically isolated.

The two problems of how to make Europe safe from the USSR and how to keep the Nato alliance together had been debated ever since the launching of the first Russian sputnik at the end of 1957 had made Europeans feel naked and exposed. Even renewed pledges of American protection by Eisenhower himself could not allay these fears. Some more meaningful co-operation was needed. De Gaulle's proposals in 1958 for a Nato directorate comprising the three powers with extra-continental interests had been made in response to an American request for ideas about this problem, but they found no favour in Washington or London where they were regarded as no more than a French claim to equality with the United States and Britain. A year later, after the installation in Europe of IRBMs under a dual control or 'two key' system, the Supreme Commander, General Lauris Norstad, stressed the need for a multi-national nuclear authority, and in 1960 the United States proposed to instal in Europe 300 mobile *Polaris* missiles on road, rail and river under American control. De Gaulle, asked to accept fifty of these, said he would do so only if France produced its own warheads, thus making French control a condition of acceptance, whereupon the Americans dropped the plan. The Russians objected that it entailed the provision of nuclear weapons for Germany. These discussions, abortive though they were, showed that Nato could not go on for ever on the basis of an American nuclear monopoly. Either the Europeans would themselves produce a deterrent force roughly equivalent to the American nuclear contribution to the alliance and so turn it into a more equal partnership, or some way must be found of creating an American–European nuclear force. The first solution – a distinct European force – presupposed a European political authority to control it, and although Europeans might have liked to have such a force, they showed no signs of evolving the necessary political authority. The solution must therefore lie on American–European lines, and there were two schools of thought, the multinationalist and the multilateralist. The multinationalists accepted national sovereign control and aimed at no more than the retractable commitment of national forces to a Nato commander, together with increased participation by all the allies in strategic planning and political consultation. The multilateralists devised a scheme for mixed forces in which nuclear weapons would be operated by units whose personnel would be drawn from different states. The American administration adopted multilateralism in 1962 not long before the British and French governments demonstrated their continuing addiction to, in the British case, multinationalism as the Americans understood it and, in the French case, a multinationalism which excluded the Americans. Since, however, the Americans hoped that multilateralism would provide the answer to the German question – i.e. how to give the Germans a satisfactory share in nuclear operations without alarming the Russians – they persisted with it despite the opposition of their other principal allies. They proposed in March 1963 a multilateral force (MLF) of twenty-five mixed-manned surface vessels, each carrying eight Polaris missiles, three-quarters of the cost to be paid by the United States and west Germany. Western Germans welcomed the scheme as a means to restore the close relations with the United States which had characterized the fifties; alarmed by the American-Russian rapprochement which produced the test ban treaty of 1963, they saw in the MLF a way of securing a special position equivalent to the possession by Britain and France of the independent nuclear deterrent which was denied them. The Russians, for the same reasons, objected stoutly to the MLF and insisted on regarding it as a case of nuclear proliferation. The French ignored it and the British were scornful of its military value but agreed, for political reasons and after strong American pressure, to participate in it. The Italians, Greeks and Turks also agreed to join. At the end of 1964 the new British labour government produced an alternative scheme without obvious appeal or virtue. Thereafter the MLF wilted because the Americans found that they no longer needed to entice western Germany away from France and because they came to believe that Russian objections were genuine and fatal to the progress of agreements to control further nuclear proliferation. So far as concerned harmony in the alliance they fell back on proposals to give the allies a bigger share in planning committees, and in 1966 such questions were temporarily submerged by a French decision to withdraw from all Nato's military organs and to expel such organs from France. France remained a member of the alliance and continued to insist on the need for it, but would have no part in its operations so long as it remained unreformed.

Restored sufficiently to semi-withdraw from the alliance, France was shaken in May 1968 by an outbreak of revolutionary violence in Paris. The causes were not peculiar to France. All over western Europe there were deep sources of discontent which overlapped and fused: urban squalor, revulsion against the horrors of the war in Vietnam, over-crowded universities and schools, the fight for higher wages in a period of inflating prices. In France de Gaulle's government irritated the young by its tone of paternalism and the liberals by its attempts to direct radio and television and to control the press: the progressive element in guallism had grown dimmer during the ten years since de Gaulle had returned to save France from fascism and military rule. The position in French universities and schools was far from being the worst in Europe (in some parts of Italy schoolchildren had to attend on a rota system because there was no room for them all at once), but it was bad enough to inflame a generation which had been attuned to political activism by the Algerian war and was politically better organized than anywhere else in Europe. Since the war the number of university entrants had been quadrupled by the rise in the birth rate and because no government had dared to change the rule that any boy or girl achieving the *baccalauréat* was entitled to go to a university. New universities were being built in Paris and out of it, but they were started too late. The resulting chaos was increased by bureaucratic centralization, the discontent by out-dated syllabuses and out-dated rules about personal conduct (sometimes enforced by the police). The new university at Nanterre on the edge of Paris became notorious for clashes between students and staff but it was typical rather than unique, and it was trouble at the Sorbonne in the heart of Paris which eventually converted such clashes into something like a revolution. After an occupation of university buildings by students the university authorities called in the police and the police behaved with such brutality that opinion in the capital, not normally on the side of students, swung massively in their favour. The troubles culminated in a night of battle in which the police (this time on government instructions) and the students fought one another for control of the Left Bank while the scenes of violence were relayed to France and beyond by radio reporters roaming the streets. The police won the battle but students continued for a time to occupy parts of the university. At the same time workers in Paris and other cities went on strike, occupied factories and set up action committees which began to look like a new government in embryo. The authority of the legitimate government was badly shaken. The prime minister, Georges Pompidou, was so alarmed that he advised de Gaulle to resign. There was talk of a new French Revolution. But a month later de Gaulle went to the polls and won a sweeping victory.

There were several reasons for this. Although a nucleus among the students had revolutionary political aims, many of them wanted no more than university reform and the strikers were not revolutionary at all. They were not trying to overthrow the government but to get better wages out of it and less unemployment. The leaders of the communist party were too much part of the system to want to risk its disruption, were afraid of the more left wing groups and had no sympathy with students. Above all de Gaulle's nerve held. Although he had to hurry back from a state visit to Romania, he did not let himself be hustled when he got back. Having assured himself by a secret expedition to military headquarters that he had nothing to fear from the army, he correctly weighed up the situation, waited for the university authorities and the trade unions to begin to recover their control in their respective spheres and then, disdaining François Mitterand's bid to replace him in the presidency, won a sweeping victory by the votes of frightened Frenchmen at the end of June and dismissed Pompidou. He then backed his minister of education, Edgar Faure, who made a radical attack on the problem of higher education in spite of some of his colleagues and of much conservative opinion. Faure introduced joint teacher-student management; abolished the centralized system under which France had in effect a single university and substituted for it sixty-five universities (thirteen in Paris), none of which was to have more than 20,000 students; and further decentralized control within each university by creating joint councils for each nucleus of 2500 students.

But de Gaulle's days were numbered. One of his aversions was the French senate. One of his pre-occupations at this point was the reform of the machinery of government by the creation of regional assemblies. He proposed to link this reform with the abolition of the senate and put the two issues together to the electorate by referendum. But the senate was not unpopular and de Gaulle's use of the referendum, coupled as it was with the implication that the rejection of what was proposed entailed his own resignation, was widely regarded as unfair tactics. A majority voted no. De Gaulle at once resigned. (He died the next year.) The president of the senate, Alain Poher, assumed the functions of the presidency in accordance with the constitution, a presidential election was held, and the gaullist candidate Georges Pompidou won comfortably in the second round. In the months following his election his words were fairer but his actions hardly softer than those of his predecessor.

This change at the top in Paris coincided with a similar change in Bonn. Adenauer's retirement had been followed by a short postlude to the Adenauer era with Ludwig Erhard as chancellor until, in 1966, he was forced out of office by his own party. From 1966 to 1969 the Christian Democrats and the Social Democrats governed in coalition with Kurt Kiesinger as chancellor and Willy Brandt as vice-chancellor and foreign minister. This government abandoned Adenauer's attitude of regarding half Europe as virtually non-existent. The sources of this evolution were détente in Europe and Washington's increasing preoccupation with establishing better relations with Moscow without as much regard for German susceptibilities as had been evinced in the past; the abandonment of the pretence that European security and the German problem were inseparable and that no European system could usefully be studied in the absence of German reunification; the growth of eastern European economies leading not only to restiveness against satellite status but also to a desire for the products of the new technology which (computers, for example) western Germany could provide; and to popular appreciation among west Germans of the barrenness of the promise of reunification via a western alliance, the realization that the road to reunification did not run through Washington. Bonn therefore entered into discussions with eastern European states and established in 1967 diplomatic relations with Romania. This eastern policy quickened after 1969 when Brandt became chancellor in a new government in which the Social Democrats were the senior partners and the Free Democrats took the place of the Christian Democrats, who went into opposition. Brandt and his foreign minister, Walter Scheel, opened discussions with east Germany, Poland and the USSR.

Progress was slow because of interlocking complexities. Besides renewing normal relations with wartime enemies (the USSR, Poland, Hungary and Bulgaria) Bonn had to negotiate agreements with Czechoslovakia which was demanding the abrogation of the Munich agreement of 1938 and with east Germany which was demanding recognition as an independent sovereign state. This last issue was complicated by the problems of Berlin, a city divided politically and physically and in which Germany's four principal conquerors still had special rights. Treaties with the USSR and Poland, which included the recognition of the Oder-Neisse line, were concluded in 1970 and ratified in 1972 after other agreements had been concluded. These included: a new four-power agreement on Berlin providing, among other things, for easier rail, road and water communication between west Germany and west Berlin and freer access for west Berliners to east Germany for a wide variety of purposes; a General Relations Treaty between the two German states, a bundle of documents whereby both signatories recognized one another's sovereignty and frontiers and promised to be good neighbours and settle disputes peaceably; and an agreement establishing diplomatic relations between Bonn and Prague and a declaration that the Munich agreement was invalid. Bonn also established diplomatic relations with Hungary and Bulgaria. Both Germanies became members of the UN (1973). A quirky postlude to these transactions was the claim in 1975 by east Germany for the return to Berlin of works of art removed during the Second World War to safer places further west – some 600 paintings by major artists including 21 by Rembrandt, over 200 drawings by Dürer and Rembrandt, Queen Nefertiti and 3000 other Egyptiaca, and more. But that the Hague Convention of 1954 could be held to apply to these circumstances was a hardly tenable proposition in law.

These various agreements concluded in 1970–73 resolved much but not all of the business which a peace conference in 1945 might have been expected to settle. Berlin in particular was not purged of its anomalies. The four powers maintained their rights in the city which remained two cities; the movement of west Berliners to the east became easier but not normal; west Berlin remained constitutionally attached to west Germany but physically contiguous only to east Germany. The reunification of Germany was not ruled out, although its attainment by force was. Brandt's *Ostpolitik* was much criticized by his countrymen and women and although he had strengthened his parliamentary position at elections in 1971, he lost ground in the ensuing years. In 1974 he was forced to resign the chancellorship by the discovery of a spy at work in his private office. His successor, Helmut Schmidt, inherited a situation in eastern Europe which had been thoroughly transformed in the five years of Brandt's chancellorship. The seal was set on this area of détente when Brezhnev visited Bonn in 1973. (Again by coincidence Brandt's departure was closely followed by change in France. In 1974 Pompidou died. In the first round of the ensuing election the socialist François Mitterand, backed by the communists, came first but without the necessary margin for election. In the second round between himself and the runner up, Valéry Giscard d'Estaing, the latter won by the narrow margin of 50.8 per cent to 49.2. The gaullist candidate came third in the first ballot and so was eliminated together with nine other candidates who received only derisory support.)

Diplomatically these moves in the east had been rendered the more delicate because they coincided with strains in the relations between western Europe and the United States. The specifically Franco-American acerbity of the gaullist decade had eased with the general's resignation and death and in 1970 French units again took part in Nato's naval exercises in the Mediterranean, but the alliance entered the seventies in some disarray. The alliance was two things. It was a military alliance directed against the USSR and it was the principal meeting ground of Americans and western Europeans. Hence arose a number of clashes, some related to the conduct of the alliance and others to wider political issues. The first of these was how the alliance was to be manned and paid for. By the seventies it was no longer a preponderantly American host with European facilities: in European theatres and waters the European allies were providing 75 per cent of the air forces, 80 per cent of naval forces and 90 per cent of land forces. The American contribution was symbolic, crucial – and financial; and the cost was beginning to hurt. American military expenditure in Europe was, by the seventies, a debit item of $1 billion in the American balance of payments, and Americans were moved to argue that Europe could not have this costly American military umbrella and at the same time obstruct American policies in other directions. The war in Vietnam had been fiercely criticized in Europe, but the war in the Middle East in 1973 raised ill will to governmental level. The United States was angered by European refusals to permit the use of airfields for the air lift to Israel and by their hurried truckling to Arab threats of an oil boycott. Europeans retorted by pointing out that they depended on the Middle East for 80 per cent of their oil, the United States for 5 per cent, and by chiding Washington for making policy on the Middle East without consulting its allies and then expecting these to assist it. Europeans were further estranged when Washington appeared to be toying with schemes for assuring the flow of oil by force of arms and they were reluctant to attend a consumers' conference proposed by the United States as a way of putting pressure on Arab producers. For similar reasons France refused to join an Energy Authority created within the OECD or to take part in a consumers' oil sharing agreement. Europeans preferred a conference between consumers and producers, negotiation rather than confrontation.

At this point the alliance was virtually in abeyance and matters were not improved by the Turkish invasion of Cyprus in 1974. Greece, blaming the United States for not taking a firmer stand against Turkey's excessive exploitation of the Greek dictatorship's inept interference in Cyprus, withdrew from active participation in Nato operations – a protest caused by events in Cyprus but also grounded in a more pervasive anti-Americanism which had grown with American benevolence towards the dictators throughout 1967–74. This Greek hostility was not offset by any countervailing Turkish sentiment, since the US Congress, taking the Greek side, voted in December 1974 to cut off aid to Turkey whereupon the Turkish government took control of twenty-four American military installations in Turkey, concluded a treaty of friendship with the USSR and accepted a large Russian loan.

At the diametrically opposite corner of Nato's territory two other members were engaged in a different conflict which too had implications for Nato installations. In 1972 the Icelandic parliament resolved to extend fishing limits to 50 miles. The act, which particularly affected Britain and west Germany, was a unilateral alteration of treaty dispositions of 1961. At the same time the Althing rejected in advance recourse to the International Court of Justice (which however ruled in August 1972 that British and west German vessels had the right to fish to a twelve-mile limit). West Germany and Iceland compromised the resulting dispute in 1975 but with Britain, whose interests were more severely affected, Iceland's action led to armed clashes as Britain provided its fishing vessels with naval protection against the armed Icelandic coastguards trying to drive them away or destroy their gear.

A two-year agreement was reached at the end of 1973, limiting the areas in which British vessels might fish and the type of vessel that might be used. This was a way of limiting the catch. Iceland, however, also declared that in 1975 it would extend its exclusive fishing rights to 200 miles. The dispute remained legally unresolved but the tensions were reduced in 1976 by a considerable British abandonment of reasonably well founded rights. For Iceland the episode was an unyielding assertion of vital economic claims assisted by the advantages of operating in home waters; the real embarrassment of the British as a whole (as opposed to the fishing community); the likelihood that the current conference on the law of the sea would in any case recommend substantial extensions of normally accepted fishing limits; and the Nato connection which could be used to bring pressure on Britain by the United States which did not wish to see Nato's strategic installations in the northern sector imperilled by Icelandic action like that of Greece or Turkey.

In the midst of these aggravating conflicts and policy disputes Nixon upbraided his allies for ganging up on the United States. Kissinger, no less irritated but more constructive, proposed in 1973 a new Atlantic Charter to define the common aims of the United States, western Europe and Japan (added because of the economic conflicts which the United States had with both Europeans and Japanese). The United States, Kissinger said, was prepared to defend western Europe and continued to approve its integration, but objected to Europeans concerting among themselves and without consulting Washington policies objectionable to the United States, which was pretty much what Europeans were objecting to in reverse. These were different ways of arriving at the fact that an alliance whose aims had been defined in the relatively simple and restricted context of a cold war in Europe could only with difficulty be held together in the context of Russo-American détente (the negation of the cold war), conflicts in the Middle East, an international economic pattern totally transformed since 1949, and numerous other changes in the world which affected the allies in differing degrees and differing directions.

Russo-American détente was the first, but not the only, field in which one partner in the alliance had gone its own way. This area of détente roused some suspicions and fears among Europeans who saw the common cause of the Nato alliance becoming subordinated perhaps to something else. The growing cohesion of certain western European governments was another factor making for the exclusion of one or more partners from the common counsels of the alliance, since the more these governments institutionalized their discussions and concerted their ideas the more they tended to decide first and tell the Americans afterwards. There was no longer a single focal point of debate and decision for all the allies on all topics. Nor should the popular anti-Americanism of the sixties be discounted.

This anti-Americanism had a variety of sources. The revival of European economies (whose stricken state had prompted the first post-war venture in American–European co-operation) revived competitiveness between European and American businesses. It also made European industries more attractive to Americans in search of wider pastures. Americans provided welcome funds and investment so long as the going was good, but they also raised resentment and some apprehension about what would happen if one day they should decide to go away again or if they should find it reasonable to concentrate research into new technologies in the United States, thus impoverishing European affiliates and subsidiaries and, at a national level, removing from European governments and parliaments decisions affecting levels of employment and investment. Secondly, political bias or strategic arguments which inclined American governments to support even so barbarous (and ultimately futile) a regime as that established in Greece in 1967 shocked and embittered many in Europe and provided confirmed anti-Americans with welcome propaganda material. No less pervasive were two extra-European spectacles.

The first was Vietnam. The failure of the Americans to finish off the war – due above all to the repetition of the old mistake of the Second World War about the effectiveness of strategic bombing – presented to the world the spectacle of the mass slaughter of a small people caught in the no-man's-land of American hostility to China. This spectacle, which would have been sufficiently harrowing in the prose of war correspondents, was illustrated week after week on the television screens in millions of European homes. The effect was unprecedented. Paradoxically it was all the greater because Europeans were convinced that the Americans would never have devastated a corner of Europe as they were devastating a corner of Asia, since Europeans were white. Even more profound, if less evident, was the impact of race riots in the United States. These riots, also brought by television into European homes, upset the picture which Europeans had of the Untited States. At the end of the Second World War western Europeans had told themselves with relief that the problems which had grown too big for European handling – including the security of Europe itself – could be left to the Americans who were mighty, sane and liberal and fundamentally the same sort of people as Europeans. In the years that followed Europe became, for all its ills, by far the most stable part of the world. Then, in the sixties, Europe was shocked to discover that American society, so far from being relatively stable too, was dangerously and sometimes nauseatingly unstable. This instability of a giant who was also a friend and a kinsman was frightening. It intensified Europe's desire to draw apart.

2. The integration of Western Europe

The defence of western Europe against the Russians by economic and military measures depended on American policy. It was effected on the one hand through the Truman Doctrine, the Marshall Plan and the joint efforts of the ECA and the OEEC, on the other hand through the Brussels treaty, Nato and the treaty complex of 1954. This American–European conjunction coincided with moves within western Europe towards integration or confederation overriding national sovereignties. In these matters British rather than American policies were at first dominant. Americans approved the integrationist trend, partly because they felt that what had been good for them must be good for Europeans too and that a United States of Europe would be a flourishing and powerful democracy, and partly because they looked forward to dealing with a single simple European political unit instead of many feeble and confusing ones. In Europe too the idea of integration had strong support during the war and after it. National governments had failed to prevent national states from being battered and their citizens from being killed, tortured or enslaved; a new start on a new and broader basis appealed especially to the younger generations; the hard practical tasks of restoration seemed to require international co-operation within Europe as well as American aid (as the Americans themselves insisted when they promoted the OEEC). The British, however, the solitary European victors apart from the USSR, enjoying an unprecedented measure of European admiration, were thinking of other things. The first steps towards European integration were therefore taken in a Europe not only sundered by the cold war but also distanced from Britain by Britain's choice.

The separation of Britain from continental Europe by the English Channel and its island status were axioms of European politics. Britain had become a maritime power and a world power. For two and a half centuries it had had no land frontiers, since even its troubles in Ireland lay beyond the sea. Its principal pre-occupations were the freedom of the seas, the movements of commerce, and peace. The first two of these objects it pursued by maintaining a naval lead over the combined strength of other substantial naval powers and by ensuring so far as possible that the European nations which dominated the world should include a number of land powers of the first rank but only one such naval power. In this context the continent of Europe was a place to which negative principles applied: it must not be allowed to distract or threaten Britain, it must not fall under the dominance of one among its principal land powers. British diplomacy was directed to maintaining a balance and preventing a hegemony in Europe; if British diplomacy failed, then British arms had to shoulder the task which, though in a sense negative, was also vital to British interests as they had evolved since the Tudors had laid the foundations for a kind of British power altogether different from the continental imperialism of the Plantagenets. The British therefore developed a state of mind which drew no distinction between the near and the far. Geographers might talk of the 'far' east and measure the distance to India in thousands of miles, but to many an Englishman Delhi and Singapore and Hong Kong were psychologically no further away than Calais; they were often more familiar, and they were of course more British.

In 1945 Britain's innate inattention to European affairs was enhanced by the fortunes of war and the prospect of peace. During the war every continental European combatant, including the USSR, had been overrun and at some point defeated or almost defeated. Britain had been terribly hard pressed and had been bombarded from the air, but it had not been invaded or occupied or defeated. In victory it vindicated its right to go on as before, since it is the prerogative of a victor to retain its past; whereas its shattered and disillusioned European neighbours were looking for a new start and not for a restoration of the old order of things which had failed. The British and continental attitudes to the past were therefore completely different, and continentals who expected British sympathy for radical political experiment in Europe were overlooking not only Britain's separate historical development but also its post-war psychology, the intent to repair and improve the structure of British life but not fundamentally to alter or find fault with it.

The advent of a Labour government in Britain in 1945 should have underlined the difference, for the Labour Party, although a reforming and not a conservative party, was no less traditionalist than the conservatives. It consisted of pragmatic radicals and socialists who wanted to make life happier for the lower classes by continuing the gradual and non-revolutionary adaptation of Britain's social structure to modern notions of social justice. It had no intention of overturning the British apple-cart and not much interest in other people's apple-carts. It was a hard-working middle-of-the-road administration which was trying, in exceptionally difficult economic circumstances (aggravated by the end of lend-lease and American insistence on the premature convertibility of sterling) to restore the British economy and reform British society and it did not wish to be diverted from these tasks by unprofitable foreign entanglements. The continent was chaotic and impoverished and, as the transfer of Britain's commitments in Greece and Turkey to the United States showed, could better struggle out of its troubles with American rather than British aid. Moreover, the new leaders in Europe were (quite apart from being foreigners) mostly conservatives and Roman Catholics; opponents it was wrongly thought of planned economies, uncomfortable partners for British socialists. In so far as they were attracted by federal ideas, these leaders were regarded as unpractical visionaries. For the British the nation state was one of those bits of the past which practically nobody questioned.

Winston Churchill had told the British during the war that they operated in three circles – the Anglo-American, the British imperial and the European – and that this triangularity gave British special opportunities and a unique position in the world. Until Harold Macmillan applied in 1961 to join the European Economic Community the European circle was the one which seemed to offer Britain the least. The most important was the Anglo-American. Britain – or at any rate

Ernest Bevin who became foreign secretary in 1945 – saw that the consolidation of Europe under the aegis of a single power could no longer be prevented by British diplomacy or British arms alone, and that if this bugbear of British foreign policy was to be avoided the Americans must be made a European power. Nato was the outward and visible sign of his success, but his endeavours to create an Anglo-American thrust in European affairs, in place of the expired British power to intervene and rectify, made him suspicious of continental federalists who might hanker after an independent European power to the exclusion of the Americans. Their policies were at best irrelevant, possibly damaging, to his aim of bringing in the new world to create a balance in Europe. Furthermore, those in Britain who were hostile to the United States or wary of its preponderance were not for the most part European federalists. In so far as there was a party in Britain which was thinking in terms of a 'third force' in world affairs, it conceived at this period a third force provided by the Commonwealth rather than by a united Europe.

Britain's change of heart did not begin to occur until some ten to fifteen years after the end of the war and even then it manifested itself much more fitfully and slowly than the comparable revolution in continental thinking which had been imposed by wartime defeats. Britain continued to think of itself as a worldwide, even if no longer an imperial, power – a somewhat uncritical adjectival substitution. One of the most striking consequences of the war was the British departure from India in 1947 (followed more rapidly than was expected by departure from Africa), but this abnegation of empire took place in such an atmosphere of self-congratulation that the attendant loss of power was overlooked. The loss of India was regarded as a victory for British commonsense, which it was, but not as a curtailment of British power, which it was too. For generations Britain had been a world power because it possessed in Asia an area where it could keep, train and acclimatize armies for use in distant parts of the globe, and this reserve of power was at least as important as the command of the seas in making Britain what it was in the world. The departure from India, coupled with the loss of wealth and strength during the war, sapped Britain's staying power in the Middle East and made Australia and New Zealand turn to the United States for their security. (The Anzus Pact of 1951, to which Britain was not a party, confirmed the lessons of the Second World War.)

Britain did not, however, draw the conclusion that the end of empire and of defence commitments in Asia, Africa and Australasia had converted Britain into a primarily European state. The empire had been replaced by the Commonwealth, a more elevating concept perhaps but one of less substance since it lacked the empire's bonds of allegiance to the British Crown, government by a ruling class which regarded itself as all one kin, mutual comprehension through a prodigal exchange of secret telegrams, and a British commitment to the defence of all its territories. The Commonwealth became an association of monarchies and republics of widely differing traditions and inclinations, requiring above all development capital which Britain could not provide, and pursuing independent and even contradictory foreign policies on the basis that this permissive latitude was a necessary price to pay for a continuing association which was still worth while. And so perhaps it was, since the Commonwealth proved to be an international organization which worked up to a point. But it contained within itself racial conflicts which posed tests of statesmanship which the British governments of this period failed to pass. In Rhodesia (see Chapter 21) Britain was credibly accused of dealing softly with rebels because they were white and at home the same government exposed itself to even more serious charges. In 1963 Britain had given Asians in Kenya the right to opt for British citizenship, which many of them took. In 1968 the most important element in this right – the right to enter Britain – was summarily removed from them by government which, in its ignorance of the true facts and figures about coloured immigration and integration, allowed itself to be panicked into slamming the door against some of its own fellow citizens. This unprecedented act, grounded in colour prejudice in a section of British society and in racial discrimination by the government, made nonsense of the Commonwealth ideal – and was later challenged and condemned in the Council of Europe. Even if Britain had in the past thought of the Commonwealth as a source of political strength, Britain's rulers in the sixties were finding it more an embarrassment than a support. Community with Europeans seemed all the more real and manageable.

Unofficial pressure groups in favour of a European union had been encouraged, not least by Churchill who spoke more than once during the war of the need for European unity and advocated in a famous speech at Zürich in September 1945 a Council of Europe. These groups organized a convention at The Hague in May 1948 which was held under the sponsorship of many of Europe's leading figures, including Churchill, and which succeeded in persuading the five Brussels powers to set up a Council of Europe consisting in the first place of themselves and Norway, Sweden, Denmark, Eire and Italy – to which were shortly afterwards added Iceland, Greece, Turkey, western Germany and Austria. The members, besides being European, were required to respect the rule of law and fundamental human rights. The constitution was a hybrid, an assembly without legislative powers yoked to a committee of ministers; the members of the assembly were appointed by national parliaments, in practice in accordance with the party representation in each parliament; the committee of ministers, which was included in the constitution on British and Scandinavian insistence against the more federalist wishes of other members, ensured that any authority which the Council of Europe might exercise should be subject to the control of national ministers responsible to their several national parliaments. In these circumstances the assembly never acquired any real authority and at the end of 1951 its president, Henri Spaak, resigned in despair.

The supranationalists turned their energies elsewhere and in May 1950 France proposed a European Coal and Steel Community (ECSC). This venture was regarded by the federalists as a first step towards the union which they desired and now hoped to attain by creating a series of functional associations which could later be agglomerated. In addition French politicians feared the revival of the Ruhr's predominance in European heavy industry. Britain was sceptical on principle and mildly hostile because it hoped that British steel would undersell European steel. There has been argument whether Britain refused to join the ECSC or France made it impossible for Britain to do so; the one view does not exclude the other. In April 1951 six states signed a treaty establishing the ECSC which came into existence in the following year. It consisted of a High Authority of nine individuals acting by majority vote with power to take decisions, make recommendations, make levies on enterprises, impose fines and generally control production and investment in the six countries; a court of justice empowered to pronounce upon the validity of the High Authority's decisions and recommendations; a council of ministers; and an assembly entitled to censure the High Authority and by a two-thirds majority to enforce the resignation of the council of the ministers. In the late fifties, when the demand for coal declined, differences arose between the High Authority and the council of ministers, and the High Authority suffered some attenuation in practice of its supranational competence.

By the early fifties the Council of Europe had been joined on the European stage by the ECSC and the incipient EDC, and in 1952 Eden proposed the amalgamation of these three bodies and their parallel institutions. The Council of Europe appointed an *ad hoc* assembly to work out a scheme on these lines, to include provision for a directly elected assembly and a European cabinet. This was an attempt to build a political association, tentatively called the European Political Community, on the twin bases of economic and military co-operation and it was to embrace most of the non-communist countries of Europe. The prospective membership was large, even though Sweden's empirical neutralism, Switzerland's doctrinaire neutralism and the unpalatable autocracies of Spain and Portugal might exclude these countries in the shorter or the longer run. But the scheme was stillborn. The demise of the EDC in 1954 killed it and even without this blow it is difficult to believe that the rudimentary institutional economic association so far achieved sufficed to support so ambitious a parliamentary structure. As the nation states of Europe recovered from their post-war blues they became less disposed to abandon their essential legislative and executive identities, even though they might be prepared for permanent international co-operation in the less obtrusive bureaucratic field.

From 1955 therefore Europe resumed its fragmentary approach to integration. The split between communists and non-communists remained; so did the ambivalence of Britain; and since the next moves were shaped by the six partners in the ECSC rather than by the larger membership of the Council of Europe or the OEEC, non-communist Europe was at first more sharply divided. The division between east and west was compounded by a division between the six and the rest.

At a meeting at Messina in 1955 the six resolved to form a European Economic Community (EEC – frequently referred to as the Common Market) and a European Atomic Community (Euratom). The relevant treaties were signed in March 1957 at Rome and both bodies came into existence at the beginning of 1958 and started to function a year later. The six set themselves to eliminate tariffs *inter se* and to establish a single external tariff within twelve to fifteen years; to eliminate quotas; to ensure mobility of labour and capital; to ban anti-competitive cartels; and to abolish subsidies which failed to conform with their general liberalizing policies. They further, if more vaguely, undertook to work out common economic and commercial policies to supplement their customs union and to equate their social policies. They also, on French insistence, agreed to give to associated territories special trading privileges (see Chapter 17). They created a council of ministers who would begin by each exercising a power of individual veto but would later take effective decisions by a 'qualified' majority of twelve votes out of seventeen (each minister having a number of votes determined in accordance with the economic weight of his country); a commission of nine, established in Brussels and reaching decisions by a simple majority; and an assembly which would function also for the ECSC and Euratom. These institutions were supplemented by adopting for the EEC the court of seven established by the ECSC treaty. By the separate treaty establishing Euratom the six undertook jointly to promote nuclear research, to construct nuclear installations, to work out a safety code, and to establish a body which would own and have pre-emptive rights over nuclear raw materials. The institutions created by this treaty were similar to those of the EEC. Their competence was restricted to the development of nuclear energy for peaceful purposes. The Messina-Rome programme kept clear of defence issues, with which the six felt unready to proceed so soon after the collapse of the EDC.

Britain had refused to join with the six because of their insistence on a common external tariff which would be inconsistent with what was left of Commonwealth preferences. Britain, with other members of the OEEC not included in the six, tried to work out forms of economic co-operation which would prevent a rift between the six and their neighbours. They proposed a free trade area, embracing the six as a unit and the remaining eleven members of the OEEC. Within this area internal barriers to industrial, but not agricultural, trade would be eliminated. There would, however, be no common external tariff and each associate would be entitled to maintain existing preferences; nor would there be any obligation to permit the free movement of labour and capital, to align general economic and social policies, or to create common political institutions like the European Economic Commission which the six were destined to establish in Brussels. Detailed discussions began at the end of 1957 in a special committee set up by the council of the OEEC under the chairmanship of a member of the Macmillan administration, Reginald Maudling. They collapsed a year later.

Throughout the late fifties France was weakened by the Algerian conflict, political instability at home, inflation and a severe drain on its financial reserves. It felt itself no match for Britain, from which it was also alienated when the Anglo-French venture at Suez in 1956 was unilaterally called off by Britain. On the other hand it was drawing closer to Germany, especially after the elimination of the last remaining Franco-German squabble by the Saar plebiscite of October 1955. A nascent Franco-German entente was encouraged by the negotiation of the treaty of Rome, particularly when France secured German agreement to the inclusion of French colonies as associated territories in the EEC on the basis that Germany should share the cost of developing their economies in return for equal access to their markets. This trend was not without its opponents on both sides of the Rhine. A *tête-à-tête* with western Germany still seemed unnatural and risky to many Frenchmen who preferred therefore to have Britain inside any European organization. In western Germany the finance minister and future chancellor, Ludwig Erhard, used economic arguments in support of a looser economic association including Britain in preference to a policy of integration which Britain was not prepared to follow. But the Algerian crisis of May 1958 and the return to power of de Gaulle clinched the argument. Two meetings between de Gaulle and Adenauer – in September at Colombey-les-deux-Eglises and in November at Bad Kreuznach – put Franco-German relations on a new footing which, in intention, was not very different from the special relationship between Britain and the United States. The second of these meetings was preceded by a blunt and unilateral French statement that the British plan for a free trade area was unacceptable. A subsequent meeting of the council of the OEEC broke up in recrimination and in 1959 Britain, together with the three Scandinavian states, Switzerland, Austria and Portugal, created the European Free Trade Association (EFTA), in which internal tariffs were to be eliminated over ten years but without any attempt to homogenize external tariffs or to establish any form of political union.

The six partners in the EEC turned to sparring over the expansion of their economic union into a political entity. In 1959 France, with Italian support, had proposed regular meetings of the six foreign ministers, backed by a secretariat to be established in Paris. The treaty of Rome was silent on political integration and it seemed to the German and Benelux members of the EEC that the French were trying to create in Paris a political organization of an international character, distinct from the institutions in Brussels and designed to bypass, throttle or even take over the supranational economic activities which were proceeding there. These suspicions were sharpened in the next year when the French elaborated their plan and proposed a council of heads of government with a secretariat in Paris. Such a 'union of states', successfully pressed by de Gaulle on Adenauer at Rambouillet in July, was clearly incompatible with federalist ambitions. The whole subject was referred by the six to a special committee (the Fouchet, later Cattani, committee) which discussed two successive plans of French origins and the objections to them. These objections amounted in sum to the contention that the plans left out all the principal features of the EEC's own constitution, since they contained no provision for a parliamentary element or for an independent executive or for eventual decision by majority vote. The Dutch insisted that Britain (whose predilections, however, were rather on the French than the federalist side) should not only be eligible for eventual membership of a political union but should participate in the preliminary discussions.

The European political discussions of 1961–62 ran parallel with negotiations for the admission of Britain to the EEC. The Macmillan government had been formed after the Suez débâcle of 1956–7 when the new prime minister's first task had been to restore Britain's position in the world. Macmillan had skilfully repaired Britain's relations – with the United States, the Commonwealth, the Africans – by a series of peregrinations, but he had not found an apt role for Britain in world affairs. His visit to Moscow in 1959 had shown him to be an honest broker but not an effective or necessary one, and the cancellation in 1960 of Britain's intermediate range nuclear missile *Bluestreak* had emphasized the difficulties of maintaining an independent nuclear deterrent with a sporadically uncontrollable economy. EFTA was at best a qualified success and the hopes entertained in some British quarters that de Gaulle would kill off the EEC had not been fulfilled. In 1961 Macmillan drew the obvious conclusion. He would bargain for entry into the gaullist EEC of sovereign states. De Gaulle, who had suggested British membership the year before, welcomed Macmillan's approach. Negotiations began in October. They were laborious but were proceeding to a successful conclusion when they were overborne by a serious Anglo–French misunderstanding. In June 1962 Macmillan visited de Gaulle at the château de Champs. What passed between them is uncertain and each may well have mistaken the intentions of the other: an interview between a devious man and a silent one can leave much unclear. It would appear, however, that Macmillan, who had made admission to the EEC a centrepiece of his foreign and economic policies, not only played down current difficulties over Commonwealth preferences and agricultural policy but also left de Gaulle with the impression that Britain was prepared to integrate with its continental neighbours in the military sphere. This integration was a matter of the first importance to de Gaulle who was looking for ways of making Europe independent of the United States but was unlikely to be able to create a credible European defence establishment without British participation.

French opinion was divided about the admission of Britain to the EEC; the tangled discussions in Brussels over food prices disturbed many Frenchmen and during 1962 the *patronat* became increasingly hostile to British admission. But for de Gaulle these were minor matters if he could get Britain into an association which would be strategic as well as economic. After June 1962 he seems to have felt confident that he could do this. The French elections of November 1962 confirmed his authority by giving him a majority in parliament and a welcome success after a setback in October when his vote in a constitutional referendum had gone down. He was aware of Macmillan's domestic difficulties when the Labour Party came out in October against joining the EEC but he probably saw little reason to suppose that the British government would be defeated. (He may have been wrong. Macmillan might have felt constrained to go to the country before so momentous a step as joining the EEC, and it is not inconceivable that he would have lost an election fought on this issue. The main arguments against the EEC, other than the national distrust of over-association with foreigners, were: that the EEC was a bureaucracy and not a democracy, constitutionally speaking an irresponsible form of government; that the EEC was devoted to free competition as opposed to planning and that entry into it meant abandoning national planning, not for international planning but for *laissez-faire*; that parliament would have to renounce its control over vital aspects of British public business; that the EEC was an inward-looking, Euro-centric organization with un-British traditions such as multi-party government and Roman-Dutch law in which British civil servants would be at a disadvantage; and that the process of government by qualified majority, i.e. by giving a power of veto to a combination of one major and one minor partner, was a sure way to create disgruntled factions.)

Towards the end of 1962, when the British and French leaders both seemed intent on getting Britain into the EEC and the American administration was blessing the union, a decision in the Pentagon started a chain of events which led to the rupture of the negotiations. This was the decision to cancel the manufacture of the air-to-ground nuclear missile *Skybolt*, which the British had contracted to buy from the United States. The decision, taken in November on the grounds of cost, deprived Britain of the instrument with which it had hoped, after the cancellation of *Bluestreak*, to maintain an independent nuclear force up to 1970. By paying half the development costs Britain might have saved *Skybolt* and its own nuclear programme, but the price was too big and in December Macmillan went to Nassau in the Bahamas to meet Kennedy and find an alternative. He did not, to de Gaulle's disgust and perhaps surprise, turn instead to France and make the failure of *Skybolt* the occasion for switching from an Anglo-American to an

Anglo-French or Anglo-European nuclear association. This demonstration of where Britain's first allegiance lay led de Gaulle to pronounce, at a gathering of the press on 14 January 1963, the exclusion of Britain from the EEC.

At Nassau Kennedy offered Macmillan the *Polaris* submarine missile in place of *Skybolt*. Macmillan accepted. Kennedy made the same offer to de Gaulle. This was a reversal of a decision in the previous year not to offer France nuclear weapons. This decision had been reached after a division between the proponents of such a deal who hoped thereby to improve Franco-American relations (a course initiated by Kennedy at a successful meeting with de Gaulle in June 1961) and its opponents who argued that it would change nothing but give a fillip to nuclear proliferation. De Gaulle refused the offer. Both Macmillan and de Gaulle were insisting on their nuclear sovereignty. De Gaulle refused to accept *Polaris*; Macmillan, while accepting *Polaris* and proposing to commit Britain's bomber and tactical air forces and *Polaris* units to Nato, insisted on ultimate British command and the right of withdrawal. The one attitude was not very different from the other, and both were essentially nationalist. The Americans, however, were looking for a supranational solution to the problem of nuclear sharing in Nato and they may have believed at Nassau that Macmillan, as opposed to de Gaulle, had agreed to fall in with their plans in return for *Polaris*.

The veto on Britain's first bid to join the Community was an affirmation that Britain was not an independent European country but, economically and militarily, a dependency of the United States. Within the Community de Gaulle's unilateral veto caused resentment, which did not however last more than a few months and was not allowed to interfere with the work of bringing the customs union into effect at the beginning of 1967, three years ahead of schedule. But the next major item, the elaboration of a common agricultural policy and in particular the fixing of a uniform price for cereals, caused dissension. It was in the French interest to accelerate this part of the programme too, and during 1963 Dr Mansholt, one of the Commission's two vice-presidents and specially charged with agricultural matters, produced a plan for fixing a common price at one fell swoop instead of by instalments. The price was to be lower than the price ruling in Germany (and Italy and Luxembourg), so that French eagerness collided with reservations in Bonn which were all the more stubborn because the direction of affairs passed in 1963 to a new chancellor, Erhard, and the new chancellor had his eyes on the general election due towards the end of 1965. De Gaulle played on the fact that Erhard, while reluctant to accelerate the common agricultural policy, was anxious to establish an agreed EEC position in relation to the coming negotiations under the GATT (General Agreement on Tariffs and Trade). These negotiations, dubbed the Kennedy Round, were part of the series of periodic swapping of tariff cuts between members of the GATT, and the six were proposing to bargain as a single team with their most important trading partners, the United States and EFTA. The American president had been empowered by the Trade Expansion Act of 1962 reciprocally to cut tariffs by as much as half but his powers to do so were to expire on 1 July 1967. The tariffs imposed by the six were mostly bunched in a band ranging from 6 to 20 per cent, whereas American and British tariffs were either much higher or zero. Consequently the EEC Commission and also the French government pressed for the lopping of the higher tariffs (*écrêtement*) rather than general cuts (in which they were eventually forced to yield when the Americans proved adamant). Some Americans and British had expected and hoped that the six would split among themselves over a common approach to the Kennedy Round but at the end of 1963 compromises were accepted in order to permit both the Kennedy Round and the common agricultural policy to proceed.

During 1964, however, differences between France and Germany, instead of evaporating, became worse with France still holding up agreement on essential preliminaries to the Kennedy Round in order not only to extract Bonn's acceptance of a uniform cereal price but also to prevent it from joining the MLF and so swinging between the European and Atlantic groupings – an attempt to get the best of two worlds which de Gaulle was determined to block. The year ended with another of the compromises for which the Community was becoming noted. The American administration having tacitly abandoned the MLF, Bonn agreed to the uniform cereal price in return for special subsidies (also payable to Italy and Luxembourg) and the postponement of the Common agricultural policy from 1966 to July 1967. This was substantially a victory for de Gaulle but it left Bonn resentful and ready to give a lead against France in the new crisis which de Gaulle's policies evoked in the next year.

The crisis arose out of proposals by Dr Hallstein, the Commission's president, to extend the authority, within the Community, of the Commission and the Assembly at the expense of the Council of Ministers and in particular to expedite the taking of decisions in the Council by majority vote instead of unanimously. These proposals were a direct challenge to de Gaulle's views and some of Hallstein's colleagues warned him that he was going imprudently fast. Moreover, by presenting his proposals first to the Assembly instead of to the Council as the rules provided Hallstein gave de Gaulle an opportunity to put his fooot down with some show of justification. The French were now in the position of opposing any alteration of the Community's constitution before 1970 while favouring the acceleration of the customs union and the common agricultural policy. Again they were successful. The west German government was keener than the French to preserve good Franco-German relations since it was afraid of becoming isolated. Always dubious of Britain's staunchness as an ally, disappointed in the United States after the withdrawal of the MLF and Washington's increasing insistence on putting relations with the USSR first, Bonn noted with alarm the special courtesies extended to the Russian foreign minister when he visited Paris in April. In the following months Franco-German meetings of foreign ministers and heads of government confirmed de Gaulle's estimate that he had little to fear from Bonn. On 1 July 1965 he broke off discussions in Brussels (the discussions were about the Community's agricultural fund but the breach was in fact due to the differences about the way the Community should function) and boycotted nearly all the Community's organs for six months – including its special committee on the Kennedy Round.

This phase ended in January 1966 when, in a series of meetings in Luxembourg (not Brussels) which were in effect a governmental negotiation between France and its five partners, the quarrel was patched up. French willingness to return to active partnership was ascribed to alarm in France at the prospect of the death of the Community and to de Gaulle's less than thunderous victory in the presidential election at the end of 1965. It can more plausibly be ascribed to the fact that de Gaulle had got what he wanted. Although the five gave away little on paper at Luxembourg, in substance they acknowledged that attempts to proceed to majority voting against French wishes would only endanger the life of the Community and had better be avoided. The Commission too, while retaining all the powers given to it by the treaty, took the point that in practice it had better tread more carefully.

France was therefore in a strong position once more when Britain decided, this time under a Labour government, to renew its application to join the Community. The new approach was markedly different from the first. Macmillan had given the impression that the main purpose of joining was to pull British economic chestnuts out of the fire, and that for Britain the economic benefits of joining would be considerable and would outweigh both the loss of sovereignty and the inconveniences of closer contacts with non-British folk. This prospectus was not an appealing one either in Britain or in the Community, and the procedure adopted to implement it was the bizarre one of sending a senior minister to Brussels to conduct protracted negotiations over details (unkindly dubbed the kangaroo tail syndrome) and without a firm policy decision on the main issue of whether Britain would in the end want to join or not. By contrast Harold Wilson told the British public that the economic disadvantages of joining would be considerable; he argued only that the advantages were in the long term more considerable. He also stated the aim unequivocally: to join the Community, accepting all its rules in advance. He himself, a convert to British membership of the Community, was much influenced by the conflict between the Community and the United States over the Kennedy Round which revealed the vulnerability of an economically isolated Britain in the event of a trade war between continental western Europe and North America. From the British point of view de Gaulle's stand against the Commission had made joining more attractive, since it had removed to the distant future, perhaps to a never-never land, the federal trappings and aspirations which scared Britain as much as they irritated the French president. The future form of a European entity had become even vaguer than before and the British liked it that way. But the chief obstacle remained. Although five of the six were ready and even eager for Britain to join, de Gaulle could still prevent it. Britain's links with the United States and its economic dependence, its recurring debits on external account, and its continuing commitments in other continents than Europe provided arguments, if arguments were needed, for classing Britain as a thing apart.

The question was whether France would continue to insist on these arguments. They had always, even in de Gaulle's mind, been counter -balanced by others, notably by France's uneasiness about a European Community in which two states – France itself and West Germany – outranked the rest and might one day confront one another on a major issue. Britain therefore had two faces. While on the one hand it was as an American appendage unacceptable, it was simultaneously as a counterweight to Germany very desirable. During 1967–69 the latter aspect began to overhaul the former, partly because of developments within the Community and partly because de Gaulle's resignation in 1969 facilitated a change of emphasis in Paris.

At the time of the renewed British application the Community found itself in an unsettled frame of mind. In July 1967 the Coal and Steel Community and Euratom were fused with the EEC. Six months later, the common market in industrial goods, with no internal barriers and a common external tariff, was completed. The common agricultural policy was well on the way to full implementation, and although food prices were high and calls on the Agricultural Fund correspondingly big, the Mansholt Plan gave promise of lower prices and lower subsidies as a result of modernization which would reduce the farming population and increase agricultural investment. But, on the other hand, the constitutional progress and economic growth of the Community had slowed down, and in 1968 France mortified the Community's headquarters in Brussels by introducing exchange controls and other measures contrary to the Treaty of Rome and without even bothering to invoke its emergency machinery. In London this confusion looked like an opportunity. The foreign secretary, George Brown, decided to replace his ambassador in Paris – a successful career diplomat – by a political personality who would, it was supposed, be able to talk more powerfully to the formidable French president, if only because he was Churchill's son-in-law. His chance came early in 1969 when de Gaulle invited him to discuss problems and in the course of a general conversation talked about closer four-power co-operation in Europe (France, Britain, west Germany and Italy) and an adaptation of the EEC to fit Britain in. These were basic gaullist ideas of long standing but as a result of a chapter of ineptitudes the interview produced a public diplomatic row when the British divulged the tenor of the talks to other governments and allowed the impression to gain ground that France was offering Britain a place in a European directory of major states in return for the suppression of the EEC and perhaps Nato too. Britain's chances of getting into the Community either by the front door or the back seemed therefore to have receded.

3. The expansion of Western Europe

By treaties signed in January 1972 Britain, Denmark and Ireland became members of the EEC on the first day of 1973. The Norwegian government, which negotiated with the EEC in company with these three countries, also agreed to join but its act was disavowed on referendum. In Denmark and Ireland a referendum held in accordance with the constitution endorsed the treaty of accession. The British case was peculiar. The treaty-making power of a British government requires no popular endorsement. Nevertheless a referendum was held, although not until two and a half years after the date fixed for Britain's accession.

Edward Heath, who became prime minister in June 1970, had been the protagonist of British membership of the EEC at the time of the first application in 1961. In December 1969 the heads of government of the six, at a meeting at The Hague, had committed themselves to British membership and Heath lost no time in confirming that France, also under new leadership, would back a second application. Heath visited Pompidou in Paris in May 1971 and the negotiations for the treaty were completed within a few months. But the Labour Party was more seriously divided than the Conservatives over the EEC and Harold Wilson, his natural ambivalence sharpened by fears of splitting his party and ruining its electoral prospects, declared that the terms secured by the Conservatives should and could be bettered. He said that when Labour returned to office these terms would be renegotiated. This was in effect a threat to denounce the treaty unless its other signatories agreed to alter its terms. Wilson also promised that revised terms would be submitted to the country as well as the cabinet. Early in 1974 Heath, having narrowly miscalculated his electoral advantage, called an election and lost it, whereupon Wilson's new administration (a minority government until strengthened by a second election in October) opened discussions with the EEC in which the main British effort, successfully accomplished, was to get new terms sufficiently different from those in the treaty to show that the Conservatives should have done better, while the main aim of the EEC negotiators was to concede as much as was necessary to retain Britain as a member but no more. The main issue was the size of the British contribution to the Community's budget, on which the foreign secretary James Callaghan obtained sizeable concessions. The British cabinet approved the new terms with few dissentients. The electorate, certainly confused by elaborate and conflicting economic arguments, probably somewhat bored by this long-drawn-out affair, and not a little impressed by the plea that it would be wrong to undo what a previous government had with all due form and propriety done, said yes to membership in June 1975 by precisely two to one. Thus, twenty-five years after it could have joined a European community on virtually any terms of its own choosing, Britain haggled its way into the Community which had been constructed without it and now embraced in a single organization the Coal and Steel Community and the Atomic Energy Community as well as the Economic Community founded at Messina.

The first effect of converting an organization of six into an organization of nine is bureaucratic complication. A new Commission of twelve was appointed in January 1973 and throughout the organs of the EEC places had to be found for British, Irish and Danish invaders. But the nature of the EEC was not basically changed. The new members belonged broadly speaking, to the same world as the founders. Nor was the EEC's unresolved constitutional problem altered since the new members lined up on either side of the debate on what the EEC was for: whether it was a mutual convenience for swapping commercial and economic advantages, pooling economic strengths and finding together new escapes from economic and social black spots, or whether it was also a political body tending towards political unification and a progressive transfer of power and decision from national centres to international. Britain, like France, looked askance and with disbelief at the political implications: without this scepticism it would probably not have joined. Denmark and Ireland on the other hand were warmer partisans of a genuine internationalism characteristic on the whole of smaller states which had become reconciled to the loss of formal sovereignty unmatched by commensurate freedom in practice. There was at the same time a second division between those who regarded a European Community as an association of European states for the better regulation of European affairs and those who saw it as an association of Europeans for the better enforcement of European views in extra-European affairs. Paradoxically the members who were most inclined, and most able, to throw some weight about outside Europe were the least keen on accelerated integration.

The conversion of six into nine made therefore quantitative rather than qualitative changes in the Community. There were, however, concurrent moves for a further enlargement which would not only horribly compound the quantitative changes but also make qualitative ones. In Brussels discussions were in progress for closer links, leading in many cases to membership, with Greece, Turkey, Malta and Cyprus (all of them already associate members) and also for agreements with Spain, Algeria and Israel: in a word, for expanding the EEC by degrees to embrace the Mediterranean, an area of vastly different economic and political complexion.

The EEC had one Mediterranean member from the start: Italy. Italy's retreat from fascism made it firmly democratic but not necessarily prosperous. Post-fascist governments inherited a situation in which 2 million out of a working population of 20 million were unemployed and nearly 50 per cent of Italy's workers were employed (or unemployed) in agriculture. By 1970 this proportion had been reduced to 20 per cent but the fundamental problems of economic overpopulation remained, for which the classic remedy was emigration (not new, since Julius Caesar had founded Narbonne in Gaul for this purpose). The chief haven, the United States, had been progressively closed by quotas and literacy tests. Some 150,000 Italians left home every year for Australia, Canada and elsewhere, but there was still not enough work for those who remained (and who, since the leavers were the younger, became a senescent population). Schemes for helping the impoverished south failed to check the widening gap between the two halves of the country, and the twin problems of surplus manpower and depressed areas became two of the mainsprings of Italy's post-war European policies. Count Sforza persuaded de Gasperi that the only cure was participation in a European confederation and so Italy joined the European Coal and Steel Community as a founder member in 1951 even though it had no coal and, outside Elba, no ironstone. Instead of growing oranges and lemons for the delectation of richer Europeans beyond the Alps Italy would emulate them, even if it had to import iron all the way from Venezuela to feed the modern steelworks being constructed at Taranto; and twenty years later Italy was exporting 20 million tons of steel a year. The discovery of natural gas in the Po valley gave Italy an unexpected boost from 1958 (described in the unscientific jargon of economists as a miracle) but supplies proved unhappily limited and this unconvenated benefit lasted only a few years. They included, however, the years when the EEC was being founded and shaped. Thereafter Italy became the poor relation among the six with occasional hints that it might be not only poor but delinquent.

Throughout the whole of the post-fascist period up to and including the elections of 1976 the Christian Democrat Party was the largest in the state and the sole begetter of prime ministers. Unrelieved by respites in opposition and unwilling or unable to produce a new generation of political leaders, it evinced a declining sense of purpose, an incapacity to master economic problems and a laxness in regard to standards of public morality which would have ensured its defeat if its main opponent had not been the communist party. The socialist left was riddled by fissures but the communists, like the Christian Democrats, maintained their unity – in spite of the shocks of 1956 and 1968 which lost them some middle-class and intellectual support but did not erode their popular following. During the brief pontificate of John XXIII (1958–63) there was a lessening of papal interference in Italian affairs but no abrogation of the Vatican's special right to intervene under the Lateran Treaty of 1929. Pius XII's excommunication of communists was lifted, there was no repetition of the abuse levelled at President Gronchi for visiting Moscow, and although the debate on civil divorce in Italy in 1969–70 led to a recrudescence of clerical intervention, the church-and-state question did not rise above the level of an accustomed, if sometimes exasperating, family dispute. Italian democracy succumbed neither to communism nor clericalism. Nor did it suffer the fate of Greek democracy although a fascist plot contrived by prince Valerio Borghese was detected in December 1970. Nevertheless by the seventies Italy was in poor health politically as well as economically. The government inspired little faith, public services were regularly breaking down, corruption was an open and even popular topic of conversation, inflation rose to 25 per cent (in 1974, the year after the oil crisis) and the deficit on the balance of payments reached an appalling $8.25 billion (of which $5 billion was for oil). West Germany and the IMF came to the rescue but Italy looked like being a permanent drain on the EEC and, particularly after the regional elections of June 1975, a political risk as the communist share of the poll edged up towards that of the Christian Democrats and Italy's allies asked themselves what they would do if the communists came into the government (they had last shared in government in 1947) or if communist successes in elections provoked the right into a coup. The problem was evaded, and thereby prolonged, when in the general election of 1976 the Christian Democrats managed to maintain a small lead over the communists but were forced to form a single-party government without a parliamentary majority.

Italy's Mediterranean neighbours to east and west were even more awkward from the point of view of membership of the EEC. Greece was even poorer than Italy and lost in 1967 its democractic regime. Spain politically and economically was, like its ruler, in a state of suspended animation. Portugal, geographically not a Mediterranean country but possessing many of the characteristics of one including poverty, seemed incurably set in its dictatorial mould until this was suddenly broken in 1974 by the strains of overexertion in Africa.

The Greek coup of April 1967 was made by a small group of army officers, a grade below the top ranks and outside the upper class crust which had normally monopolized these upper grades. They owed their advancement to the expansion of the army after the Second World War and inasmuch as this expansion had been a riposte to a communist threat they were in some sort its product. They were also fanatical, if unintelligent, anti-communist salvationists who, no less than Hitler, saw politics in black and white terms, a simple and fierce contest between good and evil. Their coup was therefore not a conservative one but a radical one, although it had at the start the acquiescence and even the support of traditional conservatives (as the Nazis had been supported by aristocrats like von Papen and by conservative industrialists). Whether the coup had also American support is doubtful. American interference in Greek affairs was undoubted and so was American suspiciousness of the centre politicians who were ousted by the coup, but of the variety of possible coups under more or less open discussion at the time the Americans may be presumed to have preferred something more traditional than the one which in fact occurred. Colonels Papadopoulos and Makarezos and Brigadier Pattakos were neither particularly eminent in the service nor particularly appealing to the public. What is certain, however, is that the Americans were widely assumed to have had a hand in the plot and behaved afterwards as though they had. Their support of a régime was, in its turn, conditioned by the balance of American and Russian forces in the eastern Mediterranean and by the continuing war in the Middle East.

Greek politics had been transformed by the communist attempt to take power in Athens at the end of 1944. This attempt was foiled by British troops and the communists in retreat committed atrocities (to some extent reciprocated by their antagonists) which seared the Greek consciousness for a whole generation. These atrocities also set Greek politics in a cold war mould before the cold war began. In place of the old strife between royalists and republicans a new pattern of communists and anti-communists was created; it not only preceded but also survived similar patterns in other parts of Europe. The government which fought the communists in 1944 was presided over by a liberal republican, George Papandreou, who had suffered at the hands of the pre-war right wing dictatorship of General Metaxas which had been supported by King George II. After the rising this same king returned and after his death in 1947 his brother Paul was widely accepted as a symbol of anti-communist unity. This pattern was reinforced by the renewal in 1946–49 of the communist rebellion which was only defeated after Yugoslavia seceded from the Stalinist block and the Americans had equipped and trained a large Greek army. The officers in this army were carefully selected and rigorously right wing. The continuing conflict of the late forties was an economic and social disaster for Greece, partly alleviated by American aid. Greece joined Nato in 1952. Already dissociated from its nearest European neighbours by the ideological right, it became also a cog in the formal alliance of western against eastern Europe. Yet it lay in eastern Europe and its alliance with western countries could comfortably continue only so long as it was democratic.

During the fifties and most of the sixties it was democratic. There was some oppression of communists and, particularly towards the end of the period, some political gerrymandering, but the conservative governments of Field Marshal Papagos and Constantine Karamanlis had solid popular support. The latter, in the course of an unprecedented eight-year period of office, stabilized the currency and achieved some economic development (especially in tourism). A scarcely disguised communist party re-entered the political arena but never got more than 15 per cent of the vote, except in the special circumstances of 1958 when its 25 per cent included a big protest vote against the government's handling of the Cyprus crisis. The Centre was fragmented by personal jealousies and out of office until, in 1963 and under Papandreou's leadership, it won more seats in parliament than any other party. During the next few years Papandreou initiated a programme of social improvement, notably in education and health, but he soon got into trouble with the palace, where on Paul's death his young, inexperienced and badly advised son Constantine now reigned, and he roused the hostility of the class of persons who equate all social reform with communism. This hostility was accentuated by the activities of the Prime Minister's son Andreas, an economist who had been induced by Karamanlis to exchange an American professorship for a non-party professional post in Athens. Andreas Papandreou was a social democrat of the type found in Scandinavia or the left wing of the American Democratic Party (he had been an active campaigner for Hubert Humphrey); his incursion into Greek politics irritated other leaders more particularly because the Centre Union led by his father was not a left wing party like the British Labour Party so much as a centre or right-centre party like the French Radical Socialists. He became a useful bogey for the Right which began to raise the cry that the country was in danger from communism, and in 1965 he was alleged to have become implicated with a left wing secret society in the army called Aspida – a society which can hardly have been very left wing if it existed in the Greek army, and a charge which was probably a put up job: after the coup expected revelations failed to materialize.

So long as king and prime minister worked in harmony there was little chance of a coup, but after an initial amicability these two fell out over the control of the armed forces. The king regarded this control as part of his royal prerogative to be exercised through a minister of defence acceptable to him. Papandreou, while retaining the palace's man in the post, believed on the contrary that the armed forces should be subordinate to civil control exercised through the prime minister and cabinet. The clash came when Papandreou sought to change the chief of staff and the minister of defence refused to dismiss him or to accept his own dismissal from the government. Papendreou decided to solve the tangle by becoming his own minister of defence but the king refused to appoint him and dismissed him from the premiership. The king had meanwhile been intriguing with some of Papandreou's party colleagues who were induced to abandon him and so bring the government down in parliament. There followed a period of squalid manoeuvres accompanied by minor demonstrations in the streets and a few strikes, until the moderate elements of both the Right and the Centre came together to put an end to an undedifying spectacle which had been started by the king's unconstitutional behaviour and to hold office pending fresh elections. But the extremists on the Right, assuming as did most people, that the Centre Union would win the election, resolved that it should not take place. This was the immediate cause of the coup.

After the coup little was heard of the communist threat which was supposed to justify it, and the seizure of the papers of the left wing party failed to produce any evidence in support. The coup was a simple seizure of power by a handful of military bigots. At the end of the year the king attempted a counter-coup which was as incompetent as the first coup was efficient; after a few hours he fled to Rome. The new régime dismantled the apparatus of the state, purged the armed forces and the Church, annulled Papandreou's social reforms, browbeat the judiciary and established strict control over the press and broadcasting. In addition it resorted to torture and brutality on a big scale and, as an international commission of lawyers subsequently found, as a deliberate instrument of policy. Torture by the police was not unknown in Greece but the extent to which it was practised and approved by the régime appalled the outside world when the facts became inescapable. As a result charges brought against Greece in the Council of Europe by the Dutch and Scandinavian governments for breaches of democratic safeguards were amended to more serious charges under the European Convention of Human Rights and Greece was forced to leave the Council in order to escape suspension from it. The American government, however, viewed these proceedings with no more than embarrassment and after a brief period of indecision gave the régime its accolade in the shape of arms supplies. Greece as a *place d'armes* for Nato seemed more important than Greece as a conforming member of the society of free and democratic nations which Nato was proclaimed to be.

The Greek dictatorship, which began as a triumvirate of colonels (George Papadopoulos, Stylianos Pattakos and Nikolaos Makarezos) was modified in 1971 when the last two were eliminated by the first; in 1973 when, following a mutiny in the navy, the monarchy was abolished; and later in that year when the army transferred effective power from Papadopoulos to Brigadier Dimitrios Ioannides, the chief of the military police. The funeral of George Papandreou earlier in the year had provided the occasion for a portentously large demonstration in Athens against the regime and students in particular continued to harass it with an indignant boldness which cost them dear. The regime collapsed in 1974 under the weight of its bungling in Cyprus (see Chapter 13) which led to a confrontation with Turkey and a military call-up for which the military rulers of the country had prepared with a farcical incompetence reminiscent of the equally empty militarism of an earlier Mediterranean *bombastes*, Mussolini. Karamanlis, who had been living in exile in Paris, returned to form a democratic coalition government and consolidated his position by winning for his party a clear majority over all others in elections held at the end of the year. The electorate also voted by two to one to abolish the monarchy.

Karamanlis was anxious to renew discussions which had lapsed between Greece and the EEC. His reasons were both political and economic. Greece needed friends. Dependence on the United States was obnoxious to most Greeks who believed that the Americans had not only supported the fallen junta but had helped it to power in the first place. There was no thought, except among the communists who had done badly in the elections, of switching to the Russian camp, and neither political nor economic profit in an association with Comecon. Karamanlis hoped, as did other democratic European leaders, that membership of the EEC would be a barrier to another fall into dictatorship in Greece, and he was also looking for allies against Turkey with which a new conflict was looming in the Aegean at the whiff of oil under the waters. Economically too Greece needed the EEC. The dictatorship had reversed the favourable economic performance of the sixties when prices in Greece had been remarkably stable and the booming economy of Germany had provided some relief for Greece's chronic state of economic overpopulation. The dictators, anxious to win support at home, had distributed favours to various classes. In order to do this they had inflated the money supply with the result that the lucky favourites had stimulated an import boom which had seriously upset the balance of payments and produced heavy and largely short-term foreign debts. Inflation reached an acknowledged 35 per cent and was certainly higher.

Furthermore Greece, as a predominantly agricultural country, faced a basic problem which was politically insoluble without the goad of foreign pressures such as an organization like the EEC might provide. Greek agriculture employed 40 per cent of the working population but contributed only 16 per cent of GNP. Like agriculture in other Mediterranean countries it was more a way of life than an economic activity. The land was owned in small and often separate parcels (the national average was about 12 acres, most holdings much smaller), Greek convention and testamentary law promoted fragmentation, and the consequent inefficiency drove peasant proprietors into the towns whence they neglected their holdings either through absenteeism or because of the family feuds which were a common consequence of the division of property enforced by law. The produce of the land went primarily to the rich foreign markets of western Europe; the domestic market got what was left over and since demand exceeded supply the Greek consumer had to pay high prices. The trade, foreign and domestic, was in the hands of middlemen who made their profits not only in exports but also at home since they bought the whole of a farmer's crop early in the year before domestic prices had begun to rise and sold it (after satisfying export markets) on a rising market. In order to appease the farmers, who were a substantial proportion of the electorate and also commanded more sympathy than middlemen, governments disbursed subsidies which condoned the structural shortcomings of the industry and paid for them out of the public purse. While economists bewailed this mismanagement, politicians could see no alternative – unless membership of the EEC were to enforce changes in practice which were incompatible with the EEC's own rules. Whether this was what the EEC was for had not been discussed among its members when in 1975 Greece formally applied for full membership.

Italy and Greece, despite the peculiar problems of each, were not special cases. Similar situations existed elsewhere in the Mediterranean even if, by the mid seventies, other countries were further back in the queue for Brussels. In regard to Spain it had become axiomatic that nothing much would happen so long as Franco lived, although the discontents of liberals, separatists and others were plain and sometimes violent, as when the prime minister, Admiral Carrero Blanco, was assassinated in Madrid in 1973. Two years later, in November 1975, Franco died in his bed and the planned transformation of Spain into a working monarchy took effect peacefully under the somewhat colourless and initially indeterminate rule of the grandson of Alfonso XIII, Juan Carlos. Unexpectedly change in Spain was preceded by change in Portugal when, in April 1974, a group of middling and junior army officers overthrew the dictatorship and installed a junta of seven under the presidency of General Antonio de Spinola, a returned and critical African governor (see the note on page III). A tussle for power followed within the dominant Armed Forces Movement and between the political parties which took shape after the coup. General Spinola resigned in September and fled the country in the following March after becoming involved in an unsuccessful anti-communist coup. A communist bid for sole or predominant power failed. Elections in April 1975 gave the socialists led by Dr Mario Soares 38 per cent of the vote and relegated the communists with 12.5 per cent to third place behind the right-centre Popular Democrats (26 per cent). Portugal seemed many times on the brink of civil war. The Armed Forces Movement and the army itself were split, but a coup in favour of the extreme left misfired and senior officers, alarmed by the prospect of anarchy, combined to support a minority socialist government and the installation of the relatively uncommitted General Ramalho Eanes first as chief of staff and then as president.

Note

Northern Ireland

Northern Ireland, frequently but wrongly called Ulster, was that part of Ireland which remained part of the United Kingdom when in 1922 the rest of Ireland broke away from the union created in 1800. During the winter of 1921–22 there were two principal issues in debate between the English and the Irish. The partition of Ireland was only the second of these since it was widely regarded as inevitable and the more heated debates, in London and among the Irish leaders themselves, were about the status of the Irish state which, the English insisted and a narrow majority of the provisional Irish parliament agreed, should be a Free State within the British Commonwealth and Empire, owing allegiance to the British crown and presided over by a British governor-general. In Ireland a republican minority pressed its case to the point of civil war but lost and Ireland, although a separate member of the League of Nations from 1923, did not become a fully independent republic until 1937.

In the north-east a border was eventually agreed in 1925. The province of Northern Ireland inherited from the Act of Union of 1800 the right to elect members for the parliament at Westminster. It had also, under the Government of Ireland Act 1920, a bicameral legislature and an executive of its own with a considerable degree of internal autonomy (extended in 1948). The province was governed from its inception until 1972 by a Protestant oligarchy dominated by land-owners but embracing in later years representatives of the more prosperous urban and professional classes, one of whom, Brian Faulkner, became its last prime minister. The power of this oligarchy rested fairly and squarely on the electorate in which Protestants outnumbered Roman Catholics by two to one. The people of Northern Ireland were divided three ways. There was, first, the, most striking and emotive religious division, a relic of the antiquated politics of seventeenth-century Europe. There was the division between those who wanted the unification of Ireland and those who opposed it and those who felt no urgent concern about it; and finally there was the division between bosses and workers, rich and poor. These divisions overlapped and the overlapping made the province's politics. The bosses were all Protestants but not all the Protestants were bosses. The partisans of a united Ireland were all Roman Catholics but not all Roman Catholics wanted Ireland united; or not immediately; or not by force. The aim of the dominant class – part of a majority in religious terms but a minority in socio-economic terms – was to remain in control, making such reformist concessions as calculation might enjoin (as to which opinions would differ). The aims of the opposition, and so their tactics, varied and in 1969 the IRA (descendants of the Irish Republican Army formed to evict the English from Ireland) split. The larger group, adopting a marxist interpretation of the situation, aimed to enlarge its base among the deprived Roman Catholic minority by enlisting the support of the poorer Protestants; this group put socialism first and abandoned violence in favour of propaganda. The other group, called the Provisional IRA, maintained the traditional policy of achieving a united Ireland by the eviction of the English (who had conveniently returned) by the traditional weapon of violence. Their interpretation of the situation was not class conflict but national war. English aims, finally, were negative. The English had lost all will to remain in any part of Ireland and regarded a united Ireland as a natural but probably remote eventuality. They felt an obligation to stand by the established order in Northern Ireland but both Conservative and Labour governments saw the need to push the provincial oligarchy into civil and political reforms, as a matter of expediency and as a matter of justice. Both believed, or acted as though they believed, that no more than this was necessary, a delusion from which they should have been disabused by the events of 1969–72.

These were the last years of the old order and in them the province had three prime ministers. Disorders, particularly on historic or religious festivals, were a normal feature of political life but not normally lethal. In 1966 disorder had been aggravated by a spate of killings by the newly formed (Protestant) Ulster Volunteer Force, but the authorities regained control until in 1969 political murder reappeared. In that and the next year the number of victims was small (thirteen and twenty respectively) but they sufficed to induce the British government to send troops. This seemingly extreme reaction was an aspect of the peculiar dilemma of the province. The local forces of law and order – the Royal Ulster Constabulary supplemented by the B-Special Constables – were composed of Protestants and were regarded by Roman Catholics as instruments of the Protestant sectarian supremacy. Their use to suppress disorders, even their continued existence, were incompatible with a policy of recognising and rectifying Roman Catholic grievances. Consequently some other force had to be imported. Conversely the dissolution of the B-Specials and the disarming of the RUC, on which the British government insisted in 1970, intensified Protestant apprehensions for their own fate and reinforced their intransigence.

Having intervened thus far the English, anxious to retire again as soon as possible, pressed the provincial executive to introduce reforms to satisfy those among the Roman Catholics who were agitating for civil rights. Successive prime ministers, Terence O'Neill and James Chichester-Clark, were willing in principle but inhibited by their own supporters who regarded reforms as a prelude to further concessions leading to the unification of Ireland with dire consequences for the plight of Protestants and the economy of the northern counties. The hold of such leaders over the Protestant majority was further weakened by the emergence of new leaders whether, like Ian Paisley, eloquent antipapalists of a kind no longer found outside Northern Ireland or, like William Craig, protagonists of the right of the majority to have its way and fight for it. Nevertheless a number of reforms were enacted. Unhappily they were years too late. They divided Protestants and no longer satisfied Roman Catholics whose attention was being diverted from civil rights to sectarianism by the Paisleyites on the one hand and the Provisionals on the other. Killings multiplied (173 in 1971) and in August a new new prime minister, Brian Faulkner, resorted to detention and internment without trial. In one night 342 persons were arrested. A number of them were clearly the wrong persons. More important, not one of them was a Protestant. This was not surprising since the object of the operation was to break the IRA.

But the operation had the opposite effect. It strengthened the Provisionals. It swung Roman Catholic opinion, which had at first welcomed British troops as protection against Protestant militants, over to the IRA and forced the official IRA to join the Provisionals in denouncing the British government, without whose endorsement Faulkner could not have acted. Stories of brutality and torture by the English, subsequently endorsed by the European Commission on Human Rights, added fuel to the flames. The Protestants were both emboldened and alarmed, a fateful combination: emboldened because Faulkner had not ventured to intern even the most militant UVF leaders and alarmed because they felt denuded in the face of increasing IRA violence and the emasculation of their own means of securing law and order. A new Protestant self-help force appeared, the Ulster Defence Association, as a counterpart to the Provisionals. The provincial executive became ineffective and in March 1972 it was suspended. The British government assumed direct responsibility.

Direct rule from Westminster involved Britain in direct confrontation with the opposition and the opposition now was not the Roman Catholic parties or civil rights movement but the Provisional IRA. Nevertheless the Heath government set to work to find a constitutional answer to Northern Ireland's problems. The policy had two pillars and they were incompatible. The one was power-sharing, that is to say an insistence on Roman Catholic participation in government at all levels including a restored provincial executive which was to be permanently a coalition and, secondly, democratic endorsement by the province's electors. By 1972 the Protestant majority of the electorate was prepared to endorse no such thing. Protestants as a whole were justly enraged by the murderous activities of the Provisionals, and Protestant militants took to killing twice as many civilians as the Provisionals (who directed their fire more particularly at the British troops). Thus the British government's policy, enshrined in a White Paper of March 1973 and apparently triumphant at a conference at Sunningdale in December, was for a second time foredoomed by unreality and the addition at Sunningdale of a gesture towards unification by the creation of a Council of Ireland (north and south) only made its rejection doubly certain. The British general election, unexpectedly called by Heath in February 1974, gave the electors in Northern Ireland a chance to show their mind and they decisively rejected the Sunningdale scheme and made it unworkable. The restored executive survived for a while but was brought down in May by Protestant demonstrations and a general strike against power-sharing, leading to the declaration of a state of emergency. London's answers were to fly in more troops and resume in May direct rule: the two things it least wanted to do.

From the winter of 1972–73 both sides within the province had produced groups which were trying to reach out to one another but they were too tentative and submerged to be much heard amid the clash of arms and rhetoric. Truces were arranged but were imperfect and short. Horrors multiplied but produced for the time being more horrors rather than revulsion. The English put a brave face on their helplessness and justified their presence by predicting, with some superficial plausibility, a blood bath if they were to leave.

Part Three

The Middle East

Chapter 7

The Arab World and Israel

In the seventh century A.D. the Arabs, united by a single tongue and a single faith, surged out of the Arabian peninsula and created an empire which stretched at its zenith from the Pyrenees, along North Africa, through what was later called the Middle East and deep into central Asia. The successors of Mahomet, or caliphs, failed to preserve the unity of this vast and increasingly polyglot realm but they imposed their religion on non-Arab peoples, so that in the twentieth century there were Muslims under Russian rule after there had ceased to be Arabs under the rule of other Europeans. This Arab empire lost first its unity and then its independence, and for something like 1000 years Arabs were subject to Kurds, Turks, British and French. But they never lost the enormously powerful links of a common language and a common faith, and when they began to recover their independence these links served to revive and give substance to visions of a renewed unity. The collapse of the Ottoman empire in Asia in 1918 offered to its Arab subjects a prospect altogether different from that offered, by the more gradual withdrawal of the same empire in Europe, to the racially and linguistically divided Christians of the Balkans.

But in 1919 the Arabs were disappointed. The Ottoman empire was virtually partitioned between the British (who already held Egypt and Cyprus) and the French, and one effect of this Balkanization of the Middle East was to foster separate Arab particularisms (Syrian, Iraqi, Jordanian etc.) and dynastic feuds at the expense of Arab unity: the Arab world was more united under the Turks than without them. The new rulers from the west, lured by international politics and by oil back to the scene of their crusading adventures, became obstacles both to Arab unity and to Arab independence, not least because of the deadening effects of their overwhelming power on the Arab will to struggle for these aspirations; a second world war was needed to get the westerners out. French rule was eliminated by the British when the French authorities in Syria and Lebanon declared for Vichy; British rule on the other hand was maintained and even temporarily strengthened in spite of powerful anti-British currents in Egypt and an attempted pro-German coup in Iraq in 1941 by Rashid Ali el-Gailani. The veiled occupation established in neighbouring Iran by Britain and the USSR did not immediately affront the Arabs, and when the war ended the British were therefore the sole surviving target of Arab nationalism, whose temper was sharpened not only by this concentration on one enemy but also by Britain's administration of the mandate over Palestine where, in consequence of Britain's endorsement in 1917 of the zionist aim of a Jewish National Home (the Balfour Declaration), a new non-Arab and non-Muslim community had gradually taken hold and was claiming the right to be not a home but a state.

Faced with this powerful and stubborn remnant of the imperialist centuries, and with the vigorous new threat of zionism, the Arabs were exceptionally divided among themselves.

At the level of power monarchs, Saudi and Hashemite, were divided by inherited rivalries; more important, there was a rift between an old order, largely monarchical and traditionalist in its views on society and religion, and a new order which, with its beginnings in Arab intellectual movements of the nineteenth century, aspired to modernize religious and political thought and forms and to reduce the huge differences between the style of living of the very rich and the very poor. This revaluation inevitably produced within the Arab world internal conflicts and strains which enfeebled the Arab capacity to remove the British or defeat the Jews. The British were able to leave in their own time, which was slow; and the Jews established their state of Israel.

The British had struggled for a generation to reconcile their pledges to the Jews and to the Arabs (the latter reinforced by Britain's desire to be on good terms with the oil-producing Arab states and to retain bases in the Arab world), but the two were irreconcilable and the attempt to find an accommodation passed imperceptibly into a hand-to-mouth evasion of the most urgent current complications until the whole responsibility of the mandatory was abandoned in 1948. At one point Britain tried partition. The Peel Commission proposed (1937) a tripartite division into an Arab and a Jewish state, leaving Britain with a mandate over a reduced area which would include the holy places of Jerusalem and Bethlehem with access to the Mediterranean. But upon closer inspection this scheme proved impracticable and Britain, forced by the approach of war in Europe to choose between the two sides, chose the Arabs and undertook, in the White Paper of 1939, to keep the Jewish element in the population of Palestine to one-third of the whole (it had risen since 1919 from 10 to nearly 30 per cent) and so to stop Jewish immigration after a further 75,000 Jews had been admitted. Thus Hitler cast upon Britain the odium of refusing asylum to Germany's persecuted Jewry because the imminence of a war against Germany made Britain even more sensitive to the need for Arab friendships: grand strategy, as well as oil strategy, dictated the terms of the White Paper.

After the 1939 White Paper zionists had switched their main effort from Britain to the United States, abandoning their hope of achieving their aims by persuasion in London in favour of an actively anti-British policy to be financed (after the war) with American money. During the war the political effectiveness of zionism was greatly enhanced in the

United States and the zionist cause was embraced by the two most powerful Americans of the forties, Franklin D. Roosevelt and Harry S. Truman. At the same time other Americans were beginning to experience the old lures of oil and strategy, with the result that the United States slid, half unsuspectingly and more than half unwillingly, into the same sort of position as Britain. Initially, and because of zionism, this American involvement set the United States and Britain in opposition to one another. The prime American concern was to persuade Britain to admit Jews to Palestine as generously and quickly as possible. On the assumption, roughly verifiable, that some 100,000 Jews had survived the Nazi abomination the United States adopted David Ben Gurion's plea, made in August 1945, for the issue of that number of entry permits. Both Churchill and Attlee, themselves men of generous disposition and proven sympathies for the zionist cause, wished to do something for the unhappy survivors and hoped, not incompatibily, to secure at the same time American support for British policies in the Middle East as a whole. But this co-operation was not to be had. The Americans wanted to help the Jews without becoming entangled in British positions of a suspiciously imperialist nature (the British only became respectable allies in these parts in American eyes in terms of a cold war threat from the USSR); they failed to appreciate the full extent of Britain's difficulties in Palestine in terms of the surrender of power in India in 1947 and the challenge to the Western position in Berlin in 1948; and they accepted uncritically the charges of anti-semitism which were thrown at the new British foreign secretary, Ernest Bevin, and which that statesman did not a little himself to promote.

The campaign to get Britain to issue the 100,000 entry permits was regarded in London as an extravaganza based on irresponsibility and ignorance and inspired by ulterior motives. American support for the campaign was resented, especially when the Jews took to terrorism in Palestine, as a section of them did immediately after the end of the war. Nevertheless the British government opted for a joint Anglo–American approach to the problem, and in October 1945 a committee of six Britons and six Americans set off to take soundings in Palestine, five Arab states and the European camps where the survivors of nazism were waiting. Its report, published in April 1946, endorsed the estimate of 100,000 homeless Jews in Europe and the plea for their immediate admission to Palestine; it also rejected partition, recommended the continuance of the British mandate and – besides urging massive Jewish immigration – proposed the abolition of existing limitations on the purchase of land by Jews. The committee had hoped to produce an acceptable package deal, but Truman endorsed only the plea for 100,000 entry permits and the Arabs and the British government rejected the proposals as a whole. The appearance of the committee's report coincided with a Jewish terrorist attack in Tel Aviv which seemed to have no other purpose but murder and which succeeded in killing seven persons. This attack provoked counter-terrorism from the British side, which indicated that the British nerve in Palestine, no less than British tempers in Whitehall, was beginning to break. While it was still widely supposed that Jewish atrocities were the independent work of special units (the Stern gang and Irgun Zvai Leumi) undertaken without the approval of the main Jewish defence force (Haganah) or established political bodies (the Jewish Agency and zionist organizations), there was already evidence that the case was otherwise and that the British authorities were faced with a concerted nationalist attempt to coerce or remove them. The extent of the violence to be used was demonstrated in June 1946 when a part of the King David hotel in Jerusalem was blown up and ninety-one persons were indiscriminately killed.

After the rejection by Britain of the report of the Anglo–American committee the idea of partition was revived. Ambassador Henry Grady for the United States and the British home secretary, Herbert Morrison, produced in July a plan for two autonomous but not sovereign provinces, and the issue of 100,000 permits a year after the establishment of this hybrid state. Truman rejected the plan and the British government next tried the expedient of a round table conference, but the Jews refused to engage in anything except bilateral discussions with the British. There was this time no American participation, and the repetition by Truman of his support for the 100,000 permits during his campaign for the presidency was not a help. Discussions nevertheless continued sporadically between September 1946 and February 1947. They were abortive. The realities of the situation were reflected by increasing terrorism and the execution by hanging of the young Jew, Dov Grüner, the first victim of British exasperation.

In February 1947 Britain announced that the problem, and possibly the territory too (though this was not clear), was to be transferred to the United Nations. In May a special session of the General Assembly created Unscop (United Nations Special Committee on Palestine) and its eleven members set off for Jerusalem. While they were there, and possibly because they were there, 4554 refugees aboard the *Exodus 1947* arrived at Haifa after having been collected by the Jewish Agency at Sète in the south of France and furnished with travel documents for Colombia. These pawns in the zionist game were refused permission to land by the British authorities and were shipped back to Sète whence, again refused permission to land, they were directed with a horrible insensitivity to a German port. In July the toll of innocent suffering was dramatically increased when two British sergeants were hanged by an Irgun band. Unable to solve their problem, or to keep order, or even to defend themselves, the British were now more than ready to go. When Unscop produced, by a majority, a new partition plan of ridiculous complexity (three Arab and three Jewish segments linked in a sort of economic union with Jerusalem under international trusteeship), they said they would do so.

The Unscop plan was adopted with modifications by the UN in November. It was accepted with misgiving by the Jews and rejected by the Arabs. It was irrelevant because the issue was to be decided by war and not by negotiation. Fighting started at once with attempts by the Jews to get control of the segments allotted to them. There were also disorders in Arab towns. The British were impotent and lost even the reputation for fairness which they regarded as one of their special contributions to public morality. On 11 December they declared that they would surrender the mandate on 15 May 1948. Fighting increased. The Jews managed to procure arms in substantial quantities, with which to meet the expected invasion by the regular armies of neighbouring Arab states. In April 1948 they contrived at Deir Yasin a massacre which set in train an exodus of refugees who were to constitute, with their as yet unborn progeny, one of the bitterest bones of contention between Arabs and Jews and one of the sorriest human spectacles of the times. 150,000 had fled by the end of the month, over half a million by the end of the year. Then and later Arab propaganda made the most of this story, while a telegram of regrets from Ben Gurion to King Abdullah of Jordan passed and remained almost unnoticed.

The last British official left Palestine on 14 May 1948. The state of Israel was movingly proclaimed by Ben Gurion who became its prime minister, embodiment and inspiration; Chaim Weizmann, the veteran leader of zionism who enjoyed worldwide respect, became the first president despite the fact that, in the previous December, the twenty-second zionist congress at Basle had marked the passing of his influence and had even exposed him to some ruderies. Truman immediately recognized the new state, followed quickly by Stalin. No less swiftly five Arab states marched, but the promptness of their reaction was no index of their keenness for a fight or their effectiveness in it. The Syrians did little and the Lebanese less; the Iraqis retired early and the Egyptians arrived late; the Jewish defence of Jerusalem, which thwarted the Jordanians, combined with the Arabs' incoherence to give Israel the victory. The UN intervened by appointing the Swedish Count Folke Bernadotte to mediate. He effected a truce which lasted from 11 June to 9 July and was followed by more fighting in which the Israelis were decisively victorious. Bernadotte was murdered on 17 September by the Stern gang; he was succeeded by a UN official, the American Negro, Ralph Bunche. The Israelis gained further successes in renewed fighting in October but by the end of the year the war was virtually over, Palestine and Jerusalem itself had been partitioned by the verdict of arms, and during the first half of 1949 armistices were effected between Israel and four of its assailants (Iraq being the absent fifth). In the second phase of the fighting the Israelis had secured their sovereign state by defeating the regular forces of Arab states as well as the Palestinian Arabs and they were ready to consolidate their gains. They wanted peace. But they could not get it. The Arabs, out of their deep humiliation and their just concern for the Arab refugees from Palestine, refused to recognize Israel's existence or make peace with it and continued the war by economic means – notably by closing the Suez Canal to Israeli shipping and to goods going to or from Israel. This action was condemned, fruitlessly, by the Security Council which also, equally fruitlessly, asserted that Israel should either re-admit the refugees or compensate them. Since these refugees outnumbered the Jews in Palestine the Israelis argued with much plausibility that they could not be expected to re-admit them so long as the Arab nations as a whole continued to proclaim their intention to eliminate the state of Israel. The Arabs themselves did little to integrate the refugees in their places of refuge since, politically, the most important point about a refugee was his refugee status and plight. From 700,000 in 1949 their numbers swelled by natural causes to over a million and a quarter by 1966.

The creation of the state of Israel was a most extraordinary political phenomenon. Israel came into existence as a result of the tenacious memories of a persecuted people whose misfortunes in various parts of the world had given them an intense addiction to the words of their holy books; as a result of atrocious crimes perpetrated against European Jewry in sight of Europe and the world; and as a result of the exertions of leading Jews who worked with vigour and intelligence to capture a piece of territory not their own, and who would probably have failed to do so if they had not believed that their end was one of those which justifies every means and had not enjoyed the advantages of working under a British umbrella. The state which they founded was almost as exceptional as its origins. By adopting the principle that the door to it must be open to all Jews everywhere, it became a mixture of tongues and cultures and unequal skills, held together by the unifying power of a Hebrew revival and by a community of race and of hope (though not of religion, since the Jewish religion meant little to many Israeli citizens). It was dependent on external aid, which it received liberally from American and other Jews and, by way of reparation, from the German Federal Republic; and its life was conditioned by external hostility, since the Arabs refused to accept its existence and insisted that, as an imperialist subterfuge for the maintenance of Anglo-American power in the Middle East, it must be dismantled. It adopted, in spite of its economic and military stringencies, a democratic form of government, and it presented to the world the unaccustomed sight of a state ruled by a governing class characterized above all by a progressive intelligence successfully applied to the diverse and taxing problems of everyday public life.

To the Arabs none of this was admirable. That the Jews had suffered at the hands of Christian Europeans through the ages seemed a poor reason for allowing them to expropriate a part of the Arab world and drive a million Muslims out of it. The failure of the armies of five Arab states to prevent the establishment of Israel was a humiliation which could only be met by rounding on the leaders who had so conspicuously failed and by declaring that the verdict of 1948 was only an interim one which would be reversed later. Those – mainly outsiders – who thought that time would heal or at any rate soften the acerbities of this conflict had to retreat to a more pessimistic view as officially sponsored Arab propaganda maintained a vicious anti-zionism and as the new generation in the refugee camps was consciously nourished on visions of a return to Palestine after a gloriously successful war which would erase Israel from the map. Zionist nationalism and zionist extremism were matched by Arab nationalism and Arab extremism. Although the situation remained frozen by external factors – in particular by the Tripartite Declaration of 1950 by which the United States, Britain and France undertook to maintain a balance of armaments between Arabs and Jews and to consult together over any infraction of frontiers – basic attitudes within the area of conflict changed little, if at all. What did change as a result of the war of 1948 was power in the Arab states immediately concerned. The defeat of 1948 accelerated the demise of some ancient régimes. In Syria Husni Zaim seized power in March 1949, held it for a few months before being ousted by Sami al-Hinnawi who was in turn ousted after a few months by Adib Shishakli who ruled until February 1954. In July 1951 Abdullah, having transformed his emirate of Transjordan into the kingdom of Jordan, was murdered as he entered the El Aqsa mosque in Jerusalem. More significant, in the following July the Egyptian monarchy was overthrown by officers who had bitterly resented the unpreparedness and ineptitude of their country's operations in 1948 and now despatched the last representative of Mohamed Ali's line into exile.

Chapter 8

Nationalism and oil in Iran

The Egyptian revolution of 1952, the dominant event in Middle Eastern politics in the first post-war generation (and the main theme of the next chapter in this book), was a nationalist response to a national defeat in Palestine and also the heir to a continuing nationalist protest against foreign domination by the British. The revolution and the subsequent negotiations with the British coincided with a nationalist attack on the British position in Iran and with negotiations in that country in which not only the British but also the Americans were involved.

History and geography made Iran wary of both the British and the Russians; oil made it specially suspicious of the British. During the war Britain and the USSR occupied Iran on the plea of strategic necessity (the Iranians resisting for three days), and enforced the abdication of the founder of Iran's new dynasty, Reza Shah Pahlavi, who was exiled to Mauritius and later died in South Africa in 1944. His son and successor, Muhammad Reza Pahlavi, had had neither the time nor the opportunity to make a mark among his people by the time that the war and the occupation ended. The treaty of 1942 which had sanctioned foreign occupation provided for the withdrawal of the British and the Russians six months after the end of hostilities. The Russians made an attempt to retain influence in the province of Azerbaijan, comparatively rich, traditionally hostile to the central government and situated on the borders of the USSR. They also lent support to Kurdish separatism and may have entertained hopes of establishing a Russian sphere of influence stretching southwards from the Kurdish republic of Mahabad through other Kurdish territories to the Persian Gulf. They were assisted by the Tudeh party, an amalgam of Marxist communists with an older liberal tradition which had infused the Constitutional Movement earlier in the century.

British troops left Iran punctually in March 1946 but Russian troops had to be manoeuvred out by the Iranian government. The astute elder statesman Qavam es-Sultaneh, who became prime minister in January 1946, visited Moscow in February on the heels of an Iranian complaint to the newly established Security Council and contrived to persuade Stalin that Russian aims in Iran could better be attained through good relations with the Iranian government than by the continued presence of Russian troops in north-western Iran. The Russians, who were at least as keen on an oil agreement with the central government as on fostering separatist movements against it, withdrew their troops only a few weeks late. Qavam entered into discussions about an oil agreement but evaded any conclusive step on the plea that, constitutionally, the ultimate decision lay with the parliament which was about to be elected; he also delayed the elections. Qavam simultaneously played a double game with the Tudeh party. Having taken some of its members into his cabinet in order to mollify the Russians, he then welcomed (to put it no higher) a revolt by powerful southern tribes which demanded the dismissal of Tudeh ministers and other Tudeh members in prominent positions. The new majlis (the lower house of the Iranian parliament) duly censured Qavam for engaging in discussion with the Russians for an oil agreement and declared it null and void. In spite of these oblique achievements Qavam was defeated and resigned at the end of the year. Having outwitted the Russians and seen the British depart too, he was embarking on a policy of co-operation with the United States, whence he hoped to get financial aid and diplomatic support in Iran's traditional search for means of keeping both the Russians and the British at arm's length.

Qavam's successors were nevertheless to be sharply engaged with Britain in a quarrel in which the United States, after some hesitation, gave Britain firm support. Although the British had left Iran in strict accordance with the terms of the 1942 treaty, Anglo-Iranian relations were soured by the existence of the Anglo-Iranian Oil Company which had a monopoly of Iran's proven oil fields and in which the British government itself held a substantial number of shares. This unusual connection gave the company a political tinge and involved the British government in commercial affairs, two developments which were, in Iranian eyes, neither natural nor welcome consequences of the grant of a concession to a private individual early in the century. Iranian discontent was further increased by the suspicion that this rich and foreign company sold oil to the British navy on unduly favourable terms, by its secretiveness about the extent of these sales and about its accounts generally, by its failure to publicize in the rest of Iran the good wages, working conditions and other benefits which it provided for its labour force. On the other hand the company's shortcomings were not all its own fault: its failure to advertise its own virtues was due to the fact that, since it was practically unique in complying with the labour laws, it could not claim credit where credit was due without casting aspersions on other employers.

The concession inherited by the company had been granted in 1901 to a certain W. K. D'Arcy and acquired by the company before the First World War. The Iranian government had bargained to receive a percentage of the company's net profits, but this bargain turned out badly for Iran since the Iranian share was rendered dependent on the level of taxation in Britain. It was further affected by the slump between the wars and in 1932 Iran purported to cancel the concession. As a result of negotiations between Reza Shah and the company a new agreement, duly ratified by the Iranian parliament, gave the company a new concession running for sixty years from 1933 (instead of sixty years from 1901) over a substantially diminished area, and gave Iran royalties to be calculated on the quantity of oil extracted. By 1950 this output was 32.5 million metric tons, three times the amount produced in 1938; Iran was the largest producer in the Middle East and contained at Abadan the largest refinery in the world.

The revenues from the oil were much needed. After the Second World War Iran embarked on economic expansion and a plan adopted by the majlis in 1947 envisaged the expenditure of $651 million of which $242 million were to come from oil. But oil revenues in 1947 and 1948 were a disappointment in spite of huge increases in the company's profits and the company, sensing trouble, entered into discussions for a revision of the agreement of 1933. In 1949 a supplemental agreement was concluded: the royalty rate was raised by 50 per cent and the company agreed to pay £5.1 million at once out of its reserves and thereafter to make further payments out of reserves annually instead of waiting until 1993, as the 1933 agreement provided. This agreement was very favourable to Iran but it was also complicated to the point of incomprehensibility and was unacceptable to a group of nationalists who wanted to terminate the concession entirely and take the management and profits of the oil industry into purely Iranian hands. General Ali Razmara, who became prime minister in 1950, refrained for a while from pressing the supplemental agreement on the majlis. When he recommended its adoption – largely on the grounds that Iran was short of qualified technicians – the majlis special oil committee demanded the nationalization of the oilfields and refinery, and the prime minister withdrew the agreement. The company, unexpectedly made aware of terms being offered by the Arab American Oil Company (Aramco) to the Saudi Arabian government – terms which were more favourable (in good years) and above all easier to understand – prepared to reopen discussions and simplify the supplemental agreement. Razmara produced a series of reports by experts who opposed nationalization but he was assassinated in March 1951 by a fanatic nationalist belonging to the semi-religious Fidayan-i-Islam. On the next day the majlis approved the oil committee's proposals and a few weeks later it nationalized the oil industry.

General Razmara was succeeded by Husain Ala, a friend and nominee of the shah who wanted to avoid appointing the chairman of the oil committee, Dr Muhammad Musaddiq, in which attempt the shah failed. Dr Musaddiq began at the end of 1951 a spell of power which lasted tumultuously until August 1953. Musaddiq was a rich and aristocratic hysteric and hypochondriac who appealed to a wide variety of emotions; he was supported by xenophobic chauvinists, by religious fanatics, by communist and non-communist radicals, by the old land-owning aristocracy to which he belonged, and by all those who distrusted the shah's attempt to resurrect the authority of the dynasty which had been abased by his father's abdication and the foreign occupation during the war. His political stock-in-trade was a blinkered nationalism which,, though it may have been intended as a screen, became the substance of his political actions. If, as seems probable, Musaddiq intended to combine the nationalization of the oil industry with the continued employment of foreign technicians and continuing foreign finance, he was soon defeated by his own extremer professions and supporters. Musaddiq became almost a figure of fun to the world at large, certainly to the Western world, but in his own country he roused genuine popularity (quite apart from the bought support of the capital's mobs) and even his political opponents were to acknowledge his success in reducing corruption in public affairs. He failed, however, to retain control over the course of the oil dispute or to retain his own confidence in himself, he became the prisoner of his own rasher attitudes, and he underrated the effectiveness of the economic sanctions which the British government was able to deploy against him.

The oil nationalization law expropriated the British company and created a new Iranian company to take its place. Throughout the ensuing controversies Dr Musaddiq insisted on British recognition of the validity of the nationalization decree as a prerequisite for any negotiations on compensation for the British company. The British on the other hand maintained that the decree was illegal and inoperative, that the company's title remained intact, and that the concession agreement of 1933 could not properly be revoked by unilateral act of one party to it even if that party was a sovereign state. Consequently Britain claimed not only compensation for the loss of the benefits secured to the company by the concession agreement but also a further sum representing damages for a wrongful breach of contract.

The controversy involved not only the British company but also the British government which was responsible for the safety of British citizens (who might be endangered by nationalist frenzy) and wished to safeguard its own financial stake in the British company; it was also concerned to stand firm in defence of British rights for fear that weakness in one part of the Middle East might provoke attacks on British interests elsewhere. During 1951 various attempts were made to negotiate with Dr Musaddiq – by the British company, by a special emissary of President Truman and by a British delegation led by a cabinet minister. The American administration chose the British side after some initial hesitation. Its sympathy for the British case was to some extent countered by its desire to attract Iran into the Western camp; since the oil dispute threatened on the contrary to separate Iran from the West, there were some Americans who were anxious not merely to mediate but to secure a settlement without necessarily getting the full measure of what London thought fit and proper. But Dr Musaddiq's extravagant histrionics alienated American sympathy and a visit by him to New York (to address the Security Council) and to Washington in October 1951 did him no good and some harm. His flirtations with Moscow and his indebtedness to Iranian communists helped to persuade the Americans to make common cause with the British and to support his internal enemies' plans to overthrow him.

The dispute was not in the last resort ruled by the legal rights and wrongs but by the British government's unwillingness to use force (except to protect British citizens); by the Iranian company's inability to sell Iranian oil in face of obstacles interposed by the British company and the lack of solidarity among producers; and by the economic collapse of Musaddiq's régime which, deprived of its revenue from the British company, was unable to find alternative sources of cash. Having failed to raise loans from the United States or the World Bank, Musaddiq called in the renowned Dr Hjalmar Schacht who judged him, after a few days' acquaintance in September 1952, to be one of the wisest men of the age but was unable to help him. Meanwhile some of Musaddiq's allies were wavering. He was reappointed prime minister in July 1952 after a routine resignation upon the convening of a new majlis, but the members showed some reluctance to grant him the full powers which he asked for. When the shah refused to give him the war ministry he resigned. But Qavam, who succeeded him, was only able to stay in office for four days and then had to take flight; the mob demonstrated in Musaddiq's favour, the majlis voted him full powers, and the throne itself seemed to be in danger. Only the army had the capacity to unseat him, and a year later it did.

Musaddiq's triumph had exposed his political dependence on the mob without lessening his financial dependence on the British, which in turn was conditioned by his dependence on the extreme nationalist mullah Kashani who had become president of the majlis and would countenance no approach to the British. By the end of 1952 Musaddiq and Kashani had fallen out. In the next year Musaddiq triumphed over Kashani and dismissed the majlis but failed to prevail over the shah. In August the shah dismissed Musaddiq and appointed General Zahedi in his place. Three days later the shah and the general were both in flight, but whereas the shah fled to Rome the general withdrew only a little distance and within a week of his original appointment he returned to put an end to the Musaddiq régime once and for all. Musaddiq was first strangled by outside forces and then removed by internal ones. His fall is an example of the effectiveness of economic sanctions.

Peace was soon made in the oil dispute. New agreements were worked out on the basis, ironically, of recognizing the validity of the Iranian nationalization decree. The Iranian oil company remained in being and in possession of the oil. A consortium of eight foreign companies – British, American and French – was created. The British company accepted, not without demur, a 40 per cent share in this consortium and received from its seven associates £214 million for the remaining 60 per cent which they bought between them. The British company was also to receive £25 million, spread over the years 1957–66, from the Iranian government in compensation for its losses since nationalization. The consortium was given effective control over the Abadan refinery and the principal oilfields for twenty-five years, with a series of options of renewal, and undertook to pay the Iranian government 50 per cent of profits. Thus nationalist doctrine was satisfied, the consumers were assured of their requirements and the producers of their revenues. Full diplomatic relations between Iran and Britain were restored early in 1954. Musaddiq spent the next two years in gaol.

The fall of Musaddiq was a victory for the shah. Musaddiq's left wing supporters were persecuted with a thorough ferocity and the shah gradually asserted the paramountcy of the throne, first through military rule which lasted until 1957 and then through a series of prime ministers who were either submissive or turned out. The death of the shah's only brother late in 1954 jeopardized the dynasty and obliged the heirless shah to divorce his second wife and marry a third, who bore him a son a year later. Thus fortified the shah began to implement a policy of land distribution and reform which proved so unpopular with the landowning classes and the majlis (in which they were well represented) that the shah dispensed with parliament for the two years 1961–63. In 1963 he felt strong enough to hold a plebiscite which confirmed his personal ascendancy and the decline of the power of the provincial notables. The world of the urban politician, the tribal chiefs and the educated young remained for diverse reasons disgruntled, but oil revenues increased and Iran's gross national product began to register annual increases of the order of 7 per cent. In foreign affairs the shah had to decide whether to join the Baghdad Pact and so identify his country with the West. He did so in 1955, after becoming the first recipient of American Point Four aid, and in 1959 he paid a state visit to London and received President Eisenhower in Tehran. After a short period of frigidity, Russo-Iranian relations improved and in 1963 President Brezhnev too was officially received in the Iranian capital, a reminder that the traditional suspiciousness between the two countries had to take account of the fact that Iran had a long undefended frontier with the USSR and looked to northern trade routes for the export of the produce of its northern provinces. The shah undertook not to permit the installation of nuclear missiles in Iran and, without abandoning Cento (as the Baghdad Pact had become), or joining the unaligned group, he moved towards a more independent position in world politics. By 1969–70 he was able to play a decisive role in shaping the political future of the Persian Gulf after the departure of the British (see chapter 12) and, relishing the role of a crowned entrepreneur, to use mineral wealth and a bounding economy to turn Iran into a military and industrial power of considerable significance. The shah's policy and bent was growth at all costs and the key was oil, although oil was not the country's only resource. (It was rich too in natural gas, other minerals and agriculture and was establishing industry as fast as 50 per cent illiteracy and a wretched educational system would allow.) When in 1973 war in the Middle East gave the oil producers the excuse to push up prices the shah insisted on maximum increases, successfully but against the wishes of more cautious Arabs who hesitated to damage western countries which were their best customers. In two years the Iranian government's revenue per barrel was multiplied by ten and its total annual oil revenues rose from $2.3 billion to $18.2 billion (38 per cent of GNP, which was rising in the seventies at rates between 10 and 17 per cent a year). Spending rose too, particularly defence spending which also multiplied by ten in the half decade and passed the $10 million mark; by 1975 Iran was spending on defence a larger proportion of GNP than any country in the world except Israel. The results of this explosion were not all happy: 1975 saw a deficit in the balance of payments of nearly $1 billion; waste and corruption flourished commensurately. Inflation took hold. Those hurt by inflation and least able to make a profession of corruption had to be compensated and wages were nearly doubled in 1974–75 with the usual cyclic nightmare: demand for goods, inadequate supply, rising prices and increased exports to fill the gaps, further price rises and further wage demands. The shah, who had dealt roughly with the landed aristocracy in the early sixties, showed signs of imperial displeasure with the new, ostentatious and corrupt rich, and toyed with schemes for handing over half the ownership and profits of industry to the workers. His regime had weaknesses – the uncertainty surrounding an autocracy with an infant heir, the opposition of the conservative mullahs, and the opposition of radical students which even one of the world's largest secret police apparatuses could not mute. In external affairs Iran cut a somewhat isolated figure. Iranians and Arabs had been saying harsh things about each other for a thousand years but in the seventies the shah improved his relations with Saudi Arabia and Egypt (facilitated by the deaths of the contrasting figures of King Feisal and Nasser) and with Iraq (consequent on the new settlement in the Gulf and hastened perhaps by Iraq's action in concluding a treaty with the USSR in 1971). To the east where Iran had frontiers with Afghanistan and Pakistan (and possible disputes with the latter in Baluchistan) the shah observed uneasily the overthrow of the Afghan dynasty and the disruption of Pakistan by the secession of Bangladesh. Further off Mrs Gandhi, although emulating his own taste for autocracy, entered in 1970 into closer relations with his most powerful neighbour, the USSR.

The Egyptian revolution and the Suez War

The titular leader of the Egyptian revolution of 1952 was General Mohamed Neguib but the real leader was Colonel Gamal Abdel Nasser who became prime minister in April 1954 and supplanted Neguib as president of the new republic a few months later. Nasser was a young man of thirty-six who had made a career in the army from origins in what might be called the lower middle class. He had the necessary impetuousness and indignation to make a nationalist revolutionary, but he had also the qualities of coolness, shrewdness and humour which keep the revolutionary sane and afloat after success. He was also sufficiently quick-witted to keep more or less abreast of the problems which assailed him when he found himself required, as head of the most important of the Arab countries, to elaborate and execute policies in world affairs. The first of these problems was the unfinished business of getting rid of the British. In addition he had to find his place in the Arab world, African as well as Asian, and take a stand in the cold war for or against the West or the Russians or neither.

The British occupation of Egypt began in 1881 with a debt-collecting expedition but its real motive was and remained strategic – to secure control of the eastern Mediterranean (threatened when British influence over the sultan's government in Constantinople was challenged by German influence), of the route to India and the east, and of the Nile valley. Egypt remained formally a province of the Ottoman empire under the hereditary rule of the heirs of Mohamed Ali, but it became in effect semi-independent under the British instead of semi-independent under the Turks. When Britain and the Ottoman empire went to war in 1914 Britain proclaimed a protectorate over Egypt which was converted in 1922, under nationalist pressure, into a treaty relationship. Britain secured in 1936 the right to station 10,000 men in the Suez Canal zone for twenty years, an arrangement which was rendered acceptable to the Egyptians because this base could serve to protect Egypt against the ambitions of Mussolini who was engaged at this very time in conquering Ethiopia. During the Second World War Churchill resolved to maintain and strengthen Britain's Middle Eastern position. The Arabs had shown certain pro-German proclivities which threatened to give Germany dominion in the Middle East after the German conquest of the Balkans and Crete in 1941. The British therefore occupied Syria, Lebanon and Iran and wooed Turkey (unsuccessfully until 1944 when Turkey severed relations with the Axis – it entered the war the following February); they also forced the pro-British Nahas Pasha on King Farouk as prime minister. Nahas hoped that in return the British would give Egypt after the war the unshackled independence which they had promised over sixty times since 1881, but the king, preferring a tougher to a waiting game, dismissed Nahas in October 1944.

At about this time Eden was preparing a post-war British position in the Middle East, based on an association of pro-British Arab states. Eden encouraged the hardened pro-British Nuri es-Said, Iraq's prime minister, to revive the concept of the Fertile Crescent as a political unit with Baghdad as its capital and embracing autonomous zionist and Maronite communities. Eden also promoted a pro-British Arab League, but in September 1944 at Alexandria Egypt, as well as Iraq, Syria, Lebanon and Transjordan, concluded the Protocol of Alexandria which preceded the treaty of March 1945 whereby these five states plus Saudi Arabia and Yemen constituted the Arab League: this larger league was not the league designed by Britain. From the beginning Egypt was much the most important member of the League by virtue of its greater population and sophistication and the influence which radiated from Cairo's universities, printing presses and radio. But the British and Egyptian interests in the Arab League were fatally crossed. For Britain the League was to be an ally and a pillar of support; Egypt, however, obsessed with the continuing British occupation not only of the Canal Zone but also of the points in Cairo and Alexandria where the Union Jack had been hoisted during the war, saw the League as an anti-British lever and not as a symbol of partnership. Britain's plight in Palestine helped to draw Arabs together in an anti-British attitude which suited Egypt and belied Eden's hopes. (Palestine, or rather Israel when it came into being, also affected the Arab League by converting it from a regional organization which, in its members' opinion, concerned nobody but themselves into an alliance with wider objectives and therefore international significance.)

After the war Britain appreciated the need for a revision of its treaty relations with Egypt – and also with Iraq and Transjordan – but had no thought of any radical departure from the Middle East. British forces were withdrawn from the Nile delta to the Canal Zone, but only tardily; it still seemed axiomatic that Britain, victorious in a war in which British exertions and tenacity in the Middle East had played a major role, was and should be a Middle Eastern power. In addition, the withdrawal from India in 1947 would have made it difficult for the new British labour government, accused by the opposition of 'a policy of scuttle' in India, to propose further substantial abdications in the Middle East. But the British position had been gravely weakened. Britain owed Egypt £400 million and Iraq £70 million; and these debts were only a part of the economic strains which were intensified by the abrupt ending of American Lend-Lease and were soon to force Britain to ask the United States to take over British responsibilities in Greece and

Turkey. In 1948 the strain would be further increased by the Palestine finale and by the need to defend the Western position in Berlin by the airlift. Such were the circumstances in which Bevin set about negotiating fresh treaties with Egypt, Iraq and Transjordan. He quickly succeeded in the last case (1946), but King Abdullah was much criticized for allowing British troops another twenty-five years' lease of Jordanian soil. With the Egyptian and Iraqi governments Bevin also succeeded in reaching agreement, but the draft treaties accepted by Sidky Pasha for Egypt and Salih Jabr for Iraq (the Treaty of Portsmouth, 1948) were rejected by their parliaments and people because they did not provide for complete British evacuation.

There followed an uneasy and unproductive period which was broken in 1951 by a clash between two rival concepts. By this time the Korean war had begun and the Western allies were anxious to create in the Middle East an anti-Russian alliance similar to Nato. With this end in view the American, British, French and Turkish governments produced plans for a Middle East Defence Organization (Medo) which would include Egypt and the Suez Canal base; the British would evacuate the base but the allies, adapting an idea once produced by Bevin, would have the right to return in certain eventualities. This scheme with its roots in the world situation ran foul of Egypt's conception of a foreign garrison on the Canal as a symbol of indignity, and since Egypt was not moved by the fear of the USSR which animated the West, Egypt rejected Medo. At the same time and for good measure Egypt denounced in October 1951 the Anglo-Egyptian treaty of 1936, which had five years to run, and began guerilla attacks on the Canal Zone. In January 1952 anti-British riots in Cairo caused extensive damage.

When therefore Neguib and Nasser seized power a few months later they were confronted not only with the traditional problem of the British, whose occupation of Egyptian soil was a standing national affront, but also with the new problem created by the desire of the West as a whole to enlist Egypt in the cold war and make the Canal Zone an anti-Russian arsenal and base. Provided they could secure total British evacuation, the new Egyptian leaders were anxious to come to terms with Britain, but they had less positive ideas about an association with the West.

In the two years after the revolution Egypt and Britain settled their outstanding differences. They began not with the Canal Zone but with the Sudan, which had been an Anglo-Egyptian condominium since its recapture from the Mahdists in 1899. Egypt wished to restore the union of Egypt with the Sudan because of the vital importance of the Nile waters and because of ancient pharaonic vistas of the unity of the Nile valley. The British, who had been effective rulers of the Sudan for half a century, insisted that the Sudanese must decide their future for themselves and the Egyptians, wrongly believing that the Sudan would opt for unity with Egypt, so agreed in February 1953. In the event the

Sudan chose independence in spite (or because) of Egyptian propaganda and pressure, and became a sovereign state in 1956. Nasser accepted this first reverse in the foreign field with a pragmatic acquiescence which he was to have to display again on future occasions.

Agreement on the Canal Zone was reached in July 1954 (and a treaty signed in October) on the basis that the British would depart in twenty months but would have the right to return if any member of the Arab League or Turkey were attacked by any outside foe except Israel. Iran was not included in the reverter clause in spite of British attempts to put it there. This treaty represented considerable, if sensible, concessions by Britain which were unpalatable to a section of the ruling Conservative Party but were accepted by the government partly on the grounds that the existence of nuclear bombs had turned the base into a death trap and partly – if less so – in response to pressure from the United States where continuing bad relations between Britain and Egypt were regarded as a serious impediment to the Middle Eastern segment of American world policies. But for Egypt the agreement of 1954 with Britain was not a preliminary to alignment with the West. Whereas the West believed during 1952–54 that better relations with Egypt implied such an alignment was not required. Consequently the better relations soon took a turn for the worse.

In 1955, the year of the Bandung conference of neutralists, Egypt became wedded to non-alignment. The issue did not arise in the first post-war years because alignment meant alignment against the Russians and there was as yet no Russian presence in the Arab world to be aligned against. The traditional Russian spheres of activity in the Middle East were the non-Arab states of Turkey and Iran, and in both the USSR had experienced and apparently accepted rebuffs at the end of the war; claims for the return of Kars and Ardahan (lost to Turkey in 1921) and for the revision of the Montreux Convention governing passage through the Straits of Constantinople were ineffective, while the attempt to subvert the régime in Iran by sponsoring the Azerbaijani republic and a Kurdish bid for independence was defeated by the unexpected astuteness of Qavam es-Sultaneh and the unexpectedly firm reactions of the United States and Britain. The prompt Russian recognition of Israel was not followed up and seemed to have been regarded by Moscow as a blind alley.

When therefore the Medo plan was first presented to Egypt, it seemed foreign and irrelevant to Egyptian interests. It was also vaguely repugnant. The Korean war, which lay behind it, was regarded by most Arabs as no concern of theirs, so much so that all the Arab members of the United Nations except Iraq refrained from voting on it in the General Assembly. Nasser himself came under the influence of Nehru, especially after the latter's visit to Cairo in August 1953 and during K. M. Pannikkar's embassy there in 1953–54. But the principal factor in Nasser's route to neutralism and the 1955 Bandung spirit was provided by the Western powers themselves.

In 1954 the Americans were arming Turkey and Pakistan. They decided to help Iraq in the same way and to brigade these countries and Iran in a new anti-Russian organization which would stretch from the Bosphorus to the Indus. The inclusion of Iraq was enthusiastically welcomed by the British who saw a way of getting a new treaty with Iraq in place of their existing treaty which was due to expire in 1957 and which Bevin's negotiations with Britain's Iraqi friends had failed to prolong. But the inclusion of Iraq was a cardinal mistake. In 1953 Dulles had decided that it was no good trying to get the Arabs to join a cold war front (the Medo policy) and that the West should therefore construct instead a non-Arab group of friends along the so-called northern tier of countries bordering on the USSR. Iraq was not a necessary member of this group, since it had no frontier with the USSR and was in any case an Arab state. Moreover, the attraction of Iraq into this northern orbit roused the deepest suspicions in Cairo both on account of existing tensions between Egypt and Iraq and as a manoeuvre by outsiders to disrupt the unity of the Arab world. The Americans were proposing to arm Iraq (and Pakistan) against the USSR, but Egypt interpreted the agreements as a strengthening of the Iraqi side in Arab politics (just as India regarded the arming of Pakistan as a threat to itself in Kashmir).

Egypt and Iraq stood for different brands of Arab unity long before the Egyptian revolution of 1952 made Egypt a socialist republic by contrast with the traditionalist monarchy which lasted in Iraq until 1958. Both before and after 1952 Egypt's leaders wished to be the leaders in the Arab world and planned to use the Arab League for this purpose; they were conscious of Egypt's natural claim to leadership and they sensed the advantages which would accrue to them in their dealings with the outside world if Egypt were the acknowledged head of an Arab commonwealth as well as an independent sovereign state. Their approach to Arab politics was Egyptian first and Arab second, and their plans stopped a long way short of Arab unity in any organic or institutional sense. The Iraqis on the other hand inherited other ideas, notably the vision of a vast Arab kingdom which had been nurtured by the British and French during the First World War and then thwarted by them. Although the sons of the sherif of Mecca – the Hashemites – came to rule in Baghdad and Amman and briefly in Damascus, they had been evicted from Saudi Arabia by the rise of Ibn Saud and had been foiled further north by the mandates system (which did not bother the Egyptians). Nevertheless the vision persisted, embracing in its changing forms – whether Greater Syria or the Fertile Crescent – Iraq, Syria, Lebanon and Palestine. But any union between Iraq and Syria would deprive Egypt of hegemony in the Arab world.

The Hashemite regent of Iraq, Abd ul-Ilah (who never forgot that he ought to have succeeded his father and grandfather as king of the Hejaz) aimed to be king in Syria when he ceased to be regent in Iraq. Had he succeeded, the Hashemites would have formed a powerful block, for

Abd ul-Ilah's young cousin Feisal became king in Baghdad and his uncle Abdullah was emir, later king, in Amman. After the first Syrian post-war revolution Husni Zaim turned to Iraq, although later in his short period of power he veered towards Egypt and Saudi Arabia; his successor, Sami al-Hinnawi, favoured an Iraqi-Syrian union but by so doing he precipitated his own fall, and his supplanter, Adib Shishakli (1949–54), the strong man of the Arab world before the advent of Nasser, rejected any close association with Iraq because it was monarchical and pro-British. The overthrow of Shishakli in February 1954 by the Syrian army, helped by Iraqi gold and by British well-wishing at the least, revived for Nasser the danger of an Iraqi-Syrian union at the moment when its other principal opponent, Ibn Saud, had just died and the Western powers were preparing their new treaty with Iraq. In the event opposition among Syrians to the Iraqi royal family and its British connections, manifested at elections in 1954, prevented the consummation of the union.

The first formal step towards the Baghdad Pact complex was the treaty of 4 April 1954 between Turkey and Pakistan. It was followed by American military aid agreements with Iraq (21 April) and Pakistan (10 May). Turkey and Iraq signed a mutual assistance pact on 24 February 1955. This was the Baghdad Pact itself and it was declared to be open to all members of the Arab League and other states interested in the peace and security of the Middle East. Britain joined on 5 April 1955, and Pakistan and Iran in September and October. But no other Arab state followed Nuri's lead into the Western camp. The Arabs rejected Nuri's belief that salvation lay in alliance with old friends in the West – partly because, to a younger generation, Britain did not appear a friend. Syria, by rejecting the pact, swung the bulk of the Arab world to Cairo and away from Baghdad, and in March 1955 a counter-alliance was formed between Egypt, Syria and Saudi Arabia. This was a victory for Nasser over Nuri and the British. It also marked the end of the period of improving relations between Egypt and the West and the beginning of violent polemics within the Arab world. Shortly after signing the treaty of March 1955 Nasser set out for Bandung where, in obedience to the prevailing anti-colonialist and neutralist wind, Iraq was censured for joining the Baghdad Pact and Pakistan for joining Seato.

Whatever the relative merits of British and American approaches to Middle Eastern problems at this time, the failure of London and Washington to find a common policy was manifest and significant. Britain may have been wise or unwise to use the Baghdad Pact for special purposes of its own in Iraq, and the United States may have been wise or unwise to join only the pact's economic and anti-subversion committees, but the most obvious consequence in Arab eyes was the discrepancy between the two Western powers and the attempt of the Americans to look un-British by not signing the pact or joining its central organs. A more forthright American policy might have persuaded the Jordanian and Saudi monarchies to join a pro-western alliance in 1954, but at that date American anti-imperialism (not yet killed in Vietnam) and Anglo-American oil rivalries were still making Washington wary of entanglements with Britain in the Middle East with the result that there was a time lag between the adoption of essentially identical policies first in London and later in Washington.

Besides the division within the Arab world Nasser was concerned with the enduring feud between the Arabs and Israel and with the fact that Israeli retaliation against Arab propaganda and provocative raids was being turned against Egypt. Shortly before the signature of the treaty of March 1955 Egypt experienced an exceptionally sharp Israeli attack in the Gaza area. The threat from Israel, where Ben Gurion returned to office (first as defence minister and then as prime minister once more) alarmed Nasser who had become aware that Israel was seeking arms from France. This Franco-Israeli association, although never enshrined in a formal alliance, became an additional prime factor in Middle Eastern politics and one of the principal ingredients in the Suez war of 1956. The tripartite declaration of 1950, which was supposed to prevent an arms race in the Middle East, was circumvented by Israel which found in France sympathizers ready to help Israel in secret. French motives were various: there was a feeling of obligation to the Jews as a people who had suffered too much; a feeling of admiration for what they had achieved in Israel: a feeling of socialist solidarity between men like Guy Mollet and Ben Gurion. These affinities were played upon by skilful Israel lobbyists who found their task much facilitated when the Algerian revolt of 1954 and Nasser's help for the rebels led many Frenchmen to conclude that a blow at Nasser was the right way to solve their troubles in Algeria – or at any rate a necessary pre-condition. In addition some Frenchmen shared Eden's view that Nasser was a menace like Hitler and must be put down before it was too late. French policy, traditionally pro-Arab, was therefore pulled in a new direction. France agreed in 1954 to supply Israel with fighter aircraft.

On his return from Bandung Nasser too began seriously to look for arms. The three signatories of the tripartite declaration refused to supply Egypt or Syria with all they requested. Syria turned successfully to the Russians who had become interested in the possibility of playing a more active role in the Middle East since the Gaza raid had exposed Egypt's weakness. But Nasser was reluctant to buy Russian. After trying Peking (where he got a hint to try Moscow) and then Washington and London once more, he finally took the Russian plunge and announced in September 1955 that he was to receive Czech arms without strings. It was now Israel's turn to be alarmed. By the Czech deal Egypt was to get a wide range of weapons including 80 MiG 15s (the fighters used in Korea), 45 Ilyushin 28 bombers and 115 heavy tanks equal to the best in the Russian army and superior to anything which Israel had. Israel pressed France to revise the agreement of 1954 by supplying Mystère 4 jet fighters instead of Mystère 2s. France complied and Israel received in April 1956 a contingent of the best fighter aircraft in Europe. (Their arrival just after the French foreign minister, Christian Pineau, had paid a successful visit to Cairo evoked an indignant anti-French outburst from Nasser and destroyed what chance there was of the Arab wind prevailing over the Israeli in the French cabinet.)

Like most countries Egypt wanted both guns and butter. Nasser had hoped to get both from the West but had been forced to buy communist arms or go without the guarantee which he was seeking. He then faced the question whether he could get economic aid from the West after accepting military aid from the communist block. The answer proved eventually to be no, but it was in doubt for some months. The test was the Aswan high dam, and it proved that not only France but also Britain and the United States were turning against Nasser.

The high dam was designed to transform Egypt's economy and society by adding 860,000 hectares to the area of cultivable land, making the Nile navigable as far south as the Sudanese frontier and generating electricity to service industrial plants which would provide some of the growing population with a living. It was to cost $1400 million, including $400 million in hard currency, of which the World Bank would advance $200 million and the United States and Britain $56 million and $14 million respectively at once and the remaining $130 million between them later. During 1955 negotiations to this end seemed to be proceeding without more than normal hitches. During the first half of 1956, however, they petered out. Britain and the United States decided not to help. Nasser's credit, in both senses of the word, was running down, especially as a result of his purchases of communist arms.

During 1956 he strengthened his enemies by recognizing the communist régime in Peking – a step which caused special irritation in Congress in Washington, even though the real reason may have been Nasser's fear that the new Russian leaders might, on their visit to London, be persuaded to join the Western powers in a new Middle Eastern arms embargo. The Czech arms deal had broken the 1950 embargo, to the general delight of the Arab world which resented the embargo as a clog on their sovereignty, but that embargo could be reimposed if the Russians were looking for inexpensive ways of showing goodwill towards the west, and in that event Peking would be the only alternative source of supply. In addition the cotton lobby in the American congress disliked laying out American money to help Egypt to grow more cotton to compete with American cotton. Egypt was blamed for not coming to terms with the other riparian states along the Nile (Sudan, Ethiopia and Uganda) and for pledging for arms purchases money which would be needed to service its foreign loans. In the United States it was argued that it was imprudent to allocate so much American money to a single project since the United States would then have to refuse all other requests for aid to Egypt for many years, leaving the Russians to step in and say yes. But behind all these reasonings lay the plain fact that Washington and London did not like Nasser and thought (like the French for a different and more specific reason) that it would be salutary to administer a snub to him and cut him down to size. This attitude was strongest in Britain where it found vent in the obsessive misinterpretations and miscalculations of the prime minister, Eden, who mistook Nasser for a fascist dictator and thought he could be easily replaced. (Eden's animosity had been sharpened in March by the dismissal of General Sir John Glubb and other British officers from Jordan's Arab Legion, of which Glubb was the commanding officer. Fortuitously this anti-British move by King Hussein coincided with a visit to Cairo by the British foreign secretary, Selwyn Lloyd, and it was therefore erroneously regarded by Eden as a deliberate affront to Britain contrived by Nasser.)

On 19 July 1956 Dulles informed the Egyptian ambassador in Washington that the Anglo-American offer to finance the dam was revoked. The French ambassador in Washington, Couve de Murville, had predicted that in this event Nasser would retaliate by seizing the revenues from the Suez Canal. On 26 July, in a speech in Alexandria, he did just that.

The Suez Canal was indubitably a part of the Egyptian state but it was also the subject of two, very different, instruments – a concession agreement and an international treaty. The former, granted to Ferdinand de Lesseps by the khedive or viceroy of Egypt, Said Pasha, and confirmed by the Ottoman sultan, conceded the right to operate the canal for ninety-nine years from its opening, which took place in 1869. The concession had passed from de Lesseps to the Universal Maritime Suez Canal Company, which was an Egyptian corporation with headquarters in Cairo and Paris and with a diversity of shareholders including the British government and a host of ordinary French *rentiers*. The concession, which was a valuable one, had twelve years to run in 1956. Thereafter the operating rights would revert to the Egyptian state. Nasser's action amounted to the nationalization of the company's rights, but since he promised compensation it was difficult to maintain that he had done anything illegal or, in the twentieth century, particularly unusual – although the company might well ask where the compensation money was to come from. Nasser would, however, be on the wrong side of the law if he broke the terms of the second relevant instrument. This was the convention made in 1888 between nine powers including the Ottoman empire, which was at that date suzerain over Egypt. The parties engaged themselves to keep the canal open to all ships of commerce or war, in times of war as well as peace, and never to blockade it. Should Nasser fail to keep the canal open he would be in breach of the convention and the signatories would be entitled to take measures to reopen it. There was some ill-judged expectation that if the canal pilots were withdrawn, the canal would cease to function and the right to intervene could be said to have arisen, but in the event the canal continued to function smoothly until bombarded by the British and French, even though the company's pilots were nearly all withdrawn as a result of pressure by outside powers.

The nationalization of the canal company gave Britain and France an excuse for the forcible action which they wished to take against Egypt. The British cabinet allocated £5 million (imperialism on a pittance) and resolved to use force within a week, only to discover that Britain's military preparedness was such that nothing could be ventured before the middle of September or without calling up the reserves. This delay enabled the United States to intervene. Eisenhower and Dulles agreed with the British and French governments in wishing to put the canal under international control but, although they had little love for Nasser, they were opposed to the use of force until all methods had been tried and had been seen to have been tried. Eisenhower, who made his position clear in letters to Eden and in public statements, was temperamentally averse to force and was also convinced that force was inexpedient because it would lead to sabotage of pipelines, would encourage other leaders (e.g. Chiang Kai-shek and Syngman Rhee) to claim American support for the use of force in their quarrels too, and would turn the uncommitted world against the west. Eisenhower sent a special emissary to London who reported on 31 July that the British were intent on using force, and thereafter a duel developed between Eden and Dulles, enemies since the crisis of 1954 in Indo-China, with Eden manoeuvring to get American sanction for a forward policy and Dulles side-stepping and playing for time.

First the British and French, with American support, convened in London a conference of the canal's principal users and presented to it a plan for a new operating board to ensure international control of the canal. The conference did not approve this plan unanimously; it was criticized as an unjustifiable infringement of Egyptian sovereignty. Nevertheless the Australian prime minister, Robert Menzies, and four other members, representing the majority view, went to Cairo to present the plan to Nasser, who turned it down and pointed out that the canal was functioning normally. Next Dulles, perhaps merely in order to keep talking and avoid shooting, propounded a Suez Canal Users' Association with the right to organize convoys and take tolls from the vessels in them. This plan appealed to the British who saw a chance of running a convoy through the canal against Egyptian opposition and so putting Egypt in the wrong in American eyes. Dulles, who was consistently pragmatic throughout this phase, then killed the scheme upon becoming suspicious that Britain and France might use it to start shooting; he pointed out that the American government had no power to force the masters of American vessels to pay tolls to the association and not to the Egyptian government. Britain and France then referred the dispute to the Security Council while explicitly stating that they reserved the right to use force. When the Council met on 5 October Egypt proposed negotiations, while Britain and France produced a plan for international control of the canal. Unofficial negotiations outside the Council made substantial progress but Egypt persisted in its refusal to accept international control and the Anglo-French plan was defeated by a Russian veto.

During these months the French became increasingly exasperated with the British. Joint Anglo-French commands had been set up at the beginning of August but the prospects of action by the slowly assembling hosts diminished as the British wavered between their desire to keep in step with the French and their anxiety not to get out of the Americans' good books. By the end of September or early October the French were reverting to their old line of co-operating with Israel, from which they had been distracted by the lure of a joint Anglo-French operation in response to the nationalization of the canal company.

Israel had excellent reasons for wishing to make war on Egypt. Raids into Israel by *fedayeen* based in the Sinai peninsula had become more audacious and more frequent. Land near the frontier was becoming too dangerous to farm and the Israeli government feared outrages even in the centres of its cities. Only a spectacular gesture could end this murderous nuisance. Further, Israel wished to break the Arab blockade of the gulf of Aqaba and so win a sure outlet to the countries of Asia and Africa from the port of Eilat which was languishing at the head of the gulf; even Israel's air links with Africa were insecure. The opening of the straits of Tiran at the entrance of the gulf would compensate Israel for the Egyptian refusal to allow ships bound to or from Israel to use the Suez Canal. But Israel's capacities were not the equal of its intentions. Egypt's new Russian bombers were in a position to bomb Israel's cities and cause panic among the newer immigrants who had not yet become tempered to life in a besieged state. Israel's air force was barely able to defend these cities even with its new French fighters, or to protect Israeli land forces operating in the open desert, and it was quite unable to bomb Egyptian airfields and so prevent the Egyptian air force from taking off. When therefore the French bethought themselves once more of the Israeli attack on Egypt for which they had been supplying arms, they found that the Israelis wanted more than arms. They wanted active French co-belligerence in the form of units of the French air force to be stationed on Israeli airfields for the defence of Israeli cities, and they also wanted British co-belligerence and the bombing of Egyptian airfields by the only locally based bombers capable of the task – which were British bombers using British bases in Cyprus.

The French set about engineering this combined tripartite operation and succeeded. During October French ministers divulged Israel's plans to British ministers; a meeting in Paris on 16 October between Mollet and Pineau, Eden and Lloyd, with nobody else present seems to have been particularly important. The British ministers, however, were reluctant to embark on any but the most furtive co-operation with Israel because of the repercussions in the Arab world. But Ben Gurion insisted on a formal commitment from the British, whom he did not trust, and this he secured at a secret meeting at Sèvres where, on 23 or 24 October, the British foreign secretary joined French and Israeli ministers, subsequently authorizing the signature of a secret tripartite treaty. At this point the Israeli commander-in-chief altered his battle orders, which had envisaged an Israeli raid in force similar to earlier raids but bigger, and proposed instead to commit his forces to the open desert upon the assumption that British attacks on Egyptian airfields would give the Israeli troops immunity from air attack.

Israel attacked on 29 October and duly received the anticipated support of Britain and France (the French also prevented the Egyptian fleet from attacking the Israeli coast), but the Egyptian air force was in any event incapacitated since the Russians, who were still in operational control of the Ilyushin 28s, ordered their pilots out of the battle area. Britain and France also issued an ultimatum to Israel and Egypt requiring both sides to withdraw ten miles from the Canal. This was a ruse intended to preserve the fiction that Britain had not colluded with Israel. Neither side paid attention to the ultimatum, Egypt because the canal was 100 miles within its own frontiers and Israel because its forces were some way from the canal and were not intended to go there. The Israeli campaign was virtually over on 2 November when its principal objectives – the clearing out of the *fedayeen* bases, the opening of the straits of Tiran and a resounding victory against Egypt – were assured.

A few hours after the initial Israeli attack the Security Council met to consider an American resolution requiring the Israelis to return to their borders. Britain and France vetoed this resolution but the General Assembly, convoked under the Uniting for Peace resolution (a procedure adopted in 1950 on Western initiative to enable the Assembly to consider and make recommendations on matters on which the Security Council was stultified by a veto), adopted in the early hours of 2 November an appeal for a cease-fire. At the UN a small group which included the secretary-general, Dag Hammarskjöld, and the Canadian minister for external affairs, Lester Pearson, worked to stop the approaching Anglo-French sea and land attack on Egypt (which, unlike the Israeli, had not yet been launched) and to recover control over an alarming situation by imposing a cease-fire and despatching an international peace force to the area. The Anglo-French attack began with a parachute drop on 5 November. On the next day a seaborne armada from Malta landed troops but on the same day Britain cried halt and France after some hesitation desisted too.

The British decision was the result of an accumulation of pressures, of which one was decisive. Britain, unlike France, was split. The parliamentary opposition, much of the press and a substantial part of the public were opposed to the government's policy. Eden's own party and a majority of the country as a whole supported him consistently except on the use of force, for which there was never a popular majority. The existence of doubts within the government itself was common knowledge. The independent members of the Commonwealth were also split; Australia and, less enthusiastically, New Zealand supported Eden, but Canada and the newer dominions did not (there were as yet no independent African members). This opposition had, however, been foreseen and discounted and for that reason the usual processes of Commonwealth consultation were omitted and Commonwealth governments, like senior advisers in Whitehall and all the pertinent British ambassadors abroad, were kept in the dark. But the decisive reason for calling off the operation was the failure to secure American endorsement and the failure to see what American opposition entailed. The attack on Egypt caused the biggest financial crisis in Britain since 1945. Britain lost on balance $400 million during the last quarter of 1956; withdrawals were probably half as much again but were partly offset by one or two exceptional influxes which were credited during the quarter. Sterling was healthy and the reserves more than adequate for ordinary purposes, but losses of this order could only be borne for a number of weeks without external aid to preserve the exchange value of the pound. It became clear that Britain would have to borrow to save the pound (which, apart from the war, was not threatened) and that neither the United States nor the International Monetary Fund would lend the necessary sums until the fighting was called off. Britain could not support an international currency and at the same time conduct independently an aggressive foreign policy.

There was in these calculations one other subsidiary element which may have had some effect on some people. This was the entry of the Russians upon the scene. Until 5 November the Russians were too much preoccupied with the suppression of the Hungarian rebellion to take a hand in Middle Eastern affairs, but on that day they proposed to Washington joint action to force Britain and France to desist and threatened vaguely to use rockets against Britain and France. They also indicated that they might allow volunteers to go to the Middle East but statements to this effect were made only after the fighting was over, except in one case when Khrushchev made, at a diplomatic party in Moscow, remarks about volunteers which were not reported in the Russian press. The Russian threat to use rockets was countered by an American threat to retaliate, whereafter no more was heard on this subject. By their intervention the Russians gained a sizeable propaganda victory in the Arab world; it is very improbable that they ever intended anything else.

Chapter 10

The decade after Suez and the third round

The Suez war raised Nasser's prestige high. He had secured the leadership in Egypt only in 1954. Suez confirmed him in it and made him a popular leader as well as a military ruler. He had kept his head and his dignity, had emerged intact from an imperialist onslaught and an Israeli invasion, and had demonstrated his power in the Arab world when even Nuri's Iraq had felt obliged to condemn Britain's action and propose Britain's eviction from the Baghdad Pact. Jordan too rejected its traditional British links and the subsidies which went with them, denounced its treaty with Britain and joined instead the Egyptian-Syrian alliance of 1955 (to which Saudi Arabia and Yemen also now belonged). Nasser kept the canal and showed he could work it and got the dam too. The Americans, who might be said to have precipitated the whole affair by abandoning the dam project, had had to come to the support of a régime which they had notoriously ceased to admire, and were left in the aftermath without a policy. The Russians were jubilantly claiming all the credit and getting much of it, and they undertook to finance the Aswan dam in place of the Americans and British.

While the debris was still flying the United States tried to make a fresh start with what came to be called the Eisenhower Doctrine. This venture proceeded from the assumptions that, with the defeat of Britain, it had become necessary for the United States to take some sort of initiative and that the decline of British power had created a vacuum which must be filled by the United States if it were not to be filled by the USSR. Between $400 and $500 million were to be disbursed in two years in the form of economic and military aid to willing recipients who would enter into agreements with the United States authorizing and inviting the use of American arms to protect the integrity and independence of the signatory if threatened with overt aggression from any nation controlled by international communism. Neither Egypt nor Syria was expected to conclude an agreement with the United States on these lines, but a special emissary was sent by President Eisenhower to tour the Middle East and get as many takers as possible. His only success was in Lebanon where, more out of courtesy than enthusiasm, a Christian leader entered into the requisite agreement – and was later to suffer for his decision. King Saud of Saudi Arabia was also polite and paid a visit to Washington but evaded signing any agreement. In Jordan there were anti-American riots. The Eisenhower Doctrine was a new version of the old plan of constructing an anti-Russian front in the Middle East, and its failure was due to the spread of neutralism among Arabs who realized, especially after the lessons of the Suez war, that they were no longer helpless against major outside powers and that the decline of Britain would be followed not by a fresh foreign domination but by none.

During the late fifties both the Americans and the Russians absorbed this lesson. For the Russians the test came in Syria and then more decisively in Iraq where events seemed to offer opportunities for intervention in a classical mode but brought instead disillusionment. Upheavals in both these countries opened for Moscow the possibility of alliances and even bases in the Middle East from which power could be exercised in imperial fashion. Syria, whence came reports of spreading communism in 1957, entered into economic and military agreements with the USSR, expelled three American diplomats and carried out a purge of the army. Turkey, disturbed by these pointers, concentrated forces on its southern borders. Egypt sent troops which were received in Damascus with acclaim. The tension was temporarily eased but in January 1958 some Syrian officers went to Egypt and asked Nasser to declare a union between the two countries in order to avert a communist takeover in Damascus. The pan-Arab nationalists of the Syrian Baath party had become alarmed at the growing influence of the Russians and of Syria's principal, and somewhat lonely, communist, Khaled Bakdash. Preferring Egyptians to communists they instigated a political move which Nasser, though embarrassed and hesitant, felt unable to reject upon being faced with the argument that an Egyptian refusal would leave no alternative to communism. The creation of a United Arab Republic, consisting of Egypt and Syria, was proclaimed on 1 February 1958. Yemen became loosely attached to it in March.

The Hashemite monarchs in Iraq and Jordan retaliated with an Arab Federation. This union was, however, insubstantial and short-lived, for on 14 July in the same year King Feisal II, the former regent and other members of the royal family, and Nuri es-Said were murdered in a military uprising led by Generals Aref and Kassim. The revolutionaries included communists whose presence at the centres of power alarmed the West and enticed the Russians. The Americans and the British, dismayed by this revolution in the centre of the Baghdad Pact, at once moved forces into Lebanon and Jordan in order to prevent the trouble from spreading, President Camille Chamoun of Lebanon invoking the Eisenhower Doctrine and King Hussein of Jordan the Anglo-Jordanian treaty. The British intervention in Jordan saved the monarchy at a time when its fall would have produced turmoil, laying it open to attack from Israel. In Lebanon there was already a civil war in progess which was threatening the religious equilibrium on which the life and prosperity of the country had been based for decades. The Lebanese government had invoked the United Nations in May but by the time of the revolution in Iraq in July the dangers of increasing civil and religious strife had become so great that the marines sent in by President Eisenhower were welcomed by a large majority. In both countries therefore foreign intervention was a stabilizing factor and was not held against the intervenors, especially as they contrived to get themselves out again rapidly with the help of Hammarskjöld. In Lebanon a new president, General Fuad Shehab, a member of an old leading family and, as a Maronite, an impartial mediator between Sunni Muslims and Christians, was able to re-establish the country's traditional equilibrium.

The Baghdad revolution looked at first sight like another link in the lengthening chain of Russian opportunities which included Arab hostility to the Baghdad pact, the Czech arms deal, the Suez war, the financing of the Aswan dam, Russian attendance at the Afro-Asian conference in Cairo in December 1957, and a visit by Nasser to the USSR in April–May 1958. Iraq left the Baghdad Pact (which was renamed the Central Treaty organization – Cento – and moved its headquarters to Ankara). But Kassim was himself no communist and his rule, which lasted until he was assassinated in February 1963, was hampered by general inefficiency and because it provoked a Kurdish revolt in the north. He was partly dependent on the communists but much less successful than Sukarno in similar circumstances in manoeuvring between the mutually hostile communist and nationalist forces which had brought him to power, and after much chaotic in-play the communists failed to consolidate or improve upon their advantages and Iraq too became more or less a neutralist state where the Russians were as unwelcome as any other major power. The Russians, who had been careful not to offend the nationalists by committing themselves to the communists, swallowed their disappointment and adapted themselves to the temper of the Arab world. They also reverted to more familiar ground. They tried (unsuccessfully) in 1959 to inveigle the shah of Iran away from the western camp, and they began to show an interest in better relations with Turkey after the fall of Menderes in 1960, in which attempt they were later assisted by Turkish disappointment over the American refusal to permit a Turkish invasion of Cyprus. The USSR recognized Kuwait in 1963 and Jordan in 1964, and the presence of Khrushchev at the opening of the Aswan dam in 1964 reasserted the usefulness of the Russian presence in the Arab world.

The Iraqi revolution also occasioned intervention by China in the affairs of the Middle East or, in Chinese terminology, west Asia. Until this time American and Russian interests in the Middle East had been openly antagonistic. Russian policies in Iran in 1945 on the one hand, and on the other the Truman Doctrine, the Baghdad Pact, American bases at Dhahran in Saudi Arabia and Wheelus Field in Libya and the US Sixth Fleet in the Mediterranean, made the Middle East look like an annex of the cold war. In 1956, however, the Americans and the Russians had found themselves in agreement on the need to thwart the

British and the French at Suez, and the Russians had even proposed joint Russo-American action; and in the aftermath of the Iraqi revolution of 1958 there appeared some prospect of an open or tacit accord between the two giant powers, an acknowledgement that both had legitimate interests in the Middle East and that some of these interests might be the same. This accord was not to the liking of the Chinese and when an international conference on Middle Eastern affairs was mooted Peking objected to the holding of such a conference without Chinese participation. The conference never took place. Although Chinese effectiveness in the Middle East was minimal, China began in 1958 to venture there. It gave exclusive support to the Iraqi communists, while the Russians were advocating a front policy; it championed Egypt's gaoled communists, to whom the Russians were turning a deaf ear; it gave some aid to the Yemeni republicans; and, more anti-Israeli than the Russians, it received the Palestinian Arab leader, Ahmed Shuqeiri, in Peking almost as a head of state and promised him military aid. Chou En-lai visited Cairo in December 1963 and April 1965. But the Chinese proved little more popular than other outsiders.

Within the Arab world itself the Iraqi revolution (which was wrongly expected to entail the early disappearance of the monarchy in Jordan) created a new pattern by shifting Iraq from the traditionalist monarchist category into the revolutionary republican one, and also by bringing to power in Baghdad socialists whose views were similar to those of the Syrian Baath party and Nasser's. But there was no following tide of pan-Arabism or of Egyptian influence. The new Iraqi régime was divided in its attitudes towards Egypt and more nationalist than pan-Arab even when the comparatively pro-Egyptian Aref became president on the death of Kassim in 1963. During the early sixties Nasser's prestige began to decline from its post-Suez peak. The fall of the senior branch of the Hashemite line had brought no gain to Egypt. The union with Syria was not a success: Egypt and Syria had no common frontier; Nasser and the Baath had too little in common beyond a superficial socialism; an influx of Egyptians into Syria and Nasser's policies of land reform and of forcing all political parties to merge in a single movement or front strained a union which had been a shot-gun marriage from the start; Syrians swung back to the idea that a union with Iraq would suit them better (especially after the Iraqi Baath helped to oust Kassim). In 1961 a (short-lived) right wing revulsion in Syria brought about the dissolution of the union.

In Yemen, loosely attached to the United Arab Republic from the start, an attempt to overthrow the imamate and install a republic led to a civil war in which Nasser backed the republican leader Brigadier Sallal without realizing that he was thereby entangling himself in Yemen for several years and to the tune ultimately of 50–60,000 troops. The imam on the other hand was supported by Saudi Arabia, so that the Yemeni civil war developed into a contest between two of the principal Arab states: After two years both sides found the effort unrewarding and in 1965 Nasser travelled to the Saudi capital of Riyadh to meet King Feisal (a relatively enlightened member of his house who had displaced his brother Saud the year before), put an end to the civil war and even effect a rapprochement between Egypt and Saudi Arabia, the protagonists of the opposing socialist and traditionalist tendencies in the Arab world. Earlier in the same year he had initiated a rapprochement with Jordan.

This re-emergence of the theme of Arab unity probably owed at least as much to apprehension about Israel's plans for diverting the Jordan's waters as to war-weariness in Yemen. An American plan in 1955 for an equitable apportionment of these valuable waters had been rejected by the Arabs on political grounds, whereupon Israel had started to construct engineering works which would take water from the Galilee region in the north to the Negev desert in the south. Israel maintained that the quantities to be pumped out of the Jordan's main stream would neither exceed the Israeli quota in the 1955 plan nor leave the lower reaches of the river unduly salty. The Arabs denied both these propositions. They also saw that the Israeli engineering works would come into operation in 1964 and in January of that year they convened a conference in Cairo, attended by traditionalist monarchies and progressive republics alike, in order to concert countermeasures. These measures included the diversion of two of the Jordan's tributaries, the Hashani in Lebanon and the Banias in Syria – the latter at points within sight and within range from the Israeli frontier; they also included the creation of a unified Arab High Command which, with a useful ambivalence, could be construed either as a means of preventing Israeli attacks on the work on the Banias or as a covert way of keeping the Syrians, the most unpredictable and volatile of the Arab allies, from starting anything on their own. And thirdly, Arab countermeasures included the promotion of the Palestinian Arabs to something approaching sovereign status with a Liberation Organization, an army and a headquarters at Gaza.

This unity was, however, imperfect. To King Hussein the pretensions of the Palestinians amounted to a threat to disrupt the Jordanian state and end the monarchy. Syria, Lebanon and Jordan all jibbed at the idea of having Egyptian troops stationed on their soil. Feisal turned out to be a dubious ally. Not only did the agreement of 1965 on Yemen come to nothing, but Feisal began to create a traditionalist or Islamic block within the Muslim world. He paid visits to the shah of Iran and to Hussein and ordered arms from the West in alarming quantities. In Iraq President Aref, one of the leaders of the revolution of 1958 and successor to Kassim upon the latter's murder in 1963, was killed in an aircraft accident in 1966: he was succeeded by his brother. The Aref brothers were comparatively pro-Egyptian but in 1968 the second was ousted by General Hassan al-Bakr who suspected the president and his prime minister of intending to restore the constitution and a parliamentary system. Al-Bakr became president and prime minister. Iraq became a prey to arrests and executions, dubiously stable and no friend to Egypt. Thus despite pan-Arab conferences at Alexandria in 1964 and Casablanca in 1965 Arab unity and Nasser's role as its leader were in decline in these years.

In the decade after the war of 1956 Israel enjoyed its gains without confirming them. The tranquillity on the Egyptian border achieved by the extirpation of the *fedayeen* was maintained and was for a while repeated on Israel's other borders. Eilat flourished, growing from a small town of fewer than 1,000 inhabitants to a flourishing port of over 13,000, trading over a large part of the world and rendering the continuing blockade in the Suez Canal harmless. Israel's warlike spirit was also kept up, and allied with its technical skills, placed Israel in a position to become a nuclear power, should it so choose. Although Arab talk of eliminating Israel went on unabated, it was believed by some to have become a mask, hiding the secret conviction that Israel had come to stay. Israel's reliance on its own might and the divisions of its enemies was reinforced, at second remove, by continuing the alliance with France which had preceded the war of 1956 and by new undertakings from the United States and Britain, as well as France, which followed it. These states declared in March 1957 that they regarded the straits of Tiran as an international waterway and would take action to ensure free passage through them into the Gulf of Aqaba. (The straits were indubitably territorial waters but international law required riparian powers to permit innocent passage for all vessels through such straits if they led to non-territorial waters or to the territory of another state.)

Until 1967 therefore there was some hope that the third round in the Arab-Israeli contest might be postponed *sine die* but by that year growing threats from Syria and from the terrorist organization *El Fatah* supported by Syria had changed the climate. An Israeli attack on Syria, leading possibly to a war with both Syria and Egypt, became a matter for practical speculation. The Israeli response to *El Fatah's* raids, which began in 1956, was to retaliate in force and by daylight with regular army units against villages in Jordan and Lebanon from which these raids originated. Forays across the Syrian border presented more difficult problems because the lie of the land favoured the Syrians and also because there were no specific limited objectives for the Israeli forces; an expedition into Syria would have been an open-ended *promenade militaire* with no precise stopping place short of Damascus. The brunt of Israel's countermeasures fell therefore on Jordan, notably in a raid on the village of Es Samu in November 1966 in which eighteen Jordanians were killed and much of the village destroyed.

The Egyptian moves which initiated the third round were to a large, if as yet uncertain, degree prompted by the state of Syrian politics. The Baath Party, founded in Syria in the early forties as a pan-Arab party of mild reform, merged in 1950 with the more left wing Arab Socialist party, dissolved (in Syria) in 1958 after the union with Egypt but re-established there in 1962, had re-established itself by an alliance with a group in the army led by General Salah Jedid, an Alawi. The Alawis are one of the principal communities in Syria, strong in the western parts of the country but distrusted by the orthodox Sunnis, by the Druzes and by the Christians. The dominant Alawi group in the army established a working partnership with the civilians of the Baath; this partnership was rendered uneasy by the marxist and atheistic elements on the left wing of the Baath, but on the other hand the military leaders found the left wing's anti-parliamentary leanings congenial and contrived in any case to secure control of much of the Baath's provincial organization. Between 1963 and 1966 the military leadership split between General Jedid and his adherents and General Hafiz Assad (another Alawi) and his. When Jedid carried out a coup against Assad in 1966 the Baath leaders sided with Jedid but became increasingly prisoners of the army at risk if Assad should ever turn the tables on Jedid. The latter's position was inherently precarious and within a year of his coup clashes with Israel laid bare Syria's vulnerability and also its isolation (Algeria was its only friend). At the same time Jedid found himself threatened by a scandal caused by the publication of an atheistic article which provoked demonstrations against his government. Anxious to deflect these attacks the government tried to lay the blame on zionists and Americans, whom it accused of fabricating lies in order to destroy it. The Russians, alarmed that Jedid's fall might entail a conservative reaction, abetted the story of an external threat to Syria. So too for similar reasons did the Palestinians. The cry was taken up throughout the Arab world and even kings Feisal and Hussein were moved to expostulate and promise aid. Israel was said to have moved troops to the Syrian border, a report which was first thought to have reached Syria from Lebanon but may have been given to the Syrians by the Russians. In Israel the Russian ambassador refused an invitation to go and see for himself that there had been no such troop movements.

Nasser had been anything but in the lead during this clamour. He did not like the Syrian government but he could not stand against the tide of Arab feeling and, as in 1958, he was ill informed about the true state of affairs inside Syria and afraid that its government might indeed be about to fall and be replaced by another that he would like even less. His standing in the Arab world had been diminished over the past years, notably by his unsuccessful Yemeni venture; he was being taunted by Jordanians and Saudis for his inactivity; gradually he became convinced that he had to do something. So he took the field. On 16 May he presented the UN commander with a demand for the withdrawal of UNEF (a step already urged by Jordan) and sent forward troops to harass UN positions in Sinai. Two days later, his demand having been rejected by the UN commander who said he had no authority to entertain it, Nasser repeated it to U Thant. After consulting his advisory committee on UNEF U Thant complied and on the

23rd UN forces pulled out of Sharm esh-Sheikh, leaving Egypt in control of the Straits of Tiran. On the previous day Nasser had declared that the straits would be closed to vessels flying the Israeli flag and to contraband of war on whatever vessel (but not to Israeli commerce in non-Israeli ships).

The moves of these days created a clear danger of war between Egypt and Israel. Syria's troubles were overtaken. In 1957 Israel had withdrawn from Sharm esh-Sheikh in reliance on western promises to guarantee free passage through the straits, the opening of which had been one of Israel's prime objectives in making war on Egypt in October 1956. Israel had stated that the closing of the straits would constitute a *casus belli* and on the day when the UN troops departed the Israeli prime minister, Levi Eshkol, publicly called on the western powers to implement their guarantee. Washington and London issued statements about international waterways and the British foreign secretary, George Brown, propounded a maritime declaration whose bearing on the crisis appeared, however, remote. De Gaulle proposed four-power talks but the Russians refused. In the early hours of the morning of the 26th the Russian ambassador in Cairo got Nasser out of bed to tell him to go carefully, but the Egyptian moves had caused a wave of enthusiasm and foolish optimism in the Arab world which carried Nasser even further forward. King Hussein arrived in Cairo to make friends with Nasser, a defence pact was signed and a joint command established, Iraq joined the pact a few days later, Egyptian troops moved to Jordan. Israel, which had viewed Egypt's first moves with equanimity, concluded that the danger of war was real, and a few hours after Iraq acceded to the Egypt-Jordanian pact, Israel – after delaying, partly under American pressure, for longer than some members of the cabinet thought prudent – struck the first blow. Victory was swift and total. Although the war has since been designated the Six Day War, Israel defeated both Egypt and Jordan within two days, annexing Jerusalem and occupying all Jordan west of the Jordan river and the whole of the Sinai peninsula. Syria was dealt with later but no less summarily. Nasser, who had moved back to the centre of the stage only to collapse even more humiliatingly than Farouk twenty years earlier, resigned but other scapegoats were found (and executed) and Nasser survived to fall in a later war.

There has been much debate over the legal correctness and political consequences of U Thant's decision to withdraw UNEF and to do so speedily. UNEF had been deployed with Egypt's agreement, which was required because the operation was launched under chapter VI and not chapter VII of the UN Charter. But Hammarskjöld had made an agreement with Nasser and the question arose whether, by this agreement, Nasser had abrogated to any degree Egypt's sovereign right to require the removal of the force. On the one hand it has been argued that the effect of the Nasser–Hammarskjöld correspondence was to make the stationing of UNEF on Egyptian soil terminable only by mutual consent. On the other hand it was said that this limitation, if and so far as any had been intended, applied only so long as UNEF was fulfilling its original role of bringing the hostilities of 1956–57 to an end, which role had undoubtedly been completed long before 1967. (It was never part of UNEF's role to keep the straits of Tiran open. This was an obligation of the western powers, if anybody's.) But whatever the true construction of the relevant documents, U Thant had to consider practical matters as well. His Advisory Council was divided, the UN's forces in the field were being forced out of their positions, two of the governments supplying forces indicated that they would withdraw whatever U Thant decided. In these circumstances it is difficult to see how U Thant had any choice. Even if he had prevaricated and delayed, as some of his critics maintained, he would probably have done no more than get some of his own forces killed.

Israel's new conquests made it safer. Although its territory was much larger, its frontiers were shorter and easier to defend. Its troops stood beside the Suez Canal and the Straits of Tiran, while in the north the commanding Golan Heights had passed from Syrian to Israeli possession. But for most Israelis this new territory was not for keeping but for bargaining with. Israel hoped that it now had the power and the counters to force its neighbours to make peace and to recognize a state of Israel with defined frontiers not very different from those existing before the war. Strategic details apart, the one gain to which Israel intended to cling with non-negotiable tenacity was the emotion-sodden old city of Jerusalem. For some months this mood prevailed but it was backed by no effective moves, even though Egypt and Jordan were thought by many observers to have signalled a readiness to negotiate. In August Arab leaders met in Khartoum. Saudi Arabia and Kuwait agreed to make good to Egypt its losses from the closing of the Canal and to Jordan its losses from the capture of all its lands west of the Jordan river, which included the revenues provided by tourists and pilgrims visiting Jerusalem. In return Egypt agreed to quit Yemen and to make no fuss about the ending of the ineffective and burdensome boycott which the oil-producing countries had applied against westerner customers. Unofficial sanction was given for separate and secret discussions by Jordan with Israel. Various peace terms were mooted, including free passage for the Israeli flag through the Straits of Tiran and the Suez Canal and eventual Egyptian recognition of Israel. But this piecemeal approach did not satisfy Israel which remained inflexibly intent on a formal peace conference and direct Arab-Israeli negotiations without intermediaries (as opposed to the so-called Rhodes formula by which each side would communicate with the other through a UN or other mediator). Fighting began again. The USSR, which had lost prestige as well as, vicariously, materials of war, decided to rearm Egypt. In October an Israeli destroyer was sunk by Egyptians using Russian weapons. As the exchanges of fire across the Canal increased Israel resolved to force Egypt to revert to a cease-fire by massive and deep retaliation but Egypt, instead of complying, called for and got more Russian help. The Russian position in Egypt was fortified; the Americans were correspondingly alarmed.

On the Jordanian front the principal changes effected by the war were, in addition to the shifting of the frontier, the influx of a further 250,000 Palestinian refugees into Jordan, a more effective organization of Palestinian guerrilla forces and the conversion therefore of Jordan into a primary target for Israeli attacks. The humiliating collapse of the regular armies of Arab states had intensified the Palestinian belief that it was futile to rely on these states for the recovery of the lands and rights which they had lost in Palestine. They resolved to fend for themselves and, because their cause had a compulsive emotional appeal throughout the Arab world, they had a degree of political influence on Arab capitals out of proportion to their military effectiveness and felt themselves to be in a position to block proposals for an accommodation with Israel which fell short of their irredentist demands. Their principal weapon was the threat to disrupt the kingdom of Jordan where, besides constituting more than half the population, they now also had armed forces. Militarily they were no serious threat to Israel – a further reason why they had to pursue their aims by threatening Jordan – but their guerrilla tactics provoked Israel to retaliations which fell upon the countries which harboured them. In 1968 a section of them took to hi-jacking aircraft. In July an aircraft of the Israeli line El Al was forced to land at Algiers where its Israeli passengers were held until released through Italian mediation, and in December the Israeli airforce destroyed thirteen aircraft on the ground at Beirut in response to an attack by Palestinians on another El Al aircraft at Athens.

In November 1967 Britain had succeeded in getting the support of the United States, the USSR and France for a resolution in the Security Council which condemned the acquisition of territory by force, re-quired Israel to withdraw from its recent conquests and advocated a settlement which would include recognition of Israel and a fair deal for the Palestinian refugees. This resolution (242/67) was endorsed by the Arabs (other than Syria) after some hesitations; it was rejected by Israel. This unaccustomed solidarity among the major powers – long but unsuccessfully sought by France – was facilitated by the fright of Washington and Moscow at finding themselves on opposite sides in a shooting war which, fortunately for them, lasted only six days. Both the super powers wanted peace in the Middle East. So long as the state of war lasted the Americans were committed, if in uncertain degree, to Israel and therefore debarred from improving their relations with Arab states. By the same token the Russians were able greatly to improve their standing as a Middle East power and their military facilities in the Middle East. The cessation of American aid to Egypt in 1966 (including free food under Public Law 480) had cast Egypt into the arms of the USSR even before the disasters of the 1967 campaign and so enabled Moscow to bring to a culminating point the capture of vantage points which it had begun after Eden, by adhering to the Baghdad Pact, and Ben-Gurion, by the Gaza raid of 1955, had initiated the Russo-Egyptian alliance. Their gains in this short period gave the Russians an interest in the stability of the Middle East where they had become something of a *status quo* power; and the emergence of an independent Palestinian power, hostile to Arab governments which were friendly to the USSR, and partly nourished by China, threatened to complicate Moscow's diplomatic problems if peace were not made. Moscow also wanted to see the Canal re-opened for the passage of supplies to North Vietnam and for its flotilla in the Indian Ocean. France, no longer dependent on Middle Eastern oil after the opening of the Algerian and Libyan oilfields, had extricated itself from the Israeli alignment into which the Mollet government had led it and, alarmed by the growth of Russian naval power in the eastern and (prospectively) western Mediterranean, tried to break the Russian monopoly in the Arab world and give Arabs some freedom of diplomatic and commercial manoeuvre by offering to sell arms to Iraq and Libya. As in 1956, so in 1967, France's main concern in the Middle East was the implications of events there upon the balance of power in the western Mediterranean. Britain, still dependent on Middle East oil and still enmeshed in the Persian Gulf, wanted peace on general grounds and particularly for the commercial convenience of reopening the Canal. But the resolution of November 1967 did not bear fruit.

In 1968–69 a war of attrition was waged on the Suez front to which Israel resolved, early in 1970, to put a stop by making air raids into Egypt to within a few miles of Cairo itself. This tactic failed because it led the USSR to bolster Egypt's defences with Russian missiles and Russian pilots and rocket crews: by the end of the year the USSR had stationed 200 pilots and about 15,000 men in missile crews in Egypt and were manning 80 missile sites in addition to earlier sites manned by Egyptians but also equipped with Russian missiles. Israel was forced to desist. Fighting was once more confined to the Canal and its environs. The United States and the USSR pressed their clients to start talking instead of fighting. Israel agreed to talk upon the basis of a withdrawal to pre-1967 limits and Nasser said that Egypt would recognize Israel. Israel agreed that talks might be indirect (through a UN negotiator, the Swedish Ambassador Gunnar Jarring) or direct. In June therefore the American Secretary of State William Rogers produced a plan for a cease-fire as a preliminary to indirect negotiations having as their goal an Israeli withdrawal and Egyptian recognition of Israel. Israel disliked this plan, as did the Palestinians; Nasser rejected it. But in July Nasser spent two weeks in Moscow, and Egypt and Israel both accepted the idea of a ceasefire. In August a ninety-day ceasefire and standstill agreement was concluded: within an area of 50 kilometres on each side of the Canal fighting would cease and no fresh units would be introduced, and talks would begin under Jarring's aegis. This agreement was renewed in November and again in February 1971, but it was immediately infringed by Egypt which moved missiles into the standstill zone. Israel responded by quitting the Jarring talks and demanding massive American aid. It got only part of its demands, waxed indignant with Washington and was forced back to the talks before the year ended.

These talks greatly alarmed the Palestinians who foresaw an Israeli-Egyptian deal, followed perhaps by an Israeli-Jordanian deal, which would leave them out in the cold. They decided to wreck the proceedings. Dr George Habash's Popular Front for the Liberation of Palestine, a small but active and extremist group among the dozen or so separate Palestinian organizations, hijacked four American and British airliners, held the passengers and crews hostage and burnt the aircraft. In Amman King Hussein, yielding to pressure from his extremist anti-Palestinian advisers, decided on a trial of strength with the Palestinians who were turning his country and his capital into an armed camp and exposing it to enemy attacks. He proved the power of his army which inflicted heavy casualties on the Palestinians but shocked the Arab world by the spectacle of fratricidal war and suffered a political rebuff when peace was restored by the intervention of other Arab states (notably Syria which invaded Jordan) and he had to sign, in the embassy of a foreign state, what was in effect a treaty of peace with the Palestinian leader Yassir Arafat, who was thus accorded the status of a head of state without the inconveniences of having territory to defend and control. The king committed himself to support the Palestinians' aims, though he soon afterwards entered into secret discussions with Israel which were unlikely to produce terms of peace acceptable both to Israel and to the Palestinians.

During the fighting in Jordan Iraqi troops stationed in that country made no move to help the Palestinians. Syria on the other hand sent a small detachment of tanks across the border but withdrew it, probably under Russian pressure induced in its turn by the prospect of Israeli or American intervention against this intervention. General Jedid's ill-fated gesture recalled his failure in 1967 to defend the Golan Heights against Israel and contributed to the overthrow of the Syrian government later in the year by its own defence minister, General Assad, a leader no less anti-Israeli than Jedid but more solicitous about good relations with Egypt and other Arab countries. More important by far, among the consequences of Jordan's internal war, was the sudden death of Nasser from a heart attack caused by his exertions in restoring peace in Jordan. He was succeeded with constitutional smoothness by vice-president Anwar as-Sadat.

The death of Nasser removed from the scene the first Egyptian to rule in Egypt since before the days of Alexander the Great. The movement which brought him to power had had complex sources It sought national emancipation, a spiritual (Islamic) revival, social reform and economic modernization. Nasser wanted to rid Egypt of a parasitic monarchy and upper class, to extinguish British domination over

Egypt and the Sudan, and to raise the miserable standard of living of the Egyptian people by a more equitable distribution of land, the extension of the cultivable area and the promotion of industries. He acquired the further aims of leading all Arabs against Israel and against Arab régimes deemed reactionary.

The revolutionary movement, in which he was at first only one among a number of leaders, was predominantly but not exclusively a military collectivity in which Nasser soon came to be the leading figure by force of personality and by the elimination of possible rivals. The enemies of the old régime had included elements – the Muslim Brotherhood on the right and the communists on the left – which constituted distinct centres of power. They were suppressed almost as quickly as the pashas of the old order. Political parties were banned. Nasser out-manoeuvred the nominal leader of the coup, Neguib, who was suspected of being insufficiently implacable against some pre-revolutionary elites. By 1954 Nasser's position had been secured. In the same year he secured Egypt's national aims by negotiating with Britain the removal of British forces from the Canal Zone and British rule from the Sudan. The stage seemed set for the economic reforms which would convert the coup of 1952 into a genuine revolution.

Egypt's economy was weak at home and abroad. Egypt had too little cultivable land, a one-crop economy (cotton), a stagnant agriculture, no mineral wealth, a very small share of international trade, little industry, little capital with which to develop industries and a population growing at the rate of 3 per cent a year. The relatively small sector of modernized industry was a foreign ownership. There was, however, a native bourgeoisie with some capital resources and Nasser aimed at first to get its co-operation in the development and diversification of the Egyptian economy. But this class had no faith in the new régime and preferred to put its money into unproductive savings at home or abroad rather than venture it in industry. By the end of the fifties massive unemployment and crushing poverty had been scarcely affected and Nasser turned to other ways. The western refusal to finance the Aswan dam and the Anglo-French attack on Egypt in 1956 had given him cause to seize the assets of foreign companies, and in the early sixties he went further and established state control over the greater part of the economy (other than retail trade). He also extended land reform from the modest and largely ineffective first steps of 1952 (when a limit of 200 feddan had been set on individual holdings, a reform which was evaded by various devices such as transferring parts of estates to relations: this reform did not apply to state or religious lands). A five-year plan for the years 1960–65 aimed to increase the gross national product by 7 per cent a year and did in fact increase it by 5.5 per cent, but this improvement was hardly felt by the working population whose numbers increased in the same years by 4 per cent.

Nasser's economic problem was never an easy one and it was made impossible by his foreign policy. He may well have intended in 1954 to devote more of his attention and resources to domestic affairs, but the resolution in that year of his differences with Britain was almost immediately followed by a more aggressive Israeli policy and by Britain's adherence to the Baghdad Pact, which Nasser interpreted as British intervention in Arab politics on the side of adversaries intent on stifling Egypt's revolution. So Nasser found himself increasingly concerned with foreign affairs instead of the reverse. The authors of the revolution had always intended to create a stronger, more efficient and better equipped army than Farouk's. This aim was not intensified by the seeming need to defend the country against Israel and the revolution against Nuri's Iraq and its British friends. Nasser's consequent search for arms – and for the means to pay for them – first pushed Egypt's defence spending up beyond all normal percentages of national income and then forced Nasser into borrowing sums which Egypt had little prospect of repaying. Aid and other resources which might have gone into development were appropriated to finance a deficit on external account which increased alarmingly from 1961 onwards. The war in Yemen made matters worse. The continuing war with Israel deprived Egypt of American aid and free food. When Nasser died Egyptians were materially hardly better off than they had been eighteen years earlier (though there had been some improvement in living conditions in towns); and Egypt itself was in pawn to the USSR.

Chapter 11

The fourth Palestinian War and the destruction of Lebanon

In 1970 the politics of the Middle East (excluding Iran) were dominated by a bipolar pattern: Israel/United States *versus* Egypt/USSR. After five years they looked very different. By 1975 the Egypt/USSR alliance had been broken. The United States, while not abandoning Israel, had ceased to regard the protection of Israel as its primary role in the Middle East. The Palestinians had acquired a new strength, only to see it gravely jeopardized. The Arab oil exporters had given a startling demonstration of the efficacy of economic sanctions. An older pattern of power was re-emerging based on the three historic capitals of Cairo and Damascus and Baghdad plus the new power centre of Riyadh. The Lebanese state was all but destroyed.

Sadat, like Nasser, found himself under pressure from Moscow to reach some accord with Israel on the assumption that Israel was under equivalent pressure from Washington. In fact both the United States and the USSR were oscillating between putting pressure on their clients and acceding at least in part to their demands for aid and arms: by the end of 1971 American aid to Israel, after being reined back for political reasons, was again substantial. After the fighting in Jordan in 1970 and the death of Nasser Egypt, Syria, Libya and Sudan had agreed to form a new federation of Arab republics, but Sadat's diplomacy was multifaceted. He wished to improve Egypt's relations with the Saudi and Jordanian monarchies and also to effect a reconciliation between Syria and Jordan, which had been within an ace of fighting one another over the Palestinians. He was well equipped for these exercises since he scared the heads of other states less than Nasser had done, and although he made the mistake of assuming and saying that he would bring the Arab-Israeli matter to the point of decision within a year, he contrived not only to establish himself at home but also to consolidate much of the Arab world while at the same time pursuing the policy of edging towards a bilateral agreement with Israel. Having inherited the cease-fire and standstill of August 1970 and the consequent talks, he offered in February 1971 to open the Canal to Israeli cargoes in return for a partial Israeli withdrawal or the convoking of a conference to be attended by the four major outside powers, but neither in this wise nor in the Jarring talks (which Israel again cold-shouldered) was any progress made during the year. In the next year Sadat twice went to Moscow, found he could not get the help he wanted, concluded that Brezhnev had betrayed Egypt by promising Nixon to keep Egypt on short commons, and with wholly unexpected boldness told the Russian specialists and advisers in Egypt to leave. They did so in a matter of weeks, leaving Moscow to look to Damascus or Baghdad for a new centre of influence in the Middle East.

In 1973 Sadat waxed even bolder. His Arab fence-mending complete and his hopes for a bilateral agreement soured by increased American aid to Israel and increased Israeli settlement of occupied areas contrary to international law, he decided to take the offensive and on 6 October Israel and the rest of the world were taken by surprise by an Arab offensive on two fronts. The Egyptian army attacked across the Canal and pierced Israeli positions, but these successes were nullified when the Egyptians ventured to operate beyond air cover and the Americans rushed aid to Israel by every available military and civil aircraft. The Russians, determined not to be left out, sent aid to Syria, Iraq and Egypt. Nine days after the first shots Israel counter-attacked, found a gap in the middle of the Egyptian front and, crossing the Canal westward, surrounded an Egyptian corps. The Egyptian stroke had been stymied and the next day Kosygin arrived in Cairo. In effect the war was over, although there was still some fighting to come. In the north it was even shorter. The Syrians, with the help of Jordanian, Iraqi, Saudi and Moroccan units, attacked the Golan heights but were held and pushed back after two days. Stalemate suited the United States and the USSR, the latter as soon as it became clear that the Arabs were not going to win and the former because, once Israel had been saved, the principal American concern was to prevent an Israeli counter-attack which would provoke a more forceful Russian riposte. Kissinger accordingly was invited to Moscow whence he proceeded to Jerusalem and the United States and the USSR jointly presented to the Security Council a resolution requiring a ceasefire, implementation of UN resolution 242/67 and peace talks under 'appropriate' auspices. Egypt and Israel accepted this resolution and it was adopted by the Council on 22 October. The Russians had privately proposed to the Americans that American and Russian troops be sent to the Middle East but Washington rejected this idea emphatically. It was, however, reintroduced by Egypt either spontaneously or at Russian instigation, and the USSR then publicly supported it. The American reaction was extreme. All American forces throughout the world were brought to the most advanced state of alert, whereupon the USSR retracted. Washington had demonstrated implacable opposition to the arrival of Russian units in the Middle East; but some European allies were disturbed by what they deemed American over-reaction, provoking in return from Kissinger some acid comments on their nerve and reliability.

There were two ways of winding up the war – a conference or diplomatic exchanges. A conference was convened at Geneva at the end of 1973 and was dignified by the presence of Kissinger, Gromyko and the Secretary General of the UN, Kurt Waldheim, but the ensuing year was devoted primarily to personal diplomacy by Kissinger while the conference was held in abeyance like a net under an acrobat. A first Israeli-Egyptian disengagement agreement was reached in January 1974; both sides withdrew and a UN force took station between them. On the northern front negotiations were slower because Israel insisted on proper notification of the numbers, names and fates of Israelis captured by the Syrians, which the Syrians either would not or could not give, and because it was impossible for Israel to withdraw more than a mile or two without endangering its entire strategic position and its settlements within range of the Golan Heights. Nevertheless Kissinger, by persistent shuttling between capitals, succeeded in getting a first agreement here too. (Both agreements were extended in November for six months and then again for another six months.) At the next stage the main crux was the status of the Palestine Liberation Organization (PLO) and its demands. Israel refused to recognize the PLO as anything but a terrorist organization or the Palestinians as anything but refugees. Israel also refused to consider territorial retreat except in the context of a general peace agreement. The PLO's proclaimed position was that it did not accept the existence of the state of Israel, but it was supposed that it might be brought to negotiate on the basis of the borders obtaining before the war of 1967. It insisted on being a principal party in negotiations as opposed to having the Palestinians represented by some Arab government. Israel wanted a series of bilateral arrangements beginning with Egypt (and side-tracking the Palestinians). Sadat was disposed to seek such an agreement provided it was quickly followed by similar agreements between Israel and its other neighbours, so that Egypt might not be accused of breaking Arab ranks or leaving the Palestinians in the lurch. Kissinger wanted an Israeli–Egyptian agreement as quickly as possible; he wanted the United States and not an international conference to be the peace-maker of the Middle East; and he wanted to fortify the American–Egyptian link without too greatly offending Israel or American Jewry: everything else could wait. Kissinger saw an Israeli–Egyptian peace as a stage towards peace in the Middle East and he did not believe that peace in the Middle East could be attained except by stages. Peace moreover was increasingly important for the United States, whose attempts to get away from a policy focused on support for Israel had been encouraged by Sadat's break with the USSR and then made urgent by the Arabs' use of oil sanctions during the war. The weakness of Kissinger's tactics was his emphasis and his dependence on Egypt which he was pressing into a bilateralism offensive to Egypt's Arab allies and into a disregard of the Palestinians whose claims remained nonetheless more central to the Arab–Israeli conflict than such purely Egyptian–Israeli questions as their common frontiers or the passage of Israeli cargoes and vessels through the Suez Canal. In order to succeed Kissinger had to divorce, and get Sadat to divorce, Egypt–Israeli issues from wider Arab–Israeli issues and above all from the Palestinian cause. He risked therefore damaging his new Egyptian friend throughout the Arab world.

The Arabs were in no mood to abandon the Palestinians, however much they might wish that the Palestinians had never been heard of. The Palestinians brought trouble and danger, but at an Arab conference in Rabat in October 1974 even their most ruthless enemy, King Hussein, who had been firing on them four years earlier, joined with everybody else in acknowledging that the PLO represented Arab Palestine; and from Rabat Yassir Arafat, chairman of the PLO executive council, proceeded to the UN General Assembly which received and listened to him as though he were a head of state and adopted a strongly pro-Palestinian resolution affirming the rights of the Palestinians to sovereignty inside Palestine and their right to be principals at a peace conference. In the winter of 1974/75 it seemed as though the PLO might declare itself a government in exile and be recognized by a majority of the United Nations, despite the lesions which weakened its claim to represent all Palestinians and despite the extremism of splinter groups whose indiscriminate kidnapping and killing shocked most people. (The PLO, formed in 1964, was virtually taken over in 1969 by Al Fatah whose somewhat more radical origins go back to the fifties and which came to prominence from 1965 onwards by staging commando operations. The more militant PFLP – People's Front for the Liberation of Palestine, political leader: George Habash – crystallized from earlier groups in 1967. From it later broke away the PDFLP – People's Democratic Front for the Liberation of Palestine – and the PFLP High Command. Al-Saiqa, the organization of the Palestinians in Syria, was created in 1966 with the support of the Syrian Baath. And there were other groups.)

If the war of 1973 gave the Palestinians a boost and a chance to recover from their drubbing in Jordan in 1970, it also boosted Arab morale and hopes in other ways. Quite apart from showing that the Egyptian army had become a match for the Israelis (at least for a week), it demonstrated Arab power against greater states. The Arab oil producers, banded together in the Organization of Arab Petroleum Exporting Countries (OAPEC, a division of OPEC), shocked the whole of the developed world by two measures – by cutting off oil and raising its price. These measures were in fact contradictory but they were in the short run very effective and there was every reason to believe that in another emergency the oil weapon would be used yet more rationally and effectively.

For the oil-producing states oil was not merely, or even primarily, a weapon. It was above all a source of revenue and for some states the only or overwhelming source. All of them were concerned to safeguard and increase their oil revenues and in 1971 they had made, at Teheran and Tripoli, agreements to secure these ends for the next five years. They also insisted through OPEC in 1972 that purchasing countries which devalued their currencies should revise the terms of these agreements so that the producers should not lose by the devaluation. They also changed their attitudes towards the way in which they would take their profit. Whereas hitherto they had done so mainly by fiscal measures, by taxes on offtake at the wellhead, they now moved towards participation or part ownership of operating companies and resolved to appropriate 25 per cent of the share capital of major companies, rising to 51 per cent by 1982. They felt moreover that what they set out to get they would get because – even before the war of 1973 – the developed world was worrying about an energy shortage amounting to an energy crisis. This crisis began to push up prices alarmingly in 1970–71 and made the producers more conscious of the advantages of restricting production: restrictions on output would prolong the life of reserves of an irreplaceable asset, put the screws on customers, and yet maintain producers' revenues if prices were raised – as they easily could be in a seller's market – to compensate for a lower volume of sales. Importing countries were vulnerable either way. Restrictions, let alone a stoppage, would jeopardize their industry and their daily life; price increases would disfigure their balance of payments. (The companies, however, were not in the same position as the importing countries. They suffered only one way. Restrictions and stoppages harmed their profits, higher prices did not.)

When the war began the Gulf producers raised their prices by 70 per cent. OAPEC threatened to cut deliveries by 5 per cent a month until Israel undertook to evacuate Arab territory and accede to the legitimate rights of the Palestinians. Saudi Arabia cut deliveries by 10 per cent; to the United States and the Netherlands, Israel's main champions, totally. Iraq nationalized parts of certain foreign companies and Libya talked of total expropriation. As a result of this multifarious, if ill-co-ordinated, Arab action oil prices in Iran, Nigeria and elsewhere shot up. Also as a result the EEC expressed its sympathy for the Palestinians, Britain stopped supplies of arms to Israel and Japan reversed its pro-Israeli proclivities. Arab threats did not fully materialize – it was, for example, not possible to boycott the Netherlands when oil despatched to other countries could be transhipped to Rotterdam – and within the Arab world there were some who feared the effects on themselves of harming western economies. But the point had been made and taken. A long-standing major factor in international affairs had been shaken. Primary producers were no longer the exploited but, where there was co-operation and shortage, could call the tune and use economic leverage for political ends. The change was so startling to public opinion in the industrial world that it was greeted with cries of blackmail. For the Middle East in particular it meant that if there were an energy crisis Arabs could not be trifled with. In a few years' time the countries round the North Sea – Britain, Norway and the Netherlands – might be able to afford a braver stance, but not yet.

Thus the Kissinger–Sadat axis was a brittle one, and although Kissinger's stage-by-stage diplomacy was admirably motivated, it was less well grounded in practical terms. The arguments which Kissinger could bring to bear on Sadat without discountenancing him in his own country were limited by the availability of so efficacious a new weapon and by the enhanced prominence of the Palestinians. Nor were the Israelis on their side to be pressured so easily. They had not been defeated. They had on the contrary satisfied themselves that in spite of initial reverses they had been on the way to another victory. But they had been severely shaken by the failure of intelligence services which, in so small a country, were vital to prevent instant obliteration. In elections at the end of 1973 the government parties lost six seats; the gains were on the right but there was increased support too for doves critical of Israel's Arab policies. The chief of staff and other senior officers resigned. Moshe Dayan, ultimately responsible for national security as Minister of Defence, lost some of his hero's image and was left out of the new government formed in April 1974 when General Yitzhak Rabin succeeded Mrs Golda Meir as prime minister. The spectacle of an American president touring Middle Eastern capitals in June was a disturbing one, even though Nixon came to Jerusalem too. The speed with which the USSR more than made up Syria's and Iraq's losses in arms was more disturbing, even though the United States did the same for Israel. At the end of 1974 Syria, by proposing a new joint military command with Egypt, Jordan and the PLO, emphasized the underlying unity among Israel's neighbours and their commitment to the Palestinians. Perhaps Israel had never been so unsettled. This was not a situation in which an American secretary of state could wield too big a stick, certainly not in public view.

Kissinger renewed his shuttle diplomacy early in 1975 with the aim of getting a further Israeli–Egyptian disengagement agreement. At first he was unsuccessful, owing mainly to Israeli obduracy. Sadat after a meeting in May with President Ford at Salzburg, announced the re-opening of the Suez Canal and in September a new agreement was reached. Fresh front lines and force levels were accepted; the keeping of the agreement was to be monitored by a string of early warning stations, some of them manned by American civilians; Israel abandoned the Mitla and Giddi passes and Egypt's oilfields in Sinai, in return for which it was promised massive American aid and the passage of Israeli cargoes (but not vessels) through the Canal. This was the crown of Kissinger's exertions and by comparison it seemed to matter little that on the northern front the greater acerbity of the adversaries and Israel's persistence in planting new settlements in occupied territory prevented any equivalent relaxation. Yet it was in this area that the next crisis was about to occur.

One of the recurrent features of Middle Eastern politics from 1919 onwards was the attempt to forget about the Palestinians. From the time when Amir Faisal and Chaim Weizmann talked at the Paris peace conference without troubling about them the Palestinians had been overlooked or worse, but they refused to disappear or lose their identity. By 1975 there were rather more than 3 million of them, of whom close on half lived in Israel, or under Israeli occupation. Of the remainder 750,000 were in Jordan, 400,000 in Lebanon, 200,000 in Syria. Through half a century they had persistently posed political problems, tugged at consciences (non-Arab as well as Arab) and resorted to violent means – including in the seventies guerrilla operations, kidnapping, murder and hijacking – in order to draw attention to themselves and their grievances. After their pounding in Jordan in 1970 the centre of these activities had been Lebanon.

Lebanon has often been called the Switzerland of the Middle East. This meant two things: first, that the Lebanese were highly successful merchants and bankers, good at making money, richer than their neighbours and rich because of the services they rendered rather than from domestic natural resources; and secondly, that the country was a patchwork of communities held together by political skill and tolerance in the service of material self-interest. The patchwork was imposed by geography as much as history, and the cohesion of the patchwork was a condition of the survival of the state. Two parallel ranges of mountains, one close to the sea and the two separated by a narrow valley, cut the country into vertical strips which are again divided by transverse barriers, and within this grid separate communities have preserved their individualities and mutual hostilities. These have been sharpened by religions – Muslim and Christian – and by further divisions within religions: Sunni, Shia and Druze; Maronite, Greek Orthodox and Greek Catholic. They have also been sharpened by varieties of economic experience, for not all Lebanese were rich. The richest group were the Maronite Christians who held in addition the presidency, given to them by the constitution and at a time when Christians as a whole outnumbered Muslims. (A decline in the Christian proportion of the population was one of the ground factors in Lebanese tensions.) The other Christian communities were neither so rich nor so powerful, but so long as Lebanon presented the appearance of a prosperous mercantile community in the guise of a state, by so much was it Christian rather than Muslim. The largest of the Muslim communities were the Shia but the Sunni, who monopolized the post of prime minister by constitutional right, were more influential politically. The Shia, many of whom had drifted from being poor countrymen to becoming poor townspeople, felt themselves to be equally neglected by Maronite Christians and Sunni Muslims. They were most exposed to Israeli incursions. The Druzes on the other hand, who still preserved much of the fierce exclusiveness which had marked their origins in the eleventh century, were confident and assertive because, though for the most part poor and frequently indignant, they formed a compact and well-knit society in an hereditary mountain homeland and under a hereditary leader, Kamal Jumblatt, who commanded their loyalties and expressed an appropriate left wing have-not philosophy.

Into this delicate cat's cradle of criss-crossing confessional and economic tensions had come in 1948 refugees from Palestine who, by 1975, numbered about 400,000, mostly housed (an ironic word) in dreadful camps. They included some five or six thousand active gunmen whose aim was the recovery of lost lands in Palestine by any effective means and the extinction – if that were necessary, as it was assumed to be – of the Israeli state. Since such an aim could never be attained by a few thousand armed men it had to be prosecuted through Arab states which had to be induced to make war on Israel. Since these states were only half willing to do so, and since when they ventured they got beaten, the Palestinians had a survival problem which led them to look even further afield for aid and sympathy, notably to the leading left wing powers China and the USSR (although the latter preferred to put its money on governments rather than on movements which were attacking governments), and to universal left wing opinion which would rally to dispossession and destitution and not be too gravely offended by the use of terror as a weapon of war. In Lebanon Palestinians could count on support, not from the political and mercantile élite which regarded them as a nuisance, but from other sections of the population which had to recognize them as fellow Arabs and fellow underdogs. By the seventies the Palestinians were more than a nuisance. Their militant organizations, encamped on Lebanese soil, regarded themselves as being at war with Israel, which was Lebanon's neighbour, and did not hesitate to strike back when attacked from Lebanon. The Maronites in particular, as conservative Christians, disliked and feared the Palestinian organizations because they were left wing, militant, Muslim and a threat to the stability of the state which gave the Maronites their wealth and their influence. It was an important coincidence that the Maronite position in Lebanon was already under some threat from the country's changing demographic balance and from the nemesis which (cf. Northern Ireland) haunts a too prosperous exclusivity.

In 1975 a group of Muslim fishermen who felt aggrieved by a concession granted to a group of Christian fishermen staged a demonstration which turned into an affray. Some Palestinians took sides with the Muslims. Christians saw in this episode a writing on the wall: the Palestinians, already a standing incitement to Israeli aggression against Lebanon, were now interfering too in the balance of internal Lebanese politics. Anti-Palestinian incidents followed, caused by the Phalange, a right wing Christian faction. Violence escalated; the government, always weak in a crisis because of conflicting loyalties implanted in it by the constitution, fell; the army, small and itself divided, failed to keep order. The disorder, which had begun as faction fights, turned into a battle for territory. The Palestinians, who had arms in plenty, became more and more involved (against the wishes of at least some of their leaders) and their opponents more and more provocative. There were innumerable truces of insignificant duration. Battle having been joined, opportunity beckoned to both sides. A left wing alliance of Druzes and Palestinians seemed set to take over the country, the Druzes in order to supplant the existing ruling groups and the Palestinians in order to make Lebanon safe for Palestinians and a base against Israel. On the other side the Maronites and their allies sensed the chance to do to the Palestinians in Lebanon what King Hussein had done to them in Jordan: expel as many as possible, kill some leaders and perhaps even, as tempers became uncontrollably bitter and destructive of life and property ruthless, exterminate them.

As the civil war threatened to entail the destruction of the state Syria had to consider what to do. Lebanon had been a part of Syria (as had Palestine) under Ottoman dominion and before, but Syria hesitated to intervene for a number of reasons. If the Syrian army were to go into Lebanon the Israeli army would very probably do so too and a new conflict would be staged, unwelcome to Syria and to Syria's Russian patrons. Nor would Jordan, with which President Assad had been improving relations for some years, take kindly to any move which looked like a step towards re-creating Greater Syria. The same argument applied at least as strongly to Iraq. Syria therefore, though inclined as a Muslim and left wing state to favour the Druze-Palestinian side, was more concerned to end the fighting and put the Lebanese state back on its feet; and after allowing Palestinians from Syria to cross into Lebanon early in 1976, Assad concentrated on finding a way of restoring the constitutional proprieties under a Maronite president (though a new one), even though this entailed attacking the Palestinians. The more militant and distant Arab states professed to be outraged by this intervention and, suspicious of Syrian designs, tried to substitute pan-Arab for Syrian management of the crisis by introducing a mixed Arab force and an Arab League mediator, but these moves had little substance, Assad chose the moment to put his own troops in and a provisional settlement was reached whereby the Maronites would retain the presidency *de jure* but the president would no longer choose the prime minister and the Muslims would have equal representation with the Christians in parliament. This was a defeat for the Druzes and Jumblatt, who had scented power only to be denied it by foreign intervention, and a defeat for the Palestinians, who had made common cause with the Druzes and other anti-Maronite elements and in doing so had backed the losing side and been battered first by the Maronites and then by the Syrians. It was also a defeat for the Russians who, having perforce shifted their pivot in the Middle East from Cairo to Damascus, saw Syria acting with a degree of independence and in a direction which were both unpalatable to Moscow. Yet Moscow gave no help to Jumblatt or Arafat; its influence in the crisis was minimal. Assad, not Arafat, had become the power behind the throne; the Syrian army and not the Palestinians had become the dominant force in the state. Lebanon itself was in ruins and in tutelage. It could eject Syria from its system only at the price of letting loose a new conflict between the private armies of Maronites and Druzes which no purely Lebanese army could control. The Palestinians, having been attacked by Jordan and by Syria, having lost their stronghold in Lebanon, and conscious that Sadat's sympathy for them was offset by the Egyptian state's contrary interest in peace with Israel, had once more nobody to rely on but themselves. Arafat had looked for support in the wrong quarter. Disillusioned with Arab governments and nervous about leftist breakaways from his own movement, he had formed an alliance with the Arab left and so became a target for Arab governments determined to annihilate the left. His policy had failed. For Israel the defeat suffered by the PLO and the rift between Egypt and Syria were a relief, although they also illuminated the extent to which Israel's peace and security depended on Arab feuds which could not safely be presumed to be perennial.

Chapter 12

The Persian Gulf, Yemen and Aden

The Arabian peninsula is a potential Saudi Arabian state bounded on three sides by the strategically important waters of the Persian Gulf, the Indian Ocean and the Red Sea and by a multitude of minor principalities, most of which had an assortment of treaty relationships with Britain. In the south-west corner of the peninsula is Yemen with a coastline stretching northwards along the Red Sea from the Bab el Mandeb (where Asia and Africa nearly meet) but with no access to southerly waters. The southern ledge of the peninsula is divided between the Aden protectorates and colony at the western end and the sultanate of Muscat and Oman to the east. From here the Indian Ocean makes a long and narrow penetration into the Middle East, dividing Arabia on the one hand from Iran on the other. This arm of the sea is at its narrowest at the strait of Hormuz. Southward lies the Gulf of Oman leading to the ocean, northward the Persian Gulf. The whole of the eastern shore of both gulfs is Iranian territory, but the opposite shore counts fourteen sovereigns. At the head of the Persian Gulf is Iraq and next to it Kuwait, separated by 350 miles of Saudi coastline from the other principalities – the island of Bahrain, the promontory of Qatar, the Trucial States and lastly the corner state of Muscat and Oman. Kuwait's political and business affinities have been with its Arab neighbours to the north and its sons have gone to Cairo or Beirut for their education, whereas the links of the remaining gulf states have been rather with Pakistan and India and their sons have gone to school in Karachi.

Britain's initial concern in these waters was to secure a monopoly or dominance over the routes to India and to protect British trade from the lawless depredations of the so-called piratical sheikhs who, at the southern end of the Persian Gulf, lived off piracy and earned for this strip of land the name of the Pirate Coast. From 1820 onwards the British imposed a maritime peace by a series of treaties or truces with these trucial sheikhs and in 1861 extended the system northwards to Bahrain by an agreement which pledged Britain to protect Bahrain in perpetuity. Later in the century Britain negotiated fresh agreements by which it assumed control over the external policies of the sheikhdoms and also of Kuwait and Qatar. Finally, as pearling and oil made the states in this area increasingly important for their own sake and not merely as pieces of territory adjoining an important trade route, a series of twentieth-century agreements gave Britain exclusive rights in the commercial exploitation of local riches but without any control over or responsibility for internal affairs.

Throughout most of this period of developing British control the landward frontiers of these states, lying vaguely in uninhabited and supposedly worthless country, were of no concern, and the obligations contracted by Britain as a part and consequence of the maritime truce remained for a long time unquestioned since Britain had additional reasons for remaining in the Persian Gulf and was undisturbed by commitments to local rulers in an area which it intended to go on policing by naval and air forces for complementary purposes. These purposes were the continuing need for communications with the east and the new traffic in oil.

The Middle East has for centuries played a major role in the communications between Europe and Asia. It must either be crossed or circumvented, and in this context the Arab nationalism of the twentieth century affected Europeans in exactly the same way as the Muslim conquests which posed the alternative ventures of the crusades and the voyages round Africa. In the heyday of British power in the Middle East the British travelled freely across it, but after the Second World War the direct central route was lost as one Arab government after another denied to Britain the special rights and facilities which it had previously enjoyed by treaty or by occupation. The withdrawal from Palestine and the Canal Zone, the revolution in Iraq in 1958 and the abrogation of the Anglo-Jordanian treaty at the time of Suez in 1956 eliminated this route and made it necessary to find a southern or a northern detour. The southern route lay through Libya and the Sudan to Aden, but in 1964 the Libyan government sought a revision of its 1952 treaty with Britain and in the same year the Sudan attached virtually prohibitive conditions to overflying rights. Going south meant flying across central Africa or even southern Africa, both routes being politically awkward as well as expensively long. The northern alternative, by Turkey and Iran and the Persian Gulf, remained therefore valuable, even though it could no longer be described as essential since technical developments were opening up a new, if arduous and expensive, route from Britain westward to Singapore.

Communications provided therefore an argument, effective though not conclusive, for staying in the Persian Gulf a little longer provided it was understood that the days of the British presence were already numbered. Oil provided only a weaker argument. The importance, even the growing importance, of Middle Eastern oil to Europe was undeniable, but the policy of ensuring supplies by a physical presence seemed increasingly dubious and anachronistic. Europe, unlike the other major consuming areas, the United States and the USSR, had become dependent on Middle Eastern oil. Britain for example, which before the Second World War imported more than half its oil from the American continent, was by 1950 importing half its needs from Kuwait alone, and it was estimated in 1965 that Europe's annual consumption of 300 million tons would rise in fifteen years to 750 million tons, despite the greater use of natural gas and nuclear power. Important discoveries of oil in the Sahara in 1956 and Libya in 1959 would decrease the proportion of Middle Eastern oil in Europe's consumption but not the total amount of Middle Eastern oil required. Oil was likely to remain cheaper than natural gas or nuclear power or submarine hydrocarbons, and Middle Eastern oil was cheaper than other oil, but this European dependence was not as frightening as it seemed to a number of European statesmen since Middle Eastern producers were on their side heavily dependent on their European customers. The oil revenues of the states concerned exceeded $2,000 million in 1964 and provided between 70 and 95 per cent of the budgetary income of the several producers. Neither the increasing demand from Japan nor the prospect of China's entry into the market on a big scale seemed likely to counter the essential need of the Middle Eastern producers to sell their oil to Europe, and if this were so military bases were as irrelevant to the flow of oil as to the supply of any other basic commodity.

There was, however, a further argument of a political rather than an economic nature. The British, it was said, had gone to the Persian Gulf to keep the peace and provide the stability without which commerce is endangered, and they had done so. A British withdrawal could be followed by disorders which would interrupt the flow of oil. These disorders might be the result of sabotage or of frontier disputes between the states of the region. Sabotage, however, is not a thing which regular military units are particularly suited to prevent, while one of the more usual causes of sabotage is nationalist resentment against the presence of foreign garrisons. Frontier disputes certainly existed: Iran claimed Bahrain; Iraq claimed Iran's province of Khuzistan and also Kuwait; Saudi Arabia had disputed frontiers with some of its smaller neighbours, many of whom were at feud with one another. So long as such disputes persisted Britain might claim to be rendering a service by remaining in the area and performing the policeman's task which it had once exercised over half the world. This argument was reinforced by an episode in 1961 from which a number of doubtful deductions were drawn.

The sheikhdom of Kuwait was unique in the Persian Gulf. It was very much smaller than Iran, Iraq or Saudi Arabia, but it was more populous, more sophisticated and much richer than the other sheikhdoms, from which it was separated by a considerable distance in space as well as by superior resources and deportment.

The British connection too was different. There was no Anglo-Kuwaiti treaty until 1899 and the making of a treaty in that year was due not to piracy or any other kind of disorder but to fears of German or Russian expansion to the Persian Gulf by means of railway concessions and Ottoman connivance. In 1961 the treaty of 1899 was amicably terminated and Kuwait became a fully independent state. At the same time Iraq, then ruled by General Kassim, repeated Iraq's traditional claims and the ruler of Kuwait, afraid of an Iraqi attack, appealed to Britain for help. A small British force was expeditiously landed, the Iraqis (who had remained a long way from the frontier) subsided, the British troops were quickly withdrawn and were replaced for a short time by contingents from other Arab states, and Kuwait became a sovereign member of the Arab League. This incident led many people in Britain and elsewhere to suppose that efficient British action had prevented general disorder and the absorption of a relatively virtuous state by a relatively wicked one; and that the British ought to remain ready to do the same thing again. British action was efficient and, in the circumstances, right, but it may not have been necessary (Iraq's intentions may have been less warlike than its words) and it was no guide to future policy since Kuwait had become in 1961 a constitutional monarchy with a parliament which was exceedingly unlikely ever to sanction a second appeal to Britain – even if membership of the Arab League and the internal suspicions of Arab states did not suffice to preserve its integrity.

In the Trucial States Britain tried but failed to promote a federation as a first step towards release from its perpetual obligations. Britain was not supposed to interfere in the internal affairs of these states but was often obliged to do so because of their mutual disputes, the shortcomings of some of their rulers and the aid which the poorer ones required. The rulers, though no longer in need of protection from the seaward, felt the need for protection against Saudi Arabia and against their own not very numerous subjects. The ruler of Qatar (which had loosely formed part of the trucial system in the early nineteenth century but had left it in the eighteen-sixties) asked for British help against internal troubles in 1963 but was refused it. The principal problem, however, was the relationship between the sheikhs and Saudi Arabia. Britain wished neither to let the sheikhs down nor to prop them up indefinitely.

Britain's relations with the Saudi royal house had been traditionally good, notably in the days of King Abdul Aziz ibn Saud, although less so after the accession of his son Saud in 1953 and the substitution of American for British influence in Saudi Arabia. Britain was also embarrassed by the apparently complete imperviousness of the Saudi régime to the slightest touch of modernity, except in the accumulation of oil royalties which were expended by the royal family with lavish uselessness. It did not seem right to abandon states once redeemed from piracy to the mercy of a big neighbour still noted for slavery. Moreover in 1955 a running dispute over the Buraimi oasis led to a minor military confrontation. This oasis, a collection of ten villages partly in the possession of the sheikh of Abu Dhabi and partly in that of the sultan of Muscat, was coveted by Saudi Arabia whose claims had been rejected by Britain for a generation. The dispute, which involved the two powerful forces of honour and oil, was referred to an arbitral tribunal at Geneva but the Saudis, having too little faith in their cause or in the tribunal, bribed witnesses on such a scale that Britain was moved to public protest. The Saudis also sent troops into the villages, whence they were forcibly expelled by the British. Yet Britain was loth to pursue the quarrel, which died down once more. In 1964 the abdication of King Saud and the accession of his brother Feisal, who belonged to the relatively progressive faction within the royal family, opened the way for better relations and ultimately for a refurbishing of the Saudi state which would enable Britain, without dishonour, to press the rulers of the Persian Gulf to negotiate with Saudi Arabia about their frontiers and their status. It was difficult to foresee how, beyond Kuwait and possibly Bahrain, the former could survive at all or the latter undiminished.

The peace of the Persian Gulf required also an understanding between Saudi Arabia and Iran, since old disputes about sovereignty could acquire a new edge if the disputed areas were proved to be rich in oil. In December 1965 King Feisal visited Iran and concluded an agreement with the shah on the ownership of the possible submarine wealth of the Persian Gulf.

In the southern part of the Arabian peninsula, where the port and base of Aden had played an even more prominent role in British imperial history than the Persian Gulf, Britain had similar problems. The port of Aden was in the possession of the East India Company and then of the government of India from 1839 to 1937, when it became a British colony. It was given a legislative council in 1947 and elected members were introduced in 1955; under a new constitution in 1958 the elected members became a majority of the council. During the period of Indian government (first as part of the Bombay presidency and finally for a few years as a separate province under the direct control of Delhi) Adenis complained that they were a neglected outpost of the Indian empire. After the transfer of their affairs to the British colonial office nationalist demands for independence appeared and waxed. Important as a port for 2,000 years, Aden also became in the middle of the twentieth century the site for a big new oil refinery and for the headquarters of Britain's Middle East Command. Conservative ministers therefore decided, and stated with incautious boldness, that nationalist aspirations could not be allowed to go to the lengths of independence. The nationalists, led by Abdullah al Asnag, the secretary-general of Aden's trade unions, proceeded to press their views by means of strikes which seriously threatened a base so dependent on native Adeni and immigrant Yemeni labour, and by boycotting the electoral processes with which Britain had hoped to satisfy local political aspirations.

The adjacent Aden protectorate consisted of twenty-three sheikhdoms divided for administrative convenience into a western protectorate embracing eighteen sheikhdoms and an eastern protectorate containing the other five. All these principalities had entered into protection agreements of some kind with Britain between 1839 and

1914, and Britain had performed a useful pacificatory role in this part of the world. After the Second World War Britain negotiated new treaties under which British political officers were appointed to advise the sheikhs who agreed to accept the advice given them except in relation to Islamic law and customs. In the western principalities the appointment of a new sheikh had to be confirmed by the British governor of the colony. The sheikhdoms and the colony constituted a geographically compact, religiously homogeneous area, but the colony differed from its surroundings in being populous, comparatively rich and hostile to the monarchical principle. The nationalists in the colony envisaged a union with the protectorate territories, and ultimately with Yemen also, but not under their existing rulers.

Aden was a little and neglected world of its own until Britain's final departure from the Suez base in 1956. In that year a British minister told the colony's legislative council, in the course of a speech which was particularly patronizing and insensitive in its references to self-government, that the British government forsaw no possibility of changes in Aden's affairs and was confident that this immobilism would be welcomed by a vast majority of its inhabitants. Later in the year the blocking of the Suez Canal by Nasser as a result of the Suez war caused unemployment, strikes and unrest in Aden. At the same time the sheikhs became aware of the threat to their way of life. In 1958 the sultan of Lahej decided to take the road to Cairo, while in 1959 six of the western sheikhs, caught between the devil of Adeni nationalism and the deep seas of Yemeni subversion, formed the federation of Arab emirates which the British had been working for in vain since 1954. This group, renamed the Federation of South Arabia in 1962, was gradually enlarged but never embraced all the sheikhs in spite of British grants fifty times bigger than those provided theretofore.

Britain, intent above all on retaining the Aden base as other bases in Kenya, Egypt and Cyprus vanished or became unreliable, decided in 1963 to attach the colony to this new federation, uniting the sheikhs and the merchant class and circumventing the nationalists. Under the British scheme Britain retained its sovereignty in the colony; it undertook not to extract the whole colony from the federation, although it might withdraw parts; during the seventh year of this symbiosis, but not before or after, the colony might of its own volition secede but if it did it would have to revert to colonial status and could not become an independent state; whereas each normal member of the federation had six seats in the Federal Council, Aden was to have twenty-four. This bizarre concoction intensified nationalist agitation in the colony, which now took two forms – a demand for independence and a demand by extremer elements for union with Yemen where an attempt to overthrow the established autocracy was in progress.

From the departure of the Turks at the end of the First World War Yemen had been ruled by its hereditary imams. Their rule was one of the least amiable or admirable in the world. By the treaty of Sana in

1934, made between Britain and the imam Yahya (1918–48), Britain recognized the imam as sovereign and accepted an adjournment until 1974 of territorial disputes arising out of Yemeni claims against the protected sheikhs and the colony of Aden. The imam Yahya's policy was to temporize but his son Ahmed revived Yemen's claims and argued that constitutional changes in the colony and in the protectorate were a breach of the treaty of Sana inasmuch as they prejudged matters which were to be settled in 1974 and created an anti-Yemeni group intended to disrupt the Yemen which Britain had recognized. Border affrays resulted and the imam concluded in 1956 the treaty of Jidda with Egypt and Saudi Arabia and in 1958 the federal association with the United Arab Republic.

In 1963 the Imam Ahmed died and was succeeded by his son, Muhammad al Badr, who in 1956 had visited Moscow and Peking. A revolution broke out immediately and a republic was proclaimed by Brigadier Sallal who invoked Egyptian help under the treaty of Jidda. The imam invoked Saudi help under the same treaty, and there ensued a mixed civil and international war, not unlike the Spanish civil war of the nineteen thirties. At Riyadh in August 1965 Nasser and Feisal agreed to discontinue their aid and withdraw their troops; the Yemenis were to install a coalition and hold a plebiscite at the end of 1966 to decide their country's form of government. But this agreement was abortive, troops were not withdrawn and Nasser later said that Egyptian forces might stay indefinitely. After the war with Israel in 1967 he had to change his mind again and withdraw them. The war ended in 1970 in compromise. The republic prevailed but royalists joined its government.

The collapse of the Riyadh agreement was a disappointment for the British who had hoped that it would ease Anglo-Egyptian relations and lead to an abatement of Egyptian aid to the extremer nationalists in Aden where terrorists were resorting to murder, inhibiting their less extreme compatriots and holding up Britain's declared intention to give the federation independence in 1968. The abandonment of Aden was not, however, intended to signal an abdication of British power and influence in this part of the Middle East, but only an alteration in the ways in which they were to be brought to bear. The United States, which had powerful naval forces in the Mediterranean and in the South Pacific, had no equivalent force in the Indian Ocean and looked to Britain to fill the gap. The British Defence White Paper of 1957, the first to appear after the fiasco of the Suez war, contained a mixture of old and new ideas. It still envisaged local forces not only in Aden and Cyprus but also in Kenya (which, however, on becoming independent in 1963 granted Britain only limited facilities by an agreement of March 1964); but it also envisaged a carrier group in the Indian Ocean. The Kuwait operation of July 1961 reinforced arguments in favour of local garrisons for acclimatizing troops, since between a quarter and a half of the men flown to the scene of that action from temperate climes had been quickly prostrated by the heat. On the assumption that such operations remained an inescapable part of Britain's lot in the world, tropical bases seemed essential.

The White Paper of 1962 reiterated the need for a British presence to assure stability and with it the need to maintain forces in Aden and Singapore. But the arguments and assumptions of the framers of Defence White Papers were challenged by those who counted the cost of these establishments (especially after the Labour victory of 1964 in the middle of a financial crisis) and by those who believed that bases in Arab territory created political ill-will out of proportion to their military usefulness. Britain was already developing an air base on Gan, an island in the Maldives about three miles long and 800 miles south of Ceylon. In 1960 the Maldives were given self-government (they became independent in 1965) and Britain took a twenty-six-year lease of Gan. Britain also created in 1965, for strategic purposes, the British Indian Ocean Territory, a new colony consisting of a string of small islands lying between the Malagasy republic and Ceylon. Most of these islands were uninhabited and detached from the Seychelles, but the most important of them, Diego Garcia, had been a dependency of the colony of Mauritius, from which it was bought in anticipation of the independence of Mauritius in 1966. In 1970 Britain and the United States resolved to build a joint naval base on Diego Garcia. (Mauritius was a French-speaking British colony with a racially mixed population in which Indians were in a majority, and with no wish to join either the neighbouring French island colony of Réunion or the more distant and much larger Malagasy republic. The Seychelles, a group of islands 1600 kilometres east of Mombasa and about twice as far from Bombay, were given a constitution in 1967, revised in 1970, and became independent in 1976 after a period of uncertainty between association with Britain and independence. In return for the islands detached to the BIOT Britain built on Mahé, the capital island, an airport to help the Seychelles become a tourist area.)

In the mid-sixties therefore Britain was preparing new positions. It proposed to withdraw from southern Arabia (but not quite yet from the Persian Gulf) and leave behind an independent South Arabian federal state. But this plan was partially thwarted by the internal inconsistencies of the federation and the rivalries of other states – Egypt and Saudi Arabia – which, still at feud in Yemen and competing for influence in the Trucial States as well, were each determined not to allow the other to succeed Britain in control of territory guarding the southern approaches to the Red Sea. The Adeni nationalists refused to co-operate with Britain or recognize the federation, turned to Egypt for help and took to terrorism to accelerate the British departure and ensure the collapse of the rest of British plans. The federated sheikhs tried to get promises of continuing British military support which the British Labour government was unwilling to give since they would virtually negate the policy of withdrawal and retrenchment and would entangle

Britain in Arab feuds: by accepting a military commitment while abandoning political power Britain would get the worst of two worlds.

For Nasser and Feisal the future of the protectorates and Aden and
Yemen was part of a complex contest which was likely to be repeated in
the Persian Gulf. Feisal, lord of the holy places of Mecca and Medina,
stood for orthodox Islam. He also represented the principle of
monarchy and traditional, antiquated social systems. In both
capacities he was a rallying point for the conservative elements in pan-
Arabism. In contrast to his extravagant brother Saud he exemplified
the sterner features of the puritanical background from which their
father, Abdul Aziz ibn Saud, had emerged to create the Saudi kingdom.
This kingdom had been very poor until the discovery of oil in 1938 but
had then become a byword for affluence and, with the departure of Britain from its last toeholds in Arabia, might hope to round off the work
of ibn Saud by acquiring the whole of the Arabian peninsula. But for all
its vast size and wealth Saudi Arabia had a serious weakness in the
smallness of its population (3.5 million) with the result that Feisal's
position was ultimately a diplomatic and not a military one. As a
diplomat he had the advantages of personal shrewdness and the opportunities provided by the distrust inspired by Nasser, which enabled him
to maintain sympathetic relations with leaders who, although not
always orthodox Muslims or monarchists or conservatives, wished to
see Egypt's influence curtailed. Saudi Arabia was in no position to lead
or consolidate the Arab world as Prussia had the German, but so long
as Nasser's aims remained obscure or alarming Feisal was a figure of
some international importance. He could get arms from Britain and the
United States; make friendly approaches to the shah of Iran who in
spite of being a reforming monarch and a heretical Muslim, was equally concerned to counter Egyptian propaganda and subversion against
the minor princes of the Persian Gulf; and hope that the emperor of
Ethiopia, although a Christian, would make common cause in checking
Egyptian influence on the African side of the narrows at the southern
end of the Red Sea.

The British Labour government of 1964–70 decided, primarily on
financial grounds, to accelerate the British departure from Aden and
the Persian Gulf. Aden and its hinterland became in 1967 the independent People's Democratic Republic of Yemen. The departure of the
British, who had provided most of the jobs, and the closing of the Suez
Canal in the same year plunged the new state into economic distress
which accentuated its inherent instability. It was also at odds with its
northern neighbour, the Yemeni Arab Republic, whence it was invaded
with Saudi help in 1972. A short war ended with talk – but no more – of
amalgamating the two Yemeni states. Passage through the Bab
el-Mandeb and the proximity of Eritrea, in revolt against Ethiopia,
gave this area international strategic importance.

In the Gulf the shah renounced the Iranian claim to Bahrain which
became in 1970 a fully independent member of the United Nations.

Populous and wealthy enough to stand on its own feet it was unwilling to become a member of the proposed new federation of Gulf states, unless it were accorded an equivalently overwhelming representation in the projected Union of Arab Emirates. This federation came into being at the beginning of 1972 but without Qatar and Ras al-Khaimar (one of the seven Trucial States), both of which chose independence. All existing treaties with Britain were abrogated. Iran, pleading strategic exigency, seized the islets of Abu Musa and the Tunbs in the narrows between the Persian Gulf and the Gulf of Oman, causing Iraq to break off diplomatic relations with Iran and expel Iranians from Iraq. The new order in the Gulf, elaborated in anticipation of the British withdrawal, rested essentially on agreement between Iran and Saudi Arabia, on the latter's inability to secure at this stage full control over the western shores of the Gulf to match Iran's control on the other side, and on the fortuitous absence of Egyptian and Iraqi voices owing to the former's defeat in 1967 and the latter's continuing war with the Kurds and other internal weaknesses, but none of these factors was necessarily permanent. The assassination of King Feisal in 1975 and the peaceful succession of King Khaled did not disturb the pattern, but in the same year Iraq began to recover its freedom of action as a result of improved relations with Iran.

In Muscat and Oman a coup in 1970 brought a new sultan to the throne. In the province of Dhofar the People's Front for the Liberation of Oman and the Arab Gulf received enough Russian and Chinese help to remain a thorn in his western side until in 1975 he succeeded in defeating the revolt with British and Iranian help.

Chapter 13

Cyprus

In 1878 Disraeli, prompted by British military opinion, contemplated the seizure of Cyprus but contrived to secure it by diplomacy. On the eve of the Congress of Berlin he entered into an agreement with the Turks to defend their empire against Russia upon being permitted to occupy Cyprus which, however much the Turks might regard it as an anti-Russian base, was for the British of those days the key to western Asia. Britain, contemplating the collapse of the Ottoman empire or alternatively the substitution of German for British influence at the Sublime Porte, was on the look-out for vantage points in the eastern Mediterranean. The occupation of Cyprus in 1878 was followed a few years later by the occupation of Egypt. The British remained in both for the best part of three generations.

Cyprus was annexed by Britain in 1914 upon the declaration of war between Britain and Turkey, and British sovereignty was recognized by Turkey by the treaty of Lausanne in 1923. Between the wars British rule was challenged by the partisans of *enosis* or union with Greece but was never seriously threatened. For the British Cyprus was a colony which could gradually be granted the degree of self-government compatible with its usefulness as a staging-post and a base in the British imperial scheme of things. For the Greek section of the population, however, the British themselves and their programme of limited democratic development were simply obstacles to a more natural scheme of things in which all Greeks were being brought together in the single nation state which had been inaugurated by the Greek revolt against the Turks in 1821. The Turkish minority was a spectator of Anglo-Greek conflict, sometimes worried and sometimes not. At the end of the Second World War the British estimate of the value of Cyprus rose as a result of the retreat from Palestine and the weakening of the British position in Egypt. The British assumed therefore that they would and should stay in Cyprus. The Greek Cypriots assumed the opposite. They expected a reward for their loyalty to Britain during the war and they regarded the British withdrawal from Egypt as a step which should logically entail a withdrawl from Cyprus and not a reinforcement of British rule there. Discussions for a constitutional advance towards limited self-government were abortive. To the Greeks they were irrelevant.

In 1946 the exiled bishop of Kyrenia returned to the island and in

1950, at the age of thirty-seven, he was elected to the archiepiscopal throne of the autocephalous church of Cyprus, which had been vacant during the years 1937–47. He took the regnal name of Makarios III, and he became at the same time the ethnarch or national leader of the Greek community. Makarios was therefore both the head of one of the most venerable of the churches within the Orthodox communion (it had been founded by the Cypriot apostle Barnabas) and also the leader of a modern nationalist movement which had fought the Turks for a century and a half and was now to fight both Turks and British on this last remaining battlefield. He and his fellow *enotists* considered that the kingdom of Greece had a sacred duty to support them, a belief shared by very many – probably most – Greeks outside Cyprus but embarrassing nevertheless to Greek governments which were reluctant to impair their good relations with Britain and even had reasons for co-operation with the traditional Turkish enemy after the admission of both Greece and Turkey to Nato. In 1950 a plebiscite organized by the church returned the inevitable (but not, as the British deludedly imagined, faked) response in favour of *enosis*; the Greek prime minister, General Plastiras, equally inevitably responded to it in a tone of mixed encouragement and moderation. About the Greekness of Cyprus no Greek bothered to think twice. Four Cypriots in five were Greek by race, tongue and religion, and called themselves Greeks. Whether they supported the left wing party AKEL or the right wing KEK they shared a common nationalism, for which they were soon to fight together in the insurrectionary movement of EOKA.

The Turkish section of the population (18 per cent) was no less alive to the Greekness of the island but it naturally drew opposite conclusions from the same facts. Although the government had passed from Turks to British, the Turks knew that they remained the principal and hereditary enemies of the Greeks, and they feared Greek rule. These fears may not have been great in the first post-war years, since the Greek record in relation to Turkish minorities was no bad one, but they were latent fears which could easily be inflamed. The Turkish state, as opposed to the Turks of Cyprus, also feared *enosis* because Cyprus was only forty miles from the Turkish coast, because post-war Greece seemed for a short while to be exposed to communism, and because Greece might still cherish the ambition to conquer Constantinople and the coasts of Asia Minor (which it had tried unsuccessfully to do immediately after the end of the First World War). Turkish governments showed, however, little inclination to intervene in Cypriot affairs until encouraged to do so by Britain.

In 1951 the Greek government sought a way of satisfying its Cypriot compatriots and its British allies by offering Britain bases in Cyprus – and also in Greece itself – in return for *enosis*, but Eden was not interested in a solution which would have been more attractive to Britain than the eventual settlement of 1959 and could have saved much bloodshed. In 1953 Eden gravely exacerbated the situation by declaring that there was no question of a British withdrawal. This statement forced Greeks to decide between an indefinite acceptance of the existing position and a resort to violence to change it. At first Makarios tried an intermediate course. In 1954 he went to Athens to try to get the Greek government to raise the Cypriot question at the UN. Eden repeated that no discussion was possible; a junior British minister with a lamentable sense of history and a notable lack of caution declared that Cyprus would 'never' be fully independent; and the colonial secretary affronted the Greek government by advancing as an extra reason for the maintenance of British rule the argument that Greece was too unstable to be allowed safely to extend its sway to Cyprus. The Greek government then raised the question of self-determination for Cyprus at the UN but half-heartedly and without pressing the case, which was shelved. The *enotists*, disappointed by this effort, reverted to the local scene and organized demonstrations which evoked an excessive British counter reaction (including measures against schoolchildren). The British in Nicosia and London believed that the *enosis* movement was a bubble blown in their faces by a small and unrepresentative group of irresponsible agitators who had succeeded in cowing the bulk of a law-abiding and pro-British population. This was, at the very least, a serious exaggeration, just as the British appreciation of the value of Cyprus as a base was also seriously mistaken: Cyprus, though valuable as a command headquarters (HQ Middle East Land and Air Forces was transferred there in 1954) and as an air staging point, was a poor country with meagre resources, a hostile population, no adequate naval base (Famagusta being too shallow) and a manifest vulnerability to Russian nuclear attack. The Suez war of 1956 proved that it had some value for the Royal Air Force but no other.

In 1955 Eden and his foreign secretary Harold Macmillan decided to fortify the British position in Cyprus by bringing the Turkish government officially into the matter. The Greek and Turkish governments were invited to a conference in London. The result was the collapse of the Greco-Turkish alliance. In Turkey hideous atrocities were perpetrated against Greek residents, and Greece boycotted Balkan Pact meetings and Nato exercises.

In Cyprus the governor and the archbishop met for the first time, and a British colonial secretary appeared in the island also for the first time. At the end of the year the governor was replaced by Sir John Harding, a field-marshal and former Chief of the Imperial General Staff. The policy entrusted to him was to separate the ethnarch-archbishop from the insurrectionary movement which had come into the open in 1954, to negotiate with the one and to extirpate the other. This policy, which was pursued until the end of 1957, was a total failure because it was based on false premises and poor information and because, at one decisive point, it was abandoned by the British government. The Harding-Makarios negotiations were proceeding early in 1956 towards a promising conclusion when the British government intervened and decreed the deportation of the archbishop to the Seychelles. Eden appears to have been swayed at this juncture by pressure from the right wing of the Conservative Party, by the dismissal of General Glubb by the king of Jordan (which Eden interpreted as a deliberate slight to his government), and by the failure to manoeuvre Jordan into his prized creation, the Baghdad Pact. These rubs roused in him the assertiveness of a weak man and he resolved to teach his enemies a lesson, foremost among them Makarios and Nasser. But Makarios was released in the following year, much to the annoyance of the Turks and without any compensating advantage since the archbishop refused to return to Cyprus and took up residence in Athens.

The British attempt to quell the insurrection was equally un-successful. This revolt was led by Colonel Grivas, an officer of the Greek army and a Cypriot by birth who set himself to evict the British by a combination of military skill, faith and ruthlessness. Grivas had fought on the same side as the British in two wars and was outraged to discover at the end of the second that, despite the UN Charter and fre-quent British promises in the past, Britain had no intention of allowing the Cypriots to choose how and by whom they should be governed. Like Cavour after the Crimean war Grivas took the view that his com-patriots had paid for self-determination with their blood, and when he saw that the British view was different, he set about shedding more blood. He decided, according to his own account, to resort to violence in 1951 but he laid his plans with considerable professional care, carried out an extensive and open reconnaissance of the terrain and waited until 1954 before making his first purchases of arms and setting up a headquarters in a suburb of Nicosia inhabited chiefly by British families. He launched his revolt in April 1955, survived a drive against him at the time of Makarios's deportation in March 1956 and im-mediately struck back. His main weapons were bushcraft, discipline and terrorism, his victims frequently Greek civilians, his armoury and front line manpower always small. He provoked the British into retaliatory measures which failed – collective fines on villages, high but ineffective bribes, hangings and torture. He defeated the policy which Harding had been sent to implement.

In the course of the year in which Makarios was in the Seychelles and the Harding-Grivas duel was taking place, the first Greco-Turkish riots also occurred and the British government began, although uninten-tionally, to transfer the initiative from London to Ankara and Athens. During 1956 Eden produced a plan by which Cyprus would be allowed self-determination after ten years of self-government, but instead of applying his scheme he submitted it for approval to the Turkish and Greek governments and accompanied it with a proposal for a tripartite treaty. The Turkish government rejected the plan and this rejection both killed it and gave Turkey a new commanding position. Later in the same year new constitutional proposals, elaborated by an eminent British judge, Lord Radcliffe, were in the same way submitted to the

Turkish and Greek governments. The Radcliffe plan rejected self-deter-mination and mentioned partition. It was accordingly rejected by the Greeks, while Turkey was emboldened to suggest that either half of Cyprus or the whole of it should be annexed to Turkey. The Greeks, thoroughly alarmed, threatened to leave the western camp. In 1957 General Ismay, the secretary-general of Nato, offered to mediate, but although the Turks were willing the Greeks were not. The Turks believ-ed that a majority of the members of Nato were sympathetic to Turkey; the Greeks believed that their cause would prevail in the UN but not in Nato. There was deadlock internationally and continuing disorder and murder locally. The government of Harold Macmillan reviewed Eden's Cyprus policy and, faced with the threat to Nato's eastern flank which had been created by it, decided that Britain no longer needed to be sovereign in the whole of Cyprus. Sovereign bases would do and the Greek and Turkish governments must be brought to accept in-dependence for the rest of the island. For Turkey independence was acceptable, since it automatically excluded *enosis*. Upon Greece in-dependence might be forced, since Greece abominated partition and was afraid that in the absence of a settlement Greeks in Istanbul and other parts of Turkey would be stripped of their property and either killed or expelled.

In December 1957 Harding was replaced by Sir Hugh Foot who produced a new plan: self-government as a colony for a period followed by self-determination with the proviso that *enosis* would need Turkish approval. The mention of *enosis* was too much for the Turks and demonstrations were organized in Ankara when Selwyn Lloyd (now foreign secretary) and Foot visited that capital. The Foot plan dis-appeared. It was succeeded by the Macmillan plan which was a further step away from undiluted British rule. Macmillan proposed to in-troduce representatives of the Greek and Turkish governments alongside the British governor and to create a mixed cabinet and separate Greek Cypriot and Turkish Cypriot local administrations. The last provision was unacceptable both to Makarios and to the Greek prime minister, Constantine Karamanlis. Their rejection of it led to fresh riots in Cyprus in which the Turks seemed to be applying pressure in order to enforce acceptance of the Macmillan plan. The revolution in Baghdad in July 1958 may have inclined the British government, threatened with the loss of its Iraqi ally and the collapse of the Baghdad Pact, to lean further to the Turkish side in Cyprus, and Macmillan set out on a tour in the course of which he slightly modified his plan, failed to reconcile Makarios or Karamanlis to it, but resolved to apply it nonetheless. Violence increased horribly.

The spreading communal hatred shocked and alarmed the Greek and Turkish governments into an accord. After exploratory contacts at the UN and Nato between their foreign ministers they conferred together in Zürich in February 1959 and announced that they had agreed that Cyprus should be independent. Britain would be accorded sovereign rights in certain areas which would be British military bases. The new state would have a Greek president, a Turkish vice-president with a veto in certain matters, and a cabinet of seven Greeks and three Turks; this 7–3 proportion would be repeated right down the administrative ladder. The Greek and Turkish states would station small armies of 950 and 600 men respectively in Cyprus. This scheme was accepted with the greatest reluctance by Makarios, who declared it unworkable. He was, however, threatened with abandonment by the Greek government and on 1 March 1959, he returned at last to Cyprus. Grivas, infuriated by the politicians' betrayal of the cause of *enosis*, was fêted, promoted and sent back to Athens. Instead of driving the British out and making Cyprus part of Greece, his campaign had ended with the British still in possession of sovereign bases and Cyprus still no part of the Greek kingdom. Cyprus became independent in August 1960, a member of the UN the following month and a somewhat strange member of the Commonwealth in 1961.

The Zürich settlement was an attempt by frightened men to prevent the situation from getting completely out of control. That was its one merit. But Makarios was right in regarding the constitution as unworkable. The Turkish Cypriots were entitled to 30 per cent of the posts in the administration, although they did not have the men to fill so many posts. Each of the five principal towns was to have two separate municipal bodies, though this concession to communal distrust produced such absurdities in practice that it was never implemented. Discussions for an improved system broke down and when the Turkish leaders in the island proposed the extension of the existing arrangements for a year, the Greek majority in parliament rejected the proposal. The constitutional court, upon being appealed to, pronounced both the Greek and Turkish cases to be wrong, and in December 1963 Makarios made proposals which were meant to force the Turks into further discussions but were taken by them to be a breach of the constitution and an attack on their safeguards. Serious fighting developed and attempts by leaders on both sides to arrange and enforce cease-fires broke down. Moreover the progenitors of the Zürich agreement had by now passed from the scene. Both the Karamanlis government in Athens and the Menderes government in Ankara had fallen. The former had been replaced by a government under George Papandreou which began its existence without a parliamentary majority, while in Turkey a military coup had overthrown the parliamentary system in May 1960, indicted over 400 people and executed fifteen of them including Menderes himself. General Gürsel, who was successively provisional head of state and then in October 1961 president, installed a coalition government, but the new military régime was assailed by an abortive coup from within its own ranks in May 1963 and by the recrudescence of Menderes's Democratic Party under the new name of the Justice Party. In December 1963, when fighting broke out again in Cyprus, the veteran Ismet İnönü had just resigned the premiership and been persuaded to retain it, albeit with a majority in parliament of only four.

Some 200 Turks were killed in this new bout. Turkish jet aircraft flew manacingly over Nicosia, a Turkish naval invasion was thwarted by the American Sixth Fleet prowling in the vicinity, the Greek and Turkish forces in Cyprus took up hostile battle positions, and the British colonial secretary, Duncan Sandys, abandoned his Christmas holiday to fly overnight to Cyprus. After four years of independence Cyprus had brought Greece and Turkey to the verge of war.

Britain tried at first to transfer the Cyprus problem to Nato. The Greek and Turkish governments were willing to accept Nato intervention but Makarios was not; nor were other members of Nato anxious to become embroiled. In February a second Turkish invasion threat was unostentatiously foiled by the American fleet and Britain accepted the need to invoke the UN. The raising of a UN force coincided with a third invasion scare, but by mid-March the Canadian advance party of a UN force reached Cyprus. It was followed by units from Eire, Sweden, Denmark and Finland which, together with British units transferred to UN command, constituted a force of 7,000 under the Indian General Gyani and subsequently under his compatriot General Thimayya and, after his death in 1966, the Finnish General A. E. Martola. This force gradually asserted control, although occasional outbursts continued to occur – and led to occasional reprisals against the Greeks in Istanbul. In addition to the peace force the UN secretary-general appointed a mediator to seek a political solution, but neither of two incumbents of this office was able to find a solution acceptable to both sides. The United States, alarmed by the consequences of a Greco-Turkish conflict, also took a hand through the former secretary of state Dean Acheson who produced a scheme for *enosis*, excluding an area in north-eastern Cyprus which would go to Turkey. The Turks thereupon asked for a larger area and so converted the plan into partition in a new form. Acheson then revised his plan and proposed that the north-eastern area should merely be leased to Turkey for twenty to twenty-five years. At this point the plan became unacceptable to everybody and the Turks, already disappointed in their hopes of Nato and frustrated by the American fleet, turned tentatively towards the Russians (who may at this time have sensed a possibility of undermining the entire Baghdad Pact since Pakistan was also disappointed by the United States and Iran was internally unstable and internationally plastic). Early in 1965 the UN mediator proposed a demilitarized independent Cyprus, debarred from *enosis*, in which the Turkish minority would be protected by a UN guarantee and a resident UN commissioner. A new government in Ankara rejected the idea. With the UN force preventing a resumption of civil war, the basic political fact reasserted itself: namely that Turkey, Cyprus's nearest neighbour and a country with three times the population of Greece, was capable of preventing *enosis* but was not capable of achieving the reconquest of the island. Hence the independent status of Cyprus, an independence resulting from a balance of external forces which was countered by an opposite balance of internal forces. Externally power lay with the Turkish state and not with the Greek state; internally power lay with the Greek community and not with the Turkish community. The power of the Greek community was limited by the power of the Turkish state, and the power of the Turkish state was limited by forces which were not native to the area itself. Cyprus therefore was an international problem-child destined, so long as these circumstances prevailed, to independence tempered by ungovernability. The UN stopped the killing but could not resolve the underlying dispute. Two UN mediators tried but failed, whereupon the Turkish and Greek governments insisted on assuming the role but did very little about it.

Year after year, and twice in each year, the mandate of the peacekeeping force was renewed by the UN who feared the consequences of saving money by removing it. Talks between the two communities were started and stopped more than once. Any whiff of *enosis* from the Greek side was met with Turkish talk of double *enosis*, a new name for partition and the attachment of northern Cyprus to the Turkish state. In 1971 Grivas was back in Nicosia. The only new element in the situation was the worsening relations between Makarios and the military junta which had seized control of Greece in 1967. The junta regarded Makarios as a troublesome red priest. They tried to force him to change his government (and did succeed in making him remove his foreign minister) and they incited his fellow bishops to bring charges of simony against him for combining the presidential and archiepiscopal offices. They were more and more anxious to score a popular victory by forcing the pace in Cyprus in order to be able to pose as Greek patriots who had united Cyprus with the Greek heartlands. But Makarios was re-elected president in 1973 without opposition, routed the bishops and had them unfrocked for good measure, and struck back at Athens in 1974 by demanding the recall from Cyprus of the officers of the Cypriot National Guard who were doing the junta's bidding and subverting rather than protecting the Cypriot state. At this point, 15 July, the junta acted. Makarios, who had already survived at least one attempt on his life, was attacked in his palace by the National Guard. He escaped in a helicopter with British help and was flown to England. The insurgents proclaimed Nikos Sampson president in his place, a choice as unwise as it was unsuitable as Sampson had been a notorious EOKA gunman and had to resign at the end of a week.

The independence and integrity of Cyprus had been guaranteed by Greece, Turkey and Britain. Greece was in the process of destroying both. Turkey saw in Greece's foolhardy action an opportunity to intervene and occupy at least a part of the island. Britain was unwilling to do anything, partly because of the difficulty of finding reinforcements for its units in the British bases but more emphatically because intervening meant intervening against Turkey and so on the side of the

Athens junta and the equally unattractive Sampson. Consequently Turkey invaded Cyprus five days after the coup against Makarios. A cease-fire was imposed two days later and the next day the junta in Athens collapsed. Constantine Karamanlis, returning from his exile in Paris, formed a provisional democratic coalition government, so that Greece became once more internationally respectable, but the Turkish army was already in Cyprus.

The three guarantors met at Geneva. Turkey's attitude was threatening but realistic: either there must be a new constitution acceptable to Turkey or Cyprus would remain *de facto* partitioned. The constitution proposed was a loose confederation not far short of independence for the components, and the proposal was accompanied by an ultimatum. The talks were broken off and the Turks again took the initiative with a fresh two-day attack and advance which put them in possession of the whole of the north coast and of Famagusta in the east. The American ambassador in Nicosia was murdered by Greeks who took American inaction to betoken sympathy for or even complicity with Turkey. The British too were criticized violently in Cyprus and in Greece for not doing more, as a guarantor, to help Cyprus escape the plight brought upon it by a Greek government. Makarios returned at the end of the year. Cyprus was in effect partitioned but nobody was prepared to say so and its affairs were therefore back to inter-community talks, hampered by the emotions of war, charges and counter-charges of atrocities, the plight of refugees, economic disruption and the unreality of any attempt to restore the integrity and independence of Cyprus with a Turkish army in control of a large part of it.

Notes

The Kurds

The Kurdish peoples trace their tribal names further back in time than any other peoples in the world and their presence in western Asia for about 4,000 years. In recent centuries they have been divided between the Ottoman, Iranian and Russian empires. Upon the dissolution of the Ottoman empire they were further divided between Turkey, Iraq and Syria. In the mid-twentieth century they numbered 5–6 million, the greater part (2.5 million) in Turkey. In Iran and Iraq they constituted important minorities of 1.4 and 1.2 million respectively. There were about 250,000 of them in Syria and perhaps 100,000 in the Armenian SSR.

Between the war the Kurds in Turkey were among the opponents of Ataturk's rule. There were Kurdish risings in 1925, 1930 and 1937 but after the Second World War – and particularly during 1950–60 when the Democratic Party was in power – relations eased. There was some recrudescence of racial hostility in the sixties but the Kurds' worst enemy was the poverty of eastern Anatolia, an area of agricultural decrepitude. In Iran the Kurds were harried by Reza Shah between the wars and then led up the garden path by the Russians who paid diligent attention to Kurdish notables during the war, fostered Kurdish nationalism and supplied a separatist movement with arms. In January 1946 the Kurds proclaimed the independent republic of Mahabad, but for the Russians the Kurdish movement was meant to be no more than an appanage of the separatist Azerbaijani republic which they had contrived in Tabriz at the end of 1945. The Mahabad republic was an expression of genuine non-communist local feelings, whereas the Azerbaijani republic was a communist artefact. Attempts to ally the two were never more than superficially successful although the Kurds, dependent on Russian support, were half tied to the Azerbaijanis. After the withdrawal of Russian troops in May 1946 the Azerbaijanis negotiated, without reference to the Kurds, a favourable agreement with the Iranian government which restored Azerbaijan to the Iranian state as an autonomous province. At this time the Iranian government was a coalition including communists, but later in the year the prime minister, Quavam es-Sultaneh, evicted his communist colleagues in Tehran and sent his army against Tabriz where the communist provincial administration was immediately overthrown with the help of the local populace. The Mahabad republic was now at the mercy of the Iranian army. It was annihilated, its leaders fleeing or being hanged.

In Iraq the Kurds were at first encouraged after the First World War to hope that the British would reward them for their anti-Turkish activities by creating an autonomous Kurdish state. The Iraqis opposed this idea and the British, after a short period of divided counsels, abandoned it. The British were concerned in the first post-war years to prevent the new Turkish republic from recovering the Kurdish area of Mosul which had been allotted by the peace treaties to Iraq, while the Iraqis were no less concerned to ensure that the Kurdish area of Kirkuk, south of Mosul and rich in oil, should not be alienated to the Kurds. After the British had failed to entrench Kurdish rights in the Anglo-Iraqi treaty of 1930, fighting broke out in which the Kurds were defeated by the Royal Air Force and temporarily dispersed. The Second World War, like the first, led the Kurds to hope for rewards from Britain for services rendered and to hope in vain. An anti-Iraqi rising under mullah Mustafa Barzani in the last years of the war was defeated by the Iraqis and some 10,000 Kurds fled to Iran, whence Barzani himself proceeded to the USSR. The revolution of 1958 in Baghdad destroyed the alliance between the three anti-Kurdish states of Iraq, Turkey and Iran and substituted for the Iraqi monarchy a republic of 'Arabs and Kurds'. Barzani returned from Moscow and was honourably and even munificently received by President Kassim, who looked with favour on the Kurds because of the left wing tendencies among them. In 1960 a Kurdish Democratic Party was allowed, but the Kurds were divided in their views on Kassim and even their left wing disliked the communist ideas and excesses which gained ground in Iraq after the revolution. After some internal dissension the Kurdish Democratic Party became definitely anti-communist, rapidly lost Kassim's favour, was persecuted and officially extinguished, even though the communists also fell from grace at this time.

In 1961 the Kurds rebelled. Kassim claimed that they were receiving military supplies from Britain and the United States. He turned for arms to the USSR, which found it opportune to forget its earlier support for the Kurds in the hope of finding a more useful ally in Kassim. The Iraqi army started a full-scale campaign against the Kurds with napalm bombs and rocket-carrying aircraft. In February 1963 Kassim was overthrown and killed and the pan-Arab nationalists of the Baath party took control of the government under the presidency of General Aref who engaged in discussions with the Kurds and gave them to understand that they would get something like autonomy. Later in the year, however, the discussions were broken off by the seizure of the Kurdish negotiators and the Iraqi army, supported in the field by the Syrians where the Baath had also come to power, embarked upon an even more ferocious campaign against the Kurds than the operations of 1961–2. But the Baath's anti-communist nationalism had alienated the communist world which raised the cry of genocide. Early in 1964 a truce was negotiated. It proved fragile, but in 1970 President al-Bakr renewed it.

The Kurdish revolt put a strain on relations between Iraq and Iran, which were in any case none too good. The shah feared the newer type of Arab régime, especially Nasser's. The Iraqi revolt of 1958 was therefore unwelcome to him, and the succession of Aref to Kassim in 1963 more so. He wanted the Shia Muslims to have an established part in the government of Iraq, and if the Shia were to be so treated, the Kurds would have to be too. He refused to help Aref's anti-Kurdish operations even when Iraqi Kurds took refuge in Iran and he gave the Kurds in Iraq surreptitious and not so surreptitious help. His rapprochement with King Feisal in 1965 encouraged him to think in terms of a Persian Gulf regulated by a Saudi-Iranian compact without the need to include or accommodate Iraq, but in 1975 he began a détente with Iraq which left the Kurds without reasonable hope of prolonging their struggle. They came to terms similar to those which they had made with the Iraqi government in 1958.

Part Four

Asia

Chapter 14

India and its neighbours

1. The Indian sub-continent

The half century preceding the departure of the British from India had seen a series of reforms, evolved by the British and leading logically and explicitly to Indian independence; the growth of divisions within India which led to the partition of 1947; and a growing awareness of world politics, in which nevertheless the new rulers were for the most part but imperfectly versed. In the nineteenth century India, though less closed to the outside world than China or Japan, had a view of the world which was vastly overshadowed by the British presence; and the principal episode of the century was the Sepoy Revolt or Mutiny of a part of Britain's subjects against British rule. This view was changing by the end of the century. The Russian advance towards Afghanistan; Curzon's preoccupation with the north-western frontier and Tibet; the extension of British Indian power into the Middle East; the alliance of Britain with Japan in 1902, followed by Japan's defeat of Russia in 1905; revolutions in Turkey, Iran and China – all these impinged upon India and turned the Indian mind or part of it outward. Although in 1947 Jawaharlal Nehru was the only member of his cabinet with any claim to expert knowledge of foreign politics, his colleagues and many others among his compatriots had grown up with the feeling that, if India's special problem was the defeat of the British raj, there were also other problems and other powers to be reckoned with, notably Russia, China and Japan. Even though many Indians misjudged the nature of the problems, deceiving themselves with the belief that their cause was the British presence and their cure would be the British departure, this mistake was a matter of misinterpretation and not of cloistered ignorance. Within India nationalism, which was one of the by-products of the Hindu and Muslim intellectual revivals of the nineteenth century and took visible shape in the founding of the Indian National Congress in 1885, was inevitably anti-British. Like most nationalist movements it came to be divided into a more militant and a less militant faction (led in this case by B. G. Tilak on the one hand and by G. K. Gokhale and then by M. K. Gandhi on the other), but unlike others it was also divided in a more enduring way before the day of victory. As independence approached, the ability of Hindu and Muslim to work together diminished until it proved impossible to maintain a single successor state to the British raj and at independence the two great religious communities feared and hated each other more than they feared or hated the British.

Britain had long envisaged the surrender of empire in India but without formulating a timetable. The Second World War imposed the timetable. At the beginning of that war the viceroy made the ludicrously inept mistake of declaring war on India's behalf, as he was entitled to do, without consulting a single Indian. Congress ministries, in office under the constitution of 1935, thereupon resigned. In 1942 Sir Stafford Cripps was sent by the British cabinet to India to offer it dominion status with the right to secede from the empire, but the exercise of this option and all other internal advances were to be postponed until the end of the war. The Congress, which may have misjudged British intentions and certainly – if recruiting figures meant anything – misjudged Indian sentiment, decided to have no part in the war and to use it to wage a Quit India campaign against the British. In 1944 Britain, now sure of victory in all theatres, appointed a new viceroy, Lord Wavell, and released Indian leaders who had been put in prison. After the general election of 1945 the Labour government sent three cabinet ministers to India to try to get agreement between the Congress and the Muslim League as a preliminary to independence, but relations between these bodies had deteriorated during the war (the reverse of the experience of the First World War) and the British attempt failed. The League and its leader Mohamed Ali Jinnah were convinced that Britain was partial to the Congress; in August 1946 Jinnah inaugurated Direct Action by the League to secure a separate sovereign state for Muslims, and the winter of 1946–7 was marked by violent communal riots. Early in 1947 the viceroy came to the conclusion that no single Indian central authority could be constituted and he accordingly advised the British government either to retain power for at least a decade or to transfer it, fragmented, to the several provinces.

The British government rejected this advice, replaced Wavell by Mountbatten and announced that Britain would abdicate in June 1948. It proposed to resolve the dilemma by neither of the methods recommended by Wavell but to partition India and hand over power to two separate central governments. The 562 princely states, which were not part of British India, were to be cajoled into one or other of the new states. Their relationship with the British Crown was regulated by the doctrine of paramountcy. Britain did not propose to transfer its paramount rights to the new India or to Pakistan but declared that paramountcy would lapse, with the result that each ruler would be free in law to accede to India or Pakistan or neither – and free in practice to accede to India or Pakistan. Junagadh made the unpractical choice of acceding to Pakistan with which it had no border; the ruler was forced to see his error, departed for Pakistan and left his state to become part of India. Three states toyed with independence: Travancore, Hyderabad and Kashmir. Travancore's ambitions were quickly seen to be illusory: Hyderabad had first to be blockaded and then (in 1949) invaded. Both became part of India. With Kashmir we shall be further concerned.

Britain's shock tactics were intensified when Mountbatten reported that even June 1948 was too late for the transfer of power. With earlier visits in mind he concluded that violence would become uncontrollable by then, and the British cabinet accepted his view. By advancing the date to August 1947 it left scant time for settling the biggest of all the issues raised, the lines of partition between India and Pakistan. It was apparent that Pakistan must consist of two widely separated areas, each containing large non-Muslim populations. A boundary commission was created, consisting of two Hindu and two Muslim judges with Sir Cyril (later Lord) Radcliffe as chairman. On most contentious points the two Hindu and the two Muslim voices cancelled each other out and Radcliffe was left to take, in two months, a series of detailed decisions on localities which he did not know and had no time to visit. One of the most important of these decisions was an award which gave India access to Kashmir. But the new borders did not serve to contain the peoples within them; probably no borders could have done so. Fear drove millions across them and in the course of this mass exodus millions were slaughtered. Sikhs, quitting the homes in the Punjab in which they no longer felt safe, attacked Muslims moving westward for the same reason; Muslims retaliated; atrocities were multiplied over a wide area reaching to Delhi itself. Probably two million men, women and children died, and this horrible feast of violence was capped in January 1948 by the assassination of Gandhi himself, Hindu apostle of non-violence killed by a Hindu fanatic.

In the new Indian state two men took control – first and foremost Jawaharlal Nehru and with him Vallabhai Patel. Nehru became Prime Minister and held that office until his death in 1964. Patel, to whom fell the task of consolidating the Indian federation of former British provinces and former princely states, died untimely in 1950. The Congress remained paramount, though divided. In 1950 it chose the right wing Purshottandas Tandom to be its president but in the following year Nehru enforced Tandom's resignation by resigning from the Working Committee which was the Congress's power house. Nehru remained president of the Congress until 1955 when he handed the office over to a reliable subordinate. In general elections in 1952, 1957 and 1962 the Congress received a slightly rising share of the vote (45–48 per cent) and a consistently massive majority in the federal parliament, despite its internal divisions and despite growing criticisms from right and left. Its principal adversary, the Communist Party, won 3.3 per cent of the vote in 1952 and around 10 per cent in the two following elections, but this vote was so concentrated as to be more effective than mere arithmetic would suggest. In the province of Kerala the communists won power on a minority vote and formed a government, but it was dismissed by the central government in 1959 and an anti-communist alliance won elections in 1960 despite a rise in the local communist vote to 42.5 per cent. The Sino-Soviet quarrel produced a rift in the party; its secretary, A. K. Ghosh, attacked China in 1961, and the Chinese invasion of India in 1962 further discomfited the party in general and its Chinese wing in particular.

But Indian political life was less disrupted by party conflict than by other divisive forces, pre-eminent among which was the language question. India's sixty-odd languages included a great many derivatives of Sanskrit, predominant in the north; a group of non-Sanskrit languages, including four principal ones, in the south; and a kind of *lingua franca* in Urdu/Hindustani. Some of these languages generated in their speakers a devotion so ardent as to provoke bloodshed. In particular Hindi, one of the northern Sanskrit derivatives, had enthusiasts who wished to make it the single official language of the country, an ambition which was opposed not only by those who realized the value of English and did not want to discourage or demote it, but also by Bengalis proud of their own tongue and by southerns who were affronted by any implied denigration of Tamil, Malayalam, Kanada or Telugu. In the south the language question became an ingredient in a Tamil separatist movement which was sufficiently weighty to cause concern though not to cause any actual disintegration, and all over India pressures grew to redraw the map on linguistic lines. A new province, Andhra, was in fact created on this basis in 1953, and in Bombay a serious crisis ensued between Marathi-speakers (who were a majority in Bombay city) and Gujarati-speakers. Feeling ran so high that the central government deemed it necessary to choose between two possible solutions; an avowedly bilingual state or the promotion of Bombay city to be a state on its own. The government chose the former course and displeased everybody, until in 1960 the Marathi-speakers were able to insist on a partition and the transfer of Bombay city to the state of Maharashtra. In the Punjab, to cite a final example with religious as well as linguistic aspects, the Sikhs campaigned for a Punjabi-speaking Sikh state which would have entailed a division of the Punjab. Despite fasts by their leader, Master Tara Singh, they were not successful.

In external affairs Nehru was determined to remain in the Commonwealth (especially if Pakistan did) while adopting a republican constitution and conducting a foreign policy which might be not merely independent of Britain's but contrary to Britain's. He succeeded in persuading the other prime ministers of the Commonwealth (as the British Commonwealth was significantly renamed at the period) that India might remain a member even though it became a republic. This was a revolutionary step. Without it the expanding post-war Commonwealth, with its strong republican tendencies, could not have taken shape. In 1949 a Commonwealth conference accepted an Indian plan to declare the British sovereign head of the Commonwealth and leave each member free to adopt a monarchical or republican form of constitution. India itself became a republic at the beginning of 1950, and within a few years there were many more republics than monarchies in the Commonwealth. The independence of each member of the British family of nations had been accepted for a generation but none had so far consistently pursued a foreign policy which ran counter to Britain's. This Nehru set out to do without impairing his good relations with London, and once more he was substantially successful. Although Britain was a committed protagonist in the cold war Nehru proclaimed that the cold war was none of India's business and that the two camps were behaving with an equally deplorable folly. Having taken a conspicuous part in bringing the Korean war to an end he went on to elaborate a policy and posture of neutralism in the hope of keeping sizeable powers out of the cold war, of limiting its evil effects and of paving the way for its eventual termination. In 1955 he visited Moscow, and India received a return visit from Bulganin and Khrushchev (who made the mistake of making the anti-British speeches which Indians were capable of making themselves but did not countenance in others). In the following year the Anglo-French attack on Egypt and the Russian intervention in Hungary confirmed Indian belief in the wickedness of all major powers, even though Nehru himself was less censorious of the Hungarian episode than of Suez (perhaps because of the latter's implications for Commonwealth solidarity). Nehru's determination that Asia should give the rest of the world an example in sanity caused him to pursue the myth of Sino-Indian friendship with an unrealistic tenacity which, when China attacked India in 1962, gravely weakened his prestige, his policy and his country.

One source of the refusal of many Indians to give the Chinese menace sufficiently serious attention was the all-consuming quarrel with Pakistan. Even India's claim against western colonial powers like France and Portugal were emotionally trivial compared with the animosity against Pakistan. (These claims were admittedly small in territorial extent. France ceded Chandernagore – virtually part of Calcutta – in 1951 and its remaining possessions – Pondicherry, Karikal, Mahé and Yanan – in 1954. Portugal adopted in India, as in Africa, the device of converting its colonies into provinces of metropolitan Portugal, but this nominal metamorphosis was of short avail and in 1961 India took the Portuguese territories – Goa, Danan and Dia – by a show of force.) Unlike India, Pakistan lost its father figure early. Jinnah, who had become governor-general on independence, died in September 1948. Moreover Liaqat Ali Khan, Pakistan's first prime minister, was assassinated three years later. For several years Pakistan wasted much of its tenuous substance on barren constitutional disputes while public figures succeeded each other in high offices, corruption became scandalous and the army wondered how long to let it go on. Khwaja Nazimuddin succeeded Jinnah as governor-general and then succeeded Liaqat Ali Khan as prime minister in 1951; in 1953 his own successor as governor-general, Ghulam Mohammad, dismissed him and installed Muhammad Ali

Bogra in his place. These changes, which involved deliberate attempts to preserve a balance between West and East Pakistan, were accompanied by a gradual collapse of authority and by rioting. In 1954 the Muslim League was severely defeated in provincial elections in East Pakistan and the central government, humiliated and jeopardized by this reverse, despatched General Iskander Mirza to East Pakistan as military governor. This appointment was the beginning of the movement towards military rule. In the next year General Mirza became governor-general on the death of Ghulam Mohammad who had been ailing for some time, and appointed Chaudri Mohammad Ali, an able and honourable civil servant, to be prime minister. He, however, resigned in 1956 and was succeeded in 1957 by Firoz Khan Noon, a distinguished veteran. A constitution was finally adopted in 1956, but in 1958 parliamentary democracy finally came to an end after the deputy speaker of the East Pakistan parliament had been hit on the head with a plank during a debate, so that he died. Martial law was proclaimed with General Ayub Khan as administrator and subsequently as General Mirza's successor as head of the state. Political parties were banned. A new constitution was introduced in 1962 based on the American presidential rather than the British parliamentary system.

Pakistan's instability gave India the excuse to justify its fears of its neighbour on the grounds that there was no knowing what governments in such straits might do next. When unstable government was succeeded by military government, Indian fears were merely transposed into a different key and it was alleged that an efficient junta was necessarily even more of a danger than an inefficient civilian régime. The ill-will between the two countries was concentrated on Kashmir, but Kashmir was not its only cause. The massacres of 1947 had given a spectacularly bad start to a relationship which was almost foredoomed in that it arose out of the inability or refusal of India's two communities to live on good terms with one another. The tendency in India to treat partition as an ephemeral aberration was an additional source of irritation in Pakistan. There were also disputes over the distribution of the waters of the Indus and its tributaries, and over the property of those – about 17 million of them – who had fled from one country into the other and found themselves unable to sell the pieces of land which they had left behind. Further, the division into two parts of what had been a single economy produced economic tensions which developed into a trade war and reached a high pitch of acrimony when India devalued its currency in 1949 in step with Britain but Pakistan refused to follow suit until 1955. But worst of all was Kashmir.

The state of Kashmir consisted of Kashmir proper; Jammu; an upper tier running from the north-west to south-east and consisting of Gilgit, Baltistan and Ladakh; and a western fringe which included the small territory of Poonch. Kashmir had been under Afghan rule when it was conquered by the Sikh prince Ranjit Singh in 1819. The same prince shortly afterwards installed Gulab Singh as ruler over Jammu, and Gulab Singh duly added Ladakh and Baltistan to his realm. In the eighteen-forties all these territories, Gilgit in the far north-west still excepted, became part of British India as a result of the two wars between the British and the Sikhs for the mastery of the Punjab. The Sikh princes remained in power as maharajahs of Kashmir and Jammu, and in 1947 the British were turning a blind eye to the notoriously unsatisfactory rule of the rich and incompetent Hari Singh. This maharajah's Muslim subjects, four-fifths of the total, were solidly opposed to his rule and so were many of the Hindu minority. Muslim opposition was divided between the Kashmir Muslim Conference, to which no Hindu could belong, and a larger organization led by Sheikh Abdullah which, following the example of the Indian National Congress, included members of both creeds.

As independence approached in 1947 the maharajah delayed and prevaricated, partly because he was toying with the notion of an independent Kashmir and partly because his interests lay in directions other than statecraft. In October the small territory of Poonch purported to secede and was immediately invaded by tribesmen from Pakistan. How far the Pakistani government had foreknowledge of these events has remained obscure. The maharajah appealed to India which refused to come to his help unless he formally acceded to India. This he did just in time to enable Indian troops to be flown into Kashmir to forestall the capture of its capital, Srinagar, by the tribesmen. The maharajah was then removed and, in 1949, deposed, and Nehru made in November the first of a number of promises to hold a plebiscite. Early in 1948 India referred the situation to the Security Council and Pakistan sent regular army units into Kashmir which recovered some of the ground which the tribesmen had lost to the Indian army. A UN mission proposed a ceasefire, which came into effect on the first day of 1949, and a plebiscite, which was never held. In effect parts of Kashmir in the west became integrated with Pakistan; these were the west including Poonch, and also Baltistan and Gilgit. The rest of the country, including Ladakh, was ruled by Sheikh Abdullah as prime minister under the nominal authority of a member of the princely house as head of state, until in 1953 the Indians, suspicious that Sheikh Abdullah too wanted an independent Kashmir, had him put in prison and replaced by Bakshi Ghulam Mohammad, with whom they proceeded to work out a new constitution for Kashmir in order to make it a fully integrated part of the Indian federation.

During the nineteen-fifties a number of abortive attempts were made to supplement the cease-fire by a political settlement. The first UN attempts were immediately unsuccessful. The American Admiral Chester Nimitz, who was appointed to supervise the plebiscite, never even went to Kashmir. A UN conciliation commission (UNCIP) abandoned its task at the end of 1949. An Australian judge, Sir Owen Dixon, was appointed UN mediator but was obliged to announce failure. Talks in 1951 between Nehru and Liaqat Ali Khan also failed. Dr

Frank P. Graham took over Sir Owen Dixon's task with the same result. After the dismissal of Sheikh Abdullah in 1953 there was a new round of talks between Nehru and Mohammed Ali but again fruitlessly. Then in 1954, at the time when Kashmir's constitution and status were being altered, a decisive event occurred. The United States and Pakistan entered into an agreement which provided for American military aid to Pakistan. From the American point of view this was an anti-Russian move, part of the American policy of containment or encirclement, but from the Indian point of view it was a powerful reinforcement of India's principal enemy. India deeply resented this American move and Nehru made it the occasion finally and explicitly to go back on his promise to hold a plebiscite in Kashmir. During negotiations in 1954–55, during which the Pakistani governor-general Ghulam Muhammad went to Delhi, Nehru refused to entertain the idea of a plebiscite. At the beginning of 1957 Pakistan asked the Security Council to order the withdrawal of all troops from Kashmir, to send a UN force there, to organize a plebiscite and to require India to abandon the new constitution which was about to integrate Kashmir in India. India opposed UN intervention and the USSR vetoed the resolution endorsing Pakistan's plan. A year later Dr Graham made similar proposals to India, which rejected them.

During the Indo-Pakistani dispute over Kashmir in the fifties it was often forgotten that Kashmir also had a frontier with China and this frontier had, since 1948, been partly in Indian hands and partly in Pakistani. In the late fifties, however, Indians became suddenly aware of hitherto unsuspected Chinese activities in Ladakh. At the same time the flight of the Dalai Lama to India attracted popular attention, and especially Indian attention, to Chinese activities in Tibet; an incident in the far north-eastern corner of India revealed a Sino-Indian clash at this point; and politics in Nepal split openly into pro-Indian and pro-Chinese strands. China became a factor in the Kashmir dispute between India and Pakistan, and likewise Kashmir became a factor in the evolving Sino-Indian dispute which ran all the way along a frontier of more than a thousand miles and involved, besides Kashmir, the small Himalayan states of Nepal, Bhutan and Sikkim and the much larger and constitutionally anomalous country of Tibet.

Since India and China are the two largest Asian countries their attitudes towards one another are a major element in the politics of Asia. In 1954, in the context of a commercial treaty about Tibet, they proclaimed five principles for the regulation of their mutual and possibly conflicting affairs. These principles, often known as the Panch Shila, were: respect for each other's sovereignty and territorial integrity, non-aggression, non-interference in each other's internal affairs, equality and mutual benefit, and peaceful coexistence. On Nehru's side the Panch Shila reflected certain basic aims of his foreign policy – to eschew war, to create an Asian order resting on the mutual trust and respect of the two leading Asian powers, to obviate anything like a cold war in Asia, and to give the rest of the world an example in international behaviour. That the context should be Tibet was partly accidental but also fitting and prophetic, for it is along common frontiers that the resolutions of states are most frequently tested.

China's subjugation of Tibet, undertaken in 1950, was a logical implementation of the determination to reunite all China's 'five races' under the control of Peking, and it brought China to the borders of India. Indians had various reasons for viewing this confrontation – a meeting, as it turned out, of ideologies as well as power – with surprising unconcern. There was first of all the determination to get on well with China, a determination which was heightened by the challenge of ideological differences and which therefore obfuscated the difficulties of doing so. Then there was a pervasive if vague belief that bad neighbourliness was a mark of capitalist power-minded states rather than a consequence of rubbing shoulders, coupled with a similar belief that many of the troubles of the past in India (including the troubles which the British had had along its frontiers) were part and parcel of an alien imperialism and had automatically been removed with the British. Finally, there was the obsession with Pakistan, so that the division of British India into two states proved not merely a weakness in the sense of a dissipation of material resources but also a weakening of the power to see things in proportion. Whether or not the Chinese were emboldened by this division, it certainly gave them opportunities, not least the opportunity to play for years a hazardous frontier game which many Indians preferred in their myopia not to notice.

The Sino-Indian border runs for about a thousand miles through some of the most daunting territory in the world. To the west Tibet marches with Ladakh, the south-eastern portion of Kashmir which, jutting eastward, thrusts a wedge between India and Tibet. The border then touches Indian territory and makes the turn to the eastward which carried it all the way to Burma by way of Nepal, Sikkim, Bhutan and the North East Frontier Agency of India (Nefa).

The Chinese claim to regard Tibet as an integral part of China had not seriously been contested by other sovereign states, however uneasy they might have been about this extension of Chinese power. The Tibetans themselves took a different view, partly on the grounds that *de facto* independence since 1911 had ripened into full independence and partly by construing vague and ancient declarations of Chinese respect as formal grants of independence and not the mere courtesies which the Chinese said they were. The Mongol Khan Kublai, grandson of Jenghiz, who became emperor of China in the thirteenth century and was converted to Buddhism, bestowed favours and rights on a lama who established in Tibet a local dynastic rule of uncertain radius. Two hundred years later a schismatic line of so-called Yellow Hat Buddhists appeared and after a further two hundred years supplanted the line installed by Kublai as effective rulers of Tibet. The chief of this line was the Dalai Lama and in the seventeenth century he received from the first Manchu emperor in China marks of respect which may or may not have amounted to something approaching sovereignty. In the next century the Chinese entered Tibet to protect the country against the Mongols and refused to go away again. They also defended it against a Gurkha invasion later in the same century and consolidated their position during the nineteenth century, aided by the tendency (sometimes described as mysterious) of the boy Dalai Lamas to die just before or soon after reaching the age to assume full powers.

The nineteenth century also witnessed the approach of the British and the Russians, and in 1903 Sir Francis Younghusband rapped on Tibet's southern door, proceeded to Lhasa and so served notice of Britain's unwillingness to leave China a free hand in Tibet. This was the period of Chinese disintegration but any British notion of taking China's place in Tibet was soon abandoned. The Dalai Lama fled in 1903 to Mongolia and thence to China, where his reception was disappointing. He returned to Lhasa in 1909 but fled again in 1910, this time in fear of the Chinese and into India. The collapse of the Chinese empire in 1911 seemed to open the way to real independence but at the Simla conference of 1913–14 between Chinese, Tibetans and British the latter proposed a recognition of Chinese suzerainty in return for a Chinese promise of Tibetan autonomy. This proposal, repeated in 1921, was never bindingly adopted. The Simla conference also propounded a frontier between India to the south and Tibet and China to the north and north-east (the so-called MacMahon line) in a document which was initialled by the Chinese but never ratified, not because China questioned the line but because its acceptance was linked with a division of Tibet into inner and outer zones and the exclusion of Chinese troops from the inner.

Upon the death of the Dalai Lama in 1934 the Chinese took the opportunity to return to Lhasa. A mission bearing condolences arrived and remained until 1949 when it was ejected as a result of the general collapse of the Kuomintang. In revenge the Kuomintang recognized as Panchen Lama a boy who had been discovered in China in 1944 and was still there. (The Panchen Lama, another Yellow Hat hierarch, was a spiritual and temporal rival of the Dalai Lama. The previous Panchen Lama had fled to China in 1923 and died there in 1937). This last throw by the Kuomintang proved useful to the communists who took over the new Panchen Lama and set him at the head of a provisional Tibetan government in exile. During 1950 there were attempts by the authorities in Lhasa to negotiate with Peking in Hong Kong, Calcutta, Delhi or wherever contact could be made, but in October the Chinese invaded and soon secured control of the capital and much of the country. Tibet appealed unsuccessfully to the United Nations and the Dalai Lama fled to India. The authorities remaining in Lhasa accepted Chinese suzerainty in return for a promise of a measure of autonomy.

The Indian government protested to China and deplored the use of force but to the Chinese argument that Tibet was a part of China the

Indian government had no reply. Nehru pursued his endeavour to reach amicable and rational solutions to current problems. After discussions in Peking during 1953 a Sino-Indian agreement on trade and intercourse in Tibet was signed in April 1954. It dealt with the rights of traders and pilgrims, transferred to China postal and other services previously operated by India as Britain's successor, provided for the withdrawal of Indian military units from Yatung and Gyantse, and enunciated the Panch Shila. India also recognized Chinese sovereignty in Tibet. Two months later Nehru and Chou En-lai met for the first time as the latter returned home to Peking from the Geneva conference on Indo-China and Korea, and in October Nehru went to Peking. The Dalai and Panchen Lamas were already in Peking where they stayed from September to December 1954.

In the next few years there were a number of incidents leading to Chinese complaints of Indian troops crossing into Tibet and Indian complaints of Chinese troops found south of the frontier. These aberrations could be accounted for by the difficulty of knowing exactly where one is in such country and the Indians in particular, anxious to prove that India and China could co-exist peaceably in Asia, were not on the look-out for more serious or sinister explanations. The possibility that the two sides had radically different ideas of where the frontier ran on the map was evaded. Yet by the mid-fifties the Chinese had entered the Aksai Chin or Soda Plains in Ladakh. This area, between the two mountain ranges of the Kuen Lun and the Karakoram, had long been disputed ground because it had never been agreed which range marked the Sino-Indian border. To the Chinese the Aksai Chin was important because it lay in the path of a road which they wished to build to link the Tibetan capital with their western province of Sinkiang. This road they now proceeded to build. Their operations can hardly have been concealed from the Indians. What is conceivable, and indeed probable, is that knowledge of what was going on did not immediately reach Nehru himself and that both locally and at the centre there was a conspiracy of silence among Indians whose animosities against Pakistan blinded them to the significance and consequences of what China was doing in territory claimed by India.

The Chinese occupation of Tibet had thus become something more than a rounding-off of the traditional domains of the Chinese empire. It was also a step towards Chinese involvement in international affairs. The continued exclusion of China from the United Nations gave China an appearance of detachment which was later reinforced by its diplomatic isolation after the breach with the USSR, but during the fifties China was prosecuting active interests in central Asia which brought it into contact with the Himalayan states of Nepal, Sikkim and Bhutan and with Kashmir and so with the Indo-Pakistani dispute. The subjugation of Tibet was an extension of Peking's authority throughout the Chinese empire in more senses than one: Tibet was reduced not only for its own sake but also as a step towards the more effective control of the great province of Sinkiang to the north and north-west of it. This was the purpose of the Tibet-Sinkiang highway and the chief cause of the flouting by China of the Panch Shila.

Sinkiang, conquered by the Manchu dynasty in the middle of the eighteenth century, had borders in the twentieth with Kashmir, Afghanistan, three Soviet Republics (the Kirghiz, the Kazakh and the Turkomen) and Outer Mongolia. It has in the past been one of those provinces where a governor exercises unusual powers by virture of his very distance from the imperial centre. He was a semi-independent proconsul who had sometimes looked to the Russian rather than the Chinese empire for help in troubles which he could not cope with himself (as, for instance, during Muslim revolts in 1930–34 and 1937). With China in disarray he could expect little from the east and needs must turn west; when, however, the Russians became fully occupied by the German invasion in the Second World War, he faced about and became the friend and ally of the Kuomintang, who were in law his suzerains. In 1944 the Russians helped to foment and sustain a revolt in the Ili district of Sinkiang where an Eastern Turkestan Autonomous Republic was proclaimed, but in the Stalin–Chiang treaty of August 1945 Moscow recognized Chinese sovereignty in Sinkiang and promised not to interfere there – a promise which seems to have been inadequately kept. During the last phase of the Kuomintang the Russians tried to extend their pre-war (1939) monopoly of civil aviation in Sinkiang and to recreate a Russo-Chinese partnership in economic opportunities. At the time of the collapse of the Kuomintang the former object had been achieved on paper but not the latter, and after the governor of Sinkiang had gone over to Mao, the Russians opened negotiations with the new régime. In March 1950 agreements were signed for the creation of joint (50/50) companies to exploit oil and non-ferrous metals for thirty years and to operate civil airways for ten. Mao was evidently in no position to hold out for complete Chinese control in the province, indubitably Chinese though it was in law, but he immediately set about improving its communications with the rest of China by rail and by road. In casting his eyes on the Aksai Chin he was, as in so many other things, following a line of policy which had occurred to his predecessors fifty years earlier. If in 1950 Mao had had to temporize over Sinkiang, in the same year he was successful in Tibet.

The later fifties were a period of mixed gains and disappointments for the Chinese in external affairs. On the credit side were Chou En-lai's appearances at the Geneva and Bandung conferences and his visits to Asian capitals; commercial agreements (1957) with Nepal and Ceylon, a Sino-Burmese border settlement and a Sino-Cambodian treaty; the failure of western policies in Laos and South Vietnam, and the progressive abrogation of democracy in Pakistan, Burma, Ceylon and Indonesia. On the debit side were the failure to take Quemoy in 1958, the quarrel with the USSR, the strains of domestic revolution and economic misfortunes. Most surprising perhaps to Peking was the uninterrupted construction of the Tibet-Sinkiang highway with its implied claim to 12,000 square miles of territory claimed by India and without any protest from Delhi. But an incident involving the capture of an Indian patrol by the Chinese in Ladakh brought the issue into the open and in 1958 the Indian government formally expressed surprise and regret that Peking had not seen fit to consult Delhi about the highway.

In 1959 Tibetan discontents mounted up into a serious anti-Chinese revolt. The Dalai Lama fled to India from Chinese retaliation. In March Nehru wrote privately to Chou to express his concern but received no answer until six months later when a public Chinese reply laid claim for the first time to extensive stretches of Indian territory. In the interval Moscow had agreed to give India financial aid and Khrushchev, before setting out for the United States, had adopted a neutral instead of a pro-Chinese posture. India likewise was maintaining a neutral position as between China and the United States and refusing to take an anti-American line. The Chinese accused India of interfering and stirring up trouble in Tibet, and in the summer the border incidents which had been going on for several years without attracting wide attention produced casualties, publicity and bitterness. In August an Indian policeman was killed at Longju at the eastern end of the Sino-Indian frontier, and in October several Indians were killed in a skirmish in the Changchenmo valley which lies about midway along the north–south border between Tibet and Kashmir and on the Kashmiri side. It was no longer possible to conceal the fact that the dispute was not about who was where on the occasion of a particular clash, but about where the frontier itself was supposed to run. Up to 1960 Nehru refused to discuss the border problem with China. In 1960–61 a conference of officials met at Peking but failed to produce agreement. Nehru neither pressed the matter nor prepared his armed forces to meet any attack in what had now become a dangerously contested area.

The eastern half of the frontier was of much less concern to the Chinese than the vital Aksai Chin, and Chinese pretensions in the east may well have been regarded by Peking as a useful lever for the extraction of concessions in the west. To India the eastern areas were more sensitive than the western, for they provided easier access into India itself; included the Himalayan principalities which were under Indian protection but would, upon any reversal of alliances, provide a Chinese springboard into India off the southern ledge of the Himalayas; and included also Nefa where the Naga tribesmen were in revolt against Indian rule, were trying up Indian forces and were damaging India's moral standing and prestige as stories of vicious Indian tactics leaked out to the world. The unratified McMahon line, the rebellious Nagas and the weak Himalayan states (where alone frontiers were defined) gave the Chinese a small orchestra of opportunities.

Sikkim, the central and smallest of the three Himalayan states, received from India in 1950 a guarantee of internal autonomy and a subsidy in return for Indian control of its defence and foreign relations. India was allowed to station troops in Sikkim. Bhutan, the easternmost of the three, agreed in 1949 to accept Indian guidance in foreign affairs in return for an Indian promise of non-interference in its internal affairs. In both cases India was continuing the policy of the British. In the background was a Chinese claim to Bhutan rejected by Britain early in the century, and the uncomfortable fact that Sikkim, governed by a minority of Tibetan stock, had been virtually part of Tibet in the eighteenth century.

Of the Himalayan states much the largest, and the only fully in-dependent, was Nepal, the home of the Gurkhas who had provided famous regiments for the armies of Britain and India. It had been a refuge for Hindus fleeing from the Moghul conquest and had become a separate unified state in the mid-eighteenth century. From the middle of the nineteenth to the middle of the twentieth century it was under the dual control of a royal family without power and the less than royal but more powerful family of the Ranas who ruled it much as the mayors of the palace ruled Merovingian France or the shoguns ruled Japan between the fourteenth century and the Meiji restoration of 1867. By the middle of the twentieth century the dominance of the Ranas was threatened by a recrudescence of the royal power and by Congresses on the model of the Indian National Congresses, of which there were two: the Nepali National Congress founded in 1947 in Calcutta and led by B. P. Koirala and his relatives, and the Nepali Democratic Congress, founded in Calcutta in 1949 by a member of the royal family. In 1950 King Tribhuvana provoked a constitutional change by fleeing first to the Indian embassy in Katmandu and then to India itself. The next year he returned, entered into an unofficial compact with the Ranas, introduced a parliamentary régime and installed a coalition govern-ment which included Ranas and Koiralas.

These dissensions were embarrassing to the Indian government whose object was to dominate Nepal politely and keep it out of the news. India recognized Nepal's sovereignty by a treaty of 1950. The Ranas had tended to look to China as a counter against India, and Nehru therefore wanted correct and amicable relations with the king. It was also important for Nehru that the king and the Koiralas should co-operate, since in any clash India's natural sympathies would be with the National Congress rather than the monarch and such a clash might induce it to turn to China.

King Tribhuvana was succeeded in 1955 by King Mahendra who proceeded to visit Moscow and Peking and to receive in his own capital not only the Indian president and prime minister but also Chou En-lai. Alive to the possibilities of exploiting his strategic position he sought economic aid from all quarters and concluded with China in 1961 a border agreement which gave Nepal the whole of Mount Everest. He also agreed to the construction of a road by the Chinese from Lhasa to

Katmandu. (He died in 1972. His son King Birendra was regarded in India as more pro-Indian.)

In the same year as its border agreement with Nepal China proposed to Pakistan negotiations for the settlment of border disputes in Gilgit and Baltistan. In the next year, 1962, it broached its Indian border questions in a very different way. In October it put troops across the McMahon line, skirting Bhutan to the west and entering a part of India which was peculiarly difficult to reach from the rest of India. (Nefa, bounded to the south by East Pakistan, has a panhandle stretching westward to Darjeeling, whence a thin corridor runs between Nepal and East Pakistan into the Indian province of Bihar.) Nehru, who had consistently admitted that the frontiers were ill-defined and needed to be discussed, refused to begin talking unless the Chinese withdrew behind the line. The Indian army in the north-east had been reinforced during 1962 but its intelligence and logistical services were conspicuously bad and when the Chinese attacked in earnest India was humiliatingly defeated and was saved from greater disasters only by the intervention of the Americans or Russians or both – or alternatively because the Chinese had had limited aims and had attained them.

China's vigorous action against India was at variance with its approach to its frontier problems with Pakistan and Nepal and surprising in the light of its domestic preoccupations. The antecedents of this operation are unclear but there are grounds for supposing that China acted as it did in response to a change of policy by India where counsels were divided. Nehru himself and his army chiefs had been opposed to a forward policy which would precipitate the issue of the disputed frontier by occupying disputed areas, but there was an opposing view which regarded forceful action as opportune and Chinese retaliation as unlikely. If, as may be supposed, Nehru became converted to this view he was quickly and bruisingly undeceived and the riddle of Chinese moderation in victory would be explained upon the hypothesis that China wanted to do no more than stop Indian infiltration into the disputed areas (by pushing forward police posts) and put the frontier problem back on ice until India was prepared to negotiate about it. China in fact offered to negotiate but the humiliation of defeat prevented Nehru from accepting: the Indian army had lost 3000 men killed and 4000 captured. Following a cease-fire at the end of the year a group of India's fellow neutralists – Burma, Ceylon, Indonesia, Cambodia, the United Arab Republic and Ghana – offered to mediate, but they did so in so neutral a spirit that many Indians were indignant, hoping for greater sympathy and support. This attempted mediation produced no resolution and the crisis simply petered out.

The coincidence of this short war with the Cuban crisis prompted speculation about deeper Chinese calculations and more dramatic international pressures behind the scenes. While it is exceedingly unlikely that Moscow took Peking into its confidence over Cuba, it is more than likely that the Chinese were kept informed by the Cubans. That being so, the Chinese could have seen in the possibility of war between the USSR and the United States an opportunity to press their claims against India and force out of Delhi a cession of the territory in Ladakh which they had occupied. Even larger motives could be imputed to them: to inflict severer defeats and losses on India, to bring Nehru's government down in chaos, to help Indian communists, to strike at India's economic planning. But for such grand designs there is no firm evidence, nor is there evidence for the surmise that China's advance was stopped by external threats. Once the Cuban crisis had been peacefully resolved the Americans were in a position to help India by bombing Chinese airfields and communications, but it is not known that they threatened to do so. The Russians, with obvious irritation against Chinese action, were willing to supply India with Russian aircraft, but whether they also threatened to cut off China's oil is another unknown.

Nehru's standing in his own country was both weakened and strengthened. He had been forced to seek military aid from the United States and Britain and his neutralism had led India into acute danger – because a neutralist, more perhaps than anybody else, needs to be prepared and strong – but he himself seemed more irreplaceable than ever and he was in no danger of losing office. The British government hoped to use this shock to India to bring about a settlement in Kashmir, but once the Chinese attack had been suspended, the shock to Indian security became less than the shock to Indian pride, so that India was in no mood to compound its differences with Pakistan, whose attitude towards India during the critical weeks had been the reverse of soothing. India moreover believed that Britain was on Pakistan's side. Conversations therefore, though initiated, produced nothing, and at the end of the year relations between the two countries were suddenly inflamed by the theft of a hair of the prophet Mahomet from its shrine at Hazratbal, near Lahore. This incident produced riots in both countries and led Nehru, aware that his life was approaching its end, to make an endeavour to resolve the Kashmir problem. In April 1964 he released Sheikh Abdullah who had talks with both Nehru and Ayub Khan. These were fruitless. In May Nehru died and was succeeded by Lal Bahadur Shastri. By the end of 1964 Pakistan, convinced that nothing short of force would serve, was preparing for war. It feared that the time for success in war was running out. On the other side India was worried by Pakistan's American arms and its overtures to China (Ayub Khan visited Peking early in 1965). Both governments were suspicious and weaker at home than they had been. Temporarily attention was diverted from Kashmir to a desolate and uninhabited mudflat called the Rann of Kutch. This unattractive area, under water for part of the year and above water for the rest, was regarded by India as part of the state of Kutch which was undeniably part of India, but Pakistan claimed that the border between Pakistan and India ran through the middle of the Rann on the principle that boundaries in water-courses lie in midstream. The dispute, in itself somewhat ridiculous, brought the two countries to the verge of fighting but abated after an offer of British mediation. (In 1968 Pakistan got by arbitration one tenth of its claim.) More serious was the arrest of Sheikh Abdullah. Since his release the Kashmiri leader had visited Britain and a number of Muslim countries and he was about to go to Peking. The Indian government, alarmed by his undiminished independence, took the view that he would be better back in prison.

On 28 August 1965 Pakistan troops crossed the cease-fire line in Kashmir which had been established and kept under UN observation since January 1949. A second attack was launched on 1 September. The Pakistani air force conducted some successful operations but the crucial land attacks were held by the Indian army and on 6 September India retaliated by invading Pakistan itself. Thereafter the fighting rapidly came to a stalemate. China delivered a threatening note to India but took no effective action in support of Pakistan. U Thant went in person to Asia and secured an (imperfectly observed) cease-fire. The USSR offered to mediate if Shastri and Ayub Khan would meet Kosygin in the Uzbek capital of Tashkent. Britain and the United States also urged both sides to stop fighting and there were at least implications that economic aid and military supplies would be stopped if they did not.

Pakistan had presumably hoped to score a quick and decisive military victory as a preliminary to negotiations from a position of strength. Its precise political aims were unknown but probably entailed the cession to Pakistan of considerable areas of Kashmir, including perhaps the central Vale of Kashmir with or without a plebiscite. These hopes were frustrated by the Indian army whose performance surprised all who were still judging it by its failures against the Chinese three years earlier. India's successes in the fighting were matched by stubbornness on the political front. Having agreed to a cease-fire India, which remained in occupation of a slice of Pakistani territory, showed no more inclination than it had after 1949 to proceed to a political settlement. Sentiment apart India had two substantive grounds for its continued refusal to treat with Pakistan. The first was strategic. The only serviceable road for the Indian army to use in order to reach Ladakh ran through the Vale with the result that the abandonment of the Vale would have crippled India in any further encounters with the Chinese in Ladakh. An alternative road skirting the Vale could be constructed but only at considerable cost and over a period of years. Secondly, Indians were genuinely averse to a setttlement on a religious basis. A plebiscite in Kashmir meant counting Muslims and Hindus and determining the political future of a territory by reference to the religion of the majority of its inhabitants. India (unlike Pakistan) was a secular state, firmly committed to a non-confessional view of politics. It could hardly accept any procedure in Kashmir which was also acceptable to Pakistan without betraying this principle and also – a matter of practical urgency – endangering the 50 million Muslims in India whose property and lives could well be jeopardized if they were regarded as adherents of Islam rather than citizens of India.

The brief war in Kashmir enabled India to re-establish its military prestige and to score a modest diplomatic point against the feeble intervention of the Chinese. India was not obliged to cede anything to Pakistan. Pakistan on the other hand failed to secure its objectives and gave its larger neighbour an opportunity to demonstrate the strength of its negative position over Kashmir. China had felt compelled to do something in support of Pakistan and had chosen to do the least. The USSR was embarrassed by a possible renewal of the Sino-Indian conflict and also by the possibility of having to take sides between India and Pakistan. India, intrinsically the more important of the two countries if only because of its size, had been cast by the USSR as a useful adjunct in the Sino-Russian conflict, was in receipt of Russian aid and had been championing the USSR's claim (rejected by China) to be an Asian country and a proper member of Afro-Asian conferences. The USSR therefore had powerful reasons for not offending India, but on the other hand it wished also to have good and improving relations with Pakistan. It disliked Pakistan's recent tendency to look for aid and comfort to Peking, from whose lukewarm cajolements Pakistan ought in Moscow's view to be weaned. Further, the Kashmir war had disenchanted Pakistan with the United States. Pakistan had accepted Seato and Washington's general alliance system but when the crunch came in Kashmir the Americans had failed to give Pakistan the support which it supposed itself to have bought and paid for. Consequently there was at least a possibility of detaching Pakistan from the American system as well as from the Chinese flirtation. More than that, the similar disenchantment of the Turks, whom the Americans had prevented from invading Cyprus, and the perennial fluidity of Iranian politics, where too the shah might be glad of a friend uncommitted to the Arabs, gave Moscow the exciting prospect of dissolving the Northern Tier. But since Russian diplomacy in Pakistan must not lose sight of more important Russian interests in India, it was essential for Moscow to reduce Indo-Pakistani animosities to the minimum. The Tashkent meeting, which took place at the beginning of 1966, was designed both to illumine the USSR in the role of peace-maker and to clear the complex channels of Russian diplomacy in Asia. The meeting stayed the expiring war and boosted Russian prestige but produced no answer to the basic problem in Kashmir. Shastri died suddenly at the end of the conference.

Britain's position during the Kashmir war was that of a friend who is so impartial that he has become useless to both sides and distrusted by both. India and Pakistan each believed Britain to be committed to the other side under a cloak of pious objectivity. In India Britain's position was made worse when Harold Wilson deplored India's invasion of

Pakistan without having previously deplored Pakistan's original act of aggression. (Although Pakistan had attacked in Kashmir and not in other parts of India it transpired that there had been a slight incursion into other Indian territory by Pakistani forces.) The Americans were in a similar position: Pakistanis judged that they had failed to live up to their engagements, Indians that they had done as little as had been expected of them.

In India itself the war in Kashmir, coming the year after Nehru's death, intensified an inevitable debate about his foreign policy. Traditionally the central point of a country's foreign policy is its own security, elaborated in national defence forces and foreign alliances. The weakness of India's foreign policy in the age of Nehru was that it decried these traditional concerns and gave more attention to the exercise of influence upon the conflicts between major powers which affected Nehru's vision but did not directly affect India's independence or integrity. In order to play this role in world affairs India needed exceptional prestige (to command the attention of the great and to collect a following of less great, without which India by itself would be of comparatively little account) and exceptional detachment. Nehru personally provided both and so succeeded in winning for himself and his country a position which, if not always popular with the great or the less great, was nevertheless gratefully used by the great on such occasions as the ending of the Korean war and the Indo-China settlement of 1954 when Indians were accepted as impartial chairmen or mediators. But Nehru's detachment, and also his refusal to allow his policy of non-alignment to be prejudiced by arms deals and alliances, was only compatible with India's own prime requirements upon the basis that its relations with its neighbours were good. And this was not the case. Both India's most powerful neighbours were hostile: China and Pakistan claimed territory under Indian control, and the attacks delivered first by the one and then by the other forced India to consider whether a policy of non-alignment between the United States and the USSR was not at least irrelevant, and possibly a hindrance, to the defence of its Himalayan borders and the retention of Kashmir. Could India be non-aligned and safe? Could it, as Nehru had believed, be safer non-aligned than dependent on one great power and forced into hostility to the other? Perhaps non-alignment remained the wisest attitude, but if so, must not India become a nuclear power as well as a neutral one?

Shastri's successor was Nehru's daughter, Mrs Indira Gandhi, and India entered a phase in which internal affairs increasingly overshadowed the world role which had so engrossed and appealed to Nehru. The contradictions within the vast Congress Party led to dissensions and splits which foreshadowed a re-formation of Indian political patterns. After elections in 1967 a number of provinces were governed by unstable coalitions and within a year five of them had been placed under president's rule. The central government faced threats to law and order from strikes, students and the continuing failure either to come to terms with the insurgent Nagas and Mizos in the north-east or to silence them.

Pakistan too was suffering internal distractions. Ayub Khan's rule had gone on too long with too few results. In East Pakistan secessionist feeling grew and the leader of the Awami League, Sheikh Mujibur Rahman, was arrested. In West Pakistan as well as East there was resentment against Punjabi domination. Leaders appeared to crystallize political and social discontents which reached sufficient proportions to force Ayub Khan to step down in 1969. He was succeeded by General Yahya Khan who proposed to guide Pakistan along much the same lines but perhaps a little faster. Elections were held in 1970 for a constituent assembly to be charged to produce a constitution within 120 days. Ayub Khan's selective democracy – a form of indirect choice based on local elections and proceeding upwards by stages by the election at each stage of delegates to the next – was set aside and universal suffrage permitted. The result in East Pakistan was an overwhelming victory for Sheikh Mujibur, in West Pakistan a somewhat less decisive victory for the People's Party led by the former foreign minister, Zulfikar Ali Bhutto. Sheikh Mujibur's victory had been predicted, though its proportions had not; they were probably inflated by a hideous cyclone which, among other things, demonstrated the incapacity of the central government to organize relief and so accentuated East Pakistan's conviction that the government in the west did not care about its problems. The success of the Awami League was primarily an expression of Bengali separatism. East Pakistan, the more populous of the two halves of the country, objected to its status (under Ayub and Yahya) as one of five provinces, the other four all being in the west; it wanted a generous measure of autonomy in a loose federation in which the central government's authority would be confined to defence, foreign affairs and some currency matters. The president and Bhutto envisaged a stronger centre. After the elections talks began between Bhutto and Mujibur. The latter was now able to point out that he was the leader of the largest party in parliament. In the background was the fact that the ultimate repository of power was the army and the army was largely western. But recourse to the army to coerce the east could mean the disruption of Pakistan.

The Bhutto–Mujibur talks got nowhere and in the east Mujibur began to act like the head of an independent administration. He was again arrested. The president gambled on stopping secession by jailing the seceders, but he provoked instead full scale fighting. It lasted two weeks. India, moved as some thought by anti-Pakistan venom but more certainly by a flood of Hindu fugitives quoted at 10 million, intervened in arms and the Pakistani forces in the east were forced to surrender: 90,000 men were taken prisoner. India also overran the Rann of Kutch and a slice of Azad Kashmir. Pakistan suffered substantial losses in men and material on land, at sea and in the air. The president resigned and Bhutto took his place. Mujibur Rahman was released to become the prime minister of the new state of Bangladesh.

The outlook for the new state was bleak in the extreme. Mujibur was popular but weak and during 1972 he was away ill in England for two months. Post-war chaos was aggravated by a catastrophic wave of disease and death, and then by general disorder, crime and corruption on such a scale that a distracted government had to proclaim a state of emergency in 1974. A year later Mujibur lost the support of the army and was murdered in a coup which was followed by a struggle for power between sections of the army. The economic activity of the country was in ruins and foreign aid ($1 billion) was quickly swallowed up. China, acting in support of Pakistan, vetoed the admission of Bangladesh to the UN for three years. Relations with Pakistan, the unravelling of the foundered association of what had been West and East Pakistan, and the release of prisoners and return of fugitives were hampered at the outset by Bangladeshi talk of war crimes trials (which never took place).

Despite the resumption of talks between Bhutto and Mujibur Pakistan found it easier to mend its fences with India than to work out a *modus vivendi* with Bangladesh. During 1972 Bhutto and Mrs Gandhi concluded a comprehensive agreement in the course of direct negotiations at Simla and by the end of the year they had fixed provisional lines of demarcation in Kashmir and begun the business of repatriating prisoners of war. Bhutto also visited Moscow and Kabul. The Bangladesh crisis had caused Mrs Gandhi to abandon India's traditional non-alignment and conclude a treaty with the USSR to offset the partiality of the USA and China for Pakistan (Washington went so far as to stop aid and denounce India for aggression). But Bhutto's most daunting problem was the creation of a new state. Pakistan had lost not only face and half its territory but also half its domestic market, a major part of its raw materials and manufactures, its overseas markets (which had been supplied by East Pakistan) and its foreign earnings; and the constitutional problem, unsolved since 1947, remained. This last problem was finally laid to rest in 1973 by the adoption of a presidential, federal constitution, but in the same year economic problems were exacerbated by disastrous floods.

In India the collapse of Pakistan was no bad thing for Mrs Gandhi and India's decisive intervention made her immensely popular. She had already defeated the opposition to herself in the Congress Party at the elections in March 1971 when she got 40 per cent of the vote and made the other half of the Congress look like clueless has-beens, but she had produced no solution to the prime needs of a huge population growing at the rate of 2.5 per cent a year or of India's industry whose growth rate was declining. The consequent stresses showed in disturbances such as those created by the Naxalites, to which were added continuing claims for the creation of yet more new states (a reorganization of the states in 1956 having done more to whet appetites than to dispose of the problem). But elections in a number of states in 1972, after the action in Bangladesh, went very well for Mrs Gandhi. They could not, however, turn the economic tide. Throughout the early seventies the problem of food was acute. It was alleviated in 1972 when the USSR supplied 2 millions tons of wheat and the USA resumed aid, but shortages continued and some basic goods and commodities disappeared altogether. A new opposition to Mrs Gandhi began to form, its chief figure being the world famous and near charismatic Jayaprakash Narayan. In 1974 India became a nuclear power in the sense that it made and exploded a nuclear device. It announced at the same time that it had no intention of making nuclear weapons. Nevertheless Pakistan was upset. In the same year India brought Sikkim more closely under its control by turning the Chogyal into a figurehead (in the name of democratization) and making Sikkim an associate state of the Indian republic with representatives in both houses of the Indian parliament. China was upset and so was Nepal. The Chogyal committed suicide two years later.

In 1975 a judge of the High Court started a train of unexpected events by ruling that Mrs Gandhi had offended against the Corrupt Practices Act in the elections of 1971 and by imposing on her the statutory disqualification from political activities for five years. The Supreme Court granted a stay and suspended the disqualification pending appeal but two days later a state of emergency was declared, hundreds of Mrs Gandhi's political opponents were arrested and stiff censorship was introduced. Mrs Gandhi explained that a conspiracy against progress and democracy had been discovered but no convincing evidence of so serious a threat was produced.

2. Sri Lanka

Ceylon gained its independence from Britain in 1948 as a consequence of the British departure from India. In 1972 it became Sri Lanka and a republic.

. It was governed alternatively by two main parties, the United National Party led in turn by D. S. Senanayake, his son Dudley Senanayake and his nephew Sir John Kotelawala, and the Sri Lanka Freedom Party, founded by Solomon Bandaranaike, a defector from the UNP, and after his murder in 1959 by his widow. The UNP governed from 1948 to 1956 and from 1965 to 1970, the SLFP the rest of the time. The most important election campaign was that of 1956 in which Bandaranaike defeated the UNP by running on a combined racial and religious ticket, pro-Sinhala and pro-Buddhist. His success was followed by persecution of the Tamil minority (a quarter of the population) and a permanent increase in the political influence of the Buddhist establishment which had subsequently to be courted by the UNP as well as the SLFP. Alongside the contest for power between these two parties opposition was provided by a variety of left wing parties of which the most notable was the Lanka Sama Samaj Party, founded in 1935 as an expression of anti-colonialism and a member of the Trotskyist international until 1963 when it joined Mrs Bandaranaike's government (this alliance was dissolved in 1975). Mrs Bandaranaike also brought the pro-Russian communist party into government and since other left wing groups had lost ground her coalition was expected to win the elections of 1965. That it did not was mainly due to an economic situation which neither main party had contrived to control but which had deteriorated alarmingly during the SLFP's years of office in the sixties.

After independence, as before, the economy of Ceylon was heavily dependent on the export earnings of tea, coconut and rubber estates owned by British companies. The revenue from these products fell steadily while at the same time the import bill rose, the largest single item being for food. This was a typical Third World situation in which the economy was dominated by increasingly less remunerative dealings with the former metropole and in increasing inability to feed the population without ruinous expenditure of foreign currency or, when that failed, foreign borrowing. The population was rising fast. It roughly doubled between independence and 1975. In the sixties alone the external debt quadrupled. Unemployment rose from around 40,000 at independence to something near to 700,000 when, at the next turn of the electoral wheel, Mrs Bandaranaike and her associates handsomely won the elections of 1970 and reformed the coalition that had been defeated five years earlier. In April 1971 it was severely shaken by a carefully prepared, well armed peasant rising.

This rising, which came as a surprise, was organized and directed by the Janatha Vinukhti Peramuna (JVP) or Popular Liberation Front, formed in 1965 as a splinter from the ailing Maoist communist party. It regarded the SFLP and UNP as two virtually indistinguishable aspects of a post-imperialist and neo-colonialist bourgeoisie which was prevented by self-interest from tackling the country's basic economic problems and social ills. The emphasis of its doctrine and its practice was on the peasants and it attempted to use the peasants to strike a direct blow at the government and the system. There was later the usual insoluble squabble about who struck the first blow, but there was no doubt about the outcome. After seven weeks the government had prevailed but the challenge to it was such that the number of people killed in the process of asserting its authority ran into tens of thousands. A most unusual constellation of states supported Mrs Bandaranaike materially or orally. They included the USA, USSR and China; India and Pakistan; Britain, Australia and Egypt.

Chapter 15

Solidarity and neutralism

The dissolution of European (other than Russian) imperialism in Asia was to all intents and purposes accomplished in the years of 1947–54. It began with the British retreat from India and its grand finale was the French defeat in Indo-China, for although in 1954 the British had not yet given independence to Malaya, Singapore and the nearby territories, and although the Indonesian claim to West Irian was unsuccessful until 1962 (when the persistence of the Indonesians triumphed over the obduracy of the Dutch because the Americans hoped to wean Sukarno away from Moscow by gratifying his special will), it was clear by 1954 that the anti-colonialist struggle was won. In the fifties post-colonialism was the greatest influence in the formation of Asian foreign policies and India, Asia's greatest ex-colonial state, the leader in forming them. During these years the two purely Asian states which were intrinsically more powerful than India (and which had not been ruled by Europeans), Japan and China, were off stage, the one recovering from defeat and occupation, the other recovering from decades of civil war and busy implementing a revolution.

Post-colonialism, together with the cold war, begot neutralism and non-alignment. In this evolution Nehru's personality and calculations were decisive. Nehru was not only India's prime minister but also a figure of fame and worldwide interest. He ruled, moreover, uninterruptedly for seventeen years. He was personally a man of catholic temper: he admired and had imbibed western liberal and democratic values and he was also attracted by communism's capacity for promoting economic growth, and likewise in his dislikes he was repelled by Stalin's tyranny and police rule but also by the crudities and stupidities of McCarthyism and by the moralistic division of the world into anti-communists and communists. (Parenthetically, and with hindsight, it is worth emphasizing the worldwide impact of McCarthyism, a domestic upheaval in the United States which seemed to betoken a sharp swing to the right in American politics, coupled with a myopically over-simplified view of world politics. McCarthy's indiscriminate charges of treason and conspiracy flourished on the shocks of the Korean war. In the United States the mood and the methods induced by these shocks were mastered when the peak of the war passed but the damage to the American image abroad persisted for much longer.)

When Nehru decided that India should remain in the Commonwealth – thereby virtually creating the Commonwealth which, without India and those which followed its example, would have become an association of white outposts protected no longer by Britain but severally by the United States – he did so upon the conditions that India should become a republic and that it should have the right to conduct a foreign policy of its own (a right conceded to the Dominions in general at the Imperial Conference of 1923). He thus stressed that political independence which all emancipated countries needed to assert, while retaining links which had economic, cultural and sentimental value. But independence, for Nehru and those placed like him, meant more than independence from the ex-imperial power. It meant also, and soon more emphatically, independence from the world's giant powers and their cold war.

These new leaders wished, first, to establish their independence beyond question; secondly, to keep their states together; thirdly, to reduce poverty, illiteracy, disease and other elementary human burdens within their countries; fourthly, to make their countries safe from aggression; and finally, to show the rest of the world that new states knew how to be friends among themselves and steer clear of other people's quarrels. Solidarity and neutralism were partly semi-mystical ends in themselves but also the means whereby to protect and develop poor states and to help to keep peace in the whole world.

Many new states were far from being nations, and such political unity as they possessed had been a function of xenophobia. Their governments were metamorphosed liberation movements which had to create the broadest possible consensus in order to prevent the new state from disintegrating or becoming ungovernable. In so far as this problem impinged on external policies it suggested the advisability of the broadest range of contacts and friendships among foreign states and the need to eschew any one precise and discriminatory alignment. Economic needs pointed the same way: no new state was so important to the world's rich powers as to be able to command from one rich power all the aid it needed; better therefore not to contract an alliance with one power which would rule out the possibility of getting aid from others. (This argument was not conclusive. Many of the small states which emerged from French rule in Africa were so weak that they had no choice but to take what they could get from France.) Similarly in the field of defence, while there was a superficial argument in favour of attachment to a particular strong protector, it was also observable that major powers wanted to keep out of the sort of local disputes in which new states wanted help – as opposed to local aspects of global conflict, in which new states did not want to get involved. Non-alignment and faith in the UN seemed therefore more appropriate than an alliance policy.

For all these reasons the new states, dependent though they were on others economically (both for the sale of their primary products and for aid) and strategically, chose non-alignment and chose it pragmatically as well as emotionally. The policy which came to be called by this name passed through a number of phases. It was rooted in the concept of neutrality. Neutrality was a general declaration of intent to remain out of any war which might occur, but it had not proved very useful to its various adherents during the Second World War and in any case the new states were not thinking of a shooting war and how to keep out of it, but of the cold war and how to behave in regard to it. Neutralism and non-alignment, therefore, as distinct from neutrality, were the expression of an attitude towards a particular and present conflict: they entailed, first, equivalent relations with both sides and, secondly – in the phase called positive neutralism – attempts to mediate and abate the dangerous quarrels of the great. In its more negative phase non--alignment involved a reprobation of the cold war, an assertion that there were more important matters in the world, an acknowledgement of the powerlessness of new states, and a refusal to judge between the two giant powers. These attitudes had first appeared embryonically among western Europeans who wished to escape from the cold war and accused the giant powers, more particularly the United States with its superior nuclear armoury, of endangering the whole of mankind for no sufficient cause, but neutralism did not become predominant in western Europe and was adopted by no government there. Only by migrating to Asia and taking root in anti-colonialist soil did it flourish.

The positive phase of neutralism represented the desires of new states to evade the cold war but not to be left out of world politics. If at first sight the post-war bipolar world seemed to leave as little scope for small powers as in the days of the great struggles between the Roman and Persian empires, on second thoughts it seemed that the neutralists might nevertheless play a gratifying honourable and sensible part. When Africa as well as Asia became independent the number of neutralists and the space they occupied round the globe became considerable. They might at the very least prevent the cold war from spreading to these considerable areas; by merely setting limits to bipolar commitment they could reduce the occasions and areas of conflict. They could too, by virtue of their combined importance, cause the great powers to woo them, thus becoming a kind of lightning conductor in world politics. More positively still, they might exert influence by the time-honoured method of holding conferences to publicize their views or by the newer method of arguing and voting in the General Assembly of the United Nations. In this last respect the Indian voice was again decisive. The new states had hesitated at first in their attitudes towards the UN, not knowing whether it might turn out to be dominated by its European members, as the League of Nations had been, or by the West or by the great powers. They feared that the new organization might be used to buttress colonialism or to subserve the purposes of the cold war, in either of which events they would have had little use for it, but after a little experience they decided otherwise and India in particular became prominent in its discussions and its field commissions and supplied for emergency operations units without which those operations could hardly have been contemplated (especially after Hammarskjöld developed the principle that major powers must not contribute fighting units to UN forces).

It is impossible to assess the precise effects of anti-colonialism, the cold war and neutralism upon one another, but it is possible to show that the policies and actions of the neutralists had some effect on states outside their ranks. In the first few years after the end of the Second World War American attitudes to Asians were deeply, and adversely, affected by two things: the need to rescue western Europe and the call to fight against an aggressor in Korea. The European Recovery Programme absorbed a great deal of American talent and American attention as well as American money and it may have made Americans less sharp about Europeans and particularly about the European colonialism which they had in the past so unequivocally decried. To Asians emerged or emerging from colonialism the American voice seemed to have become muted by concern for war-wrecked Europe and also by the need to find sure and strong allies against a Russian communist threat: in other words the cold war was perverting the American attitude on colonialism and even carrying the United States, spiritually and physically, into the imperialist camp. To the Americans the war in Korea was a major event in the conflict between communism and anti-communism, in which too few people gave too little help (no more than 10 per cent of the combat effort) and some, notably Asians, indulged in ill-timed and ill-considered criticism. The American attitude to Asian neutralism was one of righteous indignation. Thus the events of these years made Asians dub Americans imperialists and Americans dub Asians traitors. Yet the American mood changed after a few years and it did so partly because the neutralists' behaviour and activities at the UN and elsewhere showed the inadequacy of judging them by a simple criterion of communism and anti-communism.

The Russians too were made to revise their opinions. As anti-imperialists they had been equivocal, supporting communist movements but doubtful about others. What struck them most about the leaders of new states was their bourgeois character, and they attacked them accordingly as western stooges. Men like Nehru and Nasser seemed to the Russians at first no better than any western European politician who joined Nato. But the arrival of such leaders at the UN in increasing numbers converted the Russians to the idea that they constituted, and must therefore be treated as, a separate group midway between the communist block and the USSR's enemies. This transition was easier for the Russians than the Americans because the adherence of strange and distant countries to the communist block was in any case an unreal and unsatisfactory way of extending Russian influence (perhaps, as a short experience with Iraq showed, even a way of making things more difficult for Moscow), whereas the Americans were used to picking up allies all over the world and holding them together by their easy familiarity with air and sea power. In any event the neutrals succeeded in getting both the Russians and the Americans to accept them in world politics in the role which they had chosen for themselves.

Neutralism could not have been made acceptable by any state acting on its own. It owed its establishment to the effective – if transient – solidarity evinced at Asian and then Afro-Asian gatherings. The common objectives of Asian states – or the determination to find them – were reinforced by habits of co-operation which ante-dated the end of European imperialism, were cherished after it and were extended to the African states which soon afterwards emerged from the same experience of foreign overlordship. The first notable post-war Asian conference – the Asian Relations Conference held in New Delhi in March 1947 – assembled twenty-eight delegations of which only eight came from sovereign states. Its motive force was a desire to ensure that the United Nations should not become an organization dominated by European or white states and viewpoints, such as the League of Nations had been, but the tone of the discussions was not markedly anti-colonial. The conference was a gathering of Asians to discuss Asian problems including land reform, industrialization, Asian socialism and the application of non-violence in international affairs. The conference established a permanent organization which existed for eight years but did not do much else. Very soon afterwards India, Pakistan, Burma and Ceylon became independent. They did so in a world which had expected peace but not got it. There were guerrilla wars and insurrections in Burma, Malaya and the Philippines, and open fighting in Indonesia, Indo-China and Palestine. The cold war too was beginning. In domestic politics violence claimed notable victims in Burma in June 1947 with the assassination of Aung San and six colleagues, and an even more notable victim in January 1948 when Gandhi was killed.

In January 1949 another Asian conference assembled in New Delhi. The Soviet Asian Republics, which had attended the 1947 meeting, were not this time asked, and Turkey refused an invitation. Otherwise Asia, including the Middle East, was very fully represented and Australia and New Zealand sent observers. The immediate occasion for the conference was Indonesia where an Asian liberation movement was being threatened with extinction by the Dutch and where to Asian eyes the UN seemed bent on facilitating the pre-imposition of white colonial rule. In the previous December the Dutch had resorted to their second police action and had captured and imprisoned a number of Indonesian leaders. The conference demanded their release and also the immediate establishment of an interim government and independence for Indonesia by 1950 (the Security Council shortly afterwards chose 1960 as a suitable date). Like its predecessor this conference created a permanent organization which proved ineffective, partly because a number of Asian states were becoming jealous of India's predominance and did not wish to see it institutionalized. Owing to the Indonesian issue the conference had a clear anti-colonial note, but it was divided between friends of the west and neutralists. This division was accentuated in the following months when different Asian leaders took up different attitudes towards the two outstanding Asian events of the year, the victory of Mao Tse-tung and communism in China and the war in Korea. Asian solidarity was proving difficult to achieve, even on an anti-colonialist programme; the British and French campaigns in Malaya and Indo-China did not evoke the same united protest as the Dutch proceedings in Indonesia, partly because of the strong communist flavour in the Malayan and Vietnamese anti-colonialist movements.

In the fifties Asian solidarity and neutralism waxed and then wore thin. Some Asian states, putting their economic and strategic needs before their neutralism, signed not only commercial but even defence treaties with the United States or the USSR. India, by its treaty of 1954 with China embodying the Panch Shila, maintained its principles but in the same year Pakistan, Thailand and the Philippines concluded military agreements with the United States, while Afghanistan became the first non-communist country to receive Russian aid and the USSR, which already had a trade agreement with India and was about to conclude another with Burma, intensified the diplomatic and economic wooing of Indonesia which was to lead Sukarno to visit Moscow in 1956. The great powers were taking a gratifying interest in Asian affairs but one consequence of this interest was to make it more difficult for Asians to maintain a common attitude towards the great powers or to keep their distance as pure neutralism required.

During 1954 preparations were made for a conference, originally suggested by Ceylon and taken up by Sukarno and Nehru. This conference assembled at Bandung in April 1955. It was a grand assembly to stimulate co-operation among Asians and put Asia on the map. The background to it comprised the treaty between the United States and Formosa (a consequence of recent crises in the Formosa Strait and offshore islands), and the creation of Seato and the Baghdad Pact. The USSR and China welcomed what looked at first like an anti-western conference, while Washington's friends – Thailand and the Philippines – were half inclined not to go. Israel was excluded on account of Arab opinion. The twenty-nine participants included six from Africa (Egypt, Libya, Sudan, Ethiopia, Liberia, Ghana), so that Bandung became the prototype of Afro-Asian as opposed to purely Asian solidarity. It was an assembly of the needy and the indignant, not a concentration of power. Its members were divided among themselves even on the issue of non-alignment, but the timing was propitious. The cold war in Europe had, since the Berlin blockade of 1948–49 and the growth of Russian nuclear power to match the American, lapsed into a quiescent stalemate but not into a thaw. Both sides were looking elsewhere and were competing for the allegiance of states in other continents with the vague intention of building up a new preponderance by additional alliances, or of turning the enemy's flank by carrying influence and bases into new terrain. The Russians and the Chinese hoped to advance communism by exploiting anti-western nationalisms, while the Americans hoped to exploit fears of communism and of China and so create new, and if necessary heavily subsidized, military groups. American policy, freshly illustrated by the signing of the Manila Pact, ran counter to the spirit of Bandung. Chou En-lai, on the other hand, who put in a personal appearance at Bandung, went some way towards showing that Chinese communism was reconcilable with other Asian nationalisms and that at least one Chinese leader was more sensible and amenable than some current pictures of the new China suggested. The Russians had already, by accident or astuteness, taken a number of steps which brought them into closer accord with the Asian mood. The proposal to neutralize Austria was welcome to Asian neutralists, and gestures like the return of Port Arthur to China and of Porkkala to Finland heartened those who hoped that Stalin's death had changed the face of world politics. In 1955 Bulganin and Khrushchev visited Asia with tremendous acclaim (Khrushchev paid a second visit early in 1960) and the Russian campaign to win over the neutralists was so well launched that even the suppression of the Hungarian revolt of 1956 only dented it (the Anglo-French attack on Suez being invaluable to the Russians in saving their new reputation at this juncture).

For the neutralists themselves the principal achievements of the Bandung conference were that they had met and got to know one another (most of them were new to international politics); that they had laid the foundations for joint action at the UN and, through solidarity, increased their security, their status and their diplomatic weight in the world; that they had attracted new men like Nasser to the group and made it bigger; that they were making the giant powers take them seriously and treat their policies as respectable (a trend which was fortified by the admission of sixteen new members to the UN by the package deal of 1955 and still further by the big increase in African membership in 1960); and finally that they had seen one of the leaders of the new, formidable China, had found him not at all frightening and had perhaps inducted China into their pacific circle. In the summer of 1956 Nehru and Nasser visited Tito at Brioni in Yugoslavia. This event was a sign of the development of Asian neutralism into a worldwide association. With an Asian, an African and a European leading them the neutralists became more ambitious in international affairs and hoped to be able to bring pressure to bear on the giant powers in cold war matters, but this association was already passing the peak of its influence, partly because of the activities of those who wanted to turn it into an alliance of communists and black men against non-communist whites by emphasizing anti-colonialism in place of neutralism. Non-alignment became in practice anti-western non-alignment, particularly with the Afro-Asian Peoples Solidarity Movement which sponsored a variety of conferences in the late fifties.

In September 1961 a conference of the unaligned was held in

Belgrade. Whereas Bandung had been an exploratory conference, Belgrade had about it an atmosphere of crisis. The background to it included French nuclear tests in the Sahara and the resumption of Russian tests, the Bay of Pigs and the Berlin wall, the Franco-Tunisian clash over Bizerta and the grinding crisis in the Congo. A new conflict between India and China seemed to be emerging, a conflict between the USSR and China certainly was. Bandung's twenty-nine participants had been overwhelmingly Asian and not overwhelmingly anti-western. The only serious conflict over admissibility had been the Arab veto on Israel. At Belgrade the African representation reflected the division of African states between radicals and moderates, Latin American participants were selected with a similar bias and the Europeans included Yugoslavia and Cyprus but not the traditional neutrals, Sweden and Switzerland. An attempt by Nehru to concentrate on peace rather than anti-colonialism and to get Russo-American talks going met with little success, and a number of delegations displayed a partisan indifference to the nuclear explosion which the Russians set off on the eve of the conference. A proposal to fix a terminal date for colonial rule throughout the world at two to six years was enlarged during the debates to a demand for its immediate and total abolition.

After a pause plans for another conference led to a meeting in Cairo, more African than Asian, in October 1964 and to a project for a conference in Algiers in 1965. This plan was, however, vitiated by the fall of Ben Bella a few days before a preliminary meeting in June and by increasing embarrassment among the likely participants at the prospect of a local Sino-Soviet conflict. The Chinese wished to exclude the USSR and assume the leadership of the underprivileged but at a second preliminary meeting in October the invitation to the USSR was approved, whereupon the Chinese threatened to stay away. In these circumstances a majority thought it better to have no conference at all and the plans were allowed to expire. The movement seemed to be wilting but it was re-animated during 1967 by visits by Tito to Asian and African countries and in 1969 a conference in Belgrade gave it fresh impetus and paved the way for another major conference, in Lusaka, in 1970.

There remained a certain community of interests, mainly economic, between the Asian and African unaligned, but there was also a divergence as local concerns demanded more attention than global ones. India in particular felt this change of emphasis and so for different reasons did Ceylon. The Chinese attack on India, coupled with India's unpreparedness, compelled India to appeal to the giant powers from which, as the leading neutralist, it had tried to keep at arm's length. It lost a degree of its detachment and non-alignment. China on the other hand was becoming more detached. At feud for very different reasons with the United States, the USSR and India, laying claim to the office of poor man's friend and chief repository of a revolutionary dynamic that was becoming enfeebled in the USSR, China might well attract the unaligned more than its rivals supposed, and scare them less. But China's successes in this role were limited. In the winter of 1963–64 Chou set off on a tour of Africa where he made some friends – but, at any rate among most people in influential positions, he was a suspect friend because he represented a great power and because the ulterior objects of his visit were plain to see. The Afro-Asian connection was becoming more tenuous. Anti-colonialism was becoming a feebler rallying point as the colonial rulers departed. The Africans were increasingly preoccupied with the pains and problems of the African deep south which were of little real interest to Asians, who were themselves increasingly preoccupied with a Chinese threat which, at Bundung, they had hoped was illusory. After the Chinese invasion of India in 1962, Ceylon, Burma and Indonesia tried, in company with Cambodia, Egypt and Ghana, to use their good offices to effect a Sino-Indian reconciliation but their efforts were of little effect and were welcome neither in New Delhi nor Peking.

In Asia as a whole attitudes to China remained ambivalent, if only because the revolution in South-East Asia was far from consummated. This revolution had begun as a rejection of foreign rule and a reassertion of local beliefs and values. It included not only the capture of political independence but also a cultural effervescence which was partly traditionalist and partly progressive, partly directed against western ways and partly borrowing from them. Nationalists wanted to show, for example, that their ancient religions were as good as Christianity while at the same time they wanted to make their states powerful and prosperous by learning western industrial techniques. The first generation of nationalists came mostly from the upper and upper middle classes. The former included princes who normally spoke French or some other foreign language among themselves just as naturally as some of the first Arab leaders spoke Turkish; they sent their children to school in Europe and rejected little that was European except the political dominance which they had themselves taken over – without much intention of modifying the accompanying political system. Alongside them were less exalted but often more thoroughly westernized leaders who had learnt, often in Europe, western ideas on society and politics and had dreamed of applying them in their own less enlightened countries. At the next remove was an officer class which had inherited, especially from the British in India, Pakistan and Burma, the virtues of integrity, discipline and sobriety in public affairs, and were shocked by graft and incompetence and ashamed when their countries presented a poor example to the outside world. These men formed a potential second revolutionary group and also an alternative governing class in the event of any failure by the original anti-imperialist leaders to live up to the expectations which they had raised. Behind them again, though barely noticeable in the fifties and sixties, was a more completely non-western and lower middle-class stratum which was coming to take independence for granted and to think more about wealth and poverty, social justice and unfairness, and other problems which, unlike the basic problem of the first revolutionary generation, were domestic and not external. These men perceived that the real revolution was still to come. By its needs would they adjust their attitudes and their emotions towards the great powers which loomed round them, proffering money or example or understanding but always suspected of seeking an unpalatable return.

Chapter 16

South East Asia

1. Burma, Malaysia, Indonesia

The term South East Asia is used to describe the countries which lie between India, China, Australasia and the open expanses of the Pacific Ocean. Diverse by race, religion and wealth they had before the war one nearly common feature: with the solitary exception of Thailand all were ruled by foreigners. The British, the French, the Dutch, the Americans and the Portuguese had spread over the area and appropriated varying amounts of it. This state of affairs was viewed with dissatisfaction within the region and also by the Japanese, whose New Order had been expanded into the Great East Asia Co-Prosperity Scheme under the direction of a special ministry in Tokyo. When war brought the Japanese to South East Asia they came as anti-imperialist and pro-nationalist liberators, promising to remove European overlords, an operation which proved in the circumstances astonishingly easy. Three days after the attack on Pearl Harbour the Japanese sank the British warships *Prince of Wales* and *Repulse* (10 December 1941); Singapore fell in February 1942 and Corregidor in May; western dominance finished.

It was succeeded by a very short Japanese phase in the course of which the new overlords, like Napoleon in Germany, found that nationalism is not a commodity that can be turned on or off at will. Some Japanese genuinely believed in the co-prosperity theme and wished to help the peoples of South East Asia, but more were simply new imperialists or occupiers who quickly alienated the local nationalists. As the fortunes of war turned against the Japanese, so did the nationalists, preparing now to achieve their ends partly by services rendered to the former colonial powers and partly by a new strength that would not be overborne by war-weary Europeans. In Burma and the Philippines the end was easily achieved, in Indonesia less easily. In Malaya independence was delayed by an insurrection that was more communist than nationalist, and in Indo-China there followed a long war which assumed international proportions and whose settlement posed further international problems particularly in the successor states of Vietnam, Laos and Cambodia.

Throughout this region, the Philippines apart, the predominant power as the war ended was the British, represented until 1946 by the supreme commander in the South East Asia Command, Lord Mountbatten. The British expected to resume their former stations in Burma, Malaya, Singapore and smaller territories and to restore the French, Dutch and Portuguese in Indo-China, Indonesia and Timor and the white rajah of Sarawak. The intentions of the British, conditioned by the limitations set by circumstances to their actions, were, together with the ambitions of nationalist leaders backed by arms, the principal factors in a situation of considerable uncertainty.

In Burma the nationalists, a group of men without much knowledge of the outside world, pro-Japanese at the beginning of the war but later anti-Japanese and supplied with British arms, were associated together in the Anti-Fascist People's Freedom League (AFPFL). As the war came to an end there was doubt among the British whether to recognize and deal with the AFPFL. The government in London was opposed to recognition but the supreme commander, who was faced with the problems of installing a new administration without adequate resources of his own, favoured it. The Labour victory in the general election of July 1945 and the precipitate surrender of the Japanese in August operated to produce a decision to recognize. The new British governor of Burma, who wanted to arrest the nationalist leader Aung San and nearly did, was replaced, the AFPFL was treated as an embryonic government of Burma, and although Aung San and other leaders were assassinated in July 1947 their surviving colleagues achieved their goal of independence from Britain on 4 January 1948. There was no fighting. The British, strongly influenced by their own pledge to leave India and also by the belief that it was not possible to use the Indian troops of South East Asia Command against the Burmese, retired, leaving the AFPFL to struggle with its own internal divisions and with the hill peoples round the central Burmese plain whose traditional distrust of Rangoon created a string of separatist problems. The AFPFL included communists who not only split off from the main association but also split among themselves and waged separate campaigns against government; assassination had robbed Burma of a number of coming leaders during 1947 and 1948; revolt in Arakan along the west coast, added to troubles in the east (from the Karens over against the border with Thailand, the Shans wedged between Thailand and China, and the Kachins in the far north) threatened independent Burma with disintegration.

In 1950 a new danger was introduced with 4,000 Kuomintang troops who crossed into Burma from China under General Li Mi and gave rise to fears that the new Chinese régime would follow its retreating enemies. But Peking made a point of not blaming Rangoon and after a while General Li Mi and his followers were removed by air to Taiwan by the Americans. Nevertheless Burma felt it wise to edge politely and circumspectly away from its British and American connections. Although the Chinese in Burma numbered only about 300,000 Burma had a frontier with China and this frontier was straddled by the Kachins (300,000 in China, 200,000 in Burma and a small number in

India). In 1953 the Burmese government intimated that it did not wish to renew the expiring Anglo-Burmese defence treaty or retain the British military mission which had been in the country since independence; it also informed Washington that it wanted no more American aid. Chou En-lai visited Rangoon on his way back to Peking from Geneva in 1954 and the Burmese prime minister, U Nu, returned the visit later in the year. Further meetings led to the initiation of frontier discussions which were completed when General Ne Win displaced U Nu (who returned to power in 1960 but was again displaced by Ne Win in 1962 and this time imprisoned for six years). Ne Win was a general with a taste for philosophical and socialist discourse which he combined with the suppression of parliament and the imprisonment of his political opponents. In 1972 he and his senior colleagues put off their military ranks, but Burma continued to mark time under U Nu much as it had under General Ne Win. Fighting in the north became serious from 1968 and in 1971 Ne Win went to Peking and resuscitated a friendship agreement concluded ten years earlier. Thus Burma, which – like Annam – had been a Chinese protectorate in the Ming period and was now confronted with the problem of how smaller countries should conduct themselves in the context of Sino-American conflict, opted for retreat and renounced the possibilities of economic aid in preference for a quiet life on a competence.

In Malaya, a conglomeration of principalities plus small British colonial territories, even less of a unitary state than Burma, the British had no easy way out. The naval base on the adjacent island of Singapore (itself a British colony) created arguments for staying which did not exist in Burma, and the strength of the Chinese (in Malaya a substantial minority and in Singapore a majority) made many Malays less resentful of British rule than apprehensive of the local Chinese, whose leaders – replacing prosperous pre-war leaders compromised by their collaboration with the Japanese invaders – had taken to the jungle and to communism. Among the active opponents of the Japanese the largest group had been Chinese and most of these were communist rather than adherents of the Kuomintang, but by the very fact of their racial and doctrinal distinctiveness they could not claim to be a nationalist movement like the AFPFL. Their bid for power was of a different nature.

An initial and premature attempt was checked by the British after some hesitation. The British then tackled the racial problem and proposed a Malayan Union in which citizenship would be obtainable by any person who had lived ten years in the country. The Malays opposed this plan which would have made citizenship, and so political power, available to a large section of the Chinese population. The British thereupon proposed in its place, in February 1948, a Malayan Federation in which the powers of the Malay sultans were greater than in the proposed Union and the opportunities for the Chinese to become citizens were restricted.

In that year the Chinese communist insurrection began and in June an emergency was declared which was to last for twelve years during which the insurgents baffled 50,000 troops, 60,000 police and a home guard of 200,000. In 1950 General Sir Harold Briggs, the Director of Operations, realized that the key to the situation lay in the silent support given to the insurgents, often out of terror, by the great mass of the population, and he therefore made plans to assemble and protect the people in resettlement areas where they would be immune from blackmail and would cease to supply the insurgents with food. General Sir Gerald Templer, who arrived as governor in 1952 in succession to the murdered Sir Henry Gurney, continued this policy and developed at the same time political measures designed to bring the Malay, Chinese and Indian communities together as a prelude to independence. Malaya became indpendent on 31 August 1957 under a constitution which established a revolving presidency tenable by the Malay sultans in turn. Malay entered into a defence agreement with Britain but did not become a member of Seato and refused in 1962 to allow Malayan territory to be used by British units which might be called upon to help Thailand in the event of a threat to that country from Laos.

Singapore, with a population three-quarters Chinese, was set on the road to independence by the usual British process. A new legislative council with an unofficial and elected majority was installed alongside a nominated executive council. This machinery of government then evolved into a legislative assembly and a council of ministers under a chief minister, most of whose colleagues were chosen by the assembly, the governor retaining certain reserved powers. Full independence came in 1959 subject to the retention of British rights in the naval base. The prime minister, Lee Kuan Yew, was anxious for closer links with Malaya but since a union would place the Chinese in a majority the Malays were reluctant unless the union were at the same time extended to other and less Chinese territories. Such territories existed in Sarawak, North Borneo and Brunei.

In 1946 the rajah of Sarawak, Sir Charles Brooke, ceded the principality which his family had held since 1841 to the British government and in the same year Britain assumed in North Borneo the rights and responsibilities which had belonged before the war to the British North Borneo Company. Both Sarawak and North Borneo became crown colonies. Brunei, a third territory along the northern side of the island of Borneo (most of which formed part of Indonesia), resumed its pre-war status as a British protectorate.

In 1963 Sarawak and North Borneo (now Sabah) joined Malaya and Singapore to form a Greater Malaysian Union, despite protests from the Philippine Republic which had claims in North Borneo, and from the Indonesian Republic which regarded the scheme as a plan to create a western-orientated state capable of checking Indonesian growth and ambitions. Brunei refused to join at the last moment and a revolt against the sultan, who was believed to favour accession, gave the Indonesian President Sukarno the idea that the federation was unpopular and might be destroyed by inexpensive guerrilla operations, persistence and propaganda; and he might be able to add the rest of Borneo to Indonesia. The ensuing Indonesian confrontation forced Malaysia to appeal for British and Australian military help and frustrated the British intention of getting out of the region after creating Malaysia. The confrontation abated when Sukarno was demoted by his army in 1965–66, but Malaysia was a contrived constellation whose components had been forced into federation for external and adventitious reasons and upon the assumption that the territories tacked on to Malaya could not exist on their own. Brunei had questioned this assumption and Singapore was even more clearly able to rebut it. Brunei attained internal self-government in 1971, subject however to continuing British tutelage in external affairs. In 1965 the prime minister of Singapore, Lee Kuan Yew, suddenly announced its secession from the federation. This break was presented as an amicable divorce designed to prevent a conflict. Many Malays, ever fearful of the influence and economic power of the overseas Chinese, were determined to ensure that no Chinese prime minister of Singapore should become prime minister of the federation and to Lee Kuan Yew's realization of this obstacle were added temperamental tensions between the conservative Tunku Abdul Rahman in Kuala Lumpur and his more dynamic and socialist opposite number in Singapore. Within Malaya racial tensions broke surface in May 1969 after elections in western Malaya. In a country with so flourishing an economy that local needs – roads, schools, etc. – could quickly be met, the opposition found it difficult to find economic grievances on which to campaign. Racial grievances came to the fore instead. There were riots, many Chinese were killed and parliamentary government was temporarily suspended.

Beyond the British possessions in Burma, Malaya and Singapore lay the Dutch empire in Indonesia to the south and the French empire in Indo-China to the east. When the British returned to South East Asia after the defeat of the Japanese, their actions were consciously or unconsciously dominated by their decision to leave India. South East Asia (with the exception perhaps of Singapore) was for Britain an adjunct of India and it was hardly conceivable that the British could for long pursue in South East Asia policies that were plainly at variance with their chosen course in India. No such considerations affected the Dutch and the French whose positions in Indonesia and Indo-China were not regulated by any other positions in Asia. For them the question was the basic question which the British put to themselves in India – whether to go or to stay – and not the secondary question which confronted the British in Burma – whether to stay in spite of the departure from India; but since the factors affecting the British in India were quite different from those affecting the Dutch and the French further east, the first answer of the latter was also different. The Dutch and French proposed to revert more or less to their pre-war positions and they looked to their British allies to help them.

The return of the Dutch to Indonesia was generally assumed – or feared – in 1945 but for purely practical reasons the British supreme commander was unable to undertake extensive operations and dealt directly with the nationalist leader Sukarno in the key island of Java. Dutch forces arrived to take the place of the token British occupation but found themselves opposed by a comparatively well-organized and well-equipped movement under leaders of ability and sophistication whose foreign contacts and travels had given them an insight into the wider forces affecting the continuance of European rule in Asia. In this situation the British tried to mediate and by the Linggadjati agreement of November 1946 the Dutch recognized the *de facto* authority of the self-proclaimed Indonesian republic in Java, Sumatra and Madura and agreed to withdraw their forces from these areas; a union between the Netherlands and Indonesia was to be created by the beginning of 1949. But this curious and cumbrous scheme failed to please anybody, and amid suspicions and disputes the situation degenerated into chaos. In July 1947 the Dutch resorted to force in what came to be called the first police action. In January 1948 a respite was secured by the Renville agreement but fighting soon recurred, the situation was brought before the Security Council, and after a second police action in December the Dutch, who were considerably impeded by the anti-colonialism of the United States and its representatives in Indonesia, found themselves obliged by international pressures to compromise. Independence was conceded in 1949, though the Dutch still hoped for a union of some kind between the new republic and the Netherlands. Following a long conference at The Hague from August to November 1959 an independent Indonesian federation, consisting of seven states and with Sukarno as president, came into being at the end of the year. It was converted into a unitary state in the following August, although this *coup de main* by Javanese politicians was opposed, to the point of sporadic fighting and abortive secessions, in the other islands. Controversy with the Dutch continued in respect of West Irian (Western New Guinea) until 1962 when the logic of events, measured in miles from Holland, forced the Dutch to abandon a last outpost to which they had succeeded in clinging partly on the plea that the inhabitants were not Indonesians and were unlikely to get a fair deal from the Indonesians, and partly in the hope that Australian fears of the extension of Indonesian power to New Guinea (partly under Australian trusteeship and partly also Australian territory) would somehow be transmuted into a check to Indonesia.

President Sukarno became a favoured recipient of Russian aid, maintained himself in power until 1965 and held his vast country together by a dexterous manipulation of the opposing forces of communism (which had tried but failed to seize a monopoly of power by a coup at Madiun in Java in September 1948) and the army, and by the magic of his personal prestige. Indonesia was, by virtue of its size and potential wealth, a power of a completely different order from any other South East Asian state. It was regarded as a possible counter to Chinese influence and expansion, although under Sukarno it was vociferously anti-western and its communist party, led by K. N. Aidit, was one of the most effective in the world and pro-Chinese. There was therefore constant speculation about the balance of power between the communists and the army and about the likely outcome of a struggle between the two when Sukarno, frequently reported to be a sick man, should die. In September 1965 a false report of his death became the signal for a communist putsch. Six senior generals were murdered after the cruellest mutilation but others escaped and the coup failed. In a counter-coup, widely believed to have had American aid, something like half a million communists (including Aidit) or supposed communists were killed and the army established its control over Sukarno and the country. Bung Karno, or brother Karno, the creator of Indonesia, was gradually stripped of his powers: he died in 1970. His successor and the ruler of Indonesia for the next decade, General T. N. J. Suharto, kept vast numbers of his opponents and presumed opponents in detention (they were later transported to a convenient offshore island) but the national economy prospered. Although earnings from the export of rubber fell, Indonesia's oil and its enviable variety of other minerals more than redressed the balance and in the early seventies the economy as a whole was growing at the rate of 7 per cent a year.

2. Thailand

The south-east chunk of continental South East Asia consists of the four states of Thailand, Laos, Cambodia and Vietnam. The first of these had the unique experience of escaping the European conquest which embraced all the rest of South East Asia. It was left as a buffer between the British who advanced from India into Burma and the French who advanced from Annam and Tongking into Laos and Cambodia. Unlike Burma, Laos and Vietnam it had no frontier with China and it had succeeded in assimilating a substantial part of its Chinese population of 4 million (12 per cent of the total), but it shared the general apprehensiveness of all South East Asia concerning the revival of Chinese power and welcomed an American alliance as an insurance. It became the one genuinely Asian member of Seato (the Philippines and, even more so, Pakistan being but peripheral members of an alliance termed South East Asian). From 1938 to 1973 Thailand was ruled by a succession of strong men – Marshals Pibul Songgram, Thanarat Sarit and Thanom Kittikachorn – with an interlude of civilian rule (1944–46) under Nai Pridi Panomjong who, on being worsted by Pibul, retired to China and there revived his wartime Free

Thai movement which did not this time amount to much. Rich in rubber, tin, teak and rice Thailand stood in less need of foreign aid than most of its neighbours but it became expensively embroiled in the wars to the east. Threatened in 1962 by communist units on its borders with Laos it was offered and accepted the help of American troops. Two years later it permitted the establishment of American air bases for use in the war in Vietnam, and this counter-aid to the United States was gradually expanded to six major bases accommodating forces of 60,000. By the seventies the strains of war, and the awareness that the war was being lost by the Americans, fostered discontent which was accentuated by the general corruption, inefficiency and uncertain policies of military rule. The American alliance and the consequent involvement in Vietnam were increasingly criticized and after riots in 1973 civilian rule was restored. This change marked a partial reversal of external policies as well as a desire to clean up public life which had been corrupted by oligarchic government and the inflation and vices attendant on a foreign military presence. The American forces began to leave in the same year but another product of the war remained in the shape of the Patriotic Front which, with some Chinese support, had for ten years maintained guerrilla groups a few thousand strong among the Meo peoples who (numbering in all about 300,000) lived astride the Thai–Laotian frontier.

3. Vietnam, Laos, Cambodia

The most disputed post-war arena in South East Asia was Indo-China. This area, put together by the French, contained the protectorates of Annam and Tongking and the colony of Cochin-China (Annamite by race, Chinese by culture, and together called the three Kys) and the protected kingdoms of Luang Prabang or Laos, and Cambodia (Thai by race, Hindu by culture). The Khmer forbears of the modern Cambodians ruled an empire which, at its peak in the twelfth century, reached from sea to sea and included the southern parts of Burma, Siam, Laos and Annam. In Laos invading Thais had established an ascendancy in the thirteenth century. By the nineteenth Cambodia and Laos were threatened by Annam but were saved by the French.

The French established themselves in Asia later than the other European powers. Their defeats in the Franco-Prussian war of 1870–71 on their own soil had deprived them of territory, valuable resources, population, prestige and self-respect, and although recovery was surprisingly rapid, the acquisition of a new colonial empire in the eighties was in some sense a compensation. It took the form of entering the competition for whatever might be made out of the disintegration of the Ottoman and Chinese empires. Tunisia was virtually annexed as an extension of French power in Algeria, Madagascar was occupied, and in Asia Annam, Tongking and Cochin-China were made the nucleus of an

Indo-Chinese dominion which might provide a way into southern China and was extended by taking the kingdoms of Cambodia and Luang Prabang under the French wing. The acquisition of Annam and Tongking led to an unpopular war with China, while the western and Hindu-ward move brought France into competition with the British in Burma, where they were checked by the viceroy, Lord Dufferin (who feared – or perhaps invented – a French threat to India), and also into a more enduring hostility with the independent kingdom of Thailand. But French power remained substantially unshaken until 1940.

During the Japanese occupation in the Second World War the three Kys became the autonomous state of Vietnam and upon the Japanese withdrawal Ho Chi Minh, the leader of a communist dominated nationalist coalition, proclaimed the independent republic of Vietminh. Again, as in Indonesia and Korea, practical reasons of convenience dictated the course of events with more far-reaching effects that were contemplated at the time. The British took control south of the 16th parallel and the Chinese north of it; both withdrew during 1946 but the latter were not disposed, and the former not able, to do much to smooth the path for the returning French who arrived to find Ho Chi Minh in control of a sizeable area in the north and presiding over a government. The Annamite emperor Bao Dai, having abdicated in 1945, had accepted the post of chief counsellor to Ho.

The French began by recognizing Ho's government as autonomous with the French Union but refused to accept his demand for the union of the three Kys. Towards the end of 1946 French policy stiffened as a result of right wing pressures. In November Haiphong was bombarded and in December the French in Hanoi were attacked by the Vietminh, convinced that France now intended to overthrow Ho: some forty Frenchmen were killed and 200 abducted. This was the beginning of a war which lasted seven and a half years. After some hesitation the French decided to give up further negotiation with Ho and to switch instead to Bao Dai, to whom they offered the union of the three Kys which they had refused to Ho. The so-called Bao Dai experiment was an attempt to separate communists from other nationalists and to preserve with Bao Dai's complaisance a general French overlordship throughout Indo-China. An agreement signed in Along Bay in June 1948 embodied this policy (which was to be reflected in the south in the next decade by the Americans with President Diem as the anti-communist nationalist) and a new state of Viet Nam was formally constituted in June 1949. Bao Dai, who had been in France during the negotiations, returned to his own country as head of state. Viet Nam was proclaimed an Associated State in the French Union in December, and Laos and Cambodia were given the same status. Among those who refused to co-operate with Bao Dai was the Roman Catholic leader and future president of South Vietnam, Ngo Dinh Diem.

But the Vietminh did not give up and the victory of the Chinese communists across the northern border transformed the situation. The attempt of the French to retain power by the device of the semi-independent Associated State led to protracted bickering between themselves and Bao Dai and failed in the end to achieve its aim. France had not been able to nerve itself to take the extreme but simple step taken by the Attlee government in India, and the history of the next few years suggested that nothing less was of any avail. In 1950 five months of conferrring at Pau about constitutional advances exacerbated all parties, while in Indo-China the Vietminh took the field under its able general Vo Nguyen Giap. A Vietminh offensive in September was strikingly successful. Marshal Juin was sent to the scene. Bao Dai also returned. Pierre Mendès-France and others began to say that it was time for France to clear out of Asia. The French government, which had been resolutely opposed to admitting that the situation was in any sense international, relented to the extent of accepting American economic and military aid; to fight for French supremacy brought neither sympathy nor success, and the only way to continue the fight was to call it a fight against communism and invoke the aid of anti-communist friends. On this new basis General de Lattre de Tassigny was appointed high commissioner and commander-in-chief in December 1950. With a new general to raise morale (in which he was very successful), with American aid and with the negotiation of a political settlement of the status of the Indo-Chinese states within the French Union, the French made their final effort.

But the Vietminh struck first and showed that it was capable of waging open war as well as guerrilla operations. Its attack was renewed in October 1951 and a few weeks later the French lost de Lattre who was invalided home to France and died there in January. Bao Dai's Vietnamese army was coming into existence with extraordinary slowness, and the private armies which complicated the picture were not being reduced to his control. Chinese aid to the Vietminh was increasing, although the invasion which could have brought the Americans in never materialized. During 1952 French losses in men, material, morale and prestige were considerable, and in 1953 the Vietminh carried the war into Laos, threatened the royal capital of Luang Prabang and forced the French to divert forces from Vietnam to the Plain of Jars in Laos. In Cambodia King Norodom Sihanouk raised the political stakes by asking for a status in no way inferior to that of India and Pakistan in relation to Britain, and then put the French in great embarrassment by temporarily decamping to Thailand. Amid this scene of disintegration the French could do no more than offer to review the constitution of the French Union and begin yet another round of negotiations with Bao Dai as well as the Laotian and Cambodian monarchs. (Sihanouk had succeeded to the throne in 1940 at the age of eighteen. In 1955 he abdicated in favour of his father who reigned until 1960 with Sihanouk as prime minister. In 1956 Chou and Sihanouk signed a non-intervention agreement. Sihanouk visited Peking, Moscow, Prague and Belgrade; also Madrid and Lisbon. He adopted a policy – the reverse of Burma's

– of the widest diplomatic contacts and aid from as many places as possible. He seemed, however, to have a preference for China, which he again visited in 1958 and 1960. In 1960 he resumed the top place in the state with the title of Head of State.)

There was by this time nothing left for the French in Indo-China except a need to salvage pride, but since the French have quite enough to be proud of without retaining distant satrapies, they became increasingly fed up. Moreover they were now preoccupied with the revival of German strength, beside which the strength of the Vietminh seemed both inconsiderable and irrelevant to France's position in the world. If the Vietminh mattered to anybody, it mattered to the Americans (who were already paying for the war indirectly). It required only a climactic event to make France acknowledge that what it really wanted in Indo-China was to get out. This event occurred at Dien Bien Phu.

Dien Bien Phu was a small garrison or camp in a bowl in the north-west. Its possession was important in relation to the Vietminh's threats to neighbouring Laos, which were themselves important inasmuch as they demonstrated French inability to protect a protectorate and at the same time diverted French forces from the defence of the strategically and politically central Red River delta and Hanoi. Dien Bien Phu had changed hands more than once during the war. It was taken by the French in November 1953 and after some hesitation they decided to stay there.

General Navarre, now in command of French and Vietnamese forces which considerably outnumbered the Vietminh, believed that if he could force the enemy to battle he could inflict upon them a major defeat and permanently reduce their operations to minor guerrilla scale; he believed that the Achilles heel of the Vietminh was in numbers and that the Chinese or Russians, though willing to supply arms and equipment, would not send fighting men across the borders for fear of American retaliation. Dien Bien Phu was therefore to provide the setting for the battle which would cripple the Vietminh.

Early in 1954 agreement had been reached among all the principal powers concerned to hold an international conference on Indo-China and Korea, and as the preparations went ahead it became increasingly clear that the outcome at Dien Bien Phu would have a powerful influence on the course of negotiations. It also became clear that the French, so far from delivering a knock-out blow, were being surrounded and pounded by an unexpectedly large force and were in danger of having to capitulate. What was not so clear in these circumstances was whether France's allies would be well advised to make a special effort and intervene. The Americans, who had been opposed to any such involvement, began to have second thoughts and to propound the view that the loss of Indo-China would be a fatal blow to the fortunes of all South East Asia and even further afield. In January Dulles made a famous speech threatening 'massive retaliation' as a means of stopping communist expansion and aggression, and at the end of March he appealed for united international action to prevent the imposition of communism on South East Asia. Congressional leaders and allies were sounded on joint intervention in Indo-China and retaliation against China itself in the event of a Chinese counter-strike. The response was unfavourable.

The Korean war had left Americans with no appetite for Asian adventures and the allies had not recovered from their distrust of MacArthurism which they detected reviving in the views of Admiral Radford, the naval chief of staff, who advocated American air strikes. Eisenhower was prepared to give his consent to Radford's policy if Congress were to agree and the United States were not the only intervenor, but General Ridgway, chairman of the chiefs of staff, opposed intervention on the grounds that it would force the Chinese to enter the war as they had done in Korea. Eisenhower, who had campaigned for the presidency on a promise to stop the war in Korea, may have known that his conditions for intervening were most unlikely to be met, but he allowed Dulles to pursue the question of allied co-operation. Dulles discussed intervention in London and Paris on 11–14 April and returned to Washington under the impression that he had secured agreement for a general conference to devise a plan but Eden, with whom his personal relations were bad, immediately denied this interpretation of their talks and refused to send a representative to a preliminary discussion. Dulles returned to Paris later in the month with a proposal for unilateral American air intervention and Eden, who was also in Paris on his way to Geneva, flew back to London where a Sunday meeting of the cabinet refused to give its endorsement. Eden communicated this decision to Georges Bidault, the French foreign minister, at Orly airport on his way to Geneva and so acquired the reputation of being the man who saved the world from being plunged into a new world war by American temerity at Dien Bien Phu. It seems, however, truer to judge that American intervention had already been dismissed because of the opposition of the American chiefs of staff (Admiral Radford alone excepted) and American congressional and public opinion. Within a very short time the view that Indo-China was essential to the free world had been temporarily dropped and the fate of Vietnam was once more being treated as a local affair.

The Geneva conference, convened to discuss Korea and secondarily Indo-China, opened on 26 April. Dien Bien Phu fell on 7 May. The French government also fell and Mendès-France took the place of Laniel (who resigned on 13 June) with a promise to reach a settlement in Indo-China by 20 July or resign. On 23 June Mendès-France and Chou En-lai had a long private discussion in Berne before the latter set off for Peking via India and Burma during a break in the conference. At the same time Churchill and Eden visited Washington to discuss a variety of topics and repair the damage to Anglo-American relations caused by the Dulles–Eden misunderstandings of April. Soon after the conference resumed three armistice agreements were signed. Vietnam was partitioned roughly along the 17th parallel (a compromise choice), the Vietminh agreed to withdraw from Laos and Cambodia, and three armistice commissions were constituted with India, Polish and Canadian members to supervise the implementation of the agreed terms. The conference marked above all the defeat of France and its withdrawal from all the states of Indo-China. It purported to proclaim the creation of three new independent states: Laos and Cambodia, which were to be safeguarded in this condition against their hereditary enemies in Vietnam and Thailand by guarantees by China, France, Britain and the USSR; and Vietnam which had won independence but not perhaps integration.

In Laos, although the Geneva settlement provided for the withdrawal of Vietminh forces, there were other forces to keep revolt going. The Pathet Lao, created in 1949 by Ho as an adjunct of the Viet Minh and led by a member of the Laotian royal family, Prince Souvannouvong, had established itself sufficiently to be able to retain control of the two northern provinces of the country. In 1956 this prince visited Peking and Hanoi, and in the next year he entered a coalition with his half-brother Souvanna Phouma (already prime minister) on the basis that Laos would be neutralized. This experiment lasted less than a year. It was succeeded by an anti-communist phase during which Laos received an American military mission as well as the economic aid which was already flowing copiously. (American aid to Laos, totalling in the end $200 million, became a by-word for waste and the promotion of corruption.)

This right wing phase led to a two-year civil war, at the end of which Laos reverted to neutralism. The new government, making the most of North Vietnamese incursions, asked for a UN mission and a UN force. Hammarskjöld visited Laos in person and sent a special representative to observe and report and so gain time for temperatures to fall, but in December 1959 General Phoumi Nosavan staged a successful coup which had the opposite effect. It also evoked, a few months later, another coup led by Captain Kong Le, a rather naïve symbol of the irritation of ordinary men who were fed up with feuding and corruption. This coup acquired significance because Souvanna Phouma declared his support for Kong Le. The former was made prime minister once more and contrived briefly to reconcile the general and the captain, again on a neutralist ticket. But his solution did not last, largely because the Americans equated neutralism with pro-communist inclinations and were able to rebuild a right wing front under General Nosavan and Prince Boun Oum, a distant relative of the reigning family and mediatized ruler of Champassak (in the south). Souvanna Phouma fled to Cambodia, whence he was transported in a Russian aircraft to confer with his half-brother and Kong Le. He was also courted by Boun Oum and Nosavan but preferred to set off on a world tour. Meanwhile Kong Le had inflicted a defeat on Boun Oum and

Nosavan. In 1961 the three princes met in Switzerland and agreed that
Laos should become a neutralized state without military alliances. This
agreement did not, however, have any immediate effect. Fighting went
on until a further and more formal agreement was signed at Geneva in
July 1962.

The war of 1960–62 led not only to increased American intervention
in Laos (chiefly on account of the increasing involvement of North Vietnam in South Vietnam in the same years), but also to private American
disenchantment with the anti-communists in Laos and so to a determination to support the anti-communist régime in Thailand, if
necessary by a military presence. The war was brought to an end
because the United States and China reached agreement behind the
scenes on a neutralized Laos and the evacuation of foreign troops, i.e.
American troops which China feared and the United States felt to be
engaged in a worthless cause. But Laos continued to be used by Ho for
supplies into South Vietnam, the authority of the Pathet Lao spread
and the American forces were replaced by an active communist army –
part Laotian and part Vietnamese – which probably numbered 60,000
or more. In 1963 the Laotian coalition government dissolved and the
country became virtually partitioned with the Pathet Lao ruling in the
north-east and Souvanna Phouma the rest. From 1964 the United
States reversed its policy of withdrawal, gradually built up very large
ground forces and used its air forces in operations by the Laotian
government against the Pathet Lao. Laos became an important
American theatre of war, ancillary to the waging of the war in South
Vietnam and to the protection of American forces of about 50,000 men
in Thailand.

In Vietnam the 1954 Geneva settlement gave Ho Chi Minh half the
country and the expectation of the rest in less than two years if the
terms of the settlement were fully accepted and implemented. The formal agreement concluded at Geneva was an armistice agreement signed
by generals on behalf of France and the Vietminh. It drew a line
(roughly the 17th parallel), imposed a cease-fire, and made arrangements for the regroupment of military forces and the resettlement of
civilians on either side of the line. The conference also produced
a number of declarations, including a final declaration propounded
but not signed. The United States and South Vietnam dissociated
themselves in particular from this declaration's provision for elections
throughout Vietnam by the middle of 1956; they believed that such
elections were bound to transfer the whole of the country to communist
rule since the part north of the armistice line contained a majority of
the population – which was in addition likely to vote with that 90 per
cent solidarity characteristic of authoritarian régimes. The government
in South Vietnam, which had been established in Saigon by the
authority of Bao Dai before the Geneva conference, considered itself
bound by nothing that was settled there.

For the French the armistice agreement of 1954 was a means of escape. They were able to conclude a war which they were losing. Thereafter they watched with an excusable but irritating smugness as the Americans repeated in the next phase many of the mistakes which they had made between 1945 and 1954. For the Russians and the Chinese the settlement was a political arrangement which they pressed upon Ho, the Russians because they wanted France to stifle the nascent European Defence Community and the Chinese because they wanted to remove western forces and influence from a country on their borders; both may have supposed that Ho would soon rule as effectively in Saigon as in Hanoi and were faced with fresh problems when this did not happen.

For the Americans the Geneva settlement marked the end of a French presence in Asia which, however obnoxious at one time to Americans on general anti-colonialist principles, could have been rendered useful in anti-communist terms. Having decided in 1954 not to buttress French rule any longer, the United States sought an alternative anti-communist and anti-Chinese force. They disapproved of the Geneva settlement because it not only failed to constitute such a force but threatened to accelerate Chinese communist expansion by giving Ho the whole of Vietnam in two bites – the north by the armistice agreement and the south through elections: they regarded Ho as a satellite and discounted his chances of becoming the Tito of Asia. They resolved therefore to maintain the independence of the anti-communist régime established by Bao Dai in the south, and also to create a new anti-communist alliance to check China in Asia as Nato had checked the USSR in Europe and to facilitate in future the united action which Dulles had tried and failed to organize for the relief of Dien Bien Phu. Accordingly the South East Asia Collective Defence Treaty (the Manila Pact, establishing a South East Asia Treaty Association – Seato) was signed in September by three Asian and five non-Asian states: the Philippines, Thailand, Pakistan, the United States, Australia, New Zealand, Britain and France. These signatories bound themselves to take joint action in the event of aggression against any one of them in a designated area, and to consult together in the event of threats from action other than armed action (i.e. subversive activities). The designated area was the general area of South East Asia including the territory of the signatories and the general area of the South West Pacific to 20 degrees 30 minutes north; the area included therefore Vietnam, Cambodia and Laos but not Taiwan or Hong Kong.

Seato never became an impressive organization. No purely Asian state of substance joined it except Pakistan which, distant from China and not really concerned about Chinese expansion in South East Asia or anywhere else, joined for ulterior reasons – to please the United States and get American support against India. France became an increasingly cynical member; Britain became an increasingly embarrassed one, balancing the obligations of a loyal ally (with a special interest in the area so long as it retained obligations to Malaysia) against the wish to keep out of Vietnam and the temptation to criticize American mistakes there. Seato was no more than the United States writ differently. Its purpose was to ensure the independence of South Vietnam but it could not save that ill-governed country from the dilemma of either collapsing or surviving as an American protectorate. It was dissolved in 1975.

Ho had accepted the Geneva armistice reluctantly and under Russian and Chinese pressure. It may be surmised that only the prospect of elections in 1956 persuaded him to come to terms with France when he was entitled to expect not only the surrender of Dien Bien Phu but the collapse of the entire French position in any event and in the same year. He soon saw that his hopes were to be falsified and that the 17th parallel was another armistice line destined to harden into a political frontier. It was moreover a line of graver consequence than the division between the two halves of Korea, for in Vietnam the south fed the north and the perpetuation of the division entailed economic problems as well as disappointment over the denial of reunification. In the period of uncertainty between the signing of the armistice and the date fixed for the elections which were never held Ho initiated a programme of agrarian reform and sought also to expand industry and exploit North Vietnam's mineral wealth, but the agrarian reform, modelled on Chinese collectivization, provoked a peasant rising which provoked a reign of terror which got out of hand and caused at least 50,000 deaths. Industrialization required help from advanced countries such as the USSR and Czechoslovakia rather than China, and after the Sino-Russian split in the fifties Ho had to balance between Moscow and Peking. At first he allowed relations with the latter to deteriorate and in 1957 he received Voroshilov in Hanoi, but this partiality displeased some of his colleagues and may even have caused a threat to his own position. Ho himself had associations of a life-time with the USSR and Muscovite communism, and General Giap, backed by the North Vietnamese army, expressed the traditional Vietnamese distrust of China, but other leaders were reputedly pro-Chinese, including Truong Chinh whose strength lay in the Lao Dong party (founded in 1951 and essentially a communist party although it embraced a few non-communist notables). Ho spent two months in Moscow in 1959, returning to Hanoi via Peking. By this time fighting had been resumed in the south and the problem of getting rid of the French was succeeded by the far bloodier problem of getting rid of the Americans. He lived just long enough to see it happen, dying in 1969.

South Vietnam started its independent career comparatively peacefully and prosperously in spite of the arrival from the north of nearly a million refugees (two-thirds of whom were Roman Catholic Christians). The prime minister, Ngo Dinh Diem, himself a northerner and a Roman Catholic, eliminated Bao Dai, who was declared deposed in 1955, and a year later inaugurated a republic with himself as president. Although the last French troops did not leave until April 1956,

American aid was transferred from the French to the Diem government from the first day of 1955. To the Americans Diem was an anti-communist ally who would direct a new state described by them, with marvellous inexactitude, as a democracy. But they misjudged their man. Diem was an anti-French intellectual, not particularly pro-American and in no way a democrat. He treated South Vietnam as a personal or family demesne which he administered through a network of secret societies, nepotistically, intolerantly and unintelligently. He antagonised the Buddhists, the dominant religious group, and of the hill peoples who, although only a small minority of the population, inhabited more than half of the countryside in which subversive movements might be sustained. In the cities too Diem and his relatives who included five brothers, became increasingly unpopular. The cities became generators of inflation and vice while the countryside became an open field for the settlement of private grudges and for extortionate demands which drove the peasants into the arms of the communist opposition. A first coup against the régime in November 1960 failed but three months later the opposition was strong enough to attack Diem's palace from the air. At about the same time Ho decided to give material aid to the forces gathering against Diem in the countryside. Despite American pressure Diem had refused to supply food to North Vietnam in the mistaken belief that the northern régime was about to collapse under the weight of peasant revolts. Thus Ho was given an economic as well as a political motive for re-opening the war. At the time of the Geneva armistice the communists in the south, many of whom retreated to the north, had concealed their arms against a possible resumption of fighting. An active communist opposition to Diem had come into existence under the name of the Vietcong – originally a term of opprobrium, like Whig or Tory. In 1960 a National Liberation Front was formed and in 1962 the International Control Commission, an observer group established at Geneva eight years earlier, reported that North Vietnam was intervening in civil war in the south in support of the National Liberation Front.

In 1963 Buddhist hostility to the Diem régime reached a climax. Buddhist monks publicly burnt themselves to death in gruesome protest against persecution. The authorities retaliated by looting and sacking pagodas and torturing monks. The Americans cut off aid to Diem and instigated a coup against him. In November Diem and his most markedly unpopular brother, Ngo Dinh Nhu, were killed, the régime collapsed and General Duong Van Minh ('Big Minh') became the head of the first of a series of transient military governments. In the next eighteen months half a dozen coups took place. General Minh was forced into the background within two months of Diem's end. General Nguyen Khanh, more militant in relation to North Vietnam but no more secure in Saigon, was opposed by Buddhists and students demanding an end to military rule. He survived a coup against him in September 1964 but was displaced early in 1965 by the yet more militant General Tran Van Minh ('Little Minh'). From the latter part of 1965, however, the rising men were General Nguyen Cao Ky, the most militant of the generals to gain power and the most determined to carry the war beyond the 17th parallel, and General Ngyuen Van Thieu.

During the early sixties the Americans became both alive to the weaknesses of their policy of supporting weak South Vietnamese régimes and more committed to it. One of Kennedy's early decisions on taking office in 1961 had been to increase American aid in men and material but without committing combat troops. He accepted the advice of General Maxwell Taylor, a former chairman of the US chiefs of staff, to build up American forces and by 1962 American aircraft were flying combat missions, and the CIA was conducting more or less underground operations. The pretence that the Americans were in Vietnam as no more than advisers had worn desperately thin. During 1963 and 1964 the Vietcong, aided by the misrule of Diem, the confusion among his successors, and by North Vietnam and China, extended its control, until the South Vietnamese and American forces were in danger of suffering the same fate as the French in Algeria and the British in Cyprus and of being driven into a few fortified footholds. The policy, copied from Malaya, of isolating villagers from guerrillas was unsuccessful because the differences between Vietnamese villagers and Vietnamese guerrillas were insignificant compared with the differences between Malay villagers and Chinese guerrillas in Malaya. The Americans, seeing that the Vietcong was winning, decided further to increase their military effort and their control over the direction of the war, and as a result the position of the Vietcong rapidly worsened. Thereupon the government of North Vietnam, seeing that the Vietcong was losing, began to send regular divisions to its rescue. The war became, with scant disguise, a war between the United States and North Vietnam. In the south the Americans aimed to subjugate the whole country. Ultimately they failed and, with hindsight, it could be said that they would have been wiser to have adopted General Salan's strategy of holding the centres of population from which no enemy could have dislodged them, and of securing and sealing off the rich, easily defensible and ethnically distinct Cochin-China. Instead American forces were multiplied year by year: from 23,000 at the end of 1964 to 390,000 two years later and 550,000 by the beginning of 1968. When American withdrawals began in July 1969 these forces had lost 36,000 dead. At their peak the combined American, South Vietnamese and allied forces numbered one and a quarter million, backed by a mighty air force. Against them General Giap proved himself a brilliant guerrilla commander who knew how far to follow and how far to deviate from the strategic teachings of Mao Tse-tung.

The war was extended to the north in 1964. In July of that year a US destroyer, operating with South Vietnamese sea and land forces against North Vietnam was attacked by two North Vietnamese torpedo boats in the Bay of Tonkin, President Johnson used this episode, tendentiously explained, to obtain from Congress authority to use US forces in open naval combat. At the end of the same year Johnson became the elected instead of merely the accidental president of the United States. He was seduced by visions of a quick victory by the air bombardment of a fourth rate foe. In February 1965 a successful attack on an American garrison at Pleiku near the armistice line was followed by sharp American bombing reprisals. American ground forces were also now committed to the battle against the north. But the quick victory was prevented by Russian aid to Ho, notably for the anti-aircraft defence of Hanoi, and as the American bombardment became fiercer, so did opposition to the war develop within the United States.

As the American war effort was intensified President Johnson also began to bid for peace. In April he offered to treat unconditionally with North Vietnam for a cessation of hostilities on the basis that South Vietnam would be an independent and neutral state; and he offered $16,000 million in aid to South East Asia, including North as well as South Vietnam. But he was not willing to accept the Vietcong as a party to the negotiations. In reply Ho enunciated a set of conditions which were not irreconcilable with the American proposals and in July Johnson implicitly but not explicitly opened the door of the negotiating chamber to the Vietcong as well. He was, however, unwilling to stop all bombing immediately (a bombing pause in May lasted only a few days) or to agree to withdraw all American troops before negotiations began. At the beginning of 1966 Johnson conferred with Ky and Thieu in Honolulu. Bombing was interrupted for several weeks and negotiations seemed not improbable, but they remained in the event elusive and the war went on, increasing in weight and horror. Vietcong adherents and others were slaughtered by the most up-to-date weapons. They were hunted by and thrown out of helicopters, tortured, raped and murdered in cold blood. In a celebrated instance at My Lai in 1967, which later led to a criminal trial and conviction in the United States, 300 civilians were killed by a US army unit.

In 1967 Washington tried to enlist Russian aid to end the war and Johnson had a personal discussion with Kosygin at Glasboro in New Jersey. But no concrete results were forthcoming. The Ky-Thieu government split but was re-formed as a Thieu-Ky government (which lasted until 1971 when Thieu prevailed). Ky fell foul of the Buddhists, many of whom went over to the NLF. The conflict was increasingly polarized between the NLF and the Saigon regime to the advantage of the former. In a spectacular, if ultimately unsuccessful, offensive by Giap during the Tet festival at the beginning of 1968 all the main US bases in South Vietnam were simultaneously attacked, Saigon was in danger of falling to the NLF and Hue was captured and held by the NLF for two months. These events, and their presentation on television, strengthened opposition to the war in the United States, and criticism of the way in which it was being conducted. Later in the year Johnson replaced his commander-in-chief. But domestic criticism was not merely directed to the competence of generals. The use of napalm, defoliants and poison gases caused a revulsion which became not only vociferous but violent. In May 1968, after a further bombing pause accompanied this time by an American offer to withdraw, talks between the United States and North Vietnam opened in Paris. Later in the year South Vietnam and the Vietcong joined the discussions. But they led nowhere. North Vietnam had discovered that it could survive the American onslaught and maintain the supply of men and material to the south by using routes and methods which, being comparatively primitive, were never wholly disrupted by aerial bombardment. North Vietnam had also discovered that the Americans really wanted to get out and either turn the war over once more to the South Vietnamese (whose army was brought up to a strength of over one million and given the most modern equipment) or end it. The war was making Johnson so unpopular at home that, fearing defeat in the coming presidential election, he announced that he would not run. He could neither win a victory, since he was not prepared to use nuclear weapons, nor negotiate a peace, since North Vietnam preferred waiting to negotiating. Johnson was pursuing incompatible aims – to get out and to secure the existence of a separate, non-communist South Vietnam. North Vietnam was not convinced that it need concede the latter in order to get the former, and when the Democrats went down to defeat in November the new president, Richard Nixon, found himself in the same dilemma. Although he had pledged himself to end the war, little more than a year later he extended it in another vain hope to find the quick victory.

In March 1970 the ruler of Cambodia, the neutralist Prince Sihanouk, was unseated by a coup by his own prime minister, General Lon Nol. Cambodia, like Laos, had been used by North Vietnam without much regard for its neutrality and Sihanouk had been reproached by some of his compatriots for putting up with too much infringement of the country's rights. The new Cambodian government asked for American arms to defend itself against intruders. It got instead American armies, accompanied by South Vietnamese forces (hereditary enemies) and by all the devastation of which the American military machine was capable. The American command in Vietnam was justifiably anxious to counter the use of Cambodia by the North Vietnamese and unjustifiably convinced that it could capture vast communist stores and major headquarters. The operation was militarily successful, though doubtfully necessary; politically it was at best irrelevant. In 1971 the Laotian cockpit was invaded by South Vietnam with American air support but North Vietnamese forces won decisive victories. In 1972 American bombing of North Vietnam was resumed. But these operations in Cambodia, Laos and Vietnam were the last lashes of the frustrated American monster. The withdrawal proceeded steadily and only 25,000 remained at the end of 1972. Representatives of the United States, both Vietnams and the Vietcong met in Paris and reached agreement in January 1973 on a cease-fire to be internationally supervised and on the creation of a Council of National Reconciliation in Vietnam to prepare elections. These agreements endorsed the American retreat but did not bring peace. There was heavy fighting in the latter part of 1973 and throughout 1974 with Thieu expressing confidence that his new army of a million men could win the war. Instead his army and his power disintegrated in the face of 200,000 North Vietnamese and 100,000 Vietcong adversaries. The US Congress refused to sanction further aid. Thieu resigned in 1975 and Big Minh returned from the shadows to surrender what authority was left in Saigon. The war was over. About 2 million people had been killed.

In Laos the fighting stopped in 1973 on the basis that yet another coalition would be constructed and all foreign troops would be withdrawn. The new government came laboriously into existence in 1975 and perished in the same year. The monarchy perished too. Prince Souvannouvong, now president, and the Pathet Lao had won. In Cambodia the United States abandoned Lon Nol. The US Congress put a stop to the bombing of Cambodia in 1973, and the uneasy alliance of Sihanouk and the left wing Khmers Rouges slowly conquered the whole country including Pnom Penh which fell in April 1975. Lon Nol fled and, judging by reports of what happened to those who did not, was lucky that he got away.

4. The Philippines

The Americans returned to the Philippines in 1945 and gave them independence in 1946. The terms of the transfer of sovereignty included a lease of bases to the United States for ninety-nine years, reduced in 1966 to twenty-five years from that date. The central problem of the new government was authority. The country had become a gangland in which different groups, including the police, had become laws unto themselves. Violence was endemic and rose to a crescendo at or near election times. Prominent among the forces in the state were the Hukbalahaps, originally anti-Japanese guerrillas supported during the war by the Americans but, the war having ended, now expendable or worse: their leader Luis Taruc proclaimed himself a communist. He surrendered in 1974 but his movement persisted in the north with some support from the local population. There was also dissidence in the south where an established Muslim majority found itself becoming a minority, and disorder in the capital Manila where ostentation flourished alongside the debris of war.

In 1962 President Diosdado Macapagal laid claim to Sabah (North Borneo), broke off relations with Malaya and refused to recognize the new state of Malaysia, but this issue was allowed to drop by his successor Ferdinand Marcos (president from 1966), who was preoccupied with internal order and with his attempts to retain the presidency beyond the constitutional term. A referendum in 1973, following the imposition of martial law in 1972, allowed him to do this.

Notes

A. Afghanistan and the Pathans

The identity of the modern state of Afghanistan began to be formed by Ahmed Shah in the eighteenth century after the assassination of Nadir Shah of Iran whose empire had extended over Pathans, Turcomen, Usbeks and Hazares (descendants of the Mongols) who lived between the deserts of eastern Iran and what was to become the north-west frontier of the British in India. In the twentieth century it was a country governed by the Pathans of the south-east who dominated the government in Kabul with the reluctant acquiescence of other races, among whom the more important were the northerners who, though quick to stigmatize the Pathans as idlers, found in the comparative richness of their own lands and herds compensation for their disproportionately low political influence. Afghanistan was a country with few natural resources and a medieval fiscal system. Since the parliament refused to impose any but the lightest taxes on land, public revenue was derived from customs duties which were necessarily small. Smuggling was a major economic activity. King Mohammed Zahir Shah, who came to the throne in 1935, was well disposed to modest progress but obstructed by a parliament which he, unlike his neighbour the shah of Iran, was not strong enough to dismiss or manipulate. He was deposed in 1973 while on a visit to Europe, the monarchy was abolished and a republic inaugurated under the presidency of one of his relations, Mohammed Daud Khan. During the sixties foreign aid – Russian, Chinese and French – was used mainly for road building. Some of this activity, notably the road and tunnels built by Russian engineers from Mazar-i-Sharif near the frontier with the USSR and over the Hindu Kush to Kabul, was regarded with suspicion and apprehension by Pakistan.

Relations between Afghanistan and Pakistan were permanently, though not violently, disturbed by the position of the Pathans who comprise some eight or nine million Pushtu-speaking peoples living on both sides of the frontier between Pakistan and Afghanistan. After their defeat of the Sikhs in the nineteenth century the British extended their rule westward and came into collision with Amir Abdur Rahman of Afghanistan who, having consolidated his position after a time of troubles, was moving in the opposite direction. In 1893 the Durand Line, named after the foreign secretary of India and running through Pathan country, was drawn but the nature of this line was not precisely defined and successive Afghan governments denied that it was ever meant to be an international frontier. On the eve of Pakistan's independence in 1947 and after it Afghanistan tried to persuade first Britain and then Pakistan to agree to the creation of an independent Pathan or Pushtu state which would not, however, have included the Pathans living in Afghanistan (who were alleged to desire no change) but would stretch from Chitral in north-western Kashmir down to Sind and might embrace parts of Baluchistan and Sind and even Karachi. Pakistan rejected the notion. For some years there was border fighting – associated in particular with the Faqii of Ipi, a persistent thorn in Pakistan's flesh – and a series of diplomatic protests and flurries. An offer by the shah of Iran to mediate in 1950 was accepted by Pakistan but never eventuated. Shortly afterwards the dispute died down, but it continued to affect relations between Afghanistan and Pakistan and, together with the former's tradition of friendly relations with the USSR, was a factor in keeping Afghanistan out of the negotiations for the Baghdad Pact.

B. Timor

Timor, the last major island in the chain stretching between continental Asia and Australia, was divided by the Dutch and Portuguese in almost equal sections. The eastern and Portuguese half was detached from Macao at the end of the nineteenth century to become a separate Portuguese colony, which it remained after the western half had become part of the Indonesian republic. The overthrow of the military regime in Lisbon in April 1974 was expected to lead to the engulfing of eastern Timor in Indonesia, but opposition to Indonesia was manifested by two groups, the one pro-Portuguese and the other demanding independence. The latter was left wing. Civil war broke out in August 1975, the small Portuguese force left and at the end of the year Indonesia invaded and dominated the territory.

C. ASEAN

The Association of South East Asian Nations (ASEAN) was formed in 1967 by Thailand, Malaysia, Singapore, Indonesia and the Philippines who hoped, by collaboration, more effectively to attack poverty, disease and other social ills, to improve their commercial and economic bargaining powers and to keep foreign states away. Following the announcement in 1968 of British withdrawal from Malaysia and Singapore these two states concluded in 1971 with Britain, Australia and New Zealand a new and looser agreement to replace the Anglo-Malaysian defence agreement. In the same year ASEAN declared that South East Asia should be a zone of peace, freedom and neutrality – a proposition echoed by the UN General Assembly in regard to the Indian Ocean and partially implemented when Britain decided in 1974 to leave Gan and Mauritius (but not Diego Garcia).

Part Five

Africa

Chapter 17

Independence

The artificiality of dealing with political and economic affairs in terms of geographical categories is nowhere better illustrated than in Africa. The northern fringe of the African continent has been made by history a part of the Arab-Islamic civilization and is more conscious of its affinities with the Middle East than of its ancient economic or current political links with the rest of Africa. Moreover the European overlordship exercised from Casablanca to Suez through protectorates, unequal treaties, military agreements and direct annexation was different in kind from the colonial empires established by Europeans south of the Sahara. But North Africa is at the same time part of Africa: the ethnic line between the Arab-Berber and Bantu races runs through the Sudan and gives trouble there which other states on either side of the line cannot altogether ignore; Egypt and Morocco have played prominent parts in African affairs and conferences and associations; the more reticent Tunisia had a leading voice in the Congo's troubles. The desert is no longer the barrier that it used to be since the aeroplane and above all the radio have enabled men to transcend it; language is no more a barrier between Arab Africa and Bantu Africa than it is within these two areas; and religion provides points of contact between Muslims and Christians on both sides of the divide. The north therefore, though still distinct from the rest of the continent in special and enduring ways, will be classed here as more African than Asian with the sole exception of Egypt whose post-war African role has been consistently subordinated to its Asian and not the other way round.

In the nineteen-fifties and -sixties Africa produced a phenomenon of unparalleled extent – the emancipation from foreign rule of enormous areas in the form of independent sovereign states. This process had worldwide repercussions and overshadowed all other African affairs. It was on the whole unexpected. When the Second World War ended there were only three fully independent states in Africa – Ethiopia, Liberia and South Africa. The next ten years were a decade of preparation for the liquidation of the French, British and Belgian empires, and a further ten years later most of Africa was free. Since France, Britain and Belgium came to accept with versatile swiftness the need to go, these decades witnessed struggles over timetables rather than principles. Compelled by calculation rather than by force the imperial powers abandoned with unexpected ease vast areas whose governance they had acquired in the previous century with equal facility. The process of decolonization was, however, halted in the southern tip of the continent by the stubbornness of the Portuguese in Angola and Mozambique and by the ruthless determination of the semi-independent white settlers of Southern Rhodesia. The self-preservative resistance of the latter, and the refusal of the former to calculate in the same way as the French, the British and the Belgians, were decisively influenced by the existence still further south of the South African stronghold of white supremacy, where the white minority was comparatively much larger (one in four) than elsewhere in Africa and was at the same time fortified by riches, by modern technical power, by having nowhere else to go, and by a doctrinaire racialism which permitted extremities of repressive injustice and cruelty. There were also other pockets of Portuguese or Spanish rule. The Portuguese territories were the Cape Verde and Madeira islands, Protuguese Guinea and the islands of Principe and S. Tome in the Gulf of Guinea further south. Spain held Spanish Morocco, the enclave of Ifni in south-west Morocco, the Canary islands, Rio de Oro (sometimes called Spanish Mauritania and claimed by both Morocco and Mauritania – see chapter 18), south of Morocco and west of Mauritania the island of Fernando Po in the bight of Biafra, and Rio Muni, an enclave in Gabon. Spain ceded Spanish Morocco to Morocco in 1956, retaining, however, the towns of Melilla, Ceuta and three other small enclaves whose populations were mainly Spanish. In 1957 Spain sent troops to Ifni but ceded it to Morocco as far south as latitude 27° 40′ in April 1958. Fernando Po, renamed Macias Nguema island, together with Rio Muni became the republic of Equatorial Guinea in 1968.)

By 1965 then, twenty years after the end of the world war, decolonization had gone a very long way and the principal problems facing Africa were the completion of the process of liberation; the struggle against poverty; forms of government and internal stability; and external relations, including relations between African states themselves. These problems interacted upon each other.

The removal of alien and minority rule in the rest of Africa had an emotional priority in the minds of the leaders of the new states, partly because it was held to be a fraternal obligation and partly because the remaining alien rulers were the most hated. At the same time the new states were impotent and knew it. They lacked military power and economic levers, and they were frustrated by the limitations of the subversive activities for which some of them undertook to give training to refugees. They found therefore that, although independent, they were incapable of achieving the prime aim of their external policies without outside help, and they also quickly discovered that this help was not forthcoming. The debate over economic sanctions against South Africa is more fully examined in a later chapter of this book. The point to note here is that the principal economic powers of the world, which included the principal ex-colonial powers, were unwilling to impose sanctions because they had more pressing concerns in other continents, because they shrank from taking the black side against whites in a stark racial confrontation, because they feared a consequential outbreak of uncontrollable violence amounting virtually to a serious war, and because they doubted the legality of such action. To the Africans, however, it seemed suspiciously pertinent that the Portuguese were allied with the principal western powers in Nato, that South African industry produced large profits for Britons and Americans, and that successive British governments (whose anomalous position in Southern Rhodesia was not easy to grasp) seemed excessively tender in their dealings with governments in Salisbury.

The discovery that formal independence did not automatically give new states the capacity to act independently on external affairs was duplicated in another context. Next to the liberation of the rest of Africa the new African leaders were most intent upon the modernization of their countries and their economic growth. Political independence was not by itself enough; it needed to be supplemented and safeguarded by economic and social progress – less poverty and, for example, more education. Here too Africans found themselves dependent on outside help. They sought and received aid from ex-colonial and other countries in the form of financial gifts and loans, the training abroad of professional and technical persons of many kinds, the secondment to their own countries of experts and volunteers, and so forth. Besides official governmental aid they needed also investment by foreign private enterprises, and in this field in particular there arose a conflict between the urge for modernization and the sense of independence.

The enticement of the private entrepreneur, who was needed for his skills and for the plants which he might put down in African states, required a certain amount of blandishment and assurances of conditions in which businesses can operate at a profit. But a newly sensitive independence, coupled with the awareness of a galling economic dependence, sometimes produced the opposite result and set off a round of rising recriminations and suspicions for which neither side could claim to be blameless. Africans who were rough with foreign merchants or journalists or settlers, or who failed to provide the facilities and safeguards and good order to which foreign businessmen were accustomed at home, caused these businessmen to say to themselves that operations in Africa were only worth the special risks if specially large or specially quick profits could be made. They might feel that these risks justified them in charging higher prices or making unusual conditions, and as soon as they acted in this way they laid themselves open to the charge that they were exploiting the economic weaknesses of Africa and were simply out to reap an exorbitant profit and be off again. Xenophobic resentments were increased, fresh incidents would occur, the foreigner would conclude that his operations were even riskier still, and so on in a circle. Situations of this kind gave rise to charges of neo-colonialism. This term, in so far as it was meant merely to describe a state of economic dependence, expressed – if in loaded language – a truth. But it was also freely used to impute motives as well as to describe facts, and in so far as it was used to accuse ex-colonialists of deliberately seeking ways and means of restoring a lost dominance in new guise it was largely untrue and unfair. But such chances as existed of dispelling African suspicions of this kind were eliminated by the behaviour of Belgian and other financial interests in Katanga in 1960–61 and by the very imperfect compliance of western states and firms with the mandatory embargo by the UN on economic dealings with Rhodesia.

The economic plight of new states in the post-war world was extreme but imperfectly grasped, and still more marginally alleviated, by the richer countries. The dilemma of new states born into a world whose politics were dominated by a war of giants has already been discussed in the Asian context (see chapter 14). No less acute was the dilemma posed by being born into a world whose economic pattern had been laid down by the two major trading countries of the world, the United States and Britain. Before the Second World War ended these two agreed, at Bretton Woods, to apply to the international economy the principles of freer trade, no discrimination and stable rates of exchange. They devised for these purposes two new organizations: an International Trading Organization and the International Monetary Fund, the one to clear the channels of trade of physical obstacles (tariffs and quotas), the other to provide the finance for international trade and its expansion. The latter came out of the Bretton Woods conference in an American rather than a British form: in particular Britain wanted but failed to get an international currency, a variable volume of credit geared to the expansion of trade, and much larger initial reserves that the $25 billion with which the Fund actually started. The former never came into existence but was replaced by the General Agreement on Tariffs and Trade which, if it lacked the institutional permanence of the projected ITO, was nevertheless pledged to the same objectives, which it pursued by a series of meshed bilateral bargainings designed to reduce tariffs, eliminate quotas, rule out any new or increased preferences and assure the extension to all of any preference available to anyone. These organs concerned with trade were supplemented by the World Bank, also created at Bretton Woods, which was to provide funds for development.

The trading system designed at Bretton Woods presupposed a certain community of interests between all trading nations and it also supposed that tariffs and quotas were the principal barriers to commerce between states. But neither assumption was true of the economically weaker states. Although they needed to enter the international economy, they needed also to be protected in it; freedom worked against them. Further, their main problems were not tariffs or quotas but the instability of world prices for their products and the difficulty of getting into foreign markets to sell them. They were for the most part not only very poor – with an average annual income per head of $100–150, compared with over $1000 in the Nato countries, even with Greece and Turkey included – but also ill equipped for international economic competition. Many of them had inelastic one-crop economies. Their products were primary products, for which the demand (except in the case of oil) was rising less quickly than world income. Their customers were making synthetic or substitute products and, especially in the case of agriculture, were susceptible to domestic protectionist lobbies anxious to close the market to imports from overseas. The Korean war produced a boom in commodity prices from which a number of these countries benefited, but only temporarily. Another palliative was aid, that is to say, cash, credits, goods or skills given free or transmitted at less than the ruling market price. Considerable benefits were transferred in this way and the donors, totting up the yearly sacrifices, congratulated themselves on their generosity. The recipients, however, thought otherwise. They came to the conclusion that aid was the wrong answer to their problems. Apart from the fact that there was too little of it, and apart too from the realization that most of this aid was given for political purposes in the cold war, aid was condemned for a variety of reasons: because the burden of interest payments and capital repayments became a sizeable charge on export earnings; because aid was frequently tied so that the recipient, instead of using it to buy what he wanted where it could be had most cheaply, was obliged to accept schemes not at the top of his list of priorities or buy goods from the donor instead of more cheaply elsewhere; because aid perpetuated an economic pattern created in colonial times, when colonies were kept to the business of producing raw materials for their owners' needs; because, therefore, aid impeded the essential business of diversifying the post-colonial economy and making a start with industrialization in order to enable the new state to create capital. For all these reasons the weaker countries quickly found that aid was no substitute for what they really wanted – a change in the rules governing the international economy and particularly guaranteed prices for their products and ease of access to the world's more affluent markets where, if at all, these products must be sold. At a first United Nations Conference on Trade and Development (UNCTAD), held at Geneva in 1962, and a second at New Delhi in 1968, the weaker countries tried to argue the richer minority into accepting their point of view, but having little except numbers on their side they did not get very far.

In development, as opposed to trade, the World Bank also proved a disappointment to new states. The funds which the World Bank lent or invested were in the first place raised by the Bank in the world's principal money markets. Consequently the Bank, borrowing at world rates, had to lend at similar rates. But poor countries could not afford to finance their development in this way: if they could, they would not have needed the Bank. This problem was partially circumvented by the establishment, alongside the Bank, of an International Development Agency (IDA) to make 'soft' loans.

The European Economic Community provided a partial exception to these restraints on new states. When the Treaty of Rome was being negotiated France insisted on the insertion of special provisions for an associate status. It had in mind its own African territories, then all still colonies. Part IV of the treaty therefore provided that the Community might enter into arrangements with non-European states, by which these would be accorded the benefit of tariff reductions and quota extensions while being entitled at the same time to impose tariffs of their own to protect their infant industries (provided that these tariffs did not discriminate between members of the Community). The Community also established a Development Fund which disbursed $581 million in a first quinquennium and $730 million in a second. In 1964, by the first Convention of Yaounde, eighteen former French colonies took advantage of these provisions and in 1969 three former British territories – Kenya, Uganda, Tanzania – were granted the same privileges for one year (until, that is, a revised Yaounde Convention should come into operation in 1971). Nigeria too negotiated an agreement with the Community. Although at first suspicious of these arrangements as a form of neo-colonialism Nigeria could not afford to see its neighbours trading on better terms than itself with the Community, to which two thirds of its exports were despatched. Again, the relations between the Community and its African associates could be attacked on the grounds that, despite their tangible advantages, they tended to perpetuate the colonial pattern instead of modernizing and diversifying the post-colonial economy. Further, some embarrassment was caused by the fact that a minority of the members of the UNCTAD lobby had, by securing a special position for themselves, broken the solidarity of the weaker nations. In 1974 a new convention for five years was signed at Lome, this time between the EEC and forty-six African, Caribbean and Pacific states. It made provision for non-reciprocal tariff reductions, created an aid fund of $1600 million and a scheme for stabilizing export prices, and promised the Commonwealth sugar producers access to the EEC for all their sugar at the prices assured by the Commonwealth Sugar Agreement.

The third major post-independence African problem was the ordering of its new states. The nationalist leaders who became prime ministers and presidents were faced with the testing and largely unexplored problem of finding suitable political forms for their states. Both the colonial régimes and the nationalist movements which had evolved as their mirror-images were authoritarian and monarchistic, and yet it had been presumed that upon liberation the new states would adopt the home and not the export models of European polities, would dissolve their unified national movements into two or more political parties, and would convert from autocracy to democracy at the hoisting of a new flag and at the very moment when an economic revolution was to be imposed on a barely completed political one. Even the most stable and experienced government, backed by a politically sophisticated people, might have baulked at this prospect. In Africa in the fifties and sixties it was a remote and impracticable as Utopia. Successful national leaders saw to it that they remained in charge, partly no doubt because they wanted to for selfish reasons as well as good ones, but partly also because it was expected of them and because their countries would have fared worse if they had not. Their methods varied and not all of them succeeded (one of the ablest, Sylvanus Olympio of Togo, was murdered); some established an arbitrary or even a slightly crazy personal predominance; others genuinely experimented with democratic forms which might prove suitable to their circumstances; some had to cope with personal feuds and others with tribal ones; a surprising number of them survived and governed.

The outside world tended to confuse democratic experiment with personal waywardness, and the west was tempted to write off the new rulers as demagogic autocrats and their entourages as exceptionally corrupt. In addition African attempts to devise a specifically African socialism (i.e. to find ways of making deep social and economic changes in African society without simply importing semi-appropriate western socialist measures wholesale) caused westerners to label African leaders as communists and to suspect them of wishing to play an anti-western part in the cold war – although the charm of the word socialism in African ears owed at least as much to the sympathy of western European left wingers as to the example of the USSR or China – or indeed of Marx whose basic postulate of a class struggle between capital and labour, between a bourgeoisie and an urban proletariat, had little meaning in countries which had neither. The personal style of leadership, carried over from the anti-colonial struggle into the politics of independence, further alienated western opinion when it tended to degenerate into authoritarianism. Strong government is notoriously an enemy of fair government, and when strong government was equated in Africa with single-party rule, western democrats in particular with their memories of European fascism became critical. The ex-colonial powers felt that their superior values had been superciliously discarded after a cynically short interval, and the enemies of the black man spread accounts and prophecies of misrule, for which the black man himself occasionally provided material. In the west the concept of leadership had become so debased by its perversion into the *Führerprinzip* that the African democrat who was genuinely trying to use his power to hold his country together and teach it democratic practices (as for instance President Nyerere) was given scant credit. Whereas in the west a free political opposition with a genuine prospect of taking over the government was regarded as the touchstone of democracy, in new states an opposition was more often held to be – and often was – a separatist movement, tribal or religious or merely local, aiming at the disruption of the state under cover of western democratic slogans. In the west opposition was almost automatically regarded as loyal opposition; in new states it was equally automatically branded as disloyal to the concept and very existence of the state, besides sabotaging the essential tasks of peaceful economic development. It is not to be disputed that this view of opposition led in places to unjust and excessive repression, but it was wrong to generalize from these examples that the basic political philosophy was either intrinsically vicious or inappropriate to Africa. The new states were trying to evolve politically through a phase of benevolent oligarchy, steering with varied success between the perils of evil autocracy and weak democracy, between – in European terms – King Bomba of Naples and the Weimar Republic. They staged in the process frequent military coups. These occurred in the sixties on an average of about three a year. Some of them were challenges to authority to do something about a grievance (East Africa in 1964); some were serious revolts (Nigeria in 1966); many were bloodless or almost bloodless ways of changing a government which, in the absence of established constitutional machinery, was difficult to change in any other way. Despite the chaos in the Congo in 1960–64 and the horrors in Nigeria in 1966–70 independent Africa did not become the scene of carnage which some had predicted. It had been supposed that the boundaries between the new states, artificially created by the colonial powers, would not be accepted after the colonial carpet had been rolled away and that a series of border wars would break out, but in the outcome internal conflicts within over-large states proved more lethal – in Congo, Nigeria, Sudan – than disputes between states.

The relations between the new states of Africa presented a special problem because of the heritage of pan-Africanism. The nationalist movements which had become governments had been linked in a common opposition to colonialism and continued to be linked by a common opposition to South African apartheid. They also inherited a general or pan-African disposition which had its origins in ideas of the cultural community of the Negro peoples and which, after liberation, became a strand in African political thinking along with the desire to develop the new states and to extend liberation to the southern tip of the continent. This pan-Africanism was to some extent in competition with the development of African states as independent sovereign nations committed to the preservation of their integrity as well as their independence. Whereas before liberation independence meant the eviction of foreign rulers, after liberation independence and integrity implied on the one hand anti-tribalism and on the other anti-internationalism: the achievement to be defended and strengthened was the state.

Six Pan-African conferences, held between 1900 and 1945, were succeeded by meetings of African parties and African governments. The former created an All African Peoples Organization which, at conferences in Accra in 1958, Tunis in 1960 and Cairo in 1961, discussed schemes for African unity or an African commonwealth on the basis that co-operation between governments was not enough. For their part the increasing number of independent governments held a series of conferences of independent African states, beginning in Accra in 1958. At this date there were nine independent states in Africa. One of them, South Africa, declined the invitation to Accra. The others were Ethiopia, Liberia, Egypt, Morocco, Tunisia, Libya, Ghana and Guinea. They were chiefly concerned with anti-colonialism, the racial and nationalist struggles in South Africa and Algeria, and the problem of achieving some sort of African unity while at the same time respecting the independence and integrity of African states. This conference was followed in May 1959 by the Declaration of Conakry whereby Ghana and Guinea formed a union which was declared to be the starting point of a wider African union. This step was an unpremeditated retort to the ostracizing of Guinea by France, a practical demonstration of Nkrumah's pan-African principles and a lifeline for Guinea. It was followed in July of the same year by the Declaration of Saniquellie which, primarily on Liberian insistence, emphasized the independence and integrity of existing states.

By 1960, when the second conference of independent African states assembled in Addis Ababa, their number had almost doubled and their unity was about to be tested by the special strains of the Congo as well as by inherited border disputes. Fifteen states were represented. Active border disputes involved Ethiopia and Somalia, Ghana and Togo, Guinea and the Cameroons. The first of these disputes led to fighting on a not inconsiderable scale but the others did not. More serious for the prospects of African unity was a contest between Ghana and Nigeria in which Ghana urged the case for immediate steps to unity and Nigeria argued in favour of a slow approach to something like a federation. This dispute was spiced with some bitterness between the protagonists since the Nigerians resented Nkrumah's assumption of leadership and distrusted his aims, while Nkrumah feared that Nigeria intended to throw the influence of its vast size on to the side of conservatism versus socialism and of Nigerian nationalism versus pan-Africanism. In the Congo the independent African states tried, both at the UN and in a conference at Leopoldville in August 1960, to present a united front and play a constructive and pacificatory role, but they were not successful.

From this point the independent African states began to form separate groups which were later reassembled in one organization by the founding of the Organization for African Unity. The largest of these was the Brazzaville group consisting of all the former French colonies except Guinea, with the addition of Mauritania (whose claim to be independent and not a part of Morocco was accepted by the group). The Brazzaville group began as an *ad hoc* meeting at Abidjan in October 1960 when the principal topic for discussion was Algeria, but at Brazzaville in December and at further meetings during 1961 at Dakar, Yaounde and Tananarive it developed into a permanent association, discussed ways of perpetuating the co-operation and common services which had existed in the colonial period, set up an organization for economic co-operation, and considered joint institutions and defence arrangements. This group was neither pan-African nor regional, but an expression of common needs and a common outlook.

A second group took shape at a conference at Casablanca in January 1961. This group consisted of six independent African states plus the Algerian revolutionaries and Ceylon. The six African states were Morocco, Egypt and Libya (which soon afterwards transferred to the Brazzaville group) and Ghana, Guinea and Mali (which had joined the Ghana–Guinea union in the previous year). The Casablanca group opposed the independence of Mauritania and was pro-Lumumbist in the Congo, although at its second conference in May in Cairo Nkrumah strongly opposed proposals to withdraw troops from the UN force and switch them to Gizenga and prevailed upon his associates. This group too established permanent organs, including political, economic and cultural committees, a supreme command, and a headquarters at Bamako in Mali.

In August 1961 no fewer than twenty states assembled in conference at Monrovia. They included the whole of the Brazzaville group, Libya and a majority of former British territories. The Monrovia group thus subsumed the Brazzaville group and, owing to the prominence of Nigeria, acquired a specifically anti-Ghanaian and anti-Nkrumah flavour. The movement for African unity seemed to have been blocked by current problems (the Congo and, to a lesser extent, Mauritania) and by personalities. Nevertheless the idea remained alive. Even if Nkrumah's vision of a union extending into every part of the continent was unacceptable or impracticable, lesser unions might be attempted. The Ghana–Guinea union, with or without Mali, had proved of little practical consequence, but it had been a political demonstration rather than a true regional association. In the north-west Morocco, Tunisia and Algeria espoused federation prematurely, at a meeting in Tangier in April 1958. In east and central Africa there was talk of a federation between Kenya, Uganda, Tanganyika, Zanzibar, Malawi, Zambia and Rhodesia – with possible extensions in some barely visible future to Rwanda, Burundi, Mozambique and even South Africa. A Pan-African Freedom Movement of East and Central Africa (Pafmeca) came into existence in 1958, was enlarged four years later by adding 's' for South as its penultimate letter and was dissolved in 1963; these were associations for self-help in the struggle for liberation.

The French connection was at the base of a number of interstate organizations: the Entente Council (Ivory Coast, Niger, Upper Volta, Toga and Dahomey – see p. 335); the Senegal River Association (Senegal, Mali, Guinea, Mauritania – *ibid.*); a West African and a Central African Customs Union. More important than any of these was the African and Malagasy Economic Union (UAMCE) founded in 1965 by thirteen formerly French and Belgian territories and converted into the African and Malagasy Common Organization (OCAM) whose charter, signed at Tananarive in 1966, declared it to be open to all African states – provided existing members all accepted each new-comer. OCAM created a number of useful agencies which were sometimes more effective than those of the OAU, but politically its members were often divided. In the sixties it was seen as a weapon for Houphouet-Boigny of the Ivory Coast against Nkrumah and in support of Tshombe; in the Nigerian civil war, in which it tried in vain to mediate, Ivory Coast and Gabon recognized Biafra while the remainder were strongly anti-separatist; some members had diplomatic relations with China, others with Taiwan. As the colonial period receded the common French inheritance became a weaker link. There were a number of absentees from the eighth congress held at Lome in 1972 and Zaïre, feeling that it was not getting enough out of membership, resign-ed from the organization.

Although the Congo had demonstrated the difficulty of preserving unity among independent African states, it had no less demonstrated the advantages of doing so if at all possible, and a conference at Lagos in 1962 produced a draft charter for an organization of African States. At a further conference in Addis Ababa in 1963 the Organization for African Unity was born with an initial membership of thirty-two. The OAU was not a collective security organization as envisaged and en-dorsed by article 51 of the charter of the UN but an organization for the promotion of African unity and collaboration and for the eradication of colonialism. It consisted of an annual assembly of heads of state, a council of ministers and a secretariat. A projected commission of mediation, conciliation and arbitration did not materialize, although these functions were in fact performed: in border disputes between Morocco and Algeria, between Somalia and Ethiopia and Somalia and Kenya, and between Ghana and Upper Volta. In the last case, which rose out of the construction by Ghana of a school on territory claimed by Upper Volta, Ghana conceded the claim at a meeting of the OAU's council of ministers. In the other cases the OAU provided mediators and commissions of inquiry which helped to appease the disputes.

The establishment of this organization epitomized two processes which had been going on for a generation or more and had gathered force in the twenty years after the end of the Second World War. Africans ceased to be cut off from each other and they ceased to be cut off from world affairs. Their emancipation had a great variety of causes: the essential liberalism of the colonial powers, the growth of the move-ment for human rights, American and Russian attacks on colonialism, the Gandhian example, the development of roads and of international airways. While this process was taking place a new class of African, the politician, the lawyer, the intellectual, the *évolué*, was taking the place of the chief and was at the same time rejecting the models prepared for his country by the French and the British. The French had assumed that their colonies would grow into worthy pieces of France, but they had hardly noticed that their doctrine worked neither in terms of government, which was paternalistic and white, nor in terms of society, where low wages and even forced labour were too long tolerated and the favoured few tended not to become leaders in their society but to be extracted from it. The British, who had based themselves originally on paternalism and chiefs, realized the limitations of this model but planned to substitute for it an inapplicable British parliamentary system to be worked by an élite. Consequently the new states – albeit that many of their leaders had originally insisted on western democratic institutions as the best available and had expected them to work without essential modification – found that they had to innovate in theory as well as in practice. They had to find administrators, public servants, economists, teachers, doctors, accountants and trade union leaders and at the same time construct institutions and develop conventions which would reconcile the Africans' traditions with their thirst for modernity and enable them to enjoy the fruits of efficiency, liberty and justice. They looked at the outside world with a mixture of admiration and suspicion, ready to take the best of what could be learned but convinced that however much they adopted they would evolve a distinct African way of doing things and a separate African culture. This community of aim gave the new states of Africa points of contact with each other which were implicit rather than advertised and which gave their organization a kind of initial cohesion which was not be to found in the Organization of American States or the Arab League or even the European Economic Community.

Finally, in their relations with major powers Africans were inevitably influenced by the colonial past and by the support given by white men outside Africa to white rulers in Africa. France retained much influence. Although it had exercised dominion over Africans its rule had not been marked by whites-only clubs and privileges as blatantly as had been the case in other colonies. The economic weakness of many of the successor states was no doubt an advantage for France but was not by itself sufficient to explain France's comparatively good standing in Africa in the immediate post-colonial period. Britain's responsibility in Rhodesia prevented it from establishing firmly satisfactory relations. But this residual and continuing anti-western current tempted only insignificant minorities to the further step of taking sides in the cold war. For the most part Africans, like Asians and for much the same reasons, wanted to keep out of the cold war and regarded it not so much as a deep moral cosmic cleavage as an opportunity to get aid and favours from the richer members in both camps. So long as the western powers regarded neutralism in the cold war as immoral, this attitude was an additional obstacle to good relations between the new African states and the west, but it abated when the fifties gave place to the sixties and new leaders in the west began to look less frenetically on Afro-Asian neutralism.

The Russians were initially ambivalent or even hostile to neutralism, denouncing leaders like Nehru and Nasser as bourgeois western stooges, but from the mid-fifties they began to support non-communists as well as communists, partly because the former were more numerous and effective, partly perhaps because communism as an ideology mattered little to them outside Europe, and partly because in the Russian diplomatic tradition buffer states had played a prominent role which was analogous to the intermediate role of the neutralist in the ideological conflicts of the cold war and so made that role less repulsive to them than it was to Americans like John Foster Dulles. The Russians had and exploited a number of advantages. They enjoyed a reputation for having effected a remarkable economic revolution on their own and for following it after the war with even more startling technological advances. They displayed a flattering interest in African affairs, for example by the part they played at the Afro-Asian conference in Cairo in December 1957 and by establishing in 1959 an African Institute separated from the long-established Institute for Oriental Studies in which African studies had previously been lodged. They offered financial and technical aid in competition with the west and on easy terms, they organized welcome cultural exchanges and visits, and they disseminated in Africa views on disarmament and peacekeeping which Africans were glad to hear. But they remained suspect because they too were protagonists in the cold war, because they were alarmingly powerful and communist and white, and because when the test came in the Congo they tried to take independent action outside the UN and to establish a foothold in Africa by interfering in its affairs in ways no less unwelcome than those of the Belgians.

The Chinese enjoyed the advantages of being non-white, far away, uncommitted in the cold war and relatively underdeveloped. They made a favourable impression on Africans and Asians at the Bandung conference of 1955. In 1958, when their troubles with the USSR had become serious, they took their first major steps in Africa by recognizing the government established by the Algerian insurgents, extending aid to Guinea on its breach with France and making contact with rebellious dissidents in the Cameroons. The central committee of the Chinese communist party set up in 1961 an African affairs committee to develop African studies and prosecute Chinese interests in Africa. Propaganda was broadcast, literature was disseminated, scholarships were offered, and in 1963–4 Chou En-lai made an extensive tour of African states in a spirit similar to de Gaulle's tour of Latin America some months later. Loans and gifts were given to Algeria, Kenya and Tanganyika; missions were established in Burundi and Congo-Brazzaville where, on the borders of Congo-Leopoldville, guerrillas were offered practical and theoretical training; in Zanzibar China was the quickest to seize the opportunities presented by the transfer of power to a minority and won a footing on Africa's offshore island which the amalgamation with Tanganyika contained but did not eliminate. Africans responded to these Chinese moves. China became popular in

Africa and many leaders established diplomatic and personal contacts: Guinea established diplomatic relations with Peking in 1960, closely followed by Ghana, Mali, Nigeria and others; for Sekou Touré and Kwame Nkrumah were the first of many African leaders to visit Peking (in 1960 and 1961 respectively) and set a pattern of economic and cultural agreements. There were exceptions – in 1966 for example Kenyatta ejected Chinese (and Russian and Czechoslovak) diplomats and journalists and forced a breach between himself and Oginga Odinga, China's chief Kenyan partisan, as a result of which Odinga and his few followers lost their positions in government and party and were rejected by the electorate. But the list of countries gratefully accepting Chinese aid grew steadily – Zambia, Somalia, Sudan, Mali, Guinea – the more so because the aid was tactfully given. Its most notable monument, the Tanzam railway, was completed in 1976.

Chapter 18

Northern Africa

The whole of the North African coast came under European domination – French, Italian, British – during the nineteenth century or soon afterwards. The British sphere in Egypt has been considered elsewhere in this book but the rest of the area, though preponderantly Arab and Muslim, will be considered here in its geographical African context. So too will the Sudan, the country where the dividing line between Arab and African cultures is most evident.

The French invaded Algeria in 1830 and declared it a part of metropolitan France in 1848. As a consequence of their occupation of Algeria they became involved in the two neighbouring monarchies of Tunisia to the east and Morocco to the west, then under the nominal suzerainty of the Ottoman sultan. By the Bardo Treaty of 1881 they established a protectorate over Tunisia, a poor and relatively small country with a population, in 1945, of only 3 million. In Morocco the evanescence of the Ottoman sultan's power coincided with the decay of the Moroccan sultan's own authority, thus creating an invitation and an excuse for foreign intervention, but French power was not so easily substituted owing to the ambitions of other European states. In the first years of the twentieth century France obtained a free hand in Morocco by conceding the same to Italy and Britain in Libya and Egypt, by defeating a claim by Germany (which accepted compensation in central Africa) and by allowing Spain to appropriate the northern strip whence the Arabs had invaded Spain 1200 years earlier. The Treaty of Fez with the sultan in 1912 crowned these diplomatic successes and established a protectorate of the same kind as the French protectorate over Tunisia, although the whole country was not brought under effective French control until the nineteen-thirties. Tangier became an international zone and consequently a fiddlers' paradise. The Italians reaped the reward of their complaisance when they were allowed in 1911 to take Tripolitania from the Turks on the eve of the Balkan wars.

During the Second World War the whole of northern Africa became a battlefield or, in the case of Morocco, a military rear area. Equally important were the political concomitants of the war, especially the Atlantic Charter, the eviction of France from the Arab countries of Syria and Lebanon, and the appearance on the scene of the Americans, including President Franklin D. Roosevelt himself who had a much publicized interview with the Sultan of Morocco, Mohammed V ben

Yusuf. The Tunisian nationalist leader Habib Bourguiba was released from a French prison in 1943, went to Cairo in 1945 and thence to the United States, and settled in his native country once more in 1949. The Moroccan leader Allal al-Fasi, who had been in prison from 1937 to 1946, also went in 1947 to Cairo and then settled temporarily in Tangier. In 1947 the newly created Arab League established a Maghrib Bureau (Maghrib = West in Arabic; the Maghrib comprises at least Morocco, Algeria and Tunisia, sometimes Tripolitania as well), thus institutionalizing the Arab interest in the affairs of North Africa which was to become deeper and more effective in the coming years.

Both France and Italy had been defeated during the war. Both, however, ended up on the winning side. In North African terms Italy paid the price of defeat while France won the rewards of victory; Italy lost its African colonies while France was reinstated in the Maghrib.

1. Libya

The fate of Italy's colonies was to be resolved by the foreign ministers of the four principal victorious powers by September 1948, failing which the problem would be transferred to the United Nations. The British and Italian governments devised a plan, called after their foreign ministers the Bevin-Sforza plan, whereby an independent Libyan state would come into existence at the end of ten years and during the inter-val its existing three parts would be under British or Italian tutelage: the Fezzan (which was coveted by the French as an addition to Tunisia) under Italian trusteeship, Tripolitania in the middle under British administration for two years and Italian trusteeship for eight, and Cyrenaica further east under British trusteeship for the whole ten years. This plan was objectionable to the Arabs and to the Russians, who proposed a five-year UN trusteeship (they also proposed UN trusteeships of five and ten years for Eritrea and Italian Somaliland). The political committee of the Assembly accepted the Bevin-Sforza plan but the Assembly itself just failed to endorse it and there followed a period of negotiation and investigation by a UN commissioner (Dr Adrian Pelt), as a result of which the whole of Italy's North African em-pire was converted into a tripartite constitutional monarchy under the emir of Cyrenaica, Muhammad Idris as-Sanusi, as King Idris of Libya. The new state came into being on the first day of 1952 and shortly afterwards entered into an agreement with Britain which secured es-sential economic aid and arms to Libya and military rights to Britain in the small post of El Adem. The Americans subsequently established a larger base at Wheelus Field. In 1969 the king was ousted by army officers, who were disgruntled by corruption in high places. Their leader was Colonel Gadafi who disdained the conventions by interfer-ing wherever possible to help (notably the Palestinians) or harry (oil companies, communists, Israel and established governments, especially monarchical).

2. The Maghrib

In the Maghrib the French, aware of the need for changes, sought modifications within the framework of the Bardo and Fez treaties, but the nationalists aimed to terminate the protectorate status altogether. In all three territories the French had encouraged immigration, so that there was a considerable French population settled on the land or in business alongside the French administrators who ran the government of Algeria and had also come to do much the same in Morocco and Tunisia in spite of the sovereignty of sultan and bey. French education had nurtured an élite which appreciated French culture, as the French intended, but also became attracted to the idea of independence, which the French had not foreseen. These modernizing nationalists found themselves allied, if on this point only, with traditionalist malcontents who resented the French presence from a conservative and Muslim standpoint. Caught between these currents the bey of Tunis wavered ineffectually until he was more or less captured by the French, to his eventual discomfiture, while the much younger sultan of Morocco wavered more purposefully, attached himself to the nationalist movement and was exiled by the French, to his eventual benefit.

The governments of the fourth French republic were all coalitions which contained ministers who wanted to meet nationalist movements more than half-way and other ministers who did not want to make life unpleasant for the settlers. This was an impossible combination which rendered France ineffective, allowed Tunisia and Morocco to achieve their aims and drove the largest group of settlers, the Algerian, to revolt against the government of France. The first French plan was also the first French failure. The French Union, conceived in 1946, created the new category of Associated States with Morocco and Tunis, and also Vietnam, Laos and Cambodia, in mind, but whereas the Asian trio accepted this new status the African pair refused it. There were, however, reasonable hopes of a settlement with Tunisia after the return of Bourguiba in 1949 and until his arrest early in 1952. Robert Schuman, prime minister of France, spoke in 1950 of the ultimate independence of the protected states, and internal reforms of a democratic nature were seriously discussed; Bourguiba's Neo Destour party was represented in the bey's government. But many nationalists regarded the reforms as inadequate except possibly as a first step, whereas the French regarded them as a long step with no immediate next step in sight. By the end of 1951 the dialogue had turned into rivalry for the support of the bey who was himself so uncertain of his better course that he appeared sometimes to be a nationalist and sometimes a puppet of the French who were pressing him to accept the projected reforms.

At the beginning of 1962 a tougher line gained ground in Paris. Bourguiba was arrested in January and the prime minister, Muhammad Chenik, was dismissed and arrested in March. The bey accepted the French programme and a number of nationalists fled to Cairo. In Tunisia constitutional changes which had been meant to please the nationalists were imposed by authority against their will. The attempt to reach agreement bilaterally had failed, for the acquiescence of the bey was unimportant by contrast with the disagreement of the nationalists who now carried the debate into the international sphere. The next two years merely confirmed the failure and exposed its consequences. Then in 1954 Pierre Mendès-France, after his blitz peace in Indo-China, insisted that the Tunisian problem must be solved no less radically. He flew to Tunisia accompanied by the right wing Marshal Juin to propose full internal self-government. He fell from power in February 1955 before his initiative had borne fruit, but his successor Edgar Faure pursued the negotiations and in June Bourguiba accepted the French proposals as a step towards independence and returned to Tunisia. Nine months later, on 20 March 1956, Tunisia became fully independent and concluded a treaty with France which included provision for the stationing of French troops in the country.

The Moroccan case was not very different. A period of genuine negotiation revealed to both sides the gap between the French programme of democratic gradualism and the nationalists' determination to get independence very soon. The principal difference between the Moroccan and Tunisian cases lay in the temper of the ruler. Mohammad V ben Yusuf had shown signs of allying himself with the Istiqlal (Independence) party at the end of the war, and by so doing he had destroyed the basis of government in Morocco which, during the seven-year term of office of General Noguès as resident-general, had rested upon the good personal relations between the two men – the *dialogue sultan-résident*. A second major factor was the isolation of the French settlers from the outside world during the war years 1940–42, an isolation which had larger consequences in Morocco than Tunisia because the French community in Morocco was also isolated from the surrounding Muslims by Lyautey's pre-war policy of siting new French towns away from the traditional centres of Moroccan life. From 1947 to 1951 Marshal Juin was resident-general, but in spite of his somewhat forbidding presence a new *dialogue* Paris-Fez was initiated and the sultan visited the French capital in 1950. The French, however, believed that they had an alternative to treating with the nationalists, whom they and some Moroccans were tempted to write off as uncharacteristic and irresponsible townees, of less significance than traditional personages like the pro-French, and anti-sultan, pasha of Marrakesh, el Glaoui. The sultan was persuaded – he subsequently said coerced – into signing in 1951 decrees initiating the reforms which the French were prepared to introduce, but the consequent agitation in Morocco and elsewhere in the Arab world caused him to swing away from the French and for a year there was increasing uncertainty and disorder, culminating in December 1952 in violent and barbaric anti-white outbursts in Casablanca. In the following February the sultan was sent into exile. His absence, however, did not serve to restore order or strengthen French rule, while in Spanish Morocco an assembly of notables refused to recognize the exiled sultan's uncle, Muhammad ben Arafa, whom the French had placed on the throne. In 1955, following the settlement with Tunisia, the sultan was brought back and before the end of the year France had agreed to concede full independence. It took effect on 2 March 1956. Both Morocco and Tunisia became full members of the Arab League in October 1958.

By this time the Algerian revolt against France, a far more serious problem, had begun. Hostilities which opened in the Aurès mountains in 1954 were at first regarded as a fresh instalment of familiar colonial troubles but they developed into a war which involved the flower of the French army, the full panoply of military rule and censorship and terrorism and torture, three separate white French challenges to the authority of Paris, the fall of the Fourth Republic and the achievement by Algeria – uniquely in Africa – of independence by force of arms. The Algerian situation was without any close parallel in the rest of Africa. The European population had been a part of the country for much longer than any other settler community, it was nearer to the mother country, and in the main cities it was as numerous or almost as numerous as the Muslims; its services to Algeria were conspicuous. Juridically too the situation was peculiar since Algeria was constitutionally a part of metropolitan France, so that Frenchmen who failed even to envisage a severance were maintaining an unreality which was nevertheless no fiction. The legal position contributed to a stubborn psychological attitude which caused outsiders to wonder why it was that Frenchmen alone in the world were unable to see that their days as rulers in Algeria were numbered. The French moreover, like the British in the Middle East after the retreat from India, hated the thought of further surrenders after the collapse of their empire in Indo-China; just as Africans were encouraged by the ending of French and British rule in Asia, so in reverse were the French and British influenced in their African policies by their post-war experiences in Asia, making in Algeria and Egypt in particular mistakes of timing and understanding which they might have avoided if they had not felt that their descent from the first rank was proving too hasty for dignity or safety.

In Algeria, additionally, senior French officers developed in the shadow of the defeat in Indo-China a sense of mission so strong that it distorted their sense of proportion and led them in the end to jettison their oaths of allegiance. These officers convinced themselves that they belonged to the gallant and prescient category of the saviour with the sword, that they alone appreciated the full import of the communist threat to civilization, and that theirs was the honourable destiny of leading the resistance to the hosts of darkness and opening the eyes of woolly-minded sluggards to the dangers and responsibilities of the twentieth century. This apocalyptic determinism was accompanied by an almost equally passionate emotion which was local and practical instead of cosmic and visionary. The day-to-day business of administering large tracts of Algeria had become the responsibility of the army, and in the course of governing their localities officers had acquired a proficiency, knowledge and sympathy for the people in their care which, they rightly judged, would not easily be supplied by anybody else.

There was a forestaste of revolt at Sétif in 1945. Like a similar rising in Madagascar in the same year, this revolt was suppressed with brutality and many casualties; France in 1945 was in no position to do things by halves. The nationalist leader Ferhat Abbas was arrested and the French community was given the incentive and the excuse to arrogate to itself an authority which belonged rightly to the government in Paris. The weaknesses and divisions of the governments of the Fourth Republic allowed this authority to be exercised and enhanced until the return to power of General de Gaulle in 1958 put it to a test which it failed. There was, however, no effective nationalist threat to French rule during the decade between the Sétif rising in 1945 and the revolt in the Aurès mountains at the end of 1954. During these years French ministers and governors-general tried to temper the repression of nationalism with economic advancement and democratic reform, but they failed to mollify the nationalists whose aim was not reform but independence and they antagonized the European community whose preoccupation with repression left little room for anything else.

This dilemma was illustrated vividly during the first stage of the revolt. The defeat of the Faure government in November 1955 had been followed by a general election and the installation of a minority government led by Guy Mollet. The new prime minister attempted to find a way to bring the fighting to an end. Yet when he went to Algiers he was pelted with garbage by Europeans, while approaches to leaders of the insurrectionary FLN were entirely unproductive. Mollet appointed General Catroux, a widely respected and liberally minded proconsul, to the governor-generalship, but Catroux resigned his office within a week and without leaving France. In May 1956 Mendès-France resigned from the Mollet government on the grounds that it was not doing enough, while the prime minister probably felt that if he ventured more boldly he would provoke a trial of strength between Paris and the Europeans in Algeria, which Paris would not win. In October 1956 the weakness of Paris was dramatically illustrated, and its position with regard to the FLN seriously damaged, when five FLN leaders, including Ahmed Ben Bella, were kidnapped when returning by air from a meeting with the sultan of Morocco. The aircraft in which they were travelling, which was registered in France and piloted by a Frenchman although operated by a non-French company, was diverted from its destination to Algiers without the knowledge of the government in Paris. During the next eighteen months political attitudes remained irreconcilable, the French army and the FLN secured positions in which neither could defeat the other, terrorism increased on both sides and spread to Paris and other cities in France, torture became a regular instrument of government and was seen to be, and any lingering intention of applying the new compromise constitution called the Algerian Statute of 1947 was finally abandoned. The impasse seemed to be complete, politically and militarily.

In this same period Morocco and Tunisia were drawn more closely into the conflict. The sultan of Morocco had been deeply offended by the kidnapping of Ben Bella who had been his guest but an hour or two earlier, and Bourguiba was angered when the French, irritated by the FLN's freedom to use Tunisian and Moroccan soil as an asylum where they could rest and refit without fear of attack, delivered an air attack on Sakiet in Tunisia in February 1958 and killed seventy-five people; Bourguiba threatened to stop supplies to French units in Tunisia. The Moroccan monarch and the Tunisian president had met at Rabat at the end of 1957 and had offered to mediate but the French, deceived into optimism by some recent successes in the field, had declined. Bourguiba persisted in his attempts to find a peaceful solution, not without some regard to the increasing links between the FLN and Egypt with which he was on bad terms as a result of an attempt on his life for which he blamed Nasser. There was talk of a Maghribian federation to include an independent Algeria, Morocco and Tunisia.

On 28 May 1958 the last civilian prime minister of the Fourth French Republic, Pierre Pflimlin, resigned, a victim of the Algerian war for which he and five predecessors could find no solution. On 13 May Algiers had rebelled against Paris. On 30 May, so it was planned, this government would seize power in Paris by a coup. Almost the whole of Corsica, the stepping stone, had accepted the rebel régime and half the commanders of the military regions in France were believed to be disloyal. Only one obstacle to success in the capital remained – a Frenchman of enormous prestige and oustanding political skill. On 1 June General de Gaulle was invested with full powers. On 4 June he flew to Algiers.

It is only possible to guess what policy de Gaulle had in June 1958. He may have had no fixed policy but he probably saw the inevitable end. What happened was that, by a mixture of authority and ambiguity, he imposed himself upon the situation and gradually acquired the power to impose a solution upon it. This took him nearly four years. By doing enough to retain the initiative, but not too much to reveal himself, he prevented potentially hostile groups from acting against him until it was too late. He began by patching up relations with Tunisia and Morocco, agreeing to withdraw French forces from both countries (except from the Tunisian naval base at Bizerta). He next moved from Algeria many senior officers who, even were they minded to object to their postings, could not gainsay the legitimacy of an order from *the* general. General Salan, a prime rallying point for disaffection and leader of the May *putsch*, was permitted to remain temporarily in his command, but he was relieved of his civilian functions which were now once more divorced from the supreme military command. After these preliminary moves, and with cautious deliberation, de Gaulle prepared his first major statement on the future status of Algeria and made his first bid for peace with the FLN. In September 1959 he formulated a choice (not unlike his offer to France's colonies in western and central Africa in 1958) between independence, integration with France and association with France, the choice to be made within four years from the end of hostilities, defined as any year in which fewer than 200 people had been killed in fighting or by terrorism. This pronouncement precipitated a second white revolt. On 24 January 1960 the European community showed that it would oppose even de Gaulle rather than accept the independence of Algeria. The revolt was a failure. The French government, acting energetically in Algeria and at home, showed in return how the authority and power of Paris had grown during the past eighteen months. But to Algerians de Gaulle's offer in 1959 was no more than a half-way house, a solution short of true independence and by now unacceptable.

Support for de Gaulle within France, more widespread and more positive in 1960 than in 1958, was partly due to a feeling that the war hd gone on too long and partly to restiveness over the methods which were being used to wage it. henri Alleg's book *La Question* focused attention on the use of torture by units of the French army. The trial of Alleg in 1960, followed by the disappearance and (as it was correctly surmised) murder of the French communist university lecturer Maurice Audin, the trial in 1961 of the Algerian girl Djamila Boupacha, protests by the Roman Catholic cardinals occupying French sees, and a manifesto signed by 121 leading intellectuals, all contributed to turn French opinion against the French community and the French army in Algeria. Towards the end of 1960 the leaders of the January revolt were themselves put on trial. But there was still one white rebellion to come. It came in April 1961. It was led by four generals and it lasted four days. Two of the four generals, Salan and Jouhaud, were subsequently sentenced to death *in absentia* and the other two, Challe and Zeller, who surrendered, to fifteen years' imprisonment – all sentences being eventually reduced. Out of the failure of this rebellion arose the OAS (*Organisation de l'Armée Secrète*) which resorted to terrorism and, by creating among the European population fears of reprisals by an independent Algerian government, provoked – as independence became inevitable – an exodus which deprived the country of much needed skills in administration, education and other public services.

De Gaulle's victory on the white front was not at first accompanied by any improvement in the nationalist quarter. In September 1959 the FLN had proclaimed a provisional Algerian government with Ferhat Abbas as prime minister and the imprisoned Ben Bella as his deputy, and Ferhat Abbas had left Tunisia for Cairo which was to be the seat of government *pro tem*. De Gaulle, true to his general disposition, temporized after the defeat of the white revolt of January 1960, and this inactivity caused the Algerians to turn for help to Moscow and Peking. During 1960 moreover it became apparent that the movement of opinion among non-combatant Algerians was towards the FLN and its unequivocal demand for independence and not towards any middle position between the FLN and the Europeans (as de Gaulle may have hoped at the time of his pronouncement of September 1959). De Gaulle began therefore to move more purposefully towards negotiation with the FLN. A first secret encounter at Melun in June was a failure but after discussions between de Gaulle and Bourguiba, between FLN leaders and Georges Pompidou (still at this time a private banker) and between the FLN and Moroccans, Tunisians and Egyptians, a conference opened at Evian in May 1961. But suspicions and difficulties proved at this stage too great; the latter included the FLN's claim to be recognized as a government, the right of the imprisoned Ahmed Ben Bella to appear at the conference, guarantees for the French who might wish to remain in Algeria, continuing French rights in the naval base at Mers-el-Kebir, Saharan oil, and the conditions under which the proposed referendum on the status of Algeria would be held. This conference failed to reach agreement but in July de Gaulle, in a televised speech, unequivocally accepted Algerian independence. In the same month, however, Franco-Tunisian relations suffered a sharp relapse when Bourguiba, concerned about Tunisian rights in the Sahara, demanded a complete French evacuation of Bizerta (effected in October 1963 after Tunisia had laid its complaints before the United Nations, thus accentuating de Gaulle's dislike of that organization); and the FLN adopted a more assertive line when Yusuf Ben Khedda succeeded the more moderate Ferhat Abbas at the head of the provisional Algerian government, supported Bourguiba over Bizerta, and delivered some forceful speeches at the conference of non-aligned states in Belgrade in September. Still in the same month the OAS made an unsuccessful attempt on de Gaulle's life, OAS activities increased throughout France as well as Algeria, and there were rumours of the proclamation of a dissident French republic under General Salan in northern Algeria. In October Ben Khedda proposed a new round of negotiations.

The second Evian conference took place in March 1962. On 18 March a cease-fire agreement was signed. The conference also agreed on the terms for holding a referendum and, on the assumption that the result would be a vote in favour of independence, further agreed (among other things) that French troops would be withdrawn progressively over three years except from Mers-el-Kebir which France was to be permitted to occupy for at least fifteen years; that France might continue its nuclear tests in the Sahara and retain its airfields there for five years; that France would continue its economic activities in the Saharan oilfields; and that French technical and financial aid to Algeria would continue undiminished for at least three years. On 3 July 1962 Algeria became an independent sovereign state for the first time in history. But its leaders did not hold together. In the ensuing quarrels Ben Bella, returning to the scene after six years' absence in prison, won power but alienated colleagues and followers by moving too fast, by trying to reorganize the FLN on communist lines and by trying to play a leading and radical part in African and Afro-Asian affairs to the neglect of urgent domestic problems. In June 1965 he was overthrown when he was on the point of ousting his minister of defence, Colonel Houari Boumedienne, who succeeded him at the head of the government.

Boumedienne's policies included, in domestic affairs: a new structure of government, state capitalism, the nationalization of natural resources, vigorous exploitation of oil and gas deposits, and industrialization; in external affairs: cautiously good relations with the USSR, continued collaboration with France, a Maghrib entente, and active association with the Arab states against Israel. He ruled through a Council of the Revolution which was created at this point; he himself was its chairman but its further membership was undisclosed. He created in 1968 regional authorities for economic and social affairs and made them elective a year later. Dissatisfaction – sharply evinced by an abortive army revolt led by Colonel Tahar Zbiri – focused on the failure to partition all big estates at once or give workers in industry as much control in management as many of them wanted, but by the large the new government became quickly and firmly established. In the foreign field Boumedienne concluded a series of agreements with France for the development and nationalization of mining and other industries, securing both French aid and Algerian control. He also secured the return to Algeria of 300 works of art removed by the French. In 1967 France evacuated its remaining land bases in Algeria and next year the naval base at Mers-el-Kebir. Boumedienne visited Moscow soon after his accession to power, broke off diplomatic relations with Britain over Rhodesia, declared war on Israel and sent troops to fight it, and broke off relations with the United States. When a first pan-African cultural festival was held in Algiers in 1969 it was attended by the president of the USSR and the French foreign minister as well as a concourse of African and other notables.

In 1963, under Ben Bella's rule, Algeria had gone to war with Morocco over their common frontier. Morocco was also in dispute with Mauritania over frontiers. Both these conflicts were resolved in 1970, following talks between Boumedienne and the King of Morocco, Hassan II, in 1968 and a rapprochement between the king and the Mauritanian president, Ould Daddah, in 1969. The Moroccan-Algerian agreement fixed the border and provided for joint exploitation of iron ore at Tindouf on the basis that Tindouf was in Algeria. Morocco and Mauritania were drawn together by their opposition to Spain's continuing presence in Africa, a common cause which overrode the fact that both laid claim to Rio de Oro (Spanish Mauritania), a territory where the world's richest deposits of phosphates had been found in 1945. Morocco, itself heavily dependent on the export and therefore the world price of phosphates, would have liked to acquire the whole of Rio de Oro but was prepared to concede a great part of it to Mauritania rather than see there a new state, possibly with an Hispanophil monarch and extensive Spanish economic aid and tutelage. Spain on the other hand wished for a referendum which would produce a majority for independence. Morocco fought off this prospect by getting the UN to ask the World Court who had owned Rio de Oro before the Spanish got there. While the Court was deliberating Morocco and Mauritania reached agreement over the exploitation of the phosphates, and in 1975 King Hassan staged a three-day invasion which forced Spain to agree to transfer its sovereignty to these two states which thus defeated the aspirations of Algeria and the local independence movement.

3. The Sudan

The history of the Sudan in modern times is an alternation of subjection and self-rule. From 1820 to 1881 it was a part of the Ottoman empire in name and of its autonomous Egyptian pashalik in fact. From 1881 to 1898 it was ruled by the Mahdi. From 1899 to 1955 it was subject in theory to an Anglo-Egyptian condominium, in practice to Britain. In 1956 it became an independent state, and then a member of the Arab League and the United Nations.

The Anglo-Egyptian condominium reflected no Anglo-Egyptian agreement about the Sudan. The administering powers agreed in little and did not bother to co-operate. After the Anglo-Egyptian treaty of 1936 the British permitted a great degree of Eyptian penetration, but although the Sudan was coveted by Egyptian governments it attracted few Egyptian administrators. Sudanese nationalism gathered strength in the nineteen-thirties under the leadership of Ismail al-Azhari who became secretary of the Graduates General Congress, formed in 1938. Owing to the active role of Britain and the comparatively negative role of Egypt Sudanese nationalism was a first more anti-British than anti-Egyptian and indeed looked to Egypt to help displace the British. This predominantly anti-British streak was intensified during the Second World War when nationalists raised the issue of the Sudan's post-war status and received unsympathetic answers from the British who were fully occupied with present and pressing realities in the campaigns against the Italians in Ethiopia and against the Italians and the Germans in north Africa. The Egyptians sensed the opportunities in this situation and welcomed the formation by Azhari of the Ashigga Party which aimed at the union of the Sudan with Egypt. He had the support of Sayyid Ali el-Mirghani, one of the Sudan's two principal religious leaders. As a direct response a second party, the Umma Party, was created to work for the independence of the Sudan under the leadership of the Sudan's other principal religious leader, Sayyid Abd al-Rahman al-Mahdi, the posthumous son of the famous Mahdi of the eighteen-eighties. The Umma Party was suspected, or at any rate accused, by its opponents of dreaming of a revival of the Mahdist monarchy with British help.

The conflict between Britain and Egypt, which existed independently of the Sudan, was intensified by these moves and when the British administration took a step towards Sudanese self-government by creating an advisory council for the northern Sudan, the Egyptian prime minister, Mustafa al-Nahhas Pasha, resurrected the slogan of the unity of the Nile valley. The British also antagonized both the northern and the southern Sudan by omitting the south from the new councils; the south was affronted, while the north suspected Britain of a plan for detaching the south and annexing it to Uganda. This conflict, which was to lead to severe fighting on the eve of independence, was partly religious, partly racial and partly economic but fundamentally cultural in the broadest sense. The south comprised the three provinces of Bahr al-Ghazal, Upper Nile and Equatoria with a population of rather more than 3 million out of a total population of 10 million. These three provinces, bordering upon five African states (the Central African Republic, Congo, Uganda, Kenya and Ethiopia) looked to their African neighbours rather than to the Arab north. The inhabitants, although they included some 40 per cent of Muslim Africans, were predominantly negroid and pagan; some of the tribes continued to display the weaknesses inflicted by slavers from the north who had systematically removed the best men and women; the poverty of the south was worse than the poverty of the north. After the war the British, who had in the past been open to the charge that their administration accentuated the divide between north and south, adopted a policy of unification, but a conference held in 1946 contained no southern representatives and gave the south cause to complain that unification was really subordination. After a further conference at Juba in 1947 northerners claimed that the south had agreed to unification, while southerners denied this interpretation and continued to ask for separation from the north or a form of federation with guarantees.

This internal dispute was, however, partly obscured by the larger dispute between Egypt, insisting on the unity of the Nile valley, and Britain, insisting on the Sudan's right to decide for itself after a period of self-government under the British aegis. In 1947 Egypt accepted the principle of self-determination in the mistaken belief that it would produce a union of the two countries, but Britain and Egypt were still unable to agree on the immediate constitutional changes and in 1948

Britain introduced a new constitution without Egyptian concurrence. Legislative and executive councils covering the whole of the Sudan were established but the elections for them were boycotted by the pro-Egyptian parties. After anti-British demonstrations Azhari was arrested. Egypt was at this time embroiled in the Arab-Israeli war and its immediate aftermath.

In 1951 the British governor appointed a commission to consider further constitutional advances. The Sudan was plainly moving fast along the road through self-government to self-determination, and Egypt thereupon carried out a threat, uttered in 1950, to abrogate the condominium agreement of 1899 and the Anglo-Egyptian treaty of 1936. King Farouk was declared king of Egypt and the Sudan. But in 1952, as a result of the revolution in Egypt, he became king of neither.

A few months earlier Britain had produced a self-government statute for the Sudan which provided for the creation of a council of ministers, a house of representatives and a senate, and reserved to the governor only external affairs and ultimate emergency authority in domestic affairs. The new Egyptian government, whose chief, General Neguib, was half Sudanese, accepted the self-government statute, improved it (from the Sudanese point of view) and persuaded all the principal Sudanese parties to issue a pro-Egyptian declaration. The modified statute curbed the governor's authority by introducing a five-man international commission and by reducing special powers originally reserved to him in the south. It was embodied in an Anglo-Egyptian agreement of February 1953 and was intended to lead to independence not later than January 1961. Elections, preceded by vigorous Egyptian compaigning, were held at the end of 1953 and gave an overwhelming victory to Azhari's refurbished party, now called the National Unionist Party. Azhari became prime minister at the beginning of 1954. At the end of the same year Neguib was out.

The disappearance of Neguib was not the only cause of the ebbing of the pro-Egyptian tide in the Sudan. The tide had in fact not been flowing as strongly as it seemed, since the voting in 1953 had been more anti-British than pro-Egyptian. Two years after the elections the Sudan shook off both the British and the Egyptians and declared its independence, but before doing so it experienced mutiny and rebellion in the south. Disappointed by the new government's allocation of posts and by the persistent rejection of its demand for secession or a federal association, the south exploded in August 1955 as the result of an incident in which an army section turned upon its Arab officer. Disaffection spread rapidly and was only mastered when the prime minister invoked the aid of the British governor and moved substantial forces from the north into the south. The south, submitting, claimed that it had done so in reliance upon British mediation and was subsequently let down. Repression was certainly thorough and probably brutal. Southerners were executed in their hundreds and deported to the north in their thousands and fled to neighbouring African territories in their tens of thousands. The south became a closed area whence reliable information was difficult to obtain and was replaced by gruesome reports.

The revolt accelerated independence which was claimed by Azhari before the end of the year and inaugurated on the first day of 1956. It was followed by the break-up of Azhari's party, a coalition under him and then a coalition without him. New parties formed. Abdullah Khalil, who succeeded Azhari in 1956, grappled for two years with economic problems (lightened by an aid agreement with the United States in 1958) and with reviving fears of Egypt. In 1958 Egypt sent troops into two disputed areas on the Egyptian Sudanese border, but this tactless demonstration recoiled on Cairo at elections in the same year which gave the Umma Party the largest number of seats. Nevertheless Khalil was afraid of an alliance between Azhari and Nasser and he was suspected of being privy to an army coup by which he and his government and the constitution were all swept away. General Ibrahim Abboud took power with a supreme council of officers.

Military rule lasted for six years, during which the situation in the southern provinces deteriorated drastically. The Sudanese government pursued a policy of Arabization and looked with extreme suspicion on the foreign Christian missionaries whom it suspected of being not merely anti-Muslim but also active agents of a western policy of separatism. The Missionary Societies Act of 1962 restricted their activities and induced a number to leave; the surviving 300 were expelled in 1964 after the resumption of full-scale insurrection by the Anya Nya movement and brought with them to the outside world tales of extensive massacres by government troops. In October 1964 General Abboud's military régime was overthrown and after a few weeks during which General Abboud ruled in conjunction with a civilian administration he himself resigned. Ser el-Khatim Khalifa formed a transitional coalition of intellectuals and re-emergent politicians which was replaced early in 1965 by a more normal coalition of politicians in which the Umma Party had the largest voice – a position which it confirmed and enhanced at elections in April. A southerner, Clement Ngoro, held the ministry of the interior and north–south negotiations took place both in the Sudan and in Nairobi with a number of leading southern exiles. A further conference planned for February at Juba was postponed owing to a refusal by the Anya Nya to surrender in advance, but discussions were resumed in Khartoum in March. With the south demanding a federal constitution and northern politicians inveighing against separatist plots little was achieved. Fighting continued and southern opinion moved increasingly away from federation and towards independence with both sides seeking support from neighbouring states. The Sudanese government exerted itself to improve its relations with Ethiopia, Uganda and the Central African Republic, and the Sudanese African National Union appealed to African opinion through the Organization for

African Unity and its Liberation Committee in Dar-es-Salaam.

In 1969 a group of military officers led by General Nimeiry seized power and established a more left wing and pro-Egyptian government. The coincidence of similar coups in Somalia and Libya gave rise to projects for a union of all these countries with Egypt and the creation therefore of an Arab block of north-east African states. In 1970 this plan was further expanded to attract South Yemen and Syria, thus linking it with the defunct union of 1958 with Egypt as the point and common factor, but these foreign schemes came to nothing. In Sudan they were attacked by critics who argued that they were diverting attention from more urgent domestic problems, especially the dissatisfied south, where civil war dragged on until 1972.

Chapter 19

West Africa

Europeans were interested in Africa long before they occupied it. In the century after the death of the Prophet Mahomet North Africa mounted the greatest threat to European Christendom which it has ever faced, and although that threat was parried by the Frank Charles Martel and by the Byzantine emperor Leo the Isaurian, Spain remained for centuries partly under an alien rule buttressed on occasions by fresh support from Berber Africa. When the Christians finally drove the Muslims out of the Iberian peninsula, their momentum carried them on into Africa and Spanish and Portuguese adventurers, still finding it too difficult to turn east, explored and circumnavigated Africa and made Cape Horn a station on a new route to the east. In more modern times Africa became a place where Europeans got things: slaves for plantations in the west, food for industrialized countries whose peoples were leaving the land for the factory, precious minerals like gold and copper and diamonds and uranium. At first only the coastal areas were exploited, but later the rumoured wealth of the interior tempted organized expeditions to follow in the steps of adventurers and missionaries. Although checked at first by the unexpected strength of African kingdoms, white power eventually prevailed – especially when the motives of curiosity and enrichment were reinforced by inter-white competition. So, in a final phase of European penetration, Africa was partitioned by official emissaries, part soldiers, part administrators, making territorial claims and fighting for them because traders demanded protection and each European state was afraid that others would take what it did not annex for itself. Areas large but vaguely defined, were assigned to adventurers backed by, or acting in the name of, European states which had been taught by centuries of history to think first and foremost in territorial terms.

In the last quarter of the nineteenth century it became apparent that Europe had acquired a great part of Africa in a very short space of time, and that there was some danger of fights between the European states concerned as a result of the untidy and uneven distribution of the spoils. The Europeans proceeded to settle these matters reasonably amicably among themselves. There were many wars in Africa during the colonial period, but none of them was fought between European states except as an adjunct of a European war, and even the most menacing disputes (e.g. for the control of the Nile valley or the possession of Angola) were settled without the sort of conflict which in a previous century had attended the ambitions of the European powers in southern Asia and North America.

The Europeans took possession of Africa at the height of the industrial revolution. The technical disparity between Europeans and Africans was enormous. The cultural gap was no less great. Europeans remained almost without exception ignorant of African history (they often assumed there was none) and customs, while Africans acquired few of the benefits of the technically superior civilization of their new masters. There was no attempt at a partnership between the races until nearly a century later when the Europeans were in retreat and seen to be. Meanwhile very large numbers of Africans died unnecessarily and painfully, especially in the areas ruled by Belgians and Germans; the French and British versions of civilization were less lethal in spite of wars, forced labour and the pains of mineral concessions. Economically, occupied Africa stagnated until well into the twentieth century when the Second World War and the incipient successes of nationalist leaders produced some startling changes – the first by creating a demand for African raw materials and the latter by making an impact on colonial authorities who, although vaguely concerned about the welfare of their territories from the end of the First World War, did next to nothing about it until the beginning of the Second. Exceptions to this economic stagnation were provided by the gold and diamond mines of South Africa from the eighteen-seventies and by the copper of Northern Rhodesia and Katanga in the present century. Towns and their appurtenances sprang up and work was provided (at special non-European wages and in circumstances even worse than those of Victorian England) for increasing numbers of Africans. The effect of industrialization was heavily adverse for the African. The benefit to the new industrial workers was small since industry operated on cheap labour. The expectation of life among miners was low; they returned to their homes young and dying, useless and often infectiously diseased. A new class of migrant was created, the countryside was ruined, and the extremes of poverty were – as the Royal Commission on East Africa noted in 1955 – to be found in the main areas of European settlement. The European occupation had created an appalling economic problem, which itself created grave social problems (especially in cities), which in turn encouraged white observers to despise and shun the Africans. On their side the more indignant Africans began to accuse the whites of exploiting and debauching the blacks.

African political leaders drew inspiration from both India and America. They formed National Congresses in imitation of the Indian National Congress; many of them were attracted by Gandhian ideas of passive resistance; and the independence of India in 1947 had an effect in Africa which had not been foreseen by the colonial powers. From the American continent, and notably the Caribbean, Africans gained confidence and dignity and a habit of meeting together. A first pan-African conference was held in 1900, followed by a second in Paris during the peace conference of 1915. These first meetings were dominated by West Indian Negroes but the sixth, held at Manchester at the end of the Second World War, was attended by the principal African leaders – Kenyatta, Nkrumah, Akintola, Nyerere, Banda. It voiced demands for independence which would have seemed totally unreal five years earlier. A mere ten years later West Africa was leading the way to independence from European rule.

In Accra, the capital of the British colony of the Gold Coast, there were riots in 1948 started by ex-servicemen in protest against high prices. The colonial authorities were taken by surprise, and a commission of inquiry produced a radical report which said in effect that the colony's newly proposed constitution was out of date before being introduced: to give Africans a majority of the seats in the legislative council was no longer enough. A new commission of Africans, with an African judge as chairman, was appointed to devise a new constitution. These developments coincided with the appearance of a new nationalist leader, Kwame Nkrumah who, aged probably thirty-eight, had returned to his country from the United States in 1947 and was determined to press for independence more energetically than older leaders such as J. B. Danquah. Nkrumah demanded immediate self-government. He seceded from Danquah's party, formed the Convention People's party, earned the distinction of a prison sentence and won electoral victories in 1951, 1954 and 1956. After the first of these the British governor, Sir Charles Arden-Clarke, summoned him from prison and made him chief minister, thereby adopting the view that the colonial problem was not how to prolong colonialism, but how to make the best use of what time was left, to swim (not drift) with the tide and not uselessly to fight against it.

The British method, in the Gold Coast and elsewhere, was gradually to increase the elective and African elements in legislative and executive councils. Legislative councils in British territories progressed from assemblies dominated by appointed officials to assemblies containing a majority of elected members, and at the same time the governor's executive council was similarly transformed by the introduction into it of the leaders of the main party in the legislature. The governor retained at first extensive reserve powers but at a later stage this association between the colonial authority and nationalist movements was carried a stage further by converting the nationalist leader from the governor's chief minister into a prime minister of a self-governing territory. At this point the territory was on the verge of independence, and when independence was granted the governor disappeared. If the territory decided to remain in the Commonwealth, it might accept the British queen as its titular head with a governor-general as her representative on the spot, or it might become an independent republic within the Commonwealth but without any direct link with the British Crown. The new state would in any event establish diplomatic relations with the British government (as distinct from the British Crown) through representatives called high commissioners if the Commonwealth link were maintained, or ambassadors if it were not.

Given this method, the main problem was to regulate the pace. This was inevitably an uneven exercise in compromise between an irresistible flood and a removable power. The Gold Coast became self-governing in 1955, independent under the ancient name of Ghana in March 1957 and a republic in 1960. It led the way for Africans into the Commonwealth. Nkrumah, influenced by India's example, calculated also that the Commonwealth association would be a help to new states coming naked into international society.

The second West African state to become independent was French Guinea (1958). The French had been slower than the Spaniards or the Portuguese to enter Africa and less successful at first than the British or the Dutch. When in the seventeenth century they followed the new fashion their motive was emulation rather than any large expectation of gain. In the eighteenth century, however, they were participating in the slave trade on a big scale, extracting at one time as many as 100,000 slaves in a year, and after the abolition of the trade in 1851 and of slavery itself in 1848 (fourteen years after a similar prohibition in the British territories) French merchants turned from human goods to ivory and rubber and French explorers and missionaries began to penetrate inland and so stimulated ambitious dreams of a vast and compact empire stretching from the west coast to the Nile and from Morocco to the equator. In the event France acquired 3 million square kilometres by the end of the century, something between a fifth and a quarter of the whole continent. Almost the whole of the great African bulge came under French rule; it was formed into the governor-generalship of French West Africa in 1895 and comprised eventually eight separate colonies and, after 1945, the two trust territories of Togo and Cameroon. Four equatorial territories were similarly federated in 1910. Only in the valleys of the Niger and the Nile were the French worsted by the British. In 1900 French advances from Morocco in the north, from Senegal in the west and from the Congo in the south, where the great explorer de Brazza left his name, converged at Lake Chad. France also acquired in the First World War the enormous island of Madagascar; most of the German Cameroons, leaving a small slice which passed to the British who administered it with the eastern province of Nigeria; and half of Togoland, which was also originally German and was divided in 1919 between France and Britain as the owners of the adjacent territories of Dahomey and the Gold Coast.

After the fall of France in 1940 French West Africa opted for Vichy until the invasion of north-west Africa by the Americans and the British in 1942. An attempt by the Free French and the British to seize Dakar, the capital of Senegal, in 1940 failed. In Equatorial Africa, however, the governor-general Félix Eboué, a native of the Caribbean, took the Guallist side in August 1940 and introduced a number of imaginative social and political reforms. At a conference at Brazzaville in 1944 the Africans were promised more participation in mixed Franco-African councils, more decentralization and a wider franchise.

The first French constitution of 1946 was liberal from the colonial point of view but it was rejected by the French people and the second constitution of that year was less far-reaching. It created the French Union, comprising the French Republic, Associated States and Associated Territories (there were also Overseas Departments and Overseas Territories, which were part of the French Republic). ALl the West and Equatorial African territories became Associated Territories with representatives in the French National Assembly and the Council of the Republic. Representative assemblies were also established in each territory with a grand council at federal level. From 1947 to 1954 France had a succession of predominantly conservative governments, but in 1956 the Mollet government, which included Gaston Defferre as minister for overseas territories, introduced the *loi cadre* which was intended to lead to a substantial degree of internal autonomy by way of universal franchise, elected councils and the Africanization of public services. The *loi cadre* marked the abandonment of the policy of integration or assimilation in favour of a freer federation in which the African territories, while still associated with France, would increasingly order their own affairs and develop their own services and personalities. The *loi cadre* was elaborated by a series of decrees in 1957 which endowed the twelve West and Equatorial African territories with assemblies elected on a common roll and with councils of government elected by the assemblies. Considerable powers were reserved to the governors, the West or Equatorial high commissioners, or the metropolitan government, but nationalist demands had secured the elimination of special votes for whites and every constituency in every territory had a majority of black voters. The *Rassemblement Démocratique Africain*, the principal nationalist party which operated throughout French West Africa, won the ensuing elections in Guinea, Soudan, Ivory Coast and Upper Volta.

These political changes were, however, offset on the economic side where French policy remained integrationist and, in return for French aid and guaranteed markets in France, proposed to make French Africa a highly protected area serving French metropolitan economic interests. In the following years Africans became increasingly restless about economic policy in the franc zone. They claimed that a system which allowed free trade in the zone but erected barriers round it profited the stronger members rather than the weaker, impeded economic growth in the African territories, and prevented them from diversifying their economies. In addition the *loi cadre* accentuated differences among African leaders. Some, of whom Félix Houphouet-Boigny of the Ivory Coast was representative, seemed well satisfied with the French proposals, while others, among whom Sekou Touré of Guinea was the most eminent, suspected the *loi cadre* of being not a stage to sovereign independence but a device to postpone it indefinitely.

When de Gaulle returned to power in 1958 he faced the West Africans and Equatorial Africans with a choice: either autonomy with a *communauté* in which France would clearly retain control of the economic levers, or independence – which was a polite term for expulsion into a francless world. All but Guinea made the first choice. Guinea became an independent sovereign state in October 1958, humiliatingly discarded by its French mentors and forced to look to communist powers for the wherewithal to sustain its independence. But the new autonomous republics of West Africa did not long remain content with their status. In 1959 Senegal, Soudan, Upper Volta and Dahomey decided to federate under the name of Mali and ask for independence. The two latter changed their minds under French pressure and although Senegal and Soudan persisted the resulting federation lasted only a couple of months, after which Senegal too withdrew leaving Soudan with the new name of Mali; it moved into the Guinea–Ghana orbit. The idea of a Mali federation had been unpopular not only in Paris but also among French African states further south, especially in the Ivory Coast whose leader, Félix Houphouet-Boigny, riposted by forming with Niger and the detached Upper Volta and Dahomey an association called the Council of the Entente. The Entente then asked for independence by the beginning of 1960, which was conceded. Houphouet-Boigny wished to fortify the Entente by introducing dual nationality in it, but it was weakened by coups in Upper Volta and Dahomey in 1961 and by persistent suspiciousness in these and other states (including Togo which joined in 1966) of Houphouet-Boigny who was regarded as unduly hostile to Nkrumah and too partial to Tshombe. The net result of these centripetal and centrifugal forces was to solidify the several French colonies as independent sovereign states.

The independence of the Entente countries in 1960 deprived the *communauté* of any meaning although in theory it continued to exist as an association comprising France, Madagascar and the Equatorial states. These latter – Gabon, Chad, Ubangi-Shari and French Congo (the last two renamed the Central African Republic and Congo-Brazzaville) – produced a plan for a federation which was however abortive; they too became independent as separate sovereign states in 1960. In 1963 the Senegal River states (Senegal, Mali, Guinea and Mauritania) planned an association which was however frustrated by political differences: the notion was revived in the late sixties. The enduring association was the much bigger, and looser one of OCAM (see page 311).

The huge British territory of Nigeria also became independent in 1960, followed in 1961 by Sierra Leone, the British colony between Guinea and Liberia, and in 1965 by Gambia, the northernmost and last remaining British territory in West Africa, a narrow enclave within the embrace of Senegal. Of the trust territories in West Africa the French

Cameroons and French Togoland became independent republics, while the British Cameroons and British Togoland were attached to Nigeria and Ghana respectively.

In the decade after independence all these states preserved their integrity. The former French territories experienced a number of military coups (which brought them on these, but few other, occasions back into the world's press). The tale of these coups is depressing but not very bloody. Ten years after the main emancipation year, 1960, the only rulers still in power in French-speaking West Africa were Léopold Senghor in Senegal, Sekou Touré in Guinea and Houphouet-Boigny in the Ivory Coast. Modibo Keita of Mali, ousted in 1968, just failed to stay for a decade. In Togo Sylvanus Olympio was assassinated in 1963 and his successor Nicholas Grunitzky was displaced a few years later by Etienne Eyadema. In adjacent Dahomey, a country living under the shadow of Nigeria and without jobs or resources, the military were in and out of government, displacing one civilian president and installing another until in 1970 they forced three past presidents to work together on a rota system which proved to be no more than a two-year interlude before military rule. Further inland Upper Volta and Niger both suffered minor plots and upheavals, generally instigated by military dissatisfaction with the efficiency or honesty of civilian rule. These military coups were effected with a minimum of violence and amounted in effect to an accepted, if not very satisfactory, way of changing a government which had failed but which had no ready-made successor because these were one-party states without adequate machinery for changing the government in any other way.

In Chad a more serious situation developed. Chad is one of the African countries which lie athwart the dividing line between Arab and Bantu Africa. In such countries the normal friction between the centre and the regions acquires an extra racial and religious edge. President François Tombalbaye, a representative of the well educated southern élite, was well intentioned but unsympathetic towards the Muslims of the north whose opposition to his government he insisted on regarding as banditry. (It was also a threat to the tourist traffic which he hoped to encourage.) By 1966 a liberation movement, with headquarters in Libya, had been established and Tombalbaye turned for help to France with which Chad, like other former French colonies, had a defence agreement. (France had some 6000 troops in West and Central Africa in these years, distributed over thirteen states). This help began with supplies but was expanded in 1968–70 to direct intervention with paratroops and aircraft which, together with French diplomatic action in Libya, secured Tombalbaye's position, until 1975 when he was assassinated, but it also started a debate in Paris and elsewhere about whether the defence agreement covered not only the equipment and training of Chadian forces but also the intervention of French forces. France also intervened in the Cameroons to support a government against a revolt whose causes were basically economic. In Gabon too, one of the potentially rich West African states, French troops played a role when President M'Ba was deposed in 1964; he was restored but died two years later and was succeeded peaceably by his successor-designate, Albert Bongo. In the Central African Republic a coup by Colonel Bokassa was of the same order as coups in Upper Volta, Dahomey and Niger. Finally, in Congo-Brazzaville President Fulbert Youlou was overthrown by revolution, the French refusing to intervene in a case of what they regarded as genuine popular indignation. His successor suffered the same fate five years later.

The troubles of these states were small in comparison with the more spectacular troubles of the ex-British territories in West Africa. Of these only the smallest, Gambia, led an equable existence. With an economy which enabled it to dispense with British aid after 1967 Gambia experienced nothing worse than rubs in its attempts to work an 'association' with its big neighbour Senegal. Sierra Leone experienced a couple of military coups but reverted to civilian rule when the soldiers were satisfied that they had found politicians less contentious and corrupt than those whom they had ousted. Ghana and Nigeria fared worse.

In Ghana, the pioneer of West African liberation, the personal leadership of Nkrumah turned into a febrile autocracy which passed step by step beyond a struggle to maintain the unity of the new state and a struggle to modernize it, and became perverted into a struggle to assert and preserve the authority of Nkrumah himself. Upon the attainment of independence Nkrumah had three principal aims. He wished to propagate his vision of African unity by accelerating the independence of other territories and consolidating the energies of Africans and Africanism in the service of African dignity and African effectiveness in the world; but his methods and his personality did not always commend him to other African leaders, whose own pan-Africanism was filtered through their several national experiences and ambitions. Like Nasser's pan-Arabism, Nkrumah's pan-Africanism was suspect. The exuberance and vigour which had contributed so much to make him the first ruler of a sub-Saharan African republic were drawbacks in a new situation which demanded the arts of diplomacy rather than the *élan* of leadership.

Nkrumah's second ambition was to make Ghana an efficient centralized and prospering state. This ambition was impeded by a complex of regionalism, conservatism and political jealousies and also by a serious drop in the world price of cocoa, Ghana's principal source of revenue. The Convention People's Party, whose main strength was in the coastal areas, was opposed by chiefs whom it regarded as a divisive and reactionary force and by the United Party led by K. A. Busia and J. E. Appiah. Nkrumah's increasingly dictatorial and suspicious manner alienated opinion at home and abroad. The illiberality evidenced, for example, by the removal of the chief justice after the delivery of an unpalatable verdict in a treason trial, coupled with increasing corruption and spendthriftness in the administration, destroyed Nkrumah's attempts to get foreign friends and finance and created a new opposition to him in the army which, by a bloodless coup in 1966, unseated him while he was away on a visit to China.

Thirdly, in the world at large Nkrumah wished to follow a policy of non-alignment. His circumstances were exceptionally favourable. Upon independence Ghana's resources and reserves at £200 million the latter were larger than India's – gave it a material base for a measure of independence which might the more easily be maintained since the cold war had not at that date reached Africa. But in practice Ghana under Nkrumah never achieved non-aligned status in the eyes of outsiders. For half of the period 1957–66 it appeared pro-western, for the other half pro-eastern. In the first years Nkrumah sought and got western capital for development, notably for the Volta river dam. Ghana remained in the Commonwealth and was visited in 1961 by Queen Elizabeth II, but the crisis in the Congo and particularly the murder of Lumumba, for which he blamed the west, turned Nkrumah against the western world, while the elaboration in theory and practice of his 'scientific socialism' with the inauguration in 1962 of a one-party system turned the western world against him. In contradistinction to Nasser's evident pragmatism, Nkrumah became increasingly ideological and illogical, evolving a form of economic planning akin to communist models but nevertheless dependent on western capital for its success.

The new government, led by Colonel Ankrah, found that Nkrumah's extravagances had run the reserves down to £4 million and the external debt up to £279 million. Ghana also had a deficit on external account of £53 million. Colonel Ankrah and his colleagues made some improvements to this dismal tale before relinquishing power in 1969, but economic growth remained below 1 per cent a year, the population was increasing at an annual rate between 3.5 and 4 per cent, the standard of living had been cut by a severe devaluation and the first attempts of the new prime minister, Dr Kofi Busia, to secure an alleviation of the external debt were only moderately successful. By the beginning of 1972 Busia had been defeated by his predecessors' legacy, by an imprudently liberal policy which permitted an inflow of foreign goods which crippled the balance of payments, and by a drastic devaluation which doubled the external debt at a stroke. He was ousted while away in London and succeeded by an army committee calling itself the National Redemption Council under the chairmanship of Colonel I. K. Acheampong. This well intentioned group struggled, not always harmoniously, with economic problems which were being aggravated by steep rises in the price of oil and other essential imports and by consequent rises in the cost of living. Ghana's creditors gave it some relaxation on the repayment of debts but not as much as it hoped for.

Nigeria's convulsions were more terrible. Nigeria, huge and diverse, was a twentieth-century creation. The colonies of Lagos and South

Nigeria were united by the British in 1906. The former was the home of the Yorubas whose society was based partly on tribal chiefs and partly on cultivated cities. The dominant people in the latter were the Ibos who had neither chiefs nor cities but were therefore the more easily united as a nation and displayed a thrusting vigour which carried many of them long distances from their homes in eastern Nigeria and into the western and northern parts of the federation created by the British when, in 1914, they joined northern Nigeria to the two southern colonies.

The north was in a state of flux when the British reached it at the end of the nineteenth century. Early in that century the Islamicized Fulani had established their authority over a medley of pre-existing Hausa states of very varying size and had so created the empire of Usuman dan Fodio and his descendants. Conflict between Fulani and Hausa and others persisted and the British assumed the task of mastering it as a prelude to uniting all their territories in this part of the world, but the federation which they created was an uneasy amalgam of states and cultures without a national consciousness or unity. After the Second World War the southern half of the country pressed for independence, while the north hesitated for fear of being reduced to dependence upon the south with its coastal windows on the outside world's commerce, skills and manners. The north even toyed with the idea of a separate state with access to the sea either down a river corridor along the Niger or through Dahomey or the Cameroons on the one side or the other. Before independence, riots with racial and religious overtones gave manifest warning of the dangers which the new state would run, but the advantages of unity seemed to make the experiment worth while and in 1960 Nigeria became independent with a constitution based on three regions. The federal premiership went to a northerner, Sir Abubakr Tafewa Balewa. The eastern leader, Namdi Azikiwe, became president and his party co-operated with the principal northern party in the government at the centre. It was Azikiwe's belief that a country as big and heterogeneous as Nigeria could only be governed by a coalition of all its main groups within a federal structure, but the western leader, Chief Obafemi Awolowo, preferred to form an opposition in the federal parliament.

The accord between east and north did not last long, nor did the cohesion of the west. The Ibos annoyed their northern partners by trying to win parliamentary seats in the northern region. In the west Chief Akintola challenged Awolowo and succeeded in getting him and other leaders tried and imprisoned. Akintola was not satisfied with Awolowo's policy of forming an opposition at the federal level. He preferred a policy of alliance with the north, displacing the Ibos and getting for his own people a share in the power, perquisites and finances of central government. In 1963 a fourth, mid-western region was formed. In 1964 a census showed a total population for the whole country of 55.6 million, of which 29.8 million were in the north – more than half. This demographic preponderance of the north increased the attractions of an alliance with the leaders of that region and, together with charges that the census had been faked, also increased political tensions. Elections in the western region in 1965 produced allegations of flagrant malpractice and fighting. In the next year more serious fighting began in the north.

In January 1966 a group of young Ibo officers rebelled, partly in protest against bad government and partly as a demonstration against the north and its allies in the west. The federal and northern prime ministers, Sir Abubakr Balewa and the Sardauna of Sokoto, were murdered along with Chief Akintola and many more, but senior officers stepped in quickly to arrest further developments and the junior officers. A comparatively senior officer, General Johnson Ironsi, was proclaimed head of state with the mission of keeping the country from breaking up and providing competent and honest administration. General Ironsi was an Ibo. He was well intentioned but not otherwise well equipped for the delicate task of holding the country together and when in July he incautiously suggested that a unitary constitution might be better for Nigeria than a federal one, northern fears of attempted Ibo dominance flared up into another coup and he was murdered in his turn. He was replaced by Colonel Yakubu Gowon, a northern Christian, who released a number of imprisoned civilians, including Awolowo, and expressed the usual hopes for an early return to civilian rule. In September a conference at Lagos agreed on a loose fourfold federal structure, but it coincided with a counter-massacre of Ibos in the north (there had been a similar, though less severe, massacre in May) and the flight of the survivors back to the eastern region.

After the first coup in 1966 Lieutenant-Colonel Odumegwu Ojukwu had been appointed military governor of the eastern region. He now concluded that the salvation of the Ibos could only be secured by secession from Nigeria. Dissuaded from taking this step at a conference in January 1967 at Aburi in Ghana, he nevertheless proclaimed in May the independent state of Biafra and civil war began. Attempts at mediation by the OAU (at Kinshasa in 1967, Algiers in 1968 and Addis Ababa in 1969) all broke down. The federal army, expanded from 10,000 to over 200,000 men, gradually prevailed in spite of the toughness of Biafran resistance. While Britain and the USSR supplied arms to the federal government, France supplied Biafra (thereby perhaps somewhat prolonging the war) and two of France's closest African associates, Ivory Coast and Gabon, recognized the secessionist state – as too did Zambia and Tanzania in attempts to stop the killing. The suffering in Biafra, overcrowded and virtually beseiged, was appalling and widely reported throughout the world. By January 1970 it had become decisive. In that month Biafra was forced to capitulate and, as such, ceased to exist. Gowon proved a statesmanlike victor. He preached reconciliation and practised it. Nigeria's economic growth was resumed at a great pace. It became one of the world's leading producers and exporters of oil, besides being rich in coal, tin and other minerals, and in agriculture. By 1975 it was exporting 2.5 million barrels of oil a day: oil accounted for 90 per cent of exports. But the government was nonetheless overspending its revenues and internal problems were not washed away by this wealth. The rich got richer and the poor mostly stayed poor or, with inflation, got poorer. The huge army and a large police force of 30,000 became notorious for corruption, as did the more affluent sectors of civilian life. There were strikes and unemployment. The constitutional problem was unsolved. After the civil war the country was divided into twelve states (later increased to nineteen) but Gowon incautiously indicated that there might be more, on an ethnic basis which, if seriously applied, could produce up to 300-400 states. The census of 1973 returned a total population of 79.76 million, a growth of 43.5 per cent since 1963 and an average annual increase double that of the fastest growing populations in the world. Nobody believed the figures although some people in some areas liked them. The fact that increases varied widely and suspiciously from state to state forced Gowon to say that they would not be used as a basis for any political decisions. By 1974 it was announced to the relief of many Nigerians that the return to civilian rule promised for 1976 would be postponed. Gowon's too evident inability to grasp the nettle of corruption led to his displacement in 1975 while he was out of the country. He was allowed to go with his family to England. His successors Generals Murtala Mohammed (assassinated after a few months) and Olesugun Obasanjo were more vigorous in their attacks on corruption and other problems. The latter promised to cut the army by more than half and restore civilian rule in 1979.

Most of the countries mentioned in this chapter, together with others further east, suffered horribly in the seventies from appalling drought and famine which destroyed men, beasts and crops and made a mockery of hopes of progess and development. In some areas the desert advanced at the rate of a foot a year. In addition these countries' economies, often frail, were burdened by the rising world prices of fertilizers and primary products, particularly oil the cost of which began to rise significantly about 1970 and then rocketed by as much as 500 per cent as a consequence of the war in the Middle East in 1973. In many countries agricultural production failed to keep pace with increases in the population. Africa's share of world trade declined and so did the proportion of that trade which African countries did with one another. Defence spending rose. There was a drift to cities from the land. These pains and portents dictated a fresh attempt by the weaker nations to combine to bring pressure to bear on the richer and at the end of the period covered by this book a new UNCTAD conference was in preparation with plans for a 'new economic order' in which the principles of Bretton Woods would be replaced by a more protectionist mentality.

Chapter 20

The Congo

West Africa became independent without anything that could be called an international crisis. East Africa was to follow suit in the next few years. But the independence of the Belgian Congo produced not only internal chaos and civil war but also one of the principal international crises of the post-war period, in which major powers were brought to the brink of a confrontation, African states were divided among themselves, and the United Nations was called upon to play expected and unexpected roles in the course of which it was attacked by some of its principal members, its secretary-general was killed and its very existence was called in question. The sources of this catastrophe were, first, the hurriedness with which the Belgians took their departure from a colony which they had hardly at all prepared for independence; secondly, the very great size of the Congo and its ethnic and tribal diversity; thirdly, the revolt immediately after independence of the Force Publique or army, whose mutinous conduct left the new central government powerless; next, the attempt to detach the rich southern province of Katanga and make it a separate state; and finally, the fact that the United Nations was required to perform a multiplicity of barely consistent tasks and was hampered in them by the inadequacies of its own machinery and by the hostility and independent actions of certain governments, notably the Russian and the British.

The Congo is a large country of over a million square miles inhabited by many different tribes, some of which constitute tribal federations. The most prominent of these are the Bakongo in the west, including the capital of Leopoldville, and also in the neighbouring territories of Angola and Congo-Brazzaville; the Baluba in southern Kasai and northern Katanga; and the Balunda in southern Katanga. In spite of its great size the Congo touches the ocean only at the end of a corridor between Congo-Brazzaville and Angola, and its modern history begins with the ventures of explorers along the Congo river. It became famous as a result of H. M. Stanley's expedition in 1874 and was at once an object of international competition among the principal European powers. Britain, already well endowed and also busy elsewhere, did not enter the lists on its own account but pushed the claims of its old friend, Portugal. France and the three-year-old German empire were not so altruistic and in 1876 an international conference reached a temporary compromise by creating the International

African Association which was to act as a sort of composite cultural mission to enlighten the darkest heart of Africa and find out what was there. This conference met, not by accident, in Brussels and was convened by the Belgian king Leopold II.

The International African Association did not eliminate the ambitions and manoeuvres of the European powers, and in the early eighties there was widespread fear of war as a result of their jealousies and claims in West Africa from the Niger down to the Congo. In 1884 a conference in Berlin, engineered and presided over by Bismarck, sorted things out on the basis that there was enough for everybody and no need to fight: Europeans would do best to recognize each other's possessions and tacitly sanction in advance further acquisitions of anything not yet under a European flag. The Congo was handed over to the Congo International Association which was the International African Association under a new name, and in effect Leopold II in person. The king thus became the largest private estate owner in the world, although he did not yet know how rich his property was. His obligations were to extirpate the slave trade, permit free trade and secure free passage for all on the Congo river. He defaulted in his first obligation until an outcry in Britain and elsewhere compelled him to abolish the trade – and to resort to forced labour instead. His administration of his estate became one of the most notorious scandals since Cicero's denunciation of the proconsulship of Verres, and in 1908 the Congo was transferred from Leopold to the Belgian state which despatched a governor-general to rule with the help of a Belgian civil service. The interests of Africans were to have priority over the exploitation of the domain but this principle was not in practice found to involve any advancement for Africans or any but the most rudimentary mingling of the races.

Shortly before the First World War the mining of copper in Katanga began and brought with it two potent changes. Katanga gradually became twice as rich as the whole of the rest of the Congo; should the Congo ever become independent the Katangans would be in a position to demand first place in the state or to leave it and set up on their own. The second and more immediate change was the transformation of the territory into a booming partnership between the administration, Belgian finance houses and the Roman Catholic Church. And so it remained for nearly half a century. Some attention was paid to the economic well-being of the Africans but no political activity was tolerated and education above the elementary level was reserved for very few. In so far as Belgians thought about the future they imagined a slow advance by Africans to a level at which a new form of association might have to be devised, but a transfer of power to Africans did not enter into their calculations and so no steps were taken to train even an élite. So far as any practical man needed to see the Congo would remain as shut off from the rest of the world as Japan before the Meiji restoration.

This view began to be questioned in the fifties. The missionaries became alive to the pressures of nationalism and uneasy therefore about the assumptions on which the territory was being ruled by the church and its associates. In Brussels, where a left wing coalition came to power in 1954, the liberation of French and British territories could not be ignored; de Gaulle's offer of autonomy in 1958 was made at Brazzaville just across the river from Leopoldville. African leaders, some of whom met each other for the first time at the Brussels Fair of 1958, began to espouse independence in place of a somewhat less gradual evolution, and in December 1958 many of them attended the Pan-African Conference in Accra where they received encouragement from fellow Africans and were reinforced in their determination not to get left behind. A few days after the end of the Accra conference there were riots in Leopoldville.

The Belgians had recently appointed as governor-general Maurice van Hemelrijk who believed that acceleration was not the only possible policy. He advocated a parliament for the Congo by the end of 1960 and independence in 1963 (reduced, by the end of 1959, to independence in 1960). But van Hemelrijk was forced by conservative protests in Belgium to resign in September 1959. His successor, Auguste de Schryver, found he had to go even faster. Tribal fighting began before the end of the year and in January 1960 the Belgians assembled in Brussels a conference at which, to their surprise, the Africans unitedly asked for immediate independence. The Belgians agreed to leave the Congo at the end of June. Never had so much been conceded so quickly. The frontiers of the new state were to be the same as those of the colony, and when Sir Roy Welensky suggested that Katanga should leave the Congo and join the Rhodesian federation, the Belgian government was much displeased. The internal structure of the new state, whether it should be military or federal, was however left undecided, while the distribution to top posts was also unsettled pending elections which were held in May. The Belgians made some attempt to remedy their sins of omission by running a crash training programme in Brussels for Africans and by enlisting Ghanaian help in the training of more Africans in the Congo.

At this time the most prominent of the Congolese politicians, and the favourite of the Belgians, was Patrice Lumumba, one of the founders in 1958 of the *Mouvement National Congolais* which was the main non-tribal party in the Congo. Lumumba and his principal associates, who included Cyrille Adoula and Joseph Ileo, demanded the Africanization of public services and professions with a view to ultimate independence. At the Accra conference Lumumba struck up a friendship with Nkrumah and, although he became more extreme in his demands during 1959 and was eventually imprisoned, he retained his good standing with the Belgians until the eve of independence. He wanted a strong centre rather than a diffuse federation, in contra-distinction to his opponents who were essentially the modern equivalents of tribal and local chieftains: Joseph Kasavubu, the more sedate and aristocratic leader of Abako which was founded in 1950 among the Bakongo with the aim of restoring the old Kongo empire but which became converted to the idea of a Congo state provided it was a federal one; Moise Tshombe, the rich middle-class *évolué* and leader of Conakat through which the Balunda aimed to exercise power in Katanga either within a federal Congo or independently; and Jason Sendwe, whose Balubakat eyed the Balunda to the south with considerable suspicion and prevented Conakat from speaking for the whole of Katanga. Lumumba's tendency to quarrel with other leaders in his own party, and a change of attitude in Brussels, led to attempts to create an anti-Lumumba front, but the attempts failed, Lumumba's party emerged from the elections as the biggest and Lumumba was installed as prime minister of a broad coalition government with Kasavubu as president.

Independence was proclaimed on 30 June and the official celebrations lasted for four days. Forty-eight hours later there occurred the first mutinies in the Force Publique which sparked off a train of terrible disasters. The soldiers seem to have expected that independence would instantly improve their pay and open their way to the officer grades, which were entirely filled by white men. When nothing happened, they decided to replace their officers. This indiscipline was accompanied by a certain amount of violence and some rapes, much multiplied in the telling. An African sergeant, Victor Lundula, was appointed commander-in-chief and the situation seemed to have been brought under control in a couple of days. But fresh mutinies and more serious violence quickly followed; there was, however, no killing until after Tshombe's proclamation of the independence of Katanga on 11 July.

The mutiny of the Congolese army was the source of all the Congo's woes. It deprived the Congolese government of power and authority. It caused a panic among Europeans, and the Belgians announced that, with or without Congolese consent, they would return to protect their nationals. Tshombe unilaterally asked for Belgian help and declared Katanga independent. The long-term consequences of this action will be examined below. The immediate consequence was to humiliate and infuriate Lumumba who became suspicious of a Katangan-Belgian plot to subvert the independence of the new state and disrupt it by detaching its richest province. Subsequent events successively strengthened his suspicions. Although he remained for a time willing to discuss with the Belgians the maintenance of law and order, he was not willing to do what Tshombe had done and ask for their help in suppressing the mutinies. Since there was no other force immediately available to him, this rift between Lumumba and the Belgians enabled the mutinies to spread and take hold. At the same time the rift between Lumumba and Tshombe made Lumumba more anxious to maintain than to disarm the Congolese army with the result that when UN forces arrived to restore order Lumumba dissuaded them from taking the essential step of disarming the mutinous units.

These were not the only consequences. The Belgians, who occupied Leopoldville with parachute troops on 11 July in effect abrogated their recently signed treaty of friendship with the Congo and switched to Tshombe, whom they provided with a Belgian armed force and commander-in-chief. They thereby annulled not only the Belgian-Congolese association but also the unity of the Congo. This unity was already precarious and the attempts to re-establish it form one of the two principal strands in the complex story of the next three years. The other strand is the conflict over the powers and duties of the UN forces which began to arrive in Leopoldville on 14 July to restore order and displace the Belgians – but without agreement on whether the restoration of law and order included the subjection of Katanga to the authority of the central government.

On the domestic political front Lumumba and Kasavubu began working in harmony, but in September they broke with one another and Kasavubu dismissed Lumumba and appointed a new government. The parliament supported Lumumba who maintained, with some justice, that the president's action was illegal. In the ensuing crisis Hammarskjöld's representative in Leopoldville, Andrew Cordier, closed airports and radio, thereby giving an advantage to Kasavubu by denying to the more popular Lumumba the opportunity to state his case in different parts of the country or make his voice heard on the air. This action was bitterly resented within the Congo and beyond and led to fierce Congolese attacks on the UN with Russian support. Lumumba remained in Leopoldville in his official residence. Cordier's successor, Rayeshwar Dayal, refused to assist him, and he became in effect not the prisoner but the protégé of the UN (which was now attacked for being pro-Lumumba) until he fled from Leopoldville at the end of November, hoping to reach Stanleyville by car. He was overtaken a few days later with the help of aircraft and was lodged in gaol in Thysville, whence he fled to the Katangan capital of Elisabethville on 17 January, only to be captured again and murdered.

Shortly after the Lumumba–Kasavubu rift in September power in Leopoldville was seized by Colonel Joseph Mobutu, the chief of staff of the army (the commander-in-chief, Victor Lundula, was not in the capital). Mobutu ejected both the parliament and the Russian and Czech embassies and, when attempts to reconcile Lumumba and Kasavubu failed, declared for Kasavubu who acquiesced in the colonel's virtual usurpation. Mobutu was the principal ruler in the capital until the end of the year. He introduced a new constitution and some degree of order and efficiency, but although supported by the West he failed to establish the sort of military régime which other soldiers were successfully establishing in Asian and Arab states at this time. The provinces did not respond and the resources available to him – communications, trained personnel – were totally inadequate. Moreover the army itself was divided; General Lundula and the forces in Orientale province remained pro-Lumumba, as did many politicians and, so far as was ascertainable, the popular favour.

In February 1961 it was apparent that the Mobutu-Kasavubu team had failed and a new government was appointed under Ileo. It lasted six months until August when Ileo was succeeded by Adoula, who remained prime minister until 1964. During this period the Lumumbists, led by Antoine Gizenga in Stanleyville, and the Katangans, led by Tshombe and Godefroid Munongo in Elisabethville, were separate and often separatist factors in the situation. Various attempts were made to bring all three sections together but hopeful moves in the direction of Stanleyville usually caused Elisabethville to shy away, and vice versa.

The Stanleyville secession was never formalized in the same way as the Kantangan. It developed after the break between Lumumba and Kasavubu and gathered strength after the murder of Lumumba when the Russians seemed to be on the verge of recognizing the Stanleyville party as the government of the Congo and of supplying it with arms. But if the Russians were expecting to secure a foothold in Africa by exploiting the emotions roused by Lumumba's death, they miscalculated; their faces were as white as any Belgian's, their intervention was in principle as unwelcome, and instead of pleasing they shocked Africans by the ruthlessness with which, upon their arrival in Orientale, they proposed to set about the anti-Lumumbists. They were seen off by a small party of UN troops, having badly damaged their reputation in Africa. Gizenga meanwhile equivocated over his relations with Ileo, watching the state of Ileo's relations with Tshombe, but when he was appointed deputy prime minister to Adoula he accepted the post on the understanding that Adoula would use force to put an end to the Katangan secession. He accompanied Adoula to the conference of non-aligned nations in Belgrade in September 1961. The failure of the operations against Katanga, about to be related, revived his suspicions and he returned to his own base in Stanleyville, thereby re-creating the tripartite pattern. Attempts to induce him to return to the capital having failed, he was brought there under arrest in January 1962, lodged in gaol and expelled from the government.

The Katangan secession was a formal, if illegal, state of affairs with a precise beginning and a precise end. It was proclaimed by Tshombe on 11 July 1960 and renounced by him on 21 December 1961. Its inception thus coincided with the mutiny of the Force Publique and Belgian intervention, and it was accompanied by an appeal to Belgium and a refusal to allow Kasavubu and Lumumba, the federal president and prime minister, to go to Elisabethville. As a result of these moves Katanga was for the time being protected from the chaos developing in other areas, and while the UN was trying to re-establish order in Leopoldville province the Belgians did so in Katanga. They also provided Tshombe, at his request, with administrative services, and – the most important aspect of the partnership – they ran the mines and paid royalties to Tshombe instead of to the central government. These payments were a direct breach of the pre-independence agreement (the *loi fondamentale*) which had been signed by the Belgian government and accepted by, among others, Tshombe; but they enabled Tshombe to enlist and pay an army of foreigners with which to oppose his Congolese adversaries and, if need be, the UN. One of the most pregnant eventualities of the first weeks of independence was this alignment of Katanga – wealthy, relatively isolated, strongly led and able to command Belgian aid – against the rest of the Congo and its UN supporters.

The UN came to the Congo in response to three appeals by Kasavubu and Lumumba on 10, 12 and 13 July 1960. They appealed first for technical aid, including aid in the organization and equipment of security forces. In their second and third messages they appealed for help against Belgian aggression. Hammarskjöld, taking the initiative under article 99 of the Charter, on 13 July asked the Security Council to consider technical aid for the Congo and the problem of law and order. The Council authorized the despatch of military aid to the Congolese government with the proviso that force should not be used by UN troops except in self-defence. The council was divided on whether to require the Belgians to withdraw, Britain, France and China abstaining from the vote. Hammarskjöld immediately asked African states north of the Congo for military and other help, an appeal later extended to certain European and Asian members. The first troops reached the Congo on 14 July and four days later a force of 4000 had been assembled. The airlift was provided by the United States, Britain and the Soviet Union. Differences of opinion about the functions of the UN troops arose at once. General Alexander, in command of the Ghanaian contingent, immediately began disarming the mutineers of the Force Publique. Had he been allowed to continue to do so, all might have been very different, but Lumumba insisted on stopping the process, partly because he was suspicious of outside interference and partly because he wanted to use the Force Publique against Katanga.

The Security Council met again on 20 July and resolved unanimously that the Belgians should withdraw and that other states should refrain from aggravating the situation; it confirmed the authority already given to Hammarskjöld and commended what he had done. The Belgians began to withdraw on the 20th and by the 23rd they had left the Congo again – except Katanga. Ghana and Guinea then threatened to withdraw their troops from the UN force and place them at the disposal of the Leopoldville government in order to help evict the Belgians from Katanga and force the province to accept the authority of the Kasavubu–Lumumba régime. Consequently the UN had to consider most urgently whether its own force was entitled to enter Katanga to achieve these objects and, if not, whether it should now be empowered by new resolutions to do so. Hoping to bypass this difficulty Hammarskjöld flew to Brussels and the Congo to secure the entry of

UN units by negotiation and announced on 2 August that a first contingent would do so in three days' time. But the Katanga authorities said they would resist and Ralph Bunche, despatched to Elisabethville to discover if they really would, advised postponing the move. Rather than use force, and uncertain whether he was empowered to in these circumstances, Hammarskjöld returned to New York to seek further instructions from the Security Council. This check was accounted a victory by the Katangans. It further infuriated Lumumba who decided that the UN had let him down and that he should seek African support for a campaign against Katanga.

The Security Council's third meeting took place on 8 and 9 August and (France and Italy abstaining) repeated the injunction to the Belgians to leave immediately, authorized the entry of UN forces into Katanga and said once more that these forces were not to be used to influence the internal conflict. The last part of the resolution was but doubtfully consistent with the second, since the essence of the conflict was the authority of Leopoldville over Elisabethville, and the entry of UN troops into Katanga, even if designed only to compel the departure of the Belgians, could not fail to have an effect on the balance of domestic Congolese forces which were in conflict. Hammarskjöld, fortified by this resolution, returned to the Congo and to his policy of getting UN forces into Katanga bloodlessly. He entered Katanga with a token force but refused to take a representative of Lumumba with him, thus further antagonizing Lumumba who became convinced that the secretary-general was embroiled in a plot against him. For his part Hammarskjöld became convinced that Lumumba's main aim was to get rid of the UN presence. Tshombe meanwhile used the breathing space afforded by these quarrels to consolidate his position. A fourth meeting of the Security Council on 21 August produced an ominous sign when a resolution of strong support for Hammarskjöld was opposed by the Soviet Union and Poland.

Throughout August the situation in the Congo deteriorated with every prospect of a clash between the Congolese and Katangan armies. A conference of thirteen African states in Leopoldville failed to give Lumumba the support he wanted and advised against an attack on Katanga, but Congolese troops were taking matters into their own hands and contrived a massacre of Baluba who were trying to establish a state of their own between the two principal rival forces. (They had already suffered a massacre by the Balunda since Tshombe could not establish his predominance in Katanga as a whole without this radical alteration of the numerical balance.) At this point Kasavubu's resolve to get rid of Lumumba, whose unpredictability had grown alarmingly and whose reputed pro-communism was, though unfounded, embarrassing, gave Tshombe a second breathing space; the projected attack on him was called off, and his Belgian troops took the opportunity to move north and establish a second secessionary state in Kasai under the short-lived presidency of Albert Kalonji. A separate state backed by the Belgians had come into existence in the south, while in the north-east the Russians were beginning to play with the idea of another separate state backed by themselves.

The Congo seemed to be about to break up into three large and warring units, two of which would be foreign bases, and a number of smaller ones. The situation was aggravated upon the opening of the UN General Assembly in September, when Khrushchev arrived in person to attack the secretary-general and two rival Congolese delegations competed with one another for seats in the Assembly and the ears of its members.

This session of the Assembly was notable for the admission of seventeen new African members, and for the part they played. They refused to support the Russian attack on Hammarskjöld and joined with the western block to isolate the communist states. But they did not agree with prevailing western views on the Congo, nor did they remain solidly united among themselves. In Britain, France and the United States the Katangan case, propagated by an active and lavishly supplied promotion lobby which tended to put the interests of its clients before the truth, made many converts in political and business circles on the plea that Katanga was an oasis of peace and sanity in an otherwise barbarous and increasingly communist Congo. This thesis found no acceptors among Africans who unanimously condemned Tshombe and his ways, while being divided on what to do. One group turned against the UN and reverted to Lumumba's plan for a joint African invasion of Katanga. Another group remained attached to the idea of UN action, though dissatisfied with the action apparently contemplated; this group became a pressure group at the UN with the object of persuading the secretary-general and other members that a policy of reducing Katanga by negotiation was hopeless and should be replaced by direct action. A third group of Africans, consisting of recently emancipated French colonies, placed its faith for a time in the Mobutu-Kasavubu alliance and the gradual radiation of law and order from Leopoldville out into all the provinces. The decline of Mobutu, the murder of Lumumba and the installation of Ileo provided a depressing background to events in the last months of 1960 and the beginning of 1961, during which successful attempts were made by Hammarskjöld to get the Russians and the Belgians to stop their independent bolstering of Stanleyville and Elisabethville.

On 21 February 1961 the Security Council explicitly authorized the UN forces to use force in the last resort to prevent a civil war. It did not, however, authorize the use of force against Katanga, or for the removal of the Belgians, or to secure a political solution. This development marked a return to better relations between Hammarskjöld, the independent African states and the west – or at any rate the United States where Kennedy had just assumed the presidency – but it alienated not only Tshombe but also the Kasavubu–Ileo government which suspected the UN of being in western pockets, disliked any increase in its pretensions and now began to draw closer to Tshombe. At a conference at Tananarive in March Tshombe persuaded Ileo to accept a plan for a loose confederation of sovereign Congolese states. No Lumumbist had attended the conference, whose proceedings they regarded as a western ruse to give legitimacy to Tshombe by manipulating the ex-French colonies in his favour. Ileo, however, quickly repented of having moved so far in the direction of Katanga, set about repairing relations with Gizenga and the UN and, at a further conference at Coquilhatville, ordered and effected the arrest of Tshombe.

In July the Congolese parliament assembled at Lovanium, the university town near Leopoldville, in order to patch up a grand coalition. Tshombe was released, Ileo gave way to the honest and respected manager of men, Adoula (a sort of Congolese Eisenhower), and Gizenga joined the government. On the UN side the replacement of Dayal, who was weighed down by the unhappy past, by the Tunisian Khiari and the Ghanaian Gardiner helped to improve relations between the government and the UN. But the grand coalition was not achieved. Tshombe was now odd man out.

There followed the military operations against Katanga. By now Katanga was in African terms a formidable power, equipped since the beginning of the year with men, supplies and even aircraft from Belgium, France, South Africa and Southern Rhodesia. A few specified Belgians had been removed as a result of laborious negotiations, but the course of these discussions and of events convinced UN representatives on the spot that Tshombe was only playing for time and had no real intention of dismissing the Belgian and other mercenaries or of coming to terms with Leopoldville. These suspicions received blatant confirmation at the end of August. UN forces seized about 100 foreign officers who had been declared to be undesirable aliens by the Adoula government. Tshombe acquiesced but the local UN representative, Conor Cruise O'Brien, agreed that in order to minimize personal affronts the details should be handled by the Belgian consul in Elisabethville, who guaranteed the voluntary departure of the officers but then failed to honour his word. Moreover other foreign officers not in Elisabethville remained untouched. This attempt to evict some officers was doubly unfortunate for the UN since its failure encouraged Katangan obduracy while its legality was strongly attacked by British representatives in the Congo and New York and Britain became for a while as useful an ally for Katanga as Belgium or France.

In the face of this rebuff the UN had to decide whether to take further steps or to acquiesce. Khiari and O'Brien, believing that Munongo was the real kernel of resistance, hoped to separate Tshombe from Munongo and to get Tshombe to Leopoldville where Hammarskjöld would come to talk him into a more amenable and reasonable frame of mind. But Tshombe refused to be enticed and O'Brien, believing that he had Khiari's authority to use force to round up the foreign officers in

Katanga and put an end to the Katangan secession, planned a second military operation, which included the virtual kidnapping of Tshombe. It failed. The Katangans were better prepared and the British government, by refusing to allow Ethiopian jet aircraft to fly over Rhodesia to the Congo, presented the Katangans with a decisive advantage. UN forces captured the post office and radio station at Elisabethville, but Tshombe took refuge with the British vice-consul and then in Rhodesia. The UN operation had produced bloodshed which, much exaggerated in the reporting, shocked and antagonized those who thought that a peace force must achieve peace without force, and Tshombe had been let slip. Hammarskjöld arrived in Leopoldville to find an utterly unexpected situation – confusion and stalemate in katanga, stubborn and effective hostility from Britain and, if in smaller degree, from the Belgian and American governments also. He determined to seek out Tshombe and talk to him. He left for Ndola in Rhodesia by air on 17 September and was killed when his aircraft crashed *en route*.

This appalling calamity – for Hammarskjöld was one of the half-dozen outstanding personalities in post-war international affairs – was followed by a cease-fire and the return of Tshombe to Katanga. After the appointment of U Thant to serve the rest of Hammarskjöld's term of office, the Security Council returned to its familiar dilemma: whether to try to reconcile Adoula and Tshombe or to bring the latter to heel. On 24 November the Council, Britain and France abstaining, authorized the new secretary-general to use force to expel foreign mercenaries and political advisers from Katanga, thus implicitly endorsing O'Brien's policy although he himself was removed from the scene. UN forces were still in Elisabethville but they were awkwardly placed since Tshombe's mercenaries were manifestly keen to provoke a next round of fighting, in which they would surround and destroy the UN forces. The UN representatives in Katanga decided to take action in order to prevent their scattered units from being picked off piecemeal before the arrival of reinforcements, but they were again handicapped by Britain which, having promised to deliver a supply of 100-lb bombs, succumbed to right wing pressures and cancelled its undertaking. Fighting was inconclusive and when Tshombe agreed to meet Adoula, U Thant ordered a new ceasefire. On 21 December 1961, at Kitona, Tshombe renounced secession, and the Kitona agreement was endorsed by the Katangan assembly two months later.

But the troubles of the Congo were not so easily assuaged. During most of 1962 Adoula and Tshombe were engaged in a series of fruitless discussions concerning the implementation of the Kitona agreement, which was opposed in Katanga by Munongo and European secessionists. Tshombe, who interspersed his meetings with Adoula with secret visits to Welensky in Rhodesia, seemed unable to make up his mind. He eventually departed for a prolonged stay in Europe. Although Adoula took three Katangans into his cabinet in April 1963 no genuine reconciliation was brought about. The central government continued to be oppressed by problems of economics and law and order, and early in 1964 a more serious revolt broke out in Kwilu under the leadership of Pierre Mulele, who had recently made a trip to China. This outbreak was the more ominous because the UN troops were departing. The last planeload left at the end of June, the fourth anniversary of independence.

The balance sheet of these four years of international endeavour, sometimes co-operative and sometimes competitive, is not easily struck. At the very beginning the UN, through sticking to the letter of the law, desisted from disarming the mutinous Force Publique, a major source of continuing disorder. There were also mistakes and misunderstandings in the handling of relations with the legally appointed, if personally difficult, prime minister Patrice Lumumba, and the resulting suspiciousness affected not only the UN's own standing and operations but also relations among African states and relations between them and other states. Given the circumstances, however, the misunderstandings could easily have been worse. In the Katanga operations the UN earned the hostility of certain powers and suffered from the criticism that UN forces had come to secure order but had shed blood in the name of peace. Apart from the fact that all police operations must envisage the use of force as an ultimate sanction, the blame for the ambiguities over Katanga belonged primarily to the members of the Security Council whose instructions were not at first sufficiently precise; the reverses suffered by the UN in terms of public sentiment demonstrated above all the need to provide the secretary-general with more effective consultative and executive machinery. In the last resort, however, a joint operation such as the UN operation in the Congo was bound to run into difficulties as soon as there appeared among the members any serious discrepancy of aim.

The successes of the UN were considerable. It achieved almost immediately its first aim of displacing (except from Katanga) the Belgians who had returned when the Force Publique mutinied. Its intervention also prevented intervention by individual states on their own account and enforced in one case, the Russian, a retreat; fears that Africa would become a new theatre for the cold war were allayed. The UN also succeeded to a remarkable degree in keeping the Congolese economy going, providing elementary administrative services, and preventing famine and epidemics. It could take credit for staving off civil wars in the Congo which would almost certainly have been worse but for the UN presence and became worse when that presence was removed. Finally, when the UN forces departed in June 1964 Katanga had not seceded. But it was still, as it was bound to be, richer than the whole of the rest of the country, economically so dominant that its leaders were in a position either to play a separatist hand or to claim a dominant position in the central government.

The central government's lack of authority became patent immediately after the departure of the UN forces. Civil war started again. The Adoula government was first reconstituted and then replaced by a new administration under Tshombe, who returned from Europe as the UN departed. Tshombe tried to form a broad coalition and to enlist the support of the OAU, but Gizenga (whom, among others, he released from prison) formed a new opposition party and the OAU – in spite of creating a reconciliation commission under Kenyatta's chairmanship – failed to find a remedy for the Congo's ills. Tshombe was too greatly disliked to be able to control the situation except by arms and he began, soon after his return, to enlist a new force of (mainly) Belgian and South African mercenaries. This force was quickly successful and the rebels, who had taken Stanleyville in August, found themselves threatened with the loss of all their principal strongholds. They had meanwhile taken hostages, and in an attempt to rescue these hostages Belgian parachute troops were flown in October in American aircraft from the British island of Ascension to Stanleyville, which was recaptured from the rebels. About two hundred hostages were killed in spite of this operation (or, as some maintained, because of it), in addition to some 20,000 Congolese who lost their lives in the furies of this rebellion. Africans outside the Congo were divided between those who took the easy course of denouncing the Belgians, Americans and British as imperialist recidivists and those who, stifling their dislike of Tshombe, defended the right of the Congolese government to ask for outside help if it wanted to. Tshombe, who had already in July been refused an invitation to the OAU's conference of heads of state in Cairo, was kept out of the conference of non-aligned states in the same city in October. Upon his arrival in Cairo he was escorted to a hotel and kept there until he decided to return to Leopoldville.

Both in Leopoldville and in Stanleyville, the Congolese leaders were divided among themselves. Rebel unity did not survive reverses and President Kasavubu's appointment of Tshombe as prime minister had not betokened any real reconciliation. Although Tshombe was successful in elections in April 1965, Kasavubu shortly afterwards dismissed him. The president failed, however, to construct a new government without Tshombe and in November the army, in the person of General Mobutu, stepped in, dismissed the president and established military rule. With this revolution the army, which alone had had real power since independence, assumed responsibility as well. Mobutu defeated Mulele's revolt in 1966 and next year survived an attempt, assisted by mercenaries, to restore Tshombe. He broke up the political map by reducing the number of provinces from twenty-one to twelve and then to eight, and he reduced the likelihood of secession by nationalizing the assets of the Union Minière. He repaired relations with Belgium, which he visited in 1969, concluded financial and technical agreements and played host to King Baudouin in Kinshasa. Although he had to imprison large numbers in the process, he brought a semblance of peace and some prospect of economic improvement to an exhausted country. In 1970 he became president for seven years. He felt strong enough at home to give his attention to wider African problems, meeting President Ngouabi of Congo-Brazzaville (relations between the two countries began a much needed improvement) and also Presidents Kaunda and Gowon. He introduced civilians and younger men into senior government posts in place of Adoula who fell ill and Bomboko and Nendaka who were sacked. He visited the USA, Romania and Yugoslavia. He seemed bent on making his country, now called Zaïre, the Iran of Africa.

Chapter 21

East and south central Africa

1. Kenya, Uganda, Tanzania

The preponderant power in east and south central Africa had been the British, but the first Europeans to arrive were the Portuguese. Diaz touched land in East Africa on his journey from the Cape to India and back again. On this coast the Portuguese came in touch with the Arab world, establishing ports of call and repair where Arabs were already trading: Kilwa, Zanzibar, Mombasa, Malindi. The nature and extend of Portuguese rights were vague and fluctuating, and they were gradually reduced by the Arabs and then by the British and the Dutch until only the territory of Mozambique remained to them.

The British interest in East Africa has been twofold. To the dominant power in the Indian Ocean the coastal territories were a natural bait, while Britain also became a continental African power in the course of establishing control over inland regions which were deemed necessary to safeguard British strategic interests at the Cape and in the valley of the Nile. A northern thrust from the Cape bypassing the Boer republics and continuing into Rhodesia combined with a southern thrust from Egypt and the Sudan to create the strategic importance of Uganda and the route of access to it through Kenya. In a particularly colourful chapter of the history of exploration and great power competition Britain acquired Uganda and Kenya at the end of the nineteenth century, adding Zanzibar in 1890 (in exchange for giving Heligoland to Germany) and Tanganyika in 1919 as a mandated territory after Germany's defeat in the First World War.

British power was not at first territorially deployed. Preferring, as usual, the indirect approach Britain chose to exert influence on the coast through the Sultan of Zanzibar, an Arab potentate who was also Sultan of Muscat in Arabia but had moved his capital to Zanzibar in 1840. (Zanzibar and Muscat were separated again in 1861, two sons of a deceased sultan setting up separate states and dynasties as the result of mediation by the Viceroy of India, Lord Canning.) Inland, British governments left the business of expansion to commercial concerns until the last quarter of the nineteenth century when the failure of the companies chartered to exploit parts of Africa (found to be only doubtfully rewarding), coupled with the competitive expansion of European powers in Africa, induced Britain to shift to policies of territorial annexation. The failure of the British East Africa Company, for example, led Lord Rosebery's cabinet to endorse a British protectorate over Uganda, the prime minister's doubting colleagues being overpersuaded by strategic arguments about the intentions of other European powers, particuarly Italy and Belgium, in the regions of the headwaters of the Nile. After the capitulation of the Italians at Adowa in 1896 to the emperor Menelek II Britain feared that Ethiopia would make an alliance with France or with the Mahdists in the Sudan, and Lord Salisbury pressed the construction of the Uganda railway as an adjunct of his policy of reconquering the Sudan. No less important was the contest with Germany, whose determination to become an African power had been made manifest at the Berlin Conference of 1884–85.

The Germans had staked out claims in South West Africa and then in East Africa to the embarrassment of Britain which disliked German expansion in Africa but was in need of Germany's friendship in Europe and elsewhere during the period of bad Anglo-French relations from 1880 to 1904. Britain consequently acquiesced in the German occupation of South West Africa, while taking the precaution of securing Bechuanaland against possible German (or Boer) aspirations which might interfere with he railway from the Cape northwards. In East Africa Britain likewise acquiesced in a German presence and gave up using the Sultan of Zanzibar to make things difficult for the Germans in Tanganyika, while at the same time leasing from the Sultan in 1887 a coastal strip ten miles long (including Mombasa) and developing British power in Uganda and Nyasaland so that the emerging German empire might be contained within limits compatible with essential British interests. The First World War eliminated the German factor, but the early part of the twentieth century also saw, in Britain's more northerly colony of Kenya, an enterprise which was later to produce its own problems. This was the development of Kenya by white settlers. While the removal of great power complications enabled the Foreign Office to dismiss East Africa from its mind, the emergence of new complications of a different nature do not seem to have troubled the mind of the Colonial Office until too late, for whereas the Devonshire Declaration of 1923 had affirmed the primacy of African interests, the settler community assumed, and was allowed to go on assuming until the eve of independence, that its own powers and privileges were not threatened within the foreseeable future. Even in the nineteen-fifties both races believed that a white government's devotion to the principles of self-determination and majority rule would stop short at putting a substantial white community under black rule.

East African independence followed West African but – partly because it came later – was achieved by a telescoped sequence of the established pattern of evolution from nominated to mixed councils and so to the fully elected parliaments which accompanied self-government and presaged independence. Tanganyika became independent in December 1961, Uganda in October 1962 and Kenya in December

1963, but in spite of their geographical closeness the circumstances of the three territories were very different.

The special features of Uganda's progress to independence were provided by the composite political structure of the country. The Uganda protectorate included a number of monarchical entities, of which the most important was Buganda under the rule of its kabaka, Frederick Mutesa II. Others were Bunyoro, Toro, Ankole and Busogo. Moreover, between Buganda and Bunyoro there was a territorial feud of long standing. One consequence of the existence of these principalities was that Uganda had a relatively strong nationalism of a traditionalist kind which was antagonistic both to British colonial rule and to the more democratic and anti-monarchical forms of nationalism. The comparative weakness of these latter strands tended to cast the colonial administration for a progressive role in opposition to the conservatism of the kabaka, who was concerned to preserve his traditional powers and the separate identity of his principality. In 1953 a British minister let fall in London an ill-timed remark about an East African federation which was taken by the kabaka – and many other Africans – to betoken a British scheme to create a large new political unit for the better preservation of white rule. A Central African federation was being formed at this time and East Africans feared that the white settlers in Kenya were to be given throughout East Africa the powers which Southern Rhodesia's white minority was in the process of confirming in its own country and extending to Northern Rhodesia and Nyasaland. A quarrel ensued between the kabaka and the governor, Sir Andrew Cohen, and the kabaka was despatched into exile for failing to observe the Uganda agreement of 1900, by which he was obliged to accept British advice on certain matters.

The kabaka's exile lasted until 1955. A commission under Sir Keith Hancock worked out a new constitution which the kabaka accepted by the Namirembe agreement and by which he agreed to turn Buganda into a constitutional monarchy and recognize it as being an integral part of Uganda; the Buganda parliament or lukiko was to send representatives to sit in the Uganda parliament (though it began by refusing to do so). The kabaka was thus restored, but the principality to which he returned was a budding democracy within a larger democracy and the British aim to create an independent Uganda which was a unitary parliamentary democracy and not a federation had been significantly advanced.

Britain failed, however, to resolve Buganda's quarrel with Bunyoro. This quarrel went back to 1893 when the British under Lugard and the then kabaka had made war on Bunyoro. Buganda had taken from Bunyoro five counties and two parts of counties and this transfer had been sanctified by Britain in the Uganda agreement of 1900, since when Britain had turned a deaf ear to all Bunyoro complaints. In 1961, however, Britain appointed a commission of privy councillors (the Molson commission) to try to resolve the quarrel before independence.

The commission recommended a compromise which was only partially implemented by the British authorities. Buganda was confirmed in its possession of four counties which were allotted to it by the commission, but a decision on the rest of the disputed territory was postponed. In 1964, after independence, the government of Uganda conducted the plebiscite which had been recommended by the Molson commission and which conclusively restored these areas to Bunyoro.

Constitutional change in Uganda had begun in 1950 when the legislative council was given an equal number of official members (i.e. colonial servants) and unofficial members. Of the latter eight were African, four Asian and four European in recognition of an ethnic problem which did not, however, impede the advance to independence owing to the fact that the European settlers were too few to think of retaining political power and the Asians judged it expedient at an early date to conciliate rather than antagonize the African majority. A similar balance of official and unofficial members was established in the executive council in 1952. In 1954 the size of the legislative council was doubled. In 1961 Uganda was given self-government and Benedikto Kiwanuka became its first prime minister, but Bugandan separatism continued to delay full independence. The lukiko, which had petitioned the British Crown in 1957 for greater autonomy and refused in the following year to play its allotted role in a general election, even declared Buganda independent. The Uganda Peoples Congress, which had been formed by Milton Obote to fight for independence, entered into an alliance with the Bugandan home rule party, Kabaka Yekka, in order to win a parliamentry majority. Obote took Kiwanuka's place. Independence followed in October 1962. In the following year Uganda became a republic in the Commonwealth and the kabaka accepted the ornamental office of president. But the alliance between Obote and the kabaka did not last. Early in 1966 rumours of scandals in high places threatened to weaken Obote's position. He set up an inquiry and then assumed emergency powers, dismissed and arrested a number of his ministers and dismissed the president. Two months later he introduced a new constitution which precipitated a fresh clash between himself and the lukiko and made himself president. Recurrent rumours of Buganda plans to resort to force induced, or enabled, him to act first. The kabaka's palace was sacked and the kabaka, barely escaping, was driven once more into exile.

Tanganyika followed in form a similar course through official-unofficial partnership in government to self-government and independence, but the British authorities tried to give a special multiracial twist to events by espousing the equality of races as opposed to the equality of individuals. This concept was enshrined in a constitution of 1955 which provided that the electors in each constituency should all elect one member of each of the three races, but a party formed to apply it, the United Tanganyika Party, never secured much support and was eclipsed by the Tanganyika African National Union

(Tanu) formed by Julius Nyerere in 1954. In 1957 Nyerere, who had been asking for independence in twenty-five years' time, was appointed a member of the legislative council together with Rashid Kawawa, but he soon resigned in order to press the pace and urge independence by 1969. In elections spread over a period in 1958–59 Tanu won all the seats which it contested, and in 1960 it extended its victories throughout the country. The multiracial experiment was given up after a change of governor and of colonial secretary in 1959, and Tanganyika attained independence in 1961. It chose to be a republic and a member of the Commonwealth.

One of the most important elections in the history of British decolonization was held not in any colony but in Britain itself. In 1959 Harold Macmillan was returned to power by the British electorate and one of his first undertakings after this refreshing experience was a journey through Africa which made manifest a new attitude to colonial affairs. Macmillan had felt the 'wind of change' and had determined to let it blow him along. His new colonial secretary, Iain Macleod, was immediately faced with the most difficult of all the East African situations. Kenya.

In Kenya unofficial members of the legislative council began to be given ministerial appointments immediately after the end of the Second World War. They were, however, not black but white, representatives of the British settlers who had been coming to Kenya since the beginning of the century and had been acquiring and developing, in good faith and with intelligent toil, the excellent agricultural land in what came to be called the White Highlands. This community became also politically powerful. It hoped either to rule Kenya in lieu of the colonial authorities or to share in governing a multi-racial state on a scale appropriate to its wealth and sophistication rather than to its numbers. It was in other words an aristocracy with scant prospects in a democracy and it was suddenly faced with the problems, more familiar to historians than to farmers, of the aristocracy which is required by events to come to terms with a non-aristocratic future.

In 1952 this community and the colonial régime were faced with a savage outbreak in the Kikuyu tribe which lived in and around Nairobi and had long nourished grievances against the white settlers. Overtly the Kikuyu were represented by Jomo Kenyatta, one time student of anthropology at London university and president of the Kenya African Union, who had returned to Kenya in 1947. In addition the Kikuyu had formed about 1948 a secret society called Mau Mau, whose activities – known to the authorities but not made much of – were the militant expression of deep-seated nationalist or xenophobic movement. Mau Mau administered oaths and performed secret rites and cherished apocalyptic fancies, all of which were anti-European and anti-Christian. With time the society became extreme in its ambitions and barbarous in its practices. It took to murder – mostly of other Kikuyu – and finally developed a campaign of violence and guerrilla warfare. The government declared an emergency, called for military reinforcements from neighbouring territories and from Britain, arrested thousands of Kikuyu including Kenyatta (who was sentenced in 1954 to seven years' imprisonment for organizing Mau Mau), and gradually suppressed the rising. It also initiated a programme for the psychological reorientation of the detainees, although in other departments it succumbed to the infectious passions roused by the Mau Mau and became responsible for ugly beatings of detainees, notably at the Hola camp where gross inhumanities and murders were disclosed at a coroner's inquest in 1959. The African victims of Mau Mau numbered some 8,000; the number of Europeans killed was sixty-eight.

The British government realized that Mau Mau could not be made an excuse for abandoning constitutional advance and in 1956, the year of the termination of the emergency, it introduced changes in the legislative council. The guiding principle was that of multi-racialism or partnership between the races, a theory of government which found almost no support among the Africans who demanded a majority in the legislative and executive councils and refused to accept parity with the European elected members in the former or a minority of seats in the latter. To Africans multi-racialism was a device for giving the whites unfair shares. The Africans also insisted on being given a date for independence, whereas the British government, unwilling to accept the evidence of an accelerating tempo throughout Africa or to affront the Kenyan settlers by naming a date acceptable to Africans, tried to proceed towards independence at an unrevealed pace without losing control of the situation. In 1959 this policy was abandoned (along with the current colonial secretary) and Kenyatta was conditionally released; in 1961 he was given full freedom of movement and then allowed to stand for and be elected to the legislative assembly.

A constitutional conference was held at Lancaster House in London in 1960 and shortly afterwards the leader of government business in the assembly, Ronald Ngala, was up-graded to chief minister. But the African political leaders, who were now clearly destined to take power in the near future, were divided among themselves. Many of them represented tribes rather than a nation and they failed therefore to create the single unified independence movement which was characteristic of other emergent African countries. The weaker tribes combined to oppose the stronger Kikuyu and Luo and to press for a federal constitution in which important powers would reside in regions rather than with the central government. Constitutional conferences became contests between the Kenya Africa Democratic Union (Kadu), the proponents of regionalism led by Ngala, and the Kenya African National Union (Kanu), which objected that too much regionalism would make the constitution unworkable and that Kenya had neither the money nor the trained administrators to be able to afford the complications and duplications of a federal system. The advantage lay with Kanu, under the leadership of Kenyatta, who became prime minister in

June 1963, and the British government was even forced to amend in September constitutional proposals of a federal nature which had earlier been accepted by all parties. Kanu's success in elections in May enabled it to face the British government with the choice between revising the constitution on the eve of independence or seeing it changed immediately afterwards. The British preferred to give way in the hope of sparing Kenya a constitutional crisis on the morrow of independence, even though the cost of concession was a not implausible charge of bad faith from Kadu. Kenya became independent on 12 December 1963. It became a republic in 1964 when the constitution was further revised in the direction of centralism. In 1969 it lost the ablest of its leaders when Tom Mboya was assassinated. Before this Kenyatta had removed his principal left wing rival, Oginga Odinga, from the vice-presidency and then put him in detention. Kenyatta also became demonstratively anti-communist. He rejected Russian arms, expelled Russian journalists and the Chinese ambassador, and closed the Lumumba Institute.

The delay caused by the tussle between Kanu and Kadu had been a source of anxiety in Tanganyika and Uganda. Kawawa and Obote went to London in 1963 to try to persuade Britain to hurry Kenya into independence. In June the leaders in the three countries declared their intention to federate. Uganda, however, had reservations about a federation since Obote feared that Buganda would insist on being a full member of such a union instead of a component part of Uganda. Kenyatta subsequently disclaimed any serious intention to federate, declaring that the plan had been no more than a means of pressing Britain to hasten Kenya's independence. Perhaps Nyerere alone was wholehearted. The proceedings were certainly dilatory. Obote failed to attend a meeting held in Nairobi in September to discuss the scheme, and the Kenyans established an awkward system of being represented by Kanu at one meeting and Kadu at the next. There were also genuine difficulties such as the location of the federal capital, the choice of a federal president (the promotion of Kenyatta, the obvious candidate, would unleash an inopportune contest for the Kenyan presidency), the division of powers and other constitutional matters, opposition from Ghana to any regional associations likely to hamper Nkrumah's pan-African schemes, and Tanganyika's trend to the left in its domestic and its external policies. In the end Tanganyika, regretfully but firmly, insisted on a decision and the scheme thereupon collapsed.

A different amalgamation did, however, take place. On 12 January 1964 the Afro-Shirazi Union in Zanzibar seized power by a coup. This party, which represented the bulk of the African population of about 200,000 (the Arabs numbering some 44,000) had suffered a set-back in elections in 1961 which had given control to a coalition of the Zanzibar National Party and the Zanzibar Peoples Party; and in 1963 the British, ignoring warnings from Tanganyika, had transferred power to the sultan and the Arab minority with the result that Zanzibar had carried into independence an inbuilt racial conflict in which the scales had been artificially tipped in favour of a minority. The Afro-Shirazi Union wanted neither the sultan nor any kind of Arab dominance. Its leaders – Abeid Karume, Abdullah Hanga, Othman Shariff – led what was essentially an African, anti-Arab revolt and proclaimed a republic with the first two as president and vice-president. Their allies in this reversal of power included a minor Arab party, the Umma Party led by Adbul Rahman Muhammad Babu, the local correspondent of the *New China News Agency*, and a curious soldier of fortune styled Field-Marshall John Okello, who was said to have fought in Cuba but was soon sent into exile when the value of his services proved less than the embarrassment of his presence. The Afro-Shirazis and their friends were quickly branded by a startled world as tools of China.

Alarm was felt in Dar-es-Salaam too and on 17 January Nyerere, remembering perhaps Nasser's anti-communist pre-emptive action in Syria in 1958, sent his home minister and some armed police to Zanzibar, thus acquiring control of the situation. On 20 January troops in Dar-es-Salaam mutinied; a second mutiny occurred at Tabora in central Tanganyika on the following day. Similar acts of insubordination took place in Uganda and Kenya on the 23rd and 24th. In all these places order was restored with the help of British troops who were still stationed in Nairobi (they were not due to leave until the end of the year). The mutineers asked for better pay and the replacement of British officers by Africans. They were using violence to protest to their leaders, not attempting to overthrow them. But in the light of events in Zanzibar rumours circulated of a widespread communist plot, reinforced by Okello's presence in Dar-es-Salaam on the eve of the first disturbance. The British left a week after their arrival. In April Tanganyika and Zanzibar were joined together to make the new state of Tanzania with Nyerere as president and Karume as senior vice-president. The association proved most unhappy for Nyerere. He was denied all influence in Zanzibar and even access to it. Karume established an autocratic régime which, whether or not it was under Chinese control, certainly produced some extreme scandals such as the much publicized forcing of teenage girls into marriage or concubinage with the island's new élite. In 1969 Karume was able to exact from Nyerere the return to Zanzibar of political enemies who were thereby consigned to their deaths. This humiliating concession to brutality by a statesman of an uncommonly humane nature may have been due to Nyerere's fear that Zanzibar might add to his other current troubles, for he was facing discontent in the south, among former members of trade unions (which he had suppressed) and from women's organizations, junior officers and disappointed civil servants. Karume was assassinated in 1972.

The three East African territories made some attempts to integrate their economies. Under British rule they had had a common currency, and certain common services (for example, posts, railways, medical services) and had constituted a common market. Tanganyika and Uganda complained, at intervals and with some justice, that Kenya took the lion's share of the resulting benefits and in 1960 the Raisman Commission was appointed to report on these dissensions. It recommended that the links should be retained subject to some reorganization in favour of Tanganyika and Uganda. In 1964 Kenya offered further concessions in order to prevent the disruption of this partial union and in 1968, after a fresh inquiry and report by a Danish expert, the three states signed a Treaty of East African Co-operation. It became a dead letter.

Kenyatta and Nyerere brought stability, if of different kinds, to their countries. Both were still in office in 1975, the former becoming more remote and unpredictable with age and giving rise to some apprehension about what would happen when he died; the latter continuing to guide Tanzania along the road of self-reliance proclaimed by the Arusha Declaration which in 1967 pledged the country to a village socialism and participatory democracy within the framework of a single-party state. In Uganda things were different. Obote was overthrown by an army coup while he was attending a Commonwealth conference in Singapore in January 1971. In coming to power he had antagonized many traditionalists, particularly in Buganda; he had then scared the property-owning classes by mildly left wing pronouncements, and intellectuals by authoritarian scorn. After surviving at attempt on his life in 1969 he tried to curb the power of the army and its commander, Idi Amin, but failed to do so. Amin took his place. Hailed at first as a good sound army type (and boxing champion) with a respectably British background, Amin instituted a reign of terror, especially after an unsucessful attempt by Obote in September 1972 to invade Uganda from Tanzania with a force of about 1000 men. (Obote had gone first to Sudan but had had to leave as a result of the pacification of the south by Nimeiry.) Amin was not reluctant to play a part in international affairs. He proclaimed himself a friend of Israel but then changed sides and became a strong partisan of the Palestinians. He made a particular stir by giving notice to Uganda's 70,000 Asians to leave the country within three months, though he later exempted those of them who were Ugandan citizens. Since most of them were British citizens Amin's move greatly embarrassed the British government which, having foolishly failed to take up an earlier offer by Obote to discuss this problem, now found itself caught between its evident obligation to allow British citizens into Britain and the clamour against allowing them in if they were numerous and black. Amin also evicted the British military mission and High Commissioner whom he accused of complicity in Obote's attempted counter-coup. In the following year he began the take-over of hundreds of foreign, mostly British, businesses while throughout the country the roll of Ugandans, distinguished and undistinguished, who disappeared increased gruesomely, possibly into six figures.

2. Ethiopia and Somalia

The ancient Ethiopian kingdom, an amalgam of races, languages and religions, retained its independence even in the nineteenth century and therewith a certain immunity from the modernizing trends which normally accompany both colonialism and anti-colonial movements. Subjected for only five years in the twentieth century (1936–41), it resumed its hallowed way of life under its astute monarch Haile Selassie, who had first mounted the throne in 1930 at the age of thirty-eight. The emperor was a cautious innovator whose reforming proclivities were in advance of the landed feudatories and wealthy churchmen who were the most eminent and ultimately the most powerful people in his realm. An attempted coup at the end of 1960, followed by army mutinies in March 1961 and a reported conspiracy in August of that year, suggested the existence of some discontent among the educated young and junior officers who looked to Prince Asfa Wossen for more spirited progress, but the emperor re-established his control with awe-inspiring ease and continued his policy of slow internal advance. He also cultivated good relations with the emerging states of Africa (perhaps as an insurance against traditional Muslim hostility towards his predominantly Christian empire); in 1958 his capital became the headquarters for the UN Economic Commission for Africa and in 1963 the Organization for African Unity came to birth there. For both these organizations the emperor caused handsome quarters to be built.

Ethiopia's special external concern was with the neighbouring and non-Bantu Somalis who, unlike the Ethiopians, were not only conquered by Europeans in the nineteenth century but also partitioned among them. The Somalis, Muslims but not Arabs, appeared in the Horn of Africa towards the end of the European Middle Ages and subsequently joined in Muslim attacks on the Christian kingdom of Ethiopia. They were subjected in the latter part of the nineteenth century, first by the French in the sixties and then by the British and the Italians (who also took Eritrea) in the eighties. The British colony of Kenya extended northwards over a predominantly Somali area, and Ethiopia appropriated in its Ogaden province territory to which the Somalis laid claim. Relations between Ethiopia and the Somalis were therefore inherently bad and British relations with both were uneasy, since the Ethiopians suspected Britain of partiality to Somali claims against Ethiopia, while Somalis found Britain unsympathetic to their claims against Kenya.

In 1935 the Italians, dissatisfied with the barrenness of their part of Somaliland and their imperial pretensions in general, exploited an incident at Wal Wal in the disputed Ogaden in order to conquer Ethiopia. They were suspected of toying with the idea of a Greater Somalia which would annex British Somaliland, but their defeat by the British in 1941 revived the independent Ethiopean empire (to which was added Eritrea in 1952 after a period of British trusteeship) and left the Somalis still subject and divided. At the end of the war Ernest Bevin proposed at one moment a Greater Somalia consisting of British and Italian Somaliland and parts of Ethiopia, but this notion antagonized Ethiopia without profiting the Somalis. Discussions on the Ethiopian–Somali frontier proceeded sluggishly until 1959 when a conference in Oslo with Trygve Lie as arbitrator produced a compromise agreeable to neither side. In 1960 Italian Somaliland, to which the Italians had returned in 1950 to administer a ten-year trusteeship, became independent, and as this date approached the British, who had become nervous of Egyptian interference in British Somaliland, hurried their own colony forward so that it could be joined with Italian Somaliland to make the independent republic of Somalia – large but poor, racially mixed, ill prepared, and distrusted and menaced by its Ethiopian and Kenyan neighbours. A movement in French Somaliland in favour of accession to Somalia had been circumvented two years earlier when the territory's assembly voted in favour of continuing as an Overseas Territory of the French Union.

At the Lancaster House conference on Kenya in 1962 the Somalis asked unsuccessfully for a plebiscite in the Northern Frontier District of Kenya (an area of over 100,000 square miles) and its union with Somalia. Later in the same year Kenyan politicians discussed with Somalis an East African federation which would embrace not only Somalia and the British East African territories but also Ethiopia; in the event of some such development the Kenyans made it plain that they intended to keep the whole of the Northern Frontier District for themselves. In December a boundaries commission recommended that the district be divided into two regions, both to be included in the new Kenyan state. This recommendation, which was accepted by the British government, produced riots and a rupture of diplomatic relations by Somalia. Kenya was able to get other African states on its side and a Kenyan delegation walked out of an Afro-Asian conference at Moshi in Tanganyika in February 1963 when the Somalis raised the border issue. At a further conference in Addis Ababa in May a number of Africans chided the Somalis for again raising the question.

In the same year open hostilities broke out between Somalia and Ethiopia. The Somalis did not accept the treaty of 1897 by which Britain had ceded part of British Somaliland to Ethiopia; between Italian Somaliland and Ethiopia there was no established border. On independence the Somalis had refrained from challenging a neighbour which possessed American equipment. Ethiopia too, conscious of the racial divisions within its own borders, avoided a clash. But the Somali claim against Kenya alarmed Ethiopia owing to its affinity with Somali claims on Ethiopia's Ogaden province. Fighting developed unofficially along the border during 1962. In the next year the Somali prime minister, Abdirashid Shermake, visited the USSR, Egypt, India, Pakistan and Italy. He got little help or encouragement. Kenya's independence at the end of that year saw also the formal conclusion of a pre-arranged Kenyan-Ethiopian defence treaty, and a few months later open fighting began between Ethiopia and Somalia. The Russians offered their mediation and a deputy foreign minister of the USSR went to Mogadishu, thereby evincing Russian concern, if not for the Somalis, at any rate about possible American or Chinese influence in the Horn. More effective mediation was proffered by the president of the Sudan and the king of Morocco, and after talks in Khartoum hostilities were suspended. But the underlying problem was not resolved and further discussions between Kenya and Somalia in 1965 were abortive. Sporadic fighting continued until 1967 when a new Somali government asked President Kaunda to mediate. Diplomatic relations were restored the next year.

But the Horn of Africa remained an uneasy quarter: a meeting place of races and religions; a scene of territorial claims between rivals backed by outside powers – Ethiopia by the United States, Kenya presumptively by Britain, Somalia by the USSR; a bridge from Africa into Asia hardly less important than the complementary passage through Sinai at the other end of the Red Sea. In 1974 the largest of these units fell to pieces. Haile Selassie had been pressed by friends and relatives to abdicate in 1973 when he reached the age of eighty. He refused to do so and in the following year a group of army officers mutinied. This mutiny led to a further revolt by privates, NCOs and junior officers, to the dethronement of the emperor (who later died in prison, possibly murdered or maltreated) and to numerous political assassinations. The deadening influence of the aged, if once noble, emperor had produced intolerable strains (between regions and classes and even within the army) conspiracies, corruption, misgovernment and stagnation, all of which were worsened by the drought and famine which afflicted much of Africa in the early seventies and by the contrasting affluence of the court and nobles. The first mutiny was followed by a series of short-lived governments and by the formation of a Dergue or Committee whose membership seemed to be fluid and was largely unknown but which became the ultimate power in the capital. Over much of the country there was little settled authority and in Eritrea, where revolt had been sporadic but endemic since the early sixties, rebellion.

The last vestiges of direct European control in this quarter of Africa were maintained by France in the Overseas Territory (i.e. autonomous dependency) of the Afars and Issas, which contained the port of Djibouti and the west shore of the Bab el-Mandeb (through which passes much of the world's oil). In 1975 France decided to leave the territory, thus sharpening the conflict between the Afars and their cognates in Ethiopia on the one hand and the Issas, who were Somalis, on the other, at a moment when the much smaller Somali state and army had the edge over an Ethiopia weakened by revolution and disruption. These events had wider repercussions since the United States and the USSR had picked different clients in the Horn of Africa, the former having sustained Ethiopia until the fall of the emperor and the latter having lavished arms and aid on Somalia.

3. The legacy of Cecil Rhodes

Towards the end of the nineteenth century the British presence in Cape Colony, hemmed in and menaced by the German occupation of South West Africa on the one hand and the Boer republics across the Orange and Vaal rivers on the other, caused the British to venture northwards in order to rule out a junction between these two potential enemies and to secure a passage for a railway to the north through British territory. In 1884, the British government declared a protectorate over Bechuanaland, a huge and largely desert area to the north of Cape Colony, but for the rest of the century it was a British citizen rather than any British government who directed the British advance in this sector. That citizen was Cecil Rhodes and one of the principal reasons why he was able to direct policy was the fact that he was able to finance it.

Rhodes struck north from the Cape Colony into Bechuanaland with his eyes on the Zambezi river – and possibly even the Nile. His company, the British South Africa Company, was chartered by the British government in 1889 to administer Bechuanaland and he lost no time in pushing on. In 1896–7 he fought and conquered the Matebele and the Mashona and so became the ruler of what was later to be called Southern Rhodesia, but also in 1896 the failure of the Jameson raid into the Transvaal wrecked his ambition to rule in Johannesburg too and resulted in a gradual reassertion of British governmental control over policy towards the Boers: in 1899 it was the British government and not Rhodes who made the Boer War. From Southern Rhodesia he continued across the Zambezi and, by questionable methods and with questionable legality, won concessions from the sovereign or litunga of Barotseland and other African chiefs. (Lewanika, the litunga of Barotseland, had given a concession to a fortune-hunter in Johannesburg who sold it to the company. He then gave further concessions to the company in the hope of enlisting British support against the Matabele monarch, Lobengula. It seems very unlikely that the parties to the concession agreements were talking about the same things and accordingly the agreements would, in English law, be void.) Rhodes's empire was now considerable and there was no reason to suppose that it had stopped growing. Nyasaland was in fact added, although Katanga, a likely next candidate, was never reached. But the British government became restive at the prospect of having an over-mighty subject, and although the company had been allowed mineral rights (which turned out to be extremely lucrative after the opening of Northern Rhodesia's copper mines) its administrative rights were restricted. Northern Rhodesia became a British protectorate in 1924 and Nyasaland, which had been penetrated in the first place by Scottish missionaries rather than the militant pioneers from the Cape, in 1907.

In 1923 Southern Rhodesia, which had become an area of white settlement, became a self-governing colony. The British government transferred control of the colony's internal affairs to its white community and, subject only to certain safeguards and reservations, withdrew from direct participation. The alternative of uniting Southern Rhodesia with South Africa was mooted but rejected by the white Southern Rhodesians. The question of forms of association between various British territories was already in the air in the nineteen-twenties but in 1929, when the Hilton Young commission reported on this area, Northern Rhodesia and Nyasaland were expected to consort with Tanganyika rather than with Southern Rhodesia, and in 1930 the British government accentuated the differences between the two Rhodesias by declaring that in the protectorates native interests were paramount. This declaration contrasted with Southern Rhodesia's Land Apportionment Act of the same year.

At the time of the conquest by Rhodes's pioneers land had been taken from the Matabele and the Mashona. Rhodes was chiefly interested in mineral rights and, by the so-called Rudd concession signed by Kobengula, he acquired for £1,200 a year mineral rights which his company sold in 1933 to the government of Southern Rhodesia. At the same time Rhodes also acquired, indirectly from Lobengula through a man called Lippert, certain 'land' rights for £1,000 a year – and thereby gave rise to a long controversy whether his company had bought the whole of the surface of Southern Rhodesia. At the time of self-government the company, which had previously re-sold 31 million acres, transferred a balance of 45 million acres to the new government. In 1914 21 million acres had been 'reserved' for the native population and a royal commission had judged this to be enough. In 1930 the whole of the country was divided by the Land Apportionment Act into European Areas, Native Purchase Areas, Unoccupied Areas and Forests, but the division was regarded by the Africans as unjust since the Europeans, who constituted less than a fifth of the population, were allotted a slightly larger share of the whole, and all the towns; in this area no African might own land. The 1930 division therefore sharpened instead of allaying resentments about how the land had been acquired in the first place, and showed that in Southern Rhodesia native interests would be anything but paramount. The principle of racial division of the land was also a foretaste of further racial irritants on a similarly unjust and discriminatory basis.

After a preliminary conference of officials from the two Rhodesias at Victoria Falls in 1936 the Bledisloe commission was appointed in 1938 to consider closer union between them and Nyasaland. The commission rejected the idea on the grounds that divergences in native policies and the hostility of the Africans made it impracticable. It recommended no more than a Central African council consisting of the governors of the two protectorates and the prime minister of Southern Rhodesia to co-ordinate matters of common concern. This pale and tepid council was created in 1944. But the protagonists of closer union were neither discouraged nor defeated and in nine years they secured the creation of the Central African federation. Throughout these years Southern Rhodesia was pursuing a policy of association with Northern Rhodesia father having rejected the alternative of association with South Africa. It was not contemplating a separate existence on its own, although there was among the whites a group which wanted dominion status for Southern Rhodesia within the Commonwealth.

The white leaders in Northern and Southern Rhodesia realized that their interests were not the same and were wary of each other. Roy Welensky in the north, where the riches lay, suspected Godfrey Huggins in the south of wishing to take over Northern Rhodesia for the benefit of the more numerous white population of Southern Rhodesia. On the other hand Southern Rhodesia, although poorer, was freer in terms of British control over its internal affairs; it had a quasi-independence which the whites in Northern Rhodesia (excluding the colonial administrators) coveted for themselves and wished to secure through the Southern Rhodesian back door. These attitudes were clearly to the fore at a conference at Victoria Falls in 1949 which, with no Africans present, became a tussle between Huggins and Welensky with the latter falling back on the position that there should be no federation without a referendum. The northerners were at this stage suspicious of the federal idea, but the conference put it on the map and made it the central talking-point of the next few years. This conference was followed in 1951 by a conference in London of officials from the three territories and the two British departments of state concerned (the Colonial Office and the Commonwealth Relations Office). Their report, while again recognizing African opposition to federation, hoped that it would evaporate under the impact of the economic advantages which they listed. At a further conference in the same year at Victoria Falls the politicians (who included the two British secretaries of state as well as the two governors), senior officials white Rhodesian leaders accepted the greater part of the officials' arguments. This conference was also attended by Africans from Northern Rhodesia and Nyasaland, but they were less impressed by the economic advantages of a federation than by the fear of coming under the rule of the white minority in Salisbury.

A change of government in London from Labour to Conservative shifted the balance of forces in favour of federation. Whereas Labour ministers had come to look favourably on federation but were unwilling to go forward with it without first discovering more about the wishes of the African population, Conservative ministers were more emphatic in their approval, considered that it was impossible to discover what the Africans really thought, ascribed African opposition to irascible and ignorant factiousness, and believed that it was in any case the duty of government to do what was best even if some people did not yet see how good it was. Yet another conference assembled, this time at Lancaster House in London (the maternity ward for emergent constitutions). It was boycotted by the Africans of the two northern territories, though the Southern Rhodesian delegation included Joseph Savanhu and Joshua Nkomo who acted as uneasy camp-followers until the end of the conference. The outcome was a federal constitution with temporarily significant reservations. The federation was to have three separate territorial administrations and assemblies as well as a federal government and parliament, the retention of the British protectorate over the northern territories, the proviso that the federation should not be granted dominion status without the consent of a majority of the population, and the creation of an African Affairs Board with blocking powers designed (unsuccessfully as it proved) to prevent racially discriminatory legislation. The federation came into being on 1 August 1953. Huggins became the first federal prime minister with Welensky as his deputy and a cabinet of six; Huggins also became the leader of a newly formed Federal Party with branches on both sides of the Zambezi. In Southern Rhodesia Huggins was succeeded by Garfield Todd as prime minister and leader of the United Party.

The Central African federation lasted ten years. It was accepted with misgiving by some whites in Southern Rhodesia who feared cheap black labour and rightly opined that the connection with the British protecting power in the north would act as a drag on their plans for dealing with the racial situation. But on the whole federation was welcomed by the whites who believed that within it they would conserve their privileged standards of living, excitingly expand the material things which they were already doing well, and somehow find a way of fitting a small African middle class into the existing order. The idea of partnership, which was written into the constitution and salved a lot of uneasy consciences in London, meant at best a half share in power for Africans in a barely discernible future. Like the Belgians in the Congo they regarded the African as an economic man who could be satisfied with a material competence (however assessed) and, apart from a few over-educated eccentrics and professional trouble-makers, had no real interest in politics. Nationalism they greviously underestimated, and also the force of human indignation over inequality and injustice. Ideas were not their stock-in-trade and so they failed to realize that ideas were at the root of the refusal of the Africans to accept their rule. From the prime minister downwards they insulted and humiliated their black fellow citizens with remarks about living in trees and with the practical application of segregation in public places like post-offices and restaurants, and so quickly confirmed the Africans' conviction that partnership was to be not an endeavour but a pretence.

The life of the federation was violent as well as short. The Africans began the violence. Most of them were never interested in the economic aspects of federation or never understood them; the more sophisticated among them understood and saw that they were largely bogus. Despite a distinct current of non-violence in the African national movements the partisans of violence, aided by circumstances and by exaggerated white reactions, became increasingly prominent. An incident, provoked by thieves in the night, at Cholo in Nyasaland in August 1953 caused the deaths of eleven Africans and injuries to many more and led the authorities to magnify the prevalence of hooliganism and subversive activities. It was also a curtain-raiser for more significant events in Nyasaland.

Nyasaland was included in the federation because the British insisted, unwilling to keep it on their hands as a separate dependency with little hope of becoming anything but a drain on the British exchequer. It was an African country with a white population of only 1 in 500, no settlers or industry, its people dependent on Southern Rhodesia and South Africa for the jobs which did not exist and had not been created in their own country. It had been nurtured by the Church of Scotland in much the same way as Paraguay by the Jesuits. It had also a charismatic figure beyond the horizon in Dr Hastings Banda who had spent most of his life learning and practising the profession of medicine in the United States, Scotland, Liverpool, Tyneside and Ghana.

Dr Banda arrived in Nyasaland in 1958 to lead an anti-federation crusade in conjunction with nationalists of a younger generation who were glad to enlist and serve under this more famous elder figure. As in many similar cases certain differences of aim and outlook were easily submerged by the single paramount objective of seceding from the federation and establishing an independent sovereign state. In January 1959 there occurred a secret and apparently confused palaver between nationalist leaders which was afterwards represented as a murderous conspiracy to kill a number of Europeans and seize power. Banda was not present at this meeting and either knew nothing of it, or did not mind what happened at it, or knew all about it and those to turn a blind eye. Banda himself was a man of considerable even violent, oratorical powers who preached non-violence, but the situation was one of growing violence and jumpiness and in February the governor of Nyasaland asked for Rhodesian troops to help keep order. The government of Southern Rhodesia sent 3,000 troops and took the opportunity to declare a state of emergency in its own territory. The governor of Nyasaland followed suit a week later. Between 2,000 and 3,000 Africans were rounded up in the federation, the African National Congresses in all three territories were dissolved, and Banda and his chief associates were among those lodged in gaol. The British colonial secretary, Alan Lennox-Boyd, said that he had evidence of an impending massacre.

These dramatic events evoked some scepticism as well as alarm, and the British government appointed a commission under a High Court judge, Sir Patrick Devlin, to verify the allegations with which these emergency measures had been justified. The commission was unable to find evidence of any murder plot and specificially exonerated Banda. It found that the governor of Nyasaland had got into a position where he had either to abdicate or reach for emergency powers and troops, and that in consequence Nyasaland had become temporarily a police state in which it was unsafe to express approval of the policies of the Congress to which the great majority of Africans adhered. This report, by exploding a myth propagated by authorities in London as well as Salisbury, gave a fillip to the anti-federation campaign and discredited the *bona fides* of their opponents. Shortly after its appearance the Colonial Office was placed in the charge of a more liberal member of the Conservative government, Iain Macleod, and the prime minister, Harold Macmillan, began a series of devious moves designed to give British colonial policies a leftward shift. These moves were to include his tour of Africa, his 'wind of change' speech at Cape Town during that tour, the appointment of the Monckton commission, and Macleod's first visit to Kenya – all in 1960.

The federal constitution of 1953 had left the territorial constitutions untouched. It had also made clear that the federation could not hope for independence or dominion status until they were touched. In 1958 there were elections for the federal and the Southern Rhodesian parliaments. In the former Welensky, who had succeeded Huggins (now Lord Malvern) in 1956, scored an overwhelming victory; few of the qualified Africans bothered to register or vote, partly because they disliked the 'existing two-roll franchise and partly because they were afraid of the police. In Southern Rhodesia Todd was forced to resign by his cabinet colleagues who refused to accept a wage increase for Africans which had been recommended by the Labour Board. More important, they regarded the comparatively liberal Todd as an electoral Jonah and although he was allowed a seat in the new cabinet formed by Sir Edgar Whitehead he was soon dropped and in the elections his new United Rhodesia party won no single seat. Whitehead scraped in, although the Dominion Party led by Winston Field, campaigning in favour of independence by 1960, got more votes. This eclipse of Todd was in part a white reaction to the reanimation of the African National Congress by George Nyandoro and Robert Chikerema in 1957 and was also the first of a series of moves which placed the premiership in the hands of ever more extreme politicians who were gradually forced to be more explicit about the basic white demand for independence from Britain as the only way of ensuring that power would remain in white hands for as long as anybody cared to look into the future. In Northern Rhodesia a new constitution preceded elections in 1959 which gave victory to the United Federal Party (the new name for the local version of the Huggins-Welensky party); the party was, however, almost universally rejected by Africans in spite of the support it received from the whole press. These elections showed that the enchantments of federation were not working even before the alleged murder plot and the judgments of the Devlin commission.

From about 1960 there was in effect a race between the forces which wanted to extract independence for the federation out of the British government and the forces which wanted to break up the federation and establish black rule in its several parts. The British government, caught in this crossfire, resorted to the expedient of sending a commission to look into the situation. Welensky opposed this manoeuvre in private but acquiesced in public. The Africans boycotted it, as did the British Labour opposition. The commission, presided over by Lord Monckton, an eminent Queen's Counsel and former Conservative minister, produced an ambivalent report in which a majority extolled the principle of federation, but judged it unworkable. The nature of the commission's work inevitably raised the question of the right to secede from the federation, although the white leaders in Rhodesia and their friends in Britain hotly contended that the commission had no power to consider the matter and that the British prime minister had promised that it would not be raised; a majority concluded that there was no legal right to secede but that, as a matter of practical politics, the issue should be placed on the agenda of a federal review conference and that Britain should declare its willingness to permit secession after the passage of a defined trial period of federation. This was the commission's most important recommendation since it placed federation on probation. The commission's report marked in fact the turning of the tide in favour of the break-up of the federation, even though the commission gave more attention and space to reforms designed to make it work (such as parity between Europeans and Africans in the federal parliament, a broader franchise, and immediate advances towards self-government in northern Rhodesia with an African majority in the legislative council and an unofficial majority in the executive council).

A federal review conference assembled in London at the end of 1960. The federal constitution did not require such a conference at this date but in the judgment of the British government it had become necessary. Yet it achieved nothing and was adjourned *sine die*, to be followed by a Northern Rhodesia constitutional conference which produced bitter back-stage fighting in which Welensky (who, like Cecil Rhodes, relied partly on a group of members of the Westminster parliament) was worsted by Macmillan and Macleod. Each side suspected the other, perhaps correctly, of being about to use force and Welensky called up troops. The constitutional proposals which escaped from this mêlée would have made it impossible for Welensky to secure control of the Northern Rhodesian parliament. But the proposals, when embodied in a White Paper, were not allowed to pass unscathed and the British government made some slight concessions to Welensky. In so doing it angered Kenneth Kaunda and other leaders of the United National Independence Party (Unip) who accused the British of tinkering behind the scenes with the agreed outcome of the conference. There were violent demonstrations in Northern Rhodesia and the proposals were reversed. These swingings and swayings reflected the divided mind of the British Conservative party and cabinet; it was by this time reasonably clear that the federation was doomed, although nobody was prepared to say so; and although Welensky and his white followers had fervent friends in London, there was a growing body of opinion in the party which recognized the greater expediency of being friends with Kaunda and the many African states which stood behind him. A third set of proposals was eventually propounded which ensured that neither Unip nor the Federal Party could get a parliamentary majority and was in any case too complicated to be understood by anybody but a constitutional maniac. It was rejected by Kaunda.

During this same period another conference went through similar travail to produce a new constitution for Southern Rhodesia. Its proposals, which guaranteed a larger minority parliamentary representation to Africans but also removed nearly all the residual powers of the British government, were accepted by Nkomo at the conference but repudiated by him immediately afterwards because he came to believe, again probably correctly, that if he accepted the increased number of seats, the British government would immediately grant independence to Southern Rhodesia under its white rulers who would then either arrest or even reverse the advance towards African majority rule. The British government had hoped to find a formula containing a large enough element of agreement to enable it to give independence with a good conscience and get out of a hopeless situation, but African insistence on the magic formula of majority rights – echoed after all by many in Britain itself – baulked its efforts and kept it on the hook.

The following year, 1962, saw an abortive British plan to carve up Northern Rhodesia by elevating Barotseland into a separate state under its traditional and conservative ruler, the litunga, and by giving a further slice of it to Southern Rhodesia. The only effect of this bizarre and anachronistic notion was to create bad blood between the nationalists and the traditionalists. R. A. Butler was then appointed to a special office of Central African affairs. His business was to assuage the internal feuding in the Conservative Party and to wind up the federation. By the end of the year Nyasaland had been promised self-government and the right to secede from the federation. In Northern Rhodesia Unip was asked to join the government in 1962 and the right to secede from the federation was acknowledged in 1963. With the secession of Northern Rhodesia there was no federation left. It expired on the last day of 1963. Nyasaland and Northern Rhodesia became independent in July and October 1964. They became republics within the Commonwealth with Banda (who soon quarrelled with and evicted his younger colleagues) and Kaunda as their presidents.

In Southern Rhodesia the constitution of 1961 had left only one political issue between the Southern Rhodesian and British governments: independence. Winston Field had envisaged an independent Rhodesian dominion consisting of Southern Rhodesia and most of

Northern Rhodesia, with Barotseland and Nyasaland as separate states under high commissioners appointed by the United Kingdom, but this unlikely scheme had been overtaken by events. In 1963 he began negotiations with Britain on the bare issue of independence for Southern Rhodesia and was confronted with five conditions: unimpeded progress towards majority rule in Southern Rhodesia; guarantees against regressive amendments of the 1961 constitution; an immediate improvement of African rights; an end to racial discrimination; and a basis for independence acceptable to the people of the country as a whole. Ian Smith, who ousted Winston Field in 1964, tried to meet the last and most intractable of these conditions by assembling an *indaba* of chiefs, who, having been fêted by the government and even given nice trips abroad, said exactly what was expected of them – but without convincing anybody in Britain that this was a demonstration of the popular will. The advent of a Labour government in London at the end of 1964 caused despondency among whites in Salisbury and increased the demand for a unilateral declaration of independence, but the new British government, beset by a major economic crisis and possessing only the thinnest parliamentary majority, decided to keep talks with Salisbury going for the sake of talking and gaining time. There was, however, no basis for agreement since the British government was pledged to conditions which ran counter to the fundamental demand of the great majority of the white community in Rhodesia – the indefinite preservation of their minority rule. As a last resort the British government proposed the appointment of a royal commission under the Rhodesian chief justice, Sir Hugh Beadle, to examine ways of testing the popular will but this proposal was rejected by Smith and on 11 November 1965 the Smith government declared the country independent. The government was thereupon dismissed by the governor, Sir Humphrey Gibbs. It remained, however, the effective government of Rhodesia within its borders.

The British government was determined not to use force except in the event of a major breakdown of public order. Superficially the situation was one in which previous British governments had not hesitated to use force, but the Rhodesian case was in substance different in two decisive ways: because Rhodesia, although technically a colony, had been administered and in effect governed by its own white population for more than forty years and not by Whitehall, and secondly because the rebellious government was white and not black, so that a recourse to force in what the Rhodesian whites had made a racial issue would bitterly have divided opinion in Britain and could even have faced British army officers with a test of obedience which they might not have passed. The British government was left therefore with two courses, negotiation and economic coercion.

For a year it pursued both courses with the emphasis on the first. It immediately took fiscal measures against Rhodesia, imposed oil sanctions and secured the passage of a Security Council resolution against the supply of arms to Rhodesia and requesting an international economic boycott. Over forty countries besides Britain complied with this request. In April 1966 the Security Council, at British request, authorized the use of force to implement oil sanctions and in December, again at British request, it imposed mandatory sanctions over a wide assortment of commodities. Eighteen months later this ban was made total. But despite hardships, which took time to take effect or become apparent, the Smith régime was able to maintain itself thanks to the South African government (which supplied credit and goods and facilitated the export of Rhodesian products), thanks to Rhodesia's capacity to retaliate economically against Zambia (which was dependent on Rhodesia for coal for its copper mines and in other ways), and thanks also to the British government's reluctance to intensify its economic measures so long as it could go on hoping for a negotiated settlement. Rhodesia's exports were substantially blocked, its reserves were depleted, its government had to resort to internal loans, it became virtually a dependency of South Africa, but the régime was not compelled to capitulate and the economy, though damaged, adjusted itself.

In applying sanctions Britain was intent not on destroying the Rhodesian economy or even the Smith régime but on forcing Smith to come to terms. These tactics and aims did not commend themselves to most of the Commonwealth which suspected Britain of being bent on a deal with Smith even to the extent of betraying its predecessor's and its own pledges. At a Commonwealth conference in Lagos in June Britain succeeded in buying time but not in retrieving the trust of its African partners in the Commonwealth, and at a further conference in London in September Britain was obliged, by a nearly unanimous show of resolution by members from all continents, to promise to ask the Security Council to apply selected mandatory sanctions if negotiations between London and Salisbury did not produce a return to legality by the end of the year. By the first anniversary of the unilateral declaration of independence the futility of these nogitiations had become manifest, and Britain faced a lengthy economic battle which, if pursued, was bound to develop into a contest between the overwhelming majority of the United Nations on the one hand and South Africa and (less resolutely) Portugal on the other, whose policy was to keep the battle going until Rhodesia's opponents got bored and gradually ceased to enforce sanctions. Two attempts to exorcise the problem by personal negotiations between Harold Wilson and Ian Smith – the one on board HMS *Tiger* in 1966 and the second on board HMS *Fearless* in 1968 – failed, principally owing to the obduracy of Smith (or his more extreme lieutenants), but the return of the Conservatives to power in Britain in 1970 revived the prospect of a settlement – and rekindled the mistrust of the rest of Africa.

An initial and unofficial exploration of the chances for a settlement by Lord Alport produced a pessimistic answer but Sir Alec Douglas-Home, back at the Foreign Office in London, opened a dialogue with Smith through Lord Goodman and produced a plan for a return to constitutionality subject to his being satisfied that it was acceptable to the people of Rhodesia as a whole. A commission under Lord Pearce went to Rhodesia in 1972 to find the answer to this question and reported that the majority of Africans rejected the plan. The British government retired once more into the background. Inside Rhodesia guerrilla operations, which had been prematurely and unsuccessfully started a few years earlier, increased but were contained by Smith's forces with South African help. Attempts by the OAU to heal splits among black Rhodesian leaders were unsuccessful but the collapse of Portuguese rule in Mozambique transformed the situation by dealing strategic and psychological blows to the white Rhodesians (the frontiers to be defended became several hundreds of miles longer) and by posing new policy problems for South Africa (see p. 396). The leaders of neighbouring countries – Zambia, Botswana, Mozambique, Zaire, Tanzania – wanted the overthrow of Smith without a war. They were willing to talk, and to try to persuade black Rhodesians to talk, about a short transitional period before majority rule and about guarantees for the lives and property of whites. They were encouraged by the shift in South African policies, notably by a speech at the UN in which the South African representative spoke plainly about the existence of *apartheid* in South Africa, deplored it and looked forward to a time (unspecified) when it would be removed. This surprising statement was subsequently qualified, presumably for internal consumption, by Vorster, who said that it did not mean one-man-one-vote or a black parliament. Vorster's balancing act was plain for outsiders to see and Kaunda was not deterred from sending an envoy to talk with Vorster who seemed as keen as Kaunda and his colleagues to compass a change of regime in Rhodesia without bloodshed. In December 1974 Smith released the two principal detained nationalist leaders, Joshua Nkomo and Ndabaningi Sithole, as a preliminary to a cease-fire and a possible constitutional conference, and in the following September Smith, at Vorster's prompting, attended a conference with nationalists on a bridge over the Victoria Falls, Vorster and Kaunda themselves also attending. The conference was a failure, technically because of a dispute about the terms of reference already agreed between Vorster and Smith, substantially because Smith was not prepared to discuss any constitutional proposals except his own, which did not then include a transfer of power to the majority. The notion of a constitutional conference was kept alive by Smith and Nkomo but the prospects were dimmed both by white intransigence and by renewed splits among black leaders who had been temporarily persuaded into a show of unity. The collapse of the Vorster-Kaunda initiative left little in prospect except war. In Rhodesia the stalemate continued but around it two big changes had occurred. For Vorster the Rhodesian situation represented a wolf at the door, but the wolf had changed its colour. The failure of the Victoria Falls conference completed the alienation of

Vorster from Smith. The main danger for South Africa was no longer the disappearance of white rule but its persistence in hopeless circumstances and the manner of its eventual undoing. Smith was no longer a shield but an Achilles' heel. Secondly, Russo-Cuban intervention in Angola (see p. 400) must bring the United States too into a field of forces from which it had wanted to keep out. The chief American concern, besides the removal of Cuban forces from Africa and the negating of Russian influence, was stability which in Rhodesia was unachievable without the eclipse of white power. The Russo-Cuban incursion made allies of the United States and South Africa, but allies who were at the same time sundered by their racial policies. The first fruits of this exceptionally uneasy alliance were the enforced surrender of Smith in 1976 to the demands for a transfer of power from white to black.

Chapter 22

Africa's Deep South

Bantu peoples reached the southern tip of the African continent in the eighteenth century and there met the Dutch, clashed with them and were gradually subdued and turned into hewers of wood and drawers of water. The Dutch, who had followed the Portuguese to the Cape and were at first confronted only the Hottentots, enjoyed a brief dominance until, their home country having become a part of the French revolutionary empire, they became fair game for the British in the Napoleonic wars and lost their base at Cape Town which they had founded in 1652. In the eighteen-thirties they packed up and trekked and set up new independent states – successfully beyond the Orange river and the Vaal but unsuccessfully in Natal where, although they defeated the Zulus, they were again pushed on by the expanding British who annexed Natal in 1843. The British colony of the Cape grew politically, economically and demographically; it was granted constitutions in 1853 and 1872, receiving on the later occasion the right to a prime minister of its own.

In the latter part of the nineteenth century South Africa achieved an entirely unexpected prominence in British thinking for two quite separate reasons. The first of these was the discovery of its wealth – diamonds in the sixties and gold in the eighties. The second was the conviction that South Africa was a vital link in Britain's imperial communications and that therefore Britain must keep firm hold not only of Cape Town and Simonstown but also of the hinterland. This second preoccupation turned the Dutch, or Boers, into potential enemies, since they might invite other European powers to occupy the sensitive hinterland or cause trouble for the British in Cape Colony by creating an alliance with their kinsmen in the colony. Moreover attempts by the Boers to reach the coasts in Portuguese territory and to trade with the outside world through Portuguese ports were a further source of friction since these activities threatened the monopolistic profits of British traders at the Cape. The British therefore began to expand more purposefully than before. They took Basutoland from the Boers and made it a colony in 1868. They annexed Kimberley, the diamond city, in 1871 and the Transvaal in 1877. Brought up against the Bantu they fought a series of wars (notably the Zulu war of 1879) and in 1880–81 they went to war with the Boers, whom they incidentally accused of maltreating the Bantu. A British liberal government, perplexed at this same time by the graver practical and moral dilemmas of the Irish question, was divided about the right attitude to adopt towards the Boers, and after the battle of Majuba in 1881 adopted a policy of conciliation, restored the Boer republics of the Transvaal and Orange Free State and so implicitly recognized the existence of a separate and valid Boer nationalism.

Cecil Rhodes became prime minister of Cape Colony in 1890 and for a few years his voice rather than London's was the decisive one. Within the colony his policy was one of co-operation with the Boers for the paternal rule of the Africans, but any extension of this policy to form an Anglo-Boer entente in a wider field was prevented by British fears about the political and commercial policies of the Boer republics. Rhodes developed and paid for the Cape-Bechuanaland-Zambezi axis which put the Boer republics in jeopardy, countered the German threat from South West Africa and forestalled a possible anti-British alliance between the Germans and the Transvaal. In 1895 he over-reached himself. With the connivance of a part of the British government he stimulated a rising against President Kruger of the Transvaal and sent Dr Jameson raiding into Boer territory to sustain it. The result was a rebuff for the raiders and also for the British government when the German emperor sent Kruger his moral support by telegram. But although Kruger triumphed and Rhodes fell, the British government, which now resumed the dominant role, adopted Rhodes's basic thesis that the first British aim must be to prevent the emergence of a Boer South African republic comprising the Boer republics and the British colonies. By fighting and winning the Boer War in 1899–1901 Britain postponed this eventuality but did not succeed in scotching it, for it came to pass in 1961. Britain also earned the hatred of the wounded Boers but failed to appreciate its depth.

After the Peace of Vereeniging in 1902 the British pursued two barely compatible lines of policy. On the one hand they busied themselves being fair and generous to the defeated Boers, often forgetting the Africans in the process. The Transvaal and Orange Free State were granted self-government in 1906–07, and the constitution of 1908 provided for an all-white parliament which, while meant as a symbol of Anglo-Boer reconciliation, looked in retrospect more like a pledge of African exclusion. On the other hand the British had entrenched the policy of British supremacy by insisting on the extinction of the sovereignty of the republics and the dominance of the English language, so that the Boers planned for the day when the balance of power in South Africa would shift in their favour and they would be able then to turn the tables on the British. By creating the Union of South Africa in 1910 the British government tried to confederate the two self-governing Boer republics and the two British colonies as an independent dominion within the British empire, but this South African dominion was fundamentally if unperceivedly different from the three other old dominions by reason of the persistent non-British culture of the Boers (or Afrikaners) and the existence of an African majority in the shadows. When the European war broke out in 1914 the dominion joined in hostilities and sent forces overseas; the Boers however revolted, refusing – as they were to refuse again in 1939 – to be counted simply a part of a South African nation. They saw themselves as a people or Volk and not as a state.

The persistence of a distinct Afrikaner nationalism which ultimately triumphed through the electoral victories of the Nationalist Party was accompanied by the growth of an African nationalist movement which was frustrated by the Afrikaners. The Afrikaners had to resort to increasingly stringent measures and extreme ideologies in order to preserve and justify their newly won supremacy, and by the middle of the century South Africa had become an oligarchy ruled by a particular racial group without the consent of the majority of the governed who – to make matters worse – were a different colour.

The Afrikaners' attitude to colour was an extreme instance of a common prejudice. It had played a part in their decision to trek out of Cape Colony where the British were putting more liberal ideas into practice and where the coloureds (the offspring of white alliances with black servants) were given the vote in 1853 subject to certain educational tests – a right which they retained until 1956. But the African was an essential factor in the state since his labour was needed in industry and could be had cheaply owing to the scarcity of work in the native reserves (which, comprising one-tenth of the surface of the state, were supposed in theory to accommodate all the Africans but were incapable in fact of supporting more than half of them). Colour became therefore equated with economic degradation; a black man was a labourer who must and could be had for a low wage. And economic degradation led to social degradation as the Africans were crowded into slummy locations which bred self-disgust and crime. Whereas in Europe the victims of the industrial revolution were the more unfortunate members of society, in South Africa the revolution which exalted mining and heavy industry above agriculture found its victims in a separate society, alienated and increasingly hostile. Natal possessed an additional element in the Asians who first migrated there in search of work in the middle of the nineteenth century.

The Nationalist Party was built up by General James Hertzog who was supported by the Labour Party (the representatives of white labour) and opposed by the British section of the electorate and by the moderate Afrikaners led by Louis Botha until his death in 1919 and then by Jan Smuts. Hertzog was prime minister from 1924 to 1939. He and Smuts joined forces in a coalition government in 1933 but upon the outbreak of war in Europe in 1939 they again separated and Hertzog drifted back towards D. F. Malan who had founded a new Nationalist Party rather than follow Hertzog into alliance with Smuts. The Nationalists refused, however, to ally themselves with the fascist Ossewa Brandwag led by Oswald Pirow. In the first post-war elections, held in 1948, the United Party was ousted by the Nationalist Party which embarked on an extended period of power under a series of prime ministers – Malan, J. G. Strijdom, H. F. Verwoerd, B. J. Vorster – who turned South Africa into an independent republic outside the Commonwealth and a police state based on racial discrimination.

The policies of the Nationalist Party were based partly on the fears and hatreds of a minority faced by a majority of a different race and colour, and partly on a theory which was elaborated in this context. To the Afrikaner the African, especially the urban African, was an uncivilized barbarian unfit for public responsibility or private intercourse; or alternatively the African, especially the rural African, was a tame, happy and rather lazy servant whose chief desire was to remain in his undemanding, if servile, state. The mingling of the races moreover was biologically evil. Logic therefore, as well as prejudice, dictated the attempts to separate the races which collectively amounted to the policy of *apartheid*. Although the races must remain in some contact with one another for a transitional period, the aim was the segregation of the black Africans in separate territories – dubbed Bantustans – which would be social enclaves, economically self-sufficient, within a single South African polity. This theory and its elaboration were equally flawed. Scientists, including South African scientists, rejected the biological assertions at the basis of the policy of *apartheid*; economists demonstrated that the native areas could never become viable except at a cost unacceptable to the white population, and that the white community could not do without black labour: the African was to be returned to a semi-industrialized countryside while the white urban centres nevertheless craved for his services. The theory also overlooked the strength of human feelings of righteous indignation, and the political awareness of Africans who knew what was happening elsewhere in Africa. Finally, many of the protagonists of *apartheid* probably underestimated the extent to which their policies would force them to rule by violence and fraud and would attract worldwide attention and condemnation. Prisons filled, floggings became an habitual part of the process of government, executions took place at the rate of one a day, the mail ceased to be private, spies and informers multiplied, an inevitably brutalized police became a law of assault unto itself, and the régime felt itself obliged to build up a white citizen army with a potential strength of 250,000 in addition to a part-time commando force of 50,000 (based on four years' compulsory service) and a police force of 20,000 and police reserve of 6,000.

On the other side the African nationalist movement also took to violence. A Native Nationalist Congress, later renamed the African Nationalist Congress, had been formed in 1912. The object of its first leaders – chiefs and then lawyers – was to secure a place for the black African in South African society without upsetting any applecarts, but both the leaders and the rank and file began to have doubts about their prospects during the Hertzog period. The Nationalist victory in 1948 sharpened African apprehensions. The Congress leaders pursued a policy of strikes and civil disobedience to draw attention to demands which they formulated in 1955 at a conference at Kliptown. The government's response to the Kliptown Charter was to charge the leaders with treason. One hundred and fifty-six persons were indicated in a trial which lasted four years and ended wth the acquittal of all the accused. In 1957 an increase in bus fares produced a wholesale bus boycott in which Africans, by trudging long miles to work every day, demonstrated their poverty and their discipline, but violence also began to grow and in 1958 outbreaks in the Transvaal were fiercely repressed. In 1959 a section of the African National Congress broke away to form the Pan-Africanist Congress led by Robert Sobukwe.

On 21 March 1960 a crowd of Africans, probably 3–4000 strong but subsequently inflated by reports to much larger dimensions, converged on the police station at Sharpeville. It was one of a number of similar crowds which were doing the same thing all over the country in protest against the pass laws which required adult Africans always to have their identity documents upon them. In organizing this demonstration Robert Sobukwe had told Africans to leave their passes behind and present themselves at police stations in an orderly manner and unarmed. Newspaper reporters said afterwards that the crowds at Sharpeville and elsewhere were in cheerful holiday mood. At Sharpeville, where a small police force of seventy-five was nervously on duty, somebody fired a gun and within minutes dozens of Africans had been killed and many more wounded; the wounds of the victims were, according to hospital testimony, almost all in the back. At Langa in Cape Province there was a similar scene and altogether that day eighty-three Africans were killed and about 350 wounded. Sharpeville became a household word throughout the world. Statesmen of all colours denounced the bloodshed, flags were flown at half mast and formal tributes of silence were paid to the dead. In South Africa a state of emergency was declared as the protests against the pass laws continued, the militia was called up and thousands of Africans were apprehended and put in prison.

Nevertheless the principal African leaders – Chief Albert Luthuli (shortly afterwards awarded the Nobel Peace Prize), Nelson Mandela, Walter Sisulu – continued the struggle by non-violent means. A successful three-day strike in 1961 was followed by preparations for wholesale non-co-operation throughout the country and Mandela went underground in order to organize the campaign. The government was gradually placing most of the responsible leaders behind bars. As their leaders, their activities and their organizations were proscribed both Congresses produced more militant offshoots in the Sword of the Spirit and Poqo (founded in 1961 and 1962 respectively, the latter using murder as a weapon). In 1963 the government arraigned Mandela, Sisulu and others in a further mass trial at Rivonia and sentenced them to long terms of imprisonment.

The government did not hesitate to use force in return but it preferred, like any government, to provide its actions with legislative cover. Its legislative programme was extensive and cannot be considered in detail here. Its principal features, although framed within a single grand design, may be reviewed under separate headings.

In the first place there were a number of statutes affecting the individual in his private capacity. Sexual relations between Africans and Europeans had been a criminal offence since 1927. In 1950 this prohibition was extended to relations between Europeans and coloureds, and in 1949 the Prohibition of Mixed Marriages Act (unlike many other acts) did precisely what its title indicated – not without reference to the marriage of Seretse Khama of the Bamangwato to an English girl. Also in 1950 the government enacted the Popular Registration Act, described by Malan as the basis of *apartheid*, which prescribed registration and classification by race. The position of the individual before the law was also affected by the Native Laws Amendment Act, 1957, which gave the authorities power to exclude Africans from such places as churches on the grounds that they might cause a legal nuisance (the Dutch Reformed Church protested and then complied); by the Separate Amenities Act, 1953, which declared that separate amenities for blacks and whites need not be equal, as the courts had tended to insist; by the General Law Amendment Acts of 1961, 1962, and 1963 which stringently reduced the rights of the individual against the police, introduced house arrest for periods up to five years and sanctioned the indefinite detention of suspects; and by the Bantu Laws Amendment Act, 1963, which legalized the eviction of any African from any urban area no matter how long he had lived there and turned him into a squatter on sufferance who was allowed to work but not to settle.

A second category of statute fortified and formalized Nationalist control over the machinery of state. In 1949 separate Indian representation in parliament was abolished and the government then launched its attack on the coloured franchise in the Cape province. Its Separate Representation of Voters Bill, 1951, removing the Coloured voters from the common roll to a separate one, was declared unconstitutional by the courts because it took away rights which were entrenched by the South Africa Act, 1909, and could not therefore the validly removed without a two-thirds majority of the two houses of parliament sitting together. The government thereupon brought in the High Court of Parliament Bill, 1952, to give a committee of members of parliament power to override a decision of the Court of Appeal, but it too was voided by the courts. Malan then dissolved parliament, increased his majority but failed to win the two-thirds majority necessary for his purposes. He won over some United Party members in the lower house but not enough and then summoned a joint session of the two houses of parliament to consider a bill to amend the South Africa Act. This move also failed in spite of a measure of United Party support and Malan was then replaced by J. G. Strijdom who abandoned Malan's legalistic tactics in favour of packing the judiciary and altering the constitution of the senate. By these means he secured, first, the passage by the requisite two-thirds majority of the South Africa Act Amendment Act, 1956 (which validated the ill-fated Separate Representation of Voters Act, 1951) and, secondly, judicial endorsement of the Senate Act, 1956.

This long tussle stimulated extra-parliamentary but still mainly non-violent opposition to the government among liberal whites as well as among Africans. The Torch Commando, the Black Sash movement and the bus boycott were its principal manifestations; but the principal consequences were the extinction of the lesser opposition parties (the Liberal and Progressive Parties), the increasing resort to house arrest and detention without trial, and a vigorous use of the communist bogy to brand all opponents of *apartheid* as subversive agents of an international conspiracy. The South African Communist Party had, after some internal disagreement, taken up the cause of the black worker which the Labour Party refused to espouse, but the communists had been as much hampered in South Africa as elsewhere by the twists and turns of Moscow and they had not greatly prospered. In 1950, however, the Malan government secured the passage of the Suppression of Communism Act which was important, not because it proscribed communist activities and the relatively feeble communist party, but for its definition of communists and for the powers given to the executive to deal with such people. A communist was defined as any individual whom the minister of justice chose to call a communist, and in so determining the minister was to take the widest possible view since any person seeking to promote political, industrial, social or economic change by unlawful acts or omissions, or the threat of them, was to be considered a communist, as were various other broad categories of people. The act was in fact an instrument for eliminating every kind of opposition in parliament, trade unions, schools, universities and elsewhere, and at the same time a piece of propaganda meant to exaggerate the communist menace and so win support for the Nationalist régime.

In the field of labour Africans had been forbidden to form unions since 1937. A ban on strikes imposed during the war remained in force after it, and the Native Labour (Settlement of Disputes) Act, 1953, repeated these bans on unions and strikes and kept labour relations under white control.

A further category of statute was concerned with the special subject of education. The Bantu Education Act, 1953, showed the government's awareness of the crucial fact that children do not naturally adopt racial antagonisms (juvenile loves and hates being otherwise motivated), and also of the crucial need to give Africans a qualitatively different education if they were to form a permanently separate and inferior community in a society under white minority control. The act created a new division of the Department of Native Affairs which was to direct and finance Bantu education and which would displace the religious missions which were running most of the schools for Africans. Some churches handed over their schools willingly, others unwillingly;

the Anglicans preferred to close their schools in the Transvaal and the Roman Catholics decided to carry on and bear the cost themselves. In the new nationalized schools education was geared to the place of the African in South Africa, i.e. an unskilled worker in industry or a docile rustic in the special territories to be allotted to him. A further bill to permit the exclusion of Africans from universities had to be withdrawn in 1957, but two years later the university college of Fort Hare was taken over by the state and separate (but well-equipped) university colleges for Africans were created. Africans remained entitled to apply for admission to white universities if they could show that they were qualified to attend courses not available elsewhere, but in practice such pleas were always found by the authorities to lack substance and the liberalism of the universities themselves was thwarted by executive action.

The kernel of the Nationalist programme was the territorial separation of the races. In this field the Group Areas Act, 1950, prescribed racial segregation in terms of residence, business and ownership of land. One of its immediate effects (completed by the Natives Resettlement Act, 1954) was the wholesale removal of Africans from areas of Johannesburg which were needed by the whites. Some of these areas were slums, others were not; to the Africans they were areas where they had been able to own property. This act was followed in 1951 by the Bantu Authorities Act which sought to re-create chieftainship as a basis for the management of the African population. Chiefs, appointed and paid by the government, were to exercise authority in tribal areas, which would be grouped in regions, which would be grouped in territories, over which the minister for native affairs would have ultimate control. This scheme was carried a stage further by the promotion of Bantu Self-government Act, 1959, which (besides depriving the Africans of the right to elect whites to represent them in parliament) consolidated the African reserves into eight Bantustans. Six territorial authorities were established by the end of 1962, including one for the Transkei (an economically non-viable area of 16,000 square miles with a population of 2 million in the north-east of Cape province) which was equipped with a cabinet of six under Chief Kaiser Matanzima and a legislature of four paramount chiefs, sixty chiefs and forty-five elected members. Meanwhile the Tomlinson commission, appointed by the government, had reported in 1955 that the cost of implementing the Bantustan policy would by £104 million spread over ten years and that the African population in 1960 was likely to be 21.5 million. The government promised £3.5 million for the development of the Bantustans and established in 1959 a Bantu Investment Corporation with a capital of £500,000 to develop Bantu industries.

These affairs in South Africa engaged the attention of the outside world because other Africans, backed by Asians and white sympathizers, made it their business to force them into the foreground of debate at the United Nations, and also as the result of particular episodes such as the treason trial and the Sharpeville shootings.

It so happened that the Sharpeville calamity fell shortly before a meeting of Commonwealth prime ministers at which South Africa intended to seek assurances that it would be accepted as a continuing member of the Commonwealth if it became a republic. This change of status had been a prominent item in the Nationalist programme and it had not been expected to give rise to any difficulties, since the Commonwealth had already adapted itself to the presence of republics. Formally, however, the change required endorsement and there were in the Commonwealth a number of members to whom South African racial policies were so repugnant that they might grasp at an excuse to withhold their assent. Verwoerd, who had succeeded Strijdom as prime minister in 1958, was unable to attend the conference owing to an attempt on his life by a white farmer, and South Africa was therefore represented by its minister for external affairs, Eric Louw. The question of *apartheid* was with difficulty kept off the formal agenda on condition that individual prime ministers might express themselves to Louw in private. Louw, so far from making the impression which he had hoped to make on his colleagues, was forced in these conversations to appreciate the strength of their feelings and to accept a final communiqué which hinted that an application to remain in the Commonwealth, unaccompanied by reform of South African racial policies, would be rejected. Ghana, which had already voted by referendum to become a republic, was accepted as a continuing member. The Commonwealth therefore sidestepped the unpleasant and unprecedented step of expulsion and left the initiative with South Africa. A referendum was held later in the year with the expected republican result and South Africa thereupon left the Commonwealth.

Sharpeville also had repercussions at the United Nations. The General Assembly had been concerning itself with *apartheid* for some years. During its 1952–53 session it had appointed a commission to consider the racial situation in South Africa and this commission had reported that the situation was harmful to peaceful international relations. In succeeding sessions the Assembly regularly passed resolutions asking South Africa to review its policies in the light of the UN Charter and deploring its failure to do so. After Sharpeville the Security Council resolved that the situation in South Africa might endanger international peace and security, called on South Africa to mend its ways and instructed the secretary-general, in consultation with the South African government, to take measures to uphold the Charter. Hammarskjöld went to South Africa in January 1961 but his visit was as fruitless as the Assembly's resolutions. The Assembly repeated its censures in 1961 and then in 1962 asked members to break off diplomatic relations with South Africa, close their ports to South African shipping and their airports to South African aircraft, prevent their own ships from calling at South African ports, boycott all South African products and suspend exports to South Africa. The Assembly also appointed a special committee to keep the situation under review. This committee produced a series of reports and in August 1963 the Security Council recommended the suspension of all sales of military equipment. Throughout these proceedings the African members were pressing for UN action partly out of genuine attachment to the idea of collective international action as embodied in the Charter and partly because they had no prospect of achieving anything effective on their own against the vastly superior military and economic strength of South Africa. They were the more embittered by the refusal of Britain and other powers which were capable of exerting economic pressures but reluctant to do so.

The campaign for economic sanctions against South Africa developed in the sixties as the wave of independence came up against its most formidable obstacle in Africa's deep south. Here was a white minority fortified by an authoritarian and non-egalitarian theology totally different from the secular libertarianism and egalitarianism which, even if subconsciously, formed the policies of the principal European colonial powers. This minority moreover was strong and rich, and it was not a colonial offshoot but a people at home with no thought of going anywhere else. The new African states found themselves powerless to do anything about a problem to which they had given an absolute priority. They were compelled therefore to turn to those who could do something about it – in the first place Britain and secondly the United States. They hoped that these countries would be not only outraged by the enormities perpetrated by the South African régime but also convinced that *apartheid* was a danger to international peace; they wanted international economic sanctions which would either force the Nationalists to parley with the Africans and give them a share of political power, or would cause a disintegration of the régime and the emergence of something new which could in no event be worse.

The British and Americans were not prepared to agree that the practices of *apartheid* were a threat to international peace within the meaning of article 39 of the Charter. Their reasons were many. Both countries were preoccupied with problems which seemed to them more urgent. The United States gave unhesitating priority to Vietnam and to Latin American affairs at least. Britain was more intimately involved because of the old Commonwealth connection and Britain's much longer acquaintance with Africa, but in Britain's financial situation even the relatively small profit on trade with South Africa could not lightly be foregone; British exports to South Africa earned about £150 million a year, 4 per cent of total British exports, while imports from South Africa cost £100 million, 2 per cent of the import bill, leaving a favourable balance of about £50 million. In addition about two-thirds of South Africa's gold went into western reserves and was largely handled, at a profit, by the London market. In both Britain and the United States there were vested financial interests and pressure groups which, though they might not be so influential with government as was sometimes supposed, were nevertheless marginally effective owing to the articulate assiduity with which they made the case against intervention. British investments in South Africa were valued at about £1,000 million. Britain was also held back by fears of reprisals against its dependencies of Bechuanaland, Basutoland and Swaziland, by the residual importance of the right to use the naval base at Simonstown, and by a post-war mood of getting out of things rather than into them. Public opinion was largely unaroused; the committed minorities were believed to be too small to have electoral significance.

The most weighty of these various considerations was the existence of other absorbing international commitments which made both London and Washington hope that an upheaval in South Africa could be postponed, but almost equally important were doubts about the effectiveness of sanctions, about their legality in the circumstances which had arisen, and about the immediate consequences of applying them. The South African economy had not only expanded rapidly but had also become more self-sufficient; at the same time oil and other materials had been accumulated. There was no agreement among experts on the period during which South Africa could stand a virtual siege, nor was there agreement on the degree of effectiveness of the naval blockade which would be necessary for a short, and possibly for a long, time. On the legal side it was argued that the preconditions for such action laid down in article 39 of the Charter (i.e. a threat to international peace) existed and had indeed been acknowledged by the members of the Security Council who formally resolved in 1963 that the policies of the South African government 'disturbed' international peace. But the substitution of the word 'disturb' for the word 'threaten' was a precise gauge of the political temperture, for it enabled members of the Council to say one thing and yet avoid the consequences of their words. Britain and the United States could no longer bring themselves to deny the substance of the allegations made by the African states but they were determined all the same not to be embroiled with South Africa and so they insisted on using a word which was not part of the language of article 39. Nor was this simply hypocrisy, although it may have been unwise in as much as it postponed an issue which was getting worse and not better. It was not simple hypocrisy because those who had the power were unwilling to use it so long as they could see so little of its probable effects. Sanctions would require a blockade and a blockade could lead to a war. Within South Africa the collapse of the régime could produce an anarchic situation, bloodshed and misery. Ought they to take this responsibility? Since they did not want to anyhow, the question was not too difficult to answer.

The refusal of the British and Americans to be moved by the arguments in favour of sanctions on the grounds that *apartheid* constituted a threat to peace was, however, not the end of the matter. South Africa was also vulnerable on a completely different count. It was the mandatory power in South West Africa and was accused of violating the mandate agreement by, among other things, introducing *apartheid*. If this charge could be established, South Africa could be required to mend its ways in South West Africa or expose itself to legitimate intervention upon its failure to comply; and *apartheid* would be condemned in at any rate one context. The Africans went to law.

South West Africa, the most barren expanse in Africa except for the Sahara, came under German rule at the end of the nineteenth century because nobody else wanted it. In the eighteen-seventies the Cape Colony had expressly considered and rejected annexation and even the great Berlin share-out of 1884 left South West Africa as *res nullius*. In the concluding years of the century, however, the Germans moved in, first as allies of the Bantu Herrero against the Nama (an aboriginal people second in antiquity only to the Bushmen) and then as settlers and farmers. Rebellions by the Herrero and later by the Nama led to savage repressions amounting to genocide, and by 1907 the territory had been devastated, subdued and handed over to German farmers together with the surviving Africans who became little better than slaves. In the First World War it was conquered by General Botha and a South African army in a matter of weeks, but after the war it was – together with all other conquered German possessions outside Europe – placed under international mandate instead of being treated as the spoils of the conqueror. The mandate was entrusted by the Principal Allied and Associated Powers to King George V to administer through his government in South Africa. The mandate agreement provided, among other things, for the suppression of trade in slaves, arms and liquor; prohibited the establishment of military bases and the military training of Africans; guaranteed freedom of religion; and required the mandatory to submit annual reports to the Permanent Mandates Commission of the League of Nations and to forward to the League complaints and petitions from the inhabitants. In its execution of the mandate the South African government treated the new order as tantamount to annexation. Attempts were made to convert South West Africa into a fifth province of South Africa and although these attempts were successfully resisted by the League the character of the territory was profoundly altered by an influx of white South Africans who acquired land cheaply and became a ruling class complete with an elected parliament. In the north areas were reserved for Africans. White immigration was prohibited in these areas which were ruled by a governor-general appointed by South Africa acting through African chiefs who received salaries if they were complaisant but were deposed if they were not.

After the Second World War Smuts repeated pleas for the integration of the territory with South Africa on the grounds of propinquity and economic advantage; he denied that, as the mandatory, South Africa was under an obligation to negotiate a trusteeship agreement with the United Nations; and he argued that the inhabitants of the territory were happy and prosperous and wanted to be part of South

Africa. Smuts was obliged to drop his attempt to secure integration and he agreed to submit to the UN reports on conditions in the territory, but after 1948 the Nationalist government stopped the reports and also allotted six seats in the South African lower house and four in the senate to representatives of South West Africa's 53,000 European inhabitants (the non-Europeans numbered 400,000).

The International Court of Justice ruled in 1950, in an advisory opinion (which was elaborated on subordinate points in further opinions of 1955 and 1956), that the mandate was still in force, that South Africa was not obliged to place the territory under trusteeship, but that it was obliged to submit reports and transmit petitions. From this time the Herrero, Nama and Damara tribes made their views known to the world through their spokesman, the Rev. Michael Scott, who presented on their behalf a picture of their conditions and wishes very different from the official South African line. South Africa offered to negotiate with the United States, Britain and France, as the survivors of the Principal Allied and Associated Powers of the First World War, an agreement to place South West Africa under the administration of the International Court, but this novel idea was rejected by a special committee of the United Nations and was withdrawn in 1955. In 1957 the UN appointed a good offices committee of three (Britain, the United States and Brazil) which visited Pretoria the next year and recommended that either the Trusteeship Council or a new body consisting of former League members should receive reports from the mandatory, but South Africa maintained that the mandate had lapsed and that it was gratuitously continuing to administer the territory in the spirit of the mandate. South Africa next suggested a partition whereby the southern part of the territory would be annexed to South Africa and the northern part (where there were no whites) would be under South African trusteeship and administratively part of South Africa. The General Assembly rejected this scheme. The territory was in practice progressively absorbed into South Africa's administrative system and became subject also to the policies and practices of *apartheid*.

In 1959 a report by the UN Committee on South West Africa comprehensively condemned South Africa's execution of the mandate and in the following year the Organization for African Unity decided to initiate a substantive case before the International Court, claiming that the mandate agreement had been violated. Ethiopia and Liberia, former members of the League and the senior independent states of the continent, thereupon petitioned the court accordingly and engaged an eminent American lawyer, Ernest Gross, to argue their case at The Hague. In 1960 the court accepted jurisdiction by the narrow margin of eight judges to seven. After protracted and expensive proceedings the court in July 1966 non-suited the plaintiffs and, in spite of its preliminary decision in 1960, ruled by the president's casting vote (making eight against seven) that they had no standing in the matter before the court. This refusal to entertain the substance of the case caused universal astonishment and was considered all the more un-satisfactory in that the outcome was plainly due to accidents of death and ill health, without which the judgment on this point would have gone the other way. The immediate effect, besides jubilation in South Africa and some discrediting of the role of law in international affairs, was to return the South West African issue to the arena of politics (where it was bound to end up in any case);

In October 1966 the General Assembly, brushing aside the notion of further recourse to the Court, resolved by 114 votes to 2 with 2 absten-tions that the mandate was terminated and the UN must assume the administration of the territory. A special committee was appointed to consider how the second part of this resolution could be made effective. Essentially the majority in the Assembly was searching for a course of action in which Britain (which had abstained on the resolution) and the United States (which had voted for it) would participate. The com-mittee and a subsequent special meeting of the General Assembly in 1967 were divided between those who asserted, without contradiction, the enormity of South Africa's proceedings and those who asked, without reply, what was to be done about it. In 1968 the UN created a Council for Namibia (as the territory was henceforward called). This Council was not in a position to do anything.

While the case before the International Court was still in progress the South African government had appointed the Odendaal commis-sion to make recommendations about South West Africa. The commis-sion reported in 1964 in favour of dividing the territory into one white and ten black areas and spending £80 million over five years on com-munications, water and other schemes. The black areas would have certain local government powers but matters such as defence, internal security, frontiers, water and power would be reserved to the central authorities. The habitable land and the known minerals fell within the white area. The consideration of this report was postponed pending the decision of the International Court.

The collapse of the judicial offensive against South Africa and the in-creasingly evident refusal of major powers to enter upon an economic war with it coincided with the aggravation of the Rhodesian in-dependence crisis and also with the granting of independence to black régimes in Britain's three protected territories of Bechuanaland, Basutoland and Swaziland which lay on or within South Africa's borders. South Africa was simultaneously strengthened and faced with problems of external policy. The South African government aimed to preserve white supremacy by economic and military power and did not doubt its ability to do so. It had to consider whether white supremacy could be preserved beyond its own borders and, secondly, how it should conduct relations with established black states. White supremacy was strengthened by the waning of the old feud between the Afrikaner and English-speaking minorities. It was seen that the Afrikaner Nationalist victory at the elections of 1948 was irreversible. Moreover the rapid growth of the South African economy blurred the old dividing line between an Afrikaner country party and an English urban one. Afrikaners, while continuing to constitute a country party, were also penetrating in larger numbers into the upper reaches of the industrial plutocracy and sharing the bounding standard of living enjoyed by that class. This change in the fortunes of a part of the Afrikaner community created a possible dilemma for the future, when affluent Afrikaners might have to choose between the rigour of their racial doctrines and the maintenance and expansion of this standard of living by consenting to the lifting of job reservations. This prospect gave some comfort to the more optimistic liberals who hoped that economic pressures would enforce a gradual abandonment of the practices of *apartheid*. Externally the South African government appeared to conclude that white rule in Rhodesia and the Portuguese territories could not be indefinitely maintained and that the weaker black states could be induced by necessity to respond to a show of amicability and so breach the unanimity of black Africa's hostility. South Africa supported the illegal Smith régime in Rhodesia not so much because it believed in the permanence of white rule in that territory but because of the force of South African white popular sympathy for it and in order to show that the economic measures threatened against South Africa could not work even against the very much weaker Rhodesian economy. At the same time Verwoerd and Vorster pressed Smith to come to terms with Britain in the hope that the transfer from white to black rule would be delayed and that fighting so near to South Africa's own borders would be averted. To its newly independent black neighbours, and to Dr Banda's Malawi, South Africa extended its hard fist with soft gloves on. Their emissaries were invited to South Africa and treated as though their skins were as white as their economies were weak. Whether as Bantustans or as independent tributaries they could be fitted into a South African scheme of things in which South Africa, like the USSR after 1945, strong but beleaguered would look out towards a hostile world over an expanse of satellites which would one day include also a black Rhodesia, Angola and Mozambique.

In the late sixties the Nationalist Party was strong enough to afford internal dispute without risking the loss of power. A hard-line or *verkrampte* section took issue with the enlightened or *verligte* wing (a comparative term) but was severely defeated at the polls. The *verligte* majority proceeded to develop its economic relations with African states, concluded an economic agreement with the Malagasy Republic in 1970 and was encouraged by the response of such diverse African leaders as Houphouet-Boigny and Busia, Kenyatta and Bongo. South Africa also saw in 1970 an opportunity to gain credit by obtaining from the new British government a badge of respectability in the form of a reversal of the Labour government's refusal to sell it arms. Vorster perceived and played upon the Conservatives' continuing vision of world affairs in primary cold war colours and their reluctance to consummate Britain's withdrawal from military vantage points in Asia and the Indian Ocean.

This British withdrawal from the world beyond Europe had continued during the sixties. Partly because of the natural reluctance to withdraw and partly too because the British were filling a gap which the Americans were in no hurry to man, British military power had remained in evidence in the arc stretching from the Red Sea to Singapore. But after the departure from Aden in 1968 the retention of forces in the Persian Gulf seemed more than ever anomalous and transient, and in 1968 economic stringencies led the British Labour government to announce that British forces in the Gulf, and also east of it, would be withdrawn as early as 1971. This acceleration of earlier intentions alarmed Malaysia and Singapore. Singapore's prime minister, Lee Kuan Yew, went to London to contest it: he got a little money and a nine months' extension. Discussions, hitherto largely academic, for a defence agreement between Malaysia, Singapore, Australia and New Zealand were begun.

The British decision to withdraw in 1971 instead of a few years seemed at the time precipitate. Yet in another sense it was a belated recognition of the obvious and its significance rested more in the delay than in the haste, for the delay ensured that it should coincide with the growth of Russian naval power. Thus a British withdrawal which, earlier, would have forced the Americans, Asians and Australasians to fill the gap, now offered the alternative prospect of Russian naval power taking the place of British naval power in the east. Although impeded by the closing of the Suez Canal by the 1967 war, the Russians were able to extend their gains in the Middle East to the Indian Ocean where a small Russian naval force became a familiar feature, supported by bases in Socotra, Mauritius and as far east as the Andaman Islands in the Bay of Bengal. Whether or not this extension was prompted by conflict with China or by a natural tendency of major powers to be active everywhere, it redoubled American opposition to the British withdrawal and caused Britain itself, which saw withdrawal as humiliating rather than sensible, to look around for a different policy. It cast east-of-Suez strategies into a cold war, anti-communist mould.

During the British election campaign of 1970 Sir Alec Douglas-Home, the putative foreign secretary, said that a Conservative government would reverse the Labour government's policy of not selling arms to South Africa. Conservatives were not partisans of *apartheid* but wished to be friends with South Africa in spite of *apartheid* and because they could see no state nearer to the Indian Ocean that was both strong and anti-communist. After the Conservative victory one of Sir Alec's first acts was to repeat and set about implementing this declaration. He was supported by the new prime minister, Edward Heath, who resisted all arguments against this course largely, it seemed, on emotional grounds: that election promises must be kept and that British policy decisions must rest in British hands (a proposition that nobody had denied). While Heath treated arguments by African leaders as attempts to push Britain around, Douglas-Home treated African politics as a department of the anti-communist cold war. On the other side it was argued that a Russian naval threat, should it develop, could not in any event be met by a relatively small British–South African naval force; that the focus of such a threat, essentially a threat to the oil traffic, would not be in the southern oceans but round and about the southern shores of the Middle East; and that the British alignment with South Africa – a political demonstration – would create for the Russians political opportunities in Africa far greater than any military benefits likely to accrue to the anti-Russian side: just as conflict in the Middle East and the ensuing arms race in that area and the American attachment to Israel had created a Russo-Arab front, so would a British alliance with South Africa throw African countries, however reluctantly, into the arms of the USSR and perhaps make them as dependent on the USSR as Egypt had become. Having become a major power in the Middle East during the years 1955–70, the USSR could look forward in the seventies not merely to a growing role upon the high seas but in addition – and once more because of western mistakes – to a political windfall on the African continent.

South Africa itself, however, was concerned with events nearer home. J. B. Vorster, prime minister since 1966, realized that the maintenance of *apartheid* within the South African *laager* was not a sufficient or viable policy. However strong and wealthy South Africa might be, it could not ignore the disapproval of virtually the whole world including its major trading partners and potential allies; or the writing on the wall for white power in Angola, Mozambique and Rhodesia; or the dependence of its own economy on black labour, including foreign black labour; or its worsening balance of payments and consequent need to find new markets for its exports; or the all too recognizable signs and consequences of inflation and declining capital investment; or the gradual if still politically ineffectual increase in violence within its own borders. Vorster was no less wedded than his predecessors to firm and exclusive white control of the republic but he wanted also to establish correct and profitable, if not necessarily cordial, relations with as many other African states as possible. In spite of the exceedingly unpropitious political and psychological background Vorster sought to give South Africa a role in Africa, or at the least in Africa south of the Congo, similar to that which pre-war Japan had planned for itself in East Asia. He found an attentive ear in far away Ivory Coast where Houphouet-Boigny flew a kite in 1970 to test feelings about normalizing relations with South Africa. The kite flopped, Nigeria being particularly hostile because of South Africa's support for Biafra, but the reopening of the Rhodesian issue by the Conservative government in Britain forced Vorster to remain diplomatically active beyond his own borders. He was now, or soon afterwards, convinced that his role should not be unquestioning support of a régime which a Portuguese débâcle would expose to increasing armed incursion and sterner economic strangulation. Vorster told Smith that South Africa could not give Rhodesian goods priority in South African ports and he began obliquely telling his own people that white rule in South Africa must and could be preserved without white rule in Rhodesia.

The collapse of Portuguese rule was decisive. After a tentative and unsuccessful effort to intervene in Angola (see p. 400) which shocked South African opinion first because it happened secretly and then because it failed, Vorster had to live with the fact that Namibia (the former trust territory of South West Africa) had an open frontier with a new black state, while in the east he had hostages to fortune in the Cabora Bassa hydro-electric plant which was about to come into production and in the Mozambique migrants who provided South Africa with a quarter of the labour in its mines. Vorster publicly accepted Frelimo's victory and wished the new government well. He also despatched his minister for external affairs, Hilgard Muller, on a round of secret visits to African capitals and joined in the plans of Zambia and others to achieve a bloodless transition from white minority to black majority rule in Rhodesia (see p. 378).

Notes

A. Rwanda and Burundi

Rwanda and Burundi, formerly German colonies, were placed under Belgian mandate after the First World War. The population consisted of the Hutu, a Bantu people, and the Tutsi, Amharic warriors who arrived in the sixteenth century and became a semi-divine ruling caste. In 1959 the Hutu in Rwanda revolted. The Tutsi monarch, or mwami, who had succeeded upon the mysterious death of his half-brother in 1959, was deposed in 1961 and fled in the following year to Uganda. A republic was proclaimed under president Kayibanda. In the same year the Belgian mandate was terminated, Rwanda and Burundi ceased to be jointly administered, Rwanda became an independent republic and Burundi an independent monarchy. During the upheavals which followed the revolt of 1959 very many Tutsi fled to Burundi, Uganda and the Congo. Raids by some of these exiled led in April 1964 to a frightful massacre of Tutsi in Rwanda on something like a genocidal scale. In 1965 a similar onslaught was made by the Hutu on the Tutsi of Burundi who, unlike their cousins across the border, had retained their power. In 1966 the monarchy in Burundi was overthrown. In 1972 the Hutu rose and were slaughtered.

B. The Portuguese Territories

The Portuguese record in Africa and Asia is first in, last out: the first colonizers and the last imperialists. This small European country first ventured into strange continents 500 years ago and it acquired in Africa an estate twenty-three times its own size. Bartolomeo Diaz rounded Cape Horn in 1487, followed by Vasco da Gama in 1498. The Guinea trade, of which Portuguese Guinea is a relic, flourished during the sixteenth century but the Portuguese were gradually pushed out of West Africa by the Dutch, the British and the French, and they were to find their biggest prizes further south. Luanda, the capital of Angola, was founded in 1576 by a grandson of Diaz; it was held by the Dutch for a short time in the seventeenth century but was recaptured by the rich Brazilian adventurer Salvador de Sá who became its governor and restored Portuguese rule. In the seventeenth and eighteenth centuries Angola provided slaves for Brazil. The trade was abolished in 1836 and the institution of slavery itself supposedly from 1858. During the intensest phase of the European scramble for Africa Portugal was supported sporadically but ineffectually by Britain, but by nobody else. Germany coveted Portuguese territories and hoped to succeed to them by lending Portugal more money than it could repay and then foreclosing. A Portuguese dream of linking Angola with Mozambique by a land strip never materialized. Although Mozambique was settled in the twenty-five years before the First World War, the Portuguese evinced only tepid interest in Africa, while their laxity in the suppression of slavery earned them a scandalous notoriety, especially after the publication in 1906 of H. W. Nevinson's *A Modern Slavery*.

Major risings in Angola in 1922 and 1935 were ruthlessly suppressed but also nurtured nationalist movements. Lisbon began to see that its rule was threatened less by white home-rulers than by black nationalism, even though the nationalists were in the short term hopelessly hampered by illiteracy, tribal divisions and the overwhelming might of the Portuguese police and army. In 1952 Portugal's colonies were renamed overseas provinces and the fifties saw a burst of material progress in the shape of public works and development plans. The change of name enabled Portugal to claim that it was under no obligation to submit reports to the UN under article 73 (e) of the Charter, Angola and Mozambique having become not non-self-governing territories but provinces of Portugal. In this contention Portugal had the support of its American and British allies and its Brazilian kinsmen, but in 1963 a resolution of the General Assembly urging Portugal to accelerate self-determination was supported by the United States and Britain; only Spain and South Africa voted against it; France abstained.

The Portuguese practised a policy of assimilation as a means of gradually expanding the franchise, but increasing immigration from Portugal in the mid-fifties altered social and economic patterns, reinforced the colour bar and reduced many Angolans to unemployment or semi-employment. Tens of thousands of Angolans were in exile, mostly in the Congo, by 1960, and the nationalist movements established their headquarters in Leopoldville. Confidence was shaken by a dispute over the election of a northern chief, in which the Portuguese authorities acted in accordance with the letter of the law but with dubious wisdom and probity. The emancipation of the British and French West African colonies and of the Belgian Congo brought the modern African problem to Portugal's Angolan doorstep and in February 1961 there were riots in Luanda, partly stimulated by the adventures of a Captain Galvao who seized the liner *Sta Maria* and was expected in Luanda to appear off the coast in the role of liberator. These riots were suppressed but in March there were further disorders in the north and an invasion from across the Congolese frontier. The Portuguese were taken by surprise, suffered casualties of about 1,400 in killed and wou.\ded and disastrously responded to barbarities with further barbarities. African casualties were of the order of 20,000 and a stream of hideously wounded refugees – 20,000 in 1961 and a further 150,000 in the next three years – into the Congo blackened the Portuguese name, while the cost of reasserting Portuguese authority became a serious strain on Portugal's economy.

In Mozambique a guerrilla liberation movement, Frelimo, began an armed rising in 1964 and secured control over parts of the country, but it suffered in 1969 the assassination of its leader, Dr Eduardo Mondlane. The economy was hit by the blockading of Beira to implement sanctions against Rhodesia, but the Portuguese showed no signs of giving up. They embarked instead on a vast scheme to develop Mozambique's economy in association with South African, European and American concerns (which would thereby acquire a vested interest in Portuguese rule). This scheme, which centred round the building of a hydro-electric barrage at Cabora Bassa, would also entail the addition of a million persons to the white population. The political nature of the plan was barely concealed and, considering that Mozambique already had six hydro-electric schemes and needed no more, hardly could be. The political implications and lobbying by African states caused some of the participants to think again and – in the cases of Sweden and Italy – to withdraw.

In Portuguese Guinea, or Guinea-Bissao, a liberation movement started in 1956 by Amilcar Cabral led to a rising in 1959 and full scale war in 1963, in the course of which the Guineans gradually established their control over the greater part of the country. In 1970 Portugal was implicated in an invasion of the neighbouring state of Guinea. An inquiry by the UN found that 350–400 invaders had been helped by ships manned by white men and the Security Council censured Portugal. Guinea-Bissao's liberation movement (PAIGC – African Party for the Independence of Guinea and the Cape Verde Islands) had its headquarters in the Guinean capital Conakry where subsequently, in January 1973, Cabral was murdered.

By 1970 Portugal's colonial wars had forced it to allot half of its budget and over 6 per cent of its gross national product to military spending, to raise the largest armies ever raised in Portugal's history and to conscript its young men for four years. The absence of a politically active public opinion shielded the government from what had been one of the strongest, perhaps the strongest, of the decolonizing forces in London, Paris and Brussels, but ten years of costly and unsuccessful fighting in three widely separated territories sapped the will of the Portuguese armies. The liberation movement had survived and grown, winning popular support, extending their geographical control and getting arms from abroad. In response the Portuguese tried bombing and barbed wire, but bombing was inefficient against guerrillas and barbed wire failed to separate them from the populace because the latter (unlike their counterparts earlier on in Malaya) were on the side of the former. In Guinea-Bissao the governor, General Spinola, becoming convinced of the hopelessness of the struggle, resigned in 1973 and went back to Lisbon as an outspoken opponent of continuing colonial rule. His actions and writings contributed to the overthrow by the army in 1974 of the military dictatorship founded in 1926 and the Armed Forces Movement which won control in Lisbon declared itself in favour of independence for Portugal's African colonies. This was immediately achieved in

Guinea-Bissao and Mozambique but in Angola a splintering of the anti-colonial forces postponed the triumph of the MPLA (Popular Movement for the Liberation of Angola, leader: Agustinho Neto) and led to foreign intervention.

The MPLA had overplayed its hand in the 1961 rising and had suffered in consequence, but it recuperated in exile (in Congo-Brazzaville and Zambia) and recovered its effectiveness. It was, however, distracted by internal divisions at the crucial moment in 1974 and challenged by the rival FNLA (National Front for the Liberation of Angola, leader: Holden Roberto), a movement created in 1962 out of the remnants of earlier anti-Portuguese groups and supported by President Mobutu of Zaïre. A third movement, UNITA, also appeared but its only – and insufficient – assets were a certain following in and near Luanda and a prospect of foreign aid, South African or American. South Africa had so far refrained from intervening but in 1975, after the formation and break-up of a government of all three movements, it did so. In the fighting that followed the MPLA, assisted by Russian arms and Cuban troops as well as the moral support of most members of the OAU, was quickly successful. The presence of Cuban forces cast a shadow over impending events in Rhodesia and Namibia. The door to outside intervention was once more ajar in Africa, if not forced.

C. Botswana, Lesotho, Ngwane

The three territories of Bechuanaland, Basutoland and Swaziland became protectorates of the British crown in 1884, 1868 and 1890 respectively. Their transfer to South Africa, which had been envisaged in the South Africa Act 1909, was mooted by Malan during the Commonwealth conference of 1949, during a visit to South Africa by the commonwealth relations secretary, Patrick Gordon-Walker, in 1950, and again in 1951, 1954 and 1956. But the developing policy of racial *apartheid* and the intensification of police rule in South Africa eliminated such possibility as there might have been for British compliance. The Tomlinson report included all three territories among South Africa's Bantustans but Tomlinson himself acknowledged a few years later that there was no likelihood of their transfer. In 1960 a transfer under the terms of the South Africa Act became an impossibility, since that act required an order by the king in council upon the receipt of addresses from both houses of the South African parliament – an impossible procedure after South Africa became a republic. More important, the British parliament had been given assurances, frequently repeated, that there would be no transfer without a debate at Westminster and consultation of the wishes of the inhabitants.

But Britain's neglect of the territories had left them economically dependent on South Africa; Britain's traditional predilection for conservative chiefs retarded the advance of self-government without reconciling the traditionalists who, fearful of the newer type of nationalist, found some attractions in South African schemes for separate African territories based on the authority of chiefs. British weakness in regard to South Africa was demonstrated when Seretse Khama, the hereditary chief of the Bamangwato in Bechuanaland, married an English girl in 1949. Under pressure from the outraged South Africans the British banished both Seretse and his uncle, the highly talented and efficient Tshekedi Khama, on the plea that the tribe was split on the question whether to accept Seretse with a white wife as chief. Seretse remained in exile until he renounced in 1956 his claims and those of his descendants. He subsequently formed the Bechuanaland Democratic Party and after a general election in 1965 (held under a new constitution introduced in 1961) became prime minister. Bechuanaland became an independent state under the name of Botswana in 1966 but its nominal independence was even more constricted than that of most poor countries, for its poverty made it dependent either on outside aid or on its big neighbour, and in the absense of substantial aid it seemed doomed by past neglect and present stringency to become a satellite of South Africa with all the consequent threats to the moderate and democratic rule which Seretse and his party hoped to give it.

In Basutoland, entirely engulfed in South Africa, the paramount chief Constantine Bereng, who succeeded to his office in 1960 at the age of twenty-eight after an English education, led a moderate nationalist party (the Maramotlou Freedom Party) but was sandwiched between the traditionalists in the Basuto Nationalist Party led by Chief Leabua Jonathan and the more forthright nationalism of the Basuto Congress Party led by Ntsu Mokhehle. In elections in 1965 the Nationalists narrowly defeated the Congress but then appeared from the evidence of by-elections to lose ground. The opposition parties, suspicious of Nationalist links with South Africa where CHief Jonathan was regarded as the lesser evil, pressed Britain to strengthen the powers which the paramount chief would have as monarch after independence and to conduct fresh elections before independence, but the British government was unmoved by these pleas and in 1966 Basutoland became independent Lesotho with a narrow balance of domestic political forces and a tenseness in the political atmosphere which boded ill for Chief Jonathan's government and suggested that if it ran into difficulties in maintaining its authority it would have no choice but to ask South Africa for help. Riots which occurred at the end of the year gave Jonathan the opportunity to exact from King Moshoeshoe II a pledge to keep out of politics and to confine him to his palace. In 1968 some chiefs who had sided with Jonathan appeared to be switching their allegiance to the king and when Jonathan seemed to be losing the elections held in that year he cancelled the proceedings, suspended the constitution and so kept for the time being his office of prime minister. The king retreated into exile but returned in 1970.

Swaziland, the smallest of the three territories and the last to attain independence, had an elderly paramount chief, Sobhuza II, who was advised by a strongly conservative tribal council. At elections in 1964 his Mbokodo Party formed an alliance with the United Swazi party, the organ of the white farming and business community of 10,000, and routed an assorted opposition of divided and ill-prepared nationalists. Under the constitution prepared for independence in 1968 the monarch was given a dominant position: he could nominate enough members of the parliament to block measures which he did not like, he was not bound to act on ministerial advice in all matters in which a constitutional monarch is normally so bound, he was given control over Swaziland's principal asset (its minerals) subject only to advice from his traditional council and not from his minister, and his party was entrenched in power by an electoral system in which the towns, and therefore the nationalists, were submerged in large rural constituencies. Control over the minerals was, however, taken away from him on the eve of independence. Opposition was weakened because a number of nationalists joined the Mbokodo Party for opportunist reasons.

D. The Malagasy Republic

The island of Madagascar, lying off the Mozambique coast, came under French rule at the end of the nineteenth century. In 1947 a serious revolt against the post-war restoration of that rule was rudely repressed, but independence was nevertheless not long delayed. Within the island there was a conflict of interest between the Hova dominant minority, which wanted independence at the earliest possible moment, and a larger nationalist group under the leadership of Philibert Tsirinana, which preferred a short delay in order to be sure of gaining power for itself and not for the Hovas. This group succeeded in its aims. Madagascar became the Malagasy Republic in 1958, remaining in the French Union. Tsirinana became president and full independence followed in 1960. Tsirinana steered a pro-French course and became a prominent supporter of black dialogue with South Africa. Although re-elected in 1972 he was forced that year to hand over real power to General Gabriel Ramanantsava, the nominee of the army, to whom he resigned the presidency after a referendum which approved the army's action. Ramanantsava was displaced three years later by Colonel Richard Ratsimandrava who was assassinated within a week and succeeded by Captain Didier Ratsiraka. French troops left the island in 1973.

Part Six

Latin America

Chapter 23

Introductory

Latin America in the nineteenth century was isolated from world politics not – as were Africa and much of Asia – by the muffle of European imperialism but by the heritage of post-colonialism. At the same time the Latin American republics were largely isolated from each other as well as from the rest of the world. The twentieth century witnessed an accelerating reversal of this pattern, accompanied and complicated by spasmodic attempts to assimilate the democratic and industrial revolutions which were the hallmark of the experiences, and to some extent the successes, of western Europe and the United States of America: to implant, that is, democratic political forms and democratic social values in resistant narrow oligarchies, and to develop manufacturing industries where trade in primary products had hitherto sufficed for the needs of the ruling classes.

In a century and more after independence Latin America had become a by-word for political instability and could, but for widespread ignorance of its affairs, have become no less a by-word for social immobility. It was notorious for civil wars, revolutions, coups, political assassination and short-lived constitutions, while at the same time it entrenched extreme social and economic injustice. Its basic needs were the reverse of its experience, namely political stability and social and economic change. It was in these respects not unique but its ills had been aggravated by time until they posed a daunting dilemma: was it possible to get social and economic change without revolution? Was it possible to get political stability without perpetuating social and economic stagnation? The underlying conflict between the few and the many was not mediated by a middle class such as had tided western Europe over the bar of oligarchy without intolerable violence.

The government of Latin America after the end of Spanish rule devolved upon a social élite consisting of big landowners supported by the Roman Catholic Church and by a military caste aspiring to the same social status. This pattern was most notably troubled in Mexico by the revolution of 1910, but by 1945 the traditional power of the upper classes had been destroyed nowhere else and ten years later the Mexican example had still been followed nowhere except in Bolivia (1952). Nevertheless the oligarchy's props were weakening. Within the religious and military establishments there were growing doubts about the immutability and propriety of its monopoly of power and profit and some concern, expressed with varying degrees of success and sincerity, over the plight of the rural poor, the growing urban proletariat and the suppressed Indians. An awareness of gross inequalities was stirring consciences and fears and so enlisting in the service of the underdog those two powerful political forces, indignation and the recalculation of expediences. Churches began to shift their attention and their political weight somewhat to the left, and there appeared in the armed forces officers with some of the instincts of populists and a taste for demagogy.

Throughout Latin America a great part of the population was extremely poor, illiterate, unproductive and virtually outside the state. Many states were not merely run by an oligarchy but also owned by it in the sense that the land and what grew on it and what lay beneath it were the private property of a small number of individuals: in various countries 60 to 90 per cent of agricultural land was owned by a tenth of the population. Quite apart from abstract notions of fair or unfair shares, this distribution was the cause of great inefficiency. Many landowners, possessing more land than they needed to cultivate, left much of it untilled and untended, but were firmly opposed to any redistribution to other proprietors who might be more disposed to cultivate it. (Forcible redistribution produced the opposite evil of a multitude of economically intractable plots: in Colombia, for example, more than two-thirds of the land was uncultivated while much of the cultivable area had been broken down into holdings of a few acres.) Bountifully supplied with cheap labour the big landowners had no need to invest their profits in their land, modernize their methods or increase production.

The rural poor remained poor to the verge of destitution and beyond, and either endured short lives of useless and hopeless misery or drifted to towns where they were not much better off, since they were not fitted to take jobs. Public education in Latin America as a whole was so meagre that less than a tenth of the population completed a primary course and illiteracy rates of 50 per cent were not uncommon, 90 per cent not unknown. If they were Indians, the peasants who went to the towns invited incomprehension and ridicule by their strange speech and attitudes. Moreover, if the peasants had little to offer, the towns too had little to offer on their side. Industry cannot flourish in places where half the population is too poor to buy its products. Latin American industries were handicapped by the lack of a domestic market with the result that the Latin American countries continued to import goods which they could have been making for themselves. Hence the towns to which the peasants migrated, so far from needing their labour, already contained unemployment; in some of them a third of the inhabitants might be unhoused. And this unemployment was growing not only for economic reasons but also because the population explosion in Latin America was greater than anywhere else in the world: the population was in the process of doubling itself in periods of a quarter century.

There existed therefore in most parts of Latin America a

revolutionary situation. This situation was accentuated by awareness of it, since an assumption that a pattern cannot last much longer is itself a potent factor for change. The forces making for change were the relatively passive rural and urban proletariats and the active leaders who might emerge from the established social groups or the nascent middle class and who, out of dissatisfaction with the existing state of affairs, might make common cause with the masses some or all of the way towards revolution.

The growth of a Latin American middle class had been stunted by the slow pace of industrial development just as industrial development had been stunted by the self-sufficiency of a ruling class capable of maintaining its standard of living by exporting primary products and using the proceeds to import all the necessities and luxuries which it wanted from the outside world. This economic pattern had social and political consequences, since a small middle class is less likely than a large one to adopt distinctive social habits and political aims of its own, and in Latin America the small middle class, imprisoned within the oligarchic system, was relatively effortlessly seduced into gravitating into and so preserving the upper reaches of a system which it had no power to subvert. Here again Latin America was not unique, except perhaps in degree. The standing of the middle class was, however, altered by the Second World War which deprived Latin America of its habitual imports and so promoted industrial development. After a pause in the immediate post-war years the demands created by the Korean war gave a fresh fillip to industrial expansion. These wars, events external to the sub-continent's own affairs, thus altered its economic course, although they did not do so to the extent of seriously altering its social hierarchy. The industrial middle class prospered in some centres, notably in Mexico and Brazil, but for the most part it came nowhere near to supplanting the traditional ruling class in the exercise of political power.

The traditional patterns of society and government continued, if with occasional misgiving, to be supported by the most powerful element in the state, the armed services. After the wars of liberation early in the nineteenth century the new Latin American states engaged in comparatively few wars among themselves and faced with few exceptions (of which Mexico's quarrels with the United States of America were the chief example) no enemy threat from beyond the sub-continent. Their armies assumed therefore a domestic political role rather than the function of national defence. Officers, with the conservatism natural to their caste and the social ambitions which became a substitute for more serious military employment, saw themselves as the guardians or godfathers of the state – and the state as the same as the *status quo*. Unduly inefficient or corrupt politicans would be replaced by others or by a period of direct military rule, and in the exercise of this regulative function the officer class pictured itself as acting for the public weal, a habit of mind which could lead to surprising results if the army's interpretation of the public weal should change. And around the middle of the twentieth century there were indications of such a change. As armies expanded, they acquired officers from somewhat different backgrounds, so that the awareness of the need for social change and mild support for it found their way into the military establishment. The consequences of this shift were, however, ambivalent. On the one hand the insemination of a radical element into the military mind was an encouragement for the proponents of change, but on the other hand an establishment ready for no more than a small dose of change could easily be frightened back into a more rigid conservatism, if the pace of change began to outstrip the progressive officers' own cautious assessment of the need. The addition of a military element to the progressive forces could affect the pace of change in one of two ways: either by increasing it and so alienating progressive officers and bringing on a clash with the forces of conservatism, or by reducing it to a level acceptable to these officers and so alienating the more intrepid elements and producing a clash at a different point along the political spectrum.

Alongside this regrouping of domestic forces old and new, whose outcome was likely to differ from one state to the next, there was a search for new models, for political forms to replace the existing forms which were being judged and found wanting. This search led the more inquiring minds to consider two foreign models, each of which seemed to have something to contribute: western democracy with its emphasis on freedom and human rights, and communism with its reputation for economic growth. The Latin American intellectual who could discover how to get the best from both these two worlds would perhaps have found the synthetic shortcut to prosperity and justice. But he too was faced with a multiple dilemma. He knew that, for economic reasons, Latin America needed foreign aid; he knew that, for historical reasons, Latin America wanted to steer clear of foreign aid; and he had to face the fact that if, in his search for the synthetic shortcut, he looked for aid and inspiration to both the western and the communist strongholds, he would be met in each with the argument that the two models were antithetical and that he must make up his mind between them before expecting help from the guardian of either. Like Asians and Africans, although for different reasons, he would need to be non-aligned while soliciting the favours of those whose line he refused exclusively to take.

Latin America's approach to the outside world reflected the needs of countries whose economies were in a process of transition without adequate domestic resources or machinery, against a background of ill-regulated foreign aid in a previous generation. Towards the end of the nineteenth century and at the beginning of the twentieth the principal capitalist nations had lent money to Latin America to excess and at very high rates of interest to the mutual dissatisfaction of both sides – of the Latin Americans who felt that they had been exploited, and of the lenders who resented many a subsequent default and the expropriation of a number of enterprises which they had built up. (Latin

America's xenophobia was increased by the imperialist policies of the United States of America which will be described below.) But Latin America could not do without foreign capital if it was to implement development programmes, close trade gaps and meet its large (and largely short term) foreign debts. The capital required was not being produced at home. The poor were too poor to save and were getting poorer, the rich frequently invested or banked their wealth abroad, and domestic banks and other financial institutions had not developed the habits or the mechanisms for providing credit for industrial expansion. The reformers, who appreciated the need for foreign aid but were required by their environment to be anti-foreigner as well as anti-establishment, hoped to be extricated from this dilemma by getting aid from international agencies instead of foreign governments, but these agencies proved disappointing since they applied strict financial rules to their lending, insisted on currency stabilization and a reasonable prospect of profit as pre-conditions, and hesitated to come to the aid of petitioners with limited financial credentials and limited economic expertise: the post-war years in Latin America were peppered with too many economic blunders as wartime profits were dissipated on luxuries and industrialization was pursued fitfully and without discrimination.

Washington held therefore a commanding position. Washington wanted to encourage democracy, social progress and stability in Latin America; it was opposed to communism and, on the whole, to revolution. It adopted, notably in the Alliance for Progress more particularly described below, a gradualist policy in a revolutionary situation on the assumption that lavish aid could promote democracy and social progress in Latin America and at the same time ward off revolution and stifle communism. This was a very large assumption to which it was objected that in Latin America's predicament aid of this kind could hasten revolution but not prevent it, while communism was bound to be an unexorcisable element in the reform movement, as impossible to eradicate as it was in France. Washington's assumptions and policies in the middle of the century were of undeniable importance but uncertain import. They were largely influenced by the Monroe Doctrine and by special, if local, concern over the Caribbean.

Chapter 24

Populism and militarism
in Brazil and Argentina

Any attempt to generalize about a continent is open to objections so
well known that they do not need to be restated. What has been written
above must be read with the knowledge that the countries of Latin
America, whatever the similarities in their conditions, also differ from
one another no less than contiguous and homophonic countries in other
parts of the world. But before going on to consider particular events in
some of them in the years after the Second World War there is one
further generalization to be presented. Since the days of the great
liberators the traditional form of government in Latin America has
been a personalist one, dominated by a single figure not unlike the
Roman patrician with his personal following or *clientela*. These leaders
were necessarily of different kinds, but whether they were good or bad,
selfish or unselfish, efficient or inefficient, they compressed political life
into pyramids, and when the changes of the mid-twentieth century
began to make a political mark, they too produced pyramids. The
movements of protest, based on lower-class pressures for social reform,
were naturally and easily led by a paladin or a buccaneer who had
become alive to the nascent political existence of the masses or to the
racial question. The characteristic reformer or revolutionary at this
stage was the demagogue who might or might not start off with a
sincere regard for the oppressed but might equally forget about them
when in power or fail them through sheer inexperience in the business
of government. Democratic and working-class inexperience in the
business of government. Democratic and working-class organizations,
such as trade unions, were weak (except in Mexico, Bolivia and
Venezuela) and the broadly based populist revolution had little to show
until, or even after, the successes of Fidel Castro.

This tradition of personal autocracy was an outcome of an historical
process which also carried with it the genes, however recessive, of
liberal democracy. Latin America owed its independence partly to the
circumstances of the Napoleonic wars which sundered it from Spain
but also to the ideas of the Enlightenment, and although the waging of
wars of liberation favoured the establishment of autocratic and military
rule, the revulsion from European dominion was to some degree a rejection of autocracy as well as a rejection of foreigners. In Mexico, for example, the American and French revolutions and the European
revolutions of 1848 inspired a liberal trend and were reflected in the

constitution of 1857. The rule of Porfirio Díaz, who was president from 1876 to 1910 with only one four-year interlude, was a remorseless, modernizing oligarchy which nevertheless led up to the revolution of 1910. After seven years of civil war, in which the United States intervened on the side of counter-revolution and a war between Mexico and the United States was only narrowly avoided, Mexico became committed to social mobility and economic reform. Although the legislature was weak and only one party counted and the army retained a powerful political role for a further quarter-century, presidents succeeded each other decorously and constitutionally and by the end of the Second World War Mexico was a stable country under civilian rule. Its relations with the United States improved to a dignified wariness, and after 1940 a boom helped to give substance to economic and social plans. Yet progress was very slow. Although Mexico City became one of the largest and most modern cities in the world, it continued to embrace appalling poverty, and in the country as a whole the lot of the individual improved for only about one in ten, while for twice as many it grew worse.

The seniority of Mexico's revolution gave it a special standing in Latin American history, but by 1945 its impact had been lessened by time as well as by Mexico's position in the far north of the Latin American lands. Two more recent movements, both of them a blend of personalism and proto-democracy, were of more immediate significance. These were the rule of Getúlio Vargas and his successors in Brazil and of Juan Perón in Argentina from 1945 to 1955.

Brazil, the fourth largest country in the world, possesses enormous natural resources, occupies one-third of Latin America and accounts, with Mexico, for half its population and, with Mexico and Argentina, for nearly two-thirds of its products. According to the census of 1970 its population had grown by a third in 10 years and had reached 93.2 million. Its liberation was not turbulent, for it remained an empire and relatively stable until 1889, and thanks to its vast and varied resources it was able to make economic progress both before and after the First World War. Getúlio Vargas came to power democratically, and as a result of social and inter-provincial rivalries, in 1930. He began the modernization of Brazil. He strengthened the central government, nurtured industry and introduced state economic planning. He had the support of the army until he began to create an alternative power base in the poorer classes. In 1945 the army removed him. In 1950 he made a new bid for power by appealing not only to the proletariat but also to a new type of young army officer and was elected. The armed forces, hoping to control him and reluctant to flout a fair election blatantly, allowed him to take office, but by 1954 they had had enough of him and were about to evict him – on the grounds of incompetence – when he committed suicide.

The next decade saw a running down of the Vargas era under three presidents. The election of 1955 was won by Juscelino Kubitschek and

João Goulart as the presidential and vice-presidential candidates. The armed forces, divided in their attitudes towards this result, interposed no objection and indeed acted to allow the successful pair to take over. They thereby demonstrated the new president's dependence upon them, and he in return tacitly acknowledged the relationship by raising pay and providing funds for more and better military equipment. Some officers, like their counterparts in other countries, wanted more than this and hoped for a mildly reforming administration which would attack corruption, incompetence and the grosser manifestations of social injustice, but they were not willing to endorse any very radical measures nor – in the Brazilian case – did they have the satisfaction of observing a good administration at work, for President Kubitschek embarked on extravagant enterprises (such as the building of the new capital, Brasilia) and in the course of an energetically misguided administration opened up huge new opportunities for private peculation.

At the next election, in 1961, Jânio Quadros, with Goulart still as vice-president, succeeded, but he resigned after seven months leaving Goulart to take his place under the eyes of a divided and increasingly dubious army and a solidly conservative navy and air force. In these circumstances President Goulart's powers were strictly limited and he quickly reached the limits. Where Quadros had preferred to quit, Goulart chose to forge ahead; he rode for a fall. He proposed a wide extension of the franchise, land reform and a neutralist foreign policy. He appealed to the people against the armed forces and congress, accepted communist support at home, established relations with the USSR and opposed the eviction of Castro's Cuba from the OAS (but joined the United States naval blockade of Cuba during the missile crisis). These measures won him some popularity but also evoked fear and hatred, enabled communists to infiltrate into central and state administrations and trade unions and, as different provinces lined up on different sides, produced a threat of civil war, at which point the army intervened.

Having evicted Goulart the army leaders forced the congress, after a pause in which constitutional propriety was observed by recognizing the president of the chamber of deputies as president, to install General Humberto Castelo Branco as president for the remainder of Goulart's term. The general was succeeded by Marshal Costa e Silva and he by General Garrastazu Medici and in 1974 by General Ernesto Geisel. The military régime inherited runaway inflation and tackled it by such devices as wage freezes. Political parties were banned with the exception of two new ones of no independent vitality. The régime turned a hard face towards trade unions, peasants and students. It made little progress with land reform and halted literacy programmes which seemed to it dangerous: Brazil remained a country of unused land and unused talent. Faced with growing opposition it resorted to strong arm methods, including widespread and appalling cruelty to the political prisoners who were thrown in increasing numbers into the gaols.

Argentina, the second of the major states in South America, achieved

its independence from Spain at the cost of losing territories which formed the new states of Uruguay, Paraguay and Bolivia. It was only
gradually and painfully unified but from the latter part of the
nineteenth century it prospered with the development of its lands,
largely by immigrants from Europe. The government was in the hands
of upper-class conservative and radical politicians who competed for
power and sporadically permitted an admixture of democracy, especially between 1916 and 1930. The country's population, its
agriculture and its railways expanded steadily and with the introduction of refrigeration it became one of the world's major exporting countries before the First World War; but it lacked minerals and the capacity to develop industry alongside agriculture and commerce. It was
severely hit by the slump of 1929 and suffered, partly in consequence, a
revolt in 1930 in which army officers (including a thirty-five-year-old
Juan Perón) had the support of the possessing and the dispossessed
classes. This event was followed by a period of autocratic conservative
rule, buttressed by the army and by renewed prosperity. At the same
time urbanization and immigration were producing a more politically
conscious and socialist working class.

During the war the presidency was held by the ultra-conservative
Ramón Castillo, first as acting president from 1940 to 1942 and then as
president for a further year. Castillo refused to break off relations with
the Axis powers, partly because he had fascist leanings himself and
partly in despite of the United States towards which Argentina's governing classes were traditionally hostile. In 1943 the army again intervened in politics, this time in order to remove the reactionary régime of
landowners whose tenure of power since 1930 had proved that they had
learnt nothing. A series of generals occupied the presidency during the
next two years and war was declared on Germany and Japan in
January 1944. During this period Colonel Perón held government appointments and, by his awareness of the urban under-dog and his
preoccupation with social justice, acquired a large personal following
among the working classes. In October 1945 other officers, jealous of
his growing power and uneasy about his intentions, tried to secure his
removal, but they had left their attempt too late, for it provoked an upheaval in which hordes of *descamisados* invaded the political arena and
swept Perón into supreme power. Four months later, in spite of an opposition which was openly joined by the United States ambassador, he
was elected president.

Perón ruled for nine and a half years which were crammed with
legislative and other measures designed, mainly by authoritarian
methods, to turn Argentina into a modern and just country. Banks and
other enterprises were nationalized, foreign concerns were bought out
with wartime profits, public services and popular education were expanded, industrialization was accelerated, the centralized buying and
selling of agricultural products was introduced in order to cushion the
effects of price fluctuations. But the pace was too hot for the economy

and for the propertied classes, and Perón also gave grave offence to the Church. Although the programme was trimmed in the later years Perón made too many mistakes and too many enemies, and in June 1955 the navy and the air force, with the Church in the background, tried to bomb him out of the presidency. The army, however, not only remained loyal to him during the abortive coup but did not feel obliged to replace him by any other leader after it. Perón dismissed some of his ministers who were most obnoxious to the conservatives and set about safeguarding his position by organizing and arming the *descamisados*. This latter move alarmed the army which turned against him and, in September 1955, removed him by a coup which placed another general in his place.

The oligarchy had closed ranks in order to put an end to economic policies which were harming the country and social reforms which were harming themselves. They had the support of intellectuals who, although they might approve Perón's social aims, disapproved of his authoritarian methods, particularly censorship; for Perón's advocacy of social reform did not include freedom of expression. The fall of Perón halted the reform movement and, as in Brazil, raised the hopeless question of what to do when the need for reform is urgent but the readiness of the powers that be for change is restricted. The supporters of Perón – and of the vivacious Eva Duarte whom Perón had married just before his triumph in 1942 but who had died of cancer in 1952 – did not disappear. They represented a force which, if it could not be wooed away to some other movement, must either be disfranchised or be allowed to resume the *peronista* course.

Meanwhile the army ruled. It first installed General Eduardo Lonardi in the presidency, in which he was later succeeded by General Pedro Aramburu pending elections in 1958. In that year Arturo Frondizi, a representative middle-class politician, became president with army consent. The persistence of *peronista* feeling was demonstrated at elections in 1960 when, with the *peronistas* barred from putting up candidates of their own, one million abstentions were recorded. In 1962 the *peronistas* were allowed to vote once more, Frondizi gambling on his ability to win them to his side. The gamble failed conspicuously. Officers of the three services, angered by Frondizi's miscalculation, discarded him and took council among themselves on the basis that the first article of government was the continued exclusion of Perón in exile in Spain) and his like. The navy, Perón's stoutest opponents, insisted on the simple course of not having elections, and they were supported by a section of army officers known as the *gorillas*. Other army officers, however, backed by the air force, preferred to revert to the system of holding elections as required by the constitution but with the *peronistas* disfranchised. Fighting ensued and the latter group won. New elections were held but could not disguise *peronista* strength which could always be manifested either by pro-*peronista* votes or by abstentions. In the next year the moderate army group made Arturo Illía president.

The armed forces had refused to accept the electoral verdict of 1962 and had failed to find a constitutional way of excluding Perón. They had therefore resorted to unconstitutional manoeuvres and had in the process further exposed the divisions in their own ranks. In 1966 they removed Illía and substituted Juan Onganía. In 1970 they removed Onganía and substituted Roberto Levingston who was removed in his turn in 1971 to make way for General Alejandro Lanusse. None of these governments could master inflation or keep order. Disorder increasingly took the form of kidnapping for publicity and ransom – for example, the seizure and murder by a Trotskyist group of Fiat's Director-General in Argentina.

In 1972 Perón, now seventy-seven years old, returned amid speculation and apprehension. His arrival was undramatic and his stay short. He endorsed the candidacy of Hector Cámpora in the approaching presidential election and went back to Spain after a few weeks. Cámpora won the election in 1973 with 49.6 per cent of the vote and his party – the Frente Justicialista, alias *peronista* – won twenty out of twenty-two governorships and control of both parliamentary chambers. But Cámpora was unable to control the violence and kidnapping by groups which claimed a share of the peronist mantle but were disavowed by the Frente, and after a brief interval Perón reappeared, Cámpora resigned, the Frente nominated Perón and his wife Isabel for the presidency and vice-presidency and they received 61.8 per cent of the vote. Perón introduced heavy taxes, bearing specially on the rich but also – in the case of a VAT at 16 per cent – on other classes too. He died in July 1974, leaving his widow to face the problems of inflation and public order, in dealing with which she was no more successful than her predecessor. She and her government were removed in 1976 by the army which likewise could think of nothing more useful to do than imprison and maltreat its critics.

Chapter 25

Latin America and the USA: Guatemala, the Alliance for Progress, the Dominican Republic

Latin America is divided into many states. North America is not. From the days of the Liberators, when the sub-continent was Balkanized by post-imperial wars and politics, there were hankerings for the sub-continental solidarity of the great Spanish viceroyalties. A surviving cultural community and a certain geographical compactness and isolation promoted in time an inter-American system, which was enlarged in turn into a pan-American (as opposed to a Latin American) organization. But the contrast between south and north could not be eradicated. In the north the United States had shown an amazing capacity to accommodate a hotch-potch of races and preserved its unity in spite of the disruptive social and economic forces which produced the Civil War, while Canada succeeded in keeping its British and French populations under a single political roof. These two states therefore were much bigger and more powerful than any Latin American state, and the Latin Americans became fearful of United States preponderance and imperialism. Canada, which might have served as a makeweight, was reluctant to join any organization which might involve it in the conflicts between the United States and the Latin states.

The United States fed Latin American fears and suspicions. During its years of expansion the United States was uncertain of its attitudes towards its neighbours in Central America and the Caribbean, and during its years of emergence as a great power it frequently acted as though these states were something less than sovereign. Just as Britain in the twentieth century found it hard to think of Middle Eastern countries as independent or deserving independence, so the United States in an overlapping period felt much the same way about a group of states which were supposed to have a special impact on North American vital interests. When President Monroe forbade the expansion of European territorial dominions in the New World, Spain and Portugal had already lost theirs; the British, French and Dutch, who had arrived too late to get more than the pickings left over from the Hispano-Portuguese partition, had little interest in challenging Monroe's unilateral declaration and the one serious attempt to do so – France's attempt to turn Mexico into a new Habsburg empire during the American Civil War – was a catastrophic failure. By this time the United States had itself annexed one-third of Mexico, had evinced interest in an isthmian canal and was about to toy with the idea of acquiring the large islands of Cuba and Hispaniola (the latter containing the Dominican and Haitian republics).

The Monroe Doctrine, enunciated in 1823, was the basis of a policy of turning America into an island by purchases (Louisiana, Florida, Cuba, Alaska) and by barring all European powers from recovering their possessions or extending their influence in the continent. It was inspired equally by fears of Russia in the north-west and other Europeans to the south-east. For more than a century the doctrine required little exertion on the part of the United States, mainly on account of the state of Anglo-American relations, and it was not seriously called in question until, in the nineteen-sixties, the Russians dared to read in the southern area where Monroe and his cabinet had originally feared British or Spanish activity. Britain made no attempt to enlarge its West Indian empire. During the decades after the breach between Britain and the new United States British naval power served to buttress rather than to challenge the doctrine. Geography has placed no islands between the British Isles and the seaboard of the United States, so that the initial post-independence period was one of estrangement but not of conflict; it is hard to believe that conflict could have been avoided, especially during the Civil War, if the North Atlantic had been dotted with islands which the two powers would have competed to occupy. In the event the possession of a common language and common traditions was not countered by territorial disputes (except over Canada which, illuminatingly, failed to get very robust support from London), and when by the end of the century the power of the United States had grown to significant proportions, the goodwill between the two countries prevailed over occasional conflicts and led in the next century to an alliance which pulled Britain out of a European and into an American orbit. This alliance might not have been achieved but for Britain's abnegation of the role which it had once been in a position to play in central America.

In the middle of the nineteenth century, when the United States first began to think of a canal across Nicaragua to link the Atlantic and the Pacific, British assent and co-operation seemed essential. Britain had territories and claims along the nearby coast (in British Honduras, the Mosquito Coast and the Bay Islands); the United States negotiated favourable treaties with Nicaragua and Honduras. From these positions the two countries negotiated the Clayton-Bulwer treaty of 1850 whereby they agreed that neither should acquire exclusive control over any canal or special privileges in it; and further that neither should occupy or fortify or colonize or assume or exercise any dominion over any part of central America. This treaty, concluded at a time when the United States was the weaker of the two parties, became an obstacle to later plans to go ahead with the construction of a canal without British collaboration and to acquire dominion over its course and banks, but by the end of the century British interest in this part of the world was small compared with British interest in the Middle East and southern

Asia and in 1901 the Clayton-Bulwer treaty was replaced by the Hay-Pauncefote treaty which reaffirmed the principles of neutrality and free and undiscriminating use, but otherwise removed the limitations set by the earlier treaty. The United States then entered into discussions with Colombia for a grant of territory at Panama. A treaty was negotiated but rejected by the Colombian senate, whereupon in 1903 the United States promoted a revolt at Panama and the secession of the area from Colombia. A new Panamanian republic was created and, for $10 million and an annual rent of $250,000, granted to the United States perpetual sovereignty over the area to be called the Canal Zone and also the right to intervene in Panama's internal affairs. The United States made use of this right by despatching troops on a number of occasions.

More important to the United States than Panama was the large island of Cuba, closer to the United States than any other Latin American country with the sole exception of Mexico. For strategic reasons the United States tried on various occasions in the nineteenth century to buy Cuba from Spain but without success. In 1868 the Cubans rose against Spain and waged war for ten years. They were defeated but rose again in 1895. Feeling in the United States was enraged by the cruelty which the Spanish authorities used to defeat the revolt and by concern for American investments, but the government took no action until, in February 1898 and in circumstances which have remained unexplained ever since, the battleship USS *Maine* was sunk in harbour at Havana. Washington delivered an ultimatum and, although the terms were largely accepted and the war virtually over, declared war on Spain. Fighting, which extended to the Pacific, lasted three months and ended with the complete defeat of Spain and the cession to the United States by the treaty of Paris of the Philippine Islands, Guam and Puerto Rico in return for $20 million. Cuba passed in effect under the tutelage of the United States and so remained until 1933. In 1901 the United States asserted by the Platt Amendment (an amendment to the Army Appropriation Bill) that it would not withdraw its military forces unless its right to intervene for the preservation of good government were embodied in the Cuban constitution. US forces were stationed in the island in 1906–9 and 1913–21 in support of corrupt military régimes, and a naval base was built at Guantanamo.

Within a few years of the Cuban war the United States intervened in 1905 in the Dominican Republic. Fearful of European intervention as a consequence of the default of the Dominican government on its debts, President Theodore Roosevelt formulated the Roosevelt Corollary to the Monroe Doctrine, by which the United States arrogated to itself the right to intervene in Latin American countries in order to keep government in order. US forces reappeared in 1916 and for the next eight years the country was under the direct military rule of the United States with a US officer as president. A similar occupation of the neighbouring Haitian republic, also intended to forestall European creditors, lasted from 1915 to 1934. On the mainland the United States intervened openly in the Mexican revolution and civil war by a naval bombardment in 1914 and an unsuccessful army expedition in 1916–17; and US forces, sent to Nicaragua in 1911 to support a favoured president, kept the liberal opposition quiet until 1933 when, upon their departure, the dictatorship of Anastasio Somoza was inaugurated.

This United States policy of direction and control, sustained by sporadic military descents, was abandoned by President Franklin D. Roosevelt and his Secretary of State, Cordell Hull. In his first inaugural address Roosevelt promulgated a good neighbour policy based on non-intervention, and his undertaking was repeated at the Pan-American Conference of 1936 at Buenos Aires. The Platt Amendment was repealed. The right to intervene in Panama's internal affairs was abrogated by treaty. The withdrawal of US marines from Haiti was accelerated. The president accepted the right of the Mexican government to nationalize oil properties within its territory. Latin American hopes were also raised by the passing of the Reciprocal Trade Agreements Act of 1934 which gave the president power to reduce tariffs by as much as 50 per cent, and by the establishment in the same year of the Import-Export Bank for the lending of United States public funds to foreign governments.

But this amelioration of the intra-American atmosphere did not produce all that Washington desired. Before the Second World War, as after it, the United States wanted to enlist Latin American sympathies and support for wider matters, but largely failed. Before the outbreak of war Hull, mindful of Germany's attempt in the First World War to get Japan to attack the United States through Mexico, tried but failed to persuade Latin America that nazism and fascism were present dangers against which the whole American continent should take joint precautions. At Havana in July 1940 the American states agreed that no non-American state should be allowed to take over any piece of American territory, but this new and anti-German enunciation of the Monroe Doctrine was to be upheld by joint American action; the United States was given no invitation to intervene on its own against any external threat, but rather to supply its neighbours with the arms and equipment to do so. Consequently, one result of Washington's fears for the defence of the hemisphere was the strengthening of the military class throughout the area. Small Brazilian and Mexican forces were sent overseas during the war, but American military supplies affected the structure of politics within Latin America far more than they affected the course of the war.

After Pearl Harbour Mexico, Colombia and Venezuela broke off relations with Japan, Germany and Italy, and all the Central American and Caribbean republics declared war. When the end of the war was in sight the American states, meeting at Chapultepec in Mexico in February 1945, declared themselves in favour of collective defence against internal as well as external threats (this arrangement was placed on a more permanent footing by the Inter-American Treaty of Reciprocal Assistance, concluded at Rio de Janeiro in 1947), but Washington's concern to create a continental anti-communist alliance or defence system found little response among states which were still used to thinking of the United States and not the USSR as the prime intervenor in their internal affairs and were much more worried by post-war economic problems than by communism. The military classes, which were the most immediately affected by joint defence schemes, were less interested in co-operation than in strengthening their own forces. They looked to the United States for more, and more modern, equipment. The United States on the other hand became increasingly concerned with communism and increasingly trapped between policies of pre-empting communism by economic aid to its neighbours and interfering in their affairs to suppress communists or anybody who looked like a communist from Washington.

In 1951 the Mutual Security Act was extended to Latin America and from 1952 the United States concluded a series of bilateral defence agreements. If the United States (and Latin American civilians) had qualms about this further reinforcement of armies which operated most often as domestic political forces, Washington felt itself constrained by the veiled threat that armies unable to satisfy their needs in the United States might go shopping elsewhere. An inter-American police academy was established at Fort Davis in the Canal Zone in 1962 for the study and practice of techniques of counter-insurgency, but otherwise inter-American military co-operation was not noticeably fruitful or popular.

The conferences at Chapultepec and Rio were the seventh and eighth in a series of inter-American conferences which had been inaugurated in Washington in 1889. The ninth of these meetings was held at Bogotá in 1948 and created new institutions and continuing machinery for pan-American consultation and action (Canada still, by its own wish, excluded). This Organization of American States had for its objects the maintenance of peace within the area of its members, the peaceful settlement of their disputes, joint action against aggression and co-operative development of economic, social and cultural interests. For Latin America this association with the United States was welcome chiefly on account of the prospect of an economic outpouring like the Marshall Plan for Europe, but the prospect proved a mirage since Washington saw Europe and Latin America in a completely different light: Europe had been ravaged by war, was in danger of immediate economic collapse and was believed to be a defenceless bait for further Russian advances. These arguments to the hearts and heads of United States policy-makers applied little or not at all to Latin America, even had these policymakers been as much concerned with good neighbourliness as Franklin D. Roosevelt in the thirties. Latin America had not a high priority in post-war Washington. Disenchantment grew on both sides. When war broke out in Korea, in Washington's eyes an anti-communist war in which all should be prepared to stand up and be counted, Colombia alone sent troops. It appeared that collective action meant neither economic aid for Latin America nor military aid for the United States.

This discrepancy was accentuated by events in Guatemala. For over a hundred years (1838–1944) Guatemala was ruled by four military dictators with short intervals of civil government in between. In 1944 the army was divided and a group of junior officers supported a comparatively left-wing candidate, Juan Jose Arévalo, who was president until 1950. During this period the division in the army continued and was represented by the rivalry between two majors, Francisco Xavier Arana and Jacobo Arbenz Gúzman. The former was assassinated in 1949 and the latter won the election of 1950. This victory caused alarm in the United States where the new régime was regarded (disputably) as pro-communist or a forerunner of communism and therefore as presenting a threat to the Panama Canal; and also (correctly) as an enemy of foreign capitalists and especially of the United Fruit Company which, as the owner of a tenth of the country's land, exercised even more economic power in Guatemala than the Anglo-Iranian Oil Company in Iran, and stood in the way of essential land reform.

The Guatemalans, mostly of Indian stock, suffered from extremes of poverty, disease and social inattention, which were rendered the more intolerable to the thinking section by the prosperity of a small minority and by the economic omnipresence of foreign enterprises which owned not only an abundance of land but also the railways, docks and public utilities. President Arbenz accelerated his predecessor's reform programme; he nationalized uncultivated land and supported strikes against foreign concerns. These moves were interpreted in Washington as the beginnings of a fully fledged communist policy, notwithstanding that communists were greatly outnumbered by anti-communists in the Guatemalan government, parliament and civil service and that power lay with an anti-communist army. At the tenth inter-American conference at Caracas in March 1954 Dulles tried to get a condemnation of the Arbenz régime but discovered that no other state accepted Washington's interpretation of events in Guatemala. The conference passed a general resolution condemning communist domination of any American state but refused to single out Guatemala for special mention, and Dulles thereupon left Caracas abruptly and turned to conspiring with disaffected Guatemalans who were preparing to invade their country from Honduras and Nicaragua. These two countries, having complained of communist incursions from Guatemala, were themselves provided with arms from the United States, while Washington tried to prevent Guatemala from getting arms by appealing to its allies not to supply them and by trying to intercept communist shipments from Europe. The invasion took place in June and was successful. The Guatemalan government appealed to the Security Council but was frustrated by a proposal to refer the matter to the OAS. This attempt to deflect the matter was vetoed by the USSR but a week later President Arbenz was forced to resign. The leader of the invasion, Colonel Carlos Castillo Armas, succeeded him and retained office until he was assassinated in 1957. The annual rate of growth of the Guatemalan economy fell from 8.5 per cent (over 1944–54) to 3 per cent and under Castillo's successors Guatemala lived in a state of suppressed civil war.

Castillo was succeeded by General Miguel Ydígoras Fuentes. In an election in 1957 Ydígoras came second, but after some disorder and a second election in 1958 he was duly installed. His power was confirmed by a fraudulent election in 1961 but riots, repressed by the army, demonstrated a dependence which he was not wise enough to acknowledge. Military opinion turned against him on the grounds that he spent too much money on himself and too little on the armed forces. In 1962 the army defended him against an attempted coup by the air force, but he then fatally antagonized the army by allowing ex-president Juan Arévalo to return to Guatemala and campaign for the presidency. Arévalo, who seemed to be certain to win a fair election, was regarded as a reincarnation of Arbenz, and in 1963 the army under Colonel Enrique Peralta ejected Ydígoras and suspended the constitution. In 1965 the army tolerated the election of a comparatively liberal president, Julio Cesar Mendez Montenegro, but he was no more able than his more oppressive predecessors to pacify the country. A motley and frequently divided opposition, consisting of communists, trotskyists and guerrillas who were neither, staged unsuccessful risings and resorted to murder and kidnapping when their risings failed. United States forces helped the government. A United States ambassador was among those assassinated.

By abetting and indeed organizing the overthrow of the Arbenz government in 1954 the United States administration disclosed its priorities. It showed how much greater was the importance it attached to the suppression of communism than to the principle of non-intervention or to good relations with its Latin neighbours – unless it miscalculated the Latin American reaction as much as it undoubtedly misconstrued the magnitude of the communist threat. Washington also displayed its belief that its actions in the southern half of the continent need not be trammelled by great power considerations: the reaction of the USSR could be regarded, at this date, as minimal or impotent. The final lesson of the Guatemala affair was, or should have been, the impossibility of drawing a line between radical programmes which were social and therefore good and radical programmes which were communist and therefore malignant. The United States had evicted in Guatemala a reforming administration whose actions were not in themselves noxious but whose motives and further intentions were suspect. Latin America did not accept the anti-communist justification put forward in Washington.

In 1958 Vice-President Richard Nixon, on a tour of Latin American

countries, was received with insults and even violence which enlightened official and popular opinion north of the Rio Grande about some
Latin American attitudes towards the United States. In two of the
countries in his itinerary, Peru and Venezuela, dictators had recently
been displaced, but not before they had received from President
Eisenhower the Legion of Merit: Nixon found himself the target of popular indignation against the United States approval of dictators. In
1960 Eisenhower himself undertook a Latin American tour as part of a
calculated attempt to improve relations. In the interval between the two
visits the United States agreed to the creation of an inter-American
Bank and an inter-American Fund for Social Development (the latter
to finance unprofitable schemes which the World Bank was debarred
from helping); Washington had previously frowned on these institutions. Although the eleventh inter-American conference, due to be
held at Quito in 1959, was postponed, the foreign ministers of the
American states met once in that year at Santiago and twice in the
following year at San José. The first of these meetings was mainly
devoted to denouncing Trujillo and Batista, matters on which it was
not difficult to get a wide consensus. In 1960 a Venezuelan allegation
that Trujillo had instigated an attempt to murder President Betancourt
produced an inquiry, a condemnation of Trujillo and the eviction of the
Dominican Republic from the OAS, but when the United States
proposed economic sanctions and internationally supervised elections
in the Dominican Republic its associates drew back for fear of setting a
precedent for intervention in their own affairs. There was also a clash
between the United States and the rest on whether Cuba had become
decently or dangerously left wing. The conference was on the whole
anti-Cuban but was not prepared to express itself at all directly. A
proposal for inter-American mediation between the United States and
Cuba gained no ground. Nevertheless the Organization of American
States was functioning and seen to be functioning and the discords
within it were not acute, although on the perennial problem of
economic co-operation an attempt by President Kubitschek to obtain
United States aid for an 'Operation Pan-America' had produced little
response in Washington.

Chapter 26

The northern arc of South America: dictators, civilians and revolutionaries

During the late fifties there was a clatter of falling dictators, beginning with the fall of Perón in 1955. The following year saw the withdrawal of President Manuel Odría in Peru and the death of President Somoza of Nicaragua, and in 1957 and 1958 the dictators of Colombia and Venezuela, Generals Gustavo Rojas Pinilla and Marcos Pérez Jiménez, were displaced. The defeat of General Fulgencio Batista in Cuba in 1959 was not so simple an event as it at first appeared, but in 1960 and 1961 two further dictators disappeared when General Rafael Trujillo of the Dominican Republic was murdered and Colonel José María Lemus of Salvador was ousted by the middle-of-the-road régime of Colonel Julio Rivera, which embarked upon social reforms and economic development which had been of no interest to President Lemus but might have been undertaken by the extremer left with an energy indigestible in that conservative country. General Alfredo Stroessner of Paraguay seemed to have become an isolated anachronism.

The trend in these years was for the military to retire from sight. They could not abdicate real power since power inevitably was theirs. The exercise of that power in politics had become a habit partly because, with no conceivable military enemy in sight, they had nothing else to do and partly because of the defects of the rich ruling classes. The officer who is not required to prepare for a war can either opt for society or for politics. Many opted for the best society and nothing more; others for society and also for a share in the political dominance of the upper classes (to whom fundamentally the armed forces were essential); others again, having opted for politics, became dissatisfied – and, although they might despise democracy, wished to make the conduct of public affairs more efficient and less corrupt and to make a modest start with social reform. This last group came to be dubbed *nasseristas* and it was their influence which, with as yet unpredictable results, was felt in the late fifties and sixties and spread the notion that both national politics and national armies should become more professional. But if the first impact was the destruction of old-style dictators and a diminution of the prestige of old-style officers, it did not follow that government by civilians was to be the new rule, for the civilians might either fall short, in efficiency or integrity, of what was desired of them, or exceed expectations and tolerance by going ahead too fast with social reforms. In either event the military would return.

And in no event would revolutionaries be persuaded that either the military or the dominant civilian castes would make adequate reforms. In all the countries of the northern arc of South America, from Venezuela to Peru, new governments were challenged by revolution.

The first of these challenges came in Venezuela where the dictatorship of Perez Jimenez was followed by a short interlude under the young and progressive Admiral Wolfgang Llarazabal, but many of the dictator's enemies deserted Llarazabal as soon as they had got rid of Perez Jimenez and elections in 1959 and 1963 gave large majorities to the cautious Accion Democratica of Presidents Romulo Betancourt and Raul Leoni. On the expiration of Leoni's term in 1968 a Christian Democrat, Rafael Caldera, won on a split vote and raised hopes of moderate reform along the lines pursued by President Frei in Chile (see chapter 27), but the Accion Democratica remained the largest party in the Congress and a bulwark against measures unpalatable to the comfortable classes. Less easily satisfied elements, which had taken the lead in the overthrow of Perez Jimenez and had no use for the Accion Democratica, turned to revolution. After the Cuban Revolution of 1959 they received encouragement and some help from Castro and a few years later scattered risings began. Risings begot repression and *vice versa*. After initial failures various groups – communists, non-communists and dissident army officers – formed a joint Liberation Army, but unity was precarious and the communists in particular disliked guerrilla methods. From 1965 these groups were openly divided. At the end of Caldera's term in 1973 the Accion Democractica returned to power with C. A. Perez as president.

In Colombia the almost simultaneous overthrow of Rojas Pinilla, a dictator (1953–58) not wholly untinged by reformist thoughts, was engineered by the established political parties, conservative and liberal, which agreed between them on joint action to recover power and on a programme for sharing it thereafter on a roster system. Colombia experienced a period of ferocious violence during the forties and fifties, punctuated by an abortive revolution in 1948 and the assassination of the progressive president Jorge Gaitán. In 1949 the province of Marquetalia, not many miles south-west of Bogota, declared itself independent and was only recovered in the sixties with the help of the United States. The Cuban revolution led to hopes of aid for the flagging revolutionaries, but these hopes were falsified and the Colombian insurgents fared only marginally better than their Venezuelan comrades. At elections in 1974 the liberal candidate beat the conservative and an assortment of candidates of the left.

In Peru too insurgency provided no cure for social ills. Peru combines great riches with some of the worst rural poverty, urban slums (full of workless migrants from a waterless countryside neglected by absentee landowners), illiteracy and starvation in the continent. The dominant oligarchy paid no taxes, ignored the masses, obstructed government intervention in the country's economic and social affairs and allowed foreign capital to acquire the succulent heights of the economy. Peruvian politics were a contest between the upper classes and the army on the one hand and APRA, a party founded in the twenties with a semisocialist programme, on the other. APRA had been outlawed after elections in 1931 which were conducted with bloodshed, but José Luis Bustamente of APRA ruled as president from 1946 to 1948. He was then ousted by General Manuel Odría and his party was once more outlawed; its leader, Víctor Raúl Haya della Torre, took refuge in the Colombian embassy where he remained for several years before departing into exile in Italy. General Odría held power for eight years and then allowed elections to be held in 1956, as a result of which the presidency passed to Manuel Prado, a conservative politician who had held office in the thirties. During his period in office peasant risings began to occur. The poor were driven by want either to move to Lima and the coast and stage riots there or to seize lands in the interior. Their risings were scattered and easily suppressed. Once again the leaders were disunited and the communists in two minds about whether to support guerrilla action – in this case partly because the most notable guerrilla chief, Hugo Blanco, was a trotskyist and partly because they were themselves divided into pro-Russian and pro-Chinese factions, each more occupied in eyeing the other than in fighting the established order. In elections in 1962 no candidate secured enough votes to win. There were three: Haya della Torre, Odría and Fernando Belaúnde Terry, by profession an architect. The army vetoed the accession of Haya della Torre or of Odría, declared the elections fraudulent for no adequate reason, and installed a committee of four to rule pending fresh elections in 1963. The re-run election was won by Belaúnde who, although no conservative, was a safe man from the army's point of view and had had occasion to observe the president's dependence on the army's will. He proceeded to enlist the army's support for his progressive measures, which were all the more measured in consequence. Fresh risings occurred in 1965. By 1968 Belaúnde had few friends. His government was tarnished by scandals rising out of the devaluation of the currency, flagging over promised agricultural reforms (which were opposed by the land-owning class) and squeezed between the *aprista* opposition pressing for more reform and the army which was beginning to find him a burden and despatched him out of the country by air. The new régime of General Juan Velasco Alvarado proceeded to expropriate United States sugar and oil interests and to promise votes for all, including illiterates. It thus proclaimed its hostility to foreign capital and a policy of social reform from above. It seemed prepared to affront the oligarchy in order to pre-empt a revolution by the dispossessed. For the United States there appeared to be a choice between taking sanctions against the expropriation of United States corporations and accepting the notion of a military-reformist régime which might do some good in Peru and might turn to the USSR or China if the United States showed ill will. The Peruvian course from

1968 was an experiment, under strongly centralized and military direction, to introduce economic planning and a measure of social reform within a capitalist framework (from which however foreign capital had been extruded) with the emphasis on technological and managerial innovation in the service of industry and exports. Within limits the experiment was radical but from 1974 its colour became distinctly more conservative and in 1975 President Velasco was removed in the course of an extensive though bloodless purge and General Francisco Morales Bermudez was promoted from prime minister to president.

Bolivia's social configuration was rather different from its neighbours' because Victor Paz Estenssoro, after an unsuccessful attempt in 1943, had led in 1952 a successful revolt in which non-communists, communists, trotskyists and junior officers, appalled by corruption and inefficiency, injustice and poverty, had participated. His régime nationalized Bolivia's extensive tin mines, broke up large estates, introduced universal suffrage and elementary social services, and attempted to diversify the economy in order to reduce the country's dependence on mining. The régime quickly ran into economic trouble by trying to do more than its resources permitted and was forced to adopt severe stabilization measures which cut down its programmes and so produced political trouble in the form of disputes between the different components within the new order. But it ran none of the risks which undid President Arbenz because landlocked Bolivia was not so close to the United States as Guatemala and its possessing classes were not American corporations.

President Paz, who was succeeded by Hernán Siles in 1956, returned to office in 1960 but was exiled in 1964 after a coup by General Alredo Ovando Candia. In 1967 the existence of guerrilla activities was admitted and made world famous by the arrest and trial of the French marxist writer, Regis Debray (committed to prison for thirty years), and the death of Che Guevara. The government of President Rene Barrientos was weakened by splits and by conflict between him and General Ovando. In 1969, a few months after the death of Barrientos, Ovando took power, installed a purely military régime and embarked on policies partly borrowed from General Velasco's populist military régime in Peru. A year later an abortive right wing coup assisted by the United States was followed by a coup from the left led by General Juan Torres, but in 1971 the pendulum swung right again as Colonel Hugo Banzer displaced Torres.

By 1970 guerrilla activity was everywhere on the decline. The death of Che Guevara had been a blow to morale. The development of anti-guerrilla techniques under the surveillance of United States officers enabled governments to defeat movements which had never been numerically strong and were only fleetingly united. Protest found different and less romantic forms. The guerrilla *foco* was replaced by urban kidnappers – the Uruguayan *tupamoros* and their like who in Argentina, Brazil and elsewhere, specialized in the capture of diplomats as hostages. The most notable exploit of the *tupamoros* was the capture in 1971 of the British ambassador, whom they held for eight months. In elections in that year, however, the left failed, the Frente Amplio, a left wing coalition, running third to the two traditional parties of Blancos and Colorados, and after intricate and disputed calculations Colonel Juan Bordaberry of the latter party was installed president in 1972. Like his precursors he was confronted with the task of finding for Uruguay, once rich on its exports of wool, an economic future in a world which had invented rayon.

Chapter 27

Cuba: Chile

The island of Cuba, the largest of the Antilles, thrusts its western end into the jaw of the Gulf of Mexico almost midway between the peninsulas of Florida and Yucatan, from which it is separated by channels about 100 miles wide. Cuba is therefore of all the West Indian islands also the nearest to the mainland of north and central America and, as already recounted, its affairs were a special concern of the United States from the middle of the nineteenth century onwards. Its liberation from Spain at the end of the century proved (like the liberation of Arab lands from Turkish rule after the First World War) to be no more than a change of masters, and it entered upon a period of colonial rule without the benefits of a colonial administration. Far ahead of its Caribbean neighbours in educational standards and facilities, and as well endowed with a middle class as the most advanced Latin American country, it endured nevertheless a record of bad government uninterrupted from its liberation up to and including the Castro régime. The abrogation in 1933 of the Platt Amendment coincided with the end of the corrupt and odious rule of Gerardo Machado which had rested to some extent on United States support. Machado had just transferred the presidency to Manuel de Cespedes but a revolt by non-commissioned officers (including Sergeant Fulgencio Batista) and students overturned the régime and inaugurated a period of twenty years during which a number of presidents held office. Batista, who ruled from 1940 to 1944, refrained at first from infringing a constitution which prescribed four-year terms with a ban on immediate re-election, but in 1952 he made himself permanent dictator and introduced a reign of terror. On 26 July of the next year, a date which gave its name to a movement, Fidel Castro led an attack on the Moncada barracks in an unsuccessful attempt to supplant Batista. After eighteen months in prison Castro emerged to prepare in Mexico a second attempt, and in December 1956 he led an invasion band of eighty-four which was swiftly defeated. The survivors, who numbered only twelve, escaped to the Sierra Maestra, where they turned from the tactics of a *coup de main* to guerrilla warfare which they waged for two years. In March 1958 Batista attacked the growing forces of rebellion, but his campaign was a failure and served only to accelerate the disintegration of his régime. On 1 January 1959 it collapsed and Castro triumphed.

Within a year Castro's victory was seen to be a revolutionary event different from the usual run of Latin American revolutions. In the first place the reforming zeal of the new government was powerful and unrestrained. Secondly, it was meant for export. Thirdly, castroism became allied with Cuban communism, and fourthly Cuba entered into alliance with the USSR. These developments led to direct United States involvement in counter-revolution and in an invasion of Cuba in 1961, and then a year later to the direct and open clash between the United States and the USSR which has been described in an earlier part of this book.

Fidel Castro did not immediately assume any office. The presidency was conferred upon Manuel Urrutia Lleo who almost immediately sought to resign it and succeeded in doing so a few months later; he was succeeded by Osvaldo Dorticós Torrado. The premiership went in the first place to José Miró Cardona who first resigned it in a matter of days and finally resigned after a few weeks; he was succeeded by Fidel Castro. These hesitations and marks of no confidence by moderate reformers betrayed the uneasiness and uncertainty with which they observed a transfer of power which had been accompanied by summary trials and bloody revenges. In the years before coming to power Castro had issued a number of statements of a moderate character, but he and his principal lieutenant, the Argentine marxist Ernesto 'Che' Guevara, were determined to effect real reforms and not to play at reforming in the half-hearted manner of so many Latin Americans. Unlike them Castro did not bother to pay formal respect to the constitution or to hold meaningless elections. He set to work to change things. Moreover Cuba, again unlike so many Latin American republics, was a relatively prosperous country with a relatively diversified economy. Its principal weakness was its dependence on sugar, and thereby on the United States, for its foreign exchange. Castro and Guevara were therefore tempted, by circumstances as well as by their temperaments, to move fast and, relying upon a certain economic strength, to attack without delay the special link with the United States which represented a form of economic servitude and was also politically charged with memories of a generation of United States dominance. At the same time, and with an equal disregard for immediate practicalities, Castro tried to extend the benefits of revolution and reform to the peoples of neighbouring countries. He became involved in subversive activities in the Dominican Republic, Haiti, Nicaragua, Panama and Venezuela and alarmed all those whose liberal instincts were less active than their love of law and order (or at any rate order) by giving money to left wing groups and by broadcasting to Latin America a castroist message as disturbing as the voice of Nasser in the Middle East.

Castro's economic policy called for foreign aid and credits and for foreign customers to replace the United States. He made the obvious move. In February 1960 Mikoyan visited Havana and concluded a trade agreement with Cuba which, among other things, enabled Cuba to buy Russian oil. Later in the same year Guevara made a tour of eastern European countries. In May Cuba established diplomatic relations with Moscow and in June it began buying arms from the USSR and other communist governments. At the same time Castro attacked the United States rights in the Guantanamo naval base and its economic influence through the sugar trade. In June United States and British refineries refused to refine Russian oil, thereby giving Castro an excuse to take them over. The Eisenhower administration in Washington, which had been watching events with restraint, hoped to bring joint American pressure to bear but at San José in August an inter-American conference of foreign ministers, while condemning Russian and Chinese intervention in Latin America, refused to refer to Cuba by name. Washington decided to act on its own. It stopped further purchases of Cuban sugar and, after Castro had retaliated by nationalizing United States property, imposed a complete commercial boycott and in January 1961 severed diplomatic relations.

From early in 1960 the United States had been helping and encouraging Cuban refugees in two places, both under the aegis of the Central Intelligence Agency. In Florida exiled politicians were formed into a political committee which hoped to become a government of Cuba; it included men of very different views who were only held together by their common opposition to Castro and by their United States managers. In Guatemala a force was being trained against the day when it would return to Cuba in small bands and start guerrilla warfare; at first there was no thought of United States military participation in the adventure, but as time went on the original tactics were transformed from piecemeal infiltration to a single invasion thrust with United States air cover, and the exiles were further allowed to assume that the United States would back their ground operations with force rather than let them fail. When Kennedy was apprised of these activities immediately after his successful campaign for the presidency, he was troubled by them, but between that date in November 1960 and the launching of the attack on the night of 14/15 April 1961, he never translated his doubts into prohibition. The operation was already in train; the chiefs of staff, his most awe-inspiring advisers, were in favour of it; he did not want to let down several hundred Cubans, with whom he sympathized, nor did he know what to do with them if they were to be disbanded; the expectation that Castro would soon have Russian jet aircraft would make it very difficult, if not impossible, to sponsor such an invasion at a later date. Kennedy reaffirmed the ban on the involvement of United States forces but overrode the opposition of Senator William Fulbright and a few other civilian advisers who advocated the containment of Cuba in preference to direct action which would be contrary to the charter of the OAS and all too consonant with Washington's reputation for imperialism and hypocrisy in its dealings with its southern neighbours.

The invasion was a complete failure. A force of 1,400 men – nine-tenths of them semi-trained civilians – supported by B.26 bombers operating from Nicaragua with Cuban pilots landed in the Bay of Pigs only to discover that, contrary to the assurances of the CIA, the United States administration was not prepared to back them up and that expected risings in Cuba itself were not materializing. The Cuban government's riposte was more effective than had been anticipated and after forty-eight hours all was over. For good measure Castro imprisoned several thousands of his fellow citizens, thus seizing the opportunity to silence, demoralize and in some cases extinguish his opponents. His prestige beyond Cuba was greatly increased.

Nevertheless his position was in other respects unhappy. The economic measures taken by his government had, by its own admission, been ill conceived. A modish passion for industrialization led to the construction of factories for the manufacture in Cuba of articles which could be imported from abroad at less cost than the cost of the raw materials for their manufacture. In the countryside peasants displayed the worldwide dislike of their kind for co-operatives, the nationalization of land, and the enforced cultivation of crops destined for sale at fixed low prices. The middle class, which had been a more active ingredient in the revolution than the peasantry or the urban working class, became antagonized when nationalization was extended from foreign to domestic enterprises, and when the new régime took to the bad old ways of its predecessors in putting political opponents away in noisome jails. By 1962 there was an economic crisis, a general refusal to work by the peasants, food rationing and widespread disillusion, discontent and poverty.

At the end of 1961 Castro declared himself a marxist. The Cuban communist party was a distinct entity which had at the outset little or nothing to do with Castro's 'July 26' movement. It was not a party with mass support and in the Batista period it had preferred back-stage political manoeuvres which secured it a humble position on the periphery of the ruling constellation. Before the castroist victory in 1959 there were in both the castroist and the communist camps some who encouraged a rapprochement or even a fusion and others who opposed any such move. During 1961 the former groups prevailed and the parties effected a considerable degree of integration. Cuba became in consequence a part of the communist world in terms of international politics, but Castro did not become either an orthodox communist (he seemed to care little about communist teaching) or a captive of a communist machine. As independent in his way – and within the limits imposed by Cuba's need for foreign friends – as Mao or Tito, he also remained domestically the leader of a government and a movement which were only partly communist. Leaders of the Cuban communist party were promoted to office and influence but in March 1962 the most eminent of them, Anibal Escalante, was dismissed and fled to Czechoslovakia shortly before Castro set out for an extended visit to the USSR. The two parties had fallen out, the castroists prevailed and Moscow backed the winners.

Moscow's support for Castro had become an economic burden with exciting political and strategic possibilities. Keeping Castro afloat economically was probably costing the USSR more than it had bargained for in financial terms; keeping Castro afloat politically in the face of the United States determination to destroy him could be an even more costly and risky policy, but it was also an exceptionally tempting one since an effective alliance between the USSR and Cuba would give the Russians a foothold in Latin America with all its unpredictable revolutionary possibilities, and a base within a hundred miles of the United States to offset the bases with which the USSR was ringed by its antagonists. According to Cuban – and Chinese – sources the idea of sending to Cuba the missiles and jet aircraft which were first observed by United States reconnaissance in October 1962 was Khrushchev's. However that may be Cuba, which Castro had made an economic and political ward of the USSR, was converted by Khrushchev into an armed pawn. Whereas Castro had wanted to equip Cuba to defend itself against a second attack like the one in the Bay of Pigs, Khrushchev despatched weapons of an altogether different significance. The upshot has already been described and discussed. In the narrower Latin American context the results were that the OAS (which had expelled Cuba from its ranks at the beginning of the year) approved the deployment of force by the United States against the approaching Russian ships; that a number of Latin American states contributed to the blockade of Cuba instituted by the United States; that Cuba was left out of the reckoning as Kennedy and Khrushchev moved to resolve the crisis; but that Castro was given an outstandingly splendid reception when he revisited Moscow in April 1963 and won assurances of continuing Russian favour and support.

The crisis of 1962 involved for Castro a threat of extinction inasmuch as the rebuff to the USSR might carry with it an implicit freedom for the United States to work its will in Cuba and remove a government which had connived at, or even possibly instigated, an attempt to alter the balance of power in the American hemisphere more radically than at any time since the eighteenth century. But time seemed to show that Kennedy's triumph over Khrushchev was not to be so interpreted. Castro himself felt secure enough against renewed intervention by the United States to engage, towards the end of 1963, in a plot against the government of Venezuela (for which the OAS in July 1964 declared him an aggressor and recommended the severance of diplomatic and commercial connections, a step which only Mexico then refused to take); and castroism was also one of the ingredients in a rising in Andean Peru in 1965 in which desperate underdogs tried, with the help of castroist and communist supplies and moral support over the radio, to force their plight upon the attention of their government. But the ostracism of Castro in 1964 was a reminder that he was still there to be ostracized, and if he was still there part of the reason was that his state was under the protection of a major power. The Russians had been physically beaten out of the Caribbean but they retained a protective or intrusive capacity of another order. The assertion of the Monroe Doctrine had revealed its limitations. There were to be no foreign bases in the American continent but the American hemisphere's politics could no longer be sealed off from wider international politics. The United States had been harping for some time on the dangers of international communism in Latin America, but this ideological approach had missed the main point which was the opening of Latin America to the processes of non-ideological international politics, in much the same way as the Middle East and the rest of Asia and then Africa had become international magnetic fields as soon as both the major world powers decided to exercise there the powers which nobody could prevent them from exercising. In the first post-war decades it had been assumed that two areas in the world were immune from this interplay: Latin America in the penumbra of the United States, and Moscow's satellite empire in Europe in the irresistible tow of the USSR. The Cuban crisis showed that this assumption was at least an exaggeration. In the case of Latin America Khrushchev, with Castro as his eye-opener, scented that the time had come to question the unquestionable. This capacity was one of his strengths as a politician. Characteristically, however, he followed his instinct with more enthusiasm than caution and so exposed himself to a stinging tactical defeat. Characteristically too Washington, with the restraint which democracy imposes on action and even sometimes on thinking, had not come within sight of any comparable policy in Europe, thus avoiding any comparable defeat. But the principal implication of the Cuban crisis was the demolition of the theory that major powers have back gardens round which it suffices to put up notices against trespassers. Although interference in such areas remains preternaturally hazardous, the areas themselves are not enclosures where special conditions are bred, but areas where the various winds of international politics blow in different force. This revelation marked a stage in Latin America's international history as well as in the appreciation of great power politics.

For Cuba itself the experience was bitter. During the period of United States dominance up to 1933 Cuba had been a quasi-colonial territory which was permitted to contract no foreign alliances and harbour no foreign bases. Castro reversed this situation to the extreme extent of making an alliance with the USSR and turning Cuba into a Russian base. He did so on a calculation of Cuban interests which turned out to be a miscalculation, since the USSR showed by retreating in the face of Washington's challenge that Cuba's interests played very little part in Moscow's calculation of its own interests and possibilities in the western hemisphere. Although the USSR had defied the Monroe Doctrine it had not done so in support of Cuban nationalism or Cuban ambitions. Castro, who had hoped to become the Latin American equivalent of Tito, Sukarno and Nasser, at once the personification of a new national dignity and the regional leader of revolution, found himself instead the ruler of an island which had become an international curiosity rather than an international fulcrum and which was beginning to look rather bedraggled as a consequence of economic and administrative muddle. For Guevara, the Argentinian pan-American for whom Cuba's revolution (not Mexico's or Bolivia's) was to have been the real beginning of Latin America's revolution, the reassessment necessitated by the Russian retreat was even bitterer than it was for Castro, and in the course of it the two men fell out and Guevara disappeared, taking with him much of the Cuban revolution's international flavour which he tried to inject into South America until he met his death in Bolivia in 1967.

Cuba's revolution had not been the first in Latin America in the post-war years. The risings described in a previous chapter preceded it. But Castro was successful where others failed, and his success and his geographical position gave his revolution a universal as well as a continental significance. Ten years later, however, this revolution had had next to no political impact in the rest of the sub-continent. No other country followed Cuba's course: Cuba's example did not serve to alleviate the economic and social injustices which weighed on central and southern America. The confusion of castroism with communism and the economic failures of Castro's own régime (made the more prominent by Castro's long, public disquisitions on them) alienated as many people as his open personality, his intelligence and his new style in politics attracted. Cuba seemed to become more and more a phenomenon apart rather than the spearhead of continental revolution. Elsewhere change seemed more likely to come through a reforming military autocracy as in Peru for example, or perhaps even from within a no longer immobile political establishment, as in Chile.

Chile's history in the nineteenth century had been one of progress only briefly interrupted by civil war in 1891 and based on rich mineral resources and successful wars against Peru and Bolivia. In the twentieth century Chile had its share of political instability and inflation, its difficulties being accentuated by competition from artificial nitrates. The landed oligarchy lost its hold on power after the revolt of 1891 and thereafter Chile moved painfully towards a more democratic order. In 1938 elections gave power to a popular front which included communists and was not debarred from taking office by the armed forces. A period of orderly civilian government, conservative rather than radical, followed. In 1964 two progressive forces competed for the succession to President Jorge Alessandri – a popular front led by the socialist Salvador Allende and a Christian Democrat party led by Eduardo Frei Montalva. The latter won and established a progressive, anti-communist government, overtly akin to the Christian Democrat parties of Europe but ostensibly more radical.

By the end of his term Frei had to his credit a considerable advance in education, a noticeable drop in illteracy, some industrial development and new housing, and the introduction of graduated taxes. But inflation was not mastered, wages remained low, the number of landless peasants high – so high that they began to occupy lands, from which many were evicted by force and some killed. Conscious of the size of his economic problem Frei tried to avoid a direct clash with the oligarchy or the United States, but his gradualism offended on the one hand the more militant elements and on the other the more chauvinist. In 1970, in a three-cornered presidential election, Frei's designated successor, Radomiro Tomic, came bottom of the poll and amid general surprise Allende narrowly defeated the conservative Alessandri. Allende was the leader of a coalition which embraced socialists, communists and other groups on either side of these. During the campaign he played up his friendship with Castro. Although he did not win an absolute majority of the popular vote the Chilean parliament, to which the decision passed, followed the usual rule and installed him in office. Attempts to instigate an army coup to prevent him from taking over were without effect, although the commander-in-chief was assassinated by right wing extremists for keeping the army out of politics.

Allende's government began by nationalizing copper, nitrates and other minerals and the principal banks and by extending the programme of agricultural reform initiated by Frei. These measures were all but universally popular. The expropriation of US copper companies evoked no Chilean protest and the prosecution of land reform was entrusted to the expert who had prepared Frei's scheme. But Allende ran into a variety of troubles, some of his own making. Against the advice of his more cautious communist allies he wanted to press on with nationalization as fast as possible and without pausing to consolidate his first measures. He alienated the large class of medium proprietors. He also refused publicly to disavow wilder groups who were using the language of the tumbril or to insist on the disbanding of private armies, thereby laying himself open to the charge of being either fearful of or indulgent to the revolutionary left. He further alienated opinion by a style of living which was out of keeping not only with socialism but also with a usage observed by Frei, Allesandri and other presidents who had followed the Chilean tradition of living as simply in office as out of it. Allende had too a piece of bad luck. If the world price of copper had kept up he might have weathered the storms that came upon him, but the price fell and inflation rising to 300 per cent a year turned criticism and apprehension to open resistance. In the coup which followed in 1973 Allende committed suicide and Chile was given over to the very untender mercy of a right wing autocracy under General Augusto Pinochet Ugarte.

By 1975 the trend of the late fifties away from military dictatorship (see p. 424) had been clearly halted, but it would have been superficial to conclude that it had been reversed. The trend now was to one-party rule, whether military or civilian or mixed. Two things had failed.

Violent revolution, rural or urban, had achieved no success outside Cuba. Equally thwarted were those who hoped for the advance of the bourgeois liberal or social democracy familiar to Europeans of the nineteenth and twentieth centuries. Developments of this kind, though espoused by a small cosmopolitan intellectual elite, had too few roots in the political soil of Latin America where the enduring tradition was that of pre-Napoleonic Spain. Latin America did not revolt against Spain. Napoleon's subjection of Spain had simply caused Spanish power in the New World to evaporate. The liberators were therefore successors rather than liberators and they assumed, for themselves and generations to come, the centralist powers and attitudes which the Spanish crown had exported to Spanish presidencies and vice-royalties in south and central America. This was an autocratic tradition, often liberally interpreted, but not a democratic one. The new men of the second half of the twentieth century, most but not all of them military, were with rare exceptions not concerned to alter the system. They were concerned to take for themselves the positions of power and direction which had hitherto been monopolised by a different ruling class. The exception was Venezuela where, from 1959, a two-party civilian system operated to place in power by the ballot four successive presidents, all of them men of ability who, though coming from different parties, were cast in a liberal bourgeois mould. The common explanation of this phenomenon was that Venezuela, being the richest country in the sub-continent, could afford democratic politics and make them work, but since stability and tolerance are not the common experience of all rich states, further explanations have to be sought. Besides its natural resources Venezuela had a manageable population (12 million), a minimum of racial conflict, and the good fortune to possess and the good sense to elevate men with the brains and the moral standards needed to make the most of these advantages.

Economically and culturally most of Latin America remained in the shadow of foreign domination. Industrialization was weak or delayed for many reasons: ruling élites opposed import tariffs and quotas which infant industries needed but rich consumers did not like; the several domestic markets were too small and attempts to combine them rudimentary; industries which arose tended to excess capacity, their products to high costs; technology was either local and behind the times or foreign and therefore strange and expensive. Transport and other public services were poor or non-existent except near big cities. Half the population was drawn into cities of 20,000 or more, over-crowded, dirty, violent and a prey to property speculators. The economic gap between town and country was widening. The land provided status, wealth and a way of life for the few; the towns failed for the most part to become engines of new economic activity. The need for land reform was manifest and a number of countries passed relevant laws, but little practical action followed except in the wake of revolutions (Mexico, Bolivia, Cuba). Workers on the land were ill paid, under-employed and growing in numbers in spite of the drift to the towns. Without credit or adequate communications or, in many areas, water small proprietors could get neither seeds nor fertilizers nor machinery for what was economically productive land.

Notes

A. Guyana

Guyana, once British Guiana, is an almost equally divided bi-racial country in which the descendants of Indians imported by the British (after the abolition of slavery in 1838) slightly outnumber the Africans while a small Roman Catholic minority with European origins can in these circumstances be electorally important. The Indians are predominantly rural, the Africans urban. The post-war leaders of these two groups were at first divided more by temperament than policy. The Indian leader, Cheddi Jagan, a Rooseveltian liberal with a socialist American wife, joined forces with Forbes Burnham, a shrewd politician of African descent. Both men moved to the left but the former moved faster than the latter. While Jagan allowed himself to be pushed by conflict into more extreme attitudes, Burnham exercised more self-control and successfully subordinated the expression of opinions to the capture of power. They became therefore the leaders of opposing parties, separated at first by tactical considerations but increasingly racial in their confrontation. In 1961 Jagan won an election, but his radicalism, and especially his plans to unionize labour, alarmed the European planters, while local American interests were reporting him to be a dangerous communist. This view of Jagan's impact on the colony was sharpened by riots necessitating the despatch of British troops and by Jagan's leanings towards Castro's Cuba, an inclination partly temperamental but partly also economic: Cuba was one of Guyana's principal markets for its surplus rice and this market had been cut off after Castro's revolution.

With independence in the offing the United States and to some extent Britain were anxious to ensure the victory of Burnham over Jagan. Burnham cultivated the small Roman Catholic party and won the election of 1964 after the British had conveniently altered the constitution by introducing proportional representation. On a straight vote Jagan could and almost certainly would win; under proportional representation he could not. This election was followed in 1966 by independence, whereupon British Guiana became Guyana and joined the UN but not, owing to a border dispute with Venezuela, the OAS. In the next few years the victorious Burnham began to move to the left, impelled chiefly by the needs of the urban unemployed Africans and by general anti-American and anti-planter ideological imperatives.

B. The Caribbean

A federation of British colonies in the Caribbean had been under discussion since the middle of the nineteenth century. Such a federation was created in 1958 but came to grief in 1961. There have been divergent views about the causes of this failure. On the one hand it has been alleged that the delay in bringing it into being after the end of the Second World War allowed animosities to develop between the islands and that the blame for this delay rested upon the British government which, regarding West Indian leaders as much more left wing than in fact they were, slowed down the pace towards independence and therefore federation. On this view there was a genuine desire for federation, at the popular as well as the political level, despite the acknowledged difficulties – great disparities in the size and wealth of the different islands and the great distances between them. The alternative view is that, except perhaps in the smaller islands, there was no popular interest in federation or support for it and that the federation of 1958 rested therefore on a narrow base of political and trade union leaders who were liable to be undermined by a popular revulsion; and that such a revulsion was in the event stirred up by other leaders who saw in it a way to take power. This view stresses the ways of thinking of the Caribbean peoples, islanders with a keen sense of belonging to their particular islands but little sense of community with others beyond the horizon (a habit accentuated by the fact that under colonial rule each colony had been treated by the British Colonial Office as a distinct object in a series of bilateral relationships with

Britain). Shortly after federation, and before its economic benefits had had a chance to make their impact, the prime minister of Jamaica, Norman Manley, was challenged by his rival, Alexander Bustamente, to hold a referendum to see whether Jamaicans wished the federation to continue or not. The result was a narrow defeat for Manley and the federation. which Jamaica left in January 1962. Trinidad-Tobago followed suit. Both became independent members of the Commonwealth and the OAS, as did Barbados in 1966. The smaller islands became associate members of the Commonwealth, self-governing except in relation to foreign and defence policies in which Britain retained a share of responsibility. There were six of these associates: Antigua, Dominica, St Lucia, Grenada, St Vincent and St Kitts-Nevis-Anguilla. The last proved unhappily assorted and Anguilla rebelled against the government in St Kitts. It achieved a *de facto* separation which Britain, despite sympathy with Anguillan complaints, refused to endorse. Four British colonies remained colonies: Montserrat, the British Virgin Islands, the Turks and Caicos Islands and the Cayman Islands. On the mainland British Honduras moved only slowly towards independence under the shadow of Guatemala's claim to the whole territory.

In 1968 a fresh and more modest co-operative venture was launched under the name of Carifta (Caribbean Free Trade Association). It was joined by all Commonwealth states and territories except British Honduras and the Bahamas. The former joined three years later, and in 1973 changed its name to Belize. The weaker members claimed that Carifta benefited the stronger rather than themselves. All were worried by the effects of British accession to the EEC since they had, under the Commonwealth Sugar Agreement and similar schemes, an assured market and stable prices for their sugar, fruit, rum and other produce. With the exception of the solitary oil producer, Trinidad and Tobago, they were harder hit by rising oil price in the seventies which aggravated endemic unemployment and anti-government sentiment. In 1973 four states – Trinidad and Tobago, Guyana, Jamaica and Barbados – created a Caribbean Community (CARICOM), membership of which was open to all Commonwealth countries which chose to join within a year. The participation of Jamaica, which had torpedoed the federation of 1958, was vital. This new association, which replaced looser meetings of heads of government, was intended to help its members present a united front to the EEC and other economic groups and to coordinate policies as occasion might require. All the Commonwealth Caribbean states recognized the regime in Cuba in 1972.

Index

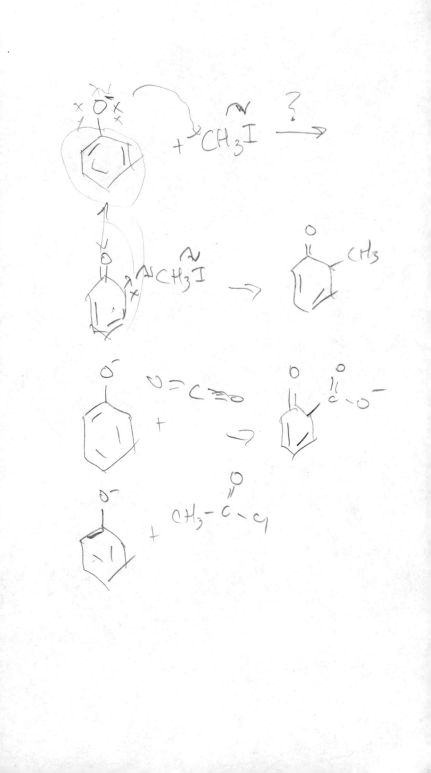